HOUGHTON MIFFLIN

English

Authors
Robert Rueda
Tina Saldivar
Lynne Shapiro
Shane Templeton
C. Ann Terry
Catherine Valentino
Shelby A. Wolf

Consultants
Jeanneine P. Jones
Monette Coleman McIver
Rojulene Norris

HOUGHTON MIFFLIN

BOSTON

Acknowledgments

For each of the selections listed below, grateful acknowledgment is made for permission to excerpt and/or reprint original or copyrighted material as follows:

Published Models

From "The Concert" from *Small Faces: Stories* by Gary Soto. Copyright ©1986 by Gary Soto. Text used with permission of the Author and BookStop Literary Agency. All rights reserved. Cover reprinted by permission of Arte Público Press.

"A Day's Wait" from *Winner Take Nothing* by Ernest Hemingway, cover painting by Ruth and James McCrea. Copyright 1933 by Charles Scribner's Sons. Copyright renewed ©1961 by Mary Hemingway. Cover painting copyright ©1970 by Charles Scribner's Sons. Reprinted with permission of Scribner, a Division of Simon & Schuster and the Hemingway Foreign Rights Trust.

"The Hummingbird That Lived Through Winter" from *The Man With the Heart in the Highlands and Other Stories* by William Saroyan. Copyright ©1968 by William Saroyan. Reprinted by permission of the Trustees of Leland Stanford Junior University.

Acknowledgments are continued at the back of the book following the last page of the Index.

ISBN: 0-618-31005-3

7 8 9 10 11 12 13 14 15 16 17 18 – DCI – 09 08 07 06

TABLE OF CONTENTS

Part 1

Grammar, Usage, and Mechanics

Part 1

Unit 2 — **Nouns** 81

Unit 5　Capitalization and Punctuation 235

Unit 6　Pronouns 297

Part 2 Writing, Listening, Speaking, and Viewing

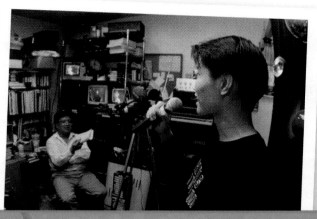

Part 2

Unit 12 — Writing a Research Report 569

SECTION 3 Narrating and Entertaining

Unit 14 Writing a Story 646

Part 3 Tools and Tips

Listening, Speaking, and Viewing

Learning from Each Other

Each of you is unique. You have your own special experiences, talents, knowledge, opinions, and observations. That makes you valuable resources for each other. As individuals you're like one-of-a-kind books full of information and ideas to share. Together as a class, you're a whole encyclopedia!

Together we can build a table, dunk a basketball, make a movie, create delicious bread to eat, and name ten constellations!

Sharing what you know and learning from others can make school—and life—both easier and more interesting. You can help each other solve problems and think of new ideas. You can offer encouragement and inspire each other to reach higher goals.

How is this done? To begin with, SPEAK, LISTEN, and VIEW! Speaking lets you share what you know. It also helps you clarify for yourself what you are thinking. Listening and viewing help you to learn from others. Here are some major purposes of speaking, listening, and viewing.

Speaking	Listening and Viewing	Examples
to entertain	for enjoyment	watching and listening to a play, telling a funny anecdote, examining a sculpture
to inform	to get information	asking for or giving directions, scanning a menu, observing someone's facial expression
to persuade	to form an opinion	recommending a movie, judging an artwork, listening to or participating in a debate

Think and Discuss

- Look back at the pictures on the previous page. What is each person's purpose for listening, speaking, or viewing?
- At what other times do you rely on listening, speaking, and viewing during the day?

Discussion Breakdown

These students are trying to decide what to plant in a class garden on the school grounds. They are using poor listening and speaking skills. What are they doing wrong?

Think and Discuss

- What is each student doing wrong in this discussion?
- What could the students do to improve their discussion?

Discussion
Breakthrough

The students are still planning a class garden. How have they improved their listening and speaking skills?

Think and Discuss

● What has each student done to improve his or her listening or speaking skills?

Being a Good Listener and Speaker

These basic guidelines will help you with listening and speaking, whether you are discussing a project with classmates, planning a Saturday with your family, or chatting with friends.

When You Listen

▶ Eliminate distractions. Shut off the TV. Turn off the music. Close the door if necessary.
▶ Make eye contact with the speaker.
▶ Listen attentively. Don't make noise or let your mind wander.
▶ If you're confused, repeat what was said in your own words. Check that you've understood.
▶ Silently summarize what you hear.

When You Speak

▶ Vary your role—participate, lead, and listen from time to time.
▶ Wait your turn. Don't interrupt!
▶ Share your ideas with the group—don't have side conversations.
▶ Make eye contact with your listeners. Speak slowly, clearly, and loudly enough to be heard and understood.
▶ Ask others what they think of your ideas. Say what you think about theirs.
▶ If you disagree, politely explain why.
▶ Stick to the subject being discussed.
▶ Occasionally summarize the main points of the discussion.

Try It Out Choose one of the statements below. Decide whether or not you agree with it. Discuss your opinions in small groups.

- There should be a law requiring people to vote in elections.
- Teenagers should be allowed to manage their own money.
- Parents should have the right to decide what their teenage kids read.

Being a Good Viewer

You can "see" something without really "viewing" it. When you see, your eyes simply pick up images. When you view, you are paying attention and really thinking about what you see. You are learning through your eyes. What kinds of information are the students in these pictures gathering by viewing?

Life in this state was sure different two hundred years ago.

That was a great move. I'd like to try it.

When You View

Viewing the World Around You

Washington, D.C., is beautiful! Hey, there's the Capitol! Those columns remind me of buildings in ancient Rome.

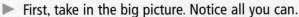

▶ First, take in the big picture. Notice all you can.
▶ Then focus. Where is your eye drawn? What are the most important parts of what you're viewing?
▶ Then refocus. What important or interesting details do you see?

Viewing Others

▶ Pay attention to body language. People often use their hands to demonstrate or to add meaning to what they are saying. A person's smile, frown, blush, yawn, or small gestures can help you figure out how he or she is feeling.

▶ Observing body language can also help you figure out how people are reacting to what you say and do.

Viewing Still or Moving Images

▶ Notice where your eye is drawn. What is the main focus of the image? What techniques did the person who created this image use to get your attention?

▶ Decide what message, if any, the image sends.

▶ Think about the purpose of the image. Is it meant to entertain? inform? persuade?

▶ Identify the target audience. Is the image meant for children? teenagers? adults? animal-lovers? sports enthusiasts? Think about how different audiences might react to this image.

Try It Out With a partner, test your skill at viewing images.

● Cut out an interesting newspaper photo that gives clues about the event it depicts. (You may also use a picture in a book, but don't cut it out. Just lay paper on the page to hide the text.)

● Take turns with your partner looking at each other's picture. Use your viewing skills to see how much you can guess about the related event.

The Writing Process

A Day in the Life of a Student

What Is the Writing Process?

The writing process helps you move step by step from a blank sheet of paper to an interesting piece of writing. The writing process gives you many chances to improve your writing.

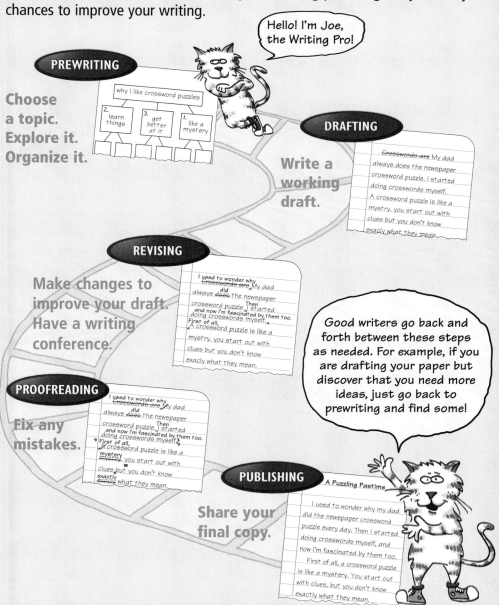

Hello! I'm Joe, the Writing Pro!

PREWRITING

Choose a topic. Explore it. Organize it.

why I like crossword puzzles

2. learn things   3. get better at it   1. like a mystery

DRAFTING

Write a working draft.

~~Crosswords are~~ My dad always does the newspaper crossword puzzle. I started doing crosswords myself. A crossword puzzle is like a mystery. you start out with clues but you don't know exacly what they mean

REVISING

Make changes to improve your draft. Have a writing conference.

I used to wonder why ~~crosswords are~~ My dad did always ~~does~~ the newspaper crossword puzzle. Then and now I'm fascinated by them too. I started doing crosswords myself. First of all, A crossword puzzle is like a mystery. you start out with clues but you don't know exacly what they mean.

Good writers go back and forth between these steps as needed. For example, if you are drafting your paper but discover that you need more ideas, just go back to prewriting and find some!

PROOFREADING

Fix any mistakes.

I used to wonder why ~~crosswords are~~ My dad did always ~~does~~ the newspaper crossword puzzle. Then and now I'm fascinated by them too. First of all, A crossword puzzle is like a mystery. ~~mystry.~~ you start out with clues but you don't know exacly ~~exacly~~ what they mean.

PUBLISHING

Share your final copy.

A Puzzling Pastime

I used to wonder why my dad did the newspaper crossword puzzle every day. Then I started doing crosswords myself, and now I'm fascinated by them too. First of all, a crossword puzzle is like a mystery. You start out with clues, but you don't know exactly what they mean.

Looking Ahead In this section, you will learn about the writing process as you write a description. To get ready, you will first read a description that was published in a book.

While visiting Mexico City with his wife, Gary Soto went to the symphony and was fascinated by the audience. What senses does he use to help you imagine the interesting people there?

Gary Soto

The Concert

from *Small Faces,* by Gary Soto

On our last night in Mexico City, we went to hear the National Symphony. I bought low-priced tickets, but when we tried to sit on the ground floor, a portly usher pointed us to the stairwell. We climbed to the next landing, where another usher told us to keep climbing by rolling his eyes toward *el paraíso*—the gallery of cheap seats. We climbed two more flights, laughing that we were going to end up on the roof with the pigeons. An unsmiling usher handed us programs as we stepped to the door. We looked around, amazed at the gray, well-painted boxes that were our seats. There were no crushed velvet chairs with ornate wooden arms, no elegant men and women with perfect teeth. Most were Indians and *campesinos,* and a few university students holding hands, heads pressed together in love.

I led Carolyn to the boxes in the front row against the rail, and together we looked far down where the others sat. Their rumblings rose like heat. They fanned themselves and smiled wide enough for us to see their teeth. We watched them until an old man touched my shoulder, said *con permiso,* and took small steps to get past me to the box on our left. When he sat down I smiled at him, as I wanted to be friendly. But he didn't look at me. He took out a pair of glasses from his breast pocket. They were broken, taped together at the bridge. I looked away, embarrassed to see that he was poor, but stole a glance when the program began: I saw his coat, slack and full from wear, and his pants with

Go to www.eduplace.com/kids/ for information about Gary Soto.

oily spots. His shoes were rope sandals. His tie was short, like a withered arm. I watched his face in profile that showed a knot of tape protruding from his glasses; a profile that went unchanged as it looked down at the symphony.

I listened but felt little as the violins tugged and pulled and scratched through an hour of performance. When the music stopped and the conductor turned around, moon-faced and trying to hide his happiness by holding back a grin, I craned my neck over the rail and watched the *elegantes* applaud and smile at one another. We applauded, too, and looked around, smiling. We were busy with an excitement that lit our eyes. But while the *elegantes* got up to stand in the foyer under torches, those around us leaned against the wall to talk in whispers.

We stayed for the second half—something by Haydn—but no matter how I tried to study the movements of musicians and conductor on his carpeted box, I couldn't help but look around the room at the Indians and *campesinos* whose faces, turned in profile in the half-lit shadows, held an instinctive awareness of the music. They would scratch a cheek or an elbow, speak quietly to one another, and sometimes squirm on the boxes. But most were attentive. It amazed me. I had never known the poor to appreciate such music, and I had lived among the poor since I was a child. These field laborers and rug weavers listened to music that was not part of their lives, music written to titillate the aristocrats who wanted so much to rise above the dirty faces of the poor. The poor sat on the fifth tier on painted boxes, bodies leaning in the direction of the music that couldn't arrive fast enough to meet their lives.

Reading As a Writer

Think About the Description

- What senses does the author use to describe the differences between the *elegantes* and the *campesinos*?
- What sensory details give you a vivid picture of the old man who sits near the writer?
- What sensory details describe the difference between the places where the *elegantes* and the *campesinos* sit?

Think About Writer's Craft

- What words in the first paragraph on page 12 describe the music? What do these words tell you about the author's feelings for the music?

Think About the Picture

- Look at the pictures on pages 11–13. In what ways does the artist use stylistic features, such as lines and color, to make the faces seem similar? In what ways does he use stylistic features to make them seem different?

Looking Ahead

Now you are ready to write your own description. Starting on the next page, you will find many ideas to help you. As you go along, you will see how one student, Bethany Braun, used the writing process to write a description of her father's restaurant.

Using the Writing Process

What Is Prewriting?

Prewriting has three parts: choosing your topic; exploring your topic; and organizing, or planning, your writing.

Start thinking about **audience** and **purpose** right away. What kind of paper will you write? Who will read or listen to your writing?

Think about how you are going to **publish** or **share** your paper. This may affect how you write your paper.

How Do I Choose a Topic?

Here are a few ways to find an idea to write about.

Ways to Think of Topics		
Try this!	**Here's how.**	
Remember your experiences.	You once entered a pizza-making contest.	• Write a **personal narrative** about what happened. • **Compare and contrast** making pizza with preparing another kind of food. • **Describe** the pizza you made.
Listen to other people.	Your aunt and uncle told you a funny story about how they met.	• Add this event to the plot of a **story**. • **Compare and contrast** your aunt's and your uncle's personalities.
Read a book.	You enjoyed a book about how money is made at the U.S. Treasury.	• Write a **research report** on how new bills are designed and printed. • **Persuade** your parents to visit the U.S. Treasury in Washington, D.C.
Reread your journal.	You wrote a journal entry about a nightmarish bus trip.	• **Describe** the inside of the bus. • Turn the entry into a **personal narrative**.
Use your imagination.	What would it be like to go skydiving?	• Write a **story** about a skydiver who is suddenly afraid to jump from the plane. • Write an **opinion essay** about high-risk sports.

Write a Description

Choosing a Description Topic

Learning from a Model Bethany wanted to write a description to submit to her school newspaper, which was publishing an issue called *Special Places*. First she made a list of ideas, and then she thought about each one.

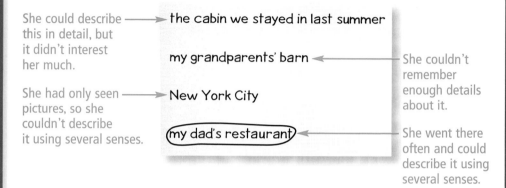

She could describe this in detail, but it didn't interest her much. → the cabin we stayed in last summer

my grandparents' barn ← She couldn't remember enough details about it.

She had only seen pictures, so she couldn't describe it using several senses. → New York City

(my dad's restaurant) ← She went there often and could describe it using several senses.

▶ Choose Your Topic

As you choose your topic, think about your **purpose**, your **audience**, and how you will **publish** or **share** your description.

❶ **List** five topics, such as a special place, an amusing pet, or a person you admire. Use the chart on page 14 to help you think of ideas.

❷ **Discuss** your topics with a partner. Which ideas does your partner like best? Why?

❸ **Ask** yourself these questions about each topic.
- Is this topic about a single person, place, or thing?
- Have I seen this or done it myself? Can I think of interesting details?
- Can I describe it using at least three senses?
- Which topic would both my audience and I enjoy?

❹ **Circle** the topic you will write about.

📁 Keep all your work for your description in one place, such as a writing folder.

Tech Tip
See page H47 for ideas for using a computer during the writing process.

What Is Exploring?

Exploring is the second part of prewriting. Explore by recalling events, gathering facts, and thinking of details to elaborate your topic.

How Do I Explore My Topic?

This chart shows different strategies you can use to explore a topic.

Exploring Strategies	
Try this!	**Here's how.**
Brainstorming a list	**Grand Canyon Trip** hiking down a trail so hot, always thirsty mules not many people
Clustering	great learning tool — NEED SCHOOL COMPUTERS — improve problem solving — need them for most jobs
Making a chart	**A Bonfire** Sight | orange, yellow, and red flames Sound | popping, crackling, and snapping
Drawing and labeling	**Our Class Trip** We were freezing! Nobody wore warm clothes.
Interviewing with a partner	How do you use your new software? What can it do?
Asking *Who? What? When? Where? Why? How?*	**Good Fishing** Where? an island on Lake Wilson, beneath a large cliff When? right after a rainstorm and just before dark
Freewriting	My favorite thing about hockey is sitting around after the game and talking about it—after a win especially. You feel tired, entire body wiped out, exhausted, still wearing your sweaty equipment.

See page H59 for more graphic organizers.

Exploring a Description Topic

Learning from a Model Bethany made an Observation Chart and brain-stormed details about the restaurant where her father works. She focused on details that appealed to different senses.

Smell	Sight	Touch
aroma right as I come through the door	dim lights	glass of cherry cola
smell of cooking food	tile floor	marble counter
I know that smell.	That floor is aging by the second.	soda bubbles popping on my tongue
the smell of lilies	statue of a tiger in the store next door	

▲ **Part of Bethany's Observation Chart**

▶ Explore Your Topic

❶ Picture what you are describing. What do your readers need to know to help them clearly imagine it?

❷ Write down as many details as possible. Use an Observation Chart.

❸ Use your five senses to brainstorm sensory words and details to add to your Observation Chart. Look at the chart of sensory words below. Use some of these, or think of your own.

Sight	Sound	Smell	Touch	Taste
gnarled	blast	pungent	gelatinous	doughy
gangly	melodious	stale	silky	antiseptic
crystalline	fizzing	mustardy	gritty	creamy
frayed	clink	musty	coarse	acrid
murky	yawn	putrid	pliable	citric
fissure	grinding	yeasty	fleecy	tart
gaudy	cough	sooty	quivering	scorched
floppy	growl	horsy	abrasive	bland
teal	clomp	greasy	spongy	saccharine
speckled	mumble	mildewy	jagged	tangy

If you can't think of many sensory words, try another topic.

What Is Organizing?

Organizing is the third part of prewriting. You plan your paper.

You choose what to include. You decide what is important to your topic.

You plan the order. You group and then sequence your ideas and details.

How Do I Organize My Writing?

Group facts, events, or ideas. Put related details into separate groups, such as a reason and its supporting details.

Choose an organization. Present the groups of details in an order that fits your purpose. It often helps to chart, diagram, or outline your plan.

Ways to Organize	
Try this!	**Here's how.**
Chronological order First Next Last	Tell events in the sequence in which they happen.
Flashback Start First Next Last	Start with an important event. Then tell the events leading up to it in chronological order.
Spatial order	Describe things in relation to each other, such as from top to bottom, right to left, or far to near.
Comparison and contrast	Group details by similarities and differences, or tell how subjects are alike and different by characteristic.
Order of importance LEAST MOST MOST LEAST	Tell the most important reason first and the least important reason last, or tell them the other way around.
Question and answer Q? A . . . Q? A . . .	Ask a question and tell the answer. Then ask another question and answer that.
Logical order	Group related details and present the groups in an order that makes sense.

Organizing a Description

Learning from a Model Bethany needed to figure out how to organize her description. She decided to group her details in the same way she had brainstormed them in her Observation Chart—by sense.

- She deleted details that were not important to her topic.
- Then she numbered each group of details in a logical order.
- Finally, she added more sensory details and exact words.

①Smell	③Sight	②Touch
aroma right as I come through the door	dim lights	gripping a glass of cherry cola
smell of cooking food with my eyes closed I know that smell.	old yellow tile floor	stroking the smooth marble counter
feeling dizzy from the smell of lilies	That floor is aging by the second.	soda bubbles popping on my tongue
	~~statue of a tiger in the store next door~~	syrup sliding down my throat
	crystal chandelier	

▲ Part of Bethany's Observation Chart

▶ Organize Your Description

❶ **Decide** how to organize your description. Use the chart on page 18.

❷ **Group** the details about your topic that belong together.

❸ **Delete** the details that aren't important to your topic.

❹ **Number** your details in the order you will write about them.

❺ **Add** any more details you think of. Use sensory words.

It's not too late for a little more brainstorming! Add any other details you think of.

What Is Drafting?

When you draft, you just get your ideas down on paper. Don't worry about mistakes or messiness because this will be a **working draft**.

- Think about your purpose and your audience as you write.
- Add more details as you go along. Good ideas can come at any time.
- If you change your mind, don't start over. Cross out what you don't like, and keep writing!

How Do I Draft My Paper?

Write sentences and paragraphs. Start with the plan you made when you organized your ideas. Turn the words and phrases into sentences. Each section should make at least one paragraph. Most paragraphs will need a topic sentence. The **topic sentence** tells the main idea.

Write a beginning and an ending. Write a beginning that introduces your topic and makes your audience want to read about it. Write an ending that tells an overall impression or makes a final comment about your topic.

Make transitions. Use transitional words and phrases to tie your sentences and paragraphs together.

Ways to Make Transitions	
Try this!	**Look at these examples.**
Show time relationships.	before, after, finally, then, next, until, when, often, soon, since, while, as, meanwhile, eventually, at last, afterward, tomorrow, Wednesday
Show cause and effect.	because, as a result, so that, therefore, if…then, thus, consequently, due to, for this reason, in response to
Show spatial relationships.	above, around, down, here, there, beside, inside, outside, over, under, in front, behind, lowest, underneath, nearest
Indicate comparison and contrast.	however, although, in contrast, similarly, unlike, instead
Show degree of importance.	above all, better, best, equally important, of less importance, worse, worst, worst of all, strongest, weakest
Introduce another idea.	also, too, another, in addition, furthermore, moreover, for example, besides, nevertheless

Drafting a Description

Learning from a Model Bethany wrote her first draft. She thought of a beginning that would make her readers curious. Then she began with the part of her Observation Chart that she had numbered *1: Smell*. She wrote a topic sentence for her first group of details. Then she used her chart to write her other sentences and paragraphs. She didn't worry about mistakes at this stage.

Do you know what my favorite place is? ~~Well I'll tell you.~~ It's Tap into your senses, and see if you can guess.

My eyes don't have to be open and I know where I am, for the smell is so familar. I walk in the door and the aroma of cooking food fills my nostrals As I take a seat at the counter, I can smell the lilies arranged in they're blue glass vase their scent makes me slightly dizzy.

I ~~get~~ ask for my usual drink, a cherry cola. I grip the glass. I stroke the smooth marble counter. I sip my soda and I can feel the bubbles ~~really~~ popping on my tongue, as the syrup slides down my throat.

▲ Part of Bethany's working draft

▶ Draft Your Description

❶ Write an interesting beginning that introduces your topic.

❷ Use your Observation Chart to write the rest of your paper. For each paragraph, think of the main idea and write a topic sentence. Write other sentences to fill in the details about the main idea. Use transitional words and phrases.

❸ End by telling an overall impression or making a final comment about your topic.

Don't worry about mistakes. Just write!

What Is Revising?

When you revise, you make changes to your draft to make it clearer or more interesting. Ask yourself the Big Questions. Don't worry about fixing mistakes yet.

How Do I Make Revisions?

Don't erase! Make changes right on your draft. Don't worry if your paper looks messy, as you can make a clean copy later. Here are ways to make your changes.

Revising: The Big Questions

- Did I say what I wanted to say?
- Did I elaborate and use details?
- Did I organize the facts, events, or ideas clearly?
- Did I write in a way that is interesting and appropriate to my audience?

> After drafting, wait a day or two before you rewrite.

Ways to Mark Your Revisions

Try this!	Look at these examples.
Cross out parts that you want to change or take out.	The music at the concert was ~~really loud,~~ ear-splittingly loud.
Use carets to add new words or sentences.	He called his parents three times ∧ from camp. *in one day*
Draw circles and arrows to move words, sentences, or paragraphs.	(Don't risk serious head injury.) Always wear a helmet while riding your bike.
Use numbers to show how sentences should be ordered.	②Did I really have to read this? ①The book seemed so long. ③Once I started it, though, I couldn't put it down.
Add attachments to show sentences that won't fit on your paper.	Laurie burst out laughing and handed the envelope to me. The note was so ridiculous. *Pretty soon we were both laughing so hard, tears came to our eyes.*

Revising a Description

Learning from a Model Bethany reread her working draft. To help her readers imagine the restaurant more clearly, she elaborated by adding exact words and sensory details. She also added a comparison.

Do you know what my favorite place is? ~~Well I'll tell you. It's~~ Tap into your

senses, and see if you can guess.

   My eyes don't have to be open and I know where I am, for the smell

      steaming soup, baking bread, and frying vegetables

is so familar. I walk in the door and the aroma of ~~cooking food~~ fills my

      sticky-sweet perfume of the

nostrals As I take a seat at the counter, I can smell the lilies arranged

in they're blue glass vase their scent makes me slightly dizzy.

I ~~get~~ ask for my usual drink, a cherry cola. I grip the glass. I stroke the

My fingers glide and then bump over a crack, like a skater tripping on ice.

smooth marble counter. I sip my soda and I can feel the bubbles ~~really~~

popping on my tongue, as the syrup slides down my throat.

▲ **Part of Bethany's revised draft**

▶ Revise Your Description

Reread your description. Use the Revising Checklist to help you evaluate your description and make changes. Don't worry about mistakes yet.

> Remember to use transitional words and phrases to connect your sentences and paragraphs.

Revising Checklist

✔ Did I introduce my topic in an interesting way?
✔ Did I write good topic sentences?
✔ Do my details support the topic sentence in each paragraph?
✔ Did I order the details in a way that makes sense?
✔ Where do I need to add sensory words?
✔ Does my ending tell an overall impression or make a final comment?

📖 See the Thesaurus Plus on page H96.

What Is a Writing Conference?

In a writing conference, a writer reads his or her paper to a partner or a group. The listeners tell what they like, ask questions, and make suggestions. Your conference partners might be a classmate, a small group, your teacher, or someone who knows about your topic.

How Do I Have a Writing Conference?

In a writing conference, you will be either the writer or the listener. Use the following guidelines to help you do your best in either role.

Guidelines for Having a Writing Conference	
When You're the Writer . . .	**When You're the Listener . . .**
• Read your paper aloud clearly. Use an appropriate volume and rate. • Pay attention to your listeners' comments and suggestions. Keep an open mind. • Take notes to remember any compliments, questions, or suggestions. • Reread your paper after the conference. • Use your notes. Make any other changes you want.	• Look at the writer. • Listen carefully. Don't let your thoughts wander. • Retell what you have heard. • Then tell two things that you like about the paper. • Next, ask questions about things you don't understand. • Finally, give one or two suggestions to help the writer. • Always be positive and polite.

That paragraph is very well organized.

I love how clearly you describe your feelings at the end.

These details are so vivid.

Always start with what the writer did well.

Having a Writing Conference

Learning from a Model Bethany had a conference with her classmate Julio.

▶ **Have Your Writing Conference**

❶ **Find** a partner or a small group, and have a writing conference. Use the guidelines on page 24.

❷ **Use** your conference notes to make any other changes you want.

What Is Proofreading?

When you proofread, you correct spelling, capitalization, and punctuation. You also check that you have used words correctly, written complete sentences, and indented paragraphs.

How Do I Proofread?

Use these ideas to help you proofread.

- Proofread for one skill at a time.
- Circle words that might be misspelled. Check spellings in a class dictionary.
- Use proofreading marks to mark your corrections.

Proofreading Marks		
Try this!	**Here's when.**	**Look at these examples.**
¶	to begin a new paragraph; to indent the paragraph	¶Filling out the job application didn't take her long. She also gave the store a list of her previous jobs.
∧	to add letters, words, or sentences	The pony careened around the pasture and jumped over the fence.
∧ (comma)	to add a comma	Because it took him so long to walk to school, Jackson was always late.
⌄ ⌄ (quotes)	to add quotation marks	"What I need," she said, "is a bike."
⊙	to add a period	Jennifer ransacked her room looking for the ring. It was gone.
~ (delete)	to take out words, sentences, and punctuation marks; to correct spelling	The closet overflowed with ~~clothes,~~ dresses, pants, and blouses.
/	to change a capital letter to a small letter	Our Principal sang a song in public.
≡	to change a small letter to a capital letter	That rocket will investigate whether there is life on mars.
∼	to reverse letters or words	The security gaurds looked bored.

Proofreading a Description

Learning from a Model Bethany made more changes after talking with Julio. After revising her paper so that it read the way she wanted, she proofread it.

¶Do you know what my favorite place is? ~~Well I'll tell you.~~ It'sTap into your

senses, and see if you can guess.

My eyes don't have to be open,and I know where I am, for the smell
is so familiar. I walk in the door, and the aroma of ~~cooking food~~ fills my
  steaming soup, baking bread, and frying vegetables
nostrils As I take a seat at the counter, I can smell the lilies arranged
  sticky-sweet perfume of the
in ~~they're~~ blue glass vase, their scent makes me slightly dizzy.
  their
¶I ~~get~~ ask for my usual drink, a cherry cola. I grip the glass, I stroke the
  ; it's slippery and damp and gives me a chill
smooth marble counter. I sip my soda,and I can feel the bubbles ~~really~~
  My fingers glide and then bump over a crack, like a skater tripping on ice.

popping on my tongue, as the syrup slides down my throat.

▲ **Part of Bethany's proofread draft**

▶ Proofread Your Description

Proofread your description, using the Proofreading Checklist. Use the proofreading marks shown on page 26.

Proofreading Checklist

Did I
- ✔ indent all paragraphs?
- ✔ use complete sentences?
- ✔ use capital letters and punctuation correctly?
- ✔ use the correct form of adjectives when comparing?
- ✔ use commas correctly?
- ✔ correct any spelling errors?

📖 Use the Guide to Capitalization, Punctuation, and Usage on page H64 and the Spelling Guide on page H80 for help.

What Is Publishing?

When you publish your writing, you share it with your audience.

How Do I Publish My Writing?

Here are some ideas for sharing your writing.

Write It Down

- Send your paper as a letter or an e-mail to friends or family.
- Submit your paper to a magazine or an Internet site that publishes student writing.
- Create a collection of writing with your classmates.
- Submit your paper to the school newspaper.

Talk It Up

- Record your paper on audiotape. Send it to a faraway friend or relative.
- Present your paper as a speech or an oral report.
- Read your paper as part of a panel discussion or a debate.

Show It Off

- Illustrate your writing with photographs or drawings.
- Read your paper aloud on a video "broadcast."
- Make a poster and attach your paper to it.
- Show slides about your topic to the class while reading your paper aloud.

Tech Tip

Make a multimedia presentation. See page H53 for ideas.

▶ How Do I Reflect on My Writing?

When you reflect, you think about what you have written. You can think about what you did well, what you could do better next time, and what your goals are for your next writing assignment.

> Reflecting is rewarding! You'll get new writing ideas, and you'll realize how much you've learned from the writing you've done.

 You might want to keep a collection of some of your writing, such as favorite or unusual pieces.

Publishing a Description

Learning from a Model Bethany made a final copy of her description and submitted it to her school newspaper.

Bethany Braun

My Second Home
by Bethany Braun

Do you know what my favorite place is? Tap into your senses, and see if you can guess.

Opening with a question makes your readers curious.

My eyes don't have to be open, and I know where I am, for the smell is so familiar. I walk in the door, and the aroma of steaming soup, baking bread, and frying vegetables fills my nostrils. As I take a seat at the counter, I can smell the sticky-sweet perfume of the lilies arranged in their blue glass vase. Their scent makes me slightly dizzy.

I ask for my usual drink, a cherry cola. I grip the glass; it's slippery and damp and gives me a chill. I stroke the smooth marble counter. My fingers glide and then bump over a crack, like a skater tripping on ice. I sip my soda, and I can feel the bubbles popping on my tongue as the syrup slides down my throat.

Great comparison! I can almost feel this myself.

The lights are dimmed. I look down and see the old yellow tile floor aging by the second. I look up and see the antique crystal chandelier glistening. Three brown ceiling fans are spinning at a brisk pace, and I wonder what it would be like to swing from one of them.

This restaurant that my father manages has in a way become my second home. I love it here. I walk out into what now seems like a boring world.

Telling how you feel makes the paper feel finished.

▶ Publish Your Description

Make a neat final copy of your description, and give it an interesting title. Then publish or share your description. Look at page 28 for ideas.

Will you keep this description? Use the paragraph on page 28 to help you reflect on your writing experience.

Part 1

Grammar, Usage, and Mechanics

What You Will Find in This Part:

Learn Grammar?

Informal Language

When you're talking with family or friends, you might use informal language that may not follow all the rules of standard English. All that matters, though, is that everyone understands each other.

Similarly, when you write journal entries, notes, or other personal writing, it doesn't matter whether every word or punctuation mark is correct.

MARCH
29

fishing with Grandpa-
6:00AM

611 Acorn Circle
Peterstown, MD 12345
February 19, 2001

...ved by last week's blizzard. Some families were
left temporarily homeless and have to stay in shelters.
Other families are in their homes; but they are struggling
without heat, electricity, or water. My classmates and
I would like to do something to help out the storm
victims. Will you allow us to have a food and clothing drive
in the town hall?

We would like to hold this event this Saturday.
Most of the students have already talked to their
parents and to the local merchants about the drive.
Everyone seems excited, and we think it will be a very
successful event. Please let us know if we can go ahead
with our plans.

Thank you for considering our request.

Yours truly,
Albert Collier
Albert Collier

Formal Language

However, in class and in many life situations, formal English is often expected. You use it when you apply for a job, speak with people in a workplace, or write for an audience.

This section of the book will help you develop your ability to use formal language when you need it.

The Sentence

Are my eyes playing tricks
on me? I see the summit.
How close it looks! Tell me
I'm not dreaming.

Kinds of Sentences

One-Minute Warm-Up

"What on earth were you doing with the cymbals during the soprano's solo?"

Make three more sentences to complete this dialogue. The first should be a statement, the second a command, and the third an expression of strong emotion.

A **sentence** is a group of words that expresses a complete thought. A sentence begins with a capital letter and ends with a punctuation mark. There are four kinds of sentences.

1. A **declarative sentence** makes a statement and ends with a period.

   Ben is a great singer.   Music is enjoyable.

2. An **interrogative sentence** asks a question and ends with a question mark.

   Isn't Ben a great singer?   Who is singing tonight?

3. An **imperative sentence** makes a command or a request and ends with a period.

   Come in, please.   Maria, don't be late.

4. An **exclamatory sentence** expresses strong feeling and ends with an exclamation point.

   What a great concert that was!   These distractions must end!

HELP
? Tip

Do not overuse the exclamation point. Too many exclamation points can make your writing ineffective.

You can make any type of sentence exclamatory by punctuating it with an exclamation point to express strong feeling.

   Music is enjoyable!   Isn't Ben a great singer!

Try It Out

Speak Up What kind of sentence is each of the following?

1. We're late for dress rehearsal.
2. Please stay calm, Anna.
3. Couldn't we start?
4. How impatient you are!

more ▶

What punctuation mark should end each sentence?
What kind of sentence is it?

5. Watch her face carefully
6. The lights are on her
7. Is her voice quivering
8. How radiant she looks

Summing Up

- **Declarative sentences** make statements and end with periods.

- **Interrogative sentences** ask questions and end with question marks.

- **Imperative sentences** make commands or requests and end with periods.

- **Exclamatory sentences** express strong feelings and end with exclamation points.

On Your Own

Write each sentence, adding the correct end punctuation. Then label each sentence *declarative, interrogative, imperative,* or *exclamatory.*

Example: Do you like the theater   *Do you like the theater?   interrogative*

9. Are you watching the play
10. Why are you making a face
11. Please pay attention
12. How great this performance is
13. Don't applaud yet
14. Good drama certainly is thrilling
15. It's exciting and entertaining
16. Try to see more plays
17. You seem to like the theater
18. Have you seen the comedy at the Plaza

more ▶

19. What an amusing play it is
20. Good comedy makes me feel terrific
21. Musicals are also fun
22. I prefer serious plays
23. They give you more to think about
24. Go see *The Juggler*
25. Tell me what you think of it
26. Will you remember to tell me

27–35. Write each of the nine sentences in this movie review, adding the correct end punctuation. Then label each sentence *declarative, interrogative, imperative,* or *exclamatory.*

Example: Believe it or not, I would see it again
        Believe it or not, I would see it again!   exclamatory

The Juggler

★ ★ ★ ½

The comedy at the Plaza is called *The Juggler* Do you think the heroine of the film is a circus performer No, she's a working mother of two young boys, living in Chicago What is her profession She's chief of police The movie centers on her struggle as she tries to fulfill home and work responsibilities Imagine the conflicts that arise The movie is brilliantly written, and the comedic acting sparkles Go see *The Juggler*

Writing Wrap-Up   WRITING · THINKING · LISTENING · SPEAKING

INFORMING / EXPRESSING

Write a Review
Write a paragraph reviewing a movie, play, or TV show you really like or dislike. Use each kind of sentence—*declarative, interrogative, imperative,* and *exclamatory*—at least once. Read your review to a partner, and discuss it together. What types of sentences does it contain? Does their variety contribute to the effectiveness of the review?

For Extra Practice see page 72.

2 Complete Subjects and Complete Predicates

One-Minute Warm-Up

Read the description of the cook below. What's wrong with it?

The cook in the Cuban restaurant next door. Smiled as he chopped the vegetables.

1. In order to express a complete thought, a sentence must have two parts, a subject and a predicate. The **subject** tells whom or what the sentence is about. The **predicate** tells what the subject is, does, has, or feels.

Subject	Predicate
People	eat.
Most people in America	eat three meals every day.

2. The **complete subject** includes a noun or a pronoun and the words and phrases that describe it. The **complete predicate** contains a verb or a verb phrase and all the words that complete its meaning.

People in some countries	eat seafood.
Prince Edward Island	is famous for its oysters.
You	should try this specialty.

3. Sometimes the complete subject or the complete predicate or both are just one word.

Fish	swim.

Try It Out

Speak Up What are the complete subject and the complete predicate in each sentence?

1. Students in every class are now preparing projects for the fair.
2. Two English classes are performing *Julius Caesar.*
3. Some of the students in Ms. Solano's social studies class have photographed flags of many nations.

more ▶

4. One of the students has built a miniature house.
5. Susan's class baked whole-wheat bread in the shapes of hearts and clover leaves.
6. Julia has designed colorful programs.
7. Students from other schools will be coming.
8. We are looking forward to the event.

Summing Up

- Every sentence has a **subject** and a **predicate**.
- The **complete subject** tells whom or what the sentence is about.
- The **complete predicate** tells what the subject is, does, has, or feels.

On Your Own

Write each sentence. Draw a line between the complete subject and the complete predicate.

Example: Every cloud has a silver lining.
Every cloud | has a silver lining.

9. The weather had been hot and dry.
10. The people of Clayville did not expect a rainstorm.
11. The first drops fell at dusk.
12. Mist turned to light rain.
13. The light rain had become a downpour by dawn.
14. A steady rain fell for almost two days.
15. The rain was extremely welcome after so many weeks of dry weather.
16. Many of the residents of Clayville had been worried about the lack of rain.
17. The heavy rainfall produced good results for the farmers and their summer crops.
18. Many plants began recovery.
19. Fruit trees produced new buds.

more ▶

20. The children of Clayville also enjoyed the results of the rain.
21. Many of the children swam in the pond for the first time this summer.
22. Cows, sheep, and goats reaped the benefits of the lush new growth of grasses.
23. Everything in the town of Clayville now looks cleaner, brighter, and practically new.
24. People with yards can return to watering their lawns, flower gardens, and vegetable patches.

25–32. Write each of the eight sentences in this paragraph from a gardening column. Draw a line between the complete subject and the complete predicate.

Example: All of Clayville breathed a sigh of relief as the rain fell.
All of Clayville | breathed a sigh of relief as the rain fell.

Clayville's Relief

Last week's long-awaited rain breathed new life into Clayville. It brought taller cornstalks and healthier tomato plants. Squash vines grew thick and strong. Some of the town's apple trees began to produce fruit. The local reservoir is full once more. All you gardeners can rejoice! Temporary restrictions on watering lawns and flower beds have been lifted. Our roses—and weeds—will thrive again.

Writing Wrap-Up

WRITING • THINKING • LISTENING • SPEAKING

DESCRIBING

Write a Description

Interview a classmate about an experience he or she has had in a storm. Write a paragraph describing that experience. Then read the description aloud to your classmate. Have your classmate select the most descriptive subject and predicate in your paragraph.

3 Simple Subjects and Simple Predicates

Find the simple subject and the simple predicate in the sentence below.

Worldwide, farmers harvest more than 26 million tons of peanuts a year.

—from *The Life and Times of the Peanut,* by Charles Micucci

1. You have learned that the complete subject contains the words that name and describe the subject. The key word or words in the complete subject are called the **simple subject**. The simple subject tells whom or what the sentence is about and is usually a noun or a pronoun.

   Peanuts in their natural state   are good for you.

   Carver's discoveries   made peanuts important.

   They   grow in shells.

2. The simple subject may be the same as the complete subject.

   Oil   is a peanut product.

   George Washington Carver   experimented with peanuts.

   He   made many products.

3. The **simple predicate** is the key word or words in the complete predicate that tell what the subject is, does, has, or feels. The simple predicate is always either a verb or a verb phrase.

   Peanut products   contain a variety of compounds.

   Peanuts   have been important for years.

   Peanuts   were used for many purposes.

4. The simple predicate may be interrupted by other words.

   We   have often wondered about the origin of peanuts.

   We   have now done research.

5. In some sentences the simple predicate and the complete predicate may be the same.

   Peanut crop pests   must be controlled.

Speak Up Find the simple subject and the simple predicate in each sentence. The complete subject and the complete predicate are separated by a line.

1. One potato | can supply half your daily vitamin C.
2. Many B vitamins | are found in a potato as well.
3. Sailors | once ate raw potatoes as prevention against disease.
4. A research institute in Peru | feeds potatoes to babies.
5. A medium potato without butter | does not have many calories.

Summing Up

- The **simple subject** is the key word in the complete subject. It is usually a noun or a pronoun.

- The **simple predicate** is the verb or verb phrase in the complete predicate that tells what the subject is, does, has, or feels.

Write each sentence. Underline the simple subject once and the simple predicate twice. The complete subject and the complete predicate are separated by a line.

Example: The potato | is a familiar vegetable.
        The potato | is a familiar vegetable.

6. This popular vegetable | first appeared in Peru.
7. Many types of potato | grew in South America.
8. It | was brought to Spain by sixteenth-century explorers.
9. The vegetable | seemed strange to Europeans.
10. It | grew particularly well in Ireland.
11. The people's diet | became dependent on the potato.
12. The potato crop | failed in the 1840s because of disease.
13. Thousands of Irish | were forced away from their homeland.

more ▶

14. Many people | left Ireland for America.
15. China | now grows more potatoes than any other country.
16. The people of Russia | call potatoes their second bread.
17. Every state in the United States | grows potatoes.
18. Most potatoes | are grown on large northern farms.

19–25. The paragraph below from a student's report has seven sentences. Write the simple subject and the simple predicate of each sentence. Draw a line between them.

Example: An amazing variety of potatoes can be found in Peru.
variety | can be found

Report

Potatoes in Peru

Some form of potato has been growing in Peru for centuries. The native language of Peru contains more than two hundred words for the potato. Inca farmers grew potatoes in the valleys of the Andes more than four hundred years ago. From the potatoes they made *chuño*. Chuño is freeze-dried potatoes. Fertile farmland is scarce in Peru. Nevertheless, Peruvian farmers still grow potatoes in many shapes and colors.

Writing Wrap-Up   WRITING • THINKING • LISTENING • SPEAKING

DESCRIBING / EXPRESSING

Write a Letter to the Editor

Suppose you have created a new and unusual recipe and served it to company. Write a letter to the food editor of a newspaper, describing your creation and your guests' reaction. In a small group, read your letters aloud.

For Extra Practice see page 74.

4 Finding the Subject

One-Minute Warm-Up

Find the subject in each of these sentences.
On the branch sits the smiling Cheshire Cat.
Remaining in the air above the branch is the cat's smile.

1. Most sentences that you write are in **natural order**: the subject comes before the predicate. Sometimes you write sentences in **inverted order**: the subject follows all or part of the complete predicate.

   Into the tree flew a bird.

   Out of the woods came the Mad Hatter.

   Lying on top of a mushroom was a caterpillar.

2. Interrogative sentences are usually in inverted order.

   Could the caterpillar speak?

   When would it speak to Alice?

3. Whenever you want to find the subject of an inverted sentence, try rearranging the words into their natural order.

   The Mad Hatter came out of the woods.

   A caterpillar was lying on top of a mushroom.

   The caterpillar could speak.

   It would speak to Alice when?

4. Most sentences that begin with the introductory word *there* or *here* are also in inverted order.

   There was a caterpillar near Alice.

   Here is a butterfly.

5. To find the subject of a sentence beginning with *there* or *here,* locate the verb, and ask the question *who?* or *what?* about it.

   What was near Alice? A caterpillar was.

6. Imperative sentences are in natural order, but the subject usually does not appear in the sentence. The subject *you* is understood. The subject remains *you* even when the name of the person is used.

   (You) Peer through the looking glass.

   Alice, (you) watch the cat.

7. Some sentences in natural order begin with words other than the subject.

> In the book a strange character appears.
>
> At the end of the story, Alice awakens.

Again, to find the subject, locate the verb first, and ask the question *who?* or *what?* about it.

Try It Out

Speak Up What is the simple subject of each sentence?

1. On a branch of the tree sat a cat.
2. Nearby lived the Mad Hatter.
3. There was the March Hare at the party.
4. Also attending the party was a dormouse.
5. How does the book end?
6. Read the book for the complete story.

Summing Up

- To find the subject of a sentence in **inverted order**, rearrange the subject and the predicate into their **natural order**, or ask the question *who?* or *what?* about the verb.

- The subject of an imperative sentence is understood to be *you*.

On Your Own

Write the simple subject of each sentence.

Example: There is my mother's copy of *Alice's Adventures in Wonderland* by Lewis Carroll. *copy*

7. Have you read Lewis Carroll's most famous book?
8. Please lend it to me.
9. When will you return it?
10. At the assembly I can give it to you.
11. Do you know the author's real name?

more ▶

12. On the back of the book's jacket, there is a picture of the author.
13. Inez, tell me his name.
14. It was Charles Dodgson.
15. Below the picture is some biographical information.
16. Read it now, please.
17. Do you see the picture of the writer?
18. What an amazing story he wrote!

19–25. Write the simple subject of each of the seven sentences in this book-jacket biography.

Example: From the imagination of an Oxford mathematician came this
classic of children's literature. *classic*

Charles Lutwidge Dodgson
(Lewis Carroll)

Charles Lutwidge Dodgson was the eldest of eleven children and grew up to become a professor of mathematics at Oxford University. He might well have been remembered for his contributions to mathematics. However, Dodgson's true fame came from writing children's books under the pen name Lewis Carroll. Among his young friends were the Liddell children. From his friendship with Alice Liddell came the idea for *Alice's Adventures in Wonderland*. Here is Lewis Carroll at his most inspired. Still unmatched in all their mad variety are the inhabitants of Wonderland.

Writing Wrap-Up

WRITING • THINKING • LISTENING • SPEAKING

PERSUADING

Write Copy for a Poster

Write some sentences for a poster advertising a book, either real or imaginary, for young people. Begin one sentence with *here* or *there*. Begin one sentence with *in* or *at*. Make one of your sentences a question. Find a partner, and read your sentences aloud to each other. Work together to name the subject of each sentence.

5 Compound Subjects and Compound Predicates

Write a single sentence, using two verbs to describe actions you see in the picture.

A sentence can include two or more simple subjects, two or more simple predicates, or both.

1. Two or more simple subjects with the same predicate form a **compound subject**.

   Pablo and Erin are running.

2. Two or more simple predicates with the same subject form a **compound predicate.**

   Sue Lee tried out and made the team. Cindy Page tried out but did not make it.

3. A sentence may also have both a compound subject and a compound predicate.

   The captain, the co-captain, or the coach ran and fell.

4. Sentences in inverted order also may have compound subjects and predicates.

   Compound Subject: Here are Aaron and Kenshiro.
   Compound Predicate: Are they laughing or crying?

5. The parts of a compound subject or of a compound predicate are usually joined by *and, but,* or *or.*

Try It Out

Speak Up What are the compound subjects and the compound predicates in these sentences?

1. Alissa and Ed ran but did not jump.
2. Martha Perkins will not practice or work on her form tonight.
3. There may be rain, sleet, or snow for tomorrow's meet.

more ▶

4. Jill and Joe left the house quite early today.
5. Here are their new track shoes and shirts for the meet.
6. Nita and Felipe have been planning a team trip for weeks.
7. Did the coach or a teacher go along?
8. Mr. Wills will go but will not stay the whole time.
9. Are the runners, the gymnasts, or the jumpers competing now?

Summing Up

- A **compound subject** is made up of two or more simple subjects that have the same predicate.

- A **compound predicate** is made up of two or more simple predicates that have the same subject.

On Your Own

Write each sentence. Underline each simple subject once and each simple predicate twice. Label each sentence *compound subject, compound predicate,* or *both*.

Example: The runner crossed the finish line and grinned.
  The <u>runner</u> <u>crossed</u> the finish line and <u>grinned</u>.
  compound predicate

10. The meet began with the coach's lengthy speech and ended with an hour-long parade.
11. On the sidelines were my parents and my cousin.
12. There, too, were my sister and her friend.
13. Would Jamal, Karen, Daryl, or Mei Ling be the winner?
14. Kelly trained, ran, and finished the race alone.
15. The parade honored the team and lasted for an hour.
16. Four bands and a juggler were part of the parade.
17. David and Keisha go to the parade every year but stay only a very short time.
18. Did Phil and Carmen give you their report on parades?
19. They gave an oral report and also showed slides.

more ▶

20. In 3000 B.C., citizens built special streets and held processions.
21. A festival or a military display was often an occasion for a parade.
22. Circus performers marched and danced in the processions.

23–28. Write the six sentences in this paragraph from a magazine article. Underline each simple subject once and each simple predicate twice. Label each sentence *compound subject, compound predicate,* or *both.*

Example: The Olympic games of ancient Greece were held on sacred land and had a religious character.
The Olympic games of ancient Greece <u>were held</u> on sacred land and <u>had</u> a religious character. compound predicate

The Glory of Greece

In 1896 King George I of Greece stood in a new stadium in Athens and opened the first modern Olympic games. The United States and many other countries sent their best athletes. Greece was well represented and hoped to excel in the revived games. Athletes from the United States, however, dominated the track-and-field competition and won nine events. Then in the marathon at the end of the games, Spiridon Loues from Greece finished first and upheld the honor of his country. The stadium and the hills around rang and echoed with cheers.

Writing Wrap-Up

WRITING • THINKING • LISTENING • SPEAKING

INTERVIEWING

Write Interview Questions

Write interview questions that you might ask a famous athlete or other celebrity. Include a question with a compound subject, a question with a compound predicate, and a question with both. Exchange papers with a partner, and write answers to each other's questions. Again, use compound subjects and compound predicates. Role-play your interviews for a small group.

 For Extra Practice see page 76.

Forming Compound Subjects and Compound Predicates

Combining Sentences Sentences that repeat the same words can sound awkward and repetitious. You can make your writing more effective by combining related subjects. Use the word *and* or *or* to form a compound subject.

The pitcher helps the team.

The shortstop helps the team too.
}
The pitcher and the shortstop help the team.

You can also combine related predicates. Use the word *and, but,* or *or* to form a compound predicate.

My soccer team jogs daily.

My soccer team also drills daily.
}
My soccer team jogs and drills daily.

> Remember to use plural verbs with plural subjects.

Apply It

1–5. Combine each pair of sentences on these cards for a bulletin-board display. Form a compound subject or a compound predicate.

Revising

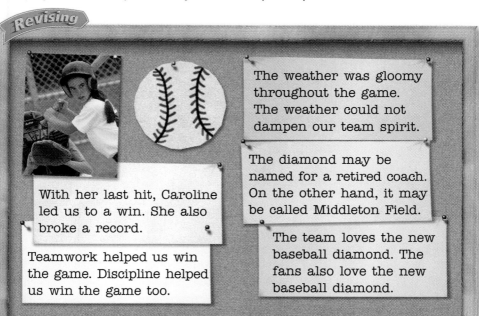

The weather was gloomy throughout the game. The weather could not dampen our team spirit.

With her last hit, Caroline led us to a win. She also broke a record.

The diamond may be named for a retired coach. On the other hand, it may be called Middleton Field.

Teamwork helped us win the game. Discipline helped us win the game too.

The team loves the new baseball diamond. The fans also love the new baseball diamond.

Elaborating Sentences Add detail to your sentences by replacing one general word with two or more exact words. You can do this by expanding simple subjects and simple predicates into compound subjects and compound predicates.

Too general:	The teams have often won regional championships.
More exact:	The football team and the field hockey team have often won regional championships.
Too general:	For the entire season, we worked together as a team.
More exact:	For the entire season, we practiced and competed together as a team.

Apply It

6–10. Revise this draft of an article for the school newspaper. Imagine you saw the game described below. Elaborate the underlined words by forming a compound subject or a compound predicate.

Revising

SPORTS CORNER

Bobcats Roar Past Eagles in 3–2 Victory

Students packed the bleachers at the soccer field. <u>Adults</u> took up whatever space was left. After the kickoff, Rosa Morales <u>got</u> the ball downfield to a teammate. Soon, Morales scored the first goal for the Bobcats. The audience <u>cheered</u>.

The Eagles, led by Heather Jones, came back with two goals in the second half. The Bobcats' coach shouted to the players. Then Jones tripped and fell. She <u>left</u> the field. The Bobcats pushed ahead for the win. <u>Several things</u> helped them achieve victory.

Rosa Morales about to score

Compound Sentences

Will Sam perform well? forget his lines? trip on his long robe? lose his voice?

Take turns making sentences about Sam's first acting experience. Each sentence must have the word *and, but,* or *or*.

Simple Sentences

1. A **simple sentence** expresses one complete idea.

   The main characters in ancient Greek dramas were at the mercy of their fate.

2. A simple sentence can have a compound subject, a compound predicate, or both.

   Clotho, Lachesis, and Atropos were the goddesses of fate. (compound subject)

   They created the fabric of each life and scheduled its end. (compound predicate)

   Clotho, Lachesis, and Atropos spun, decided the length of, and cut the thread of life. (compound subject and compound predicate)

Compound Sentences

1. A **compound sentence** expresses two or more complete ideas that are related and are equal in importance. If a sentence is compound, it can always be separated into two or more simple sentences.

   The Trojan War lasted ten years, and Troy was destroyed.

2. Connect the simple sentences in a compound sentence with a conjunction, or connecting word, such as *and, but,* or *or*. Use a comma between the joined sentences unless the sentences are very short and closely related.

   Helen was the wife of a Greek king, and Paris, a prince of Troy, kidnapped her.
   She was freed and he was killed.

3. You may also join simple sentences with a semicolon alone.

   A champion among warriors fought for the Greeks; his name was Achilles.

Speak Up Identify each sentence as *simple* or *compound.*

Homer

1. Homer was a Greek poet; he probably lived around 700 B.C.
2. Homer's two epic poems became the basic textbook for every young Greek.
3. In the mid-1200s B.C., Greece and the city of Troy fought a war.
4. Several centuries later, Homer wrote the *Iliad,* and he also wrote the *Odyssey.*
5. The *Iliad* describes three weeks of battle during the Trojan War; its subject is the rage of Achilles.
6. Achilles is a very angry man and has only one real friend.
7. Patroclus, the friend of Achilles, is killed, and the warrior's wrath explodes.
8. Athena, goddess of war, sides with Achilles and helps him defeat Troy.

Summing Up

- A **compound sentence** is made up of two or more **simple sentences** joined by a conjunction such as *and, but,* or *or.*
- A comma usually separates the parts of a compound sentence.

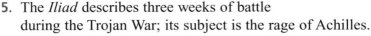

Identify each sentence as *simple* or *compound.*

Example: The *Odyssey,* Homer's other epic poem, tells of the wanderings of the king of Ithaca. *simple*

9. In the *Odyssey,* Homer describes what happens to Odysseus, another Greek hero of the Trojan War.
10. After the war, Odysseus wants to go home to his wife in Ithaca, but first he must travel for ten years.

more ▶

11. The goddess Circe tempts Odysseus with luxury, and he stays with her one year.
12. The Sirens call to him with an offer of knowledge of the future, but he has himself tied to his ship's mast and resists their call.
13. Then he stays with the goddess Calypso for seven years, and she offers him immortality.
14. At last, Odysseus leaves Calypso; he chooses to be human and rejoins his family.

15–18. Rewrite this paragraph from a speech in a Greek drama. Correct the four errors in punctuation.

Example: Mothers and daughters laughed near the washing pools and they were happy.

Mothers and daughters laughed near the washing pools, and they were happy.

Proofreading

ACHILLES AND HECTOR

Once there was peace and beauty in Troy but the war has changed all that. The Greeks attacked, they showed no mercy. Hector fought Patroclus in a furious battle; he killed Patroclus. Then Hector tried to avoid Achilles's revenge. The goddess Athena offered her help to Hector but she was secretly on Achilles's side. Alas, brave Hector was slain by Achilles and his body was dragged in the dust.

Writing Wrap-Up WRITING • THINKING • LISTENING • SPEAKING

CREATING / EXPRESSING

Write Dialogue

Write several lines of dialogue for a conversation between friends as they leave the movie theater. Use only compound sentences. Working in groups of three, read one another's pieces aloud. Is the dialogue effective? Does it sound like real people talking? Are all the sentences compound?

7 Conjunctions

One-Minute Warm-Up

Read the sentences. Notice whether each verb is singular or plural.

Either a lady or a tiger is behind the door.

Neither a lady nor a tiger is behind the door.

Both a lady and a tiger are behind the door.

Explain what each sentence says about whether a lady or a tiger is behind the door.

You have seen how a connecting word, or a conjunction, connects two or more simple sentences in a compound sentence. You can also use conjunctions to join words. A **conjunction** is a word that joins words or groups of words. A **coordinating conjunction** connects related words or word groups that have the same function in a sentence.

Compound Subject:	Carol and Brian have arrived.
Compound Predicate:	Carol may dance but will not sing.
Compound Modifier:	The guests are happy yet quiet.
Compound Sentences:	Ron will sing, for Carol will play piano.
	Sam will not dance, nor will he juggle.
	Maria is artistic, so she will decorate.

Coordinating Conjunctions						
and	but	or	nor	for	yet	so

Like coordinating conjunctions, **correlative conjunctions** join words or word groups. Correlative conjunctions appear in pairs and are more forceful and precise than coordinating conjunctions.

Neither Lin nor Thom has arrived.

Either the car will start, or Jim will jump-start it.

Whether it rains or snows, we will go.

Correlative Conjunctions	
either . . . or	not only . . . but (also)
neither . . . nor	whether . . . or
both . . . and	just as . . . so

Speak Up What are the conjunctions in these sentences?

1. The molar tooth of an elephant measures about a foot and weighs eight or nine pounds.
2. Most cow elephants and bull elephants have tusks.
3. An elephant may eat over five hundred pounds of food and may drink fifty gallons of water a day.

Write conjunctions to complete the sentences.

4. The two species of elephant are Indian _____ African.
5. The Indian elephant is about nine feet tall, _____ the African elephant can be as tall as thirteen feet.
6. Both Indian _____ African elephants are very intelligent.
7. Elephants are in great danger from habitat destruction, _____ conservation measures are necessary.

Summing Up

- **Coordinating conjunctions**, such as *and, but,* and *or,* join words or word groups that have the same function.
- **Correlative conjunctions**, such as *neither . . . nor,* are pairs of conjunctions that connect related words or word groups.

Write the conjunctions from these sentences.

Example: Tigers once roamed much of Asia, but now some species are extinct.   *but*

8. Their numbers have decreased, yet some tigers survive.
9. Tigers usually live near water and can swim very well.

more ▶

10. Many people admire tigers and work to protect them.
11. However, people not only admire but also fear tigers.
12. Tigers can live both in tropical rain forests and in cold evergreen forests.
13. There are tigers in Thailand, India, and Siberia.
14. Tigers are solitary animals, and they rarely venture into open country.
15. Tigers' coats are a mixture of browns and yellows and black stripes, and this coloration makes the animals almost invisible in their habitats.
16. Since the 1970s, wildlife groups have been trying to save tigers, and the number of tigers is growing.

17–20. Replace the four underlined conjunctions to correct the errors in this travel-journal entry.

Example: Not only the rain forests of Southeast Asia <u>or</u> the cold Siberian mountains are habitats for tigers. *but (also)*

Proofreading

DATE: April 2   **PLACE:** Java

We have traveled to <u>either</u> continental and island parts of Asia in search of tigers. At last our search was rewarded, <u>yet</u> we saw a tigress with her two cubs, swimming in the river. Neither she <u>or</u> the cubs took any notice of our van, which was stopped some distance away. We dared not approach any closer, <u>for</u> we did get great photos.

Writing Wrap-Up   WRITING • THINKING • LISTENING • SPEAKING

NARRATING

Write a Story
Imagine that you are an animal confronting a person. Write an attention-getting story beginning about what you see, hear, feel, and smell. Use both coordinating and correlative conjunctions. Volunteers can read their paragraphs to the class. Have your classmates identify the conjunctions.

8 Complex Sentences

One-Minute Warm-Up

Find the two clauses in the sentence below. Which clause can stand alone? Which clause cannot?

It flailed its branches and twisted itself around like an enormous octopus, as if it were angry at Dexter for some reason.

—from *The Great Dimpole Oak,* by Janet Taylor Lisle

A **clause** is a group of words that has a subject and a predicate. One kind of clause that you already know is a simple sentence. A simple sentence has a subject and a predicate and expresses a complete thought. A simple sentence that is joined to another clause is called a main clause, or **independent clause**. When you join two independent clauses together, you form a compound sentence.

                            indep. clause   indep. clause

Compound Sentence: A tree matures, and it bears fruit.

A clause that does not express a complete thought is a dependent clause, or **subordinate clause**.

    When a tree matures,

1. A subordinate clause depends on an independent clause to complete its meaning. One or more subordinate clauses joined to an independent clause form a **complex sentence**.

                            sub. clause   indep. clause

   Complex Sentence: When a tree matures, it bears fruit.

2. Subordinate clauses can be in different places in a complex sentence. Always use a comma after a subordinate clause that begins a sentence. Do not use a comma before a subordinate clause that ends a sentence.

    When you go to the library, read about trees.

    Read about trees when you go to the library.

3. Subordinate clauses often begin with words like *although, when,* and *after.* Such words that connect subordinate clauses to independent clauses are called **subordinating conjunctions**.

Common Subordinating Conjunctions				
after	as long as	if	unless	where
although	as though	since	until	whereas
as	because	so that	when	wherever
as if	before	than	whenever	while

4. You can combine related simple sentences with subordinating conjunctions to form complex sentences.

Simple Sentences	Complex Sentence
All trees produce sap.	Although all trees produce sap, not all
Not all sap produces syrup.	sap produces syrup.

Different conjunctions express different relationships.

After I climbed the tree, Charles whistled.

Whenever I climbed the tree, Charles whistled.

While I climbed the tree, Charles whistled.

If I climbed the tree, Charles whistled.

Be sure to use the subordinating conjunction that expresses the meaning you intend.

Try It Out

Speak Up Is each sentence *simple, compound,* or *complex?* Identify each subordinating conjunction and subordinate clause.

1. Some kinds of trees produce rings every year whereas other kinds of trees don't.
2. Because some trees do not produce rings annually, their age cannot be determined exactly.
3. Although no one has counted more than 3,200 rings on a tree, some trees may be even older.
4. The largest trees in the world are in California.
5. These trees are nearly three hundred feet tall and thirty-five feet in diameter.
6. The fruit of some trees is hard and dry, but the fruit of others is soft and fleshy.
7. Some fruit weighs as much as forty pounds while other fruit weighs less than an ounce.

California redwood tree

more ▶

Try It Out continued

Which clauses are independent, and which are subordinate? Add an independent clause to each subordinate clause to form a complex sentence. Where do commas belong?

8. when the snow falls
9. although we will get there early
10. the trees don't have leaves yet
11. wherever squirrels are
12. if you look closely at this tree
13. Harriet will collect nuts and fruit
14. as soon as it gets warmer

Summing Up

- An **independent clause** can stand alone.
- A **subordinate clause** cannot stand alone.
- A subordinate clause has a subject and predicate and often begins with a **subordinating conjunction**.
- A sentence with one or more subordinate clauses and an independent clause is a **complex sentence**.

On Your Own

Write *simple, compound,* or *complex* to describe each sentence. Write each complex sentence, underlining the subordinate clause once and the subordinating conjunction twice.

Example: Some maple trees are grown for wood while others are cultivated for their sap.   *complex*
Some maple trees are grown for wood <u>while others are cultivated for their sap</u>.

15. The Norway and Japanese maples are decorative trees.
16. Since some hard maple trees have a beautiful grain, they are selected for furniture.
17. The wood of soft maples is good for small wooden articles.

more ▶

18. The big-leaf maple can be one hundred feet tall, and its leaves are sometimes one foot wide.
19. Although the silver maple has beautiful leaves, it is susceptible to diseases.
20. The maple tree has more varieties than most people imagine.

21–28. Write the eight subordinate clauses, and underline each subordinating conjunction in this travel advertisement.

Example: The trees are aglow with color when autumn comes to New England.   *when autumn comes to New England*

Autumn in New England

At the peak of the foliage season, as you enter the Berkshires, you see a riot of color on the mountainsides. In warm golds and russets, the trees announce the end of summer. The maples sport brilliant reds and oranges whereas the rocky mountainsides are deep violet and gray. When the sky is cloudless, the contrasts are breathtaking. After you drive northeast for a few hours, you arrive in the White Mountains of New Hampshire. Where the steep-sided, rugged mountains rise into the clouds, the landscape is forbidding but beautiful. Rivers run through the narrow valleys separating the mountains. Continue driving north until you reach Mount Washington. It is the highest point in New Hampshire. Evergreens and snowcaps accent the autumn colors wherever you look. Before the trip is over, you will have memories and pictures to last a lifetime.

Writing Wrap-Up

WRITING • THINKING • LISTENING • SPEAKING

DESCRIBING

Write a Travel Guide
Write a paragraph for a travel guide, describing a beautiful or interesting place you know about or have visited. Use several complex sentences. Read your paragraph aloud to a few classmates. Then ask them to choose the sentence that best describes the place.

   For Extra Practice see page 79.

Forming Compound, Complex, and Compound-Complex Sentences

Combining Sentences: Compound and Complex Sentences

You can combine short, simple sentences to make your writing smoother and easier to understand. Try using both compound and complex sentences.

To make a compound sentence, join simple sentences with a comma and a conjunction (such as *and, but,* or *or*).

I went to Arizona this summer. I bought some petrified wood.	}	I went to Arizona this summer, and I bought some petrified wood.

You can also combine two sentences to make a complex sentence. To do this, you must turn one simple sentence into a subordinate clause. A subordinating conjunction (such as *because, when,* or *although*) begins a subordinate clause.

Petrified wood was once actual wood. Mineral-rich water turned it into rock.	}	Although petrified wood was once actual wood, mineral-rich water turned it into rock.

Apply It

1–6. Look at this student Web site about a trip. Combine each pair of underlined sentences to create a compound or a complex sentence.

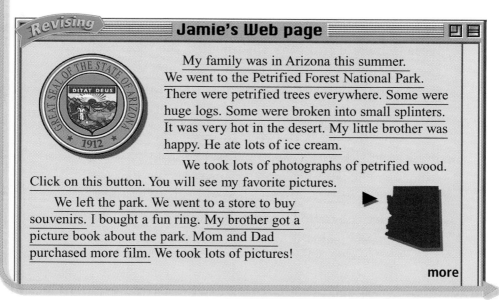

Revising

Jamie's Web page

My family was in Arizona this summer. We went to the Petrified Forest National Park. There were petrified trees everywhere. Some were huge logs. Some were broken into small splinters. It was very hot in the desert. My little brother was happy. He ate lots of ice cream.

We took lots of photographs of petrified wood. Click on this button. You will see my favorite pictures.

We left the park. We went to a store to buy souvenirs. I bought a fun ring. My brother got a picture book about the park. Mom and Dad purchased more film. We took lots of pictures!

more

Combining Sentences: Compound-Complex Sentences A group of short, related sentences can be combined to make a compound-complex sentence. This type of sentence can help organize your writing by linking related information. It also helps you vary sentence length.

A **compound-complex sentence** has at least two independent clauses and at least one subordinate clause.

A lush forest once stood on this land.
The area is now desert.
It has no living trees.
} Although a lush forest once stood on this land, the area is now desert, and it has no living trees.

Apply It

7–10. Revise these paragraphs from a draft of a research report. Combine each set of underlined sentences to make a compound-complex sentence. Use the subordinating conjunction in parentheses.

Petrified wood was formed by a natural process. The Triassic period ended. Layers of silt covered the trees. Minerals from the silt replaced the trees' cells. (after) Millions of years passed. Wind and water eroded the sediments. The petrified logs were exposed. You can see them now in Arizona. (as)

Petrified wood is colorful. Different minerals are present in the wood. Some pieces are deep red. Others are mostly brown. (because) People like to collect these stones. Visitors cannot take petrified wood from the national park. Pieces can be bought at shops. These beautiful ancient trees are fascinating to study. (although)

9 Fragments and Run-ons

What's wrong with this description? What would you do to fix it?

Along the side of the canoe.

We tipped the canoe, I sat down quickly, it righted itself.

The capital letter and end punctuation of a sentence show where a thought begins and ends. You can confuse your reader if you use end punctuation for an incomplete thought or if you run your sentences into each other.

Sentence Fragments

A **sentence fragment** is any word group that does not have both a subject and a predicate or does not express a complete thought. Most fragments leave the question *who?* or *what?* unanswered.

In the river. *(Who did what in the river?)*

Because I like water. *(What did you do?)*

Notice how each fragment below is corrected by adding a subject or a predicate or by completing a thought.

Fragment	Corrected Sentence
Went to the lake.	We went to the lake.
But he likes boats.	Joe doesn't row, but he likes boats.
After the race.	Prizes were awarded after the race.

Try It Out

Speak Up Is each group of words a sentence or a fragment?

1. Canoed on the ocean.
2. Although it was an important means of transportation.
3. But it is also a lot of fun.
4. While they floated down the rapids.

more ▶

Try It Out continued

Which item below is a sentence? Which items are fragments? How would you correct the fragments?

5. Canoeing a popular sport.
6. Because he likes adventure.
7. Bob doesn't plan to do any canoeing next weekend.

Run-on Sentences

Be careful not to run your sentences together. A **run-on sentence** consists of two or more sentences that are run together with commas or without any punctuation.

> Dean looked, he didn't see the flashlight. He looked again the flashlight had appeared from nowhere.

You can correct a run-on sentence in one of three ways.

1. Divide it into separate sentences by using end punctuation and a capital letter.

> Dean looked. He didn't see the flashlight.

2. Rewrite it as a compound sentence, using a comma and a coordinating conjunction.

> Dean looked, but he didn't see the flashlight.

3. Rewrite it as a complex sentence, using a subordinating conjunction.

> Although Dean looked, he didn't see the flashlight. When he looked again, the flashlight had appeared from nowhere.

Try It Out

Speak Up Which two items below are run-on sentences?

8. Sonja Henie won medals for figure skating in the Winter Olympics of 1928, 1932, and 1936.
9. Later Miss Henie became an actress, she skated in films.
10. She made more than ten films she died in 1969.

Sonja Henie

more ▶

How would you correct the following run-ons?

11. Mimi stood up on the ice for the first time she felt unsteady.
12. She felt nervous, she didn't fall.
13. Slowly she glided over the ice LaToya smiled at her.
14. She knew she needed a lot of practice, LaToya agreed.
15. Mimi went home happy, she would skate again tomorrow.
16. LaToya would be there to help her they were good friends.
17. They had known each other since childhood they lived next door to each other now.
18. They weren't in the same class, they always ate together.

Summing Up

- A **sentence fragment** does not have both a subject and a predicate or does not express a complete thought.

- A **run-on sentence** is two or more sentences that run together. Rewrite a run-on as separate simple sentences, as a compound sentence, or as a complex sentence.

On Your Own

Rewrite the items, correcting the fragments.

Example: The sport of rowing.
The sport of rowing goes very far back in history.

19. In 1839 the first Henley Regatta.
20. Held yearly at Henley-on-Thames in England.
21. Now an Olympic sport for men and women.
22. Sculling and sweep-oar rowing.
23. A popular sport at large and small schools alike.
24. When a team prepares for a race.
25. A workout for a racing team.
26. Learn to use the oars.

more ▶

Rewrite the items below, correcting the run-on sentences.

Example: Rowing "shells" usually have eight oars, "sculls" have two to four oars.
Rowing "shells" usually have eight oars, and "sculls" have two to four oars.

27. One old race is the "Doggett Coat and Badge" it began in the 1700s in England, it is still held.
28. Professional oarsmen used to row small ferries, some transported businessmen to meet trans-Atlantic ships.
29. Intercollegiate rowing races have been popular for many years the first Harvard-Yale race was held in 1851.

30–34. This boating guide excerpt has five sentence errors. Rewrite the paragraph, correcting all sentence fragments and all run-on sentences.

Example: Rafting can be challenging. When the river flows fast.
Rafting can be challenging when the river flows fast.

Proofreading

Rafting Guidelines

Many rivers are excellent for beginning rafters, there are also certain rivers. Where the sport can be quite dangerous. For the rapids are long and swift. For example, beginners need a guide on Maine's Penobscot River. The guide can steer the raft from the back. And give orders to other people paddling. Paddlers should stay low in the raft. Because the swift water can easily tip a raft over. Just remember the five commands: "Right paddle," "Left paddle," "Back paddle," "Front paddle," and "Jump!"

Writing Wrap-Up   WRITING • THINKING • LISTENING • SPEAKING

NARRATING

Write a Letter to a Friend
Write a paragraph of at least five sentences describing an adventurous trip. Check your paper carefully. Working with a partner, read your paragraph out loud. Then ask him or her to read your paragraph and mark any fragments or run-ons.

          For Extra Practice see page 80.

Enrichment

Dog Dollars

You are a representative to the town council and propose increasing the cost of dog licenses. These currently cost $5.00, and the town issues approximately 300 a year. Make a bar graph showing how the town's income would increase if the price were raised by 10%, 20%, and 30%. Write a summary of your findings and a statement telling what you recommend. Use coordinating conjunctions where possible, and underline them. Also include at least one pair of correlative conjunctions.

Challenge Another representative objects to the proposal. Write his or her argument and alternative proposal.

Recycled Comics

Clip a comic strip from the newspaper and paste it onto a sheet of paper. Cover the speech balloons by pasting small scraps of paper over them. Then create a new dialogue for the characters. (To give yourself room to write, let your new speech balloons extend onto the sheet of paper.) Include all four sentence types—declarative, interrogative, imperative, and exclamatory. Also include a compound sentence and a complex sentence.

1 **Kinds of Sentences** *(p. 34)* Write and punctuate each sentence. Label it *decl.*, *int.*, *imp.*, or *excl.*

1. What a thrill it is to go to Washington
2. I leave here next Saturday morning
3. Have you ever been there at cherry blossom time
4. Come to the airport with me

2 **Complete Subjects and Complete Predicates** *(p. 37)* Write each sentence. Draw a line between the complete subject and the complete predicate.

5. The first excursion will be next week.
6. Both experienced and inexperienced hikers are invited.
7. Flat, comfortable shoes are needed.
8. The trails can be steep and rocky.

3 **Simple Subjects and Simple Predicates** *(p. 40)* Write the sentences. Underline the simple subject once and the simple predicate twice.

9. Japan is composed of many islands.
10. The northern islands can be cool in the summer.
11. Most summers are hot and humid in the south.
12. The city of Tokyo lies near the middle of Japan.

4 **Finding the Subject** *(p. 43)* Write each simple subject.

13. How do you find the area of this triangle?
14. Please pay attention to the problem, Bob.
15. There are no tricks to this problem.
16. Is the base equal to the height?

5 **Compound Subjects and Compound Predicates** *(p. 46)* Write each sentence. Underline each simple subject once and each simple predicate twice. Label each compound subject and each compound predicate.

17. Kathy and some other students made plans for their report.
18. They went to the library and borrowed some books.
19. Each person read one book and wrote a short summary of it.
20. Lin and Brad reported on the solar system and showed slides.

6 **Compound Sentences** *(p. 51)* Write each sentence and identify it as *simple* or *compound.* Underline the connecting word, or conjunction, in each compound sentence.

21. The swimmers gathered, and a storm broke.

22. Some looked glum, but others were cheerful.
23. The rain had to end, or the coaches would cancel the meet.
24. Ten minutes later, the meet began in mixed sunshine and clouds.

7 Conjunctions *(p. 54)* Write each conjunction.

25. Lei Ping and I like to make big tuna sandwiches for picnics.
26. We add either grated carrots or chopped celery to the tuna.
27. There are fancier picnic foods, yet I like tuna best.

8 Complex Sentences *(p. 57)* Write each complex sentence. Underline each subordinate clause once and each subordinating conjunction twice. Add commas where needed.

28. Whenever I am tired from homework I take a quick jog.
29. If I continue my work my mind wanders.
30. I dash out of the house before I grow too sleepy.
31. After I've jogged for ten minutes I feel refreshed.

9 Fragments and Run-ons *(p. 63)* Rewrite the sentences, correcting the fragments and run-ons.

32. India has a variety of climates they follow a pattern.
33. Cool, hot, and rainy seasons.
34. During the rainy summer.

Mixed Review 35–42. Write this paragraph from a magazine article, correcting the eight errors.

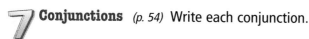

Proofreading Checklist

✔ incorrect punctuation of compound and complex sentences
✔ sentence fragments
✔ run-ons
✔ incorrect conjunctions

From its source in Lake Itasca in Minnesota, the Mississippi River flows south across the continent it enters the Gulf of Mexico southeast of New Orleans. A total distance of more than 2,300 miles. Although it begins as a clear stream the Mississippi picks up huge quantities of silt as it is joined by tributaries. Especially the sediment-laden Missouri River. The Missouri unites with the Mississippi above St. Louis and the Ohio joins it at Cairo, Illinois. After the Mississippi has reached its full glory it is a brown flood more than a mile wide. From bank to bank. Both the Amazon or the Congo, however, discharge a much greater volume of water than does the mighty Mississippi.

 See www.eduplace.com/kids/hme/ for an online quiz.

✔ Test Practice

Write the numbers 1–8 on a sheet of paper. For questions 1–4, read each sentence. Choose the underlined part that is the simple subject of the sentence. Write the letter for that answer.

1 <u>Mrs. Arnold</u> <u>will be</u> visiting my <u>family</u> next <u>week</u>.
     A   **B**   **C**   **D**

2 Much <u>laughter</u> was <u>heard</u> from the <u>auditorium</u> during the <u>show</u>.
       F   **G**   **H**   **J**

3 Do <u>you</u> <u>remember</u> the last <u>verse</u> of that <u>song</u>?
     A   **B**   **C**   **D**

4 <u>Across</u> the rolling <u>waves</u> <u>sailed</u> the three <u>ships</u>.
    F   **G** **H**   **J**

For questions 5–8, read each sentence. Choose the underlined part that is the simple predicate of the sentence. Write the letter for that answer.

5 The <u>students</u> in Mrs. Ross's <u>class</u> <u>have borrowed</u> our <u>microscopes</u>.
       A   **B**   **C**   **D**

6 You <u>included</u> some <u>vivid</u> <u>details</u> in your <u>description</u>.
      F   **G** **H**   **J**

7 <u>Most</u> of the <u>passengers</u> on the <u>plane</u> <u>slept</u>.
    A   **B**   **C** **D**

8 The <u>tour</u> of the <u>White House</u> <u>was</u> the most interesting part of our <u>trip</u>.
     F   **G**   **H**   **J**

Now write numbers 9–14 on your paper. Read the passage and look at the numbered, underlined parts. Choose the answer that shows the best way to capitalize and punctuate each numbered part. If the part is already correct, choose the last answer, "Correct as it is." Write the letter for the answer you choose.

About two hundred people enjoyed the annual fourth of July cookout at
                                                          (9)
Red oaks park on Monday. Although the weather was hot and muggy. Nobody
     (10)   (11)
seemed to notice. Adults and children enjoyed good food and a friendly game

of softball, a popular local band provided musical entertainment. The mood
   (12)
was happy and relaxed as the sun set. Then at nine o'clock the fireworks
                 (13)
display started it was a dazzling ending to a splendid day.
        (14)

9 A Fourth of July
   B Fourth Of July
   C Fourth of july
   D Correct as it is

10 F red oaks park
   G Red oaks Park
   H Red Oaks Park
   J Correct as it is

11 A muggy nobody
   B muggy, nobody
   C muggy; nobody
   D Correct as it is

12 F softball. a
   G softball a
   H softball. A
   J Correct as it is

13 A relaxed, as
   B relaxed. As
   C relaxed; as
   D Correct as it is

14 F started. It
   G started, it
   H started, it,
   J Correct as it is

(pages 34–36)

1 Kinds of Sentences

- **Declarative sentences** make statements and end with periods.
- **Interrogative sentences** ask questions and end with question marks.
- **Imperative sentences** make commands or requests and end with periods.
- **Exclamatory sentences** express strong feelings and end with exclamation points.

● Write *declarative, interrogative, imperative*, or *exclamatory* to describe each sentence.

Example: Why is opening night so exciting? *interrogative*

1. An actor's voice is an important tool.
2. Performers must learn to speak loudly and clearly.
3. Could the audience understand you?
4. Don't slam the door.
5. Watch out for falling scenery!

▲ Write each sentence, adding the correct end punctuation. Label each sentence *declarative, interrogative, imperative*, or *exclamatory*.

Example: Mime is an expressive form of acting
   Mime is an expressive form of acting.   declarative

6. The actors tell their stories with gestures instead of sound
7. Use your hands and face to show your feelings
8. How amazing he is
9. Have you ever seen a mime with white face makeup

■ Rewrite each sentence to make the kind of sentence shown in parentheses. Use the correct end punctuation.

Example: Was Agatha Christie a mystery writer? (declarative)
   Agatha Christie was a mystery writer.

10. Did she write sixteen plays? (declarative)
11. Have you seen *The Mousetrap*? (imperative)
12. It is one of London's longest-running plays. (interrogative)
13. That was an obvious clue. (exclamatory)
14. Is Miss Marple your favorite character? (declarative)

(pages 37–39)

2 Complete Subjects and Complete Predicates

Remember

- Every sentence has a **subject** and a **predicate**.
- The **complete subject** tells whom or what the sentence is about.
- The **complete predicate** tells what the subject is, does, has, or feels.

● Write each sentence. Draw a line between the complete subject and the complete predicate.

Example: About one hundred million Americans ride bicycles.
About one hundred million Americans|ride bicycles.

1. Bicycles are almost everywhere.
2. Many city streets have special lanes for bicycles.
3. The earliest bicycle was made of wood.
4. This bicycle had a huge front wheel and a small rear wheel.

▲ Write each sentence. Draw a line between the complete subject and the complete predicate.

Example: People of all ages ride bicycles.
People of all ages|ride bicycles.

5. Many people ride bicycles for exercise.
6. The Olympic Games include bicycle racing.
7. The parts of a bicycle have now become more complicated.
8. Bicycles all over the world often have multiple speeds.

■ Write *complete subject, complete predicate,* or *sentence* to describe each group of words. Write each incomplete sentence, adding a subject or a predicate to complete it. Draw a line between the complete subject and the complete predicate.

Example: Bicycle competitions.
complete subject   Bicycle competitions|are popular.

9. Most bicycle races.
10. Are held on public roads and highways.
11. Often cover more than fifty miles.
12. Special bicycles are used.
13. The annual Tour de France.
14. The name of the most popular road race of all.

(pages 40–42)

3 Simple Subjects and Simple Predicates

- The **simple subject** is the key word in the complete subject. It is usually a noun or a pronoun.
- The **simple predicate** is the verb or verb phrase in the complete predicate.

Remember

● The complete subject and the complete predicate are separated by a line in each sentence. Write the simple subject and the simple predicate for each sentence.

Example: People in colonial times|ate one hot meal a day.   *People   ate*

1. Dinner|was their main meal.
2. They|ate it in the early afternoon.
3. Hot, healthy food|gave workers energy for the afternoon.
4. Supper|was the last meal of the day.
5. The usual supper|was bread and soup.
6. Most people|now eat a big hot meal at night.

▲ Write each sentence. Draw a line between the complete subject and the complete predicate. Underline the simple subject once and the simple predicate twice.

Example: The style of breakfast has changed over the years.
   The style of breakfast|has changed over the years.

7. A colonial breakfast was often oatmeal or mush.
8. Mush was made with cornmeal and hot milk.
9. Large breakfasts were once popular.
10. People of today may not have time for big breakfasts.
11. A healthful meal at the start of the day is important.
12. A well-balanced breakfast will give you energy for hours.

■ Rewrite the sentences, expanding each subject and predicate with additional words and phrases. Underline the simple subject once and the simple predicate twice.

Example: Colonists farmed.   *The early colonists farmed the land.*

13. They harvested wheat.
14. Corn grew.
15. Cattle grazed.
16. Disease existed.
17. Times have changed.
18. Machinery was invented.
19. Oil is used.
20. Medicine has improved.

(pages 43–45)

4 Finding the Subject

- To find the subject of a sentence in inverted order, rearrange the subject and the predicate into their natural order, or ask the question *who?* or *what?* about the verb.
- The subject of an imperative sentence is understood to be *you.*

Remember

● Write the simple subject of each sentence. If the subject *you* is understood, write *(you).*

Example: Lying on my desk is a notebook.   *notebook*

R. L. Stevenson

1. Under it is a book.
2. Hand it to me, please.
3. Here is the title of the book.
4. Is it *The Strange Case of Dr. Jekyll and Mr. Hyde*?
5. Have you read this book by Robert Louis Stevenson?
6. There are other good books by the same author.

▲ Write the simple subject of each sentence. If the subject *you* is understood, write *(you).*

Example: Did Stevenson write in the late 1800s?   *Stevenson*

7. Where do you keep your adventure stories?
8. Show me one of the books, please.
9. Here is a well-known book by Stevenson.
10. There are many exciting adventures in it.
11. Is *Kidnapped* your favorite book by Stevenson?

■ Rewrite each sentence, following the directions in parentheses. Change the word order, and delete words if necessary. Write the simple subject.

Example: Three books are on your desk. (Begin with *There.*)
    There are three books on your desk.   *books*

12. You have read all of them. (Make interrogative.)
13. You should finish them one at a time. (Make imperative.)
14. You have a favorite author. (Make interrogative with *Do.*)
15. You should read many different authors for variety. (Make imperative.)
16. My library card is in my wallet. (Begin with *In.*)
17. A reading room is located in the library. (Begin with *Located.*)
18. The library is closed on Saturday. (Make interrogative.)

(pages 46–48)

5 Compound Subjects and Compound Predicates

- A **compound subject** is made up of two or more simple subjects that have the same predicate.
- A **compound predicate** is made up of two or more simple predicates that have the same subject.

● Write the sentences. Underline the compound subjects once and the compound predicates twice.

Example: Washington and Lincoln were born in February.
Washington and *Lincoln* *were born in February.*

1. Abraham Lincoln became President in 1861 and was in office until 1865.
2. Lincoln was shot and killed in 1865.
3. There were fewer people and no cars.
4. Thirteen stripes and thirty-five stars were on the flag.

▲ Write each sentence. Underline each simple subject once and each simple predicate twice. Then label the sentences *compound subject* or *compound predicate* or *both*.

Example: Has Ada or Don written or spoken about Lincoln?
Has Ada or *Don written* or *spoken about Lincoln?* *both*

5. Lincoln's boyhood was hard but does not seem unusual for that time.
6. Lincoln first lived in Kentucky but moved to Indiana.
7. There were few schools or books in those days.
8. Lincoln and other children studied alone and wrote on boards.

■ Rewrite each sentence. Add one or more subjects or predicates to make a compound subject or a compound predicate. Underline each simple subject once and each simple predicate twice.

Example: Pioneer men in Lincoln's day grew their food.
Pioneer men and women in Lincoln's day grew their food.

9. Horses were the primary means of transportation.
10. There were few railroads before the 1840s.
11. Families in covered wagons traveled west.
12. Can you imagine a world without modern technology?

(pages 51–53)

⑥ Compound Sentences

Remember

- A **compound sentence** is made up of two or more simple sentences joined by a conjunction such as *and, but,* or *or.*
- Usually a comma separates the parts of a compound sentence.

● Write *simple* or *compound* to describe each sentence.

Example: Greece is a small country, but it has a long history.   *compound*

  1. Artists and scientists lived in Greece about two thousand five hundred years ago.
  2. The writers were brilliant, and we still read their works.
  3. Socrates lived in the fourth century B.C., and he was a great teacher.
  4. He was first a sculptor, and he later became a teacher.
  5. His questions and answers challenged Athenian society.

▲ Write each compound sentence correctly. If the sentence has no errors, write *correct.* Add commas or semicolons where necessary. Underline any conjunctions.

Example: The Greeks were athletic and they loved sports and games.
    The Greeks were athletic, <u>and</u> they loved sports and games.

  6. Each town had a place for sports and that was the gymnasium.
  7. Government by the people flourished in Athens and Athenian democracy was direct rather than representative.
  8. Every citizen of Athens was a member of the government but not everyone was a citizen.
  9. Free men could be citizens but women and slaves could not.
 10. Athens was defeated by Sparta in 404 B.C. Sparta had a strong army.

■ Add a sentence to each simple sentence to form a compound sentence. Use the conjunctions *and, but,* and *or* at least once each.

Example: Greece is a beautiful country.
    Greece is a beautiful country, and tourists flock to it.

 11. Faraway places interest most of us.
 12. Events of long ago are fascinating too.
 13. I have never been to Greece.
 14. Can modern visitors see the ruins of Troy in Turkey?
 15. I would like to read the *Iliad*.
 16. The language of ancient Greece was different from modern Greek.

(pages 54–56)

7 Conjunctions

- **Coordinating conjunctions**, such as *and, but,* and *or,* join words or word groups that have the same function.
- **Correlative conjunctions**, such as *neither...nor,* are pairs of conjunctions that connect related words or word groups.

● Write the coordinating or correlative conjunctions from each sentence.

Example: A camel can go for many days not only without food but also without water. *not only . . . but also*

1. The camel's hump does not carry water, but it stores fat.
2. A camel can hear but often disregards commands.
3. Camels are sometimes mean, yet they can be very gentle.
4. Camels may bite or spit at their owners.
5. Not only one but two sets of eyelashes protect the camel's eyes.

▲ Write the best coordinating conjunctions to complete these sentences. Some sentences have more than one answer.

Example: Gorillas eat leaves, buds, bark, _____ fruits. *and*

6. Gorillas have broad shoulders, long arms, _____ short legs.
7. Gorillas look fierce, _____ they are actually shy.
8. A gorilla will harm a human only if provoked _____ attacked.
9. Humans may think that gorillas are not intelligent, _____ a gorilla named Koko has learned sign language.

■ Write the best correlative conjunctions to complete these sentences.

Example: _____ protection of wild animals _____ management of their environment are necessary.
Both protection of wild animals and management of their environment are necessary.

10. _____ the destruction of habitat _____ the reduction of animals' food supplies threaten wildlife.
11. _____ we practice conservation efforts _____ else we will lose many of our natural resources.
12. _____ land animals _____ sea animals can escape the effects of human activities on their environment.

(pages 57–60)

8 Complex Sentences

- An **independent clause** can stand alone.
- A **subordinate clause** cannot stand alone.
- A subordinate clause has a subject and predicate and usually begins with a **subordinating conjunction**.
- A sentence with one or more subordinate clauses and an independent clause is a **complex sentence**.

● Write the subordinate clause from each complex sentence.

Example: Although some people dislike cities, others are happy there.
Although some people dislike cities

1. Some people enjoy a city where life is constantly busy.
2. When you live in a big city, you can always find entertainment.
3. People and traffic surround you wherever you go.
4. As long as you don't mind noise, you will enjoy city life.

▲ Write each complex sentence. Underline the subordinate clause once. Underline the subordinating conjunction twice. Add a comma where necessary.

Example: After the leaves change color they fall from the trees.
After the leaves change color, they fall from the trees.

5. The trees in New England are beautiful when the leaves have turned.
6. When the weather is sunny and cool the colors are very bright.
7. If the weather is warm and wet the colors are muddy and dull.
8. The red maple received its name because its leaves turn red in the fall.

■ Write a complex sentence by adding a subordinate clause to each sentence. Use appropriate subordinating conjunctions, and underline them. Add commas where necessary.

Example: Ida lived on a farm.
Before she went to Chicago, Ida lived on a farm.

9. Her father preferred the country.
10. The family visited the nearby city often.
11. Everyone always enjoyed the visits.
12. The family also welcomed the peace of the country.

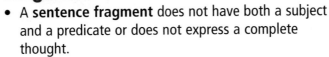

(pages 63–66)

⑨ Fragments and Run-ons

- A **sentence fragment** does not have both a subject and a predicate or does not express a complete thought.
- A **run-on sentence** is two or more sentences that run together. Rewrite a run-on as separate simple sentences, as a compound sentence, or as a complex sentence.

● Label each item *fragment, run-on,* or *sentence.*

Example: Made up of rocks or the remains of animals. *fragment*

1. If you see very black soil.
2. Plants and crops grow on it, soil produces most of our food.
3. Although soil is deep in some places, it is shallow in others.
4. When you are in Georgia.
5. Each layer of soil has color and thickness.
6. A mixture of soil and sand makes sandy loam, it is good for plants.

▲ 7–15. Rewrite this passage to correct all fragments and run-ons.

Example: Soil supports the growth of plants, it is important.
Soil supports the growth of plants. It is important.

    If the soil cannot produce good crops. Not enough food will be produced. Rain and wind wash soil away, it takes a long time to make more. Rocks erode over the years, they become soil. Wind blows sand against rocks, the rocks wear down. When a river runs over rocks for years. Wears them away. Water freezes in cracks in rocks. And breaks them apart.

■ 16–22. Rewrite this passage to correct all fragments and run-ons.

Example: Although we depend on soil to grow food. We have not always taken proper care of it.
Although we depend on soil to grow food, we have not always taken proper care of it.

    Soil is built up over hundreds of years. But rain and wind can carry it away quickly. The early colonists and later pioneers. Did not know how to care for the soil. They overused the soil they failed to fertilize it. When they cleared land for their farms. They cut down trees that had protected soil from water and wind.

Bold reds, warm oranges, and bright yellows *are* New Mexico!

Nouns

Kinds of Nouns

Two horses approach the finish line. Tell what happens next. Use at least three nouns, one of which names something other than a physical thing.

A **noun** names a person, a place, a thing, or an idea.

Bob visited Fresno and saw an exhibition of horses.

Person	Mr. Gomez, friend
Idea	love, labor
Thing	pencil, Statue of Liberty
Place	Utah, crossroad

HELP ? **Tip**

Many nouns, such as *box* or *picture*, also function as verbs.

Common and Proper Nouns

All nouns are either proper or common. A **proper noun** names a particular person, place, thing, or idea. Always capitalize a proper noun. If it consists of more than one word, capitalize only the important words. A **common noun** names a general class of person, place, thing, or idea.

Proper: The National Horse Show was held in April in New York.

Common: The annual horse show was held last month in the city.

Try It Out

Speak Up What are the common nouns and the proper nouns in these sentences? Which nouns should be capitalized?

1. A parade began the ohio horse show.
2. Horses feel tension.
3. A pony lost a shoe.
4. His name was gremlin.
5. Lynn held the reins.
6. A smile hid her fear.
7. Teams from utah competed.

Concrete and Abstract Nouns

All nouns are also either concrete or abstract. **Concrete nouns** refer to material things, to people, or to places. **Abstract nouns** name ideas, feelings, or qualities.

Concrete: This pony is small.
Abstract: Lin wept in sorrow.

Concrete: people, Mexicans, Mount Hood, book, *Tom Sawyer*
Abstract: love, relief, patriotism, language

Nouns, therefore, have several classifications. All nouns are either proper or common and either concrete or abstract.

Blue Nile: proper, concrete   happiness: common, abstract
heroism: common abstract   box: common, concrete

Try It Out

Speak Up What are the concrete nouns and the abstract nouns in these sentences?

8. Where do you keep your horses?
9. Rain leaked through the roof of the stable.
10. Lynn told us her ideas for the new stalls.
11. Show horses must have the right spirit.
12. What day is the big race?
13. Jan shivered in anticipation.
14. Hopes are made of dreams.
15. The team will visit Kentucky next.

Summing Up

- **Nouns** name persons, places, things, or ideas.
- **Common nouns** name general classes of things.
- **Proper nouns** name particular things and are capitalized.
- **Concrete nouns** refer to material things.
- **Abstract nouns** name ideas, feelings, or qualities.

Write each noun. Label it *common* or *proper,* and *concrete* or *abstract.* Capitalize the proper nouns.

Example: Is your class studying history?

class	*common*	*concrete*
history	*common*	*abstract*

16. What is your idea of justice?
17. The statue of liberty symbolizes freedom.
18. The colonists opposed taxation without representation.
19. Did john hancock sign the declaration of independence?

20–35. Write the sixteen nouns in the research report below. Label each one *common* or *proper,* and *concrete* or *abstract.* Capitalize the proper nouns.

Example: Racehorses are bred for speed and endurance.

racehorses	*common*	*concrete*
speed	*common*	*abstract*
endurance	*common*	*abstract*

Thoroughbreds

Three horses are named in the pedigree of every Thoroughbred. The first sire of this breed was the byerley turk, a seventeenth-century warhorse known for a proud spirit. The second stallion was the darley arabian, known for beauty and grace. The third ancestor was the godolphin arabian. His distant offspring included the beloved man o' war.

Writing Wrap-Up   WRITING • THINKING • LISTENING • SPEAKING

NARRATING

Write a Narrative Paragraph

Write the first paragraph of a story about a horse. Use each kind of noun—*common, proper, concrete,* and *abstract*—at least once. Remember to capitalize all proper nouns. Exchange paragraphs with a partner and check that your partner has used each kind of noun at least once. Then try to guess what will happen next in your partner's story.

    For Extra Practice see page 107.

2 Compound and Collective Nouns

Can you detect the spelling errors in the sentences below?

A water proof flash light was found at the crimescene.

The policechief believes the finger prints belong to the defendant.

Compound Nouns

A noun of two or more words is a **compound noun**.

White House   software   Mrs. Wu

high school   forget-me-not   Professor Woodman

Some compound nouns are written as one word, some are written as two or more words, and some are written with hyphens. Check your dictionary to be sure of the spelling.

One Word	Separate Words	Hyphenated Words
bookcase	Edgar Allan Poe	father-in-law
bridegroom	commander in chief	half-moon
porthole	postage stamp	stick-in-the-mud
sportscast	music box	runner-up
headache	water ballet	kilowatt-hour

Try It Out

Speak Up Which nouns are compound?

1. airplane
2. happiness
3. lunchtime
4. sister-in-law
5. backpack
6. playpen
7. imitation
8. classroom
9. high school
10. sorrow
11. houses
12. sadness

Collective Nouns

A **collective noun** names a group or a collection of people, animals, or things considered as a unit.

Common Collective Nouns					
crew	orchestra	committee	flock	fleet	group
class	chorus	family	herd	jury	team

Speak Up Which nouns are collective nouns?

13. The team played poorly.
14. The crowd sounded like a herd of elephants.
15. Overhead we saw a flock of geese.
16. The band played the national anthem.
17. The staff included professionals and nonprofessionals.

Summing Up

- A **compound noun** is a noun that is made up of more than one word. Some compound nouns are written as one word, some as separate words, and some as hyphenated words.

- A **collective noun** names a group of people, animals, or things considered as a unit.

On Your Own

Write a collective noun or a compound noun from the box to complete each sentence.

Example: The _____ included many actors. *cast*

folktale	playwright	jury	snowstorm	pack
bridegroom	cast	council	woodsman	class

18. The eighth-grade _____ put on the play.
19. The play is based on a Russian _____.
20. A _____ goes to claim his bride, whose family has opposed him.

more ▶

21. He loses his way in a blinding _____.
22. The sound effects include a _____ of wolves, howling off-stage.
23. At the edge of the forest, he enters the cottage of a _____.
24. To his dismay, he finds the village elders sitting in _____, discussing his fate.
25. They are acting as both judge and _____.
26. How will the _____ end this tale?

27–35. Write the nine collective and compound nouns from the list of courtroom rules below. Identify each as either compound or collective.

Example: The jury will refrain from chewing gum. *jury   collective*

 ## Courtroom Rules

- When the court is in session, there will be order at all times.
- If there is any disorder, the courtroom will be cleared.
- The lawyers for the state will be seated to the left of the judge.
- The defense team will be seated to the right of the judge.
- The names of eyewitnesses will be given to the judge.
- The press may not use cameras or tape recorders.
- Gentlemen will wear suits. Ladies will wear suits or shirtwaists.
- There will be no animals in the audience.

Writing Wrap-Up

WRITING • THINKING • LISTENING • SPEAKING

PERSUADING

Write an Editorial

Write an editorial for the school newspaper explaining what school rule you would like to change and why. Use at least three collective nouns and three compound nouns. Exchange paragraphs with a partner and work together to identify the collective and compound nouns. Circle what you think is the most persuasive argument offered by your partner.

Writing with Nouns

Combining Sentences: Appositives An appositive is a noun or noun phrase that identifies, describes, or renames the noun that it follows. You can combine two related sentences by turning one of them into an appositive.

Use commas to set off most appositives from the rest of the sentence. Commas show that the appositive gives extra information. It could be left out without changing the meaning of the sentence.

Belle is a search-and-rescue dog.   Belle, a German shepherd, is a
Belle is a German shepherd.   search-and-rescue dog.

Sometimes an appositive identifies a noun and is central to the meaning of the sentence. Do not use commas to set off such an appositive.

Unclear

Belle's littermates are also   Belle's littermate is also a search-
search-and-rescue dogs.   and-rescue dog.

One littermate is named Sampson.   **Clear**
Another littermate is named Blue.   Belle's littermate Sampson is also a
                                     search-and-rescue dog.

Apply It

1–4. Revise this draft of a student's persuasive fundraising letter. Use appositives to combine the four pairs of underlined sentences.

Big Mountain Search Dogs

Dear Sir or Madam:

     Hello! I work at Big Mountain Search Dogs. It is a dog-training facility. Our dogs do important work. The police use our dogs to rescue lost hikers or skiers after an avalanche or a big storm. An avalanche is a slide of either rock or snow. How do our dogs find lost people? Our dogs are expert sniffers. The names of the expert sniffers are Tobey and Mack.

     We need your help. A Newfoundland eats twenty-five pounds of dog food each week! The Newfoundland is a dog often used in rescue work. Your donation will help us care for our dogs.

                         Sincerely,

                         Mikaylah Simms

Elaborating Sentences: Appositives Appositives can add detail to your sentences. In the following sentences, appositives provide precise information to elaborate the nouns.

> A dog uses alerts to indicate a discovery.
>
> A dog uses alerts, a bark and a sharp pull on its lead, to indicate a discovery.
>
> The trainer taught Belle many search-and-rescue skills.
>
> The trainer Lucy Juarez taught Belle many search-and-rescue skills.

Apply It

5–10. Revise these captions from a student's research report on search-and-rescue dogs. Add appositives to elaborate the six underlined words. Look at the photographs to find details. Write the new sentences.

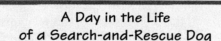

A Day in the Life of a Search-and-Rescue Dog

A Rescue Dog Goes to Work

This <u>dog</u> has been trained to find lost people. The dog and three <u>searchers</u> work together to locate trapped people. The searchers wear special <u>equipment</u>.

Another Successful Rescue

A rescue dog relies on its <u>senses</u> to find people. It can take years to find a dog with the right <u>qualities</u> to succeed as a rescue dog. After each rescue, a search dog is given a <u>reward</u>.

3 Singular and Plural Nouns

One-Minute Warm-Up

Find the nouns in the sentence below. How many are singular? How many are plural?

Their nests are huge, weigh up to half a ton (4,500 kilograms), and crown the tops of dead trees, power poles, and nesting platforms near water.

—from *Ospreys,* by Dorothy Hinshaw Patent

Most nouns change form to show number. A **singular noun** names one person, place, thing, or idea. A **plural noun** names more than one. You form the plural of most nouns by simply adding -*s* to the singular. Many other plural forms involve spelling changes. Look up a word in your dictionary when you are not sure of its plural form. The rules listed below will serve as handy references for deciding how to write the plural forms of many nouns. Remember, though, that the rules might not apply to every noun in a spelling pattern.

Regular Forms

Rules for Forming Plurals		
Add -s to form the plural of these nouns:		
Most singular nouns	globes	Michaels
Most nouns ending in *o* preceded by a vowel	radios	stereos
Many nouns ending in *o*	pianos	altos
Nouns ending in *y* preceded by a vowel	donkeys	valleys
Proper nouns ending in *y*	Bradys	Malloys
Some nouns ending in *f* or *fe*	roofs	safes
Add -es to form the plural of these nouns:		
Nouns ending in *s, x, sh, ch, z*	boxes	buzzes
Some nouns ending in *o* preceded by a consonant	echoes	heroes
Nouns ending in *y* preceded by a consonant (change *y* to *i* first)	fly—flies	
Some nouns ending in *f* or *fe* (change *f* to *v* first)	calf—calves	

Speak Up What is the plural form of each noun?

1. Harry	9. belief	17. Selena
2. veto	10. mess	18. valley
3. monkey	11. tax	19. rope
4. soprano	12. tornado	20. month
5. ax	13. clay	21. potato
6. Ron	14. bush	22. guy
7. life	15. history	23. solo
8. bunch	16. safe	24. leaf

Irregular Forms

Some nouns have unusual singular or plural forms. Check your dictionary.

Unusual Noun Forms

1. Some plurals are formed by irregular spelling changes.

 child—children foot—feet mouse—mice

2. Some nouns have the same singular and plural forms.

 deer sheep grapefruit

3. Some nouns are used only in the plural form.

 clothes scissors pants

4. Some nouns end in *s* but have a singular meaning.

 physics measles news

5. Some nouns from other languages are made plural as in the original language.

 analysis—analyses alumnus—alumni

6. Compound nouns usually are made plural by adding *-s* to the most important word in the compound.

 commanders in chief brothers-in-law

7. Compound nouns that are written as one word or do not have a noun part are made plural by adding *-s* at the end.

 cupfuls forget-me-nots

8. Letters, numbers in mathematics, symbols, and words used as words are made plural by adding an apostrophe and an *-s* (*'s*).

 a's *8*'s *&*'s *but*'s

Speak Up What is the plural form of each item?

25. mouse
26. basis
27. salmon
28. *?*
29. *3*
30. stimulus
31. deer
32. grapefruit
33. series
34. patch
35. story
36. cupful

37. maid of honor
38. crisis
39. *and*
40. analysis
41. bookcase
42. physics
43. German measles
44. sister-in-law
45. goose
46. tablespoonful
47. lady's slipper
48. *&*

HELP **Tip**

Use your dictionary if you are not sure how to spell a plural noun.

Summing Up

- A **singular noun** names one person, place, thing, or idea.
- A **plural noun** names more than one.
- The plurals of nouns are formed in different ways. Check your dictionary if you are unsure about the spelling of a plural noun.

Write the plural form of each item. If it is already plural, write *plural*.

Example: echoes *plural*

49. bucketful
50. turkeys
51. *20*
52. *+*
53. grandchild
54. crash

55. briefcase
56. church
57. great-aunt
58. cousin
59. trophies
60. foxes

61. odds
62. potato
63. torpedoes
64. leaves
65. clothes

more ▶

66–80. The field-guide entry below has fifteen incorrect plural nouns. Find them and write them correctly.

Example: Blackbird is the name given to some thrushs.   *thrushes*

Proofreading

Red-winged blackbirds spend most of their lifes in marshs and fields. They are seven to nine inchs long. Males are all black with red-and-yellow patchs on their shoulders. The males often spread their winges to display the bright colors when they sing in the spring. Females are brown and look like large sparrowes with sharp bills.

The females are striped lightly over the eyes and heavily over the rest of their bodys. From the eggs that each female lays every year, three to five babys hatch.

Red-winged blackbirds eat insectes, seeds, and berrys. They do not eat mouses, however. You can see these birds as they sit on tree branchs, fence postes, or cattails by the roadside. They travel and roost in large flockes. Tricolored blackbirds in the Pacific states are western cousines of the red-winged blackbird.

Writing Wrap-Up

WRITING • THINKING • LISTENING • SPEAKING

COMPARING / CONTRASTING

Write a Journal Entry

Write a journal entry in which you compare yourself to your favorite animal. What do you have in common? How are you different? Use as many noun plurals as possible. With a small group, read your journal entries aloud. Together decide who used the most unusual noun plurals. Were they spelled correctly?

4 Possessive Nouns

One-Minute Warm-Up

Write a sentence or two about the picture. Use two nouns with apostrophes that show possession.

You already know how to make nouns plural. You can also make them possessive. **Possessive nouns** show ownership or relationship. A possessive noun always has an apostrophe (').

Jade's scissors (the scissors that belong to Jade)

the dog's whiskers (the whiskers of the dog)

the workers' demands (the demands that the workers made)

Mike's new address (the new address that Mike has)

Rules for Forming Possessive Nouns	
Most singular nouns: Add an apostrophe and -s ('s).	Mr. Bass—Mr. Bass's Tom—Tom's
Plural nouns ending with s: Add only an apostrophe (').	girls—girls' babies—babies' Joneses—Joneses'
Other plural nouns: Add an apostrophe and -s ('s) to the end.	children—children's geese—geese's
Compound nouns: Add an apostrophe and -s ('s) to the end.	sister-in-law—sister-in-law's (singular) sisters-in-law—sisters-in-law's (plural)

If two or more people own a single thing, place the apostrophe after the last person's name.

Miguel and Scott's basketball

If each owns a thing separately, make each noun possessive.

Miguel's and Scott's basketballs

Try It Out

Speak Up How would you change each word group into another word group that has a possessive noun?

1. the bikes that Ted and Nick each has
2. the color of the rabbits
3. the cat that Javis and Yolanda own together
4. the German shepherd that the Johnsons have
5. the apartment building of Mr. Dix
6. the glances of the passersby
7. the tractor trailers of her son-in-law
8. the jack-in-the-box that the children own

Summing Up

- A **possessive noun** shows ownership or relationship.
- To form the possessive of a singular noun, a plural noun not ending in *s*, or a compound noun, add an apostrophe and -*s* ('*s*).
- To form the possessive of a plural noun ending in *s*, add an apostrophe only (').

On Your Own

Rewrite each word group as another word group with a possessive noun.

Example: the photographs that the Rogerses have
the Rogerses' photographs

9. the clocks that my brother-in-law owns
10. the spaghetti dinner that my cousins made
11. the application that Alison made
12. the wedding bouquet that my mother had
13. the request that our teachers made
14. the old computer of the instructor
15. the mathematics book that my brother has
16. the meow of the cat

more ▶

17. the car that my mother and father own
18. the pets that Jerry and Eva each has
19. the paintbrushes that belong to Carlos
20. the front paws of the bears

21–28. Write correctly the possessive form of the eight nouns spelled incorrectly in the weather report below.

Example: Hurricane Marthas' winds will diminish tonight.   *Martha's*

proofreading

Web site

Northwestern Texases line of damaging squalls punched eastward this afternoon across Louisianas heartland, where the wind gusts damage included toppled trees and power lines. Hail is likely tonight in Arkansas' mountains. Several thunderstorm's paths threaten the weekends ball games in the mid-South.

Despite a few scattered showers in Georgia and Alabama, however, these state's prospects are for more dry days. Relief is promised next week as a cold frontes leading edge slides southward. Florida's long drought may well be over.

WEATHER

Forecast for the Week

Zoom in on Area

National Weather

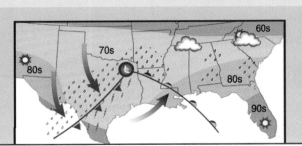

Writing Wrap-Up

WRITING • THINKING • LISTENING • SPEAKING

DESCRIBING

Write a Friendly Letter

Write a letter or an e-mail to a friend describing your favorite kind of weather. Include at least four possessive nouns. Read your letters, one at a time, to a small group. Ask volunteers to spell the possessive nouns.

Writing with Possessive Nouns

Combining Sentences Possessive nouns show ownership. They can also help tighten your writing. Use possessive nouns to combine short, repetitive sentences.

Nicola had a softball.
The softball was signed
by every teammate.

Possessive noun
Nicola's softball was signed
by every teammate.

Jeremy and I play tennis.
We listen to the radio that
Jeremy brings with him.

When Jeremy and I play tennis,
we listen to Jeremy's radio.

> Sometimes you must change the wording when you combine sentences. Make sure that your new sentence makes sense!

Apply It

1–5. Revise this journal entry. Combine the five pairs of underlined sentences by using possessive nouns.

Revising

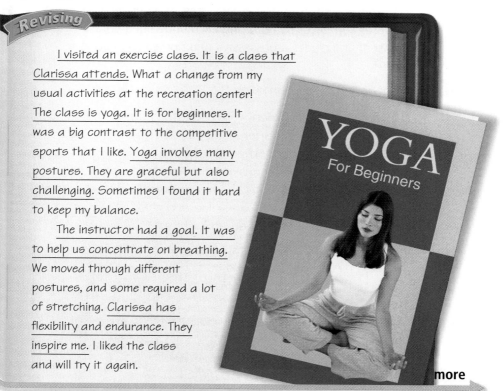

I visited an exercise class. It is a class that Clarissa attends. What a change from my usual activities at the recreation center! The class is yoga. It is for beginners. It was a big contrast to the competitive sports that I like. Yoga involves many postures. They are graceful but also challenging. Sometimes I found it hard to keep my balance.

The instructor had a goal. It was to help us concentrate on breathing. We moved through different postures, and some required a lot of stretching. Clarissa has flexibility and endurance. They inspire me. I liked the class and will try it again.

YOGA
For Beginners

more

Writing Concise Sentences Good writers avoid using wordy sentences. They can be hard for a reader to figure out and can slow the pace of reading. Sometimes you can change a long, wordy phrase into a possessive noun.

I am wearing the old jersey that belonged to my mom.

I am wearing my mom's old jersey.

You can also replace a string of rambling words with a strong noun.

Too Wordy

A good workout gives me a feeling of being really energized and happy and glad I did it.

When I play a lot of basketball, I gain more control over where I want my feet to go and how I handle the ball.

More Concise

A good workout gives me a feeling of exhilaration.

When I play a lot of basketball, I gain more coordination.

Apply It

6–12. Read this excerpt from a student's draft of a personal narrative. Revise the seven wordy sentences by replacing each underlined phrase with a shorter phrase that includes a possessive noun or a strong noun.

Revising

This summer, I went to a basketball camp that is run by Southwest Recreation. I improved my game using the drills of my coach. My team got three wins in a row because of the amazing skill belonging to the players. Playing so well is a thing that you accomplish after lots of hard work. Our mascot was blue and gold. The mascot of the opposing team was red and white.

On the last day of camp, the coaches passed out trophies. All the people who had gone to the camp that summer were there. The trophy from Coach Green was given to the most improved player.

Exact Nouns

Less Exact Nouns

The students collected food and clothing for their community service project.

More Exact Nouns

The students collected canned soup, coats, sweaters, and mittens for their community service project.

Use exact nouns to present your ideas clearly so that readers will understand them. By choosing a variety of nouns, you will also make your writing interesting and provide important details.

Apply It

1–10. Revise this ad about your class collection drive for a community service project. Use a more exact noun in place of each underlined noun. Delete any words that no longer make sense after you have substituted exact nouns.

WANTED

Our grade 8 class is collecting things for a local place. We are doing this as a project for a time. We need to get clothes for a variety of people. Since some are children, we also need things they can play with. Please be sure the stuff you bring is in good condition. We hope to deliver everything on a holiday. Please bring your donations to the school next week.

Enrichment

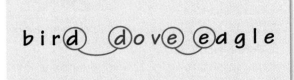

Nouns!

The Noun Connection

Players: 2

Materials: paper, pencil

To play: One player writes down a general category of concrete noun, such as *bird*. Using a different-colored pencil, the other player writes down a more exact noun, such as *dove*, that belongs in that category. The second noun must begin with the last letter of the first noun. Players take turns adding exact nouns that begin with the last letter of the previous noun.

bir**d** **d**ov**e** **e**agle

If a player is stumped, that player skips his or her turn. When both players are stumped, they start again with another general concrete noun.

Scoring: Each correct noun scores one point.

Challenge Try the game using only abstract nouns. Each noun may begin with any letter in the previous noun. Some categories might be *emotion, time, trait, condition, quality, ideal,* and *belief.*

TIME LINE

Choose a century that you have learned about recently. Make a horizontal time line showing several major events that occurred during that period. Beside each date, write a sentence about what happened. Use an appositive in each sentence.

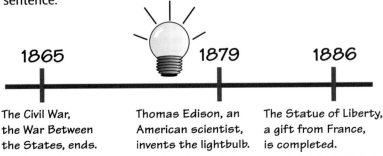

1865 — The Civil War, the War Between the States, ends.

1879 — Thomas Edison, an American scientist, invents the lightbulb.

1886 — The Statue of Liberty, a gift from France, is completed.

1 **Kinds of Nouns** *(p. 82)* Write each noun, and label it either *common* or *proper* and either *concrete* or *abstract*. Capitalize the proper nouns.

1. bridge
2. sadness
3. thanksgiving day
4. stripe
5. gulf of mexico
6. emma
7. north america
8. cousin
9. salt
10. sir francis drake
11. honor
12. truth
13. argentina
14. cucumber
15. detroit
16. year
17. joy
18. paper

2 **Compound and Collective Nouns** *(p. 85)* Write the compound nouns and the collective nouns. Label each one *compound* or *collective*.

19. Mrs. Romero is the best teacher of mathematics in our junior high school.
20. Yesterday she discussed geometric solids with our class.
21. After an engaging demonstration, Mrs. Romero passed out some math problems to the captivated audience.
22. We divided into small groups and worked on the problems.
23. Our teachers served as onlookers and checked our worksheets.
24. Even members of our math club thought that some problems were difficult.

3 **Singular and Plural Nouns** *(p. 90)* Write the correct form of the incorrectly spelled singular or plural nouns in these sentences. If a sentence has no incorrectly spelled word, write *correct*. Use your dictionary if you need help.

25. When you work with computers, you learn new wayes to use common words.
26. You have heard of a program and a window, but computer programes and windowes have very specific meanings.
27. Old-fashioned printers had daisy wheels, which looked a little like daisys or like spokes that have tooths on them.
28. Daisy wheels functioned like typewriter keyes.
29. Almost all professions have uses for the computer.
30. Doctors can use them to compare reactions to stimuluses.
31. Computers make it easier for doctors to make diagnosises.
32. Earth scientists might even use computers to analyze the different layers of rocks.
33. Farmers can keep track of their sheeps, pigs, and oxes.
34. Using a computer, a women's college would know where its alumnas lived and worked.
35. Be sure that the factes you put into computers are correct.
36. A saying of computer science is "Garbage in, garbage out."
37. The computer is a wonders of modern science.

Possessive Nouns *(p. 94)* For each singular noun, write the plural form, the possessive form, and the plural possessive form. Use your dictionary if you need help.

38. Iris
39. deer
40. father-in-law
41. gentleman
42. Bernstein
43. librarian
44. great-aunt
45. whale
46. hostess
47. author
48. Chong
49. firefighter
50. German shepherd

51. studio
52. Caroline
53. bird
54. Paco
55. chief
56. Ross
57. finch
58. Brock
59. mouse
60. editor
61. bass
62. teacher
63. May

64. Max
65. soprano
66. alto
67. baby
68. Estrada
69. sheep
70. ox
71. Victoria
72. Penny
73. beetle
74. alumnus
75. O'Malley
76. chorus

Mixed Review 77–86. Ten of the nouns on this shopping list have errors. Write each of the incorrectly written nouns correctly.

Proofreading Checklist
✔ capitalization of nouns
✔ plural forms of nouns
✔ possessive forms of nouns
✔ punctuation of appositives

Shopping List

oat puffs

cat food

sponges'

Mrs. Mains pie's

5-lb. bag of flours

tomatoes fresh and canned

spaghettis

juice boxs

yeast

orange's

honey

bananas

Baking Powder

Quinns oil soap

See www.eduplace.com/kids/hme/ for an online quiz.

Test Practice

Write the numbers 1–8 on a sheet of paper. Read each group of sentences. Choose the sentence that is written correctly. Write the letter for that answer.

1 A Jolene has been doing research at the Public Library.

   B She is preparing an oral report for her History class.

   C In her report Jolene will discuss the Middle Ages.

   D She is especially interested in the lives of Knights.

2 F The lights of the City look beautiful at night.

   G Which of those Skyscrapers is the tallest?

   H We'll take a cab to your Apartment Building.

   J Meet me in front of Johnson Towers in an hour.

3 A The cows and their calfs had gotten out of the pasture.

   B We saw the prints of their hoofs along the muddy path.

   C The herd had wandered into the woodses near the farm.

   D They were munching happily on fernes and bushs.

4 F In two monthes Nicole will be getting married.

   G Her two future sister-in-laws will be her bridesmaids.

   H Her friend Elena will sing two soloses during the ceremony.

   J Who will catch Nicole's bouquet of forget-me-nots?

5 A Mr. Hatchs' truck broke down on the highway.

   B The truck's engine started smoking.

   C Then Mr. Hatch saw a police cruisers' flashing lights.

   D Mr. Hatch was glad to have a police officers assistance.

6 F On Sunday we will celebrate my grandparent's anniversary.

   G We invited all of Grandma and Grandpa's friends.

   H The guest's invitations were mailed last week.

   J The grandchildrens' gift will be a special quilt.

7 A Germans shepherd make good guide dogs.

   B Do bears usually live in family groups?

   C The deers don't seem afraid of people.

   D The sheeps will be sheared tomorrow.

8 F Mr. Lopez teaches a physic class in the middle school.

   G The class activitys are interesting and challenging.

   H The students must use mathematics too.

   J Lucy gets mostly Bs' on her assignments for him.

Now write numbers 9–20 on your paper. Read each paragraph. Choose the line that shows the mistake. Write the letter for that answer. If there is no mistake, write the letter for the last answer.

9 A This flashlight's
   B batterys don't work. Please
   C buy some new ones today.
   D (No mistakes)

10 F After Mayor Curtis's
   G speech, about six reporters
   H asked questions.
   J (No mistakes)

11 A We made pie dough
   B with two cupful of flour, a
   C bit of cooking oil, and water.
   D (No mistakes)

12 F Hannah can sit besides
   G Jermaine, or she and Bree can
   H sit together in the next row.
   J (No mistakes)

13 A We should rehearse our parts
   B for the play. I think we should
   C practice during lunch time.
   D (No mistakes)

14 F The dance is tonight. I want
   G to wear my favorite pair of
   H pant. I hope they're clean.
   J (No mistakes)

15 A We are having a dry
   B summer. Since May only two
   C inches of rain in the area.
   D (No mistakes)

16 F Jasmine borrowed my
   G only pair of jeans and spilled
   H paint all over them.
   J (No mistakes)

17 A Will writes so good. I
   B like his funny stories, but the
   C serious ones are even better.
   D (No mistakes)

18 F That magician does an
   G amazing disappearing trick.
   H Nobody have figured it out.
   J (No mistakes)

19 A The awards banquet is
   B tonight. Ms Pou our principal
   C will present the trophies.
   D (No mistakes)

20 F Mr. James's history class
   G is my favorite. This month
   H we're studying the Civil War.
   J (No mistakes)

Unit 1: The Sentence

Kinds of Sentences *(p. 34)* Write each sentence, adding the correct end punctuation. Label each sentence *declarative, interrogative, imperative,* or *exclamatory.*

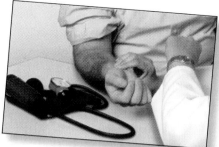

1. Put these two fingers on your wrist
2. Can you feel your pulse
3. What a strong pulse you have
4. Your heart works like a pump
5. Blood moves through your arteries
6. How does oxygen travel to your heart

Subjects and Predicates *(pp. 37, 40, 43, 46)* Write each sentence. Draw a line between the complete subject and the complete predicate. Underline each simple subject once and each simple predicate twice. Label the *compound subjects* or the *compound predicates.*

7. Alexander Hamilton, John Jay, and James Madison published *The Federalist.*
8. *The Federalist* is a series of eighty-five essays.
9. These essays explained republican government and encouraged acceptance of the Constitution.
10. Hamilton wrote most of the essays.
11. These essays argued against the existing government.
12. The strongest argument for acceptance of the Constitution must have been the need for law and order.

Compound Sentences, Conjunctions, and Complex Sentences *(pp. 51, 54, 57)* Write each sentence, and label it *simple, compound,* or *complex.* Underline each subordinate clause once and each subordinating conjunction twice.

13. Byron's friend is a dancer, and she is performing on Friday.
14. I would like to go, but I don't have the money.
15. If you lend me the money, I shall go.
16. Byron's friend is a talented dancer and singer.
17. Her skill has increased because she has practiced for years.
18. When she dances, she looks so graceful.
19. You practice, but you should practice more.
20. Most ballet dancers are lean, yet their muscles are well developed and finely conditioned.

See www.eduplace.com/kids/hme/ for a tricky usage or spelling question.

Fragments and Run-ons *(p. 63)* Rewrite these sentences, correcting each fragment and run-on.

21. A triangle has three sides a quadrilateral has four sides.
22. Because there are different kinds of quadrilaterals.
23. A square has four equal sides they join at right angles.
24. A rhombus has four equal sides. But no right angles.
25. Which quadrilaterals have right angles which ones do not?
26. A triangle with a right angle.
27. A scalene triangle has three sides. That are unequal.
28. An obtuse angle is more than ninety degrees, a triangle can have only one obtuse angle.
29. An angle less than ninety degrees.

Unit 2: Nouns

Kinds of Nouns *(p. 82)* Write the nouns. Label each one *concrete* or *abstract* and *common* or *proper*.

30. Sailors greet a lighthouse with respect.
31. Keepers of these buildings lead solitary but useful lives.
32. The light warns boats of the danger of rocks or reefs.
33. Ancient Libyans hung baskets of burning coal from towers.
34. Boats on the Mediterranean received these warnings.
35. Now the operation of these lights is automatic.
36. The structures often use computers that send out signals.
37. Most lighthouses today are not operated by people.
38. The romance of the lonely lighthouse still inspires poets and artists.

Singular, Plural, and Possessive Nouns *(pp. 90, 94)* For each singular noun, write the plural, singular possessive, and plural possessive forms. Use a dictionary if you need help.

39. moth
40. son-in-law
41. fly
42. Gus
43. Willis
44. May
45. America
46. squirrel

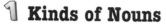
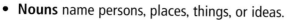

(pages 82–84)

1 Kinds of Nouns

- **Nouns** name persons, places, things, or ideas.
- **Common nouns** name general classes of things.
- **Proper nouns** name particular things and are capitalized.
- **Concrete nouns** refer to material things.
- **Abstract nouns** name ideas, feelings, or qualities.

Remember

● Write each noun. Then label it either *common* or *proper* and either *concrete* or *abstract.*

Example: horse *common concrete*

1. beauty	6. Chicago	11. molar
2. rider	7. Ms. Ling	12. cousin
3. trophy	8. idea	13. elegance
4. July	9. love	14. kindness
5. table	10. tuba	15. Lake Erie

▲ Write each noun, and label it either *common* or *proper* and either *concrete* or *abstract.*

Example: The Olympics include gymnastics.
   Olympics proper concrete   *gymnastics common concrete*

16. These exercises develop balance and strength.
17. The gymnast did a cartwheel with ease.
18. Silence filled the room, and the tension grew.
19. Shannon Miller won a medal.
20. The whistles, shouts, and applause were deafening.
21. The woman from China performed with confidence.

■ Write each sentence. Underline the nouns. Capitalize the proper nouns. Add the kind of noun in parentheses to complete each sentence.

Example: My favorite event in the olympics is _____. (concrete)
   My favorite event in the Olympics is archery.

22. It takes _____ to perform in front of a crowd. (abstract)
23. The swimmers dived with style and _____. (abstract)
24. A(n) _____ from japan won a medal for judo. (concrete)
25. The winner cried tears of _____. (abstract)
26. The runners jumped over the _____. (concrete)

(pages 85–87)

2 Compound and Collective Nouns

- A **compound noun** is a noun that is made up of more than one word. Some compound nouns are written as one word, some as separate words, and some as hyphenated words.
- A **collective noun** names a group of people, animals, or things considered as a unit.

● Write each underlined noun. Label it *compound* or *collective*.

Example: A <u>group</u> of hikers walked up the path.   *group collective*

1. The hikers walked through <u>Yellowstone National Park</u>.
2. A <u>flock</u> of birds called noisily in the branches overhead.
3. The birds sounded like a <u>band</u> of trumpets.
4. Was that a <u>crowd</u> of skiers in the distance?
5. The hikers were approaching the <u>mountaintop</u>.
6. They could see a faint <u>half-moon</u> in the sky.

▲ Write the compound nouns and the collective nouns. Label each one *compound* or *collective*.

Example: A crowd was gathering near the bandstand.
             crowd collective   *bandstand compound*

7. A team of horses for the carriages stood near the bikeway.
8. A German shepherd and a cocker spaniel slept under a bench.
9. The moonlight shone through a cluster of surrounding trees.
10. The woodwinds in the orchestra began to play.
11. New York City is always pleasant in the springtime.

■ Write a compound noun or a collective noun to complete each sentence. Label the noun *compound* or *collective*.

Example: Today is Charles's fourteenth _____.   *birthday compound*

12. His parents and the rest of his _____ are coming to dinner.
13. Charles's older sister is a student at _____.
14. A _____ of her friends has just returned from a camping trip.
15. They carried their belongings in _____ on their shoulders.
16. At night they slept in the outdoors in a public _____.

(pages 90–93)

3 Singular and Plural Nouns

Remember

- A **singular noun** names one person, place, thing, or idea.
- A **plural noun** names more than one.
- The plurals of nouns are formed in different ways. Check your dictionary if you are unsure about the spelling of a plural noun.

● Write the correct plural noun from each pair. Use your dictionary if you need help.

Example: memorys, memories   *memories*

1. foxes, foxs
2. radioes, radios
3. heros, heroes
4. stories, storys
5. tooths, teeth
6. bushs, bushes
7. chiefs, chieves
8. leafs, leaves
9. alumnuses, alumni
10. childs, children
11. cupsful, cupfuls
12. 5es, 5's

▲ Write the plural form of each noun in parentheses. Use your dictionary if you need help.

Example: Two _____ in the chorus brought their _____. (alto, cello)
       altos cellos

13. Use these _____ to cut those _____ of bread. (knife, loaf)
14. All the _____ ran, but the _____ walked. (child, man)
15. Did you catch many _____ on your fishing trip? (trout)
16. Two of the _____ escaped over the _____. (thief, roof)
17. _____ flew around the _____ of the _____. (Bee, hoof, donkey)

■ Rewrite each sentence, correcting the spelling errors in the plural nouns. Use your dictionary if you need help.

Example: The sopranoes gave forget-me-nots to the alumnuses.
       The sopranos gave forget-me-nots to the alumni.

18. My great-uncles raise gooses and turkies on their farms.
19. My sister-in-laws have won many trophys at the state fair.
20. They grow the best tomatos, zucchinis, and beetes.
21. Our sheep and lambes lead peaceful lifes.
22. The womans carried bucketsful of water to the horseses.

(pages 94–96)

④ **Possessive Nouns**

- A **possessive noun** shows ownership or relationship.
- To form the possessive of a singular noun, a plural noun not ending in *s,* or a compound noun, add an apostrophe and *-s* (*'s*).
- To form the possessive of a plural noun ending in *s,* add an apostrophe only (').

● Rewrite each word group, adding an apostrophe where necessary to form a possessive noun.

Example: peoples choice *people's choice*

1. sheeps wool
2. foxs color
3. Besss idea
4. ladies hats
5. the Smiths house
6. childrens toys
7. calves feet
8. mouses claws
9. flys wings
10. sisters-in-laws gloves
11. thieves goods
12. womens blouses

▲ Rewrite each word group, using a possessive noun.

Example: sneakers of the boy *boy's sneakers*

13. swim team for boys
14. clothing for men
15. words of Alex
16. voice of the alto
17. sweater of Tess
18. cold of James
19. room of Hank and Jack
20. house of the Evanses
21. desks of the girls
22. success of Mr. Tory
23. successes of the Torys
24. reign of King Charles
25. work of the doctor
26. poems by Pound and Frost

■ Rewrite each incorrect phrase correctly. If a phrase has no errors, write *correct.*

Example: this firefighters' helmet *this firefighter's helmet*

27. a man's sock
28. my sister Beths lunch
29. Uncle Boris' wig
30. that ladys' goldfish
31. the maid of honor's dress
32. the two girl's records
33. foxe's tail
34. one jurys' decision
35. three mens' beliefs
36. the bosses' assistants
37. a heros' welcome
38. the geeses' honks
39. each boys' shoes
40. the three lawyerses cases

Dart, sail, bolt, zip—
Fly, race, speed, rip!

Verbs

Kinds of Verbs

Read the sentences below. Find the verb that expresses a physical or mental action and the verb that expresses a state of being.

The earth smelled ripe. Now and again the wind blew in like the wheeze of an old horse.

—from *The Barn*, by Avi

Action and Being Verbs

You know that every sentence has a verb. The verb tells what the subject *has, does, is,* or *feels.*

Ed and Iris raise vegetables.   They feel happy.

1. Verbs express action or being. An **action verb** tells what the subject *has* or *does.* An action verb can express **physical** or **mental action**. Verbs like *run* and *look* express physical action. Verbs like *think* and *dream* express mental action.

   Physical: Farmers plow fields. Gardeners plant seeds.
   Mental: Farmers fear drought. They hope for rain.

2. A **being verb** does not refer to action but describes a state of being. It tells what the subject *is* or *feels.* Verbs such as *be, feel, appear, become,* and *seem* express being.

   The crop is ready for harvest.   The tomatoes feel soft.
   The beans look healthy.   The onions smell.

Try It Out

Speak Up Find each verb. Does it express mental action, physical action, or being?

1. Ed fed the seedlings.
2. The plants became bushy.
3. The pumpkins looked ripe.
4. Ed picked a pumpkin.
5. Iris dreamed of pumpkins.
6. Ed hoped for more pumpkins.
7. The squash was ripe too.
8. They put it into their basket.

Linking Verbs

A verb that expresses being is called a **linking verb** when it links the subject with a word in the predicate. The word in the predicate describes or identifies the subject.

Dill is an herb.   It looks feathery.

You can think of linking verbs as equal signs.

Pepper is a spice.   (Pepper = a spice)

Pepper tastes spicy. (Pepper = spicy)

Here are some common linking verbs.

appear	feel	remain	smell
be	grow	seem	sound
become	look	stay	taste

Some linking verbs can also be used as action verbs. If you can substitute a form of *be* for the verb, it is a linking verb.

Linking	Action
The tomato grew moldy. (The tomato was moldy.)	Jim grows tomatoes. (Jim is *not* tomatoes.)
The beans taste salty. (The beans are salty.)	The cook tasted the beans. (The cook is *not* the beans.)

Try It Out

Speak Up Find the verbs. Which ones are linking?

9. He looked at the recipe.
10. It looked difficult.
11. Chicken tastes delicious.
12. It was his favorite food.
13. Raymond became brave.
14. He plunged ahead.
15. He followed the recipe.
16. He smelled the garlic.
17. It smelled so good.
18. His task was successful.

Summing Up

- A **verb** expresses *action*—physical or mental—or *being*. Being verbs are sometimes linking verbs.
- A **linking verb** expresses *being*. It links the subject with a word in the predicate that describes or identifies the subject.

On Your Own

19–28. Write the ten verbs from this part of a restaurant review. Label each verb *action* or *linking*.

Example: The chef at Federico's understands Mexican food.
understands   action

Restaurant Review

Federico's Place remains one of the most authentic Mexican restaurants in our town. The head chef is Federico Carlos Dias. Federico lovingly recalls his grandmother's kitchen and her delicious tortillas. Like hers, his tortillas are handmade. His unique sauces taste and smell delicious. He uses a wide variety of fresh chili peppers, onions, and tomatoes. Then he adds his own herbs and spices. Frederico also imports poblano peppers from his native village in Mexico. With these, he makes one of the tastiest dishes on the menu, chiles rellenos.

Writing Wrap-Up   WRITING • THINKING • LISTENING • SPEAKING

COMPARING / CONTRASTING

Write a Food Review

Write a paragraph comparing and contrasting two meals—one that you really liked and one that you disliked. Use both linking verbs and action verbs. Exchange paragraphs with a partner, and label the linking and action verbs.

2 Verb Phrases

Find the verbs in the sentence below. Identify which are main verbs and which are helping verbs.

> I had smoothed my socks when I put on my shoes, but now with each step I could feel wrinkles beneath my toes...

—from "The Assault on the Record," by Stephen Hoffius in *Ultimate Sports: Short Stories by Outstanding Writers for Young Adults,* edited by Donald R. Gallo

You often use more than one word to make up a verb.

Heidi has gone to the meet.

She might not return until late, but we will wait.

1. A **main verb** expresses action or being. A **helping verb** helps complete the meaning of the main verb. One or more helping verbs and a main verb together form a **verb phrase**.

Helping Verb	Main Verb
Heidi is	running well today.
Soon she will have been	running for an hour.
Maybe she will	be a winner.

Common Helping Verbs

be, am, is, are	have, has, had	can, could	will, would
was, were, been	do, does, did	shall, should	may, might

2. You can use forms of *be, have,* and *do* as both main verbs and helping verbs.

Main: Heidi is not tired. She has an athlete's strength.

Helping: She is running now. She has run eight miles.

Sometimes a helping verb is hidden in a contraction.

She's running well today. (She's = She is)

Soon she'll be ready for the race. (she'll = she will)

3. Sometimes other words interrupt a verb phrase. These words are never part of the verb phrase.

Do you see any signs?   I can't find the map.

I cannot learn this route.   I shall never learn it.

Speak Up What is the verb phrase in each sentence? Which is the main verb, and which is the helping verb or verbs?

1. Fatuma has trained regularly for months for the first marathon race of the track season.
2. She's paced herself well throughout the race.
3. This marathon has always been twenty-six miles long.
4. Fatuma is now winning marathons.
5. She will fly across this finish line well ahead of most of the other runners.
6. Fatuma has finally been rewarded for her many months of hard work and dedication.
7. Will she compete in the next marathon?
8. She's already thinking about her preparations for next week's fifteen-mile race.

Summing Up

- A **verb phrase** includes a main verb and one or more helping verbs.
- The **main verb** expresses the action or being.
- The **helping verb** or verbs help complete the meaning of the main verb.

Write each verb phrase. Underline the main verb in each verb phrase.

Example: People have held athletic competitions since the time of the ancient Greeks.   *have held*

9. Ever since the days of ancient Greece, athletes have been competing in many sports.
10. Track-and-field events have been very popular for a long time.
11. In one type of track event, an athlete must leap over hurdles.
12. A good hurdler should have speed, rhythm, and balance.
13. A successful hurdler should also move with long strides.

more ▶

14. Of course a hurdler will have practiced for many hours before an important race.
15. Other great athletes may have trained for years for a specific track event.

16–26. Write the eleven verb phrases in this biographical sketch. Underline the main verb in each verb phrase.

Example: Jesse Owens is remembered for his courage as well as his speed.
is <u>remembered</u>

Web site

Jesse Owens: Olympic Hero

James Cleveland Owens was born in Alabama in 1913. He was called Jesse by his friends and family. In his early years, Jesse had often suffered respiratory problems. Yet, as a high school student, he was already setting records in track-and-field events. Soon he would be competing with world-class athletes.

To many people, Jesse's participation in the 1936 Olympic games in Nazi Germany might have seemed ironic. As an African American, Owens was not especially welcomed by the Nazis. Many people had boycotted the games because of Hitler's racist policies. Jesse Owens's ability, however, could not be denied. At the end of the games, he'd won four gold medals. Jesse Owens had dramatically contradicted Nazi theories.

Home   Forward   Back

Writing Wrap-Up

WRITING • THINKING • LISTENING • SPEAKING

EXPRESSING

Write a Testimonial

Write a paragraph about an athlete or some other person who has influenced your life. Use main verbs and helping verbs in your sentences. Volunteers can read their testimonials aloud to the class.

---

3 Tenses

Make up several sentences about a performer forgetting lines or saying them wrong. With your verbs, show the passage of time from the rehearsals (past) to the performance (more recent past or present).

Time is shown by the **tense** of a verb. You use different tenses of verbs to express different times.

Past Tense:	Last week we rehearsed all day every day.
Present Tense:	Now we rehearse in the afternoons.
Future Tense:	Next week we will rehearse in the mornings.

Principal Parts

To form tenses of verbs, you use **principal parts**. The principal parts of regular verbs follow a pattern.

The first principal part is the **base form** of the verb, for example, *jump*. The second principal part is the **present participle**. To form the present participle, add *-ing* to the base form of the verb: *jumping*. Use a form of the helping verb *be* with the present participle: *is jumping*.

The other principal parts are the **past** and the **past participle**. To form these principal parts of regular verbs, add *-ed* or *-d* to the verb: *jumped*. Use a form of the helping verb *have* with the past participle: *has jumped*.

Here are spelling rules for forming regular verb parts.

1. For a one-syllable verb ending with a single consonant, double the final consonant before adding *-ing* or *-ed*.

   chop—chopping—chopped

2. For verbs ending with *e,* drop the *e* before adding *-ed* or *-ing.* You might also say that the past and past participle of such verbs are formed simply by adding *-d.*

   type—typing—typed

3. For verbs ending with a consonant + *y,* change *y* to *i* before adding *-ed.*

   cry—crying—cried

Speak Up What are the principal parts of each verb? How do you spell them?

1. close
2. try
3. expect
4. compare
5. plan
6. carry
7. stop
8. inspect
9. trim
10. hurry
11. inspire
12. scan
13. glue
14. tumble
15. clarify
16. hum

Simple Tenses

Verbs have three **simple tenses** in English.

Tense	Use	Example
Present walk(s)	For situations that exist now; for repeated actions	She walks daily. They walk daily.
Past walked	For situations that occurred in the past	Yesterday she walked. Yesterday they walked.
Future will walk	For situations that will occur in the future	Later she will walk. Later they will walk.

Speak Up What are the forms for the three simple tenses of each verb used with *she* and with *they?*

17. mix
18. turn
19. step
20. survive
21. worry
22. pour
23. taste
24. cry
25. lift
26. drop

Perfect Tenses

The three perfect tenses are the **present perfect**, the **past perfect**, and the **future perfect**.

Tense	Use
Present Perfect has, have rehearsed	For something that took place in the past and may still be going on
Past Perfect had rehearsed	For something that took place before something else in the past
Future Perfect will have rehearsed	For something that will take place before something else in the future

Present Perfect:	He has rehearsed every day this week.
Past Perfect:	He had practiced before we came.
Future Perfect:	He will have finished when the bell rings.

Try It Out

Speak Up What are the forms for the three perfect tenses of each verb with *he* and with *they?*

27. cry
28. wash
29. scrape
30. clean
31. drop
32. paint

Summing Up

- Every verb has four **principal parts**: base form, present participle, past, past participle.
- Verbs have different **tenses** to express different times.
- Use the principal parts of a verb to form its tenses.

Write the four principal parts of each verb.

Example: skip *skip skipping skipped (has) skipped*

33. hop
34. look
35. pry

36. walk
37. receive
38. paint

39. wipe
40. spell
41. decide

42. select
43. name
44. rely

45–54. Write the correct verbs for the ten sentences in these paragraphs from a job application letter. For each verb, use the tense in parentheses.

Example: I _____ your advertisement in the newspaper *Variety*.
(notice—present perfect) *have noticed*

HELP WANTED
We are looking for
a creati...

    I _____ to apply for the advertised position as director of your Broadway company. (wish—present) In the past, I _____ many responsibilities as a director. (perform—present perfect) At the end of this year, I _____ the Tinytown Players for two years. (direct—future perfect) If I _____ how good I would be at directing, I would have started even sooner. (suspect—past perfect) Now I _____ a job in the big time. (want—present)

    In preparation for our present production, *Our Town,* I first _____ the script carefully. (study—past) Now we _____ auditions. (complete—present perfect) The cast _____ rehearsals tonight. (start—present) Over the next few weeks, I _____ numerous rehearsals. (direct—future) We confidently expect the same enthusiastic applause from an audience of dozens that we _____ in the past. (receive—present perfect)

Writing Wrap-Up   WRITING • THINKING • LISTENING • SPEAKING

INFORMING

Write a Letter of Application

Write a letter applying for a job. Emphasize your past accomplishments, either imaginary or real. Use at least four tenses, including two perfect tenses. Volunteers can read their letters aloud.

4 Forms of *be, have,* and *do*

What is wrong with these sentences? How can you fix them?
My mother's maiden name were Mary Beatrice Reilly.
As a child she liked beets, so she have the nickname Mary Beets.

Be, have, and *do* are verbs that you use very often. You can use forms of these verbs as main verbs and as helping verbs.

Main Verb	Helping Verb
Beets are delicious.	We are growing beets this year.
Beets have edible roots.	We have grown them every year.
Beets do well in loamy soil.	Do you like beets? I really do like beets.

All three verbs can form contractions with *not:* for example, *isn't, aren't, hasn't, haven't, doesn't,* and *don't.*

Dana **doesn't** like beets.   Shaun **isn't** a gardener.

Be, have, and *do* have different forms for different subjects and for different tenses. The chart below shows present and past forms of *be, have,* and *do.*

Subject	*be*	*have*	*do*
Singular Subjects			
I	am, was	have, had	do, did
you	are, were	have, had	do, did
he, she, it (or singular noun)	is, was	has, had	does, did
Plural Subjects			
we	are, were	have, had	do, did
you	are, were	have, had	do, did
they (or plural noun)	are, were	have, had	do, did

Speak Up Which verb form in parentheses completes each sentence correctly?

1. The weather (is, are) very dry this year.
2. The Dunns (does, do) not know what they will do if it (does, do) not rain soon.
3. The crops (do, did) well last year.
4. Animals (have, has) problems when the weather (is, are) dry.
5. Last year the Dunns (have, had) a healthy harvest.
6. This year their neighbor (has, have) a new irrigation system.
7. (Do, Does) wheat require a lot of water?
8. When (did, do) Mr. Cato plant his crops?
9. I (am, are) interested in farming.
10. How much rain (do, does) the crops need?
11. We (haven't, hasn't) had rain for weeks.
12. According to the radio, a storm (is, are) coming soon.

Summing Up

- You can use *be, have,* and *do* as main verbs and as helping verbs.
- *Be, have,* and *do* have different forms for different subjects and for different tenses.

Write each sentence, using the correct form of the verb.

Example: The crops (have, had) no rain for weeks.   *had*

13. The vegetable crops (has, have) wilted from lack of rain.
14. The Dunns (do, did) everything they possibly could do.
15. (Does, Do) the sky look dark?
16. (Am, Is) I imagining it, or are those rain clouds?
17. I (does, do) believe I see raindrops.

more ▶

18. (Do, Does) you see them too?
19. We (wasn't, weren't) expecting rain.
20. No one (has, have) listened to a weather report today.
21. (Are, Is) the crops going to be all right?
22. A heavy rain (are, is) what the crops need.
23. The farmers (is, are) happy to see the rain.
24. We will (have, has) a healthy harvest after all.
25. I (am, are) looking forward to eating fresh vegetables.

26–34. Write correctly the nine incorrect forms of *be*, *have*, and *do* from this part of a letter to a friend.

Example: Has you ever seen a white eggplant?   *Have*

Proofreading

> I had discovered a vegetable I really like to eat. When I first saw it at the supermarket, it does not look as if it would taste very good. It looked as if it have a burned purple skin. I thought it is some huge, ugly egg. Vegetables is not my favorite foods, anyway. I usually does not really enjoy eating them. I found out at dinner, however, that the eggplant have a delicious taste. It are now among my favorite things to eat. It were everything vegetables should be—tasty and good for you.

Writing Wrap-Up

WRITING • THINKING • LISTENING • SPEAKING

DESCRIBING

Write a Letter

Write a short letter to a friend describing a new vegetable you plan to genetically engineer. Use *be*, *have*, and *do* both as helping verbs and as main verbs. Exchange letters with a partner. Identify the helping verbs and main verbs in each other's letters.

   For Extra Practice see page 176.

5 Irregular Verbs

Use the verbs *cast, catch,* and *hurt* in two or three sentences describing what you see in the picture. In your sentences use an *-ing* form of one verb and a helping verb with another.

To form the past and past participles of regular verbs, you follow a certain rule: you add *-d* or *-ed* to the base form of the verb. **Irregular verbs** do not follow any rules. You must learn the principal parts of each one. It may help you to use the verb forms in short sentences such as these.

Today I speak.   Yesterday I spoke.
Now I am speaking.   Often I have spoken.

You have just learned some forms of the verbs *be, have,* and *do.* Here are their principal parts.

Verb	Present Participle	Past	Past Participle
be	(is) being	was, were	(has) been
have	(is) having	had	(has) had
do	(is) doing	did	(has) done

The following irregular verbs are arranged in related groups. Some irregular verbs have the same form for the verb, the past, and the past participle.

Verb	Present Participle	Past	Past Participle
burst	(is) bursting	burst	(has) burst
cast	(is) casting	cast	(has) cast
cost	(is) costing	cost	(has) cost
cut	(is) cutting	cut	(has) cut
hit	(is) hitting	hit	(has) hit
hurt	(is) hurting	hurt	(has) hurt
let	(is) letting	let	(has) let
put	(is) putting	put	(has) put
set	(is) setting	set	(has) set

Some irregular verbs have the same form for the verb and the past participle.

Verb	Present Participle	Past	Past Participle
become	(is) becoming	became	(has) become
come	(is) coming	came	(has) come
run	(is) running	ran	(has) run

Some irregular verbs have the same form for the past and the past participle.

Verb	Present Participle	Past	Past Participle
bend	(is) bending	bent	(has) bent
bring	(is) bringing	brought	(has) brought
buy	(is) buying	bought	(has) bought
catch	(is) catching	caught	(has) caught
feel	(is) feeling	felt	(has) felt
find	(is) finding	found	(has) found
hold	(is) holding	held	(has) held
lay	(is) laying	laid	(has) laid
lead	(is) leading	led	(has) led
leave	(is) leaving	left	(has) left
lend	(is) lending	lent	(has) lent
lose	(is) losing	lost	(has) lost
make	(is) making	made	(has) made
pay	(is) paying	paid	(has) paid
read	(is) reading	read	(has) read
say	(is) saying	said	(has) said
seek	(is) seeking	sought	(has) sought
sell	(is) selling	sold	(has) sold
shine	(is) shining	shone	(has) shone
sit	(is) sitting	sat	(has) sat
sleep	(is) sleeping	slept	(has) slept
stand	(is) standing	stood	(has) stood
sting	(is) stinging	stung	(has) stung
swing	(is) swinging	swung	(has) swung
teach	(is) teaching	taught	(has) taught
tell	(is) telling	told	(has) told
think	(is) thinking	thought	(has) thought
win	(is) winning	won	(has) won

Speak Up What are the four principal parts of these irregular verbs?

1. burst
2. have
3. swing
4. buy
5. lose
6. run
7. set
8. become
9. say
10. be
11. hit
12. come
13. cut
14. do
15. shine
16. hold

Summing Up

- **Irregular verbs** do not follow rules for forming the past and past participles. You must learn the principal parts of irregular verbs.

Write each sentence, using the correct form of the verb in parentheses.

Example: I had _____ a few books about a great new sport.
    (buy—past participle)
    I had bought a few books about a great new sport.

17. I first _____ interested in fishing by watching a nature program on television. (become—past)
18. I never _____, however, that I would land a rainbow trout. (think—past)
19. I had _____ my friends that I wanted to try this sport someday. (tell—past participle)
20. I don't know how my father _____ out about my interest. (find—past)
21. My father _____ me a rod, line, hooks, and bait. (lend—past)
22. Then he _____ me some basic skills. (teach—past)
23. Finally, the day had _____. (come—past participle)
24. I was _____ at the edge of the dock. (stand—present participle)

more ▶

25. I _____ the rod back in a wide arc. (swing—past)
26. Then I _____ the line into the water. (cast—past)
27. The hook _____ the water lightly. (hit—past)
28. In a few seconds, I _____ a nibble on the line. (feel—past)
29. Dad and I were _____ the fish in with a net when I realized something. (bring—present participle)
30. I had _____ my first rainbow trout. (catch—past participle)

31–38. Write correctly the eight incorrect verbs from this student journal. All of the errors are verbs in either past or past participle form.

Example: Last summer, no one felted the changes in the cod fishing industry more than my father. *felt*

Proofreading

Last year, the government sayed that commercial cod fishing must slow down off New England's shores. It reported that overfishing had cutted the fish population. My father is a fisherman and has catched cod for twenty years. At first he telled himself that the government was wrong, but he could not break the law.

Mom says that cod fishing has ran Dad's life for twenty summers. I saw how it hurted him when he put his boat in dry dock. The insurance on the boat costed more this year than his income from fishing. Now my dad has became a ship's carpenter and he repairs boats.

Writing Wrap-Up   WRITING • THINKING • LISTENING • SPEAKING

CREATING

Write a Poem
Write a poem describing your favorite time of day. Use the principal parts of some of the irregular verbs from this lesson. Share your poem with a partner. What does your choice of "favorite time of day" say about you?

6 More Irregular Verbs

One-Minute Warm-Up

What is wrong with these two sentences? How can you fix them?

Unfortunately, Yang choosed the steeper bike path.

Now, he has fell off his bike into a prickly bush!

Here are two more groups of irregular verbs to learn.

The vowel in some irregular verbs changes from *i* in the verb and present participle to *a* in the past and *u* in the past participle.

HELP ? Tip

If you are not sure whether a verb is regular or irregular, you can find the principal parts in your dictionary.

Verb	Present Participle	Past	Past Participle
begin	(is) beginning	began	(has) begun
drink	(is) drinking	drank	(has) drunk
ring	(is) ringing	rang	(has) rung
sing	(is) singing	sang	(has) sung
sink	(is) sinking	sank	(has) sunk
spring	(is) springing	sprang	(has) sprung
swim	(is) swimming	swam	(has) swum

Other irregular verbs have past forms that follow no pattern and past participle forms that end with *n, en,* or *ne.*

Verb	Present Participle	Past	Past Participle
blow	blowing	blew	blown
break	breaking	broke	broken
choose	choosing	chose	chosen
drive	driving	drove	driven
eat	eating	ate	eaten
fall	falling	fell	fallen
fly	flying	flew	flown

Verb	Present Participle	Past	Past Participle
forget	forgetting	forgot	forgotten
freeze	freezing	froze	frozen
give	giving	gave	given
go	going	went	gone
grow	growing	grew	grown
know	knowing	knew	known
lie	lying	lay	lain
ride	riding	rode	ridden
rise	rising	rose	risen
see	seeing	saw	seen
speak	speaking	spoke	spoken
take	taking	took	taken
throw	throwing	threw	thrown
wear	wearing	wore	worn
write	writing	wrote	written

Try It Out

Speak Up What are the four principal parts
of each of these irregular verbs?

1. eat
2. go
3. ring
4. take
5. write
6. swim
7. choose
8. know
9. break
10. wear
11. fly
12. throw
13. begin
14. forget
15. speak
16. blow

Summing Up

- You must learn the principal parts of irregular verbs.

Write the principal parts of each verb.

Example: blow *blow blowing blew blown*

17. drive
18. fall
19. give
20. sink
21. ride

22. freeze
23. see
24. drink
25. sing
26. spring

27–36. Write correctly the ten incorrect verbs in this entry from a travel journal. All of the errors are in either past or past participle forms.

Example: On hot days we always laid in the shade. *lay*

Proofreading

We have saw and done a lot here in New Mexico. Yesterday, we swum in the Rio Grande. The current taked us from our diving rock southward to a hot spring. We eaten taquitas and apricots in the noon sun. Then, we lain on the rocks in the shade.

We can boast now that we have rode horses on Native American land. We can say that we have sang Native American songs at a powwow. At the trading post, I choosed Apache moccasins, and my sister bought some Hopi silver earrings. My mom worn her cowboy hat everywhere. (What can I say? She's embarrassing, but I have knowed her a long time, and I love her.)

Writing Wrap-Up WRITING · THINKING · LISTENING · SPEAKING

REFLECTING

Write a Journal Entry

Write a paragraph describing when you feel most in touch with nature. Use at least three of the irregular verbs from this lesson. Exchange your journal entry with a partner. Ask your partner to give the four principal parts of one of the verbs you used.

7 Progressive Forms

One-Minute Warm-Up

How can you change the verb in this sentence to show that the action is taking place right now? to show that it will continue to take place in the future?

Dolphins swim in the waters off the Outer Banks of North Carolina.

The **progressive form** of a verb shows that the action is continuing. Study the verbs in the following sentences. When is the action taking place?

Tillie collects seashells.   Tillie is collecting seashells.

The sentence on the left tells you that Tillie collects seashells often or regularly. The sentence on the right tells you that Tillie is collecting them right now. The action is *in progress*. The verb *is collecting* shows a progressive or continuing action. The progressive form of a verb is the present participle combined with a form of *be*. Each of the six verb tenses has a progressive form. Forms of the helping verb *be* show the tense.

Present Progressive:	The trained dolphin is performing now.
Past Progressive:	It was performing yesterday.
Future Progressive:	It will be performing tomorrow.
Present Perfect Progressive:	It has been performing all day.
Past Perfect Progressive:	It had been performing for an hour when we arrived.
Future Perfect Progressive:	It will have been performing for four hours when we leave.

Try It Out

Speak Up What is the form of each of the verbs in parentheses?

1. Brad and I _____ a skin-diving course together. (take—present perfect progressive)
2. We _____ about such a course since last summer. (think—past perfect progressive)

more ▶

Try It Out continued

3. We _____ about special equipment for the sport.
   (learn—present perfect progressive)
4. One day we _____ a slide show when a real diver came in.
   (watch—past progressive)
5. The diver _____ a face mask and breathing through a snorkel.
   (wear—past progressive)
6. While he was instructing us, we _____ strokes and discussing safety.
   (practice—past progressive)
7. One day next week we _____ for the first time.
   (dive—future progressive)
8. Experienced divers _____ us on our first dive. (accompany—future
   progressive)
9. Brad and I _____ forward to our first dive since the beginning of the
   class. (look—present perfect progressive)
10. By the time we go on vacation, we _____ about this sport for a
    month. (learn—future perfect progressive)

Summing Up

- Each tense has a **progressive form** to express continuing action.
- Form the progressive with an appropriate tense of *be* plus the present participle.

On Your Own

Write the six progressive forms of each verb.

Example: fly   *is flying*   *was flying*   *will be flying*
                has been flying   *had been flying*   *will have been flying*

11. make	14. speak	
12. sell	15. win	
13. cut	16. write	

more ▶

17–26. Write each of the ten verbs in this Web site article on deep-sea diving. Use the verb and the progressive form given in parentheses.

Example: Divers _____ all the time for treasure aboard sunken ships.
(look—present progressive)   *are looking*

Every day, somewhere in the world's oceans, divers (find—present progressive) a different world under the surface of the sea. People (dive—present perfect progressive) underwater for centuries. Scientists (test—past progressive) underwater equipment already in the eighteenth century. Before that, divers (use—past perfect progressive) no special equipment. Since 1900, inventors (solve—present perfect progressive) many technical problems. In 1915, a large number of divers (use—past progressive) ordinary air. By

1939, however, they (try—past progressive) mixtures of helium and oxygen.

By the year 2000, divers (explore—past perfect progressive) the deep for six thousand years. Future divers (explore—future progressive) the sea floor at ever greater depths. When they rise to the surface, they (stay—future perfect progressive) underwater longer than any divers before them.

Writing Wrap-Up   WRITING • THINKING • LISTENING • SPEAKING

DESCRIBING

Write a TV Program Description
Write several sentences describing the setting of a made-for-television movie. Use several progressive verbs and at least two different verb tenses. Read your sentences aloud to a partner. Work together to identify the progressive forms of each verb.

   For Extra Practice see page 179.

Writing with Verbs

Using Tenses Consistently Verb tenses show the time of an event. When you write, use tenses carefully. Put verbs in the same tense to write about events occurring at the same time.

Incorrect

On Friday I went snorkeling for the first time, and it is exhilarating.

The instructor was pointing at his snorkel and mask. He tells me to get ready to dive.

Correct

On Friday I went snorkeling for the first time, and it was exhilarating.

The instructor was pointing at his snorkel and mask. He was telling me to get ready to dive.

Apply It

1–7. Read the message on the post card below. Rewrite the sentences, putting each verb in the correct tense.

Revising

Three days ago, my family takes a boat trip to a cove, where we snorkeled. I saw many fish, and a bass even swims right by me. It is huge. It was as big as my arm.

Then we went back to the marina. There were many crabs around the docks. Mom gives us special rods to catch crabs, and guess what? We catch a dozen crabs in an hour. That night, dinner tastes really good as we ate all the crabs we caught.

The next day, we went to the beach because it is sunny. Mom and Dad read books while we swam in the ocean.

PLACE STAMP HERE

Tara Smyth
121 Cottage Street
Oakville, MD 20019

more

Telling Exactly When Sometimes you will write about events that happened at different times. Use the correct tense to tell exactly when each event occurred.

Incorrect	Correct
I <u>raise</u> tropical fish in an aquarium. I <u>own</u> some of my fish for five years.	I <u>raise</u> tropical fish in an aquarium. I <u>have owned</u> some of my fish for five years.
Last week I <u>had bought</u> a black molly. It <u>lives</u> for years if I <u>keep</u> the aquarium clean.	Last week I <u>bought</u> a black molly. It <u>will live</u> for years if I <u>keep</u> the aquarium clean.

Apply It

8–14. Revise these excerpts from a science journal. Use the correct tense to tell exactly when each event occurred.

Revising

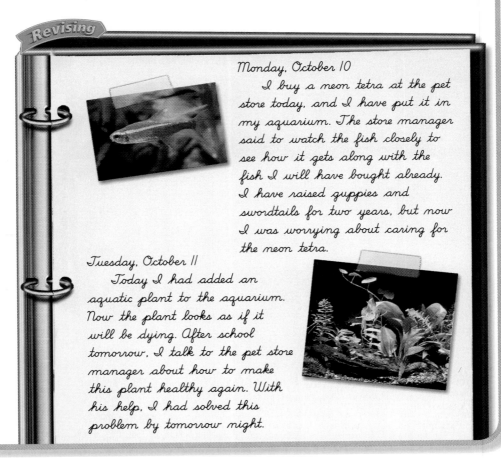

Monday, October 10

I buy a neon tetra at the pet store today, and I have put it in my aquarium. The store manager said to watch the fish closely to see how it gets along with the fish I will have bought already. I have raised guppies and swordtails for two years, but now I was worrying about caring for the neon tetra.

Tuesday, October 11

Today I had added an aquatic plant to the aquarium. Now the plant looks as if it will be dying. After school tomorrow, I talk to the pet store manager about how to make this plant healthy again. With his help, I had solved this problem by tomorrow night.

136 Unit 3: Verbs

8 Transitive and Intransitive Verbs

One-Minute Warm-Up

Find the two verbs in the sentence below. Which verb takes an object? Which verb does not?

The birds sang only gray songs and the road wound back and forth in an endless series of climbing curves.

—from *The Phantom Tollbooth*, by Norton Juster

1. Most verbs express action. Often that action is directed toward another word in the predicate. A verb that directs action toward something or someone named in the predicate is called a **transitive verb**.

> **Transitive:** The mechanic had repaired the truck.
> The owner paid the mechanic.

The word in the predicate to which the action of the verb is directed is the **object**. A transitive verb always has at least one object. If you can answer the question *what?* or *whom?* after an action, then you know that the verb is transitive.

> **Transitive:** The mechanic watched the *driver*. (Watched *whom?* The driver.)
> The driver unlocked the *cab*. (Unlocked *what?* The cab.)

2. An **intransitive verb** does not have an object. There is no "receiver" of the action.

> **Intransitive:** The truck was running well.   The driver turned left quickly.

Often words following an intransitive verb answer the questions *how?*, *when?*, or *where?*

> The driver drove away. (Drove *where?* Away.)
> The truck ran smoothly. (Ran *how?* Smoothly.)

Sometimes, though, an intransitive verb is the only word in the predicate.

> The driver continued.

3. Some verbs can be used either transitively or intransitively.

> **Transitive:** He opened the window.
> **Intransitive:** The window opened easily.

Linking verbs are always intransitive. They do not express action, and they cannot, therefore, have objects.

Linking Verbs: The driver looked comfortable.
The trip became a pleasure.

Try It Out

Speak Up Find each main verb. Is the verb transitive or intransitive?

1. First, Wing Fai put some tape on the wall.
2. He gently hammered a nail into the tape.
3. The picture felt heavy to him.
4. He attached strong wire to the back of the picture frame.
5. Finally, he lowered the picture over the nail.
6. Wing Fai stepped back from the picture.
7. It looked a little crooked to him.
8. He pushed the corner of the picture frame down slightly.
9. Finally, the picture appeared level.

Summing Up

- A **transitive verb** expresses action that is directed toward a word in the predicate.
- The word to which the action is directed is the **object** of the verb.
- An **intransitive verb** does not have an object.
- Linking verbs are always intransitive.

On Your Own

List each main verb. Label it *transitive* or *intransitive*.

Example: Heavy rains had destroyed part of the road.
had destroyed   transitive

10. The damage to the road had occurred over a week ago.
11. Ruts and holes in the road had disrupted traffic for several days.   **more ▶**

12. People in the neighborhood called the city highway department.
13. Some people were angry about the road's condition.
14. Drivers moved slowly around the deep ruts in the road.
15. One man could not exit his driveway because of the damage.
16. A road crew arrived at the washed-out part of the road.
17. The workers shoveled dirt into the uneven places.
18. At lunchtime they ate their sandwiches under nearby trees.
19. Several hours of work remained for the crew.
20. Lightly at first, the rain began again.
21. They worked in the rain during the late afternoon.

22–26. List the five verbs from this entry in a construction supervisor's log. Label each verb *transitive* or *intransitive*.

Example: The leveling machine came to the site. *came—intransitive*

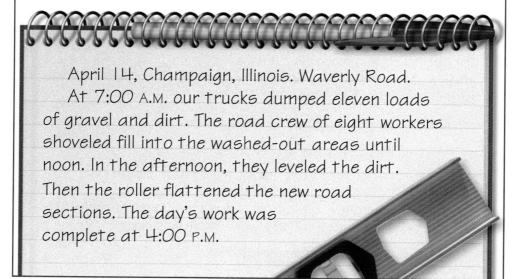

April 14, Champaign, Illinois. Waverly Road.
At 7:00 A.M. our trucks dumped eleven loads of gravel and dirt. The road crew of eight workers shoveled fill into the washed-out areas until noon. In the afternoon, they leveled the dirt. Then the roller flattened the new road sections. The day's work was complete at 4:00 P.M.

Writing Wrap-Up
WRITING • THINKING • LISTENING • SPEAKING

EXPLAINING

Write Instructions
Write instructions for repairing or taking care of something such as a bicycle, a pet, or a computer. Exchange instructions with a partner. Read each other's instructions aloud and decide whether transitive or intransitive verbs occur more frequently.

9 Direct and Indirect Objects

Make up a sentence using three nouns that the picture might suggest. Does any noun in your sentence directly receive the action of the verb? If so, which one?

Direct Objects

You know that transitive verbs are action verbs. Transitive verbs have objects.

Arlene has the ball.

The umpire annoyed the catcher.

The outfielders grabbed their mitts.

HELP

? Tip

Be careful not to mistake the object of a preposition for an object of the verb.

1. The **direct object** is a noun or a pronoun in the predicate to which the action of the verb is directed or done. The direct object answers the question *whom?* or *what?*

    Transitive: The pitcher noticed me. (noticed *whom?* me)

    The pitcher threw the ball. (threw *what?* the ball)

    The shortstop swung his bat. (swung *what?* his bat)

2. As you know, intransitive verbs do not take objects. Do not be confused by words in the predicate that tell how, when, or where an action happens.

    Intransitive: The ball swerved suddenly. *(how?)*

    We will play again tomorrow. *(when?)*

    We'll all meet here. *(where?)*

Direct objects may be compound.

The catcher wanted his mask but not his mitt.

Did the manager ask the umpire or the third-base coach?

The batboy dropped the ball and the bat.

Speak Up Find the verbs. What are the direct objects of the verbs?

1. Ezra's new uniform had grease on it.
2. Ezra washed the uniform first in cold water.
3. Plain soap and water did not remove the dirt.
4. Finally, Ezra tried a commercial cleaner.
5. The local dry cleaner had recommended the product highly.
6. Ezra just sprayed the liquid onto the uniform.
7. The product dissolved the filth instantly.
8. Ezra wrote a letter to the manufacturer.
9. Could he do a commercial about his dazzling uniform?

Indirect Objects

A sentence may have more than one kind of object.

Ezra <u>wrote</u> the manufacturer a letter.

1. An **indirect object** tells *to whom, for whom, to what,* or *for what* the action of the verb is done. The indirect object comes between the verb and the direct object. The indirect object is always a noun or a pronoun.

           IO   DO   IO   DO

   Jay's homer <u>gave</u> the team a lead. The team <u>awarded</u> him a trophy.

2. When *to* or *for* appears before a noun or a pronoun, the noun or pronoun is not an indirect object.

                                       IO   DO

   Indirect Object: The manufacturer <u>sent</u> him a letter.

                                     DO

   No Indirect Object: He <u>sent</u> a letter to him.

3. Like a direct object, an indirect object may be compound.

                 IO   IO   DO

   The coach <u>gave</u> the pitcher and the batter some advice.

            IO   IO   DO

   He <u>told</u> Sam and Jim a joke.

Speak Up Find each verb and its object or objects, if any. Is each object a direct or an indirect object?

10. The catcher gave Johnson the signal for a curve ball.
11. Johnson threw the batter the ball.
12. The batter delivered a fly ball to the left fielder.
13. The fielder caught it, and the batter was out.
14. The batboy handed the next player a bat.
15. Johnson threw the batter his most famous pitch.
16. The knuckle ball caught the air currents and danced wildly.
17. The batter held the bat out and tapped the ball forward.
18. He sent the pitcher a bunt.

Summing Up

- The **direct object** of a sentence is a noun or a pronoun in the predicate to which the action of the verb is directed or done.

- The **indirect object** is a noun or a pronoun in the predicate that tells *to* or *for whom* or *to* or *for what* the action is done. The indirect object comes between the verb and the direct object.

Write each verb or verb phrase. If it is transitive, write its object. Label each object *direct object* or *indirect object*.

Example: The players are showing the crowd an exciting game tonight.
        verb: are showing   indirect object: crowd   direct object: game

19. The announcers are giving the radio audience a play-by-play report.
20. The umpire has just handed the players his decision.
21. Certainly this will teach the visitors a lesson.
22. Browning's play probably gave this boisterous crowd the thrill of a lifetime.

more ▶

23. Now the excited spectators are giving this great pitcher a loud cheer.
24. Will this stunning victory bring Browning a new contract next season?
25. The team's pitching coach must have shown him some new strategies.
26. The two teams will meet again in Toronto tomorrow night.
27. Jack Torres should pitch an exciting game.

28–38. Write the eleven verbs or verb phrases in this television sports announcers' dialogue. Label each object *direct object* or *indirect object*.

Example: The crowd gave the home team a warm reception today.
　　　　verb: gave　indirect object: team　direct object: reception

> **Al:** Stratton has just slammed his bat and cap onto the ground. The batboy gives him another bat.
>
> **Jason:** Now Stratton hits the first pitch into left field. Whoops, Gilmore misses the catch but recovers the ball! This slugger is giving fielders and fans a scare today.
>
> **Al:** Stratton reaches first base. Safe! Now Evans is coming to the plate. The pitcher delivers Evans a curve ball right over the plate.
>
> **Jason:** Whoa, Evans pops a high fly to Fox, and the game is over!

Writing Wrap-Up

WRITING • THINKING • LISTENING • SPEAKING

NARRATING

Write Dialogue

Write the dialogue between two news announcers giving a live report on an important baseball game. The dialogue is part of a larger story recounting the rise of a championship baseball team. Use both direct objects and indirect objects. Take the role of one announcer, and have a partner take the role of the other announcer. Discuss with your partner how you could make your dialogue more effective.

10 Predicate Nouns and Predicate Adjectives

Name the nouns in the sentence below that refer to the subject of the sentence, *breakfast*.

In India breakfast is often yogurt, bread, lentils, and tea.

—from *Passport on a Plate: A Round-the-World Cookbook for Children*, by Diane Simone Vezza

A linking verb links, or connects, the subject to a word in the predicate. This word in the predicate always refers to the subject.

Cheese is good for you.   Edam is a cheese.

Cheese is a popular food.

Certain cheeses are very expensive.

1. Sometimes the word that is linked to the subject is a noun that renames the subject. It is called a **predicate noun**.

   Cheese is a dairy product. Cheddar remains my favorite cheese.

2. Sometimes the word that is linked to the subject is an adjective that describes the subject. This word is called a **predicate adjective**.

   Cheese tastes delicious.   Some cheeses smell strong.

3. Be sure that you do not confuse the linking verb *be* with the helping verb *be*.

   Helping Verb: Daniel is making blueberry yogurt.   (*Yogurt* is a direct object.)
   Kim is buying a pound of imported cheese.
   (*Pound* is a direct object.)

   Linking Verb: Yogurt is a tasty, healthy food.   (*Food* is a predicate noun.)
   This cherry yogurt tastes very sweet.

4. Like other parts of a sentence, predicate nouns and predicate adjectives may be compound.

   Blue cheese is moldy but healthful.

   Roquefort is a village in France and a cheese.

Speak Up What are the subjects and the linking verbs in these sentences? Is the underlined word a predicate noun or a predicate adjective?

1. Cow's milk is the <u>base</u> for most of our cheeses, yogurts, and ice creams.
2. Cheeses from the milk of goats are not only <u>available</u> but also <u>delicious</u>.
3. In parts of Asia, buffalo milk remains the major <u>ingredient</u> of some cheeses.
4. Cheese from reindeer's milk seems <u>similar</u> to Swiss cheese.
5. Cheese from camel's milk is <u>popular</u> in certain areas of central Asia.
6. Sheep's milk has long been <u>common</u> in the Middle East.
7. Cheeses from these animals may be <u>mild</u> or <u>strong</u>.
8. Cheese is the favorite <u>food</u> of many people.
9. Cheese and crackers is a tasty <u>snack</u>.
10. A diet of only cheese and carbohydrates would be <u>fatty</u> and <u>unhealthful</u>.

Summing Up

- Predicate nouns and predicate adjectives follow linking verbs.

- A **predicate noun** identifies or renames the subject.

- A **predicate adjective** describes the subject.

Write each verb or verb phrase. If it is a linking verb, write and label the predicate noun or the predicate adjective.

Example: About four hundred cheeses are available.
linking verb: are   predicate adjective: available

11. The manufacturing processes are alike for all cheeses.
12. The curd is the solid part of the milk.
13. The liquid part is the whey.

more ▶

14. The cheesemaker separates the curd from the whey.
15. Curd thickens with the addition of rennet and certain bacteria.
16. Rennet is an extract made from the lining of a calf's fourth stomach.
17. The cheesemakers next press the curd together.
18. Slowly, the curd becomes more solid.
19. The thickened mass eventually becomes cheese.
20. The cheese manufacturers sell the cheese to food stores.

21–26. Write the six verbs or verb phrases in the paragraph from a newspaper food column below. If a verb is a linking verb, write and label the predicate noun or the predicate adjective.

Example: Cheese has become extremely popular.
linking verb: has become   predicate adjective: popular

Cheese's Growing Popularity

People are including cheese with breakfast, lunch, and dinner. Cheese can be an appetizer, a recipe ingredient, or a snack. It enhances pizza, cheeseburgers, and tacos. Soft cheeses, such as Brie, are creamy and substantial. Mozzarella, Monterey Jack, and Muenster cheeses seem mild to most tastes. A sharper cheese, such as Gorgonzola, is delicious for the more adventurous cheese lover.

Writing Wrap-Up   WRITING • THINKING • LISTENING • SPEAKING

PERSUADING

Write an Ad
Write two or three sentences from an advertisement describing your favorite meal. The meal can be a common one or one that you invented yourself. Use several linking verbs. Volunteers can read their ads aloud and invite reactions from the class.

    For Extra Practice see page 182.

Active and Passive Voices

Do these sentences seem awkward? How can you change them to emphasize the doer of the action?

The engine was raced by the mechanic.

Then the spark plugs were disconnected by him.

In most sentences the subject performs the action, and the verbs are in the **active voice**. In the **passive voice**, the subject receives the action.

Active: Electric motors run high-speed trains.

Passive: High-speed trains are run by electric motors.

1. The object of the verb in the active voice becomes the subject of the verb in the passive voice.

                                             verb   DO

Active: Magnets in the motor and the track create a <u>force</u>.

                subject   verb

Passive: A <u>force</u> is created by magnets in the motor and the track.

2. To change a verb from the active voice to the passive voice, use the corresponding tense of the verb *be* and change the main verb to its past participle.

The magnetic force moves vehicles. (present tense of *move*)

Vehicles are moved by the magnetic force. (present tense of *be* + past participle of *move*)

3. The performer of the action does not always appear with a verb in the passive voice.

The original model has been perfected.

4. Only transitive verbs—verbs that have objects—can be in the passive voice. If there is no object of a verb in the active voice, then there is nothing to become the subject of the verb in the passive voice.

Intransitive: Dr. Sato <u>travels</u> by train often. *(no object)*

                                    DO

Transitive: Dr. Sato <u>developed</u> a train. *(active)*

              subject

A train was developed by Dr. Sato. *(passive)*

5. The passive voice in general is weaker and more awkward than the active voice. Use the passive voice when the doer of the action is unknown or unimportant. Use the active voice when you want direct, forceful sentences.

> **Passive:** This train was tested. (Sentence emphasizes the fact that this train has been tested.)
>
> **Active:** Engineers tested this train. (Sentence emphasizes who tested the train.)

Try It Out

Speak Out Which verbs are in the active voice? Which are in the passive voice?

1. Cars are used by nearly everyone.
2. Future drivers are given safety tips.
3. Everyone considers fuel conservation important.
4. Air quality has been improving recently.

How would you change the active to the passive voice? How would you change the passive to the active?

5. Government programs promote safety on the highways.
6. Safety features are put into new cars by manufacturers.
7. Cars now need less gas than before.
8. Less noisy engines are developed by engineers.

Summing Up

- The subject of a verb in the **active voice** performs the action.
- The subject of a verb in the **passive voice** receives the action.
- Use the passive voice when the doer of an action is unimportant.
- Use the active voice for direct, forceful sentences.

On Your Own

Write the verb or verb phrase in each sentence. Label each verb or verb phrase *active voice* or *passive voice*.

Example: The train was replaced by the automobile.
was replaced—passive voice

9. Today people seek other methods of transportation.
10. Subways and buses are often used by people in cities.
11. Bicycles are ridden by many people everywhere.
12. Walking to work is preferred by some people.
13. Students often ride buses to school.
14. Many people still drive cars.

15–20. Rewrite each of the six sentences in this student's report. Change the passive to the active voice and the active to the passive voice.

Example: Commuter trains are boarded by workers, tourists, and families.
Workers, tourists, and families board commuter trains.

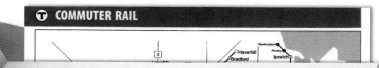

Ⓣ **COMMUTER RAIL**

Newburyport
Haverhill   Rowley
Bradford   Ipswich

The commuter rail line is used daily by passengers from Boston's surrounding towns. Towns as far away as Providence, Rhode Island, are reached by Boston's commuter trains. Fifty miles could be traveled in one trip by a commuter going to work.

Growing populations demand communities farther and farther from centers of business. Commuter services are required by workers and their families. As a result, Boston and many other cities are building more rail lines.

Writing Wrap-Up

WRITING • THINKING • LISTENING • SPEAKING

CREATING

Write a Mock Traffic Report

Write a report on a traffic jam for the TV program *Comedy News.* Include at least one verb in the passive voice and one verb in the active voice. Find a partner and read your reports to each other. Together, evaluate which parts of your reports were the funniest.

Writing with Verbs

Writing Clearly with the Active Voice Using the active voice will make your sentences strong and direct. You should use the active voice most of the time.

> This sentence is stronger when written in the active voice.
>
> **Passive voice:**   Henry Ford's first automobile was built by him in 1896.
>
> **Active voice:**   Henry Ford built his first automobile in 1896.

Apply It

1–6. Read this part of a student time line. Six sentences use the passive voice. Rewrite them using the active voice.

Revising

Henry Ford and Mass Production

1895

1905 ➤

The automobile was not invented by Henry Ford. The methods and procedures needed to build and sell thousands of cars a month were developed by Ford, however.

1913 ➤

Beginning in 1913, interchangeable parts were introduced by Ford in his factory. Assembly lines were also used by him. However, the work was made difficult by mass production. During 1914, about half of his workers quit every month. Wages were doubled by Ford in order to keep workers.

Using the Passive Voice Effectively Good writing includes both the passive voice and the active voice. You should know when to use the passive voice effectively.

You can use the passive voice when you do not know who performed the action.

> The gasoline-powered engine was invented during the 1870s.
> Historians are not sure who built the first automobile with one.

You can use the passive voice when the most important part of the sentence is what happened to the subject.

> Henry Ford was born in Michigan on July 30, 1863.

You can also use the passive voice to discuss an unfortunate event without blaming anyone.

> Mistakes were made, and Ford's first automobile company closed after less than two years.

Apply It

7–12. Rewrite this excerpt from a student report. Decide whether the active voice or the passive voice is more effective for each of the six underlined verb phrases. Revise the sentences that need the active voice.

Revising

Document

The Ford Motor Company <u>was founded</u> on June 16, 1903. The money for the company <u>was provided</u> by Alexander Malcolmson. Ford and Malcolmson argued over whether to build an inexpensive car for ordinary Americans. The problem <u>was solved</u> in 1906, when Malcolmson sold his share of the company. The inexpensive Model T first <u>was produced</u> by Ford in 1908. Thousands of these cars <u>were sold</u> in the first year. Through hard work and determination, success <u>had been achieved</u> by Ford.

12 Subject-Verb Agreement

Make up a sentence that tells how these two animals are alike. Then make up a sentence that tells how the one on the left is different from the one on the right. Identify the subjects and the verbs. How does the subject of each sentence affect the verb?

Singular and Plural Subjects

In every sentence you write, the verb must agree with its subject in number. Use a singular verb with a singular subject and a plural verb with a plural subject.

Singular: The <u>kitten</u> plays.
            The <u>dog</u> barks.
Plural: The <u>kittens</u> play.
            The <u>dogs</u> bark.

Singular	Plural
I run	we run
you run	you run
he, she, it runs	they run

Singular	Plural
I see	we see
you see	you see
he, she, it sees	they see

Try It Out

Speak Up Which verb agrees with each subject?

1. The red fox (live, lives) alone most of the year.
2. In the spring, however, pairs (make, makes) dens in burrows that other animals have left.
3. In this lair three to nine cubs (is, are) born.
4. After sunset a fox (hunt, hunts) rabbits and rodents in woodland areas.
5. In folk tales the fox (has, have) a reputation for cleverness.
6. In fact, foxes (avoid, avoids) capture in very clever ways.

Compound Subjects

A compound subject may have a singular or a plural verb, depending on the conjunction you use. If you use *and* to join the parts of a compound subject, use a plural verb.

Shrews, moles, and toads eat insects.

A mole and a toad were in my garden last night.

If you use *or, nor, either...or,* or *neither...nor* to join the parts of a compound subject, the verb agrees with the nearer subject.

Plural: Neither pandas nor koalas are in our zoo.

Plural: Either a panda or two koalas live in that zoo.

Singular: Two koalas or a panda is coming later.

Try It Out

Speak Up Which verb agrees with each subject?

7. Like a true bear, the koala and the panda (has, have) stout bodies, short legs, round heads, and big paws.
8. Actually, neither the koala nor its relatives (is, are) bears.
9. The koala and the kangaroo (belongs, belong) to the same order.
10. Neither kangaroos nor koalas (is, are) related to the panda.
11. The red panda and the raccoon (is, are) closely related.

Summing Up

- A subject and its verb must agree in number.
- Use a plural verb with a compound subject joined by *and*.
- Use a verb that agrees with the nearer of two subjects joined by *or*.

On Your Own

Write each sentence, using the correct verb.

Example: A white badge, or mark, (give, gives) badgers their name.
A white badge, or mark, gives badgers their name.

12. Skunks, minks, badgers, and otters (is, are) in the weasel family.
13. Intruders often (provoke, provokes) a surprised skunk to spray.
14. Zorilles and marbled polecats also (discharge, discharges) a smelly liquid.
15. In cold climates, some weasels (turn, turns) white.
16. This kind of weasel (are, is) called an ermine.

17–22. Write correctly the six incorrect verbs in this field guide entry.

Example: Otters and minks has sleek, lustrous fur.   *have*

River Otter

River otters has the same body type as any weasel—
lithe and slim, with short legs. They feeds on fish, other
small aquatic animals, and small mammals. The river
otter of North American lakes and streams are sometimes
called the land otter or the Virginia otter. Both young and
adult otters likes to play. Riverbanks
or even a snowbank make a good
slide for an otter. A wild animal
rarely respond to training, but the
young otter is an exception.

WRITING • THINKING • LISTENING • SPEAKING

COMPARING / CONTRASTING

Write an Advice Column

Write an advice column answer to someone who wants help
selecting a pet. Compare two kinds of pets you know about. Use a
variety of compound subjects joined with *and, or*, or *nor*. Read your
answer aloud to a small group and ask them to evaluate your advice.

Grammar/Usage

13 More About Subject-Verb Agreement

One-Minute Warm-Up

What is wrong with these sentences? How can you fix them?

Shakespeare's *Romeo and Juliet* take place in Italy.

Next year our class are going to study Italian history.

Titles, Names, and Nouns Ending with *s*

A title or a name takes a singular verb form, even though the title or name may look plural. A noun ending with *s* or nouns joined by *and* can actually refer to one person or thing.

<u>Antony and Cleopatra</u> [a play] was written by Shakespeare.

<u>The United States</u> [a country] is more than two hundred years old.

<u>Davis, Wu, and Lee</u> [a store] sells quality clothing.

1. Certain nouns ending with *s* always take a singular verb.

   Singular: <u>Mumps</u> is no longer a common disease.
   The <u>news</u> was encouraging today.

2. Other nouns ending with *s* always take a plural verb.

   Plural: These <u>scissors</u> cut well.
   Those <u>pants</u> are in the washing machine.

Try It Out

Speak Up What is the correct verb in each sentence?

1. *The Two Gentlemen of Verona* (is, are) a play by Shakespeare.
2. Shorts (was, were) worn in Shakespeare's day.
3. The Blackfriars theater (was, were) where some plays were performed.
4. *The Merry Wives of Windsor* (is, are) also by Shakespeare.
5. News of a performance (spreads, spread) quickly even today.

William Shakespeare

More Subject-Verb Agreement **155**

Collective Nouns and Nouns of Amount

A **collective noun** names a group acting as a single unit.

Common Collective Nouns			
team	collection	clan	group
herd	Congress	committee	student body
flock	Senate	orchestra	crew
family	legislature	club	jury

1. Usually you use a singular verb with a collective noun. You must use a plural verb with a collective noun that refers to the individuals in the group.

   Singular: The <u>team</u> is playing well tonight. *(whole team together)*

   Plural: The <u>team</u> are putting on their helmets. *(each team member)*

   Singular: My <u>family</u> is going to the seashore for the summer.

   Plural: My <u>family</u> are all going to different places this summer.

2. Terms that refer to amounts—such as money, time, weight, measurements, or fractions—are usually singular when thought of as a single unit. When terms that refer to amounts are thought of as separate items or units, they are plural, and they require a plural verb.

   Singular: <u>Ten dollars</u> is too much for that hat. *(one amount)*

   Plural: <u>Ten quarters</u> are divided among six cups. *(ten separate coins)*

   Singular: <u>Twelve years</u> seems like a long time. *(one time period)*

   Plural: Those <u>twelve years</u> are each important ones. *(twelve separate years)*

Try It Out

Speak Up What is the correct verb in each sentence?

6. For weeks the cast (has, have) been rehearsing their lines.
7. The group (has, have) been working together productively.
8. Eight weeks (is, are) usually enough time to rehearse a play.
9. Those eight weeks (is, are) usually scheduled one by one.
10. After all expenses, only two quarters (is, are) left in the cash box.
11. Five dollars (is, are) a reasonable ticket price.

more ▶

12. The stage crew (has, have) completed the scenery.
13. During dress rehearsal, the cast (was, were) performing well.
14. The orchestra (is, are) tuning up one by one.
15. The audience (was, were) whispering to one another during the opening scene tonight.
16. As the curtain opens for the second act, the whole audience (seem, seems) attentive.

A teacher checks a student's model stage set.

Summing Up

- Use a singular verb with a title or a name of a single thing, with a collective noun referring to a whole group, and with a noun of amount when thought of as a single unit.

- Use a plural verb with a collective noun referring to the individual members of a group and with a noun of amount referring to the individual units.

On Your Own

If the underlined verb is correct, write *correct.* If it is not correct, rewrite the sentence correctly.

Example: Shakespeare's *Romeo and Juliet* <u>was</u> written over three hundred years ago.   *correct*

17. Three hundred years <u>are</u> a long time.
18. Those three hundred years <u>has</u> included countless productions of Shakespeare's plays.
19. In the play, Romeo's family <u>has</u> hated Juliet's family for years.
20. Juliet's family <u>have</u> a deep hatred of Romeo's family.

more ▶

21. The cast of *Romeo and Juliet* <u>speak</u> to one another in verse.
22. Even today the audience <u>are</u> moved by the timeless story.
23. The Royal Shakespeare Company <u>performs</u> Shakespeare's plays.
24. *Antony and Cleopatra* <u>are</u> one of its recent productions.

25–30. Write correctly the six incorrect verbs in the encyclopedia entry below.

Example: Three centuries of popularity are a great tribute to an author. *is*

Proofreading

encyclopedia

fter James I came to the throne in 1603, Shakespeare's theater company were known as the King's Men. As the name suggests, female roles was played by young men or boys. The troupe was sometimes summoned to act before the king and court. Most often, however, the group were busy performing at the Globe and other public playhouses before all classes of citizens. Twelve pennies were the highest cost of a theater seat.

The Globe Theatre

Politics was an influence on the theater of Shakespeare's time. After a rival troupe were forced to leave the private Blackfriars theater for putting on plays that offended the king, the King's Men was invited to play at that higher-priced indoor theater as well.

Writing Wrap-Up   WRITING • THINKING • LISTENING • SPEAKING

CREATING

Write Interview Questions
Write questions you might ask your favorite author or actor about his or her work. Use at least one title, one collective noun, and one noun of amount. Read a partner's questions aloud. Discuss whether the subjects and the verbs agree.

14 Agreement in Inverted and Interrupted Order

What is wrong with these sentences? How can you fix them?

Ducks in a pond swims together.

Why does a duck and her ducklings walk in single file?

Inverted Order

1. A sentence in **natural order** begins with the subject, which is followed by the verb.

   subj. verb
   Four ducks live by the pond.

   A sentence that begins with all or part of the predicate is in **inverted order**.

   verb subj.
   By the pond live four ducks.

2. No matter where the subject is in a sentence, the subject and the verb must agree. Pay particular attention to subject-verb agreement when the subject does not appear first in a sentence. First, find the subject. Then make the verb agree with it.

   verb subj.
   In the zoo live deer.

   verb subj.
   There are two roads to the zoo.

   verb subj.
   Where is the fox?

   subj. verb
   Among the trees a deer eats quietly.

   verb subj. verb
   Have you ever seen a red fox?

You determine the form of the verb by first identifying the number and the person of the subject. A singular subject takes a singular verb. A plural subject takes a plural verb.

Try It Out

Speak Up What is the subject of each sentence? Which verb form agrees with it?

1. In the world's oceans (is, are) dolphins.
2. (Have, Has) you ever studied their behavior?
3. There (is, are) many theories about their communication.
4. Through their speech dolphins (show, shows) feelings.
5. How (do, does) researchers study dolphin behavior in the wild?

Interrupted Order

The verb does not always agree with the nearest noun. This noun may be part of a phrase between the subject and the verb. A sentence is in **interrupted order** when a word or a phrase interrupts the subject and the verb. First, find the subject, and then make the verb agree with it.

> The mice in that cage are growing very fast.
> Bebo, one of the smallest mice, is the oldest.

Try It Out

Speak Up What is the subject of each sentence? Which verb form agrees with it?

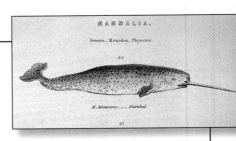

6. The whales of the toothed-whale group (has, have) blowholes and teeth.
7. The narwhal, one of these whales, (has, have) a long tusk.
8. The tusk of this species (is, are) actually a sensitive tooth.
9. Usually only male adults of this group (has, have) tusks.
10. No expert on whales (knows, know) the function of the tusk.

Summing Up

- A sentence is in **inverted order** when all or part of the verb comes before the subject.
- A sentence is in **interrupted order** when a word or phrase comes between the subject and the verb.

11–20. Correct the ten errors in subject-verb agreement in this paragraph from a science Web site. Underline the subject of each sentence, and be sure the verb agrees with the subject.

Example: In the ocean lives many kinds of whales

In the ocean live *many kinds of whales.*

Proofreading

Web site

Back   Forward

There are two groups in the whale family. In the whalebone whale group is ten species. In this group is the right whale and the razorback whale. Also in this group is the blue whales.

Which one of the whalebone whales are the largest? Largest of any of the world's creatures are the blue whale. The length of some blue whales reach almost 100 feet. The weight of these giants approach 150 tons. Five elephants, standing end to end, is not as big as a blue whale. Blue whales at maturity consumes two tons of food a day. This whale, like other kinds of whales, fill its mouth with food while swimming.

Writing Wrap-Up   WRITING • THINKING • LISTENING • SPEAKING

PERSUADING

Write a Persuasive Paragraph

Do animals have emotions or personalities? Write a paragraph that gives your viewpoint on this question. Use inverted order for some of the sentences. Read a partner's paragraph aloud. Do subjects and verbs agree?

15 lie, lay; rise, raise

What's wrong with these sentences? How can you fix them?

Will you raise up early to exercise or lay in bed late?

Will you rise your sleepy head from the pillow and then lie it down again?

The verb *lie* means "to rest or to remain." It is intransitive: it never takes a direct object. The verb *lay* means "to put or to place." It is transitive: it takes a direct object.

Rise means "to get up or to move upward." It is intransitive and does not take a direct object. *Raise* means "to lift or to grow." It is transitive: it takes a direct object.

HELP ? Tip

If you are not sure which form to use, try saying the sentence aloud.

        DO

Susan will lie down. First, she will lay her <u>book</u> down.

        DO

Soon she will rise. She will raise her <u>hands</u>.

See Lessons 5 and 6 for the principal parts of *lie, lay*, and *rise*.

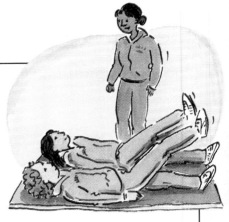

Try It Out

Speak Up Which verb correctly completes each of these sentences?

1. She said to the class, "Please (rise, raise)."
2. "(Lie, Lay) the mats on the floor for warm-up exercises."
3. Beth (laid, lay) her mat next to Gina's.
4. Gina had (raised, risen) early that morning.
5. Ms. Jonas continued, "Now (lie, lay) down for exercises."
6. The gymnasts (lay, laid) down and then (rose, raised) their legs.

Summing Up

- Use *lie* for "to rest or to remain." *Lie* is intransitive.
- Use *lay* for "to put or to place." *Lay* is transitive.
- Use *rise* for "to get up." *Rise* is intransitive.
- Use *raise* for "to lift or to grow." *Raise* is transitive.

On Your Own

7–16. Write each sentence in this entry from a gymnast's diary, correcting the ten incorrect verb forms.

Example: My team raised early.   *My team rose early.*

The equipment had been risen to regulation height. Mats had been lain everywhere. We lay our sweatsuits on the benches. All of us laid on the floor for warm-ups. Even the coach laid down for the exercises. After several sets of sit-ups and push-ups, we raised and went to use the equipment. My friend Josh laid on a mat and practiced a floor exercise. I decided to lay down and raise my legs to stretch. Finally ready, I raised up onto the parallel bars. I slowly rose my legs above the bars.

Writing Wrap-Up

WRITING • THINKING • LISTENING • SPEAKING

DESCRIBING

Write an E-Mail Message

Write an e-mail message to a friend describing an exercise session. Use the verbs *lie, lay, rise,* and *raise.* In a small group, read your messages aloud. Discuss which description was liveliest.

16 affect, effect; accept, except

What is wrong with these sentences? How can you fix them?

If we except skateboards in the park grounds, the skateboarders will be safer than they are on the street.

But how will skateboarders effect the safety of hikers on the park's trails?

Words that sound alike may be especially confusing. The verb *affect* means "to influence." The word *effect* can be used as a noun or a verb. *Effect* as a noun means "result of action." As a verb, *effect* means "to cause to happen."

The new law will affect many people.

The effect should be felt in several months.

Congress will effect the law next month.

Accept is a verb meaning "to receive willingly." *Except* is usually a preposition meaning "excluding, other than."

Congress accepted the proposal.

All except the last item passed.

Try It Out

Speak Up Which word is correct in each sentence?

1. Their clean-up work should (affect, effect) the condition of our parks.
2. The new plan will have an (affect, effect) on all of us.
3. Which neighborhoods will be most (affected, effected)?
4. The major (affect, effect) will be more beautiful parks.
5. Park visitors must now (accept, except) the new rules.
6. All visitors (accept, except) park employees must register.

Summing Up

- The verb *affect* means "to influence."
- The verb *effect* means "to cause to happen."
- The noun *effect* means "result."
- The verb *accept* means "to receive."
- The preposition *except* means "excluding."

On Your Own

7–14. Write correctly this political speech shown on a teleprompter. It contains eight incorrect uses of *affect, effect, accept,* and *except.*

Example: Better planning will be the affect of this law.
Better planning will be the effect of this law.

Proofreading

The new zoning regulations should significantly effect our community. Who will most feel the affects of these new regulations? Developers will be most affected.

The height of new buildings will be effected most by the zoning change. Developers will have to except limits on height. Town officials accept for the fire chief have expressed dismay. Most citizens, however, except the law. They believe that this zoning law will affect an improvement in our environment and will effect our lives for the better.

Writing Wrap-Up

WRITING • THINKING • LISTENING • SPEAKING

INFORMING

Write Rules

Write rules to be posted at the entrance to a city park or playground. Use *affect, effect* (noun and verb), *accept,* and *except* at least once. Exchange lists with a partner and discuss whether you have used *affect, effect, accept,* and *except* correctly.

Exact Verbs

One verb choice:

As the team assembled, I spoke to get their attention.

More exact verb:

As the team assembled, I yelled to get their attention and told them that we had to return to camp by sunset.

The verbs *say* and *ask* are often overused. If you choose exact verbs, your writing will be more interesting, and your readers will understand the precise shades of meaning you intend.

Apply It

1–6. Rewrite this personal narrative. Replace the underlined verbs, *said* and *asked,* with more exact verbs from your Thesaurus Plus. Delete any words that no longer make sense after you have substituted exact verbs.

Revising

We stopped a park ranger and asked about the best trail to the summit. She said, "I'm about to hike in that direction. I can guide you to the beginning of the trail."

As we hiked, the ranger said that there were recent changes in the landscape. When we passed some charred trees, she said to herself, "The fire damaged these pines." Looking serious, she asked us about our knowledge of fire-safety techniques in the wilderness. The ranger then stopped at the beginning of a steep trail. "This is the way," she said.

Enrichment

Verbs!

Principal Parts Play

Players: 2–4

Materials: 1 open manila folder (for gameboard); for each player, 7 index cards and 1 game piece (such as a button)

To play: Make a gameboard like the one to the right, using some of the irregular verbs from pages 125, 126, 129, and 130. Use some verbs from each page. Each player writes *1, 2, 3, 4, present participle, past,* and *past participle* on index cards. Stack all

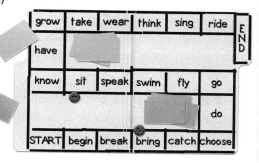

the cards with numbers facedown in one pile. Stack the rest of the cards facedown in another pile.

One player draws a number card and moves his or her game piece the number of spaces shown on the card: 1, 2, 3, or 4. The player then draws from the other pile and says aloud the indicated principal part of the verb on which he or she has landed. If the name for the principal part is incorrect, the player returns to his or her previous space.

Scoring: The first player to reach *END* wins.

Challenge Players must use the principal part of the verb in a sentence. Helping verbs must agree with the subject.

Get a Job!

Suppose you want one of the following jobs at a summer day camp: assistant recreation instructor, kitchen helper, or junior counselor. Write a letter to the camp director, telling why you are interested in the job and what qualities and experience you have that would qualify you. Underline every action verb once and every linking verb twice.

1 **Kinds of Verbs, Verb Phrases** *(pp. 112, 115)* Write each verb phrase. Underline the main verb once and the helping verb or verbs twice. Then label each verb phrase *action* or *linking*.

1. Have you seen the newspaper yet?
2. It does look especially fat today.
3. I must pay special attention to the constantly breaking news about my town.
4. We shall have finished the paper before noon.
5. I couldn't have understood those dense articles without your kind and patient help.

2 **Tenses, Forms of *be*, *have*, and *do*** *(pp. 118, 122)* Rewrite each item, using the verb and tense in parentheses.

6. they (have—past perfect)
7. we (do—future perfect)
8. I (have—present perfect)
9. she (do—future)
10. he (be—past)
11. we (rely—past perfect)
12. you (regret—present perfect)
13. they (state—future)
14. we (hail—present)
15. you (annoy—past perfect)

3 **Irregular Verbs** *(pp. 125, 129)* Rewrite each sentence, adding the verb and tense in parentheses.

16. Election time, you might have noticed, _____ up on us again. (creep—present perfect)
17. I _____ to you this year seeking the office of student body president. (come—present perfect)
18. I _____ much praise for the job that I did as treasurer last year. (get—past)
19. I assure you that by the end of the next year, I _____ equal praise for my work as president. (get—future perfect)
20. My support _____. (grow—present perfect)
21. I _____ costs and saved money for the class by eliminating needless expenses. (cut—past)
22. At times I _____ myself out. (wear—past)
23. I _____ my best effort to the important job of being your president. (give—present perfect)

4 Progressive Forms *(p. 132)* Write the progressive form of each verb and tense in parentheses.

24. The rehearsal _____ well. (go—past perfect)
25. Julio _____ tired. (grow—past)
26. He _____ for hours. (rehearse—present perfect)
27. He _____ soon. (stop—future)
28. By this coming Monday, Julio _____ with us for a month. (work—future perfect)

5 Transitive and Intransitive Verbs, Direct and Indirect Objects, Predicate Nouns and Predicate Adjectives *(pp. 137, 140, 144)* Write each verb, and label it *transitive* or *intransitive.* Then write each object, and label it *direct object* or *indirect object.* Write each predicate noun and predicate adjective, and label it *predicate noun* or *predicate adjective.*

29. Hand me that atlas!
30. Many country music stars record their songs in Nashville.
31. For a short time areas like Jonesboro and Knoxville were part of another state.
32. Its name was Franklin in the eighteenth century.
33. Cotton is king in the city of Memphis.
34. Farmland has now become urban.
35. Tennessee produces an enormous amount of marble.

6 Active Voice and Passive Voice *(p. 147)* Rewrite each sentence, changing the active voice to the passive voice or the passive voice to the active voice.

36. A gifted guitarist accompanied the singer.
37. The audience applauded both performers.
38. Their concerts are attended by thousands of Europeans, Asians, Americans, and Australians.
39. Their records are played often by Jasper.
40. Students around the world know all of their songs.

7 Subject-Verb Agreement; Inverted and Interrupted Order *(pp. 152, 155, 159)* Write each sentence, using the correct verb.

41. A group at my school (is, are) showing a movie today.
42. The movie, three hours long, (tell, tells) of a prince.
43. Either the custodians or Mr. Wu (has, have) the projector.
44. Seated in their chairs, the audience (quiet, quiets) down.
45. Both the students and their teacher (seem, seems) endlessly fascinated.
46. In the audience (is, are) two stars of the movie.

lie, lay; rise, raise; affect, effect; accept, except
(pp. 162, 164) Write the verbs that correctly complete these sentences.

47. (Lay, Lie) everything down, and (lay, lie) on the floor.
48. (Raise, Rise) your legs as high as possible.
49. This exercise (affects, effects) your muscles.
50. You may feel the (affects, effects) tomorrow.
51. Now please (raise, rise), (accept, except) those in front.
52. Come forward to (accept, except) the award.
53. This is the (affect, effect) of your hard work.
54. (Lay, Lie) the award down near the trophy case.

Mixed Review 55–66. Write these paragraphs from a human-interest article, correcting the twelve errors with verbs.

Proofreading Checklist
✔ subject-verb agreement
✔ incorrect tenses of regular and irregular verbs
✔ usage problems

Proofreading

The Lost Kitten, *continued...*

Jayne and her daughter, Robin, has recovered a very lucky kitten. They first miss Frodo around noon yesterday. Nine hours later, they almost had give up hope of finding him. Robin laid down and began to cry. As Jayne held the girl and comforted her, Robin becomed quiet. Out of the silence come a scratching sound from the bathroom wall.

Quietly they creeped to the wall and listened. Jayne realized that the plumber had removed the drywall panel while he is fixing the bathtub drain that morning. There was nineteen screws holding the panel. After ten minutes of frenzied work, they pry the panel back. There set the dusty kitten.

Test Practice

Write the numbers 1–8 on a sheet of paper. Choose the best way to write the underlined part of each sentence. Write the letter for that answer. If the part is already correct, write the letter for the last answer.

1 The tickets <u>costed</u> too much, and we didn't buy them.

   A cost

   B costs

   C costing

   D Correct as it is

2 Tani <u>has forgot</u> her knapsack and her jacket.

   F have forgotten

   G has forgetted

   H has forgotten

   J Correct as it is

3 Tomorrow evening my class-mates and I <u>will be performing</u> our play.

   A is performing

   B have been performing

   C are performing

   D Correct as it is

4 Neither the music nor the words <u>is</u> familiar to me.

   F am

   G was

   H are

   J Correct as it is

5 *Great Expectations* <u>were written</u> by the English novelist Charles Dickens.

   A was written

   B was writed

   C were wrote

   D Correct as it is

6 The members of the committee <u>has thought</u> about the problem.

   F has been thinking

   G have thought

   H is thinking

   J Correct as it is

7 The captain of the team usually <u>except</u> the trophy.

   A accept

   B excepts

   C accepts

   D Correct as it is

8 Last week the supermarket man-ager <u>rose</u> the price of many food items.

   F rise

   G raised

   H risen

   J Correct as it is

✓ Test Practice *continued*

Now write numbers 9–14 on your paper. Look at the paragraph. Choose the correct way to write the underlined part in each numbered line. Write the letter for that answer. If the part is already correct, write the letter for the last answer, "Correct as it is."

---

(9)   Left-handed people in our society <u>is always facing</u> challenges. Almost

(10) everything around us is made for right-handers. <u>Doorknobs zippers and car controls</u>

(11) are just a few examples. Most left-handed people can use these <u>items the</u> adjustment

(12) often feels <u>awkwardly and unnaturally</u>. Because the world seems so right-handed,

(13) parents of a left-hander may try changing their <u>child's</u> hand preference. This change,

(14) according to doctors, <u>are</u> a bad idea. Many doctors believe that parents should leave left-handers alone.

---

9   **A** is always faced
    B are always facing
    C has always faced
    D Correct as it is

10 **F** Doorknobs zippers, and, car controls
    G Doorknobs, zippers and car controls,
    H Doorknobs, zippers, and car controls
    J Correct as it is

11 **A** items, but the
    B items, or the
    C items; but the
    D Correct as it is

12 **F** awkwardly and unnatural
    G awkward and unnatural
    H awkward and unnaturally
    J Correct as it is

13 **A** childs
    B childs'
    C childs's
    D Correct as it is

14 **F** is
    G were
    H have been
    J Correct as it is

(pages 112–114)

1 Kinds of Verbs

- A **verb** expresses *action*, physical or mental, or *being*. Being verbs are sometimes linking verbs.
- A **linking verb** expresses *being*. It links the subject with a word in the predicate that describes or identifies the subject.

Remember

● Write each underlined verb. Label it *action* or *linking*.

Example: Thanksgiving dinner <u>is</u> my favorite meal. *is   linking*

1. The turkey <u>looks</u> delicious.
2. You <u>carve</u> it easily with a sharp carving knife.
3. I <u>smell</u> the aroma of bread baking in the wood-burning stove.
4. It <u>smells</u> absolutely wonderful to me.
5. I <u>baked</u> some butternut squash as a vegetable side dish.
6. This <u>was</u> my contribution to the meal.
7. Todd <u>prepared</u> potatoes, peas, and cauliflower.

▲ Write each verb. Label it *action* or *linking*.

Example: Herbs are important to a good cook. *are   linking*

8. People use different herbs in different countries.
9. Some herbs smell wonderful, like mint and parsley.
10. I smell garlic in this tasty chicken dish.
11. I tasted herbs in the lettuce and tomato salad.
12. I added some more spices to the spaghetti sauce.
13. The onions and spices changed the flavor of the sauce.
14. The taste of the onions remains strong even in the sauce.

■ Complete the sentences, using the given subjects and adding the predicate, using the kind of verb in parentheses.

Example: On the stove the spaghetti sauce _____. (action)
    On the stove the spaghetti sauce bubbled.

15. Some spices such as cinnamon and nutmeg _____. (linking)
16. Too many spices in the sauce _____. (action)
17. The smell of the clam chowder _____. (action)
18. The golden whole-wheat bread in the oven _____. (linking)
19. The addition of wheat germ, bran flakes, or oatmeal _____. (action)
20. The taste of slow-rising yeast bread _____. (linking)

(pages 115–117)

2 Verb Phrases

- A **verb phrase** includes a main verb and one or more helping verbs.
- The **main verb** expresses the action or being.
- The **helping verb** or verbs help complete the meaning of the main verb.

● Write the underlined verb phrase. Underline the main verb once and the helping verb or verbs twice.

Example: Scientists <u>have been studying</u> earthquakes for years.
    have been studying

1. Winds, waves, cars, and volcanoes <u>can</u> all <u>cause</u> vibrations.
2. Real earthquakes <u>are caused</u> by other conditions.
3. Rock <u>may seem</u> quite hard.
4. It <u>may</u> even <u>snap</u> under a great deal of pressure.
5. This <u>will produce</u> vibrations or waves for miles around.
6. Cracks in the ground <u>may become</u> the paths for these waves.

▲ Write each verb phrase. Underline the main verb once and the helping verb twice.

Example: For many, earthquakes are connected with the West.
    are connected

7. Actually, earthquakes have occurred in many different places.
8. In 1755 Boston was struck by a strong quake.
9. Northern New York may suffer frequent quakes.
10. Even rockbound Manhattan has trembled on several occasions.
11. The South has not remained free of earthquakes either.
12. Charleston, South Carolina, did have an earthquake once.

■ Write each sentence, adding a verb phrase to complete it. Underline all main verbs once and all helping verbs twice.

Example: _____ you _____ the cause of earthquakes?
    Do you know the cause of earthquakes?

13. Earthquakes _____ *tectonic* or *volcanic*.
14. A tectonic quake _____ by a flaw in the earth's crust.
15. A sudden movement of lava below the earth's surface_____ a volcanic quake.
16. _____ you _____ earthquakes in geography class?

Remember

3 Tenses

(pages 118–121)

- Every verb has four **principal parts**.
- Verbs have different **tenses** to express different times.
- Use the principal parts of a verb to form its tenses.

● Write the tense of the verb phrase in each sentence.

Example: They had not started yet. *past perfect*

1. They live nearby.
2. Nothing will happen.
3. You carried the bags.
4. We had ordered tickets.

5. You have opened the door.
6. He will have waited.
7. You have not started.
8. They had checked the roof.

▲ Write each sentence, using the correct form of the verb and tense in parentheses.

Example: Lana _____ of stardom. (dream—past perfect)
  Lana had dreamed of stardom.

9. Lana _____ all her energy for the performance. (need—future)
10. The cast _____ for months. (work—present perfect)
11. They _____ until midnight last night. (rehearse—past)
12. The critics _____ the play by tomorrow morning.
    (review—future perfect)
13. Everyone _____ for good reviews. (hope—present)
14. Broadway audiences _____ fresh talent. (recognize—future)

■ Write each sentence, using an appropriate tense of the verb in parentheses. Label the verb tense.

Example: Popcorn _____ for a long time. (exist)
  Popcorn has existed for a long time.   present perfect

15. Native Americans _____ corn thousands of years ago. (pop)
16. People _____ popcorn before then, however. (use)
17. Popcorn already _____ in 3600 B.C. (exist)
18. By 1900 Mr. Cretors _____ the popping machine. (invent)
19. Today Americans _____ over 500,000,000 pounds of popcorn each year. (consume)
20. Experts speculate that between this year and the end of next year Americans _____ more than 600,000,000 pounds of unpopped corn. (purchase)

(pages 122–124)

4 Forms of *be, have,* and *do*

- You can use *be, have,* and *do* as main verbs and as helping verbs.
- *Be, have,* and *do* have different forms for different subjects and for different tenses.

● Write each sentence, using the correct verb form in parentheses.

Example: What (do, does) you know about corn?
What do you know about corn?

1. We (is, are) learning about corn in social studies class.
2. Corn (is, are) a very important crop in the United States.
3. It (has, have) always grown in North and South America.
4. Farmers (has, have) developed bigger and better corn.
5. Today they (has, have) big machines and large fields.

▲ Write each sentence, using the correct verb form in parentheses. Then label that verb *main* or *helping.*

Example: People (has, have) grown corn for thousands of years.
People have grown corn for thousands of years.   helping

6. It (was, were) around before Columbus sailed.
7. Corn always has (been, be) an important crop.
8. Manufacturers (has, have) hundreds of uses for corn.
9. Some paper (is, are) made from corn.
10. Corn products (is, are) used in glue, starch, and fabrics.

■ Write each sentence, using the form of *be, have,* or *do* that best completes it. Then label that verb *main* or *helping.*

Example: In Great Britain corn _____ called maize.
In Great Britain corn is called maize.   helping

11. Grains such as wheat and oats _____ called corn.
12. For centuries people _____ enjoyed corn in different ways.
13. How many ways _____ you know?
14. I _____ two ears of corn in my refrigerator right now.
15. Latin Americans probably _____ the most uses for corn as food.
16. They _____ many wonderful things with corn.

5 Irregular Verbs

(pages 125–128)

- **Irregular verbs** do not follow rules for forming the past and past participles. You must learn the principal parts of irregular verbs.

Remember

● Write each sentence, using the principal part of the verb in parentheses.

Example: The Tylers _____ an interesting thing. (do—past)
The Tylers did an interesting thing.

1. They _____ some large pots to the roof. (bring—past)
2. Then they _____ soil and seeds in the pots. (put—past)
3. After a week, tiny green shoots _____ through. (come—past)
4. They _____ into blossoms. (burst—past)
5. The blossoms _____ beautiful strawberries. (become—past)
6. Some birds _____ the berries that same day. (find—past)
7. They _____ no berries for the Tylers! (leave—past)
8. The Tylers _____ out more plants. (set—past)

▲ Write the present participle, the past, and the past participle forms of the verbs. Include helping verbs.

Example: pay   *is paying   paid   has paid*

9. make	12. set	15. be	18. win
10. read	13. find	16. run	19. hold
11. stand	14. become	17. have	20. do

■ Write each sentence, using the correct past or past participle of the verb in parentheses.

Example: Many birds _____ overhead. (be) *Many birds were overhead.*

21. Jeff and Randy _____ under a huge, old oak tree. (sit)
22. Had the two men really _____ their way? (lose)
23. They had _____ to the lake with some other friends. (come)
24. They all had _____ the cottage an hour ago. (leave)
25. They _____ the way back to the cottage. (seek)
26. The sun had already _____ an hour before. (set)
27. Shortly, they _____ their compass. (find)
28. Jeff _____ the compass steadily on the way back. (hold)
29. Finally, the men _____ to the cottage. (come)
30. They had never _____ so happy in their lives. (be)

(pages 129–131)

⑥ More Irregular Verbs

• You must learn the principal parts of irregular verbs.

● Write each sentence, using the principal part of the verb in parentheses.

Example: Sam had _____ the juice. (drink—past participle)
Sam had drunk the juice.

1. The *Titanic*, a ship, _____. (sink—past)
2. The parade is _____. (begin—present participle)
3. Marcy had _____ across the lake. (swim—past participle)
4. The ice is _____. (freeze—present participle)
5. The telephone has _____ five times. (ring—past participle)
6. Brad _____ down for a rest. (lie—past)
7. Donna is _____ the snowmobile. (drive—present participle)

▲ Write each sentence, choosing the correct principal part. Use your dictionary if you need help.

Example: A scientist (spoke, spoken) to us about the desert.
A scientist spoke to us about the desert.

8. He had (took, taken) many trips to deserts around the world.
9. Wind had (blew, blown) sand into many shapes and patterns.
10. People (rode, ridden) camels in the hot deserts.
11. These people (wore, worn) scarfs for protection against the sand.
12. The barrel cactus (drank, drunk) its fill of rainwater.
13. Its sharp spines (gave, given) it a dangerous appearance.
14. I had not (knew, known) that deserts grow cold at night.

■ Write each sentence, using the past or past participle form of the verb in parentheses. Then label it *past* or *past participle*.

Example: My family _____ a trip through the Grand Canyon. (take)
My family took a trip through the Grand Canyon. *past*

15. I had never _____ a mule before this trip. (ride)
16. The mules _____ a trail along the edge of the river. (choose)
17. Our raft _____ it through the white water. (make)
18. The mules _____ down the south side of the canyon walls. (go)
19. Large boulders had _____ on the trail. (fall)
20. We had _____ all our meals by a small fire. (eat)

(pages 132–134)

7 Progressive Forms

Remember

- Each tense has a **progressive form** to express continuing action.
- Form the progressive with an appropriate tense of *be* plus the present participle.

● Write the progressive form from each sentence.

Example: Harry had been watching birds.   *had been watching*

1. Grace is watching seagulls at the beach.
2. She was watching them all last week too.
3. Grace has been looking for unusual gulls for two weeks.
4. She had been listening to the radio for reports first.

▲ Write each sentence, using the correct progressive form of the verb and tense in parentheses.

Example: Marine biologists _____ sea life for many years.
(study—present perfect progressive)
Marine biologists have been studying sea life for many years.

5. Scientists _____ more and more about the sea all the time.
(learn—present progressive)
6. A famous ocean exploration ship, the *Calypso,* _____ the sea since 1951. (explore—past perfect progressive)
7. An expedition led by the late Jacques Cousteau _____ the Red Sea when they discovered a ship from the third century B.C.
(study—past progressive)
8. People _____ to protect the sea. (work—present perfect progressive)
9. Our conservation efforts _____ marine life for future generations.
(preserve—future progressive)

■ Write each sentence, replacing each underlined verb with its progressive form.

Example: The storm <u>had brewed</u> for several hours.
The storm had been brewing for several hours.

10. The waves <u>crash</u> onto the rocks.
11. The temperature <u>has dropped</u> steadily during the past hour.
12. Storm clouds <u>had gathered</u> in the sky since 6 A.M.
13. All small boats <u>returned</u> to the safety of the harbor.
14. The radio <u>will broadcast</u> reports about the storm all day.

(pages 137–139)

⑧ Transitive and Intransitive Verbs

- A **transitive verb** expresses action that is directed toward a word in the predicate.
- The word to which the action is directed is the **object** of the verb.
- An **intransitive verb** does not have an object.
- Linking verbs are always intransitive.

● Write each underlined verb. Label it *transitive* or *intransitive*.

Example: People <u>need</u> shelter. *need   transitive*

1. Today many people <u>construct</u> large houses.
2. Builders on a construction site <u>work</u> quickly.
3. First, workers <u>pour</u> a foundation for support of the building.
4. They usually <u>raise</u> beams or columns next.
5. The beams or columns <u>form</u> the skeleton of the house.
6. The final structure <u>looks</u> quite different from the skeleton.

▲ Write each verb. Label it *transitive* or *intransitive*.

Example: Water wells draw water from the ground. *draw   transitive*

7. Ground water from rain flows into the wells.
8. The water is sometimes hundreds of feet down.
9. Scientists locate good sites for wells with modern equipment.
10. In earlier times, people found water by means of a forked branch.
11. The main stem pointed down to an underground water supply.
12. People were seldom successful with this method.

■ 13–25. Write each main verb. Label it *transitive* or *intransitive*.

Example: A modern skyscraper can spring up within one year.
   spring   intransitive

First, an architect designs the building. Next, the construction company plans carefully. Before the construction starts, engineers test the soil. Finally, bulldozers appear on the site. They level the earth for the foundation. Work begins on the skeleton of the building. Workers bolt pieces of steel together. Then they weld the steel permanently. At last the builders apply the outside walls. They do this work quickly, and interior decoration begins next. The skyscraper looks grand.

(pages 140–143)

⑨ Direct and Indirect Objects

- The **direct object** of a sentence is a noun or a pronoun in the predicate *to which* the action of the verb is directed or done.
- The **indirect object** is a noun or a pronoun in the predicate that tells *to whom, for whom, to what,* or *for what* the action of the verb is done. The indirect object comes between the verb and the direct object.

● Write each underlined object. Label it *direct object* or *indirect object*.

Example: All mystery writers offer <u>readers</u> the same basic <u>plot</u>.
          readers   indirect object   plot   direct object

1. Writers use different <u>details</u> and <u>characters</u>, of course.
2. All mystery stories solve the same <u>problem</u>.
3. The hero or heroine discovers the guilty <u>person</u>.
4. Edgar Allan Poe presented the <u>problem</u> in 1841.
5. He gave the <u>world</u> its first mystery <u>story</u>.

▲ Write the verbs and their objects. Label each object *direct object* or *indirect object*.

Example: The criminal left Detective Green an important clue.
        verb: left   indirect object: Detective Green   direct object: clue

6. The maid brought Detective Green one gold earring.
7. The maid's friend Margo had lent the victim the earrings.
8. Margo had owed the victim some money.
9. The single missing earring offered Green a hint.
10. Green offered her the chance to confess.

■ Write the sentences, adding objects as shown in parentheses. Use articles where you need them. Remember to place your objects correctly.

Example: The phone awakened _____. (direct)
        The phone awakened the detective.

11. She grabbed her _____ and listened to the message. (direct)
12. Who had so abruptly sent _____? (direct and indirect)
13. Suddenly she remembered _____. (direct)
14. Would she find _____ in time to prevent disaster? (direct)
15. Had someone given _____? (direct and indirect)
16. In a short while, she would know _____. (direct)

(pages 144–146)

10 Predicate Nouns and Predicate Adjectives

Remember

- Predicate nouns and predicate adjectives follow linking verbs.
- A **predicate noun** identifies or renames the subject.
- A **predicate adjective** describes the subject.

● Write each underlined word. Label it *predicate noun* or *predicate adjective*.

Example: Milk is the first <u>food</u> for many babies. *food   predicate noun*

1. With milk, children will grow <u>strong</u>.
2. Cows are the main <u>source</u> of milk in this country.
3. Goat milk and sheep milk are <u>common</u> elsewhere.
4. Milk must remain very <u>clean</u>.
5. Otherwise, milk drinkers can become <u>ill</u>.
6. Dairy farming is an important <u>industry</u>.

▲ Write each linking verb. Then write each predicate noun and predicate adjective. Label it *predicate noun* or *predicate adjective*.

Example: Milk directly from the cow is warm.
    linking verb: is   predicate adjective: warm

7. It becomes a home for germs if not refrigerated.
8. Dairy farmers are careful about cleanliness.
9. The barns, the cows, and the equipment are very clean.
10. Milk drinkers in the United States feel safe and secure.
11. Milk is a product of many areas of the United States.

■ Write each sentence. Underline the linking verb. Add a predicate noun or a predicate adjective and label it.

Example: Cows were a _____ of milk five thousand years ago.
    Cows <u>were</u> a source of milk five thousand years ago.
    predicate noun

12. Half of the milk from dairy farms becomes other dairy _____.
13. Examples of such products are _____ and _____.
14. Milk from different cows doesn't look _____.
15. Milk bottles appeared in the 1880s and became quite _____.
16. Now, coated paper containers have grown more _____.

(pages 147–149)

11 Active and Passive Voices

- The subject of a verb in the **active voice** performs the action.
- The subject of a verb in the **passive voice** receives the action.
- Use the passive voice when the doer of an action is unimportant.
- Use the active voice for direct, forceful sentences.

● Write each underlined verb. Then label it *active* or *passive*.

Example: Cars and airplanes <u>are steered</u> by their drivers.
are steered   passive

1. Railroad trains <u>are pulled</u> by locomotives.
2. Passenger trains still <u>run</u> along many routes.
3. Many railroads still <u>run</u> passenger trains.
4. Most trains in the United States today <u>carry</u> products.
5. Many cities in Europe <u>are served</u> by high-speed trains.

▲ Rewrite each sentence, changing the passive voice to the active voice or the active voice to the passive voice.

Example: The earliest trains were pulled by men or horses.
Men or horses pulled the earliest trains.

6. Wagons full of coal were pulled up from mines by miners.
7. These wagons were guided along by two wooden rails.
8. Later the rails were covered with iron for more strength.
9. Meanwhile the steam engine was being developed by inventors.
10. The English constructed the earliest engines.

■ Rewrite each sentence, changing the passive voice to the active voice or the active voice to the passive voice. Label the new sentence *active* or *passive* to describe the verb.

Example: A horse and a locomotive ran a race.
A race was run by a horse and a locomotive.   passive

11. The locomotive had been built by Peter Cooper of New York.
12. Cooper had given it the name of Tom Thumb.
13. The race was almost won by the little locomotive.
14. A horse and a locomotive had made history.
15. Trains were called "iron horses" by many people.

(pages 152–154)

12 Subject-Verb Agreement

- A subject and its verb must agree in number.
- Use a plural verb with a compound subject joined by *and*.
- Use a verb that agrees with the nearer of two subjects joined by *or*.

Remember

● Write each sentence, using the correct verb in parentheses.

Example: The walrus (lives, live) in northern oceans.
        The walrus lives in northern oceans.

1. Only orcas (is, are) the natural enemies of walruses.
2. Its four flippers (makes, make) the walrus a good swimmer.
3. Its long ivory tusks (grows, grow) forty inches and (weighs, weigh) nine pounds.
4. Both the male walrus and the female walrus (has, have) tusks.
5. Neither seals nor sea lions (has, have) tusks like walruses.

▲ Write each sentence, using the correct verb in parentheses.

Example: A wallaby (is, are) a small kangaroo.
        A wallaby is a small kangaroo.

6. Wallabies (lives, live) on the continent of Australia.
7. This animal also (lives, live) on Tasmania.
8. Both the kangaroo and the wallaby (leaps, leap) high into the air.
9. A baby wallaby (is, are) called a *joey*.
10. A newborn joey (measures, measure) only about one inch.
11. Wallabies (carries, carry) their young in pouches.
12. A joey (leaves, leave) the pouch after six months but (returns, return) at any sign of danger.

■ Write each sentence, using the present tense of the verb in parentheses.

Example: Kenya _____ famous for its wildlife. (be)
        Kenya is famous for its wildlife.

13. Elephants, giraffes, and zebras _____ in game reserves. (roam)
14. Neither a giraffe nor a zebra _____ a meat-eater. (be)
15. Both giraffes and zebras _____ plants. (eat)
16. This movie _____ many colorful animals of Africa. (show)

13 More About Subject-Verb Agreement

(pages 155–158)

- Use a singular verb with a title or a name of a single thing, with a collective noun referring to a whole group, and with a noun of amount.
- Use a plural verb with a collective noun referring to the individual members of a group and with a noun of amount when the individual units are referred to.

Remember

● Write each sentence, using the correct verb in parentheses.

Example: The store Jones and Bailey (sells, sell) seats.
The store Jones and Bailey sells seats.

1. *Romeo and Juliet* (is, are) a play by Shakespeare.
2. The Neighborhood Players (is, are) performing it tonight.
3. Romeo and Juliet (is, are) two young people in love.
4. Romeo's family (has, have) quarreled with Juliet's family.
5. The couple (faces, face) difficulties throughout the play.
6. Two dollars (is, are) the price of a student ticket.

▲ If the underlined verb form is correct, write *correct*. If it is not correct, rewrite the sentence, using the correct form.

Example: The panel has <u>chosen</u> a play for next season. *correct*

7. *The Boys from Syracuse* <u>is based</u> on a play by Shakespeare.
8. Jim said that $154 <u>was spent</u> on one costume alone.
9. The chorus <u>sing</u> different parts.
10. Six dollars <u>are</u> the cost of each ticket.
11. The National Theatre in London <u>perform</u> Shakespeare's plays.
12. Dramatics <u>is</u> exciting to take part in.

■ Write each sentence, using a verb in the present tense. Label each verb *singular* or *plural*.

Example: In any play scenery _____.
In any play scenery is important. singular

13. The audience always _____.
14. Twelve years _____.
15. The Drama Club _____.
16. Dressmakers' shears _____.
17. The cast _____.
18. The group _____.
19. Trousers _____.
20. Thousands _____.

(pages 159–161)

14 Inverted and Interrupted Order

Remember

- The subject of a sentence in **inverted** order follows all or part of the verb.
- First, find the subject. Then make the verb agree with it.

● Write each sentence, using the verb form in parentheses that agrees with the underlined subject.

Example: <u>People</u> of the world (shares, share) information.
People of the world share information.

1. There (is, are) many different <u>ways</u> of communicating.
2. The <u>expressions</u> on your face (sends, send) messages to others.
3. A <u>movement</u> of your hand also (says, say) something.
4. The <u>ring</u> of telephones (means, mean) someone is calling.
5. <u>Notes</u> of music (expresses, express) emotions.

▲ If the underlined verb form is correct, write *correct*. If it is incorrect, rewrite the sentence, using the correct form.

Example: Smoke signals <u>is</u> a kind of language.
Smoke signals are a kind of language.

6. Pictures on a cave wall <u>communicate</u>.
7. Long ago a string of pictures <u>were</u> used to tell a story.
8. In one story <u>was</u> many pictures.
9. The details in the pictures <u>was</u> hard to draw.
10. Soon one group of lines <u>were</u> used for one idea.

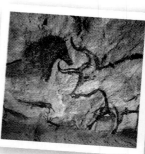

■ Write each sentence. Underline the subject and use the past tense form of *be* that agrees with it.

Example: The invention of alphabets _____ a great step forward.
The <u>invention</u> of alphabets was a great step forward.

11. In the Middle East _____ people who first used an alphabet.
12. The sounds in their speech _____ written with pictures.
13. A combination of pictures _____ used for a word.
14. An important development for human beings _____ the more recent letter alphabet.
15. There _____ no longer a different symbol for each word.
16. There _____ only a short list of symbols.

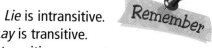

(pages 162–163)

15 *lie, lay; rise, raise*

- Use *lie* for "to rest or to remain." *Lie* is intransitive.
- Use *lay* for "to put or to place." *Lay* is transitive.
- Use *rise* for "to get up." *Rise* is intransitive.
- Use *raise* for "to lift or to grow." *Raise* is transitive.

Remember

● Write each sentence, using the correct verb in parentheses.

Example: The principal (raises, rises) the flag each morning.
The principal raises the flag each morning.

1. John (raised, rose) to ask a question.
2. In our meeting, Ann has (raised, risen) an interesting issue.
3. We will (lie, lay) the question before the Student Council.
4. Carl nervously (raised, rose) his hand.
5. He (lay, laid) his glasses down for a moment and looked up.

▲ Write each sentence, using the correct verb in parentheses.

Example: The curtain (rises, raises) on a cabin in the woods.
The curtain rises on a cabin in the woods.

6. Then the lights are (raised, rose) to show early morning.
7. Smoke is (raising, rising) slowly up the chimney.
8. A hunting dog is (lying, laying) near the kitchen stove.
9. Only a few of the family members have (raised, risen).
10. Several small children are still (lying, laying) in bed.

■ Write each sentence, choosing first the correct verb and then its correct form for the tense indicated in parentheses.

Example: I _____ early for the rehearsal. (raise/rise—past)
I rose early for the rehearsal.

11. The backstage crew _____ a couch in the center of the stage. (lay/lie—past)
12. Two of the crew _____ on the couch. (lay/lie—past progressive)
13. The curtains _____ and the play begins. (raise/rise—present)
14. We _____ a carpet down for the first act. (lay/lie—future)
15. The stagehands _____ for the applause. (raise/rise—past)
16. Some helium balloons for decoration _____ to the ceiling. (raise/rise—past perfect)

(pages 164–165)

16 *affect, effect; accept, except*

Remember

- The verb *affect* means "to influence."
- The verb *effect* means "to cause to happen."
- The noun *effect* means "result."
- The verb *accept* means "to receive."
- The preposition *except* means "excluding."

● Write the sentence, choosing the correct word.

Example: The use of computers has (affected, effected) students' grades.
The use of computers has affected students' grades.

1. National test scores are certainly (affected, effected) by student use of computers.
2. The greatest (affect, effect) was on math scores.
3. All classes (accept, except) social studies are using computers.
4. The school will (accept, except) the gift of new computers.
5. The teachers will (accept, except) late computer homework.

▲ Write each sentence, choosing the correct word.

Example: The debate team (accepted, excepted) a challenge.
The debate team accepted a challenge.

6. (Accept, Except) for Sharon, all members will participate.
7. Sharon was not (accepted, excepted) for the debate because of lack of experience.
8. We (accepted, excepted) the argument in favor of computers.
9. John said that computers (affect, effect) education in a positive way.
10. Geeta will argue that computers have a bad (affect, effect).

■ Write each sentence, using *accept, except, affect,* or *effect* correctly.

Example: I corrected all my mistakes _____ one.
I corrected all my mistakes except one.

11. Computers have _____ business and office practices.
12. A major _____ has been the processing of greater amounts of information.
13. Typists' skills, _____ for proofreading, have been _____.
14. Office workers have _____ computers as an improvement.
15. Most workers' skills have been _____ by using computers.

Modifiers

Both its exotic habitat and
the dramatic colors of the
blue ribbon eel are
positively eye-popping!

¹ Adjectives

One-Minute Warm-Up

Find the adjectives in the sentence below, including articles.

To the rebellious young American dancers of the time, the traditional European ballet seemed decadent and undemocratic.

—from *Martha Graham: A Dancer's Life,* by Russell Freedman

You can use **modifiers,** or words that describe, to make your language clear and colorful. One kind of modifier is an adjective. An **adjective** modifies a noun or a pronoun.

A dancer performed on the bare stage.

He was strong and graceful.

Adjectives tell different kinds of details about the words they modify.

Which:	the, that, those, other, my, which, Jeb's
What kind:	young, happy, deserted, yellow, aging, uneven, famous
How many:	three, some, several, few, little, half, many, much

1. Possessive nouns function as adjectives.

Mr. Gerry's son is an actor.   The boy's love is theater.

The theater's stage is deep.   Jean's play broke records.

2. Other kinds of words can work as adjectives in sentences.

That director is famous.   The book is his script.

The grinning actress fell.   The completed script arrived.

We entered the movie theater.   They used a cardboard prop.

3. The words *a, an,* and *the* are special adjectives called **articles**. *A* and *an* are called **indefinite articles** because they refer to any person, place, or thing. Use *a* with a noun or a pronoun beginning with a consonant sound. Use *an* with a noun or a pronoun beginning with a vowel or vowel sound.

A dancer can be tall or short. (any dancer)

An actress came to see the tryouts. (any actress)

A harp provides the music. (any harp)

The is called a **definite article** because it points out a specific noun or pronoun.

The dancer on stage is tall. (a specific dancer)

The actors from *Annie* arrived. (particular actors)

4. You can form **proper adjectives** from many proper nouns. Capitalize proper adjectives.

French drama   Mexican art   Russian ballerina

5. Most often you use adjectives before the noun or pronoun that they modify.

that long, dark alley   an exciting new play

6. Sometimes you may want to place adjectives after a noun or a pronoun for special emphasis. Use commas to set off such adjectives.

The dancers, hot and flushed, rested in the wings.

Adjectives used in this way can also come before a noun.

Hot and flushed, the dancers rested in the wings.

A **predicate adjective** follows a linking verb. As you know, a predicate adjective always describes the subject.

The dancers were hot and flushed from their efforts.

Try It Out

Speak Up Which words are used as adjectives? Include articles in your answers. Which words do they modify?

1. A large autographed photograph of this actor is in our local theater.
2. Kind and generous, he has sponsored many young actors.
3. He is calm and patient with all children.
4. This new theater runs our favorite French films.
5. Several Spanish tourists took pictures of the film's expensive set.
6. The comedian, funny but unsmiling, amused every member of the receptive audience.
7. Each performance at this modern theater was fresh, alive, and entertaining.
8. The six players discussed their next few roles.
9. The mirrored wall reflected their dancing silhouettes.

more ▶

10. The acting troupe rehearsed for a radio play.
11. Eager and smiling, the lead spoke the first words.
12. The audience grew still as he uttered his hushed speech.
13. Crashing noises came from the left wing of the stage.
14. A figure, enormous and shadowy, appeared on stage.
15. Was this an unexpected visitor or a surprise twist in plot?

Summing Up

- An **adjective** describes, or modifies, a noun or a pronoun.
- An adjective formed from a proper noun is a **proper adjective**. Capitalize proper adjectives.
- A **predicate adjective** follows a linking verb and describes the subject.

On Your Own

Write each word used as an adjective, including articles. Then write the word it modifies.

Example: Handwritten manuscripts were the main records of human
history for many centuries.
Handwritten—manuscripts   the main—records
human—history   many—centuries

16. In ancient times many manuscripts were written on papyrus.
17. Papyrus was made from a tall, needlelike Egyptian plant.
18. Connected papyrus sheets were formed into long rolls.
19. Some rolls were six meters in length.
20. Parchment, another ancient material, was an improvement over papyrus.
21. Parchment was stronger, smoother, and cheaper than papyrus.
22. Vellum, smooth and precious, is parchment of high quality.
23. The invention of modern paper was a Chinese contribution to the craft of bookmaking.
24. The Chinese carved each page from a wooden block and spread ink over the raised surface.

more ▶

25. The oldest known book was printed in China, using block printing, in 868.
26. About 1045 Pi Sheng, a Chinese printer, made the first movable type from a baked, hardened mixture of clay and glue.
27. In the fifteenth century in Germany, Gutenberg invented a printing press that used movable metal type.
28. An important part of Gutenberg's invention was the production of large numbers of identical metal letters.

29–54. Write the twenty-six adjectives, including articles, in the following sentences from a research report. Then write the word each adjective modifies.

Example: Early printers converted cheese presses into printing presses.
Early—printers   cheese—presses   printing—presses

Research Report

Books in Print

The first printed English book appeared in 1475. In the 1500s Paris and the northern Italian city of Venice became important bookmaking centers. By the 1700s printers were producing portable and inexpensive books. Paperback books became popular in the 1800s. Today, book publishing has become mechanized and computerized. Over the course of five centuries, books have changed the world. Literacy has become the right of the many, rather than of the fortunate few.

Writing Wrap-Up

WRITING • THINKING • LISTENING • SPEAKING

NARRATING

Write a Mystery Story

Can you hook your readers in three to four sentences? Write the opening paragraph of what will be your next best-selling mystery. Use various kinds of adjectives. Share your opening paragraph with a partner and together discuss what worked best.

Writing with Adjectives

Combining Sentences Use adjectives to make your writing clear and colorful. You can also combine sentences by moving an adjective.

> Ernesto surveyed the landscape.
>
> It was bleak and rocky.
>
> Ernesto surveyed the bleak, rocky landscape.

You can also change some words into adjectives to combine sentences.

> Ernesto looked at a storm cloud.
>
> It floated in the sky.
>
> Ernesto looked at the floating storm cloud.

Apply It

1–6. Rewrite this excerpt from a student's science-fiction story. Use adjectives to combine each pair of underlined sentences.

Revising

> Lin walked down the street. It was deserted and eerie. Where was everyone? She noticed barrels scattered about. They leaked.
>
> She wanted to find out what had happened. The city had been abandoned. There was no sign of people anywhere. The city had once been a metropolis. It had thrived.
>
> Lin stepped into the park. The park was gloomy and empty. Then she stopped short. She thought she saw a shadow against the wall. The shadow was moving.

Elaborating Sentences Use adjectives to clarify or add detail to your writing. Precise, vivid adjectives can help you elaborate your sentences and make them more interesting to read.

Dirk put the paper in the bin.

Dirk put the notebook paper in the recycling bin.

You can vary the position of adjectives in your sentences too.

Dirk put the folded and tied newspapers outdoors for curbside recycling.

Dirk put the newspapers, folded and tied, outdoors for curbside recycling.

Apply It

7–16. Revise this editorial for a school newspaper. Add adjectives to modify the underlined words.

Revising

The Neatnik Speaks

Have you seen the <u>stacks</u> of paper that get used every day at our computer stations? Some <u>students</u> print out every <u>change</u> that they make in a <u>report</u> or a <u>letter</u>. They keep testing different <u>margins</u> and <u>fonts</u>. Please, test these things on the computer screen! Then print your <u>work</u>. This will cut down on <u>waste</u> and will also keep the <u>bins</u> from overflowing and causing a <u>mess</u>! Your cooperation will make the Neatnik very happy.

2 Comparing with Adjectives

What's wrong with these sentences, and how can you fix them?

The most tall building in Japan is the Landmark Tower in Yokohama. The most oldest building is the Horyu Temple.

Degrees of Comparison

You can use adjectives to compare two or more persons, places, or things. To do this, you use different forms, or **degrees**, depending upon how many things you are comparing.

Degree	Example
Positive (basic form): Makes no comparison.	The Empire State Building is a tall structure.
Comparative: Compares two.	The World Trade Center is taller than the Empire State Building.
Superlative: Compares three or more.	The Sears Tower is tallest of the three.

Try It Out

Speak Up What is the correct form of each adjective in parentheses? Is it positive, comparative, or superlative?

Fallingwater

1. Frank Lloyd Wright is often said to be the _____ architect of the twentieth century. (great)
2. Wright was _____ than Louis Sullivan, who was his employer and teacher. (young)
3. Sullivan was _____, but Wright was _____. (great, great)
4. Wright had a _____ interest in nature than Sullivan. (strong)
5. Wright's designs were _____ than those of other architects. (bold)
6. His Fallingwater may be the _____ house ever built. (fine)
7. He also wrote _____ articles and books about his work. (long)

Forms of Comparison

You can make comparisons by adding -er and -est or more and most to adjectives. The chart shows you how.

Adjectives	Positive	Comparative	Superlative
One syllable	warm	warmer	warmest
Two syllables	pretty famous	prettier more famous	prettiest most famous
Three or more syllables	reliable	more reliable	most reliable

Check your dictionary about whether to use -er and -est or more and most with an adjective of two syllables.

1. When you want to show less rather than more, use *less* to form the comparative and *least* to form the superlative.

   Positive: Sullivan was enthusiastic about skyscrapers.

   Comparative: His partner, Adler, was less enthusiastic than he was.

   Superlative: Wright was least enthusiastic of the three.

2. You need to follow certain spelling rules when you add -er and -est to adjectives.

   One-syllable adjectives ending with one vowel and a consonant:
   Double the final consonant. Then add -er or -est.   thin—thinner—thinnest

   Adjectives ending with a consonant and y:
   Change the y to i. Then add -er or -est.   happy—happier—happiest

   Adjectives ending with a consonant and e:
   Drop the e. Then add -er or -est.   cute—cuter—cutest

3. You must learn the irregular forms of a few adjectives.

Positive	Comparative	Superlative
good	better	best
bad	worse	worst
many, much	more	most
little (quantity)	less	least
far	farther	farthest

4. Use *little, less,* and *least* with things that cannot be counted. Use *few, fewer,* and *fewest* with countable things.

    Uncountable: Is there less interest in Sullivan than in Wright?

    Countable: Are fewer skyscrapers being built now?

5. Use *much* with uncountable things. Use *many* with countable things.

    Uncountable: Wright's work created much excitement.

    Countable: Many architects follow his example.

6. Avoid using *more* or *most* with *-er* or *-est.*

    Incorrect: Wright was more greater. Was he most happiest?

    Correct: Wright was greater. Was he happiest?

Try It Out

Speak Up What is the correct comparative or superlative form of the adjective in parentheses?

Philip Johnson and Glass House

  8. Who is the _____ of all modern architects? (prominent)

  9. Is Philip Johnson a _____ architect than Louis Kahn? (good)

10. Johnson designed _____ glass buildings than brick ones. (many)

11. One of Johnson's _____ works of all was his design for the new wing of the Boston Public Library. (good)

12. His Glass House, however, is _____ than the library. (famous)

Summing Up

- Use the **comparative degree** of an adjective to compare two things.
- Use the **superlative degree** to compare three or more things.
- Form the comparative degree with *-er* or *more.*
- Form the superlative degree with *-est* or *most.*

Write each sentence, using the correct comparative or superlative form of the adjective in parentheses.

Example: Many of the _____ cities were in the Middle East. (old)
Many of the oldest cities were in the Middle East.

13. Architecture was considered a _____ field than many. (honorable)
14. Were the Greeks _____ builders than the Romans? (good)
15. Is a Greek temple _____ than a Roman one? (fine)
16. The interior was _____ than the exterior. (impressive)

17–22. Rewrite each sentence in this part of a lecture comparing Greek and early Roman architecture. Correct the six errors.

Example: The lovelyest Greek temple ever built is the Parthenon.
The loveliest Greek temple ever built is the Parthenon.

The Greeks built the beautifulest temples. Early Romans, on the other hand, spent their most greatest efforts building cities. They built less temples and more public buildings, theaters, and stadiums. The more impressive of the earlyest structures still to be seen in Rome is the ruin of the Colosseum. Built in the first century A.D., it was the biggest outdoor theater of its time.

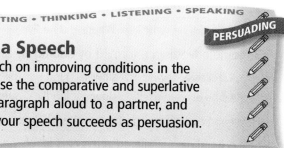

WRITING • THINKING • LISTENING • SPEAKING

PERSUADING

Write a Speech

Write a paragraph for a speech on improving conditions in the school cafeteria. In your speech use the comparative and superlative forms of adjectives. Read your paragraph aloud to a partner, and together discuss whether or not your speech succeeds as persuasion.

3 Adverbs

Find the three adverbs in the riddle. Which word does each adverb modify?

What book was once owned only by the wealthy, but now everyone can have? In addition, this book is free.

(A telephone book)

Identifying Adverbs

Adverbs modify verbs, adjectives, or other adverbs.

Modifies verb: Jules Verne wrote clearly and colorfully.

Modifies adjective: He is quite popular with many readers.

Modifies adverb: He handled his subjects remarkably well.

Adverbs tell *how, when, where,* and *to what extent.*

How: Sam read the novel carefully.

When: We read that story yesterday.

Where: Verne's books are read everywhere.

To what extent: I am very interested in science fiction.

1. Many adverbs that tell *to what extent* are **intensifiers**—they add to the meaning of the words they modify.

almost	least	most	really	terribly
awfully	less	quite	slightly	too
extremely	more	rather	so	very

Verne's style is quite realistic. He writes extremely well.

2. The words *how, when, where,* and *why* are adverbs.

How did he write?   Where did he live?

3. Some adverbs are formed by adding *-ly* to adjectives.

Adjective: wise   slow   kind   awful

Adverb: wisely   slowly   kindly   awfully

However, not all words that end with *ly* are adverbs.

Adjectives: Phileas Fogg seems lonely and friendly, not ugly.

Speak Up Identify the adverbs, and tell which words they modify. Which adverbs are intensifiers?

1. How could I pass the time indoors?
2. I looked very hard for a really good book.
3. I read almost steadily for a few hours.
4. I exercised rather vigorously here and there.
5. I ran up and down repeatedly and rested afterward.
6. I became extremely hungry and made a very large pot of soup.

Position of Adverbs

You can place most adverbs that modify verbs in different positions in a sentence. Use a comma after most adverbs that begin a sentence.

Thoughtfully, Jan read the book.
Jan thoughtfully read the book.
Jan read the book thoughtfully.

Moving some adverbs may change their function and the meaning of a sentence.

Only Verne worked in France. (*Only* describes *Verne* and is an adjective. No one else worked there.)
Verne only worked in France. (He lived elsewhere.)
Verne worked only in France. (He did not work elsewhere.)

Be careful to place words like these as close as possible to the words they modify.

almost	hardly
even	just
nearly	only
merely	scarcely

You should place most adverbs that modify adjectives and adverbs close to the words they modify. Misplaced modifiers may confuse your readers or convey unintended meaning. Make sure that the position in which you place an adverb lets you communicate the exact meaning you want to express.

Misplaced: Deeply Phileas Fogg was grateful. (*Deeply* seems to modify *Phileas Fogg.*)

Corrected: Phileas Fogg was deeply grateful.

Speak Up Which adverbs should not be shifted? Which adverbs can be shifted? Shift those adverbs to another part of the sentence. (There may be more than one correct way to change some sentences.)

7. Actually, science fiction can be traced back to myths.
8. A Greek writer merely rewrote myths as science fiction.
9. In the 1600s, modern science was just developing.
10. Modern science fiction developed also at this time.
11. Probably Jonathan Swift produced the first enduring science fiction in his 1726 satire *Gulliver's Travels*.

Gulliver

Summing Up

- **Adverbs** modify verbs, adjectives, or other adverbs. Adverbs usually tell *how, when, where,* and *to what extent.*
- **Intensifiers** are adverbs that tell *to what extent.*
- Some adverbs should be placed as close as possible to the modified words.

Write the adverbs and the words that they modify. Label the intensifiers.

Example: H. G. Wells wrote science fiction brilliantly and intelligently.
brilliantly   intelligently—wrote

12. Why did his books sell so well?
13. At first, Wells mainly wrote fiction.
14. He then developed rather naturally into a bold forecaster.
15. In 1909 he realistically described modern airplanes and submarines.
16. Long trips aboard these vehicles seemed highly improbable then.
17. People read Wells's works excitedly.   more ▶

18. Later, Wells became quite deeply involved in world events.
19. He went everywhere and spoke often against certain political beliefs.
20. He firmly believed that these beliefs were driving humanity downward.
21. Wells sometimes used science fiction to present his views.

22–26. Shift the adverb to a better position in each of the five sentences in this paragraph from a biographical essay. (There may be more than one correct way to change some sentences.)

Example: Wells did not only write science fiction.
Wells did not write only science fiction.

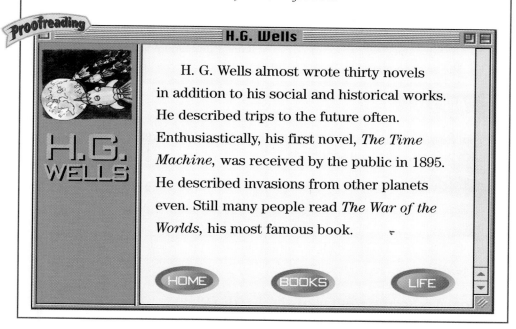

H.G. Wells

H. G. Wells almost wrote thirty novels in addition to his social and historical works. He described trips to the future often. Enthusiastically, his first novel, *The Time Machine*, was received by the public in 1895. He described invasions from other planets even. Still many people read *The War of the Worlds*, his most famous book.

HOME   BOOKS   LIFE

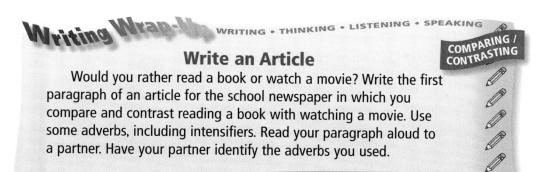

WRITING • THINKING • LISTENING • SPEAKING

COMPARING / CONTRASTING

Write an Article

Would you rather read a book or watch a movie? Write the first paragraph of an article for the school newspaper in which you compare and contrast reading a book with watching a movie. Use some adverbs, including intensifiers. Read your paragraph aloud to a partner. Have your partner identify the adverbs you used.

Writing with Adverbs

Combining Sentences An adverb can modify a verb, an adjective, or another adverb. Sometimes you can use adverbs to combine sentences. In this example, the writer moved an adverb from one sentence to the other to modify an adjective. This saves a lot of words!

I watched the scary movie.

The movie was awfully scary.

} I watched the awfully scary movie.

You can also combine simple sentences by changing an adjective into an adverb. (This will not work with all adjectives.)

verb
Carlita studied the scene.

adjective
She was thorough.

} adverb modifies verb
Carlita thoroughly studied the scene.

Apply It

1–6. Rewrite this excerpt from a student's essay. Use adverbs to combine each pair of underlined sentences.

Revising

My Favorite Movies

I like science-fiction movies. I really like them. My parents let me rent one science-fiction video. They let me rent one monthly. Here are my favorites:

Journey to the Center of the Earth (1959)

I watched this old movie. I was doubtful about it. I thought it might be dumb, but it wasn't. I have watched this movie several times. I was eager each time.

The Andromeda Strain (1971)

This movie is thrilling. It is so sus-penseful that I could not look away for even a moment. It was nominated for two Oscars and deserved the nominations. It definitely deserved them.

Elaborating Sentences Use adverbs to make your writing clearer and more specific. Precise, vivid adverbs can help you elaborate when you write.

Use adverbs to clarify meaning or to add detail.

The movie scared me.

The movie scared me terribly.
The movie slightly scared me.

The main character seemed real.

The main character seemed frighteningly real.
The main character seemed pleasantly real.

Replace vague adverbs with precise ones.

Vague: The acting was very good.

Clear: The acting was extraordinarily good.

Apply It

7–14. Read this excerpt from a student video script. Revise the script by adding precise, expressive adverbs to modify the underlined words.

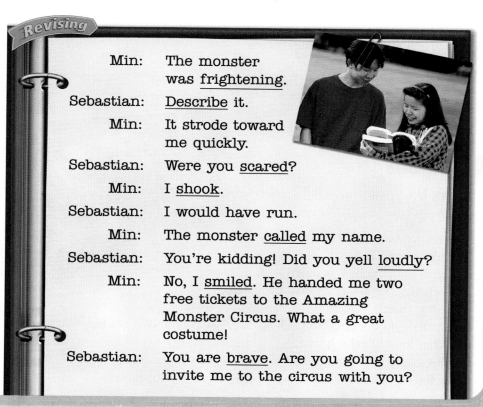

Revising

Min: The monster was frightening.

Sebastian: Describe it.

Min: It strode toward me quickly.

Sebastian: Were you scared?

Min: I shook.

Sebastian: I would have run.

Min: The monster called my name.

Sebastian: You're kidding! Did you yell loudly?

Min: No, I smiled. He handed me two free tickets to the Amazing Monster Circus. What a great costume!

Sebastian: You are brave. Are you going to invite me to the circus with you?

4 Comparing with Adverbs

One-Minute Warm-Up

What's wrong with this sentence? How can you fix it?

Not only did Joe run faster than the chicken, he ran further.

Degrees of Comparison

You can use adverbs to compare the actions of two people or things. Like adjectives, adverbs have three **degrees**.

Degree	Example
Positive (basic form): Makes no comparison.	Cars travel fast.
Comparative: Compares two.	Trains travel faster than cars.
Superlative: Compares three or more.	Planes travel fastest of all.

Try It Out

Speak Up What form of the adverb completes each sentence correctly? What is its degree?

1. Modern bicycles travel _____ than older ones. (fast)
2. Years ago, cyclists pedaled _____ on their wooden bicycles than cyclists do today. (hard)
3. Cyclists do not need to push so _____ on lightweight bicycles. (hard)
4. What kind of bike lasts _____ of all? (long)
5. Obviously, metal bikes last _____ than wooden ones. (long)
6. A six-day bicycle race will be held here _____. (soon)

Forms of Comparison

Adverbs change form to show comparison.

Adverb	Positive	Comparative	Superlative
One syllable	soon	sooner	soonest
Two or more syllables	early clearly	earlier more clearly	earliest most clearly

Most adverbs of two or more syllables form comparisons with *more* and *most*. Check your dictionary if you are not sure.

1. Use *less* and *least* to show less rather than more.

Positive:	The pilot flew skillfully.
Comparative:	The trainee flew less skillfully than the pilot.
Superlative:	The beginner flew least skillfully of all.

2. You must follow certain spelling rules when you add *-er* or *-est* to adverbs.

Adverbs ending with a consonant and *y*: early—earlier—earliest
Change the *y* to *i*. Then add *-er* or *-est*.

Adverbs ending with a consonant and *e*: late—later—latest
Drop the *e*. Then add *-er* or *-est*.

3. Some adverbs have irregular forms.

Positive	Comparative	Superlative
well	better	best
badly	worse	worst
much	more	most
far	farther	farthest
far	further	furthest
little	less	least

4. Use *farther* and *farthest* when you talk about physical distance. Use *further* and *furthest* in all other cases.

A jet travels farther than a glider.

Let's look further into this problem.

5. As with adjectives, you should avoid using *more* or *most* with adverbs ending in *-er* or *-est*.

Incorrect:	This train travels more faster than that one.
Correct:	This train travels faster than that one.

Try It Out

Speak Up What comparative or superlative form of the adverb in parentheses completes each sentence correctly?

7. A wooden bicycle without pedals came _____ of all. (early)
8. Pedals were added about twenty years _____. (late)
9. Today's bicycles do perform _____ than older ones. (good)
10. You can certainly travel _____ in comfort than before. (far)
11. People now ride bicycles _____ than they used to. (much)
12. Of all sports, many people enjoy bicycling _____. (much)

Summing Up

- Use the **comparative degree** of an adverb to compare two actions.
- Use the **superlative degree** to compare three or more actions.
- Form the comparative degree with *-er* or *more*.
- Form the superlative degree with *-est* or *most*.

On Your Own

Write each sentence, using the correct comparative or superlative form of the adverb in parentheses.

Example: In 1897 people rode bicycles _____ than they had done before. (frequently) *In 1897 people rode bicycles more frequently than they had done before.*

13. Then people began to drive cars _____ than they rode bicycles. (often)
14. They could go _____ in a car than on a bicycle. (fast)

more ▶

15. They could also go _____ than on a bike. (far)
16. Today the bicycle is again one of the _____ used vehicles of all. (commonly)
17. Bikes move _____ in traffic jams than cars do. (well)
18. In city traffic a bike may arrive _____ than a car. (early)
19. A cyclist who obeys traffic laws _____ than another will be safer in the long run. (carefully)

20–26. Correct the seven incorrect adverbs in these paragraphs from an Internet movie summary.

Example: I rented this old favorite movie earlyest of anyone in the biking club.
   earliest

Proofreading

Web site

Location: http://www.movieclassics.com/breaking.away

Movie Classics

Breaking Away

In the film *Breaking Away,* the main character admires Italian bicyclists most than any others. He is excited about being in a race with them until one pushes him off his bike, and he arrives latest at the finish line than he otherwise would have. Worse of all, he feels ordinary. His situation becomes much better, however.

He still believes that he and his friends can bicycle further and fastest than other teams. He decides to prove that working-class boys can ride more better than the local university students can. By the end of the film, he understands clearer that friendship makes winning possible.

Writing Wrap-Up WRITING • THINKING • LISTENING • SPEAKING

EXPLAINING

Write Director's Notes

Write a list of directions for actors in a film about a bicycle race or other race. Use some comparative and superlative forms of adverbs. Exchange your list with a partner. Find the adverbs and together check that their forms and spellings are correct.

5 Negatives

Make up an excuse for not cleaning your room.

A **negative** is a word that means "no" or "not." The word *not* is often used as an adverb. You often join *not,* or its contraction *n't,* with a verb. *Not* or *n't* makes a verb negative.

Shirley has not spotted an oriole yet.

I cannot find the birds.

They can't have flown away.

Other words are also negatives.

I have never seen such a mess as this one.

I can hardly move around in this room.

There's nowhere I can go from here.

No one seems to hear me.

Nothing is happening in this house.

A **double negative** is the use of two negative words to express one negative idea. Be careful to avoid double negatives. Most negative words have positive forms. You can usually use positive forms to correct double negatives.

Negative	Positive	Negative	Positive
neither	either	none	any
never	ever	no one	anyone
no	any, a	nothing	anything
nobody	anybody	nowhere	anywhere

Incorrect: Won't nobody help me clean up?

Correct: Won't anybody help me clean up?
Will nobody help me clean up?

Incorrect:	I can't find the soap nowhere.
Correct:	I can't find the soap anywhere.
	I can find the soap nowhere.

The words *hardly, scarcely,* and *barely* are negatives. Do not use them with another negative to express a negative idea.

Incorrect:	I can't hardly see the floor.
Correct:	I can hardly see the floor.
Incorrect:	There's barely no light in here.
Correct:	There's barely any light in here.
Incorrect:	There is scarcely nobody around.
Correct:	There is scarcely anybody around.

Try It Out

Speak Up Change the sentences to avoid double negatives. (There may be more than one correct answer.)

1. I didn't see nothing I liked in the store.
2. There isn't anything at home neither.
3. There aren't no sweaters in the closet.
4. Isn't there an Irish knit sweater nowhere in this room?
5. I can't find hardly any shirts in the drawer.
6. My brother can't find nothing either.
7. Doesn't nobody know where we can find a simple white shirt?
8. Brenda hasn't scarcely begun to look for me.

Summing Up

- A **negative** means "no" or "not."
- A **double negative** is the use of two negatives to express one negative idea. Avoid double negatives.

Rewrite each sentence correctly. (There may be more than one correct way to change a sentence.)

Example: There isn't scarcely any firewood left.
There is scarcely any firewood left.

9. Didn't nobody bring some into the house?
10. We can't cook nothing unless we get some wood.
11. We can't keep warm neither.
12. I've never gone nowhere that's colder than this.
13. You can't hardly expect any heat in the mountains.
14. There isn't nothing we can do unless we have help.
15. Won't nobody go out and get some wood?

16–22. Rewrite each sentence in this part of a story, correcting the seven errors. (There may be more than one way to correct a sentence.)

Example: There weren't no experienced mountaineers in our group.
There were no experienced mountaineers in our group.

Proofreading

We didn't have no electricity in the cottage. There wasn't no heat either. That night we all decided there couldn't be no wood in the shed out back. You can't barely see at night out there. No one didn't want to leave the cottage. We didn't have nothing for supper but peanut butter sandwiches. There wasn't nowhere to go but into our sleeping bags until morning.

Writing Wrap-Up   WRITING • THINKING • LISTENING • SPEAKING

REFLECTING

Write a Journal Entry
Write a journal entry about something important you forgot to do and what happened as a result. Include some negatives in your journal entry. Share your entry with a partner and together discuss methods you use to remember important things.

     For Extra Practice see page 233.

6 Adjective or Adverb?

What's wrong with this sentence, and how can you fix it?

Sandy played good yesterday, which was lucky because it was a real important game.

You have learned about adjectives and adverbs and how to make comparisons with them. You must be careful not to confuse adjectives and adverbs.

Incorrect: Today the girls' tennis team played good.

Correct: Today the girls' tennis team played well.

Incorrect: The team members felt badly about losing to their rivals last week.

Correct: The team members felt bad about losing to their rivals last week.

Remember what adjectives and adverbs do.

Adjectives: Modify nouns and pronouns

Which one	that person
What kind	red hat
How many	five men

Adverbs: Modify action verbs, adjectives, and other adverbs

How	played well
When	came yesterday
Where	lived upstairs
To what extent	really well

Adjective: Our top player, Trina, had a powerful serve.

Her serve was powerful.

Adverb: Our top player, Trina, served powerfully.

1. Use *good, bad, sure,* and *real* as adjectives. Remember that adjectives (not adverbs) follow linking verbs.

Trina felt bad about her backhand.

She was sure it was her weakest shot.

Her other shots were good.

Her worries were real.

2. Use *well, badly, surely,* and *really* as adverbs.

Trina knew her opponent well. (*not* good)

Lydia didn't play badly. (*not* bad)

She was surely swift and strong. (*not* sure)

She was really steady too. (*not* real)

3. *Well* is an adjective when it refers to health.

Lydia had been ill but was now well again.

Try It Out

Speak Up Which words in parentheses correctly complete the sentences?

1. It's (real, really) strange that Albert Einstein didn't do (good, well) in school as a boy.
2. He did (bad, badly) in history and languages.
3. Mathematics and science came (easy, easily) to him.
4. By his teens he was (sure, surely) of his abilities.
5. However, he was not a particularly (good, well) student at the Polytechnic Institute either.
6. His (real, really) wish was to study and expand his ideas on his own, which he eventually did.
7. He (sure, surely) developed into a brilliant scientist.
8. His scientific contributions are (real, really) important.

Summing Up

- Use *good, bad, sure,* and *real* as adjectives to modify nouns or pronouns and after linking verbs.
- Use *well, badly, surely,* and *really* as adverbs to modify verbs, adjectives, or other adverbs.
- Use *well* as an adjective when you mean "healthy."

Rewrite each sentence, using adjectives and adverbs correctly.

Example: To some people math comes easy.
To some people math comes easily.

9. Other people become real nervous when they are faced with math problems.
10. They would do good if they relaxed.
11. Math anxiety has been discussed good in many books.
12. Many people are not real sure of themselves with numbers.
13. They feel so uncomfortably before a math test.
14. Something sure can be done about math anxiety.

15–20. Rewrite each sentence in this part of a talk on math anxiety, correcting the six errors in the use of adjectives and adverbs.

Example: Not everyone does bad in math.
Not everyone does badly in math.

Proofreading

Good coaching will sure help anyone with math anxiety. Teachers are becoming real good at recognizing the problem. More confidence and less nervousness sure are the answers. Teachers must be real encouraging of students' natural abilities. Many people can do good in math if they relax. Then, instead of feeling badly before a math test, they will feel confident.

Writing Wrap-Up WRITING • THINKING • LISTENING • SPEAKING

EXPLAINING

Write an Advice Column

Write a brief request for advice on how to deal with some anxiety—either about schoolwork or about something else. Then write a response giving advice. Use adjectives and adverbs, such as *good*, *well*, and *badly*. With a partner read your advice aloud. Did you both give good advice? Did you use adjectives and adverbs correctly?

Choosing Different Adjectives and Adverbs

The purpose of modifiers is to make your writing precise and vivid. Don't get into the rut of using the same adjectives and adverbs over and over. Try to vary your writing with less-used modifiers.

Adjective Choice: The movie was exciting.

Better Adjective Choice: The movie was riveting!

Adverb Choice: very interesting characters

Better Adverb Choice: exceptionally interesting characters

Exciting and *very* are overused modifiers. Choosing a variety of adjectives and adverbs will add important details to your writing and eliminate repetition of words.

Apply It

1–8. Revise this movie review. Replace the eight underlined words—the adjective *exciting* and the adverb *very*—with different adjectives or adverbs from your Thesaurus Plus.

Revising

Have you seen this new movie? I thought it was really great! The main characters are two teenagers who slip into a confusing time warp. They meet some very exciting people. As you know from her other movies, the director is very skilled at building an exciting plot. All the characters are exciting, and the dialogue is exciting. During the exciting conclusion, I was on the edge of my seat. Even the sound track was exciting.

Enrichment

Modifiers!

Cinquains

A cinquain is a five-line poem with a set number of syllables in each line. The syllables per line follow this pattern: two, four, six, eight, two. Write a cinquain of your own on any subject. Use both adjectives and adverbs. Underline adjectives (including articles) in red and adverbs in blue.

Challenge Write a poem of two or more stanzas. Make each stanza a cinquain.

```
2   I stand.
4   Blue water winks
6   its silver eyes at me.
8   I spring high, arch smoothly downward.
2   I dive.
```

Scrambled Modifiers

Players: 2

Materials: paper and pencils

To play: Each player writes ten sentences in a list. In five of the sentences, include an adjective that has scrambled letters. In the other five, include a scrambled adverb. (Mix up the adjective and adverb sentences in your list.)

Players exchange papers, unscramble each other's scrambled words, and label them *adj.* or *adv.* When both players are finished, exchange papers again and check each other's words and labels.

This pizza tastes nasticaft!

Scoring: Each correct word earns one point; each correct label earns two points.

fantastic, adj.

1 **Adjectives** *(p. 190)* Write the adjectives, including the articles, and the words that they modify.

1. The long, narrow canoe glided through the smooth waters.
2. Two men, quiet and serious, concentrated on their actions.
3. They dipped their paddles in a slow, steady rhythm.
4. The shore, wooded, dark, and unfriendly, appeared at last.
5. The men beached the canoe beneath a large willow tree.

2 **Comparing with Adjectives** *(p. 196)* Write each sentence, using the correct form of the adjective in parentheses.

6. Deserts may be the _____ places in the world to live. (hard)
7. The Sahara is _____ than the Mojave Desert. (dry)
8. The Empty Quarter in Saudi Arabia may be _____ of all. (arid)
9. Death Valley, California, is the _____ place in the United States. (hot)
10. Azizia, Libya, though, is _____ than Death Valley. (hot)
11. Not all deserts are _____. (hot)
12. The Gobi in central Asia is a _____ desert than most. (cold)
13. Sometimes it is one of the _____ places on earth. (cold)
14. Some deserts are _____ than others. (pretty)
15. A few are among the _____ regions of all. (spectacular)

3 **Adverbs** *(p. 200)* Write the adverbs and the words that they modify. Underline the intensifiers.

16. The day had begun quite satisfactorily.
17. In only one hour, Ted Rizzo had nearly finished his chores.
18. Now the smells of breakfast floated outdoors invitingly.
19. He sniffed appreciatively, and he walked homeward.
20. He suddenly felt quite hungry, and he rushed into the house.
21. On the table was a very small glass of orange juice.
22. Ted was greatly disappointed by this.
23. Shortly his mother appeared with a plate of warm bread.
24. "So that's what smelled so good," he said.
25. She said, "You've been working so hard that today I decided to bake you some bread."
26. Ted was really delighted, and he thanked her.
27. Soon Mrs. Rizzo brought a puffy cheese omelet into the room.
28. Ted ate quickly and enthusiastically.
29. "The white part is the plate," said Mrs. Rizzo jokingly.
30. Then Ted gratefully thanked his mother and left briskly.

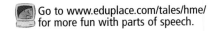
Go to www.eduplace.com/tales/hme/ for more fun with parts of speech.

4 Comparing with Adverbs (p. 206) Write each sentence, using the correct positive, comparative, or superlative form of the adverb that is in parentheses.

31. Computers can solve many complicated problems _____ than people can. (rapidly)
32. Years ago, most computer programmers worked _____ than they do now. (slowly)
33. Programmers worked _____ of all on aspects of program development. (hard)
34. They learned _____ that routine computer tasks could be stored in the machine's memory. (quickly)
35. Programs are now stored _____ in the computer's memory than on magnetic tape. (often)
36. After this development, programming was done _____ than before. (easily)
37. Programming languages resemble human language _____ than they resemble machine language. (closely)
38. A list of these languages would _____ include Visual BASIC, Pascal, C++, PERL, and Java. (likely)
39. Recently, computer scientists have gone _____ of all in developing computer languages. (far)
40. The newer languages can produce programs _____ than older ones can. (readily)
41. Computer science is taught at colleges and universities _____ than before. (much)

5 Negatives (p. 210) Rewrite each sentence correctly.

42. We had hardly never seen such an extraordinary storm, and it appeared so suddenly.
43. By afternoon we didn't have no power.
44. Nobody on the whole street had no light or heat.
45. There isn't no warm place anywhere in the house.
46. I couldn't hardly stand the freezing weather, and every location seemed unbearable.
47. There didn't seem to be no blankets anywhere, but we had just bought some last week.
48. Neither of my sweaters was not warm enough, and my teeth were chattering uncontrollably.

6 Adjective or Adverb? *(p. 213)* Rewrite each sentence correctly.

49. Antonio looks especially well today in that shirt.
50. His new wool pants are real light.
51. He sure has excellent taste in all his clothing.
52. Does he feel badly about getting ketchup on his jacket?
53. He certainly doesn't feel well about it.
54. The sleeve is stained bad.
55. I've never had salmon near this good.
56. Those old recordings sound well for their age.
57. Maeve and Andre surely dance good.
58. They can do some real complicated dance steps.

Mixed Review 59–65. Write this entry from a student's science journal, correcting the seven errors.

Proofreading Checklist
✔ incorrect adjectives and adverbs
✔ incorrect comparatives and superlatives
✔ double negatives

Proofreading

August 14

    Tonight I was lying out on the grass watching for the Perseid meteor shower on the most starriest night of this year. At first there wasn't nothing unusual. Then the shooting stars started up sudden, and it was more better than anything I could imagine. It was the excitingest event of the summer. These meteor showers occur once a year. They are debris from the orbiting Swift-Tuttle comet. You can see them real good if the night is clear. When they enter Earth's atmosphere, they emit light as they burn. Most of them don't never hit the ground because they burn up completely.

Test Practice

Write the numbers 1–8 on a sheet of paper. Read each group of sentences. Choose the sentence that is written correctly. Write the letter for that answer.

1
- **A** Those sets of nesting dolls are Russian.
- **B** Some dolls are bright painted and in traditional costumes.
- **C** Other sets are much moderner.
- **D** Of all my nesting dolls, my most favoritest are the ones painted to look like the Beatles.

2
- **F** The runners tense and silent waited for the starting signal.
- **G** Kayla shouted real loud as the favorite surged ahead.
- **H** Mara Holliday hadn't never won this event before.
- **J** Painfully, Tim gasped for air.

3
- **A** Dinah's throat is more painful today than it was yesterday.
- **B** The doctor says her right tonsil is swollener than her left.
- **C** There isn't no medicine she can take for this illness.
- **D** The doctor promises that she'll get better quick if she rests.

4
- **F** Bessie Coleman certain was an amazing woman.
- **G** She was the first African American woman pilot.
- **H** Coleman couldn't take no flying lessons in the United States because of her race.
- **J** She was real stubborn and learned to fly in France.

5
- **A** I think Charlie Chaplin is the funiest of all comedians.
- **B** Did you know that this famous star was british?
- **C** I couldn't hardly stop laughing at that factory scene.
- **D** Chaplin dreamed up great gags, and he moved very gracefully.

6
- **F** My big brother cooks better than either of my parents does.
- **G** The turkey golden and crisp made everyone's mouth water.
- **H** Most people can cook good if they follow a recipe.
- **J** The pie was finished earlyer than we expected.

7
- **A** Jared tries littler than any of the other members of the team.
- **B** Matt throws the ball more accurate than Austin.
- **C** Unfortunately, Marshall sprained his ankle last week.
- **D** Mr. Stein, fair but strict, is the most great coach of all.

8
- **F** Nita can scarcely see the board.
- **G** She is terrible frustrated.
- **H** Fortunately the teacher lets her move to the front row.
- **J** Now she can read the german vocabulary words.

Now write numbers 9–12 on your paper. Use the paragraph to answer the questions. Write the letter for each answer.

⁹When my mother was a girl, measles was a common and fairly serious disease in the United States. ¹⁰Mom caught the measles when she was seven, and she had to lay in bed for a week. ¹¹The long days spent in bed were boring, but the nights were even worst. She stared feverishly up at the ceiling where strange shapes danced spookily. ¹²Because of her illness, she couldn't except that the monsters were just shadows.

9 Which is the best way to rewrite Sentence 9?

A When my mother was a girl, measles were a common and fairly serious disease in the United States.

B When my mother was a girl measles was a common and fairly serious disease in the United States.

C When my mother was a girl, measles was a common and fairly seriously disease in the United States.

D Best as is

10 Which is the best way to rewrite Sentence 10?

F Mom catched the measles when she was seven, and she had to lie in bed for a week.

G Mom caught the measles when she was seven, and she had to lie in bed for a week.

H Mom caught the measles when she was seven and she had to lay in bed for a week.

J Best as is

11 Which is the best way to rewrite Sentence 11?

A The long days spent in bed were boring, or the nights were even worst.

B The long days spent in bed were boring, but the nights were even more bad.

C The long days spent in bed were boring, but the nights were even worse.

D Best as is

12 What is the best way to rewrite Sentence 12?

F Because of her illness, she couldn't accept that the monsters were just shadows.

G Because of her illness she couldn't except that the monsters were just shadows.

H Because of her illness, she couldn't accept that the monsters was just shadows.

J Best as is

Write numbers 13–16 on your paper, and do this page the same way you did the previous one.

¹³In the southern part of England stand an arrangement of large stones. The name of this ancient monument is Stonehenge. ¹⁴Workers probably begun to construct this unusual monument about four thousand years ago. ¹⁵Nobody can't figure out how the workers transported the enormous rocks. ¹⁶The bigest stones weigh 50 tons! Some experts believe that Stonehenge was used to track the position of the sun and keep track of time during the year.

13 Which is the best way to rewrite Sentence 13?

  A In the southern part of england stand an arrangement of large stones.

  B In the southern part of England stands an arrangement of large stones.

  C In the southern part of England stands an arrangement of largely stones.

  D Best as is

14 Which is the best way to rewrite Sentence 14?

  F Workers probably began to construct this unusual monument about four thousand years ago.

  G Workers probably will begin to construct this unusual monument about four thousand years ago.

  H Workers probably beginned to construct this unusual monument about four thousand years ago.

  J Best as is

15 Which is the best way to rewrite Sentence 15?

  A Nobody can figure out how the workers transported the enormous rocks.

  B Nobody can figure out. How the workers transported the enormous rocks.

  C Nobody cannot figure out how the workers transported the enormous rocks.

  D Best as is

16 Which is the best way to rewrite Sentence 16?

  F The most big stones weigh 50 tons!

  G The bigest stones weigh 50 tons?

  H The biggest stones weigh 50 tons.

  J Best as is

✅ Test Practice *continued*

Write numbers 17–20 on your paper, and do this page the same way you did the previous two pages.

[17]When Ben checked the pond on Thursday he found that the water had froze.[18]The wind must of been blowing when the temperature dropped because the ponds icy surface was wrinkled. [19]Some rushs raised out of the ice, creating a spiky affect. A single duck circled in a few feet of open water. [20]Ben felt badly for the duck; it looked like the loneliest creature in the world!

17 Which is the best way to rewrite Sentence 17?

  A When Ben checked the pond on Thursday he found that the water had frozen.

  B When Ben checked the pond on Thursday, he found that the water had froze.

  C When Ben checked the pond on Thursday, he found that the water had frozen.

  D Best as is

18 Which is the best way to rewrite Sentence 18?

  F The wind must have been blowing when the temperature dropped, because the pond's icy surface was wrinkled.

  G The wind must of been blowing when the temperature dropped because the ponds' icy surface was wrinkled.

  H The wind must have been blowing when the temperature dropped because the pond's icy surface was wrinkled.

  J Best as is

19 Which is the best way to rewrite Sentence 19?

  A Some rushs rose out of the ice, creating a spiky effect.

  B Some rushes rose out of the ice, creating a spiky effect.

  C Some rushes raised out of the ice, creating a spiky effect.

  D Best as is

20 Which is the best way to rewrite Sentence 20?

  F Ben felt bad for the duck; it looked like the loneliest creature in the world!

  G Ben felt badly for the duck, it looked like the loneliest creature in the world!

  H Ben felt bad for the duck; it looked like the most loneliest creature in the world!

  J Best as is

Unit 1: The Sentence

Subjects and Predicates *(pp. 37, 40, 43)* Write each sentence. Draw a line between the complete subject and the complete predicate. Underline the simple subject once and the simple predicate twice.

1. The ginkgo has survived for millions of years.
2. Many people refer to this tree as a living fossil.
3. A ginkgo can grow to a height of 100 feet.
4. Its different types of flowers do not grow on the same tree.
5. The roasted nut of the ginkgo is a delicacy in the Far East.

Conjunctions, Complex Sentences *(pp. 54, 57)* Write and label the coordinating, correlative, and subordinating conjunctions.

6. When you visit New York City, you should see the Empire State Building or the World Trade Center towers.
7. Actually, a visit to both the Empire State Building and the World Trade Center is nice if you have enough time.
8. Be sure to go to the tops because the views are magnificent.
9. Don't bother going if the day is overcast.
10. Although these buildings are tall, the Sears Tower in Chicago is taller.

Fragments and Run-ons *(p. 63)* Rewrite each item, correcting the fragments and run-ons.

11. The Library of Congress in Washington.
12. Because it is the biggest library in the United States.
13. The library collects materials from all over the world the materials are in 468 languages.
14. The papers of twenty-three presidents.
15. It is a huge place, it is located in several buildings.
16. Millions of maps, recordings, and photographs in the library.

Unit 2: Nouns

Kinds of Nouns *(pp. 82, 85)* Write the nouns. Label each one either *concrete* or *abstract* and either *common* or *proper*. Label the compound and collective nouns.

17. Afghanistan is a mountainous nation with valleys and deserts.
18. This country in Central Asia is slightly smaller than Texas.
19. The people are known for their bravery.
20. They have often fought against invaders to keep their freedom.
21. The land is covered with snow in winter and dust in summer.

See www.eduplace.com/kids/hme/ for a tricky usage or spelling question.

22. Spring is beautiful, with colorful flowers all over the land.
23. Snow leopards and mountain goats are found there.

Singular, Plural, and Possessive Nouns *(pp. 90, 94)* For each singular noun, write the singular possessive, the plural, and the plural possessive forms. Use your dictionary if you need help.

24. octopus
25. pony
26. doe
27. tuna
28. butterfly
29. Roy
30. chickadee
31. Filipino
32. son-in-law
33. Diaz
34. Dailey
35. buffalo

Unit 3: Verbs

Verbs, Verb Phrases, Tenses *(pp. 112, 115, 118)* Write the verbs. Label them *action* or *linking*. Then label the tense.

36. Galileo died in 1642, the same year as Isaac Newton's birth.
37. At the time of his death at age 85, Newton had changed the way that people thought about the universe.
38. Newton's works are masterpieces of scientific writing.
39. Sir Isaac Newton also invented a new kind of mathematical analysis.
40. Explanations of the natural world had been imprecise before.

Italian astronomer Galileo Galilei

Irregular Verbs *(pp. 122, 125, 129)* Write the principal parts for each verb.

41. teach
42. write
43. read
44. become
45. think
46. speak
47. put
48. lay
49. be
50. sink
51. bring
52. freeze
53. lie
54. rise
55. do

Direct and Indirect Objects, Predicate Nouns and Adjectives *(pp. 140, 144)*
Write each sentence. Label the direct and indirect objects, the predicate nouns, and the predicate adjectives.

56. I have just finished a book by Ved Mehta.
57. The book taught me an important lesson.
58. Overcoming an obstacle is not impossible.
59. Mehta was blind from the age of three.
60. Nevertheless, he met this challenge with determination.
61. He attended college, and he also became a writer.
62. He did numerous surprising things.
63. He hitchhiked across America, played chess, and rode a bike.
64. He is really a wonderful writer too.
65. People without sight can sometimes sense the presence of objects.
66. Vicente gave me a book about blindness.

Subject-Verb Agreement *(pp. 152, 155, 159)* Write each sentence. Underline the subject. Use the correct form of the verb.

67. That pile of baseballs (is, are) for us.
68. That is fine, but there (is, are) no bats.
69. Behind the dugout there (is, are) two of them.
70. The other team, the Bobcats, always (use, uses) our equipment!
71. My trousers (is, are) quite dirty from the mud on the mound.

Unit 4: Modifiers

Adjectives, Adverbs *(pp. 190, 200)* Write the words used as adjectives, and the adverbs. Do not list any articles. Then write the words that the adjectives and the adverbs modify.

72. The Sumerians created the first civilization.
73. In ancient times, they settled in a land between two rivers.
74. This rich land, which was called Mesopotamia by the Greeks, was ideally suited for agricultural cultivation.
75. The Sumerians probably first used irrigation successfully.
76. They built impressive cities from natural, bricklike materials.
77. They made very effective bronze tools and weapons.
78. Most significantly, they created one of the world's finest legal codes.

Comparing with Adjectives and Adverbs *(pp. 196, 206)* Write each sentence, using the correct form of the word in parentheses.

79. In addition to water and oxygen, food is one of our _____ daily needs. (important—superlative)

80. Humans must satisfy this need as _____ as possible. (nutritiously—positive)

81. A balanced diet is _____ than one lacking in essential nutrients. (beneficial—comparative)

82. A snack can sometimes provide good energy, but a balanced meal provides _____ nutrition. (good—comparative)

83. Proteins, carbohydrates, fats, vitamins, and minerals are the _____ building blocks for the body. (necessary—positive)

84. For a long time, people thought that animal protein was the _____ kind of protein. (good—superlative)

85. Soybeans are now a _____ source of protein than they used to be. (popular—comparative)

86. Nutrition experts suggest that Americans should eat _____ fat than we do. (little—comparative)

87. Experts also say that we should get _____ of our nutrients from fresh fruits and vegetables. (some—comparative)

Adjective or Adverb? *(p. 213)* Write each sentence, choosing the correct modifier.

88. Oh, Marlene, do you feel (bad, badly) today?

89. You look (terrible, terribly)!

90. Did the loud thunder prevent you from sleeping (good, well) last night?

91. I hope you won't do (poor, poorly) on the exam in Mr. Alberti's biology class.

92. I (hard, hardly) worry about Mr. Alberti's tests because I am always prepared.

93. His tests (sure, surely) are fair.

94. I always do (real, really) well on them.

95. Of course, if I feel bad I can't do my best on any exam no matter how (good, well) I've studied.

(pages 190–193)

1 Adjectives

- An **adjective** describes, or modifies, a noun or a pronoun. **Remember**
- An adjective formed from a proper noun is a **proper adjective**. Capitalize proper adjectives.
- A **predicate adjective** follows a linking verb and describes the subject.

● Write the adjectives, including the articles.

Example: Most summer theaters are small. *Most summer small*

1. The final rehearsal for the show is next Tuesday.
2. Every performer seems nervous.
3. The graceful dancers stand on the empty stage.
4. Which person will be successful in ten years?
5. That tall and attractive actor is dreaming about fame.
6. Those singers are resting for the next song.
7. The busy director enters and announces a script change.

▲ Write each adjective and the word it modifies. Include articles.

Example: In summer theater many performers are young and eager.
summer—theater many young eager—performers

8. The cast members perform many different tasks.
9. One day a bright, talented actor will sweep the stage floor.
10. The previous day that person may have painted some scenery.
11. A strong, slim dancer helps a hesitant performer with her lines.
12. For the weary but satisfied actors, the work was worthwhile.

■ Rewrite each sentence, adding adjectives.

Example: Has the tourist seen a play?
Has the Italian tourist seen a Broadway play?

13. People were waiting in line to buy tickets.
14. The line wound around one block.
15. Some sailors from a country were talking to a man.
16. One group of children made everyone else in the crowd smile.
17. Boys sat on the curb while a teacher waited.
18. A car came around the corner and pulled up to the door.
19. The crowd watched as the actor entered the theater.
20. The box office opened, and the crowd bought tickets.

(pages 196–199)

2 Comparing with Adjectives

Remember

- Use the **comparative degree** of an adjective to compare two things.
- Use the **superlative degree** to compare three or more things.
- Form the comparative degree with -*er* or *more*.
- Form the superlative degree with -*est* or *most*.

● Write the titles for three columns: *Positive, Comparative,* and *Superlative.* Copy the adjectives below into the *Positive* column. Then write each comparative and superlative form.

Example: cold   *comparative: colder   superlative: coldest*

1. red
2. comfortable
3. bad
4. noisy
5. large
6. terrible

▲ Write each sentence, using the correct positive, comparative, or superlative form of the adjective in parentheses.

Example: A building must withstand the _____ weather of all. (bad)
   A building must withstand the worst weather of all.

7. Builders of the past had _____ technology than we have today. (little)
8. The _____ builders of all used timber, stone, or mud. (early)
9. Wood and stone were _____ in some areas than in others. (scarce)
10. Therefore, the _____ material of all was mud. (popular)

■ Write each sentence, using the correct positive, comparative, or superlative form of the adjective in parentheses. Then label the adjective *positive, comparative,* or *superlative.*

Example: The Romans were _____ users of the arch. (creative)
   The Romans were creative users of the arch.   positive

11. The arch spanned _____ distances than posts and beams had spanned. (great)
12. It also required _____ stones or bricks than posts and beams. (few)
13. In a _____ period than this, the Middle Eastern arch was brought to Europe. (late)
14. Pointed arches were used in the _____ structures of all in the Middle Ages, the cathedrals. (wonderful)

(pages 200–203)

3 Adverbs

- **Adverbs** modify verbs, adjectives, or other adverbs. Adverbs usually tell *how, when, where,* and *to what extent.*
- **Intensifiers** are adverbs that tell *to what extent.*
- Some adverbs should be placed as close as possible to the modified words.

● Write the adverbs in these sentences.

Example: Jules Verne looked ahead to certain inventions clearly.
  ahead   clearly

1. He predicted airplanes and guided missiles accurately.
2. Surprisingly, his books remain popular today.
3. Verne cleverly used realistic details in his fantastic tales.
4. Verne's books were very successful.
5. People were quite interested in science in the 1800s.
6. That most certainly added to the popularity of Verne's books.

▲ Write the adverbs and the words that they modify. Underline the adverbs that are intensifiers.

Example: Jules Verne took his readers almost everywhere.
  <u>almost</u>—*everywhere   everywhere—took*

7. *Twenty Thousand Leagues Under the Sea* is quite famous.
8. A rather mad sea captain travels happily under the ocean.
9. *Around the World in Eighty Days* takes readers farther away.
10. Phileas Fogg travels around the earth in only eighty days.
11. Eighty days seemed like an extremely short time then.

■ Rewrite each sentence, adding two or more adverbs.

Example: Science fiction is popular.
  Science fiction is currently very popular.

12. The interesting plots involve space travel or time travel.
13. Marvelous inventions are another theme.
14. Many science fiction stories are set in the future.
15. They may be set in the present or in the past.
16. Science fiction is different from fantasy.
17. Fantasy relates impossible events.
18. Science fiction writers have a solid background in science.

(pages 206–209)

4 Comparing with Adverbs

- Use the **comparative degree** of an adverb to compare two actions.
- Use the **superlative degree** to compare three or more actions.
- Form the comparative degree with -*er* or *more*.
- Form the superlative degree with -*est* or *most*.

● Write the titles for three columns: *Positive, Comparative,* and *Superlative.* Copy the adverbs below into the *Positive* column. Then write each comparative and superlative form.

Example: soon   *comparative: sooner   superlative: soonest*

1. early	3. frequently	5. well	7. speedily	9. badly
2. quickly	4. late	6. far	8. little	10. loudly

▲ Write each sentence, using the form of the adverb in parentheses that best completes it.

Example: In the 1780s ships sailed _____ than before. (far)
In the 1780s ships sailed farther than before.

11. A merchant wanted a ship that went _____ than other ships. (fast)
12. For years, clippers sailed _____ of all the kinds of ships. (fast)
13. The British worked _____ on steamships than on clippers. (much)
14. Eventually steamships crossed the ocean _____ than clippers. (speedily)
15. Of all countries, England built the luxury liner the _____. (early)
16. Passengers were treated _____ than ever before. (well)
17. Of ways to travel then, people enjoyed liners the _____. (much)

■ Write each sentence, using the form of the adverb in parentheses that best completes it. Use the *comparative* or *superlative* forms and label each one.

Example: People always want to move _____ than usual. (fast)
People always want to move faster than usual. comparative

18. Does moving the _____ mean moving the _____? (fast, well)
19. Let us examine the matter _____ than this. (far)
20. Most people try to advance _____ than other people. (quick)
21. We do _____ if we go _____ than usual. (well, slow)
22. Those who do _____ of all are those who can relax. (well)

(pages 210–212)

5 Negatives

- A **negative** means "no" or "not."
- A **double negative** is the use of two negatives to express one negative idea. Avoid double negatives.

Remember

● Write each sentence, choosing the correct word.

Example: I don't (never, ever) remember a hotter day.
I don't ever remember a hotter day.

1. Nobody wants to do (nothing, anything) in this heat.
2. Even the mosquitoes (can, can't) scarcely move.
3. There's no breeze (anywhere, nowhere).
4. The fan doesn't do (no, any) good.
5. It (can, can't) barely push the heavy air around.
6. Doesn't (anybody, nobody) have air conditioning?

▲ Rewrite each sentence to correct the double negative. (There may be more than one way to correct each sentence.)

Example: There isn't scarcely anyone here yet.
There is scarcely anyone here yet.

7. Didn't no one put the juice in the refrigerator?
8. There won't be nothing cold to drink.
9. I can't find my CDs nowhere.
10. Eva can't find her cassette tapes neither.
11. You can't hardly hear the music in the other room.
12. Isn't Chris bringing no CDs for us to listen to?

■ Rewrite each sentence that has a double negative. (There may be more than one way to correct a sentence.) If there is no double negative, write *correct.*

Example: They haven't done nothing about fixing the bike.
They haven't done anything about fixing the bike.

13. Wasn't anybody at the repair shop?
14. Nobody never answers the telephone there.
15. No one can drive to the repair shop this afternoon.
16. We don't have no spare time right now.
17. You shouldn't never leave your bike in the driveway.
18. Hardly no one could see it lying there.

(pages 213–215)

⑥ Adjective or Adverb?

- Use *good, bad, sure,* and *real* as adjectives to modify nouns or pronouns and after linking verbs.
- Use *well, badly, surely,* and *really* as adverbs to modify verbs, adjectives, or other adverbs.
- Use *well* as an adjective when you mean "healthy."

Remember

● Write each sentence, using the word in parentheses that correctly completes it.

Example: Chester is (real, really) happy about his summer job.
Chester is really happy about his summer job.

1. He was not (sure, surely) that he would get it.
2. Chester is normally a very (good, well) swimmer.
3. He did not swim (good, well) for his lifesaving test, however.
4. When he took his test, he was not feeling (good, well).
5. He was certain that he had done (bad, badly) on the test.

▲ Rewrite each sentence correctly.

Example: The dancer did not look well in her costume.
The dancer did not look good in her costume.

6. She looked real good in strong colors.
7. Pale pink made her look ill even when she felt good.
8. She was not surely what to do about the costume.
9. The director knew that the problem was real serious.
10. If she felt uncomfortable, she might dance bad.

■ Rewrite each incorrect sentence correctly. Label each corrected word *adjective* or *adverb*. If a sentence is already correct, write *correct*.

Example: The new restaurant seems to be doing good.
The new restaurant seems to be doing well. well adverb

11. Everything smells and tastes well.
12. The meal we had last night sure was delicious.
13. The table looked really good too.
14. Unfortunately, Tom was not feeling well last night.
15. He skated bad at the hockey game and then went home.
16. He felt badly about missing such a good meal.

"Listen, Liz. You may be Taft Middle School's mascot, but that doesn't give you the right to run wild on Panther Field and scare all those poor football players!"

Capitalization and Punctuation

Interjections

What's happening in this picture? What is each student feeling? Make up a sentence to go in each character's speech balloon. Consider which punctuation marks you would use.

You know that an exclamatory sentence expresses strong feeling, indicated by an exclamation point. Certain words can also be exclamatory. A word or a group of words that expresses feeling is called an **interjection**. Interjections express emotions such as anger, surprise, pain, happiness, and relief.

Common Interjections				
ah	goodness	oh dear	ow	uh oh
aha	hey	oh my	phew	well
bam	hooray	oh yes/no	pow	whee
bravo	hurrah	okay	shh	whoops
good grief	oh	ouch	ugh	wow

An interjection is not a sentence and has no grammatical relationship to the other words around it. Use an exclamation point after an interjection that expresses strong feeling. Use a comma after an interjection that expresses mild feeling.

Wow! That was a great play!

Hooray! I got the part.

Shh! I can't hear.

Whoops, I dropped the book.

Oh, I forgot my lines.

Okay, let's continue.

An interjection may represent a sound.

Bam! That was a loud noise.

Aha, now I understand the story.

Ow! I hurt my finger.

Like exclamation points, interjections should not be overused. Too many interjections make your writing or speaking ineffective.

Hooray! I got the part.

Speak Up Find the interjection in each sentence.
How should each sentence be punctuated?

1. Hey do you know her name?
2. Wow She dances so brilliantly.
3. Oh I'll never be able to dance like that.
4. Goodness she's spinning so gracefully.
5. Bravo She's terrific.

Summing Up

- An **interjection** is a word or a group of
  words that expresses feeling or represents
  a sound. Use an exclamation point after an
  interjection that expresses strong feeling.
  Use a comma after an interjection that
  expresses mild feeling.

Rewrite each sentence, adding the correct punctuation. Underline each interjection.

Example: Hey there's a baseball game on Saturday.
   Hey, there's a baseball game on Saturday!

6. Great let's go to the game.
7. Well the team is quite good this year.
8. Hooray Chico is at bat.
9. Bam The bat really whacked the ball.
10. Wow That ball is out of here.
11. Pow It went right over the pitcher's head.
12. Whoops Phil shouldn't have swung at that one.
13. Phew The catcher almost tagged Sara out at home plate.
14. Ugh The umpire really missed that call.
15. Oh dear Did you see the other team's new pitcher?
16. Wow He really throws the ball fast.

more ▶

On Your Own continued

17–24. Write and punctuate the eight sentences that contain interjections in the following story. Underline the interjections.

Example: Shh Did you hear that?   _Shh! Did you hear that?_

Proofreading

"Okay the score is tied, there are two outs, and it's the ninth inning," said the Stars' coach. "Luckily, our best hitter, Jason, is batting."

"Uh oh look who's pitching," groaned some of the Stars, pointing to the field. The Comets' best pitcher, Karl Li, had just trotted onto the pitcher's mound. It was Jason against Karl.

"Hey Karl's good, but he's not invincible," said the coach.

The first pitch was a strike. Jason swung at the next pitch and hit a high foul ball, which drifted out of reach. "Phew that was a close one," said Maria. She was standing in the dugout with the rest of the Stars.

Both teams watched tensely as Karl Li wound up for the next pitch. "Well here it comes," thought Maria. Just then Jason swung hard. "Pow The ball exploded off his bat. From the dugout Maria cried, "Oh yes That ball is out of here!"

The Comets' outfielder ran toward the fence. At the last second, he jumped. The ball sailed inches over his glove and over the fence for a home run. "Hooray We've won!" yelled the Stars.

Writing Wrap-Up   WRITING • THINKING • LISTENING • SPEAKING

PERSUADING

Write a Radio Ad

Write a radio ad describing and promoting a new piece of athletic equipment guaranteed to make you a success in a particular sport. Use at least one interjection. Read your ad to a partner. Together discuss which parts of your ad are most effective.

2 Sentences and Interjections

What is wrong with these sentences? How can you fix them?

Boy. I wish Sir Arthur Conan Doyle had written more Sherlock Holmes books?

to me, Holmes is the most interesting mystery character.

Every sentence begins with a **capital letter** and ends with a **period**, a **question mark**, or an **exclamation point**.

Declarative:	I read a book.	**Imperative:**	Read it.
Interrogative:	Did you read it?	**Exclamatory:**	It's great!

As you know, an interjection is a word such as *oh, wow,* or *bravo.* When an interjection expresses strong feeling, an exclamation point follows it. When an interjection expresses milder feeling, a comma follows it.

Wow! I just solved the mystery.   Oh, tell me about it.

Try It Out

Speak Up How would you correct these sentences?

1. who wrote the story
2. Edgar Allan Poe wrote it
3. what a creative writer he was
4. don't tell me the ending
5. oh I wouldn't do that

Summing Up

- Begin every sentence with a **capital letter**.
- Use a **period** at the end of declarative and imperative sentences.
- Use a **question mark** at the end of interrogative sentences.
- Use an **exclamation point** at the end of exclamatory sentences and after an interjection expressing strong feeling.
- Use a **comma** after an interjection expressing milder feeling.

Write each sentence, adding the appropriate capitalization and punctuation.

Example: who was Charlotte Brontë   *Who was Charlotte Brontë?*

  6. Charlotte Brontë was born in England in 1816
  7. please tell me the name of her most famous novel
  8. is the title *Jane Eyre*
  9. hey that's one of my favorite novels
 10. did Charlotte's sister write the novel *Wuthering Heights*
 11. both sisters also wrote poetry
 12. wow those sisters were really talented

13–20. Write the riddle below, correcting the eight errors in capitalization and punctuation.

Example: great I guessed the answer.   *Great! I guessed the answer.*

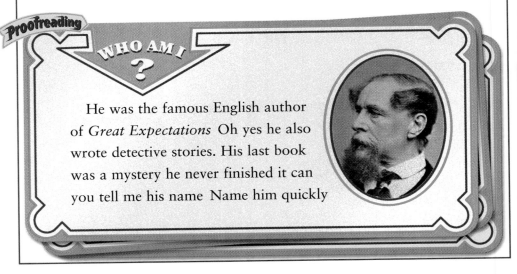

Proofreading

WHO AM I
?

He was the famous English author of *Great Expectations* Oh yes he also wrote detective stories. His last book was a mystery he never finished it can you tell me his name Name him quickly

Writing Wrap-Up   WRITING • THINKING • LISTENING • SPEAKING

INFORMING

Introduce a Speaker

You won a contest and your favorite writer is coming to speak at your school. Write a brief speech introducing him or her to the audience. Include at least one sentence of each type and one interjection. Proofread your work. Then, with a small group, read your introduction aloud and invite comments.

3 Proper Nouns and Proper Adjectives

Find the proper noun in the riddle.

What was the highest mountain before anyone measured Mount Everest?

(Mount Everest)

Geographical Names

You know that a **proper noun** names a particular person, place, or thing and that a proper noun always begins with a capital letter. Therefore, you must capitalize proper nouns from geography. Do not capitalize small words like *the* and *of*.

1. Capitalize cities, states, countries, and continents.

Chicago   Texas   Austria   South America

2. Capitalize bodies of water and geographical features.

Ohio River   White Mountains   Gulf of Mexico

3. Capitalize the names of areas. Do not capitalize directions.

the Southwest   the Middle East   Central Asia
We traveled south along the coast, then east.

4. Capitalize streets and highways.

Route 66   Wall Street   Avenue of the Stars

5. Capitalize buildings, bridges, and monuments.

Fort Knox   World Trade Center   Brooklyn Bridge

You can form a **proper adjective** from a proper noun. Capitalize proper adjectives.

Proper Nouns	Proper Adjectives
Mexico	Mexican art
North America	North American birds
Paris	Parisian fashion
Jefferson	Jeffersonian democracy

Speak Up Which words should be capitalized?

1. The egyptian museum in cairo has many treasures.
2. Egypt and the suez canal are part of the middle east.
3. Aswan is a city in the nile valley in southern egypt.
4. I visited the institute of africa on elm road.
5. An exhibition of african art included carved masks.

Titles, Organizations, Dates, and Subjects

Other proper nouns that you should capitalize include titles, names of organizations, historical events and periods, certain dates, and certain subjects.

1. Capitalize titles for people. Do not capitalize titles if they are used alone as common nouns.

   Captain Ahab   Dr. Kaplan   Father
   The doctor will see you now.   My uncle is the president.

2. Capitalize organizations, institutions, and businesses.

   United League   Dallas Symphony   Hirsch Institute
   Tampa High School   Ted's Garage   Branford Company

3. Capitalize languages and specific school subjects followed by a number. Do not capitalize general school subjects.

   English   Biology I   Algebra 2
   social studies   science   math

4. Capitalize historical events, periods of time, and documents.

   Boston Tea Party   Revolutionary War   Age of Reason
   Roaring Twenties   Gettysburg Address   the Constitution

5. Capitalize days, months, and holidays, but not seasons.

   Monday   November   Fourth of July
   spring   autumn   winter

Speak Up What words should be capitalized?

6. In history 1, we are studying the civil war.
7. The gettysburg address was delivered by president lincoln.

more ▶

8. Jefferson davis was the president of the confederacy.
9. General lee appeared at appomattox court house in april 1865.
10. Lee became president of washington college after the war.

Summing Up

- A **proper noun** begins with a capital letter.
- You can form **proper adjectives** from proper nouns.
- Capitalize proper adjectives.

On Your Own

Write the incorrect sentences, adding capital letters where needed. If a sentence is already correct, write *correct.*

Example: The museum of science on barberry road has a new exhibit.

The Museum of Science on Barberry Road has a new exhibit.

11. The exhibit runs from thursday, september 4, through tuesday, december 30.
12. The museum of science will remain open on memorial day.
13. Every fall and spring, the museum has a special exhibit.
14. It is held by the world ocean society on clinton avenue.
15. The current exhibit is on the world's natural waterways.
16. Research by the national science foundation is included.
17. Interest in science increased in the middle ages.
18. Today professor wyman is taking the geography 101 class of bentley university to the exhibit.
19. Other geography classes will visit during the spring break.
20. The atlantic ocean is half the size of the pacific ocean.
21. The atlantic was named for the atlas mountains in africa.
22. There are mountain ranges under the ocean.
23. The tallest mountains on land are the himalayas.
24. The george washington bridge spans the hudson river.
25. From the bridge, you can see the world trade center.

more ▶

Proper Nouns and Proper Adjectives **243**

On Your Own continued

26–35. Write each sentence in this part of a pamphlet for a guided tour. Correct the eight errors in the use of capital letters and the two errors in the use of proper adjectives.

Example: Meet the Brazil people in the exciting region of bahia.
Meet the Brazilian people in the exciting region of Bahia.

Proofreading

Welcome to
Rio de Janeiro

When you land in the South America country of Brazil, you first will visit beautiful rio de janeiro. There, you will be welcomed by a friendly people who speak the Portugal language. Our trip to iguaçu falls will begin the next day. These spectacular falls on the border between argentina and brazil are four times wider than niagara falls.

Writing Wrap-Up
WRITING • THINKING • LISTENING • SPEAKING

EXPRESSING

Write a Journal Entry

If you could visit any part of the world, where would you go first? Write a journal entry in which you discuss where you would like most to travel and why. Use at least one proper noun and one proper adjective. Share your journal entry with a partner, and check that proper adjectives and proper nouns have been used correctly.

For Extra Practice see page 287.

4 Uses for Commas

Why is each comma in this sentence necessary?

Even mumps, measles, or whooping cough could kill the weakened, hungry children.

—from *Restless Spirit: The Life and Work of Dorothea Lange,* by Elizabeth Partridge

1. You often use commas to separate items in a series. A **series** is three or more related words, phrases, or clauses.

   Words: Leon photographed cities, people, and parks. (nouns)
   He aimed, focused, and took the picture. (verbs)
   The tree was old, twisted, and leafless. (adjectives)

   Phrases: People often take photographs during sports events, on vacations, and at parties. Leon took photographs in the morning, at dusk, and in the evening every day.

   Clauses: Leon developed the photos, I enlarged the best ones, and Tim put them in frames.

2. Use a comma between two or more adjectives that come before a noun.

   Leon photographed the dilapidated, rusty jalopy.

3. Do not use a comma with two or more adjectives if the adjectives are used together to express a single idea. To decide whether to use a comma, try reading the adjectives with *and,* or reverse the adjectives. If the sentence sounds awkward, do not use a comma.

   Awkward: Leon uses an expensive and Japanese camera.
   Awkward: Leon uses a Japanese expensive camera.
   Correct: Leon uses an expensive Japanese camera.

4. You know that a compound sentence is made up of two or more independent clauses. Use a comma to separate these clauses. You may omit the comma if the clauses are short.

   I brought a camera, Leo brought film, and Inez brought a flash.

   We wanted a picture of the sunrise, but it rained that day.

   The rain stopped and the sun came out.

Speak Up Where should commas be used in these sentences? Which sentences do not need commas?

1. Photographers view the scene set the camera and shoot.
2. Modern cameras are complicated but many of them are automatic.
3. Some impressive American cameras develop pictures instantly.
4. Cameras are useful entertaining and relatively inexpensive.
5. You can take pictures anywhere with sensitive color film.
6. Inexpensive cameras can take clear lifelike pictures.

Summing Up

- Use a comma to separate items in a **series**.
- Use a comma between two or more adjectives that come before a noun. Do not use a comma if they express a single idea.
- Use a comma to separate the simple sentences in a compound sentence.

Write the incorrectly punctuated sentences, adding commas where needed. If a sentence needs no commas, write *correct*.

Example: Large bulky cameras have just about disappeared.
Large, bulky cameras have just about disappeared.

7. Modern cameras are compact light and durable.
8. Good amateur photographers are becoming more common.
9. A camera some film a good eye and an interesting subject are the basic requirements for photography.

more ▶

10. Photography may seem like a recent invention but people have been taking photographs for more than 150 years.

11. A practical French inventor produced the first sharp photograph in 1839.

12. His impressive exciting achievement caused a sensation.

13–20. Write the sentences in this part of a Web site for a museum of photography. Add or delete commas as needed. There are eight errors.

Example: Pictures of people buildings and landmarks were now possible.
Pictures of people, buildings, and landmarks were now possible.

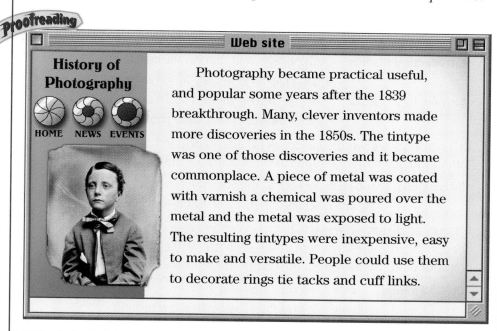

Web site

History of Photography

HOME   NEWS   EVENTS

Photography became practical useful, and popular some years after the 1839 breakthrough. Many, clever inventors made more discoveries in the 1850s. The tintype was one of those discoveries and it became commonplace. A piece of metal was coated with varnish a chemical was poured over the metal and the metal was exposed to light. The resulting tintypes were inexpensive, easy to make and versatile. People could use them to decorate rings tie tacks and cuff links.

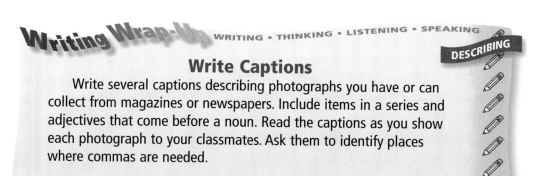

Writing Wrap-Up   WRITING • THINKING • LISTENING • SPEAKING

DESCRIBING

Write Captions

Write several captions describing photographs you have or can collect from magazines or newspapers. Include items in a series and adjectives that come before a noun. Read the captions as you show each photograph to your classmates. Ask them to identify places where commas are needed.

For Extra Practice see page 288.
Uses for Commas   **247**

5 More Uses for Commas

What is wrong with these sentences? How can you fix them?

Marco do you need a new printer?

Since my project is done I'd be glad to help with yours.

1. Use commas after words, phrases, and clauses that come at the beginning of a sentence.

Introductory Words:	Oh, I need a sharper pencil.
	Yes, they are in the supply cabinet.
Introductory Phrases:	Arriving late, Walt sat near the door.
	During the long meeting, he fell asleep.
Introductory Clauses:	After the session ended, I spoke to Hal.
	While I waited, I made some phone calls.

2. **Interrupters** are words that break up a sentence and add emphasis. Use commas to separate interrupters from the rest of the sentence.

Interrupters:	You know, of course, the purpose of this meeting.
	We will meet again next week, by the way.

3. A **noun of direct address** is the name of a person or persons spoken to directly. It can come anywhere in the sentence. Use commas to separate nouns of direct address from the rest of the sentence.

Direct Address:	John, I will need your help with this.
	Come into my office, Janice, for a few minutes.
	Staple these pages together, James.

4. As you know, an **appositive** adds information about the noun that directly precedes it. Use commas to separate an appositive only if it is not necessary to identify the noun.

Appositive:	The president, Harold White, will present the award.

If the appositive is necessary to explain or identify the noun, do not use commas.

The documentary *Space Exploration* won an award.

My friend Patrick has seen the movie.

Speak Up Where are commas needed in these sentences? Which sentence does not need any commas?

1. If the office is modern you will see few typewriters or pens.
2. Wooden desks and bookcases Flora are things of the past.
3. Looking around you notice that everything is steel or plastic.
4. Of course John the photocopy machine is always in use.
5. The most important office tool the computer commands people's attention.
6. In a small room the noisy printer rolls out page after page.
7. The pamphlet "Your Friendly Computer" sits on everyone's desk.

Summing Up

- Use commas after words, phrases, and clauses that come at the beginning of sentences.

- Use commas to separate **interrupters**, **nouns of direct address**, and unnecessary **appositives** in a sentence.

Write each incorrectly punctuated sentence, adding commas where needed. If a sentence needs no commas, write *correct*.

Example: ENIAC the first electronic computer was built in 1946.
ENIAC, the first electronic computer, was built in 1946.

8. Yes everyone is affected by a computer in some way.
9. When you dial the phone a computer connects your call.
10. At the local supermarket a computer speeds your checkout.
11. Regulating electricity the computer supplies constant power.
12. Meteorologists scientists who study weather rely on computer information.
13. Although computers are changing our lives they are only tools.
14. No my friend they are not smarter than humans.
15. They were in fact created by humans.

more ▶

16. Like any other tool the computer helps us do things Peter.
17. The first computers built were huge.
18. Susan compare those old computers with a modern desktop model.
19. The book *Computers in Your Life* gives the history of this invention.
20. Today's computers marvels of speed and compactness use tiny silicon chips an invention of the 1970s.

21–28. Write the sentences in the e-mail letter of complaint below, correcting the eight errors in the use of commas.

Example: According to the warranty you must assist me Mr. Janus.
   According to the warranty, you must assist me, Mr. Janus.

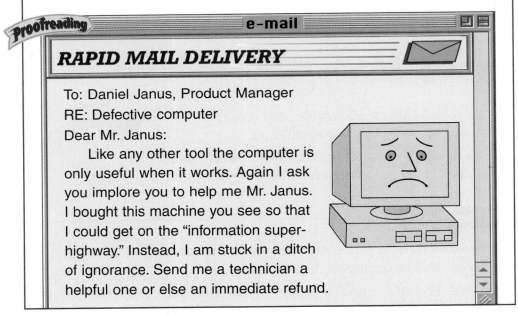

proofreading

e-mail

RAPID MAIL DELIVERY

To: Daniel Janus, Product Manager
RE: Defective computer
Dear Mr. Janus:

Like any other tool the computer is only useful when it works. Again I ask you implore you to help me Mr. Janus. I bought this machine you see so that I could get on the "information super-highway." Instead, I am stuck in a ditch of ignorance. Send me a technician a helpful one or else an immediate refund.

WRITING • THINKING • LISTENING • SPEAKING

PERSUADING

Writing Wrap-Up

Write a Letter of Complaint

Write a letter of complaint expressing your dissatisfaction with something you have bought and demanding action. Include sentences with introductory words, introductory phrases, introductory clauses, and interrupters. In a small group, read your letters aloud. Then decide who wrote the most persuasive letter of complaint.

Writing Sentences with Commas

Combining Sentences: Words and Phrases in a Series By now you know that too many short, choppy sentences can distract your reader. One strategy for fixing them is to combine words or phrases in a series. This will trim away extra words and streamline your writing.

I was happy about this job opportunity.
I felt excited too.
I was surprised to find it!

} I was happy, excited, and surprised to find this job opportunity.

In the series above, each item is a single word. Don't mix single words with phrases. When you combine phrases in a series, each phrase should have a similar structure.

I am a hard worker.
I learn quickly.
I cooperate well.

Correct Series

I am a hard worker, a quick learner, and a cooperative person.

OR

Awkward Series
I am a hard worker, learn quickly, and I am cooperative.

Correct Series

I work hard, learn quickly, and cooperate well.

Apply It

1–5. Revise this excerpt from a job-application letter. Combine sentences by placing words or phrases in a series.

Help Wanted
Delivery person. Hard worker needed with own transportation. Bikes okay! Must know area well. Please respond

Revising

    I am a good student. I also learn swiftly, and I am reliable. I have lived here all my life. I know every street and shortcut. I know every business. I have a safe, reliable bike. It has twenty-one speeds. It also has a light and a basket.

    If you need help in your store, I can greet customers or sweep the floors. I am also good at stocking shelves. If you'd like, I can get references from teachers and neighbors. I am diligent. I am loyal. Finally, I am punctual!

more

Combining Sentences: Clauses in a Series You can combine sentences to make a longer compound sentence by grouping related ideas.

You know that a compound sentence is made up of independent clauses. A series contains at least three independent clauses. Use commas to separate them, and place a conjunction before the last clause.

In Florida, shrimp and lobster boost the fishing industry. Rich farmland enhances agriculture. Mineral deposits support the mining industry.

In Florida, shrimp and lobster boost the fishing industry, rich farmland enhances agriculture, and mineral deposits support the mining industry.

Each clause in a series should have a similar structure. In the awkward sentence below, the clauses begin with unrelated nouns. In the smoother revised sentence, each clause begins with a noun about regions.

Awkward Series

Some regions of Florida contain titanium ore, phosphate rock is in other regions, and you will find brick clay in still others.

Correct Series

Northeast Florida contains titanium ore, central Florida produces phosphate rock, and other regions provide brick clay.

Apply It

6–8. Revise this student report. Combine sentences by using words, phrases, or clauses in a series. Use a similar structure for items in a series.

Revising

Career Opportunities in Florida

Agriculture is only one of Florida's industries. The real estate business continues to grow. Financial services thrive. Retail stores offer a variety of goods. Perhaps the most fascinating business is the hospitality industry.

The hospitality industry serves business travelers. It provides food and lodging for vacationers. It employs many workers. Resorts and amusement parks attract many tourists. These businesses need managers. They need lifeguards. They need chefs as well as landscapers.

Help Wanted

6 Dates, Addresses, and Letters

Think of a sentence or two telling where you were on the first day of this century. Include the date, the city, and the state.

Without commas, these items can be confusing to read.

July 4 1776

Philadelphia Pennsylvania

7 Walnut Drive Marion Ohio

1. With dates, use commas to separate the month and the day from the year, and the year from the rest of the sentence. Do not use commas if you are giving only the month and the year or only the month and the day.

   July 4, 1776, is the day our nation was born.

   July 1776 was an important time in history.

   Holiday traffic on July 3 is usually heavy.

2. In an address, use a comma between the names of the city and the state. If the address is within the sentence, also use a comma after the name of the state.

   Philadelphia, Pennsylvania, is our nation's birthplace.

3. When an address appears within a sentence, use a comma to separate each item in the address except the Zip Code.

   Send the bill to 4 Hall Street, Miami, Florida 33142.

   Do not use a comma between items in an address that are joined by a preposition.

   We visited my uncle at 215 High Street <u>in</u> Middletown, New York.

   Anna's family is driving to Mineral Point <u>in</u> Wisconsin for the holiday.

4. You probably already know the parts of a friendly letter. In addition to the items within the writer's address and the date, a friendly letter includes a greeting and a closing. Use a comma after the greeting in a friendly letter and after the closing in both a friendly letter and a business letter.

   Dear Betty,   Your friend,   Sincerely yours,

1–10. Where are commas needed?

48 Kent Drive
Lexington KY 40511
January 29 2001

Dear Alissa

   Your letter of May 30 2000 just got here! Because you didn't include the Zip Code or the name of the state, the letter was delivered to Lexington Massachusetts 02173. I have no idea how the post office finally figured out where to send it.

   Anyway, I'll write more later about the upcoming Valentine's Day party. I'm looking forward to seeing you there. The address of the party is 12 Lee Road Boone Kentucky. See you on February 14 2001.

Your friend

Olivia

Summing Up

- Use a comma to separate the month and the day from the year.

- Use a comma between the city and the state. Use a comma after the state if the address is within the sentence. Use a comma to separate each item except the Zip Code.

- Use a comma after the greeting in friendly letters and after the closing in both friendly and business letters.

11–26. Write this friendly letter, adding commas where needed. Sixteen commas are missing.

Example: September 6 1620 is when the Pilgrims left England.
September 6, 1620, is when the Pilgrims left England.

Proofreading

1320 Adams Road
Stillwater Oklahoma 74074
March 27 2001

Dear Aunt Jessie

    April 7 2001 is when I will finally be in Boston!
I can't wait to see you and Uncle Raymond. Except for visits
to Tulsa Oklahoma in November 1997 and to Houston Texas
in January 1998, I've never been away from Stillwater.
    I've been studying some history. April 19 1775 was the
first battle of the American Revolution in Lexington,
Massachusetts. Can we visit the site of the Boston Tea
Party, which occurred on December 16 1773 in Boston
Harbor? My Boston tour book lists addresses of other
historical sites, including the home of Paul Revere at 19
North Square Boston Massachusetts 02113. Is that far
from the Museum of Science at Science Park in Boston? I am
looking forward to my visit!

             Your nephew
             Leo

Writing Wrap-Up WRITING • THINKING • LISTENING • SPEAKING

REFLECTING

Write a Letter
Write a letter to a friend in which you tell about something important you learned that didn't come from a book. Using the letter above as a model, tell when you learned this important thing. Exchange letters with a classmate. Discuss whether you have used commas correctly.

7 Quotation Marks

What is wrong with these sentences? How can you fix them?

Grandfather told me that Waltzing Matilda is an Australian song about hoboes who tramp the roads. He said, It is Australia's unofficial anthem.

Direct Quotations

When you write a **direct quotation**, you write a speaker's exact words. Use quotation marks to set apart a speaker's words from the rest of the sentence.

"Please open your books now," said Mr. Emory.

Then he said, "We're ready to begin."

1. Notice that you begin a direct quotation with a capital letter. You use a comma to separate the quotation from the rest of the sentence.

2. Place question marks and exclamation points that belong to the quotation inside the quotation marks. Place question marks and exclamation points that do not belong to the quotation outside the quotation marks. Always place periods and commas inside the quotation marks.

"Where is Tasmania?" asked the teacher.

Ralph said, "I don't know where it is."

Did Denise say, "It is near Australia"?

3. The example below shows how to punctuate a divided quotation that is all one sentence. The first letter of the second part of the quotation is not capitalized. Notice, however, that when a divided quotation is two separate sentences, you must capitalize the first word of the second part.

"Here," Kim replied, "is Tasmania."

"Here is Tasmania," she said. "It is off the southeastern coast of Australia."

4. An **indirect quotation** tells what someone said without using the speaker's exact words. Do not use quotation marks around indirect quotations.

Kim said that Tasmania is off the coast of Australia.

Ralph asked if he could look at the map.

Speak Up Where are commas, quotation marks, and capital letters needed? Which sentences are already correct?

1. Mr. Romero asked is Australia a country?
2. Yes replied Lauren.
3. Mr. Romero asked is Australia a continent?
4. Howard answered I'm not sure.
5. Please reply said Mr. Romero if you know the answer.
6. Anna said that Australia has had an unusual history.
7. That's right said Mr. Romero. It is a country and a continent.
8. Did Mr. Romero say tell me more about Australia?

Titles of Short Works

You also use quotation marks around titles of short works. The first, last, and all important words in a title are capitalized. Do not capitalize any unimportant word such as *the, a, and, of, for,* or *to* unless it is the first or last word in the title.

Short Story:	"Jug of Silver"
Poem:	"Jabberwocky"
Chapter of a Book:	"Writing Business Reports"
Magazine Article:	"How to Ask for a Raise"
Song:	"The Star-Spangled Banner"

Speak Up How would you capitalize and punctuate these items?

9. looking for the kiwi (short story)
10. the extraordinary animals of australia (magazine article)
11. waiting for the boat to take me there (song)
12. in the station (poem)
13. the raising of sheep in australia (book chapter)
14. all about new zealand (magazine article)
15. coming of age in the outback (book chapter)
16. australia and tasmania (poem)

A New Zealand kiwi

more ▶

17. the first people to settle australia (book chapter)
18. the ballad of botany bay (poem)
19. the voyages of james cook (magazine article)
20. the kangaroo hop (song title)
21. australia's mammals with pouches (magazine article)
22. scent of the eucalyptus (short story)

Summing Up

- Use quotation marks to set off **direct quotations** from the rest of the sentence.
- Use quotation marks around the titles of short stories, poems, book chapters, magazine articles, and songs.
- Capitalize all important words in a title.

On Your Own

Write each sentence. Capitalize and punctuate it. If a sentence is already correct, label it *correct*.

Example: The national anthem is entitled advance australia fair.
   The national anthem is entitled "Advance Australia Fair."

23. Name some Australian animals said Mr. Romero.
24. Judy answered the kangaroo and the koala are Australian.
25. Did Howard say I discovered that the platypus is an Australian mammal that lays eggs?
26. Mr. Romero held up an article called the animals of Australia.
27. Here he said is a picture of two birds, the emu of Australia and the cassowary of New Guinea.
28. Neither of these birds flies he added. You'll notice that the emu looks very much like an ostrich.
29. Lauren said that she had once read a funny poem that was called the emu and you in the zoo.
30. The kookaburra is another Australian bird that is known for its harsh call read Mr. Romero.

more ▶

31. Jeffrey exclaimed what a strange name that is!
32. Lauren asked Mr. Romero what a wombat is.
33. It's a marsupial, along with kangaroos, koalas, and wallabies piped up Joshua.

34–50. Write correctly these sentences from a transcript of a classroom discussion. There are seventeen errors in punctuation and capitalization.

Example: Our assignment was the chapter called australia's animals.
Our assignment was the chapter called "Australia's Animals."

Proofreading

"Does anyone know what a marsupial is " Mr. Romero asked?

Marsupials carry their young in pouches" said Elizabeth. She referred to an article called kangaroos and koalas.

Does anyone know, asked Mr. Romero, of any other unusual Australian animals besides the marsupials? Several people said that "they didn't know of any."

"Isn't there a bird," asked Miguel, that builds structures on the ground and then decorates them?

Mr. Romero exclaimed, "that's right! The male bowerbird builds twig bowers and decorates them with colorful objects to impress the female."

Writing Wrap-Up WRITING • THINKING • LISTENING • SPEAKING

COMPARING / CONTRASTING

Write a Dialogue

Write a short dialogue between two people who are comparing two kinds of pets or other animals they know about. Check to be sure you have applied the rules for quotation marks correctly. Role-play your dialogue with a partner.

For Extra Practice see page 291.

8 Titles of Long Works

Explain why italics are used in this sentence.

She would present new tests, taking her examples from stories of amazing children she had read in *Ripley's Believe It or Not*, or *Good Housekeeping*, *Reader's Digest*, and a dozen other magazines she kept in a pile in our bathroom.

—from *The Joy Luck Club*, by Amy Tan

You know that the titles of short works are enclosed in quotation marks. In print, the titles of long works such as books, magazines, newspapers, movies, TV series, and musical works appear in italics. **Italics** is a special kind of slanted print that looks like this: *italics*. The titles of works of art, such as paintings and sculptures, also appear in italics. When you write or type, you underline the titles of long works to represent italics. (On the computer you can make italics.)

Book:	*A Summer to Remember*
Magazine:	*Sports Illustrated*
Newspaper:	*Denver Post*, *The New York Times*
Play:	*The Butler Did It*
Movie:	*The Black Stallion*
TV Series:	*The American Experience*
Painting:	*Sunflowers*
Musical Works:	*Symphony No. 5*, *The Marriage of Figaro*

Notice that the first word, the last word, and all important words in each title begin with a capital letter. Do not capitalize a word like *a, the, of, for, to,* or *and* unless it is the first or last word in the title. Do not underline or italicize *the* with newspaper titles unless *the* is part of the title.

Try It Out

Speak Up What words in each of these titles should be capitalized?

1. *the wizard of oz*
2. *alice in wonderland*
3. *the barber of seville*
4. *minneapolis star tribune*
5. *the world of national geographic*
6. *road and track*

more ▶

7. *los angeles times*
8. *the house of dies drear*
9. *call it courage*
10. *house and garden*
11. *symphony no. 9*
12. *singing in the wilderness*
13. *great expectations*
14. *a night at the opera*
15. *a street in tahiti*
16. *as you like it*
17. *the diary of anne frank*
18. *riders to the sea*

Anne Frank

Summing Up

- Underline the titles of major works such as books, magazines, newspapers, plays, movies, paintings, and long musical works to represent **italics**.

On Your Own

Rewrite these titles of long works, capitalizing them where necessary.

Example: *on a clear day you can see forever*
On a Clear Day You Can See Forever

19. *a bug's life*
20. *a day of triumph*
21. *the dallas weekly*
22. *our town*
23. *the wonderful world of disney*
24. *san francisco chronicle*

25. *out of the blue*
26. *museums of the world*
27. *portrait of a woman*
28. *the old man and the sea*
29. *the hobbit*
30. *the prague symphony*

more ▶

31–38. Write the eight titles in these paragraphs from an autobiographical essay. Underline the titles of long works, and put quotation marks around the titles of short works. Capitalize the titles correctly.

Example: I recently read the book a treasury of music.

<u>A Treasury of Music</u>

Proofreading

Document

My father is a musician. He plays in a jazz band and works for a music magazine. He knows almost every popular song ever written, but summertime is his favorite. He often travels to interview musicians for his magazine, blue notes. Sometimes I go along, and in the car we sing This Land Is Your Land and other favorite folk songs.

My main interest is in musical theater, and I have performed in a local production of west side story. Before auditioning for this show, I studied its inspiration, Shakespeare's play romeo and juliet. It was interesting to see how the Renaissance setting of Shakespeare's play was transformed to the modern streets of New York City.

Other kinds of music are beginning to interest me. Recently, I saw the Italian opera rigoletto. Before going to the performance, I read the book stories of operas. Interviews with opera stars on television series such as biography reveal the powerful personalities of these famous singers.

Writing Wrap-Up   WRITING • THINKING • LISTENING • SPEAKING

INFORMING

Write Web Site Text

Write a paragraph about yourself for your new Web site. Include titles of your favorite music, art, books, movies, newspapers, and magazines. Check capitalization, quotation marks, and underlining for correctness. Exchange paragraphs with a partner, and talk about them. How are your choices alike? How are they different?

9 Colons and Semicolons

What connects these two sentences?

The dancers were still not a formal company; many performers came and went as their work schedules allowed.

—from *Alvin Ailey, Jr.: A Life in Dance,* by Julinda Lewis-Ferguson

1. You know that you use a comma after the greeting in a friendly letter. Use a **colon** after the greeting in a business letter.

   Dear Mrs. Tomasello: Dear Sir:

2. When you write the time, use a colon to separate the hour from the minute.

   8:40 A.M.   6:30 P.M.

3. Use a colon before a list of items in a sentence. Words like *the following* or *these* often signal the use of a colon.

   In music class we study these composers: Copland, Ives, and Barber.
   Bring the following: your book, a notebook, and a harmonica.

4. However, you should not use a colon after a verb or after a preposition.

   Bring a music book, a harmonica, and a notebook to class.
   The program consists of a solo, a duet, and a trio.

5. You know that a compound sentence is made up of two related complete thoughts that are joined by *and, but, or, nor, for,* or *yet.*

   I practiced for three hours, and now I'm ready.

   You can use a **semicolon** in place of the conjunction when the relation between the two clauses is very clear.

   I practiced for three hours; now I'm ready.
   This music is very difficult; it is written for an advanced student.

6. Also use a semicolon to join two independent clauses when the second clause begins with an adverb such as *however, therefore, consequently, besides, moreover, furthermore,* or *nevertheless.*

   I played my best; however, I still need more practice.
   The piano needed tuning; therefore, I couldn't play it today.

7. Use a semicolon to separate two independent clauses that have commas within one or both of them. The semicolon shows your reader where the complete thoughts begin and end, thus avoiding confusion.

> Tom plays the clarinet, the saxophone, and the piccolo; and his brother plays the piano and the flute.

Try It Out

Speak Up Where are colons and semicolons needed?

1. Dear Ms. Delaney
2. The West Indian concert will be held at 730 P.M. on Friday.
3. We will hear the following school groups the Glee Club, the Folk Singers, and the Steel Band.
4. You study both classical and popular music therefore, we recommend this concert.
5. The guests of honor are Jim Evans, Elena Cruz, and Carlos Flores and additional groups are Star, Flash, and Fire.

Summing Up

- Use a **colon** after a greeting in a business letter, between the hour and the minute in time, and before a list.
- Use a **semicolon** to connect independent clauses that are closely related in thought or that have commas within them.

On Your Own

Rewrite each sentence, adding colons and semicolons where needed.

Example: Music history is difficult however, I like the class.
> *Music history is difficult; however, I like the class.*

6. The class meets on Monday morning and lasts from 1025 to 1110.
7. We're studying these musical forms sonatas, concertos, and fugues.

more ▶

8. We've written two papers moreover, we've also done a group project.
9. My group includes Ben, An, and Nicki and our project was on Bach.
10. We studied symphonies now I enjoy listening to them.

11–18. Write this part of a business letter, adding (or deleting) semicolons and colons where necessary. Eight corrections are needed.

Example: The concert starts at 1030 it will last for an hour.
The concert starts at 10:30; it will last for an hour.

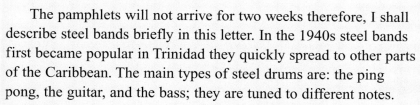

Dear Mr. Marley

You have requested information about steel bands consequently, I am sending you several pamphlets. They include the following *The Steel Band, Beating the Drum,* and *West Indian Music.*

The pamphlets will not arrive for two weeks therefore, I shall describe steel bands briefly in this letter. In the 1940s steel bands first became popular in Trinidad they quickly spread to other parts of the Caribbean. The main types of steel drums are: the ping pong, the guitar, and the bass; they are tuned to different notes.

The Jamaica Steel Band concerts are Monday, Tuesday, and Wednesday the time is 815 P.M.

Writing Wrap-Up   WRITING · THINKING · LISTENING · SPEAKING

INFORMING

Write an Announcement
Write an announcement for a school event. Include the date, the time, the place, and a list of items that participants should bring. Read your announcement aloud with a small group. Have the group identify places where colons or semicolons are needed.

Writing Sentences with Semicolons and Colons

Combining Sentences with Semicolons The end of a thought is usually signaled by a period. However, you can use a semicolon to combine two closely related independent clauses.

> We surveyed eighty-seven students. ⎫ We surveyed eighty-seven students;
> More than half listen to the radio. ⎭ more than half listen to the radio.

When the second clause begins with an adverb such as *however, therefore, consequently, besides, moreover, furthermore,* or *nevertheless,* remember to place a comma after the adverb.

> Our survey showed that more boys than girls listen to music while working out; however, more girls than boys listen to music when relaxing.

Sometimes you'll want to combine clauses in a series. If such clauses already contain commas, use semicolons to separate the clauses.

> It also showed that most boys like rap, pop, and jazz music; most girls like hip-hop, pop, and classical music; but both girls and boys like loud, rhythmic music.

Apply It

1–5. Revise the survey results below. Use semicolons to combine sentences.

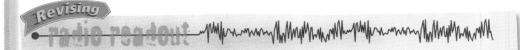

Revising
radio readout

We surveyed students about radio-listening. Our findings surprised us.

Ten students, mostly boys, always listen at lunchtime. Twenty students, mostly girls, sometimes listen at lunchtime. Forty students, an even mix of girls and boys, never tune in then.

The most popular programming was music. However, sports came in a close second. Twenty students enjoy comedy shows. Another ten like news programs. Fifteen often listen to call-in shows. Furthermore, some students call stations to share their views.

Combining Sentences with Colons Sometimes you can use a colon to combine two related independent clauses when one of the clauses contains a list. Use the colon to introduce the list.

I am selling many things.
I am selling CDs, tools, a bicycle,
and a keyboard.

I am selling the following things:
CDs, tools, a bicycle, and a keyboard.

Do not use a colon, however, after a verb or a preposition.

Last year, my sister <u>sold</u> comic books, in-line skates, and dolls.
Merchandise for our moving sale consists <u>of</u> clothes, furniture, and appliances.

Apply It

6–10. Revise this draft of a flier. Combine each set of sentences by using colons to introduce lists.

Revising

Come to the Lincoln School Fundraiser!

- Ms. Raine's class is selling many things. It is selling brownies, cookies, cakes, and cupcakes.

- The library will sell books. It will sell science-fiction novels, mysteries, and horror stories.

- Mr. Biddle's class is selling the following. These items are used CDs, second-hand guitars, and fantastic sheet music.

- See Mr. Washington ride a burro! His Spanish class will be selling lots of goodies. His class will sell homemade piñatas, candy, and photos.

- Last but not least, Ms. Cohen's class will sell these things. Tree seedlings, flowers, and tomato plants.

10 Abbreviations and Numbers

What abbreviations and numerals could you use in the following sentences?

The track meet started at eleven-thirty in the morning. In all, one hundred and five students took part. Three uninvited dogs also participated. One of them won the two-hundred-meter event.

Abbreviations

A shortened form of a word is called an **abbreviation**. Initials are a form of abbreviation. Titles used before a person's name as well as the names of states and months can be abbreviations. Most but not all abbreviations begin with a capital letter and end with a period. If you are unsure of an abbreviation, you can check a dictionary.

 HELP

Tip

Abbreviations often appear in written works. In general, however, you should not use abbreviations in formal writing.

Names	Mr.—Mister Mrs.—married woman Ms.—any woman Dr.—Doctor	Sr.—Senior Jr.—Junior James K. Polk—Knox Gen.—General
Addresses	St.—Street Rd.—Road Ave.—Avenue	P.O.—Post Office H.S.—High School Apt.—Apartment
Businesses	Co.—Company Inc.—Incorporated	Corp.—Corporation Ltd.—Limited
Organizations	NATO—North Atlantic Treaty Organization SBA—Small Business Administration	
State Names	ME—Maine	IL—Illinois
Days	Mon.—Monday	Thurs.—Thursday
Months	Jan.—January	Aug.—August
Units of Measure	mph—miles per hour l—liter	hp—horsepower in.—inch or inches
Time	A.M.—midnight to noon	P.M.—noon to midnight

Note these additional facts about abbreviations.

1. To save space in addresses and names of businesses, you can use abbreviations for some words.

2. Periods do not usually appear after abbreviations for organizations, and all the letters are capitals.

3. The United States Postal Service uses a capitalized two-letter abbreviation with no period for each state. See the list of abbreviations in the Capitalization/Punctuation/Usage guide at the end of the book.

4. Do not abbreviate the months of May, June, and July.

5. Do not capitalize or use periods after abbreviations for units of measure. The only exception is the abbreviation for *inch,* which is followed by a period.

6. If you use the abbreviation for a unit of measure, then you should use a numeral with it.

Try It Out

Speak Up How would you use abbreviations in each item?

1. High School 89
2. Thursday
3. April 9
4. Mister Logan
5. Route 189
6. Data, Incorporated
7. February 14
8. John Ray Jenks Senior
9. 8 feet
10. Grand Boulevard
11. Arlington, Texas
12. 9 inches
13. Doctor Peter J. Shea
14. Mount McKinley

Mount McKinley, Alaska

Numbers

1. When writing sentences, always spell out numbers under one hundred. Use numerals for numbers over one hundred except for even hundreds.

   There are eighty-two students present.
   There are 182 students in my school.
   There were two hundred students last year.

2. Always spell out a number that begins a sentence.

   One hundred thirty-five students attended the meeting.

3. Spell out expressions of time when you use the word *o'clock*. Use numerals, however, when the time is followed by A.M. or P.M. or is used alone as an exact time.

> Let's meet at seven o'clock.   The taxi came at 6 P.M.
> We took the 2:15 train.   It arrives at 2:45.

4. Use numerals to refer to large sections of writing or lines within the sections.

> Chapter 6   Unit 10   line 13

Try It Out

Speak Up Which numbers in these sentences should be spelled out? Which should be written as numerals?

15. Aren't there more than 45 people in the tour group?
16. Everyone must catch the bus at 3 o'clock exactly.
17. We leave in 25 minutes, according to page two of the schedule.
18. 7 minutes later, 12 additional people had arrived.
19. All 61 were there by 3:23 P.M., 2 minutes before the bus left.
20. The bus arrived at the park at five P.M., and we joined one hundred and twenty other people for the tour.
21. About 400 people have taken the tour over the past 3 weeks.

Summing Up

- Most **abbreviations** begin with a capital letter and end with a period.

- Spell out numbers under one hundred and numbers at the beginning of a sentence. Use numerals for numbers over one hundred and for sections or lines of writing.

Write these items, using correct abbreviations.

Example: 60 miles per hour   *60 mph*

22. Mister Chan
23. Barstow, California
24. Wednesday
25. Apartment 4B
26. Jenkins Company
27. Rand High School
28. Mister Jon Ross Senior
29. December 30
30. thirteen inches
31. 8 feet
32. Saturday, January 14
33. Central Intelligence Agency

34–42. Write the newspaper report below, correcting errors in the use of numbers. Use abbreviations where you can. You should find six errors in the use of numbers and three opportunities to use abbreviations.

Example: The track meet began at eleven thirty-five in the morning.
The track meet began at 11:35 A.M.

Proofreading

A total of 9 schools were represented at Saturday's track-and-field meet. 18 students from Cass Central made up the largest single group of contestants. One of the smallest schools—Possum Creek High School, with only one hundred and eighty students in all—took highest honors, winning first place in 5 different events. Possum Creek's coach, Doctor Joe Jackson, said that he was thrilled but not surprised.

The only serious threat to Raoul Ramirez Junior, winner of the final race, came from one unidentified mutt who nipped at his heels most of the way. Then the dog raced ahead to finish the 200 meters alone, but she was disqualified for running under the tape. By four-fifteen P.M., the annual meet was over.

Writing Wrap-Up · WRITING · THINKING · LISTENING · SPEAKING

DESCRIBING

Write a Newspaper Report

Write a paragraph for a school newspaper describing an athletic event, field trip, or other school activity. Use as many abbreviations and numbers as possible, following the rules you have learned. With a partner, read your reports aloud. Then read each other's papers, and circle any abbreviations or numbers that are incorrect.

11 Apostrophes

There's a mistake in the riddle. What is it? How can you fix it?

What do you use to redecorate a babys bathroom?

(infantile)

1. You have already learned to use an apostrophe to show possession and to replace letters that you drop in contractions. Remember that to form a possessive noun, you add an apostrophe and *s* to most singular nouns and plural nouns not ending in *s*.

   girl—girl's   children—children's
   Mrs. Ross—Mrs. Ross's   Tom—Tom's

2. You add only an apostrophe to most plural nouns ending in *s* to make them possessive.

   girls—girls'   Johnsons'

3. Remember that possessive pronouns, such as *its, hers,* and *theirs,* never contain apostrophes.

4. To form contractions with verbs, you use an apostrophe to replace the missing letters.

   does not—doesn't   have not—haven't   would not—wouldn't

5. To form contractions with pronouns and verbs, you also use an apostrophe to replace dropped letters.

   you are—you're   they would—they'd   she will—she'll

6. Use an apostrophe and *s* to form the plural of letters, numerals in mathematics, and symbols.

   i's   *p*'s and *q*'s   7's   4's   *'s   #'s

7. Follow the same rule to form the plural of words used as the names of words.

   The judge would not listen to any *if*'s, *and*'s, or *but*'s.

8. Do not use an apostrophe to form the plural of years or decades.

   the 1890s   the sixties   in her twenties

Speak Up Where are apostrophes needed in each sentence?

1. The class assignment isnt difficult.
2. Theyre studying my geography teachers map.
3. The *s on their map indicate capitals.
4. Marys error in the spelling of *Mississippi* is understandable.
5. Dont forget that there are four ss, four is, and two ps.
6. Youre remembering your ss in *Tennessee*, arent you?
7. Rays problem is remembering the Canadian prime ministers name.

Summing Up

- Add an apostrophe and *s* to singular nouns and to plural nouns not ending in *s* to show possession. Add an apostrophe to plural nouns ending in *s* to show possession.

- Add an apostrophe and *s* to form the plural of letters, numerals, symbols, and words used as the names of words. Use an apostrophe in contractions to replace missing letters.

Write the sentences, adding apostrophes where necessary.

Example: The childrens drawings arent very accurate.
   The children's drawings aren't very accurate.

8. Theyre drawing maps of South American countries.
9. What do the #s mean on Nicholass map?
10. Arent they the boundaries of the Andes Mountains?
11. Carlas mountains have +s all around them.
12. Dont you know that the Andes are the longest mountain range?
13. Two students maps have different colors.
14. Youre using a lot of red in your map, arent you?
15. Andreas name hasnt been spelled correctly on this list.
16. Hectors map is finished, isnt it?

more ▶

17. Why are there so many *South*s on Harrys map?
18. *Chile* doesn't have two *l*s, Miranda.
19. Use **s to mark the capital of each country.
20. Argentina isnt on Lionels map.
21. Jennys map doesn't show the capital of Brazil.
22. Didnt Beas map show all of South America?
23. Can we abbreviate all the *and*s and the *but*s?

24–32. There are nine errors in the use of apostrophes in this paragraph from an advertising brochure for a schoolroom atlas. Write the paragraph correctly.

Example: Peoples understanding of geography is growing.
People's understanding of geography is growing.

Look at any past years atlas. The newest countries probably aren't on it's maps. The former Soviet Unions' countries are examples. So are the regions in the Balkan's. Our students must develop their understanding of other countries geography. We should all be aware of other nation's borders and land formations. That way, well understand these nations better and communicate with them more successfully. Youll find classroom uses for the world trade map on page 40, marked with red **s to show new countries.

Writing Wrap-Up

WRITING • THINKING • LISTENING • SPEAKING

EXPRESSING

Write a Journal Entry

Where was your favorite place to play when you were a child? Write a journal entry describing this place. Include some contractions, possessive nouns, and plurals of symbols or numerals. With a partner, read your journal entries aloud, and then check each other's use of apostrophes.

 For Extra Practice see page 295.

12 Hyphens, Dashes, and Parentheses

One-Minute Warm-Up

What is wrong with these sentences? How can you fix them without adding commas?

There were only twenty three chairs instead of twenty four at the anniversary party. Nevertheless, the cake was gorgeous, and it had the couple's marriage dates 1991–2001 written in chocolate icing.

1. Use a **hyphen** to divide a word at the end of a line. Only words with more than one syllable can be divided. Do not leave a single letter at the end or at the beginning of a line. Longer words can be divided in more than one place.

HELP ? Tip

If you are not sure where to divide a certain word, check your dictionary.

   Incorrect: e-lection   librar-y

   Correct: elec-tion   li-brary   **Correct:** porcu-pine   por-cupine

2. Use a hyphen in compound numbers from twenty-one to ninety-nine and in fractions used as adjectives.

   thirty-two   a two-thirds majority   one-half teaspoon

3. You have seen hyphens in some compound nouns. When two or more words expressing one thought act as an adjective before a noun, use a hyphen to connect them.

   long-range plans   up-to-the-minute report   well-known man.

4. Use a **dash** to set off a sudden change of thought or an afterthought, or to mean *namely* or *in other words.*

   Tom and Alex are very close—most brothers are.

   The game—it went into overtime—was really exciting.

5. **Parentheses** indicate another type of interruption. They enclose information that isn't necessary to the meaning of a sentence or information that some readers may already know.

   Charles Lindbergh (1902–1974) was a pioneer in aviation.

   The president (Cooper Smith) presented the award.

In some cases you may find that either dashes or parentheses will work.

Speak Up Use hyphens and dashes correctly in these sentences.

1. One of the best known pieces of furniture is the bed.
2. A king size bed the largest size is wider than a double bed.
3. How do you divide *furniture, fur niture* or *furni ture?*

Where are parentheses needed in these sentences?

4. A double bed is four and a half feet 1.37 meters wide.
5. French beds of the Empire period early 1800s were large.

 Summing Up

- Use a **hyphen** to divide a word at the end of a line, to join the parts of compound numbers, and to join two or more words that work together as one adjective before a noun.
- Use **dashes** to show a sudden change of thought.
- Use **parentheses** to enclose unnecessary information.

Write each sentence, adding hyphens or dashes where needed.

Example: Early people hardy souls slept on leaves.
Early people—hardy souls—slept on leaves.

6. A very rough bed is often called a *bunk* perhaps a shortened form of *bunker.*
7. American colonists usually stuffed their beds with whatever was plentiful corn husks, wood chips, or straw.
8. Could a bed be one third husks and two thirds straw?
9. The bedroom rarely a separate room could be in a corner.

more ▶

10. Many children slept with their parents or in a trundle bed a bed pushed under the parents' bed during the day.
11. Privacy a sought after condition was almost impossible.
12. How is *privacy* divided, *priv a cy* or *pri va cy*?

13–20. Write these sentences from an encyclopedia entry on Early American furniture. Correct the eight errors by adding parentheses or dashes where necessary.

Example: Have you studied furniture its history and uses?
Have you studied furniture—its history and uses?

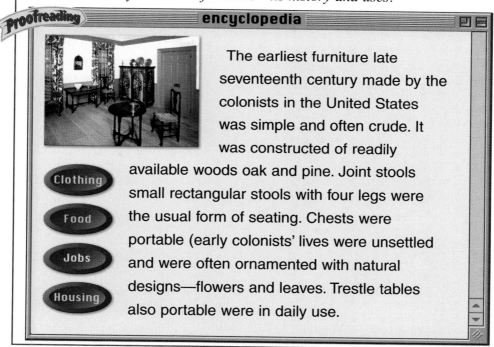

encyclopedia

The earliest furniture late seventeenth century made by the colonists in the United States was simple and often crude. It was constructed of readily available woods oak and pine. Joint stools small rectangular stools with four legs were the usual form of seating. Chests were portable (early colonists' lives were unsettled and were often ornamented with natural designs—flowers and leaves. Trestle tables also portable were in daily use.

Clothing

Food

Jobs

Housing

Writing Wrap-Up

WRITING • THINKING • LISTENING • SPEAKING

PERSUADING

Write an Ad

What is your vision of the ideal room? Pick a room in your home that you would like to remodel for yourself. Write an ad describing this room and its furnishings. Include hyphens, dashes, and parentheses as appropriate. Volunteers can read their comparisons aloud and invite comments.

Enrichment

Famous Quotes

You are a newspaper reporter who has witnessed a famous speech, such as Lincoln's Gettysburg Address, or the signing of an important document, such as the Declaration of Independence. Write a brief news article about the historic event. Include at least two direct quotations and two indirect quotations. Be sure to punctuate correctly.

$4 \text{ score} + 7 = ?$

Challenge You are also working on a novel set during the time of the historic event that you have witnessed. Write a dialogue between two characters that suggests how the event has affected their lives.

Dear Author

Write a letter to an author explaining why you liked his or her book. Revise your letter, proofread it, and copy it neatly, adding your address at the top right. Address an envelope to the author in care of the publisher. (Look for the name and city of the publisher on the title page of the book. You can find the complete address in the library.) Include your return address, and use abbreviations in both addresses. Stamp the envelope and mail the letter.

FAMOUS AUTHOR AT WORK

1 Interjections *(p. 236)* Rewrite each sentence, adding one of these interjections: *oh, hey, hurrah, wow, well.* Use each only once, and capitalize and punctuate each interjection.

1. _____ Have you seen *Galaxy* yet?
2. _____ it is so exciting!
3. _____ What a terrific ending it had!
4. _____ we hardly ever see such good movies.
5. _____ We are going to see it again!

2 Sentences and Interjections *(p. 239)* Write each sentence, adding the correct capitalization and punctuation.

6. am I going to fall
7. signal when you're ready
8. wow I'm standing up
9. oh no I'm losing my balance
10. it was certainly fun
11. do you like skiing

3 Proper Nouns and Proper Adjectives *(p. 241)* Rewrite each sentence, capitalizing all proper nouns and proper adjectives.

12. The doctor that I go to for my eyes is dr. lessell.
13. His office is at the patrick t. wellington hospital.
14. That hospital is located on charles street.
15. I see him each spring and autumn, usually in may and november.
16. I ordered some new french eyeglass frames after my last visit.

4 Uses for Commas *(pp. 245, 248)* Write these sentences, adding commas where needed.

17. One Portuguese prince Henry the Navigator started the era of global exploration in the fifteenth century.
18. Prince Henry himself of course never sailed on such a voyage.
19. At Sagres Portugal Prince Henry founded a naval observatory.
20. This center drew scholars astronomers and sailors.
21. Yes Portugal led the way for later discoveries.

5 Dates, Addresses, and Letters *(p. 253)* Rewrite each item, adding the correct punctuation.

22. Please call me on Tuesday March 22 2001 before noon.
23. Myra's address is 12 Rancho Road Las Vegas Nevada 89107.
24. Why don't we meet in Cleveland Ohio tomorrow?

25. Dear Maxine   Your brother
26. The correct address is St. Croix Falls WI 54024.

6 **Quotation Marks** *(p. 256)* Rewrite each sentence. Capitalize and punctuate it correctly. Use quotation marks where necessary.

27. What asked Miss Valdez is our national anthem?
28. The Star-Spangled Banner is by Francis Scott Key.
29. Frieda inquired when was it written?
30. The words were written in 1814 Joe answered when the British attacked Fort McHenry in Baltimore.
31. Jerry added the music, however, was an old English tune.

7 **Titles** *(pp. 257, 260)* Write the sentences. Underline the titles of long works. Use quotation marks for the titles of short works. Capitalize the titles correctly.

32. Did you read the article recordings take new forms?
33. I read in Time about a new recording of A London Symphony.
34. For more information about the symphony, read the book recorded music.
35. That TV show called national nightly news isn't very good.
36. One national newspaper is entitled the wall street journal.

8 **Colons and Semicolons** *(p. 263)* Write these items, adding semicolons and colons where needed.

37. Dear Ms. Floyd-Smythe
38. The beginning sewing classes will meet at 1030 A.M.
39. You may take the following tailoring, embroidery, or cutting.
40. Bring these items scissors, thread, and material.
41. Sewing machines are available for all students in addition, needles and thimbles will be supplied for handwork.

9 **Abbreviations and Numbers** *(p. 268)* Write the sentences, using abbreviations where possible and the correct form for numbers.

42. Pick up your packages after 3 o'clock on Monday, November 10.
43. They are being stored in Cheesequake, New Jersey.
44. Ask for Mister Malfitano, who can locate them for you.
45. Coast Storage Incorporated closes at five-thirty.
46. You will be billed for two hundred fifty cubic feet of space.

10 **Apostrophes** *(p. 272)* Write the sentences, adding apostrophes where needed.

47. Teenagers volunteer to teach children their *abc*s.
48. Two girls tables are here, and the childrens books are there.

49. Use the materials on your tables; dont use theirs.
50. Tracy no longer confuses *b*s and *d*s.
51. Jesss spelling should continue to improve in the future.

Hyphens and Parentheses *(p. 275)* Write the sentences, adding hyphens and parentheses where needed.

52. Bernardo O'Higgins 1776–1842 was a remarkable Chilean hero.
53. He was a well respected liberator.
54. O'Higgins a man with an Irish name worked hard to free Chile.
55. He died in exile at the age of sixty six.

Mixed Review 56–68. Write this list of tourist destinations in Texas, correcting the thirteen errors in capitalization, punctuation, and numbers.

Proofreading Checklist
✔ capitalization
✔ commas and end punctuation
✔ quotation marks and apostrophes
✔ form of numbers

Proofreading

- Austin the state capital and home of the university of Texas
- Rio grande, known in Mexico as Rio Bravo
- san Antonios' famous River Walk
- Dont miss the Johnson Space center in Houston!
- Houston Ship Channel, 51 miles long
- Corpus christi, settled in 1839
- Matagorda Bay, inlet of the gulf of Mexico
- "Remember the Alamo!
- Padre island National Seashore, sixty five miles of beaches

✅ Test Practice

Write the numbers 1–10 on a sheet of paper. Find the part of the sentence that needs a capital letter or letters, and write the letter for that part. If no part of the sentence needs any capital letters, write the letter for "None."

1. We entered Vermont / and drove west / toward lake Champlain. / None
   A   B   C   D

2. Mr. Lee / went to the library to / borrow *Life on the mississippi.* / None
   F   G   H   J

3. My cousin / thinks that december 1 / is the first day of winter. / None
   A   B   C   D

4. The doctor moved / her office to Crown Square / last Monday. / None
   F   G   H   J

5. For english class, / Miss Cho assigned a poem / called "The Raven." / None
   A   B   C   D

6. Over the weekend, / Jeremy listed the member nations / of Nato. / None
   F   G   H   J

7. In World War II, / Britain's Royal Air Force / defeated the Germans. / None
   A   B   C   D

8. Sue signed up for algebra I / but didn't take art / or music classes. / None
   F   G   H   J

9. In 1215 King John / signed a document / called the magna carta. / None
   A   B   C   D

10. Atlanta, Georgia, / is an important city / in the Southeast. / None
    F   G   H   J

Now write numbers 11–16 on your paper. Read the letter and look at the numbered, underlined parts. Choose the correct way to write each underlined part. If the part is already correct, choose the last answer, "Correct as it is." Write the letter for the answer you choose.

---

(11)   566 River Road

(12)   Olmsted Falls Ohio 44138

July 8, 2001

(13) dear uncle joshua

I just received your most recent letter. I was absolutely thrilled to hear that you were made

(14) manager of waffle wonderland the famous restaurant. I can just imagine you surrounded by mountains of

(15) fluffy golden waffles and cupfuls of luscious syrup.

(16) Since I have never ate a waffle in my life, I am looking forward to visiting you at the restaurant.

Your niece,

Albinia

---

11 **A** 566, River Road
    B 566 River road
    C 566, River road
    D Correct as it is

12 **F** Olmsted Falls, Ohio, 44138
    G Olmsted Falls Ohio, 44138
    H Olmsted Falls, Ohio 44138
    J Correct as it is

13 **A** Dear Uncle Joshua,
    B Dear Uncle Joshua;
    C Dear uncle Joshua,
    D Correct as it is

14 **F** waffle wonderland the
    G Waffle Wonderland, the
    H waffle wonderland, the
    J Correct as it is

15 **A** fluffy, golden, waffles, and cupfuls
    B fluffy, golden waffles and cupsful
    C fluffy, golden waffles and cupfuls
    D Correct as it is

16 **F** Since I have never eated
    G Since I have never eaten
    H Since I have never aten
    J Correct as it is

Now write numbers 17–22 on your paper, and do this page the same way you did the previous one.

15 Kootenai Street
Boise, Idaho 83712
(17) February 6 2001

Dear Rachel,
(18) Today school was canceled; I will lay around all
(19) day and watch TV. My mother says that I am the most laziest
kid she knows. She thinks that I should go out and shovel snow!
(20) I say you shouldn't never make life harder than you need to.
(21) Besides, I'm not so terrible lazy. I plan to watch
The Grapes of Wrath, a movie classic in black and white.
I bet most of my classmates are watching really bad
daytime TV.
(22) your friend
Jane

17 **A** february 6 2001
B February, 6 2001
C February 6, 2001
D Correct as it is

18 **F** canceled, I will lay
G canceled; I will lie
H canceled, I will lie
J Correct as it is

19 **A** I am the laziest
B I am the lazyest
C I am the lazier
D Correct as it is

20 **F** you should ever make
G you shouldn't ever make
H you shouldnt ever make
J Correct as it is

21 **A** so terrible lazily
B so terribly lazy
C so terribly lazily
D Correct as it is

22 **F** Your friend,
G your friend,
H Your friend
J Correct as it is

(pages 236–238)

1 Interjections

- An **interjection** is a word or a group of words that expresses feeling or represents a sound. Use an exclamation point after an interjection that expresses strong feeling. Use a comma after an interjection that expresses mild feeling.

● Write the interjections.

Example: Oh dear, I'm always so nervous before a performance. *Oh dear*

1. Shh! The curtain is about to go up.
2. Oh no, I lost my wig!
3. Good grief! You'll miss your entrance!
4. Hey! Someone help look for her wig.
5. Phew, that was a close call.
6. Well, let's hope nothing else unexpected happens.
7. Ugh! Something always seems to go wrong.

▲ Rewrite each sentence, adding the correct punctuation. Underline each interjection.

Example: Oh I hope I get the part! <u>*Oh!* I hope I get the part.</u>

8. Hey are you going to try out for the school play?
9. Hooray I'll be a star at last.
10. Oh no Spare me the details for a change.
11. Goodness I will never memorize this speech.
12. Wow this scenery is really quite heavy.
13. Bravo You got them right.

■ Rewrite each sentence, adding an appropriate interjection from the box. Punctuate and capitalize your sentences correctly.

Example: You are a very good actor. *Bravo! You are a very good actor.*

14. Think about the personality of your character.
15. I can't say the line that way.
16. I don't understand this speech.
17. Why would your character say that?
18. I understand this now!
19. I'll speak these lines in a deep voice.
20. That was really terrific.

aha	oh no
okay	oh yes
bravo	goodness
hey	wow
well	hooray

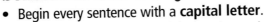

(pages 239–240)

2 Sentences and Interjections

- Begin every sentence with a **capital letter**.
- Use a **period** at the end of declarative and imperative sentences.
- Use a **question mark** at the end of interrogative sentences.
- Use an **exclamation point** at the end of exclamatory sentences and after an interjection expressing strong feeling.
- Use a **comma** after an interjection expressing milder feeling.

● Write the kind of sentence shown in parentheses. Begin it with a capital letter, and add the correct punctuation.

Example: wow what a great story that was (exclamatory)
Wow, what a great story that was!

1. have you ever heard of Miss Marple (interrogative)
2. she solved mysteries in Agatha Christie's books (declarative)
3. how simple and innocent Miss Marple was (exclamatory)
4. lend me your book by Agatha Christie, please (imperative)

▲ Write the sentences. Capitalize and punctuate them correctly.

Example: aha what a surprise that ending was
Aha! What a surprise that ending was!

5. mysteries became very popular in the 1900s
6. were the mysteries always solved by detectives
7. no many of the crimes were solved by amateurs
8. didn't one series of detective stories feature a doctor
9. wow what a clever idea that was

■ Rewrite each sentence as the type of sentence shown in parentheses. Change, add, or omit words if necessary. Add the correct capitalization and punctuation.

Example: are there women detectives (declarative, exclamatory)
There are women detectives. There are women detectives!

10. how typical is the female detective (declarative, exclamatory)
11. women detectives appeared in fiction over a hundred years ago (exclamatory, interrogative)
12. you did tell me about the first female writer of detective stories (interrogative, imperative)

3 Proper Nouns and Proper Adjectives

(pages 241–244)

- A proper noun begins with a capital letter.
- You can form proper adjectives from proper nouns.
- Capitalize proper adjectives.

Remember

● Write these sentences, capitalizing the underlined words if necessary. If a sentence is correct, label it *correct.*

Example: What countries are on the continent of <u>north america</u>?
What countries are on the continent of North America?

1. Mexico was a <u>spanish</u> colony for three hundred years.
2. Mexicans celebrate their <u>independence day</u> on September 16.
3. The capital of this country is <u>mexico city</u>.
4. Wasn't <u>grandfather</u> born in <u>mexico</u>?
5. Yes, he and <u>uncle</u> Pedro were both born there.
6. They have lived in <u>pasadena</u> now for twenty years.

▲ Write each sentence, using capital letters where necessary.

Example: The month of july has some interesting days.
The month of July has some interesting days.

7. On july 4, 1776, the declaration of independence was signed.
8. It was signed in philadelphia, pennsylvania, by the continental congress.
9. A hero of the american revolution, captain john paul jones, was born in july.
10. Emma lazarus wrote the poem that is on the statue of liberty.
11. A copy of the statue stands on the seine river in paris.

■ Write each sentence, using capital letters only where needed. If the sentence is correct, label it *correct.*

Example: Which Continent is larger, Europe or north america?
Which continent is larger, Europe or North America?

12. The North american continent is larger than the european continent.
13. In both size and population, asia is the largest continent.
14. The japanese ruler Hirohito was emperor from 1926 until his death in 1989.
15. A past ruler of India was Prime Minister Indira Gandhi.
16. Yasunari Kawabata was the first japanese to win the Nobel Prize for literature.

(pages 245–247)

④ Uses for Commas

Remember

- Use a comma to separate items in a series.
- Use a comma between two or more adjectives that come before a noun. Do not use a comma if they express a single idea.
- Use a comma to separate the simple sentences in a compound sentence.

● Write these sentences, adding commas where needed to the underlined parts.

Example: Mathew Brady was a <u>famous successful</u> photographer.
Mathew Brady was a famous, successful photographer.

1. Photographs became a <u>common popular</u> feature of American life.
2. Brady was a good <u>photographer and</u> he was also a businessman.
3. Brady was <u>talented ambitious and industrious.</u>
4. Before he was <u>twenty-one</u> he already had his own studio.
5. <u>Senators presidents and famous people</u> came to his studio.
6. Then the <u>Civil War began and</u> Brady wanted to photograph it.
7. His <u>dramatic clear</u> photographs have become pieces of history.

▲ Write each sentence, adding one or more commas where needed. If the sentence needs no commas, write *correct*.

Example: Wet-plate photography was messy limited and crude.
Wet-plate photography was messy, limited, and crude.

8. Some important new photographic discoveries began in 1871.
9. A dry-plate process was invented and it changed the photographer's job.
10. Exposure time was faster and cameras could be hand-held.
11. The new plates were dry clean and effective.
12. Professional photographers previously had made their own plates and developed them.

■ Add a word, a phrase, or a clause, as shown in parentheses, so that the sentence requires one or more commas. Write the new sentence.

Example: Today's cameras are small and light. (word)
Today's cameras are small, light, and convenient.

13. You can take a camera to the beach or to a party. (phrase)
14. Some photographers take pictures of people. (clause)
15. Photographs are exhibited in studios and homes. (word)
16. A photograph can change our way of seeing its subject. (clause)

5 More Uses for Commas

(pages 248–250)

Remember

- Use commas after words, phrases, and clauses that come at the beginning of sentences.
- Use commas to separate interrupters, nouns of direct address, and unnecessary appositives in a sentence.

● Write the sentences, adding commas to the underlined parts where necessary.

Example: <u>Lisa</u> do you ever make long-distance calls?
Lisa, do you ever make long-distance calls?

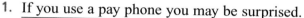

1. If you use a <u>pay phone</u> you may be surprised.
2. <u>After a few clicks</u> you will hear a voice.
3. <u>Sounding a bit strange</u> the voice will tell you the cost.
4. Do not <u>however</u> talk to the voice.
5. There is not a real person on the other end <u>my friend</u>.
6. <u>Although it sounds like a person</u> the voice is from a computer.

▲ Write each sentence, adding commas where needed.

Example: How does a computer work Mrs. Chun?
How does a computer work, Mrs. Chun?

7. A computer Dennis can be programmed.
8. Because it is programmable we can tell it what to do.
9. Using a different program the computer can do a different job.
10. A home computer for example can help you budget your money.
11. You can use another program a word-processing program to write your history essay.

■ Write each sentence, adding an interrupter, a noun of direct address, or an introductory word, phrase, or clause as shown. Use commas correctly.

Example: Describe the future factory. (noun of direct address)
Describe the future factory, Janet.

12. Future factories may be run by one person. (interrupter)
13. Labor will be done by robots. (noun of direct address)
14. This may eventually happen. (clause)
15. Robots are taking over many tasks. (phrase)
16. Most robots are not shiny metal people. (word)

(pages 253–255)

⑥ Dates, Addresses, and Letters

- Use a comma to separate the month and the day from the year.
- Use a comma between the city and the state. Use a comma after the state if the address is within the sentence. Use a comma to separate each item except the Zip Code.
- Use a comma after the greeting in friendly letters and after the closing in both friendly and business letters.

● Rewrite the items. Add commas where needed in the underlined places. If an item is correct, label it *correct.*

Example: My cousin lives in <u>Redding California</u>.
My cousin lives in Redding, California.

1. <u>781 Fourth Avenue</u>
2. <u>Santa Fe New Mexico 87501</u>
3. <u>August 15 2001</u>
4. <u>Dear Marissa</u>
5. On <u>September 9 2001</u> I'll be arriving in California.

▲ Rewrite the items, adding commas where necessary.

Example: The San Francisco California quake was in April 1906.
The San Francisco, California, quake was in April 1906.

6. 1190 Grand Boulevard
7. Springdale Arkansas 72764
8. May 23 2000
9. Dear Uncle Lyle
10. The worst forest fire ever occurred on October 8 1871.

■ You and your friend Desmond have been quizzing each other on little-known facts, and you have the answers to his questions. Write this part of a letter to him, putting the information in sentences. Use commas correctly.

Example: February 16, 1948—first daily TV news show
February 16, 1948, was the date of the first daily TV news show.

11. First United States telephone book—New Haven Connecticut February 21 1878
12. First parking meter—Oklahoma City Oklahoma July 16 1935

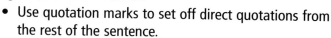

(pages 256–259)

7 Quotation Marks

- Use quotation marks to set off direct quotations from the rest of the sentence.
- Use quotation marks around the titles of short stories, poems, book chapters, magazine articles, and songs.
- Capitalize all important words in a title.

Remember

● Write each sentence. Add quotation marks where needed.

Example: Anna asked, What do you know about Australia?
Anna asked, "What do you know about Australia?"

1. Josh said, Here's a book about Australia.
2. Josh went to the chapter called Strange and Surprising Facts.
3. What are some of the facts? asked Anna.
4. Well, said Josh, here's something interesting.
5. Listen, he said. Australia has more sheep than people.

▲ Write the sentences. Capitalize and punctuate them where necessary. If a sentence is correct, label it *correct*.

Example: Many nations are crowded Josh said but not ours.
"Many nations are crowded," Josh said, "but not ours."

6. Josh was reading an article called the tourist in Australia.
7. Anna asked have you learned anything new from that article?
8. Yes Josh replied there are a few new facts in here.
9. He continued do you know where most Australians live?
10. Josh said that over half the people live in six cities.

■ 11–18. Rewrite the passage. Capitalize and punctuate it.

Example: Who wrote the Australian national anthem asked Anna.
"Who wrote the Australian national anthem?" asked Anna.

Josh told Anna that he had become very interested in Australia. He had just finished an article called the people of australia.

What sorts of people are Australians? asked Anna.

Well, many of the first settlers of Australia Josh replied were British prisoners.

Anna asked were they the first people there?

No answered Josh they weren't. *Aborigines* had been living there for thousands of years. Josh showed her a story called life down under.

Extra Practice

(pages 260–262)

⑧ Titles of Long Works

- Underline the titles of major works like books, magazines, newspapers, plays, movies, paintings, and long musical works.

● Write the titles, underlining them and using capital letters where necessary.

Example: david and lisa (movie) _David and Lisa_

1. green mansions (book)
2. car and driver (magazine)
3. star wars (movie)
4. the century (TV series)
5. the daily news (newspaper)
6. maids of honor (painting)
7. the firebird (musical work)
8. raisin in the sun (play)

▲ Write each sentence. Capitalize the titles and add quotation marks or underlining where necessary.

Example: Is the play the importance of being earnest by Wilde?
　　　　　 Is the play _The Importance of Being Earnest_ by Wilde?

9. Jake had been reading the magazine young people's digest.
10. He decided to write a poem and name it our favorite things.
11. A tale of two cities was one of his favorite books.
12. Oklahoma! was his mother's favorite song.
13. It was in the play and the movie oklahoma!
14. In his clinton herald, Jake saw a beautiful painting reproduced.
15. His favorite painting by Renoir was entitled the dance at bougival.

■ Complete each sentence with a correctly written title of your choice.

Example: Have you read the book _____?
　　　　　 Have you read the book _A Wrinkle in Time_?

16. Yesterday I read an interesting article called _____.
17. It was in the _____, a newspaper that I often read.
18. The last movie I saw was _____.
19. The TV series _____ is one of my favorites.
20. _____ is a poem I memorized because I wanted to.
21. _____ is a song I like to sing frequently.
22. I would like to name my best painting _____.
23. _____ is the book I have read most often.
24. I would like to write a story called _____.

(pages 263–265)

⑨ Colons and Semicolons

- Use a **colon** after a greeting in a business letter, between the hour and the minute in time, and before a list.
- Use a **semicolon** to connect independent clauses that are closely related in thought or that have commas within them.

● Write the items. Add the needed colons and semicolons to the underlined parts.

Example: I enjoy silent <u>films therefore,</u> I have seen many.
I enjoy silent films; therefore, I have seen many.

1. Dear Mr. <u>Greenberg</u>
2. *City Lights* will be shown at <u>445, 630, 815, and 1000</u> P.M.
3. No one talked in silent <u>films however,</u> there was music.
4. *City Lights* will be accompanied by <u>musicians two</u> violinists and a cellist.
5. Charlie Chaplin became <u>famous his</u> name is still known.

▲ Write the items. Add the needed colons and semicolons.

Example: I heard my favorite song it was on at 335 P.M.
I heard my favorite song; it was on at 3:35 P.M.

6. Dear Mrs. Ruiz
7. Hit songs are nothing new they have existed for centuries.
8. The song "Greensleeves" was a hit in the sixteenth century moreover, many people still know it today.
9. Some hits of the eighteenth century were the following "All Through the Night," "Yankee Doodle," and "Rule, Britannia."

■ Rewrite each item to include a colon or a semicolon. Change the wording, the capitalization, and the punctuation where necessary.

Example: We sang "Yesterdays," "Swanee," and "Ida."
We sang the following songs: "Yesterdays," "Swanee," and "Ida."

10. Dear Mr. Singer,
11. Early movies were very emotional, silent, and black and white. They were very popular anyway.
12. The first "talkie" was *The Jazz Singer*. It starred Al Jolson.
13. A song came from the screen. The voice sounded like Jolson's.
14. Viewers were suspicious. They looked behind the screen.
15. *The Jazz Singer* is at ten-thirty A.M. and eight-thirty P.M.

(pages 268–271)

10 Abbreviations and Numbers

Remember

- Most abbreviations begin with a capital letter and end with a period.
- Spell out numbers under one hundred and numbers at the beginning of a sentence. Use numerals for numbers over one hundred and for sections of writing.

● Rewrite each item, using abbreviations for the underlined words.

Example: Carl Raymond Smith Senior   *C. R. Smith Sr.*

1. August 22
2. Sentix, Incorporated
3. Senator Russell
4. 12 liters
5. Portland, Maine
6. American Medical Association
7. 16 inches
8. Chapter 9
9. Wednesday, February 9
10. United Nations
11. Route 192
12. James Roger Perl Junior

▲ Write each item, using correct abbreviations where possible. For the items containing numbers, keep the numerals if they are correct. Otherwise, spell them.

Example: Finally, 6 o'clock arrived.   *Finally, six o'clock arrived.*

13. Doctor Carla Fay Jones
14. Better Business Bureau
15. 12 pounds, 4 ounces
16. Winston John Remo Senior
17. six centimeters
18. 65 plants were sold.
19. Is it 8 o'clock yet?
20. Are there 57 books?
21. No, there are 157.
22. 10 liters

■ If an item contains an incorrect abbreviation, rewrite it correctly. If it is correct, write *correct.*

Example: Novem. third at 6 o'clock   *Nov. 3 at six o'clock*

23. Sat. at four-eighteen P.M.
24. Doc. J. M. Reilly
25. the 5:29 o'clock train
26. 99 students
27. 5 m
28. Jun. 11
29. Mar. 14 at nine o'clock
30. Unicef meeting
31. M. F. Bidwell
32. 250 ft. 4 in.
33. Apart. A
34. Seattle, WASH
35. Sun., Dec. 8, at 10 A.M.
36. Unit Twelve

11 Apostrophes

(pages 272–274)

- Add an apostrophe and *s* to singular nouns and to plural nouns not ending in *s* to show possession. Add an apostrophe to plural nouns ending in *s* to show possession.
- Add an apostrophe and *s* to form the plural of letters, numerals, symbols, and words used as the names of words. Use an apostrophe in contractions to replace missing letters.

Remember

● Write each sentence. Add an apostrophe to each underlined word.

Example: We heard Mr. <u>Gosss</u> lecture on Europe.
We heard Mr. Goss's lecture on Europe.

1. <u>Ronas</u> report on the Industrial Revolution was interesting.
2. Other countries followed <u>Englands</u> lead in industry.
3. <u>Peoples</u> interest in freedom increased after 1700.
4. <u>Youre</u> going to report on that, <u>arent</u> you?
5. <u>Its</u> easier to read when you <u>dont</u> use symbols.
6. <u>Theyll</u> listen to two <u>students</u> reports each day.

▲ Write each sentence, adding apostrophes where needed.

Example: Its true that our history is connected with Europes.
It's true that our history is connected with Europe's.

7. Im writing my report on Europes languages.
8. Isnt it true that some countries have four or five languages?
9. Rosss report is on the history of Germany from 1930 to 1945.
10. Russias alphabet is Larrys subject.
11. Its different from ours, and hes including examples.
12. The Russians *r*s look like *p*s, and their *s*s look like *c*s.

■ Write each sentence, adding apostrophes where needed.

Example: Thats an interesting fact about the worlds languages.
That's an interesting fact about the world's languages.

13. Spains main language and Italys are different, but theyre related.
14. Use *and*s instead of &s or +s in your report, please.
15. There are too many *I*s, *my*s, and *me*s in Boriss report.
16. Spaniards have *ñ*s and *ch*s in their alphabet, dont they?

(pages 275–277)

12 Hyphens, Dashes, and Parentheses

- Use a **hyphen** to divide a word at the end of a line, to join the parts of compound numbers, and to join two or more words that work together as one adjective before a noun.
- Use **dashes** to show a sudden change of thought.
- Use **parentheses** to enclose unnecessary information.

Remember

● Write the sentences. Add the punctuation in parentheses to the underlined parts.

Example: Chippendale <u>1718–1779</u> was a furniture designer. (parentheses)
Chippendale (1718–1779) was a furniture designer.

1. Chippendale's <u>well designed</u> pieces are prized. (hyphen)
2. Furniture <u>chairs, tables</u> can be works of art. (dashes)
3. The golden age of English furniture <u>1714–1820</u> is famous. (parentheses)
4. Chippendale <u>probably the most famous</u> wrote a book. (dashes)

▲ Write each sentence, adding the punctuation in parentheses.

Example: Tudor furniture 1500–1600 features large scale pieces.
(parentheses, hyphen)
Tudor furniture (1500–1600) features large-scale pieces.

5. Ancient Egypt's New Kingdom 1570–1090 B.C. has given us examples of well designed furniture. (parentheses, hyphen)
6. Symbols of strength and power lions' paws or oxen's hoofs were often carved on furniture legs. (parentheses)
7. A fifty page article in *Today* features furniture. (hyphen)
8. Ten pages a significant amount show pieces from ancient Rome. (dashes)

■ If a sentence has an error, rewrite it correctly. If it is correct, write *correct*.

Example: A well thought of furniture maker was Duncan Phyfe.
A well-thought-of furniture maker was Duncan Phyfe.

9. Duncan Phyfe 1768–1854 was a Scotland born colonial.
10. Machine made furniture became fashionable earlier than you might think as early as 1820, in fact.
11. How is *fashionable* divided, *fa-shion-able* or *fash-ion-able*?
12. The first real furniture factory was built in Michigan Grand Rapids and was the start of an important American industry.

We have no problem posing for the camera. Who wouldn't be wearing a permanent smile on a class trip like this?

Pronouns

Personal and Possessive Pronouns

Find the personal and possessive pronouns in the sentence below.

"She lets me read her poems. I let her read mine. She is always sad like a house on fire—always something wrong."

—from *The House on Mango Street,* by Sandra Cisneros

Personal Pronouns

You can replace nouns with **pronouns** to make your speaking and writing flow more smoothly.

Nouns: Don and *Don's* brother like books. *The brothers* read whenever *the brothers'* schedules leave *the brothers* some time.

Pronouns: Don and his brother like books. They read whenever their schedules leave them some time.

1. Pronouns such as *they* and *them* are called **personal pronouns**. Personal pronouns have different forms to show person, number, and gender.

2. Personal pronouns show **person**. A pronoun in the **first person** shows who is speaking. A pronoun in the **second person** shows who is being spoken to. A pronoun in the **third person** shows who or what is being spoken about.

    First Person: I want to go to the library tomorrow.

    Second Person: Do you have any books to return?

    Third Person: She returned them yesterday.

3. Personal pronouns also show **number**. **Singular** pronouns refer to one person or thing. **Plural** pronouns refer to more than one.

    Singular: He chose three books.   **Plural:** They worked on the class report.

4. Third person singular pronouns show **gender**. *She* and *her* are **feminine**. *He* and *him* are **masculine**. *It* is **neuter**.

    Feminine: Ask Annie what she thinks about that topic.

    Masculine: Rob says he found a useful book.

    Neuter: The book has two chapters about it.

Personal Pronouns		
Person	**Singular**	**Plural**
First	I, me	we, us
Second	you	you
Third	he, him, she, her, it	they, them

Try It Out

Speak Up What are the person and number of each underlined pronoun? Is each third person singular pronoun masculine, feminine, or neuter?

1. Sharon and <u>I</u> work with <u>her</u>.
2. <u>We</u> collect plastic containers on Saturdays.
3. Do all of <u>you</u> know that plastic is a valuable product?
4. When <u>it</u> is recycled, energy is saved.
5. If people knew that, <u>they</u> wouldn't throw milk jugs away.

Possessive Pronouns

1. You have learned that possessive nouns show ownership. You can use **possessive pronouns** to replace possessive nouns.

<u>Ben's</u> book is a biography.   His book is a biography.
<u>Lisa's</u> book is science fiction.   Her book is science fiction.

Possessive Pronouns		
Person	**Singular**	**Plural**
First	my, mine	our, ours
Second	your, yours	your, yours
Third	his, her, hers, its	their, theirs

2. Most possessive pronouns have two forms for each person. One form describes a noun, as an adjective does. Use *my, your, his, her, its, our,* and *their* before nouns. The pronouns *mine, yours, his, hers, ours,* and *theirs* are used alone.

Used before a noun	**Used alone**
That book is not my book.	That book is not mine.
That was her magazine.	The magazine was hers.

3. Do not confuse possessive pronouns and contractions. A possessive pronoun never has an apostrophe.

The book has lost its cover.   It's coming apart.
Your book is broken.   You're going to repair it.

Possessive Pronouns	Contractions
your	you're (you are)
its	it's (it is)
their	they're (they are)
theirs	there's (there is)

Try It Out

Emily Dickinson

Speak Up What possessive pronoun completes each sentence pair?

6. She and he bought a new book. It is _____.
7. That poem is by Emily Dickinson. It is _____ poem.
8. That poem is by Emily Dickinson. The poem is _____.
9. This one is by Robert Frost. The poem is _____.

What is the correct form to complete each sentence?

10. Can this possibly be (you're, your) signature?
11. The envelope is missing (it's, its) contents.
12. Have they picked up (they're, their) mail yet?

Robert Frost

Summing Up

- A **pronoun** is used to replace a noun.
- **Personal pronouns** have different forms to show person, number, and gender.
- A **possessive pronoun** can replace a possessive noun.

Write the correct pronoun for each sentence pair.

Example: The Library of Congress belongs to us. It is _____.   *ours*

13. In 1812 we lost the library. _____ nation's library burned.
14. Thomas Jefferson helped. He sold _____ books.
15. There were about 7,000 items. _____ filled the library.

16–20. Write this part of a guide's talk for a tour of the New York Public Library. Correct the five errors in pronoun form or spelling.

Example: The library entrance hall is beautiful. Its marble.   *It's marble.*

Proofreading

The New York Public Library is a landmark for New Yorkers. It's central location at Fifth Avenue and 42nd Street makes it easy to find. Its a favorite spot for New Yorkers to meet there friends. The steps of the library are guarded by two lions. They're carved from marble. During the holiday season, they're necks are hung with wreaths. People often call they Patience and Fortitude.

Guide Pass
129076
Signature
Sarah Johnson

Writing Wrap-Up   WRITING • THINKING • LISTENING • SPEAKING

EXPRESSING

Write a Note of Congratulations

Your favorite author has just won a literary prize for his or her latest novel. Write a note in which you congratulate the author and explain why you think he or she deserved to win the prize. Use at least five pronouns from this lesson. With a partner, read your notes aloud, and together check that pronouns have been used correctly.

2 Pronoun Antecedents

What is confusing about
the second sentence?
How can you fix it?

Lawanda interviewed the woman who won the Pulitzer Prize
for the best play. She said it would not change her life at all.

Agreement with Antecedents

You know that a pronoun takes the place of a noun.

Shane spoke to the audience. He read the news.

1. The noun that the pronoun replaces is called an antecedent. The prefix *ante-*
means "before," and the root *-ced-* means "go." An **antecedent** usually
goes before a pronoun and names the person, place, or thing to which the
pronoun refers. Sometimes the antecedent is in an earlier sentence.

   The radio is old, but it works well.

   Lucas listened to his radio.

   The speakers should be on the shelf. Are they there?

   The tapes were left uncovered. Are they dusty?

2. The antecedent does not always go before the pronoun. Sometimes the
antecedent comes after the pronoun.

   Although she was late, the announcer walked slowly.

3. The antecedent of one pronoun may be another pronoun.

   By seven o'clock, I had turned off my radio.

4. A pronoun must always agree with its antecedent in number and in person.
A pronoun that is third person singular must agree with its antecedent in
gender as well.

   Third Person Singular

   Masculine: Keith finished his work.

   Feminine: Evelyn completed her assignment too.

   Neuter: The report is in its folder.

5. When the antecedent is two or more nouns joined by *and,* use a plural pronoun.

> James and Clark will give **their** report next week.

6. When the antecedent is two or more nouns joined by *or,* use a pronoun that agrees with the noun nearer the pronoun.

> **Singular:** Did Leon or Roy forget **his** cue?
>
> **Plural:** The sportscaster or the reviewers will give **their** reports on the game.

Try It Out

Speak Up What is the correct pronoun in each sentence? What is each pronoun's antecedent?

William Spooner

1. She or Mary is writing about William Spooner in (her, their) report for class this week.
2. Spooner was known for his slips with language. (He, They) gave our vocabulary a new word.
3. Once, when escorting a lady to her seat, Spooner said, "Let me sew you to (her, your) sheet."
4. This was one of (his, her) most famous "spoonerisms."
5. Don't laugh! A tongue-twister may play (its, their) tricks on you some day!
6. Lucy or the twins will give (her, their) report on language in English class next week.

Clear Antecedents

1. You can use pronouns to make your writing more interesting and smooth. However, you must make sure that the pronouns you use have clear antecedents.

> **Unclear:** They say that trash can be used as a source of energy.
> They present a lot of ads on radio.
> It says that liftoff will be at dawn tomorrow.
> He learns from some TV shows.

The sentences above contain pronouns with unclear antecedents. Who are *they, it,* and *you*? Try to avoid writing or saying sentences like these. Use nouns or different wording instead.

> **Clear:** Experts say that trash can be used as a source of energy.
> Sponsors present a lot of ads on radio.
> The newspaper says that liftoff will be at dawn tomorrow.
> Stanley learns from some TV shows.

2. Be sure also that the antecedent for each pronoun that you use is clear.

    Unclear: Dan interviewed Greg when he was in town.
                 (Was Dan or Greg in town?)

    Clear: Dan interviewed Greg when Dan was in town.
                 Dan interviewed Greg when Greg was in town.
                 When Dan was in town, he interviewed Greg.

Try It Out

Speak Up How would you correct the unclear pronoun antecedents in these sentences?

7. They say that only one main rule for writing headlines exists.
8. They must tell a story accurately.
9. It should not, however, tell the whole story.
10. You should want to read past the headline.
11. If the headline of a story is too long, it spoils it.

- An **antecedent** is a noun or pronoun to which a pronoun refers.
- A pronoun must agree with its antecedent in person, number, and gender.

On Your Own

Write each sentence, using the correct pronoun. Underline its antecedent.

Example: A newspaper rarely raises (its, their) price.
          A newspaper rarely raises its price.

12. How do newspapers get (their, its) money?
13. (They, You) get money from ads and daily sales.
14. My brother and I enjoy reading the daily paper. (He, We) would like to be reporters.
15. In (his, their) dreams, my brother writes about world events.   **more ▶**

16. I, however, think that (our, my) specialty would be sports.
17. Sheila and Nancy think that (she, they) would write about basketball.
18. This is my favorite newspaper. (Their, Its) sports page is the best!

19–24. Rewrite correctly the sentences from this part of a journalist's career talk to a school newspaper staff. Four pronouns do not agree with their antecedents or have unclear antecedents.

Example: You can see a variety of stories in the newspaper.
Readers can see a variety of stories in the newspaper.

Seattle
GAZETTE

   Beat reporters cover everyday news stories. They have to be short and informative. They must collect facts and write their stories by the deadlines. They are set to allow enough time to print the newspaper.
   A reporter's assignment might be a crime story, a disaster, or a meeting. Reporters use her intelligence and persistence. They might talk to many people for one story. Often his interviews are by telephone. It should always add details to the published story.

WRITING • THINKING • LISTENING • SPEAKING

Writing Wrap-Up

EXPRESSING / PERSUADING

Write a Letter to the Editor
   Write a letter to the editor objecting to the newspaper's account of a sports event, a concert, or a movie. Assume that you witnessed the event yourself, and give your own version of it. Use pronouns and be sure that they have clear antecedents. Volunteers can read their letters aloud. Which letters expressed an opinion most persuasively?

Writing with Pronouns

Using Pronouns Well You can use pronouns to make your writing smoother. Just make sure that the reader can easily tell which noun a pronoun refers to. Replace an unclear pronoun with a noun.

Unclear

Paul, Ramona, and Junko ran for class president. She won because her campaign speech rallied student voters.

They all promised to hold open planning meetings.

Clear

Paul, Ramona, and Junko ran for class president. Junko won because her campaign speech rallied student voters.

The candidates all promised to hold open planning meetings.

Apply It

1–5. Read this draft of a school news bulletin. Revise the unclear pronouns so that the meaning of each sentence is clear.

Revising

New Officers Take Charge

President
Alberto Montaldi

Treasurer
Deanna Wade

Secretary
Derrick Robins

   Eighth-grade voters elected a new president, a treasurer, and a secretary on Wednesday. Because he could not make the assembly, he made a speech on Thursday about how he'll fulfill his duties as secretary.
   Although he defeated Jack for president, he did not gloat. Alberto wanted to have a big celebration party, but she was already keeping a close eye on the budget. In their first order of business, they compromised on a pizza party to be held during lunch period next Friday.
   The new officeholders will be available at lunch today, so we can visit and discuss concerns.

Avoiding Pronoun Overload Overuse of pronouns in your writing can make your sentences sound flat. Try replacing some pronouns with their antecedents or with other exact nouns or noun phrases.

> TV advertising is important to car manufacturers. They use it because it sells products for them.

> noun phrase
>
> Television advertising is important to car manufacturers. These wealthy companies use TV advertising because it sells products for them.
>
> antecedent

Apply It

6–10. Revise this part of a student report. Replace the unclear pronouns with antecedents or nouns that are more exact.

Revising

Report, revision 1

Make Your Sales Easier

As a small business, how can you make an effective print advertisement to sell a product? You can plan a beautiful design for it. Catchy wording and humor can help get the attention of readers. However, they won't mean much if it doesn't motivate them to make a purchase.

First, think about what they need. How will the product meet the needs of your audience? How can you best communicate to consumers the value of it? How can you persuade consumers that the product is essential to improving the quality of life? Remember that the combination of images and words can be the most powerful way to promote it.

3 Pronoun Case

What is wrong with these sentences? How can you fix them?

The only one who has seen my painting is me, but I might show them to Julio. When Maria and him came over to visit, he asked to see my work.

Subject and Object Pronouns

You have learned that pronouns replace nouns and that nouns can be used as subjects or objects in a sentence. Pronouns have different forms, called **cases**, that show whether they are being used as subjects or as objects.

1. Pronouns used as subjects or as predicate pronouns, which replace predicate nouns, are called **subject pronouns**. They are in the **nominative case**.

> I love art.   A great artist is he!

2. Pronouns used as direct or indirect objects or as objects of the preposition are called **object pronouns**. They are in the **objective case**.

> Art fascinates me.   I'll lend him two brushes.   These two are for him.

Subject and Object Pronouns		
Nominative Case		
I	we	We admired Cara's artwork.
you	you	The artist was she.
he, she, it	they	
Objective Case		
me	us	Cara called us.
you	you	She showed them her work.
him, her, it	them	They are pleased with it.

3. Notice that the pronouns *you* and *it* are the same in the nominative and objective cases.

Speak Up Is each underlined word or phrase used as a subject, a predicate noun, a direct object, or an indirect object? What pronoun can replace each word or phrase?

1. Yesterday <u>the class and I</u> studied a painting.
2. <u>The painting</u> is called *Children's Games*.
3. Mr. Lei gave <u>the class and me</u> a task.
4. Find ten familiar games. Can you list <u>the games</u>?
5. Now tell <u>Janice</u> all the games, please.
6. The painter's initials are P. B. Can you name <u>the man</u>?
7. Was it Pieter Brueghel? Yes, it was <u>Pieter Brueghel</u>.
8. <u>Brueghel's paintings</u> can be found in museums around the world.

Pronouns in Compounds

1. Many sentences have compound subjects or objects.

Tracy and I will be at the museum.   Will you join Tracy and me?

When a pronoun is part of a compound subject or a compound object, be sure to use a pronoun in the correct case.

Pronouns in Compound Sentence Parts	
Nominative Case Compound subject	Tom and she design the sets. He and she design the sets.
Compound predicate noun or predicate pronoun	The designers are Tom and she. The designers are he and she.
Objective Case Compound direct object	The artist drew Len and her. The artist drew him and her.
Compound indirect object	We gave Sue and him a sketch. We gave her and him a sketch.

2. If you are not sure which case to use in these compounds, say the sentence with the pronoun alone.

William and (she, her) painted in New York.
She painted in New York.
William and she painted in New York.

(He, Him) and (she, her) lived there.
He lived there. She lived there.
He and she lived there.

Please show (he, him) and (I, me) the art.
Please show him the art. Please show me the art.
Please show him and me the art.

Pieter the Elder

Speak Up What is the correct pronoun form?

9. We have been studying Pieter Brueghel the Elder. (He, Him) and two of his sons are very famous painters.
10. (He, Him) and several of his relatives were successful Flemish artists.
11. Still popular are Jan the Elder, Pieter the Younger, and (he, him).
12. Five Brueghels in all created important art. Their admirers include Sue and (I, me).
13. Mr. Lei assigned Sue and (I, me) to write a report next week on this famous family.

Summing Up

- Subject pronouns are in the **nominative case**.
- Use the nominative case for pronouns used as subjects and predicate pronouns.
- Object pronouns are in the **objective case**.
- Use the objective case for pronouns used as direct objects and indirect objects and as objects of prepositions.

Write the pronoun form that correctly completes each sentence. Label it *nominative* or *objective*.

Example: Tell me again about Brueghel. Who was (he, him)?
    he   nominative

14. By "Brueghel" I mean Pieter the Elder. The class liked (he, him) best.
15. The Brueghel born around 1525 was (he, him).
16. His sons, grandsons, and (he, him) all became well-known artists.
17. (They, Them) were people who painted in the 1500s and the 1600s.

18–24. Study the sentences in this part of a student's oral report on a visit to an art exhibition. Correct the seven errors in pronoun case.

Example: This artist's work appeals to my sister and I.   *my sister and* me

ABOUT THE ARTIST
Henri de Toulouse-Lautrec

Proofreading

    Marco, Julie, and me visited an exhibition of late nineteenth-century French art. All of we agreed that we liked Henri de Toulouse-Lautrec's work. Julie and Marco asked about Toulouse-Lautrec's life, and the guide gave she and he a pamphlet about the artist. It was him who so effectively portrayed the entertainers of Paris, showing great insight into their feelings. His own severe leg injuries may have made he sympathetic to lonely, isolated people. Although the artist's oil paintings appealed to I, an amateur painter, Marco and Julie preferred his posters. Him and her liked them best.

Writing Wrap-Up

DESCRIBING

Write an Advertising Flier
Write a brief description for an advertising flier of the work of a visual or musical artist you admire. Use at least five pronouns in the nominative and objective cases. In a small group, read your descriptions aloud, and identify together the case of each pronoun.

4 Interrogative Pronouns

Who turned out the lights?

Who's voice is that?

To who am I speaking?

One of these sentences is correct. What's wrong with the other two sentences? How can you fix them?

When you ask questions, you use another kind of pronoun.

Who said that?   What did he say?   Which do you mean?

1. A pronoun used to form a question is called an **interrogative pronoun**. The antecedents of interrogative pronouns are the words that answer the questions.

Who said that? Holmes said that.

What did he say? He said, "Aha!"

Which do you mean? I mean the mystery.

2. If the words *which* and *what* come directly before nouns, they act as adjectives, not as pronouns. If *which* and *what* stand alone, they act as pronouns.

Adjectives: Which picture do you like? What plan will you follow?

Pronouns: Which do you like? What is your plan?

3. The interrogative pronoun *who* has different forms to reflect case depending on how you use it in a sentence.

Nominative Case: who (subject pronoun)

Who knows the story? He knows.

Objective Case: whom (object pronoun)

To whom did you give a book? I gave a book to her.

4. To help you decide whether to use *who* or *whom,* turn the question into a statement. Substitute *he* or *she* for *who,* and use *him* or *her* in place of *whom* to see which case is correct.

Question: (Who, Whom) will we pick?

Statement: We will pick (who, whom). We will pick (he, him).

The objective case is correct here, so *whom* should be used.

5. When the interrogative pronoun shows possession, use *whose,* the possessive form of *who.* Do not confuse the pronoun *whose* and the contraction *who's,* which sound alike. *Who's* means "who is."

Possessive Pronoun: Whose are these glasses?
Contraction: Who's at the door?

Speak Up Which pronoun or contraction is correct?

1. (Who, Whom) did the mystery author Carolyn Keene create?
2. (Who, Whom) is her most important character?
3. (What, Who's) is the most popular mystery series of all time?
4. (Which, Whom) is it—the one about Nancy Drew or the one about the Hardy Boys?
5. (Who, Whom) is the best teen-age investigator?
6. (Who, Which) do you prefer?
7. (Who, Whom) does Paul like the best?
8. (Who's, Whose) going to solve the mystery first?
9. (Whose, Who's) are these books?
10. (Who, Whom) should we ask?
11. (Who, Whom) in my class reads mystery books?
12. (Whom, Which) would you choose as your favorite author?

Summing Up

- The **interrogative pronouns** *who, which, what, whom,* and *whose* ask questions.

- Use *who* as a subject, *whom* as an object, and *whose* as a possessive.

- Do not confuse the interrogative pronoun *whose* with the contraction *who's.*

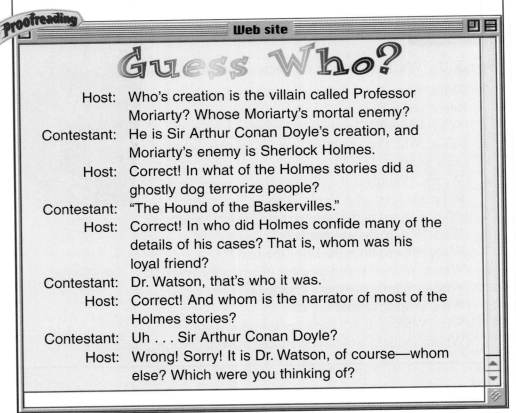

On Your Own

13–20. Correct each sentence in this part of a transcript from a TV quiz show. There are eight errors in the use of interrogative pronouns.

Example: Whose the famous author of *The Red-Headed League*?   *Who's*

Proofreading

Web site

Guess Who?

Host: Who's creation is the villain called Professor Moriarty? Whose Moriarty's mortal enemy?

Contestant: He is Sir Arthur Conan Doyle's creation, and Moriarty's enemy is Sherlock Holmes.

Host: Correct! In what of the Holmes stories did a ghostly dog terrorize people?

Contestant: "The Hound of the Baskervilles."

Host: Correct! In who did Holmes confide many of the details of his cases? That is, whom was his loyal friend?

Contestant: Dr. Watson, that's who it was.

Host: Correct! And whom is the narrator of most of the Holmes stories?

Contestant: Uh . . . Sir Arthur Conan Doyle?

Host: Wrong! Sorry! It is Dr. Watson, of course—whom else? Which were you thinking of?

Writing Wrap-Up
WRITING • THINKING • LISTENING • SPEAKING

INFORMING

Write a List of Questions

You are working out the plan for your first mystery novel. Write at least five questions you will need to answer in your novel. (You do not need to write the answers, just the questions.) Use interrogative pronouns. Exchange questions with a partner. Do you both agree on what the important questions are? Did your partner use interrogative pronouns correctly?

For Extra Practice see page 340.

5 Demonstrative Pronouns

One-Minute Warm-Up

Find the pronouns in the sentences below. Which pronoun points out a person, place, or thing?

> Keeping away from Salamandastron, they moved south and stalked the swampland fringes for toads, frogs and birds. When these were not available there were always plants and roots.
>
> —from *Salamandastron: A Novel of Redwall*, by Brian Jacques

You can use another kind of pronoun to point out persons, places, things, or ideas.

> This is a weasel.   Those are its babies.

A pronoun that points out something is called a **demonstrative pronoun**.

1. A demonstrative pronoun must agree in number with the noun it points out or with its antecedent.

   Singular: This is a mink.   That is a polecat.

   Plural: These are minks.   Those are polecats.

2. Use *this* and *these* to point to things nearby. Use *that* and *those* to point to things farther away.

   This is a white weasel.

   These are weasels with long tails.

   That looks like a weasel over there.

   Those are probably weasels with short tails.

3. Like *which* and *what*, the words *this, that, these,* and *those* may function as adjectives or as pronouns in a sentence. When they come directly before a noun, they are demonstrative adjectives. When they stand alone, they are demonstrative pronouns.

   Demonstrative Adjective

   I don't like this cage.   These cages are small.

   Demonstrative Pronoun

   I don't like this.   These are small.

4. You should avoid the expressions *this here* and *that there. This* already means "the one here," and *that* already means "the one there."

> This is a beaver. (*not* This here)
> That is a cute animal. (*not* That there)
> These are not mice. (*not* These here)
> Those must be moles. (*not* Those there)

Try It Out

Speak Up Which words are correct in the following sentences? To which nouns do the words refer?

1. (These, These here) are my favorite animals in the animal reserve.
2. (That, Those) are the zebras we saw yesterday.
3. (That, That there) is a beautiful old camel.
4. (This, That) must be a water buffalo down there.
5. (These, Those) are lions over there.
6. (That, This) is certainly an interesting trip!
7. (Those, Those there) are cheetahs, the world's fastest animal.
8. (This, That) gazelle near the side of our jeep looks very young.
9. (That, That there) elephant is using its trunk to tear off the leaves of a tree.

Summing Up

- A **demonstrative pronoun** points out something.
- *This* and *that* refer to singular nouns or pronouns.
- *These* and *those* refer to plural nouns or pronouns.
- *This* and *these* point out things that are close.
- *That* and *those* point out things that are farther away.

Write each sentence, using the correct demonstrative pronoun. Underline the noun it points out.

Example: (This, That) is a monkey in the far corner.
That is a <u>monkey</u> in the far corner.

10. Is (this, that) its baby right here?
11. (This, These) could be chimps.
12. (This, These) must be the mother chimpanzee.
13. (That, Those) cannot be real gorillas.
14. (These, Those) must be baboons in the next room.

15–22. Write each sentence correctly in this story opening. There are eight errors in the use of demonstrative pronouns.

Example: They prefer that there. *They prefer that.*

Proofreading

My cocker spaniels, Arlo and Dixie, are those sitting demurely beside me here. This here is Arlo's tug-of-war toy. This is his Frisbee™ over in the corner. These here are Dixie's squeaky toys next to this here chew bone. That are the dogs' favorite possessions and the cause of all the trouble during the groomer's last visit. This was a disaster. I can't forget that there afternoon.

Writing Wrap-Up

WRITING • THINKING • LISTENING • SPEAKING

NARRATING

Write a Narrative

Write the opening paragraph of a story about human beings told from the point of view of an animal. The animal observes humans and then describes what the humans are doing. Use demonstrative pronouns. Exchange papers with a partner, and read each other's paragraphs aloud. What do you think will happen next in your partner's story? How would you continue it?

6 Indefinite Pronouns

Find the pronoun in the sentence below.

Near the dikes the people had time for nothing but work.

—from *The Journey Back*, by Johanna Reiss

Kinds of Indefinite Pronouns

Words such as *someone* and *something* refer to a person or thing that is not identified. Such pronouns are called **indefinite pronouns**.

Someone is arriving.   Something delayed the flight.

1. An indefinite pronoun that refers to only one person or thing is singular. An indefinite pronoun that refers to more than one is plural.

    sing.   pl.
    Everyone enjoys travel.   Many of us love to fly.

2. Some indefinite pronouns can be either singular or plural, depending on what they refer to in a sentence.

    sing.   pl.
    All of the fuel has been used. All of the flights have been canceled.

Singular			Plural	Either
another	everybody	nothing	both	all
anybody	everyone	other	few	any
anyone	everything	one	many	most
anything	neither	somebody	ones	none
each	nobody	someone	others	some
either	no one	something	several	

3. Some words that can function as indefinite pronouns can also act as adjectives modifying nouns.

    Adjective: Each plane is ready.

    Indefinite pronoun: Each of the planes is ready.

Speak Up Identify each indefinite pronoun. Is it singular or plural? Not every sentence has an indefinite pronoun.

Houses in Delft

1. Last year some of the boys and girls in Mrs. Leyden's class traveled with her to the Netherlands.
2. Did you know that all of western Holland is below sea level and that *nether* means "low"?
3. Not everyone, however, took all of the tours that were planned for each day.
4. Naturally, no one wanted to miss the trip to a chocolate factory.
5. Many of us spent hours traveling up and down the narrow canals of Amsterdam.
6. The trip had something to offer everyone.
7. One day we visited the pottery factory at Delft, where we saw the workers hand-painting some vases.
8. Both Mrs. Leyden and her daughter were born in The Hague, but neither of them had much time to visit relatives.
9. Some of the most magnificent flowers anybody had ever seen appeared in the flower exhibit in Dam Square in Amsterdam.
10. None of us will ever forget the Anne Frank House, where Anne's family and several friends hid for two years.

Agreement with Indefinite Pronouns

1. You know that verbs must agree with their subjects in number. When an indefinite pronoun is the subject, the verb must agree with it.

   Singular: Someone is traveling to China.

   Plural: Several in this row <u>have</u> tickets to London.

The chart on the preceding page shows you whether an indefinite pronoun is singular or plural. Some pronouns, however, can be either singular or plural. The meaning of the pronoun in the sentence determines its number. The words that follow the pronoun will tell you whether the meaning is singular or plural. If the pronoun refers to something that cannot be counted, it is singular.

Singular: Most of the <u>food</u> has been eaten.

Plural: Most of the <u>passengers</u> have finished their meals.

In the first sentence, *most* refers to a single, uncountable amount of food. Therefore, *most* has a singular meaning here. In the second sentence, *most* refers to several passengers. In this case, then, *most* has a plural meaning.

2. You have also learned that pronouns and their antecedents must agree in number. When an indefinite pronoun is the antecedent of a personal pronoun, the personal pronoun must agree with it.

Singular: Everything has been put in its place.

Plural: Both have been put in their places.

3. Most singular indefinite pronouns can refer to either males or females. There is no agreement problem, however, if the gender is made clear by other words in the sentence.

Each of the two <u>women</u> raised her hand.

Neither of the <u>brothers</u> has packed his bags.

When the gender is not clear, try to avoid awkward constructions. If possible, use plural pronouns instead. If you cannot rewrite the sentence easily, use *his or her*, not *his* alone.

> **HELP**
> **?** **Tip**
>
> Remember that the words *everyone* and *everybody* are singular and indefinite pronouns. Do not use the personal pronoun *their* with *everyone*.

Acceptable: Everyone on the plane had his or her luggage.

Better: All on the plane had their luggage.

Try It Out

Speak Up Which word in parentheses is correct?

11. None of us (has, have) been to the museum, so some of us (is, are) going one day while others (is, are) going the next.
12. Everybody (want, wants) to pack (his or her, their) suitcases before the last day of the trip.
13. All of our luggage (has, have) grown smaller since we arrived!
14. Each of the men (is, are) stopping in Frankfurt, Germany, on the way to (his, their) destination.
15. Both of the customs officials (has, have) finished checking most of the passengers.

more ▶

16. (Has, Have) all of them brought (his or her, their) passports?
17. All of the jobs (is, are) done.
18. None of the tickets (has, have) been picked up yet.
19. Everybody on the overseas flight (was, were) delayed.
20. Few in the last hour (was, were) able to land.
21. Many in the room could not find (his, their) bags.

Summing Up

- An **indefinite pronoun** does not refer to a specific person or thing.
- Verbs must agree in number with indefinite pronouns used as subjects. Pronouns must agree with indefinite pronouns used as antecedents.

On Your Own

Write each sentence. Underline each indefinite pronoun and label it *singular* or *plural*.

Example: Everyone reported on several of the books.
everyone—singular   several—plural

22. Have all of you read *Hans Brinker, or The Silver Skates,* which is one of my favorite books?
23. Anyone who has not read it has missed a really great story.
24. In the winter, most of the canals freeze throughout the Netherlands.
25. Many of the people throughout the Netherlands enjoy ice-skating on the frozen canals.
26. None of us can ice-skate as well as the character Hans Brinker could.
27. A few of my friends have heard of the book.
28. Some of my classmates have seen an old movie based on the book.
29. Neither of us remembered to bring some refreshments for the book report party.

more ▶

30. Everyone did some research, but no one had spent much time on it.
31. Nevertheless, most of us participated in the discussion, and several shared original artwork.

32–40. Correct the errors in this e-mail letter. There are nine errors in the use of indefinite pronouns.

Example: Each of the days of our trip were memorable.
            Each of the days of our trip was *memorable.*

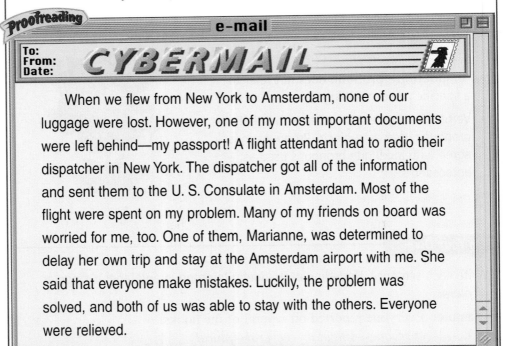

Proofreading

e-mail

CYBERMAIL

To:
From:
Date:

When we flew from New York to Amsterdam, none of our luggage were lost. However, one of my most important documents were left behind—my passport! A flight attendant had to radio their dispatcher in New York. The dispatcher got all of the information and sent them to the U. S. Consulate in Amsterdam. Most of the flight were spent on my problem. Many of my friends on board was worried for me, too. One of them, Marianne, was determined to delay her own trip and stay at the Amsterdam airport with me. She said that everyone make mistakes. Luckily, the problem was solved, and both of us was able to stay with the others. Everyone were relieved.

Writing Wrap-Up   WRITING • THINKING • LISTENING • SPEAKING

PERSUADING

Write an Ad
Write a few paragraphs for an advertisement describing a new airline. Try to convince readers that this airline will offer benefits unavailable on other airlines. Use at least five indefinite pronouns in your advertisement. Share your advertisement with a small group, and together check that indefinite pronouns have been used correctly.

7 Reflexive and Intensive Pronouns

Make up a caption for this picture. Use one of these pronouns: *himself* or *myself*.

You often use pronouns that end in *-self* or *-selves*. These forms are either reflexive pronouns or intensive pronouns. Although their spellings are the same, their uses in sentences are different.

Reflexive: Harry splashed himself with water.
Intensive: The children made that rug themselves.

1. A **reflexive pronoun** has as its antecedent the subject of the sentence. It completes the meaning of a sentence and generally cannot be left out.

   Burton knows himself very well.   Did you teach yourself music?

2. An **intensive pronoun** is used to emphasize another word, its antecedent. An intensive pronoun may or may not refer to the subject of the sentence. It can usually be left out without destroying the meaning of the sentence.

   Sid himself hung the picture.   The landscape was painted by Sid himself.

3. Both reflexive and intensive pronouns must agree with their antecedents in person, number, and gender.

   I will fix myself lunch in a while.   Jack can fix a sandwich himself.

Reflexive and Intensive Pronouns	
Singular	**Plurals**
myself	ourselves
yourself	yourselves
himself, herself, itself	themselves

4. Do not use reflexive or intensive pronoun forms in place of personal pronouns.

   Ron and I repaired the lamp. (*not* Ron and myself)

   This is between you and me. (*not* between you and myself)

5. Never use such incorrect forms as *hisself* or *theirselves*.

Mr. Gilman built the house himself. (*not* hisself)

His family lived there themselves. (*not* theirselves)

Try It Out

Speak Up Find the antecedent of each underlined pronoun. Is the pronoun reflexive or intensive?

1. Hubert found <u>himself</u> in the middle of a flood.
2. We met the plumber <u>herself</u>.
3. The oven cleaned <u>itself</u>.
4. Let's try to fix the sink <u>ourselves</u>.
5. I will call the painters <u>myself</u>.
6. Don't slip and hurt <u>yourselves</u>.

How would you correct each of the following sentences?

7. The painters protected theirselves from fumes.
8. Mrs. Sullivan and myself found the source of the leak under the sink.
9. Her son can repair pipes hisself now.
10. Herself and Russell will fix the sink tomorrow.

Complete each sentence with an appropriate pronoun. Is it reflexive or intensive?

11. Her brother has taught _____ much about house repair and maintenance.
12. The painters should see _____ in those funny hats.
13. We _____ aren't sure of the color we should use.
14. You should learn to repair things _____.
15. The work _____ is not difficult.

Summing Up

- A **reflexive pronoun** ends in *-self* or *-selves* and refers to the subject of the sentence. It generally cannot be left out of the sentence.

- An **intensive pronoun** ends in *-self* or *-selves* and emphasizes another word in the sentence.

- Avoid using pronouns with *-self* or *-selves* in place of personal pronouns.

Write the reflexive or intensive pronoun in each sentence. Label it *reflexive* or *intensive*.

Example: The painters saw themselves in the mirror.
themselves   reflexive

16. They themselves knew they looked funny.
17. One had painted himself green.
18. Another had decorated herself with blue spots.
19. The paint itself was splattered all over the floor.
20. The painters thought themselves very comical.
21. I myself had to try hard not to laugh.

Rewrite each sentence correctly. Underline the corrected word.

Example: Many people like to fix things theirselves.
Many people like to fix things themselves.

22. My brother and myself tried to fix something once.
23. My brother fooled hisself that time.
24. Himself and I tried to fix a clock.
25. Between you and myself, we ruined the job.

Rewrite each sentence, adding an appropriate reflexive or intensive pronoun.

Example: You should prepare _____ properly for repair jobs.
You should prepare yourself properly for repair jobs.

26. First, you should read the directions _____.
27. Several professional repair persons _____ gave me that advice.
28. Repair manuals _____ also provide the amateur with excellent advice and tips about working.
29. I _____ found out about repair manuals the hard way.
30. One night last week, my mother and father had given _____ an evening out.
31. Meanwhile, I decided to repair my broken alarm clock _____.
32. My brother Patrick said, "You can't do that _____."
33. He decided to help me _____.
34. As it later turned out, Pat and I could have saved _____ much time and trouble.
35. The clock _____ needed only a new battery!

more ▶

On Your Own continued

36–42. Rewrite each sentence correctly in this part of a how-to article. There are seven errors in the use of reflexive or intensive pronouns.

Example: You might ask you, How can I do this job best?
You might ask yourself, How can I do this job best?

Proofreading

Plumbing Made Easy

With a little forethought and planning, you can prepare you to do simple plumbing jobs easily and enjoyably. Trust myself when I tell you to begin by making sure you have the right tools. Naturally, the tools itself won't do the job for you. However, you will be frustrated if you find yourself halfway through a complicated job and missing the right tool. Professionals prepare theirselves by double-checking their tools and supplies. A well-equipped and well-organized toolbox will pay for themselves many times over.

Now let's take those tools in hand and fix that leaky pipe ourself! In the next section of this article, you will learn the process for making this common household repair theirselves.

Writing Wrap-Up
WRITING • THINKING • LISTENING • SPEAKING

EXPLAINING

Write Instructions
Write instructions on how to do something, make something, or repair something. Your instructions could be a list of steps or simply a paragraph. Be sure to arrange the steps in the correct order. Use both reflexive and intensive pronouns. Find a partner and read each other's papers aloud. Were your partner's instructions clear? Were pronouns used correctly?

 For Extra Practice see page 343.

8 Choosing the Correct Pronoun

What do these two diary entries really mean? Match each entry to the proper description below.

1. To Ruby, her piano comes first, before anyone, including me.
2. I like Ruby's piano, but I don't love it as much as she does.

Dear Diary,
Ruby loves her piano more than me.

Dear Diary,
Ruby loves her piano more than I.

Using we and us with Nouns

1. Occasionally you may need to use the pronoun *we* or *us* with a noun for identification or special emphasis.

   The dancers want music, but we readers want silence.

   The dancers won't let us readers have peace.

2. If you are using *we* or *us* with a noun, use the pronoun case you would use if the noun were not there. With a subject or a predicate pronoun, use the nominative case. With a direct or indirect object, or with the object of a preposition, use the objective case.

   Nominative: We girls will sing soon.

   Objective: You should join us altos in the back row.

HELP ? Tip

If you can't decide whether *we* or *us* with a noun is correct, say the sentence aloud both ways without the noun.

Try It Out

Speak Up Which sentences are correct? If a sentence is incorrect, how should it be corrected?

1. The bus will pick up us violinists to go to the workshop.
2. We students will listen to professionals.
3. Us amateurs will certainly benefit from the experience.
4. The conductor directed we violinists to our places.
5. Us lucky ones will never forget the workshop.

Pronouns in Comparisons

You often use pronouns when you make comparisons.

> I like the viola better than she.

> Suki plays as well as he.

These comparisons are incomplete. If you are not sure which pronoun to use, add words to complete the comparison.

> I like the viola better than she likes it.

> Suki plays as well as he plays.

The pronoun used in a comparison may change, depending on the meaning that you have in mind.

> He likes music as much as her. (He likes music as much as he likes her.)

> He likes music as much as she. (He likes music as much as she likes music.)

Try It Out

Speak Up Choose the correct pronoun. If a sentence has two possible answers, explain your choice.

6. Why is Rose a better musician than (I, me)?
7. Brad and I practice more than (she, her).
8. We know our music as well as (she, her).
9. People listen to Rose more than (we, us).
10. Brad gives me more advice than (she, her).
11. I should listen to her more than (he, him).

Summing Up

- If you use *we* or *us* with a noun, use the pronoun case that you would use if the noun were not there.

- To decide which pronoun form to use in an incomplete comparison, add words to complete the comparison.

Rewrite each sentence correctly.

Example: Us students talked about talent today.
> *We students talked about talent today.*

12. Genius fascinates we less talented people.
13. Us amateurs practice long hours with small results.
14. Why did Bach or Mozart have more talent than you or me?
15. Why is another student a better musician than you or him?
16. These questions annoy we music students.

17–22. Write the sentences correctly in this part of a biography. There are six errors in pronoun case.

Example: Mendelssohn's sister is said to have been as talented as him.
> *Mendelssohn's sister is said to have been as talented as he.*

Proofreading

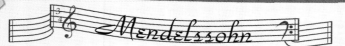

The Mendelssohn children studied literature and painting as well as music; few families were as cultivated as them. Felix Mendelssohn's sister, Fanny, composed music as readily as him. Felix often said that Fanny played the piano better than him. However, he became much better known than her. People remember him, not she, although she composed about 500 pieces. Still, not many siblings were as close as they, and she was his musical adviser until he left home. Her letters and diaries have provided much valuable information to we scholars.

Writing Wrap-Up WRITING • THINKING • LISTENING • SPEAKING

COMPARING / CONTRASTING

Write a Comparison
Working with a partner, compare and contrast what you like or dislike in music. Then write a paragraph comparing your likes and dislikes with those of your partner. Make at least five statements of comparison. Use *we* or *us* with a noun in at least one sentence. Read your paragraph aloud in a small group, and invite discussion. Ask the group members to be sure your pronoun cases are correct.

Homophones

The words *You* and *Ewe*, *Their* and *They're*, and *fourth* and *forth* are all homophones. The pairs of words have the same pronunciation but different spellings and meanings. Make sure to keep your writing clear and easy to understand by using the correct homophone. Here are some other homophones.

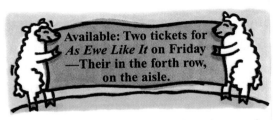

Available: Two tickets for *As Ewe Like It* on Friday —Their in the forth row, on the aisle.

Word	Meaning
base	located at the bottom
bass	having a deep tone
capital	a city that is the seat of government
capitol	a building in which a state legislature meets
cite	to quote as an example
sight	something worth seeing
choral	performed by a chorus
coral	a rocklike formation in the sea
knead	to mix or shape with the hands
need	something required or wanted

Apply It

1–6. Rewrite the messages in these ads. Find and correct each incorrect homophone.

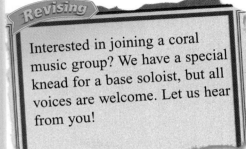

Revising

Interested in joining a coral music group? We have a special knead for a base soloist, but all voices are welcome. Let us hear from you!

Student Trip: Ride the bus to the state capitol and see all the cites along the way. Guided tour inside the capital included.

Enrichment

Pronouns!

Pronoun Ticktacktoe

Players: 2

Materials: 24 index cards, pencil, paper

To play: Each player writes the following twelve pronouns on cards: *I, me, she, her, he, him, you, it, we, us, they, them.* Put all twenty-four cards together, shuffle them, and stack them facedown. Draw a ticktacktoe board.

One player draws two cards, uses both pronouns in a sentence, and tells if the pronouns are being used as subjects or objects. If the pronouns are used correctly and correctly identified as subject or object, the player marks an *X* in a square. Then the other player has a turn and marks an *O* if correct.

Scoring: The first player to mark three squares in a row wins.

Challenge Each player crosses out the personal pronouns on four of the cards and replaces the personal pronouns with the interrogative pronouns *who, whom,* and *whose,* and the contraction *who's.* One player draws a card and must use the word correctly in a question before putting a mark on the board.

UNDERSEA WORLD

Many extraordinary creatures live in the sea. Choose one that interests you, such as an octopus, a sea horse, or a hammerhead shark. Look up information in a reference book, and write at least five interesting facts about the creature. Use at least one possessive pronoun (pp), one reflexive pronoun (rp), and one indefinite pronoun (ip). Underline these pronouns and label them with the initials shown above in parentheses.

Jellyfish may be transparent, and some glow at night.
_{ip}

Checkup: Unit 6

1 Personal and Possessive Pronouns *(p. 298)* Write the pronouns in each sentence. Identify the person and number of each one, and write the gender of all third-person singular pronouns.

1. I have found many clamshells on the beach near my house.
2. Did you know that they can dissolve in water?
3. They are made of calcium carbonate.
4. It is carried by the water and can harden into calcite.
5. Calcite can mix with particles and cement them together.
6. We tried an experiment with clamshells in science class.

2 Pronoun Antecedents *(p. 302)* Rewrite the sentences, using pronouns and antecedents correctly and clearly.

7. A supermarket must pay attention to how they display goods.
8. People with pets, for example, want to find everything for it in the same aisle.
9. The market should have their detergent and bleach together.
10. They should also be an attractive place to shop.
11. Let's go into this market and see what they have.

3 Pronoun Case *(p. 308)* Write the pronoun that correctly completes each sentence.

12. Both you and (I, me) think Jenny Lind was a great singer.
13. Many people would agree that it was (she, her).
14. P. T. Barnum managed (she, her) in the United States.
15. (He and she, Him and her) worked together for two years.
16. I think you and (I, me) could choose (she, her) as the subject of a report.

4 Interrogative Pronouns *(p. 312)* Write the pronoun that correctly completes each sentence.

17. (Who's, Whose) is this bicycle?
18. (Who, Whom) left this racing bike here?
19. (Who's, Whose) going to enter the race?
20. (Who, Whom) won the grand prize last year?
21. (Who, Whom) did the winner have to beat?

5 Demonstrative Pronouns *(p. 315)* Rewrite each sentence, using demonstrative pronouns correctly.

22. (This, These) are geodes, hollow rocks with crystals inside.
23. (These here, These) are purple, but (those there, those) are green.
24. (That, Those) are quartz crystals.
25. Could (this, these) be geodes?
26. We'll have to crack (this here, this) open to find out.

Go to www.eduplace.com/tales/ for more fun with parts of speech.

6 Indefinite Pronouns *(p. 318)* Write each sentence. Underline each indefinite pronoun and the verb or pronoun that agrees with it.

27. Everybody in Westwood schools (has, have) to study history.
28. All in the eighth grade (studies, study) European history.
29. Each of the teachers, Mr. Rose and Mr. Nakamura, has (his, their) specialty.
30. Both of them (teach, teaches) modern history.
31. Neither of them (teach, teaches) ancient history.
32. Each of these two teachers is famous in (his, their) field.

7 Reflexive and Intensive Pronouns *(p. 323)* Rewrite each sentence, using reflexive and intensive pronouns correctly.

33. My brother and I considered us excellent cooks.
34. The family members convinced theirselves to let us cook dinner.
35. My brother hisself admits that the dinner was not a success.
36. He and myself burned the turkey.
37. We had forgotten about it while we busied us making the mashed potatoes.

8 Choosing the Correct Pronoun *(p. 327)* Rewrite each sentence, correcting pronoun errors.

38. Clarkson does better than us in swimming.
39. Our teams competed last week, and us juniors won.
40. Corky Bancroft swims with us, and no one is better than him.
41. I suppose us swimmers can never hope to be as fast as he.
42. He amazed all of we swimmers.

Mixed Review 43–48. There are six pronoun errors in this paragraph from a student's book review. Write the paragraph correctly.

Proofreading Checklist
✔ lack of agreement between pronouns and antecedents
✔ incorrect pronoun case
✔ incorrect use of interrogative pronouns
✔ incorrect use of personal and possessive pronouns

Proofreading

> Agatha Christie is a well-known mystery writer. No one is better than her at planting false clues. Readers, however, get weary of this tactic, and he or she longs for good clues. Who has Christie chosen to be the villain in this book? It's villain is someone we never hear of until the end! The smug detective Hercule Poirot and me have come to the end of our long acquaintance. Now its Sherlock Holmes for me.

Test Practice

Write the numbers 1–8 on a sheet of paper. Choose the best way to write the underlined part of each sentence. Write the letter for that answer. If there is no mistake, write the letter for the last answer.

1 The bus driver apologized to James and <u>myself</u> for being so late.

   A I

   B me

   C my

   D (No mistakes)

2 Did Ana or Stacey forget <u>her</u> ballet shoes?

   F their

   G hers

   H herself

   J (No mistakes)

3 The millionaire farmer insisted on fixing the broken tractor <u>hisself.</u>

   A himself

   B theirself

   C heself

   D (No mistakes)

4 The individuals who played that particular prank are <u>he and herself.</u>

   F him and her

   G himself and herself

   H he and she

   J (No mistakes)

5 After swimming in the sea, we washed <u>ourself</u> in the outdoor shower.

   A us

   B we

   C ourselves

   D (No mistakes)

6 To <u>whom</u> did the municipal authorities award the building contract?

   F who

   G whose

   H who's

   J (No mistakes)

7 <u>This here</u> is a rare orchid.

   A That there

   B This

   C These

   D (No mistakes)

8 <u>Who's</u> half-eaten frankfurter is sitting on the picnic table?

   F Whose

   G Who

   H Whom

   J (No mistakes)

Now write numbers 9–12 on your paper. Read the passage all the way through once. Then look at the underlined parts. Decide if they need to be changed or if they are fine as they are. Choose the best answer from the choices given. Write the letter for each answer.

My family is renting an apartment in Paris for <u>August; all of the Parisians has left</u> for the month.
(9)

9 A August all of the Parisians have left
   B August; all of the Parisians have leaved
   C August; all of the Parisians have left
   D (No change)

<u>Many has gone</u> to country
(10)
homes in the mountains or near the beaches of France. Others are traveling to more distant locations, such as the United States.

10 F Many have gone
    G Many has went
    H Many have went
    J (No change)

While we are here, we want to see the <u>following, the eiffel tower,</u>
(11)
the Louvre, and Notre Dame. We also plan to gorge ourselves on delicious French food.

11 A following; the Eiffel Tower,
    B following: the Eiffel Tower,
    C following: the Eiffel tower;
    D (No change)

We are staying in the part of Paris called <u>Montmartre the</u> apart-
(12)
ment is small but very attractive. We will take lots of photos to show you when we return.

12 F montmartre? The
    G Montmartre; the
    H Montmartre: the
    J (No change)

Write numbers 13–16 on your paper, and do this page the same way you did the previous one.

"The merry wives of Windsor"
<u>(13)</u>
<u>are</u> a play by William Shakespeare.

This play is

13 **A** *The Merry Wives of Windsor*
   is
   B *The merry wives of windsor*
   is
   C "The Merry Wives of
   Windsor" are
   D (No change)

classified as <u>a farce a comedy</u> full
<u>(14)</u>
of extremely absurd situations. It

was written around 1600

14 **F** a farce; a comedy
   G a farce, a comedy
   H a farce. A comedy
   J (No change)

when Shakespeare <u>was in his 30s</u>
<u>(15)</u>
<u>and</u> had already written twenty-one

other plays.

15 **A** was in his thirties, and
   B was in his 30's and
   C was in his thirties and
   D (No change)

This is one of <u>the most fre-</u>
<u>(16)</u>
<u>quently</u> acted of all Shakespeare's

plays. Its success is partly due to its

hero, the fat rogue Sir John

Falstaff.

16 **F** the most frequent
   G the most frequentliest
   H the frequentliest
   J (No change)

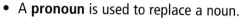

(pages 298–301)

1 Personal and Possessive Pronouns

- A **pronoun** is used to replace a noun.
- **Personal pronouns** have different forms to show person, number, and gender.
- A **possessive pronoun** can replace a possessive noun.

● Write *personal* or *possessive* for each underlined pronoun.

Example: <u>We</u> have newspapers in every room of <u>our</u> house.
We—personal   our—possessive

1. My brother and <u>I</u> work in a newspaper office.
2. <u>We</u> have worked there for three months now.
3. <u>He</u> wants to become a reporter.
4. News reporting is also a goal of <u>mine</u>.
5. Is anyone in <u>your</u> family in the news business?
6. How did <u>he</u> or <u>she</u> become interested in <u>it</u>?
7. Billy got <u>his</u> job through an ad in the newspaper.

▲ Write each pronoun. Label it *personal* or *possessive*.

Example: He has finally made up his mind about the news job.
He—personal   his—possessive

8. She told us about it last week, and then we told him.
9. Three other students work at the newspaper, but you do not know them.
10. They bring their lunch with them every day.
11. If I had my choice, I would have a job like yours.
12. If your office is near ours, why not visit us someday soon?
13. Would you recommend the work for all people?
14. No, news work has its advantages, but it is very hard.

■ Rewrite the incorrect sentences. Write *correct* if a sentence has no errors.

Example: Its always busy in a newsroom. *It's always busy in a newsroom.*

15. Your always racing against time.
16. The editor and Mr. Carey told us how they're computers help.
17. You're daily paper, for example, may be in color.
18. A few years ago, your paper was entirely black and white.
19. Now theirs a satellite that can give us news instantly.
20. Your right; its an amazing world we live in.

Extra Practice

(pages 302–305)

2 Pronoun Antecedents

- An **antecedent** is a noun or pronoun to which a pronoun refers.
- A pronoun must agree with its antecedent in person, number, and gender.

● Rewrite each sentence, choosing the personal or possessive pronoun that agrees with the underlined antecedent.

Example: TV is popular, but radio still has (its, their) fans.
TV is popular, but radio still has its fans.

1. Many <u>people</u> listen to (his, their) radios during the day.
2. <u>Anna</u> has a clock radio next to (her, their) bed.
3. Anna's <u>parents</u> listen to the news as (it, he, they) dress for work.
4. With (his, its) own money, Anna's <u>brother</u> bought a radio.
5. Does <u>Anna</u> or her <u>mother</u> use a headset with (her, their) radio?

▲ Rewrite each sentence, choosing the correct personal or possessive pronoun. Underline its antecedent.

Example: I prefer radio to TV, for I can use (my, its) imagination.
I prefer radio to TV, for I can use my imagination.

6. When my sister graduates from college, (she, he) plans to work in radio.
7. Although (it, she) has a nice voice, my sister will not be an announcer.
8. She and a friend have (her, their) hearts set on being radio producers.
9. Even though (he, they) are not heard, producers are important.
10. A producer lines up guests and prepares (it, them) for the show.
11. Has your sister or her friend gotten (her, their) first job yet?

■ Rewrite each incorrect sentence, correcting pronouns and antecedents as necessary so that each sentence can stand alone. If a sentence has no errors, write *correct.*

Example: They say we have a new writer starting next week.
The editor says we have a new writer starting next week.

12. The reporters returned to her radio newsroom quickly.
13. Their evening news stories were being prepared by the writers.
14. The news editor and the producer were reviewing her notes.
15. Would Eva's story or Joe's story ever be on the air?

338 **Unit 6:** Pronouns

(pages 308–311)

③ Pronoun Case

- Subject pronouns are in the **nominative case.**
- Use the nominative case for pronouns used as subjects and predicate pronouns.
- Object pronouns are in the **objective case.**
- Use the objective case for pronouns used as direct objects and indirect objects and as objects of prepositions.

Remember

● Write *subject* or *object* to describe each underlined pronoun.

Example: Who were Georgia O'Keeffe and Alfred Stieglitz?
They were artists. *subject*

1. <u>She</u> and <u>he</u> worked in different fields.
2. O'Keeffe admired <u>him</u> greatly.
3. Eventually, her teacher was <u>he</u>.
4. Stieglitz encouraged <u>her</u> in her art career.
5. O'Keeffe's work was bold. <u>It</u> startled people.

▲ Write the correct pronouns to complete these sentences. Label each pronoun *subject, predicate pronoun, direct object,* or *indirect object.*

Example: Todd and (I, me) are working on a photography project.
I—subject

6. (He, Him) and Jennie used to work together.
7. The only ones in the class are (we, us).
8. Mr. Chan gave Todd and (I, me) some instructions.
9. (He, Him) and an associate visited (we, us).
10. (We, Us) told (they, them) the steps in the procedures.

■ Rewrite any incorrect sentences. If a sentence has no errors, write *correct.*

Example: Leah and me are making a statue. *Leah and I are making a statue.*

11. The process has interested her and me for a long time.
12. Our teachers gave her and I some directions.
13. First, Leah and I prepared a clay model.
14. Then the teachers asked us to prepare a mold.
15. When unmolding time came, them and us held our breath.
16. The most delighted were her and I!

(pages 312–314)

4 Interrogative Pronouns

- Interrogative pronouns like *who, which, what, whom,* and *whose* ask questions.
- Use *who* as a subject, *whom* as an object, and *whose* as a possessive.
- Do not confuse the pronoun *whose* with the contraction *who's.*

● Write the interrogative pronoun in each sentence.

Example: Who is writing a story? *Who*

1. Who likes mystery stories?
2. Whom did the witness see clearly?
3. Who stole the diamond necklace?
4. Who's hiding something under a newspaper?
5. Whose was the emerald necklace?
6. Whom did the police arrest?
7. What happens next?

▲ Rewrite each sentence, using the correct interrogative pronoun or contraction.

Example: (Who, Whom) knows the answer to this question?
Who knows the answer to this question?

8. (Who, Whom) in the story did you suspect?
9. (Who, Whom) did you like?
10. (Whose, Who's) was the better ending?
11. (Who, Whom) guessed the ending?
12. (Who's, Whose) going to write the next mystery story?
13. (Who, Whom) will be the victim?
14. (Who, Whom) will you make the guilty person?

■ Rewrite each incorrect sentence. If a sentence has no errors, write *correct.*

Example: Whose your favorite mystery writer?
Who's your favorite mystery writer?

15. Whom has heard of the writer Agatha Christie?
16. Whom has been able to guess any of the endings?
17. Whom has read the whole book?
18. Who thought it was exciting and surprising?
19. Whose going to see the play made from that book?
20. Who does the play have as its star?

(pages 315–317)

5 Demonstrative Pronouns

- A **demonstrative pronoun** points out something.
- *This* and *that* refer to singular nouns or pronouns.
- *These* and *those* refer to plural nouns or pronouns.
- *This* and *these* point out things that are close.
- *That* and *those* point out things that are farther away.

● Write the demonstrative pronoun in each sentence.

Example: This is an interesting museum. *This*

1. That is a beaver.
2. Those are large front teeth!
3. These are its kits over here.
4. Those are waterproof coats on the kits.
5. This is its den right here, with its underwater entrance.
6. These are the logs it cut with its strong teeth.

▲ Write each sentence, using the correct demonstrative pronoun. Underline the word that it points out.

Example: (Those, Those there) are striped tree squirrels.
    Those are striped tree squirrels.

7. (This here, This) is a very young squirrel.
8. (This, These) are very industrious animals.
9. (This, These) is a picture of flying squirrels.
10. Isn't (that, that there) a very bushy tail on that squirrel?
11. Is (this, that) its nest in the elm tree over there?
12. (This, That) is its pile of nuts and seeds right here.

■ Write each sentence, using a correct demonstrative pronoun. Underline the word that it points out.

Example: Is _____ a molehill over there? *Is that a molehill over there?*

13. _____ is a strange-looking creature in the far corner.
14. _____ are very tiny eyes it has.
15. _____ is a very impressive tunnel down there.
16. Is _____ the place where the mole lives over there?
17. _____ are earthworms, beetles, and slugs here!
18. _____ is the diet of the well-fed mole.

(pages 318–322)

⑥ Indefinite Pronouns

Remember

- An **indefinite pronoun** does not refer to a specific person or thing.
- Verbs must agree in number with indefinite pronouns used as subjects. Pronouns must agree with indefinite pronouns used as antecedents.

● Write each sentence. Use the word in parentheses that agrees with the underlined indefinite pronoun.

Example: Somebody in our family (is, are) flying to England today.
Somebody in our family is flying to England today.

1. Everybody (is, are) happy for Terry.
2. Many of us (is, are) going to the airport with him.
3. Nobody in the family (has, have) been to England before.
4. Several (has, have) relatives in the city of London.
5. Most of us would like to visit (his, our) London relatives.
6. All of the trip (has, have) been carefully planned.

▲ Write each sentence correctly. Underline each indefinite pronoun and the form that agrees with it.

Example: Everybody in London (seems, seem) to be in a hurry.
Everybody in London seems to be in a hurry.

7. Everyone in the tour group (has, have) boarded a special bus.
8. Does everybody have (his or her, their) camera ready?
9. Most of the city (is, are) filled with traffic.
10. Few of the streets of the city (is, are) empty.
11. None of the people on the bus (seems, seem) to mind, however.

■ Rewrite each incorrect sentence. If a sentence has no errors, write *correct.*

Example: Most of the passengers have fastened his seat belts.
Most of the passengers have fastened their seat belts.

12. Everybody in the aisles are being directed toward a seat.
13. Several of the passengers are tucking their hand luggage away.
14. Others still hasn't finished reading the instructions.
15. Some of the seats is leaning back and must be straightened.
16. Most of the work have now been done.

(pages 323–326)

7 Reflexive and Intensive Pronouns

Remember

- A **reflexive pronoun** ends in -*self* or -*selves* and refers to the subject of the sentence. It generally cannot be left out of the sentence.
- An **intensive pronoun** ends in -*self* or -*selves* and emphasizes another word in the sentence.
- Avoid using pronouns with -*self* or -*selves* as personal pronouns.

● Write each sentence, using the correct pronoun.

Example: Should David paint his room (hisself, himself)?
  Should David paint his room himself?

1. He asked (hisself, himself) whether he could do it.
2. Then he asked if I could help (him, himself).
3. We bought (us, ourselves) paint and rollers.
4. David and (I, myself) just had to mix the paint.
5. David wanted to do the ceilings (himself, hisself).
6. He finished and handed (myself, me) the roller.

▲ Write each sentence, using the correct pronoun. Underline its antecedent.

Example: Mr. Best taught (hisself, himself) to braid rugs.
  Mr. Best taught himself to braid rugs.

7. Mr. and Mrs. Best made (theirselves, themselves) two rugs.
8. Jim and I had planned to buy (us, ourselves) a rug.
9. Mr. Best taught Jim and (me, myself) to make one instead.
10. I found (me, myself) surrounded by strips of fabric.
11. I divided the strips (theirselves, themselves) into groups of three.
12. In a few weeks, Jim and I had made (us, ourselves) a rug.

■ Write each sentence, using a reflexive or intensive pronoun. Label the pronouns *reflexive* or *intensive,* and underline their antecedents.

Example: Pam and Jack were cooking dinner _____.
  Pam and Jack were cooking dinner themselves. intensive

13. First they decided to make _____ a big salad.
14. Pam cut the cucumbers and green peppers _____.
15. Then they cooked _____ some delicious lasagna.
16. We helped _____ to seconds on everything.

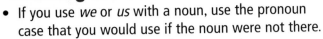

(pages 327–329)

⑧ Choosing the Correct Pronoun

Remember

- If you use *we* or *us* with a noun, use the pronoun case that you would use if the noun were not there.
- To decide which pronoun form to use in an incomplete comparison, add words to complete the comparison.

● Write each sentence with the correct pronoun.

Example: Mrs. Davis showed (we, us) students an old viola.
Mrs. Davis showed us students an old viola.

1. (We, Us) students all asked the age of the instrument.
2. The answer surprised (we, us) eighth graders.
3. It was over two hundred years older than (we, us) students.
4. Mrs. Davis told (we, us) curious students to think of an Italian name.
5. Brad came up with an answer sooner than (I, me).
6. "The name begins with *S*," Brad told (we, us) slowpokes.

▲ Rewrite each sentence, correcting pronoun errors.

Example: Us students tried to guess who made the viola.
We students tried to guess who made the viola.

7. Brad gave we students a good clue.
8. "His nickname rhymes with mine, but he is more famous than me."
9. Brad gave we classmates another clue.
10. He told we slowpokes that the name ends in *i*.
11. Us brave students named Stradivari.
12. Stradivari was not the maker.

■ Write each sentence with the correct pronoun.

Example: _____ students had not heard of Lorenzo Storione.
We students had not heard of Lorenzo Storione.

13. An Italian like Stradivari, Storione was born a century later than _____.
14. Then Mrs. Davis showed _____ musicians her own viola.
15. _____ students compared it with the Storione.
16. Brad and she played. He plays as well as _____.
17. Mrs. Davis asked _____ students to guess the age of her viola.
18. We guessed that it was older than _____.

Are the fish biting in this
part of the lake?

Phrases

Prepositional Phrases

Make up one or two sentences describing what is about to happen in the picture. Use three of these words: *across, onto, into, by, beside,* and *over.*

A **preposition** is a word that shows the relationship between a noun or a pronoun and another word in a sentence. Some prepositions are made up of more than one word. Different prepositions convey different meanings.

My friend Elena sings in the opera house.

My friend Elena sings near the opera house.

My friend Elena sings outside the opera house.

My friend Elena sings behind the opera house.

Common Prepositions			
about	beneath	in place of	over
above	beside	inside	past
according to	besides	in spite of	since
across	between	instead of	through
after	beyond	into	throughout
against	but	like	to
along	by	near	toward
among	despite	next to	under
around	down	of	underneath
as	during	off	until
aside from	except	on	unto
at	for	on account of	up
because of	from	onto	upon
before	in	out	with
behind	in back of	out of	within
below	in front of	outside	without

1. In a sentence a preposition is always followed by a word called the **object of the preposition**. The object may have one or more modifiers.

The opera will be performed on a large stage.

2. A preposition followed by more than one object has a **compound object of the preposition**.

> Between City Hall and the library is the opera house.

3. A preposition, its object or objects, and any modifiers form a **prepositional phrase**. A phrase is a group of words that functions as a single unit.

> Elena sang the high notes with ease.

Many sentences have more than one prepositional phrase. Each phrase includes a preposition and its object or objects along with any other accompanying words.

> During the performance, we sat in back of Paul.
> At the end of the opera, people in the audience cheered.

4. When the object of a preposition is a pronoun, you must be careful always to use the objective case.

> Sheila attended the opera with them and me.

5. You may have noticed that many prepositions are words that can also function as adverbs. Remember that a preposition always has an object. An adverb does not have an object.

Preposition:	We went inside the opera house.
Adverb:	We went inside.

Try It Out

Speak Up What are the prepositional phrases in these sentences? Identify each preposition and each object.

1. One opera by Richard Wagner is based on legends from earlier centuries.
2. The name of this famous opera is *Lohengrin*.
3. The events of the complicated plot take place in the tenth century.
4. During the first act, a boat drawn by a swan comes into view.
5. According to legend, a marriage takes place between a knight and a princess.
6. The famous melody of the "Wedding March" from this opera is often played at weddings.

more ▶

Choose the correct pronoun to complete each sentence.

7. That hit play was written by (she, her).
8. Between you and (I, me), I found the plot confusing.
9. Instead of (he, him), Alan Ellis played the lead.
10. Without the efforts of you and (they, them), this play would not have been so successful.

Summing Up

- A **preposition** is a word that shows the relationship between a noun or a pronoun and another word in a sentence.

- A **prepositional phrase** includes a preposition, its object or objects, and all of the modifiers of the object.

- When a pronoun is the object of a preposition, use the objective case.

On Your Own

Write each prepositional phrase. Underline the preposition once and its object or objects twice.

Example: Stravinsky was known as a composer of great ballet music.
    as a composer   *of great ballet music*

11. Igor Stravinsky, the composer, was born in Russia but left before the beginning of World War I.
12. He lived in France for many years, and then he moved to the United States in 1939.
13. Some of his scores were based on Russian legends.
14. He first gained fame with his music for *The Firebird*.
15. It tells about the capture of a fantastic bird by a prince.
16. Through the gratitude of the firebird, the prince wins a battle and gains the love of a princess.

more ▶

17. Stravinsky often depended on Russian folklore for the themes in his early music.
18. Later he became well-known as a composer of very modern music.

19–25. There are seven pronoun errors in this diary entry. Write the entry correctly.

Example: Could there ever be a ballet about my brother and I?
Could there ever be a ballet about my brother and me?

Proofreading

The Nutcracker

December 21

Tonight our aunts went with Darryl and I to see <u>The Nutcracker</u>, a ballet with music by Tchaikovsky. It was a first for he and I. To our aunts and I the dancing and music were marvelous. Darryl was fidgety at first, but soon the costumes and the story appealed to he also. In the story—at a holiday party with candy, toys, and dancing dolls—a sister and brother quarrel (what else is new?) over a nutcracker given to her by a magician. Late at night the sister, Clara, comes downstairs to find fierce mice attacking and the nutcracker leading the toy soldiers in battle against they and their king. With Clara's help the toy soldiers finally win, the nutcracker changes into a prince, and the Sugarplum Fairy dances before he and Clara.

Writing Wrap-Up

WRITING • THINKING • LISTENING • SPEAKING

CREATING

Retell a Legend

Write a brief story, retelling in a modern setting a legend, myth, or fairy tale that you know. Include prepositional phrases. With a small group, read your stories aloud and identify prepositional phrases you used. Discuss what you liked best about each story.

2 Prepositional Phrases as Modifiers

Look at the picture. Then use the following words to continue the directions given below: *until, next to, on, over,* and *beyond.*

To get to the pond, continue on this road for about two miles . . .

You know that a phrase is a group of words used as a single unit. Prepositional phrases always act as modifiers.

1. A prepositional phrase that modifies a noun or pronoun is an **adjective phrase**. It tells *which, what kind,* or *how many.*

   Go to the beach near the road.

   One of the lifeguards from the town will be there.

2. A prepositional phrase that modifies a verb, an adjective, or an adverb is an **adverb phrase.** An adverb phrase tells *how, when, where,* or *to what extent.*

   We went on the ferry. They met us later in the afternoon.

3. You may use prepositional phrases either before or after the words they modify as long as the meaning of the sentence is clear. Sometimes another word or phrase comes between the modified word and the prepositional phrase.

   The lone runner jogged steadily along the deserted beach.

   For years people worked hard on fishing boats.

4. To be clear, you should always place an adjective phrase next to the word it modifies. Place an adverb phrase as close as possible to the word or words it modifies, or place it at the beginning or end of the sentence.

   Unclear: A man rescued a dog in a rowboat. (Who was in the rowboat?)

   Clear: A man in a rowboat rescued a dog.

Speak Up Find each adjective phrase. What does it modify?

1. A cape is a point of land.
2. Cape Cod in Massachusetts has the shape of a hook.
3. Beaches for swimmers and sunbathers attract visitors.
4. Cod is a kind of local fish.

Find each adverb phrase. What does it modify?

5. By the early summer, Cape Cod is full of visitors.
6. Each year, many foreign tourists come to Cape Cod.
7. In early times, Norsemen may have fished near Cape Cod.
8. An Englishman first sailed around Cape Cod in 1602.

Summing Up

- Prepositional phrases always function as modifiers.
- **Adjective phrases** modify nouns or pronouns.
- **Adverb phrases** modify verbs, adjectives, or adverbs.

Write each adverb phrase. Then write the word or words it modifies.

Example: Martha's Vineyard is not far from Cape Cod.
  from Cape Cod   far

9. The island was discovered in 1602 and claimed by New York.
10. After some years it was given to Massachusetts.
11. Famous authors come to the island for peace and quiet.

more ▶

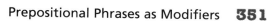

12. Many people travel to Martha's Vineyard from the mainland in the summer.
13. Because of the weather, few people visit the island during the cold months of winter.
14. You can reach the island only by boat or plane.

15-26. Write this part of a travel brochure. It contains twelve adjective phrases. Underline each one and draw an arrow to the noun or pronoun it modifies. Do not underline adverb phrases.

Example: In winter, islanders enjoy the calm of the island.

In winter, islanders enjoy the calm <u>of the island</u>.

Martha's Vineyard

The island of Martha's Vineyard is located near the mainland of Cape Cod. Its permanent population of around fourteen thousand is increased in summer by thousands of tourists. Many visitors rent cottages on the beaches or in the towns. Your ferry to the island may land at the charming town of Vineyard Haven. At Edgartown you can find traces of the whaling and fishing industries of past centuries. Don't miss the long view of the sea from the multicolored cliffs.

Writing Wrap-Up

WRITING • THINKING • LISTENING • SPEAKING

DESCRIBING

Write a Guidebook Description

Write a paragraph for a guidebook describing a beautiful or interesting place you know about, either local or far away. Use at least five prepositional phrases. Find a partner and read your descriptions to each other. Then exchange papers and underline the adjective phrases once and the adverb phrases twice.

For Extra Practice see page 387.

Writing with Prepositional Phrases

Combining Sentences: Prepositional Phrases Sometimes you can improve the flow of your writing by using prepositional phrases to combine related sentences.

I took a trip.
I went to my aunt's house.
My aunt lives in Corpus Christi, Texas. }

I took a trip
to my aunt's house
in Corpus Christi, Texas.

To avoid writing unclear sentences, place a prepositional phrase as close as possible to the word or words it modifies.

Does the party really take place on horseback?

Unclear

My cousins and I rode on horseback. }

My cousins and I rode to my aunt's house for a party on horseback.

Clear

We rode to my aunt's house.

My cousins and I rode on horseback to my aunt's house for a party.

We were going for a party. }

On horseback, my cousins and I rode to my aunt's house for a party.

Apply It

1–5. Revise these descriptions for a student's scrapbook. Use prepositional phrases to combine sentences.

Revising

My cousins and I are standing near the USS Lexington. The USS *Lexington* is in Corpus Christi, Texas. We walked around to look at the ship. We read the plaques. The plaques tell about the ship's battles. The battles took place during World War II.

We went to the Texas State Aquarium. We went there for the afternoon. We learned about marine conservation. The aquarium featured many exhibits. The exhibits of fish were in huge tanks. Many of these creatures are native to the Gulf of Mexico. We could look at jellyfish. We could look at sharks. We could see them through the glass.

more

Elaborating Sentences Prepositional phrases can add information to sentences. You can elaborate your sentences with prepositional phrases that act as adjectives and adverbs.

> Every morning, sea lions appear.
>
> Every morning, sea lions appear on the floating docks at Fisherman's Wharf.
>
> Children watch the sea lions playing.
>
> Children on the pier watch the sea lions playing in the water.

Avoid writing silly sentences—place prepositional phrases correctly.

Silly
My brother saw wax figures of famous people in a museum in costume.

Better
In a museum my brother saw wax figures of famous people in costume.

Apply It

6–12. Rewrite this part of a letter. Elaborate the underlined sentences by adding prepositional phrases. Use the picture and your imagination to supply details.

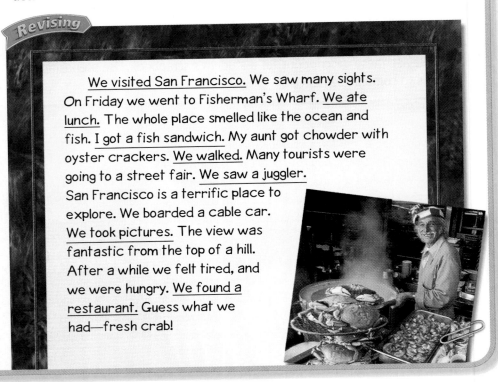

Revising

We visited San Francisco. We saw many sights. On Friday we went to Fisherman's Wharf. We ate lunch. The whole place smelled like the ocean and fish. I got a fish sandwich. My aunt got chowder with oyster crackers. We walked. Many tourists were going to a street fair. We saw a juggler. San Francisco is a terrific place to explore. We boarded a cable car. We took pictures. The view was fantastic from the top of a hill. After a while we felt tired, and we were hungry. We found a restaurant. Guess what we had—fresh crab!

3 Choosing Correct Prepositions

What is wrong with these sentences? How can you fix them?

> Beside Ralph, no one was willing to dress up as the chicken mascot, and Ralph was too big to fit into the costume. Finally, the production manager said, "Among Juan and Julie, I want one of you to volunteer to dress up as the chicken."

Choosing *between* or *among*

Many people confuse the prepositions *between* and *among*. When the object of the preposition refers to two people, things, or groups, use *between*. When it refers to more than two, use *among*.

The lines were divided between the actor and the actress.

The lines were divided among the six cast members.

Relations between the actors and the producers were good.

Relations among the entire crew were good.

Try It Out

Speak Up Which preposition correctly completes each sentence?

Oklahoma!

1. The school drama club decided on one musical (among, between) many different shows.
2. The final choice was (among, between) the two most popular shows, *Oklahoma!* and *Carousel*.
3. Similarities exist (among, between) the two musicals; both were written by Rodgers and Hammerstein.
4. An agreement about the show was reached (among, between) the club members.
5. The production duties from now on will be split (among, between) the director and the stage manager.

Using beside and besides

The prepositions *beside* and *besides* have different meanings. *Beside* means "next to."

> Please come sit beside me.
> I always keep a book beside my pillow.

Besides means "in addition to" or "except for."

> Is anyone besides Jeff going skating?
> Besides my sisters, I've invited three friends.

Try It Out

Speak Up Which preposition correctly completes each sentence?

Rodgers (left) and Hammerstein

6. A book on the Rodgers and Hammerstein musicals lies (beside, besides) my lamp.
7. (Beside, Besides) this book I have read nothing today.
8. Few popular composers deserve a place (beside, besides) them.
9. They wrote many musicals (beside, besides) *Carousel.*
10. (Beside, Besides) musicals, Rodgers wrote music for a TV show.
11. Who (beside, besides) Oscar Hammerstein composed musicals with Richard Rodgers?
12. (Beside, Besides) Hammerstein, a man named Lorenz Hart worked with Rodgers.

Summing Up

- Use *between* with two persons, things, or groups.
- Use *among* with more than two persons, things, or groups.
- Use *beside* to mean "next to."
- Use *besides* to mean "in addition to" or "except for."

13–20. Write each sentence in this part of an interview correctly. Eight prepositions are incorrect.

Example: "Put the comfortable chair besides me for our guest, please."
"Put the comfortable chair beside me for our guest, please."

Proofreading

Music

Interviewer: Between all the shows you have starred in, which was your favorite?

Broadway star: *My Fair Lady* and *Gigi* were my two favorites—I really can't choose among them.

Interviewer: Beside Richard Rodgers, do you like any other Broadway composers?

Broadway star: Lerner and Loewe, who wrote *Camelot*, are between my other favorites.

Interviewer: Beside you, I have never interviewed a star of musicals who once sang in operas. Do you have a preference among the musical and the opera?

Broadway star: Does anyone on Broadway beside me prefer opera? Just between you and me, I would rather attend an opera than any other musical performance. I keep tapes of great opera performances on the shelf right besides my favorite current recordings.

Writing Wrap-Up   WRITING • THINKING • LISTENING • SPEAKING

COMPARING / CONTRASTING

Write a Review

Write a movie or concert review in which you compare and contrast the work of two actors or musicians. Use *among, beside, besides,* and *between* at least once in your review. In a small group, read your review aloud. Then discuss the strong points of one another's work. Check that prepositions were used correctly.

4 Verbals: Participles

Find all of the adjectives in the sentence below.

Most teams agree that a crowded mountain is a dangerous mountain.

—from *Within Reach: My Everest Story,* by Mark Pfetzer and Jack Galvin

You know that verbs tell what the subject of a sentence does or is. You can use certain forms of verbs in another way, too, as verbals. A **verbal** is a word that is formed from a verb but is used as an adjective, a noun, or an adverb.

There are three kinds of verbals: participles, gerunds, and infinitives. Notice how forms of the verb *climb* are used as verbals in these sentences.

Participle: Pat's climbing friends get together regularly. (adjective)

Gerund: Climbing is Pat's hobby. (noun)

Infinitive: She is happy to climb all day long. (adverb)

1. A **participle** is a verb form used as an adjective. You have learned about the principal parts of verbs. You can use the present participle and the past participle forms as verbals.

Verb	Present Participle	Past Participle
climb	climbing	climbed
burst	bursting	burst
pay	paying	paid
think	thinking	thought
spring	springing	sprung
break	breaking	broken
know	knowing	known
take	taking	taken

2. Since participles act as adjectives, they modify nouns or pronouns.

The blinding storm kept the climbers indoors for several more days.

The trained guide went out into the snow.

His forgotten pick lay on the table.

A participle can come either before or after the noun or pronoun that it modifies.

Chilled and exhausted, most of the climbers returned home after an hour on the mountain.

Those remaining left shortly afterwards.

Try It Out

Speak Up What is the participle in each sentence? Which word does it modify?

1. A challenging mountain offers excitement to a climber.
2. Experienced climbers look for new mountains to climb.
3. Spiked boots are one necessary piece of equipment.
4. Climbers also use ropes, axes, and specialized tools.
5. Good climbers, tiring, will rest where they can.
6. Those resting will check their equipment and their route.
7. Returning groups of climbers carefully unpack and examine their gear.
8. Climbers who find damaged equipment must repair or replace such gear.

Summing Up

- A **verbal** is a word that is formed from a verb but used as an adjective, a noun, or an adverb.
- A **participle** is a verbal that is used as an adjective. You can use the present participle or past participle form of a verb as a verbal.

9–20. Write the twelve participles in this part of a mountain-climbing guidebook. Then write the words they modify.

Example: Among the leading areas for climbs in the United States are Mount Rainier and the Rocky Mountains. *leading   areas*

Some mountains challenge even skilled climbers. Although most mountain climbers follow carefully mapped routes, still the climbers must anticipate disturbing events. Climbers sometimes confront falling rocks or blocked paths.

Prepared mountain climbers generally have safer and more successful outings. Less experienced climbers are often forced to turn back before reaching their destinations.

Those climbing require special gear, such as rope to tie themselves together and special boots to help them move securely on rocks or ice. Most climbers carry backpacks loaded with dried food and other supplies. Their backpacks also contain emergency medical supplies. Climbers on long trips may even carry flares. Forgotten or broken equipment can bring a climb to a sudden halt.

Writing Wrap-Up
WRITING • THINKING • LISTENING • SPEAKING

EXPLAINING

Write Instructions

Write a paragraph or a list of instructions explaining how to do something—anything you know about. How do you build a campfire? How do you wash a dog? Can you explain how to make pancakes or scan photographs into a computer? Use several participles in your instructions. Underline the participles and circle the words they modify. With a small group, take turns reading your instructions aloud and discussing them.

For Extra Practice see page 389.

5 Participial Phrases

What is wrong with this sentence? How can you fix it?

Blinking, buzzing, and beeping wildly, the inventor tried to repair the computer.

Sometimes a participle is accompanied by other words that complete its meaning.

Amazed by his success, the scientist continued his work.

1. A participle and its accompanying words make up a **participial phrase**. A participial phrase, like a participle alone, modifies a noun or a pronoun.

   Sitting in his office, he reread the instructions.

2. The words that complete a participial phrase may be one or more prepositional phrases.

   Thomas Edison, experimenting with different materials in his laboratory, eventually improved the light bulb.

   A participial phrase may contain a direct object, and it may contain an adverb that modifies the participle.

   participle DO
   Fearing failure, the scientist almost abandoned his work.

   adverb participle DO
   Then, steadily gaining confidence, he succeeded.

3. You will not confuse the main verb of a sentence with a participial phrase as long as you first identify the subject and the simple predicate of the sentence.

   subject simple predicate   DO   participial phrase
   The crowd was watching the inventor testing his new creation.

4. A participial phrase may come before or after the word it modifies. If too many words come between the participle and the word it modifies, however, the meaning becomes unclear.

   Misplaced: John created a robot experimenting in his lab. (Who was experimenting, the robot or John?)

   To be clear, place a participial phrase near the word it modifies.

   Correct: Experimenting in his lab, John created a robot.

5. Use a comma after a participial phrase that introduces a sentence. Also use commas to set off a participial phrase following the subject if the phrase is not necessary to the meaning of the sentence.

> Struck by joy, Dee laughed.   Dan, waving good-bye, drove away.

Try It Out

Speak Up Identify each participial phrase. Which word does it modify?

1. How could someone photograph objects moving rapidly?
2. In the 1870s this was a serious question facing inventors.
3. Meeting the challenge, one photographer found a solution.
4. The photographer and his assistants worked with twenty-four cameras neatly arranged in a row along a racetrack.
5. Running past the row of loaded cameras, a horse caused each camera to shoot a picture.
6. For the first time, people saw something moving in a picture.

Summing Up

- A **participial phrase** is made up of a participle and its accompanying words.
- Participial phrases may contain direct objects, prepositional phrases, and adverbs.

On Your Own

Write each sentence. Underline each participial phrase and double-underline the word it modifies. Add commas as needed.

Example: The tin can invented in 1812 kept food from spoiling.
> *The tin <u>can</u>, <u>invented in 1812</u>, kept food from spoiling.*

7. In the Civil War, food sealed in cans was given to soldiers.
8. Troops in the hot South could now eat totally unspoiled food.

more ▶

9. Pork and beans canned in tomato sauce became a popular meal among the soldiers.
10. Many soldiers returning from war asked local shopkeepers for canned food.
11. Canning everything from milk to cherries canners were selling thirty million cans a year by 1870.
12. Inventors noting the success of the tin can turned to other methods of food preservation.

13–16. Write each sentence in this part of a documentary script. Move the four misplaced participial phrases close to the words they modify. Add or delete commas where necessary.

Example: Experimenting with frozen meat in 1626, history actually records one early inventor.

History actually records one early inventor experimenting with frozen meat in 1626.

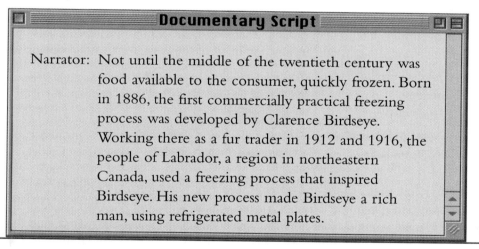

Documentary Script

Narrator: Not until the middle of the twentieth century was food available to the consumer, quickly frozen. Born in 1886, the first commercially practical freezing process was developed by Clarence Birdseye. Working there as a fur trader in 1912 and 1916, the people of Labrador, a region in northeastern Canada, used a freezing process that inspired Birdseye. His new process made Birdseye a rich man, using refrigerated metal plates.

Writing Wrap-Up

WRITING • THINKING • LISTENING • SPEAKING

INFORMING

Write a News Article

What real or imaginary invention would you like to see developed? Write the opening paragraph for a newspaper report on such an invention. Include some participial phrases. Volunteers can read their paragraphs aloud to the class. Then exchange papers with a partner. Underline the participial phrases and the words they modify.

6 Verbals: Gerunds

One-Minute Warm-Up

Find all of the nouns in the sentence below.

High prices have prevented some fans from collecting.

—from *Collecting Baseball Memorabilia,* by Thomas S. Owens

You have learned that a participle is one kind of verbal. Another kind of verbal is a gerund.

Bowling is a very old sport.

Gardening is a satisfying hobby.

Collecting baseball cards can be a lucrative pastime.

1. A **gerund** is the present participle of a verb (the -*ing* form) used as a noun. In a sentence a gerund can function in all of the ways that a noun does. Here are some examples.

Subject:	Reading is my favorite activity.
Direct Object:	I enjoy reading.
Object of Preposition:	Today is a good day for reading.
Predicate Noun:	My favorite activity is reading.

2. You know that a word ending with -*ing* might be a verb, a participle, or a gerund. To determine whether a word ending with -*ing* is a verb, participle, or gerund, you must see how the word is used in the sentence. First, find the simple subject and the simple predicate. They will help you to know whether a word is a gerund.

Cora and Andy are running in tomorrow's big race. (*Running* is part of the verb phrase *are running.*)

The running water overflowed. (*Running* is a participle here, modifying the subject *water.*)

Running is both a fun and healthful exercise. (*Running* is the subject of this sentence. It is a gerund.)

Speak Up Find each gerund in these sentences. Is it used as a subject, a direct object, an object of a preposition, or a predicate noun? Some sentences have no gerund.

1. Sketching is fun for me.
2. Marya exercises every day by swimming.
3. Her other leisure activity is painting.
4. She and I are singing in the chorus tonight.
5. Of all my interests, I care most about reading.
6. Traveling comes second or third on my list of favorites.
7. What is the most interesting hobby for you?

Summing Up

- A **gerund** is the present participle of a verb used as a noun.
- A gerund functions in all of the ways that a noun does.

Write each sentence. Underline the gerunds. Then write *subject, direct object, object of a preposition*, or *predicate noun* to tell how each gerund is used. Write *none* if a sentence does not have a gerund.

Example: Walking and running are Harris's favorite outdoor activities.
  Walking and *running* are Harris's favorite outdoor activities.
  subjects

8. A hobby can be anything from fishing to painting.
9. Few things are better for relaxing than a satisfying hobby.
10. Some people enjoy gardening whereas others prefer reading.
11. Gardening gloves protect the hands of those who do yard work.
12. Many people find pleasure in painting, sculpting, or carving.
13. Practical hobbies include sewing, building, and cooking.
14. Skating, skiing, and swimming are some healthful hobbies. **more ▶**

15. Reading about faraway places is satisfying to many people.
16. People of all ages relax and get in shape by jogging.
17. In fact, running has become a hobby as much as an exercise.
18. Winston Churchill, a former Prime Minister of Great Britain, liked painting and writing.
19. Collecting was President Franklin D. Roosevelt's hobby, and he acquired an amazing stamp collection.
20. President Dwight D. Eisenhower's favorite kind of exercise was golfing.

21–28. The sentences in this bulletin board notice contain eight gerunds. Write each gerund, and then write *subject*, *direct object*, *object of a preposition*, or *predicate noun* to tell how each gerund is used.

Example: Sledding is my only winter sport. *Sledding—subject*

ACTIVITIES

Winter Sports Club Meeting

Find out about the club by coming to the library on Friday at 4:00 P.M. Welcoming new members is our favorite activity, so don't be shy.

Next Saturday our sports will be skating, sledding, and skiing at Prospect Park. Afterward, at the lodge, refreshments will be served, and music for dancing will follow. We enjoy tobogganing, too, and will schedule a trip to Blackbird Hill in the near future. Planning is part of the fun, so be there on Friday to share it.

Writing Wrap-Up

WRITING • THINKING • LISTENING • SPEAKING

PERSUADING

Write an E-Mail Message

Write an e-mail message to persuade a friend to participate in your favorite sport or hobby. Use several gerunds. With a partner, read your message aloud. How persuasive is your message? Then, identify the gerunds and tell how each is used.

7 Gerund Phrases

Find the two sentences with errors.

Jake hates my singing.
Jake hates me singing.
Anna loves my guitar.
Anna loves me guitar.

Gerund Phrases in Sentences

1. Like a participle, a gerund can sometimes be accompanied by other words that complete its meaning. A **gerund phrase** consists of a gerund accompanied by an adjective, an adverb, a direct object, or a prepositional phrase.

   Wearing tight shoes hurts. (gerund + direct object)
   Long-distance running is fun. (adjective + gerund)
   I like dancing on ice. (gerund + prepositional phrase)
   Performing alone is his dream. (gerund + adverb)

2. Gerund phrases, like gerunds alone, function as nouns in sentences. Like a noun, a gerund phrase can be a subject, a direct object, an object of a preposition, or a predicate noun.

Subject:	Preparing for a concert takes time.
Direct Object:	Lane began practicing his flute.
Object of Preposition:	Before playing the music , he studied it.
Predicate Noun:	His big challenge was walking onstage.

3. Be careful not to confuse a gerund phrase with a participial phrase. If the phrase functions as a subject, an object, or a predicate noun in the sentence, it is a gerund phrase. If it serves as an adjective, it is a participial phrase.

Gerund Phrase:	Singing softly was difficult. (subject)
Participial Phrase:	Singing softly, he calmed the baby.
Gerund Phrase:	We began singing the song. (direct object)
Participial Phrase:	The girl singing the song is Pat.

Speak Up Identify each gerund phrase and participial phrase. Does each gerund phrase act as a subject, a direct object, an object of a preposition, or a predicate noun?

1. Singing opera, they use their voices in special ways.
2. Bart received the prize for being the best tenor.
3. Being the best tenor, Bart had many solo parts.
4. You should try singing high C.
5. Humming in the background, the chorus set a mood.
6. Appearing with a professional cast was Kristen's dream.
7. Facing the audience can be the hardest part.
8. Practicing day and night is a necessary ingredient for succeeding as an opera singer.
9. Taking their seats, the members of the orchestra began tuning their instruments.
10. Accompanying the singer, the violin section slowly played the tragic melody.

Possessives in Gerund Phrases

1. Sometimes a noun or a pronoun comes before a gerund.

   Michael's leaving is a disappointment.

   I can't imagine his going away.

2. Always use the possessive form of a noun or pronoun before a gerund.

   Because of Roger's being the director, our class play was very successful.

   His directing is unequaled.

3. When you are in doubt about which form to use before a gerund, substitute another noun for the gerund. You know that you need to use a possessive form before a noun. Because a gerund functions as a noun, only a possessive form is correct before a gerund, as well.

   Because of Roger's skill, our class play was very successful.

   His talent is unequaled.

Speak Up Which word correctly precedes the gerund phrase in each sentence?

11. I warned Gino about (them, their) being late.
12. I don't appreciate (him, his) talking back to me.
13. (Fran, Fran's) leaving will solve the problem.
14. (Me, My) being there was a help.
15. That ended (Martha, Martha's) disrupting the rehearsals.
16. We are delighted by (Joe, Joe's) sensitive acting.
17. (Him, His) continuing with the show is essential to its success.
18. (Us, Our) agreeing on how the other minor roles should be handled was also important.

Summing Up

- A **gerund phrase** can be a subject, a direct object, an object of a preposition, or a predicate noun.

- Use a possessive noun or a possessive pronoun before a gerund.

Write each gerund phrase and underline the gerund. Then write how the gerund is used in the sentence: *subject, direct object, object of a preposition,* or *predicate noun.*

Example: A program for helping young artists has begun.
helping young artists—object of a preposition

19. The program's goal is providing students with a variety of artistic opportunities.
20. Few question the benefits of encouraging talent.
21. The problem is obtaining the necessary money.
22. People find different ways of raising funds.
23. Asking for funds is an important activity.

more ▶

24. Supporters must continue advertising the program.
25. Now the group will try campaigning on a large scale.
26. Starting such a campaign is a challenging task.
27. Requesting funds and other forms of assistance from large corporations will be the first strategy.
28. Contacting firms is the director's role.
29. Companies find different ways of being helpful.
30. Helping young artists is a worthwhile cause.

31–36. Write the sentences in this journal entry, correcting the six errors in nouns and pronouns used with gerunds.

Example: Them holding the meeting was for a special purpose.
Their holding the meeting was for a special purpose.

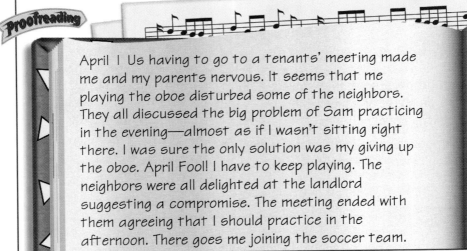

Proofreading

April 1 Us having to go to a tenants' meeting made me and my parents nervous. It seems that me playing the oboe disturbed some of the neighbors. They all discussed the big problem of Sam practicing in the evening—almost as if I wasn't sitting right there. I was sure the only solution was my giving up the oboe. April Fool! I have to keep playing. The neighbors were all delighted at the landlord suggesting a compromise. The meeting ended with them agreeing that I should practice in the afternoon. There goes me joining the soccer team.

Writing Wrap-Up   WRITING • THINKING • LISTENING • SPEAKING

INFORMING

Write an Advice Column

Give advice to a teenager who has to perform in a play and has stage fright. Use some gerund phrases in your sentences. Include a possessive noun or a possessive pronoun before the gerund in at least one sentence. In a group of three, read your advice columns aloud. Who gave the most useful advice? Then check that gerund phrases were used correctly.

For Extra Practice see page 392.

Writing with Participial and Gerund Phrases

Combining Sentences: Participial Phrases

To make your writing more interesting, vary the length of your sentences. You can use participial phrases to combine short sentences into longer, more engaging ones.

> When a participial phrase begins a sentence, set it off with a comma.

Participial phrases function as adjectives.

I could hear Della.
She was practicing the violin.
I was listening from my room.

Listening from my room, I could hear Della practicing the violin.

When you combine sentences, place a participial phrase as close as possible to the word or words that it modifies. Putting the phrase in the wrong place can make your meaning unclear.

Mike was playing a trumpet solo.
The audience was impressed.

Unclear
Playing a trumpet solo, the audience was impressed by Mike.

Clear and Smooth
Playing a trumpet solo, Mike impressed the audience.

Apply It

1–5. Rewrite this draft of a concert announcement. Combine each set of underlined sentences by using participial phrases.

Revising

Come to the spring concert. <u>The student musicians will amaze you. They will be playing violins, violas, cellos, and basses.</u>

<u>Drama club students will be ushers. The drama club students will be wearing green T-shirts.</u> Arrive early! <u>A few latecomers were not happy last year. They were turned away at the door.</u> We ran out of room!

The concert will cap a great school year. <u>It will feature a surprise soloist. We will put on an electrifying performance. We have practiced for months.</u> We are excited about this concert.

more

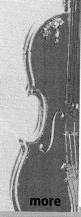

Combining Sentences: Gerund Phrases You can also combine sentences by using gerund phrases. Like sentences with participial phrases, sentences with gerund phrases can be used to vary your writing style.

Remember that gerunds are words that end in *-ing*. Gerunds and gerund phrases function as nouns.

I play folk songs.

That's my hobby.

gerund phrase

Playing folk songs is my hobby.

Apply It

6–10. Rewrite this draft of a report about folk music. Use gerund phrases to combine each set of underlined sentences.

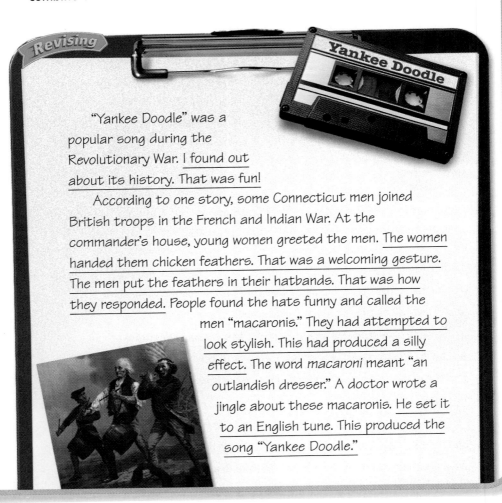

Revising

Yankee Doodle

"Yankee Doodle" was a popular song during the Revolutionary War. I found out about its history. That was fun! According to one story, some Connecticut men joined British troops in the French and Indian War. At the commander's house, young women greeted the men. The women handed them chicken feathers. That was a welcoming gesture. The men put the feathers in their hatbands. That was how they responded. People found the hats funny and called the men "macaronis." They had attempted to look stylish. This had produced a silly effect. The word *macaroni* meant "an outlandish dresser." A doctor wrote a jingle about these macaronis. He set it to an English tune. This produced the song "Yankee Doodle."

8 Verbals: Infinitives

One-Minute Warm-Up

What word is missing from these sentences? In how many places is the word needed?

Shaina wants learn how drive a car.

Her father is going teach her.

You have learned about participles and gerunds and how they are used. The third kind of verbal is the infinitive. An **infinitive** is made up of the word *to* and the base form of the verb.

Paul wants to leave.

It is necessary to go.

To exit, use the side door.

It is best to arrive in the early morning.

You can use infinitives as nouns, adjectives, or adverbs.

Uses for an Infinitive	
As a noun: subject direct object predicate noun object of a preposition	To leave would be rude. I want to leave. His decision is to leave. I want nothing except to leave.
As an adjective: modifies a noun modifies a pronoun	Now is the time to leave. She is someone to follow.
As an adverb: modifies a verb modifies an adjective modifies an adverb	To leave, use the back door. We are ready to leave. He is well enough to travel.

Be careful not to confuse infinitives with prepositional phrases that begin with *to.*

| **Infinitive:** | Is this the road to take? |
| **Prepositional Phrase:** | Is this the road to the store? |

Speak Up Find each infinitive. Is it used as a noun, an adjective, or an adverb?

1. Do you want to study?
2. When you need to concentrate, look for peace and quiet.
3. Many people go to some quiet corner or room.
4. Playing soft music may make it easier to concentrate.
5. Probably the best time to study is before you become too tired.
6. To learn, you should summarize the information that you are studying.
7. To summarize is to explain the important ideas.

Summing Up

- An **infinitive** is formed with the word *to* and the base form of the verb.
- An infinitive can be used as a noun, an adjective, or an adverb.

Write each infinitive. Then label it *noun, adjective,* or *adverb* to tell how it is used in the sentence. Write *none* if a sentence has no infinitive.

Example: To learn, you must find a good way to study.
>   *To learn—adverb   to study—adjective*

8. To study, you must apply your mind to a subject.
9. To question and to think are important parts of studying any subject.
10. One way to study is to memorize.
11. You may not find most things difficult to memorize.
12. To understand, however, is much harder.

more ▶

13. Knowledge of some kind is important to everyone.
14. To acquire that knowledge, you usually need to study.
15. Not everyone knows the best way to learn.
16. To read, you should have good light.
17. Go to a quiet place without distractions.
18. Important materials to have include pencil and paper.

19–32. There are fourteen infinitives in this e-mail letter from an older sister. Identify each infinitive and label it *noun, adjective,* or *adverb,* according to how it is used.

Example: A good thing to do is to ask yourself questions.
        to do—adj.   *to ask—noun*

DIGITAL MAIL DELIVERY

    To confess is good for the soul, little brother, so I want to say that I miss you like crazy. I'm ready to give you the advice about studying that you asked for. That way, you'll be smart enough to come to college and visit me next year.

    Sometimes you may want to do anything except schoolwork. The thing to do is to persist. You need to organize your work. Take notes to review later, and remember to make an outline for every paper you write. If you have trouble finding information, it's time to call a well-informed friend (me, for example). At college the librarian is the one to see. To succeed, study only when you feel alert. Don't try to study all night before a test. It doesn't pay.

Writing Wrap-Up
WRITING • THINKING • LISTENING • SPEAKING

REFLECTING

Write Resolutions
    Think of five goals you want to accomplish within the next year, and list them in sentence form. Use infinitives in your sentences. Volunteers can read their goals aloud to the class. Then exchange lists with a partner. How is each infinitive in your partner's list used?

For Extra Practice see page 393.

9 Infinitive Phrases

One-Minute Warm-Up

ORACLE BONES, STARS, AND WHEELBARROWS
Ancient Chinese Science and Technology
FRANK ROSS, Jr.

Find the phrase that contains an infinitive in this sentence.

Literally thousands of substances were used by the pharmacists of ancient China to formulate medicines.

—from *Oracle Bones, Stars, and Wheelbarrows: Ancient Chinese Science and Technology*, by Frank Ross, Jr.

1. An **infinitive phrase** is made up of an infinitive and the words that complete its meaning. The phrase may include direct objects, predicate nouns, predicate adjectives, prepositional phrases, or modifiers.

     infin.   DO   infin. prep. phrase
To invent a machine is not easy to do in a hurry.

     infin.   PN   infin. PA   infin.   adverb
To be a good inventor, it is important to be calm and to concentrate carefully.

2. Infinitive phrases, like infinitives alone, can be used as nouns, as adjectives, or as adverbs.

Uses for an Infinitive Phrase		
As a noun:	subject	To discover a new continent must have been exciting for an explorer.
	direct object	About 1500 B.C. the Egyptians started to use metal rings as money.
	predicate noun	Thomas Edison's goal was to improve the electric light bulb.
	object of a preposition	Some people want nothing except to have a long, healthy life.
As an adjective:	modifies a noun modifies a pronoun	It is time to try your invention. I need someone to help me.
As an adverb:	modifies a verb	The teacher wrote to the patent office to register his invention.
	modifies an adjective	His chemistry students were all eager to hear about his project.
	modifies an adverb	Russ is well enough to continue work now that he is using crutches.

3. Remember that an infinitive phrase is different from a prepositional phrase.

infin. phrase

Columbus tried to reach China. (*to* + a verb)

prep. phrase

Columbus sailed to America. (*to* + an object)

Try It Out

Speak Up Identify each infinitive phrase. Is it used as a noun, as an adjective, or as an adverb?

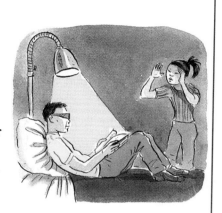

1. The watt is used to measure power.
2. Have you ever stopped to look at the number on a light bulb?
3. The number is meant to show the power requirement in watts.
4. I intend to buy a two-hundred-watt bulb.
5. I plan to use it in the floor lamp.
6. I need a stronger light to read by.

Summing Up

- An **infinitive phrase** is made up of an infinitive and the words that complete its meaning.

- Infinitive phrases act as nouns, adjectives, or adverbs.

On Your Own

Write each infinitive phrase. Label it *noun, adjective,* or *adverb* to tell how it is used in the sentence. Write *none* if a sentence does not have an infinitive phrase.

Example: We turn to a clock or watch to find out the time.
to find out the time—adverb

7. People have always wanted to know the time.
8. To tell time, people once depended on the sun.

more ▶

9. Early clocks were hard to read accurately.
10. Later, clocks were able to keep more accurate time and were easier to read.
11. Until the nineteenth century, only wealthy people could afford a high-priced clock.
12. A person might go to an inn to check the time.
13. Clocks on buildings were easy to see clearly.
14. Soon everyone wanted a device that would enable them to know the exact time.

15–20. Write each of the six infinitive phrases in this magazine advertisement. Label each phrase *noun*, *adjective*, or *adverb* to tell how it is used in the sentence.

Example: By the 1870s, people used alarm clocks to wake up on time.

to wake up on time—adverb

To find beauty in technology, look at a fine old clock. In the 1780s, cuckoo clocks were first brought to this country. In the 1800s, many companies began to make clocks—our company among them. Today, as then, to make a beautiful timepiece is an art, a matter of personal attention and care. Here in Geneva, New York, a small, talented group of clock-makers knows the way to bring beauty and technology together. Our skilled artisans will work together to craft a beautiful, reliable timepiece for you. Isn't it time to have the time of your life?

Writing Wrap-Up
WRITING • THINKING • LISTENING • SPEAKING

PERSUADING

Write an Advertisement
Write a magazine advertisement for a discovery or invention—old or new, real or imaginary. (Illustrate it if you wish.) Use several infinitive phrases. With a partner, read your advertisements aloud. Exchange papers, underline your partner's infinitive phrases, and tell how each is used.

For Extra Practice see page 394.

Idioms

The phrase *in a pickle* is an **idiom** because it has a meaning different from the meanings of its separate words. To be in a pickle is to be in a difficult situation. Idioms can make speech and informal writing colorful, but they are frequently overused and are inappropriate in formal writing.

To be in a pickle is to be in a difficult situation.

Apply It

1–8. The box shows the meanings of the underlined idioms in the paragraphs from a business letter below. Rewrite the letter, replacing each idiom with its meaning.

hurry	very nervous and anxious	had no effect on me	ecstatic
thrilled	making plans too early	be patient	in trouble

Revising

I was beside myself when I saved enough money to buy your CD-Plus Player with a microphone. As soon as I sent in my order, I promised to be the DJ for our next school dance. My parents warned me that I might be counting my chickens before they hatched, but their words went in one ear and out the other.

The dance will be held next Friday, and I'm up a tree. My friends have advised me to keep my shirt on and wait for your delivery. However, I am sitting on pins and needles, wondering whether the CD-Plus Player will be here on time. I trust now that you will shake a leg and get the player to me before Friday. If it arrives on time, I'll be sitting on top of the world.

Enrichment

Haiku

A haiku is a poem that consists of three lines and seventeen syllables. Line 1 has five syllables, line 2 has seven, and line 3 has five. A haiku usually describes a specific event in nature and expresses the emotion that this event stirs in the poet. Write a haiku of your own. Include two or more verbals and underline them. Label them *participle, gerund,* or *infinitive*.

<u>Flying</u> is her dream.
gerund

The baby crow tries <u>to soar.</u>
infinitive

<u>Trembling,</u> she looks down.
participle

Challenge Write another haiku using two infinitives. Label each infinitive *noun, adjective,* or *adverb* to show how it is used.

GEOMETRIC SHAPES

Draw three different geometric shapes. Use a ruler, a compass, and a protractor; be exact. On another piece of paper, write directions for drawing each shape. Assume that the person following the directions will not know what the shapes are. Use prepositional, participial, gerund, and infinitive phrases. Then give the directions to a classmate. Do not tell what the shapes are. If your classmate cannot draw all three shapes, revise your instructions to make them clearer.

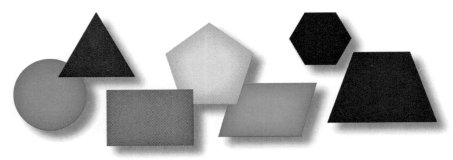

See TE margin for answers.

1 **Prepositional Phrases** *(p. 346)* Write each prepositional phrase, under-lining each preposition once and each object twice.

1. *Xerography* refers to a process of duplication.
2. This process was invented by Chester Carlson in 1938.
3. *Xerography* comes from the Greek words for "dry" and "write."
4. The process was crude at first, but the first copier was sold around 1950.
5. With xerographic copiers we can make copies of anything from printed matter to color photographs.

2 **Prepositional Phrases as Modifiers** *(p. 350)* Write the prepositional phrases and the words that they modify.

6. Badlands National Park in South Dakota is famous for its fossils.
7. Badlands are formed in dry areas with loose soil on top of rock.
8. The ground is unprotected by plants.
9. Water from rain or snow cuts into it.
10. The land is quite useless for farming or development.
11. The beauty of the landscape attracts many to the area.

3 **Choosing Correct Prepositions** *(p. 355)* Write each sentence, using the correct preposition.

12. (Between, Among) baseball's best sluggers was Josh Gibson.
13. The showdowns (among, between) Gibson and pitcher Satchel Paige are legendary.
14. No other American player (beside, besides) Gibson has ever averaged as many home runs per times at bat.
15. Gibson's performance can be ranked (beside, besides) Hank Aaron's.
16. Which catchers (beside, besides) Gibson are in the Baseball Hall of Fame?

4 **Participles and Participial Phrases** *(pp. 358, 361)* Write each sentence. Underline each participle or participial phrase once and the word or words it modifies twice.

17. Atlantis was a legendary continent located in the Atlantic Ocean and inhabited by a perfect society.
18. Setting out to conquer neighboring lands, the inhabitants of Atlantis were defeated by the Athenians more than ten thousand years ago.
19. Atlantis, sunk by earthquakes and floods sent by the legendary Greek gods, has aroused the interest of many.
20. Exploring a Greek island, scientists in 1967 discovered a buried city.
21. Is this city the civilization lost centuries ago?

 See www.eduplace.com/kids/hme/ for an online quiz.

5 **Gerunds and Gerund Phrases** *(pp. 364, 367)* Write each gerund or gerund phrase. Then write *subject, object of a preposition,* or *predicate noun* to show how it is used.

22. Gesturing is visual signaling with the body.
23. Much gesturing is the same around the world.
24. Wagging an index finger can tell a small child not to do something.
25. In some cultures people say "Okay" by forming a circle with two fingers.
26. Waving with the palm forward can mean good-bye.
27. A particular style of walking may show how a person feels.

6 **Infinitives and Infinitive Phrases** *(pp. 373, 376)* Write each infinitive or infinitive phrase. Then write *noun, adjective,* or *adverb* to show how it is used.

28. In 1970 Dave Kunst's goal was to walk around the world.
29. Walking so far, Dave, of course, had obstacles to overcome.
30. He returned home midway to recuperate from an attack by bandits.
31. When he was forbidden to cross China, he sailed to Australia.
32. To cross Australia takes as many steps as to cross China.
33. Eager to get home, Dave completed his trek in 1974.
34. Was he the first one to walk around the world?

Mixed Review 35–40. Write this part of a letter, correcting the six errors related to phrases.

Proofreading Checklist
✔ incorrect prepositions
✔ incorrect pronoun as object of preposition
✔ incorrect pronoun before gerund phrase
✔ incorrect punctuation or placement of participial phrase

Proofreading

Dashing around New York on my class graduation trip I couldn't decide what to see first. I had a hard time choosing between all the great cultural events, but finally Sal and I bought tickets to the ballet. *Swan Lake* was super! The first appearance of the swans was exciting for Sal and I. Us being unfamiliar with the ballet made the dancers' entrance even more thrilling. (None of the others beside us saw a ballet—they all went to see *Cats*.) We saw wild turkeys among many other birds riding the train home.

Test Practice

Write the numbers 1–6 on a sheet of paper. Read each group of sentences. Choose the sentence that is written correctly. Write the letter for that answer.

1
  A Rodneys masquerading as a foreign student was the highlight of the school fair.

  B It was difficult to locate Alyssa among the hordes of similarly dressed girls.

  C A teacher stood next to the stage wearing a funny T-shirt.

  D The captain of the girls' field hockey team waited for her parents besides the food booth.

2
  F The flight attendant wants to comfort the crying toddler.

  G The food cart is stuck among rows 18 and 19 of the airplane.

  H A group of travelers sit in the first class section from Greece and Turkey.

  J Beside supper, the passengers will be served a complimentary snack.

3
  A Butterfly gardening is Lian's new hobby.

  B She has planted a row of yellow day lilies besides the barn.

  C She roams between all four of her gardens and searches for exotic butterflies.

  D Because of she being such a good gardener, her new hobby is already a success.

4
  F Emery hurls herself into the ocean and swims happily among the sand bar and the shore.

  G She surfing is very skilled.

  H A towering wave rises behind her, and she decides to dive.

  J Beside being a good surfer and swimmer, Emery is an accomplished diver.

5
  A To find cheap entertainment, people used to go to music halls.

  B Beside listening to singers, audiences could watch jugglers and acrobats.

  C Eating snacks were acceptable in a music hall.

  D Watching TV shows are a more common form of amusement today.

6
  F A firefighter can rescue trapped victims in a special waterproof suit.

  G The flames spread rapidly between the five rooms.

  H Fighting fires requires special equipment, such as ladders and water pumps.

  J Spraying the fire extinguisher the cook quickly put out the grease fire.

Now write numbers 7–10 on your paper. Use the paragraph to answer the questions. Write the letter for each answer.

> [7]Psychologists' analysises of newborn babies have begun to explain much about the earliest stage of human development. Infants adjust very quickly to the world around them.[8]Gazing around the newborn prefers their mothers face to the face of another women. [9]Most newborns responds intelligently to sound, turning to inspect unusual noises. [10]Newborns can distinguish between many kinds of scents, they smile at pleasant odors and turn away from nasty ones.

7 Which is the best way to rewrite Sentence 7?

A Psychologist's analyses of newborn babies have begun to explain much about the earliest stage of human development.

B Psychologists' analyses of newborn babies have began to explain much about the earliest stage of human development.

C Psychologists' analyses of newborn babies have begun to explain much about the earliest stage of human development.

D Best as is

8 Which is the best way to rewrite Sentence 8?

F Gazing around, the newborn prefers his or her mother's face to the face of another woman.

G Gazing around the newborn prefers his or her mother's face to the face of another women.

H Gazing around, the newborn prefers their mother's face to the face of another woman.

J Best as is

9 Which is the best way to rewrite Sentence 9?

A Most newborns respond intelligent to sound, turning to inspect unusual noises.

B Most newborns responds intelligently to sound, turning to inspect unusually noises.

C Most newborns respond intelligently to sound, turning to inspect unusual noises.

D Best as is

10 Which is the best way to rewrite Sentence 10?

F Newborns can distinguish among many kinds of scents, they smile at pleasant odors and turn away from nasty ones.

G Newborns can distinguish among many kinds of scents; they smile at pleasant odors and turn away from nasty ones.

H Newborns can distinguish between many kinds of scents; they smile at pleasant odors and turn away from nasty ones.

J Best as is

Write numbers 11–15 on your paper, and do this page the same way you did the previous one.

¹¹Wow that new girl certain has an amazing hairdo! ¹²The rest of we girls have long hair, or she has a shorter cut. ¹³The hair around her face are jagged, creating a wild affect. ¹⁴The strands on top of her head has been gathered into smooth round knobs. ¹⁵Although the girl looks odd she also looks charmingly.

11 Which is the best way to rewrite Sentence 11?

A Wow! That new girl certainly has an amazing hairdo!

B Wow! that new girl certainly has an amazing hairdo!

C Wow, that new girl certain has an amazing hairdo!

D Best as is

12 Which is the best way to rewrite Sentence 12?

F The rest of we girls have long hair, but she has a shorter cut.

G The rest of us girls have long hair, but she has a shorter cut.

H The rest of us girls have long hair, but she has a more short cut.

J Best as is

13 Which is the best way to rewrite Sentence 13?

A The hair around her face is jagged, creating a wild affect.

B The hair around her face are jagged, creating a wild effect.

C The hair around her face is jagged, creating a wild effect.

D Best as is

14 Which is the best way to rewrite Sentence 14?

F The strands on top of her head has been gathered into smooth, round knobs.

G The strands on top of her head have been gathered into smooth-round knobs.

H The strands on top of her head have been gathered into smooth, round knobs.

J Best as is

15 Which is the best way to rewrite Sentence 15?

A Although the girl looks odd; she also looks charming.

B Although the girl looks odd, she also looks charming.

C Although the girl looks odd, she also looks charmingly.

D Best as is

(pages 346–349)

1 Prepositional Phrases

- A **preposition** is a word that shows a relationship between a noun or a pronoun and another word in the sentence.
- A **prepositional phrase** includes a preposition, its object or objects, and all of the modifiers of the object.
- When a pronoun is the object of a preposition, use the objective case.

● Copy the underlined prepositional phrase. Underline the preposition once and each object twice.

Example: You may think of operas <u>as very serious music</u>.
as very serious <u>music</u>

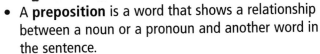

1. Some operas are based <u>on fairy tales</u>.
2. Do you know the story <u>of Hansel and Gretel</u>?
3. <u>According to the tale</u>, they are brother and sister.
4. There is an opera <u>about these two young people</u>.
5. <u>Because of its lively music</u>, the opera is quite popular.

▲ Write each prepositional phrase. Underline the preposition once and each object twice.

Example: Opera was born in the Italian city of Florence.
<u>in</u> the Italian <u>city</u>   <u>of</u> <u>Florence</u>

6. Opera was first performed in the late sixteenth century.
7. An opera is a combination of a story and music.
8. The story is sometimes ignored on account of the music.
9. You may be pleased with an opera despite its silly plot.
10. In many good operas, the drama is heightened by the music.

■ Write each sentence, supplying a pronoun as the object of the preposition. Underline the prepositional phrase.

Example: Tickets for the opera were sent to Jane and _____.
Tickets for the opera were sent to <u>Jane and him</u>.

11. Are the opera tickets for you and _____?
12. *The Magic Flute* was seen by Ronald and _____ last week.
13. According to Evan and _____, the opera was by Mozart.
14. Everyone except Maria and _____ enjoyed the opera very much.

(pages 350–352)

2 Prepositional Phrases as Modifiers

- Prepositional phrases always function as modifiers.
- **Adjective phrases** modify nouns or pronouns.
- **Adverb phrases** modify verbs, adjectives, or adverbs.

Remember

● Write the adjective phrase or the adverb phrase that modifies the underlined word in each sentence.

Example: Another <u>word</u> for a cape is a point.   *for a cape*

1. Cape Fear is a <u>point</u> in North Carolina.
2. Cape Fear <u>extends</u> into the Atlantic Ocean.
3. It is an interesting <u>part</u> of the state.
4. It <u>got</u> its name for a very good reason.
5. During September, fierce storms often <u>hit</u> the area.
6. The <u>ocean</u> around Cape Fear becomes quite rough.

▲ Write the adjective phrases or the adverb phrases in each sentence. The word in parentheses tells you which kind to look for. Then write the words that the phrases modify.

Example: A cape near the tip of Africa is quite famous. (adjective)
　　　　near the tip—cape   of Africa—tip

7. The Cape of Good Hope is a place of great interest. (adjective)
8. Because of its location and history, it is famous. (adverb)
9. It was discovered in 1488 by a Portuguese explorer. (adverb)
10. The weather around the cape was stormy. (adjective)
11. The explorer from Portugal named it the Cape of Storms. (adjective)

■ Write each prepositional phrase. Label it *adjective* or *adverb*. Then write the word or words that it modifies.

Example: Cape Horn lies at the southern tip of South America.
　　　　at the southern tip—adverb—lies
　　　　of South America—adjective—tip

12. The cape is on Horn Island in Chile.
13. The island was named after the city of Hoorn in Holland.
14. Ships went around Cape Horn from the Atlantic to the Pacific.
15. The slow trip around the cape was filled with many dangers.
16. Then the Panama Canal was built as a link between the oceans.

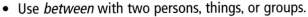

Extra Practice

Remember

(pages 355–357)

3 Choosing Correct Prepositions

- Use *between* with two persons, things, or groups.
- Use *among* with more than two persons, things, or groups.
- Use *beside* to mean "next to."
- Use *besides* to mean "in addition to."

● Write each sentence, adding the preposition in parentheses that correctly completes it.

Example: Who (beside, besides) Dora is trying out for *Carousel?*
Who besides Dora is trying out for Carousel?

1. The director must choose (between, among) many actors for the part of Billy Bigelow in *Carousel*.
2. (Beside, Besides) Billy, there are other important male roles.
3. The play is about the love (between, among) Billy and Julie.
4. They stand (beside, besides) each other and sing a duet.
5. (Beside, Besides) "If I Loved You," another famous song from *Carousel* is "You'll Never Walk Alone."

▲ If a preposition is incorrect, rewrite the sentence correctly. If the sentence is correct, write *correct.*

Example: The club is choosing among *South Pacific* and *42nd Street*.
The club is choosing between South Pacific *and* 42nd Street.

6. The people sitting right besides Gino want *42nd Street*.
7. Between the other six members of the cast, *South Pacific* is the favorite.
8. Does *42nd Street* have any big numbers besides the title tune?
9. Isn't there a dance routine among the male lead and the female lead?
10. Beside Rose and Gino, who can dance well enough for the show?

■ If a preposition is incorrect, rewrite the sentence correctly. If the sentence is correct, write *correct.*

Example: Respect between all members of the cast is essential.
Respect among all members of the cast is essential.

11. When I stood besides Kim to sing our duet, I was thrilled.
12. A duet makes the ties between two characters clearer.
13. Performers should have musical talent beside acting ability.
14. The people in this play are among the most talented that I know.

(pages 358–360)

4 Verbals: Participles

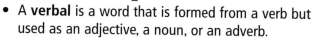

- A **verbal** is a word that is formed from a verb but used as an adjective, a noun, or an adverb.
- A **participle** is a verbal that is used as an adjective. You can use the present participle or past participle form of a verb as a verbal.

Remember

● Write the underlined noun or pronoun. Then write the participle that modifies it.

Example: Many people enjoy organized <u>hikes</u>.   *hikes   organized*

1. A challenging <u>hike</u> is good exercise.
2. Years ago, a traveling <u>person</u> would usually walk or ride.
3. Sitting in a moving <u>car</u> provides no exercise.
4. Many recreation departments offer planned <u>hikes</u>.
5. <u>Those</u> leading are usually expert guides.
6. Attentive <u>hikers</u>, listening, can learn about nature from the guides.

▲ Rewrite each sentence, adding a participle formed from the verb in parentheses to modify each underlined noun or pronoun.

Example: Can we enjoy a <u>walk</u> in the woods? (relax)
Can we enjoy a relaxing walk in the woods?

7. <u>Hikers</u> are finding fewer places worth exploring. (dedicate)
8. Forests are being replaced by <u>areas</u>. (develop)
9. Many problems can arise from <u>forests</u>. (disappear)
10. <u>Trees</u> produce oxygen and help to clean the air. (grow)
11. The <u>number</u> of forests threatens our world. (decline)
12. <u>People</u> can do much to improve this situation. (interest)

■ Rewrite each sentence, adding a participle to modify at least one noun or pronoun.

Example: Forest fires are a cause of forest damage.
Forest fires are a leading cause of forest damage.

13. Flames kill not only trees but other things in the forest.
14. Ashes on streams can kill fish and pollute the water.
15. As a result of a forest fire, floods can occur.
16. The plants and trees that absorb rainwater are destroyed.
17. Schools can teach fire prevention to students.
18. Firefighters are happy to share their knowledge with others.

Extra Practice

(pages 361–363)

5 Participial Phrases

- A **participial phrase** is made up of a participle and its accompanying words.
- Participial phrases may contain direct objects, prepositional phrases, and adverbs.

Remember

● Each participle is underlined. Write each sentence, and underline all the words that make up the participial phrase.

Example: <u>Standing</u> on the corner, Dan waited for a green light.
Standing on the corner, Dan waited for a green light.

1. Traffic lights, <u>developed</u> a century ago, are now widespread.
2. The first lights <u>directed</u> the flow of carriages <u>pulled</u> by horses.
3. <u>Installed</u> in London in 1868, a very early signal had mechanical arms for daytime and a gaslight for nighttime.
4. <u>Seeing</u> a need for improvement, cities developed better lights.
5. Early lights <u>operated</u> by hand required an attendant.
6. Automatic lights <u>controlling</u> busy streets appeared in the 1920s.

▲ Write each sentence. Underline each participial phrase once and the word or words it modifies twice.

Example: Wanting some milk, I reached for a glass.
Wanting some milk, I reached for a glass.

7. The first glass was a material formed by volcanoes.
8. The first glass made by people appeared about 4,500 years ago.
9. People using fire may have discovered glass by accident.
10. Sand, soda, and lime melted together, form glass.
11. With a tube dipped in molten glass, glassblowers made bottles.

■ Write each sentence. Underline each participial phrase once and the word modified twice.

Example: Used first only in China, the umbrella is now common.
Used first only in China, the umbrella is now common.

12. An umbrella decorated with jewels showed wealth and power.
13. Becoming popular in the late 1700s, the umbrella developed opposition.
14. Drivers of horse-drawn cabs, fearing a loss of business, wanted to dispose of umbrellas.
15. Staying dry with umbrellas, people did not need cabs so often.

390 Unit 7: Phrases

(pages 364–366)

⑥ Verbals: Gerunds

Remember

- A **gerund** is the present participle of a verb used as a noun.
- A gerund functions in all of the ways that a noun does.

● Write each underlined gerund. Then label it *subject, direct object, object of a preposition,* or *predicate noun* to tell how it is used in the sentence.

Example: Some people, like squirrels, enjoy <u>collecting</u>.
     collecting—direct object

1. Have you ever tried <u>drawing</u>?
2. One restful activity is <u>reading</u> books and magazines.
3. <u>Relaxing</u> is important for everyone.
4. Some people relax by <u>dancing</u>.
5. You might like <u>singing</u> in a small madrigal group.
6. Another possibility is <u>acting</u> in school plays.

▲ Write each gerund. Then label it *subject, direct object, object of a preposition,* or *predicate noun* to tell how it is used.

Example: Singing is one kind of performing.
     Singing—subject   performing—object of a preposition

7. Two very popular hobbies are singing and acting.
8. Dancing can be an entertaining activity too.
9. More and more people are enjoying dancing.
10. Looking for a new activity, you might investigate juggling.
11. Activities like juggling can be demanding, however.
12. Practicing and performing can take a lot of time.

■ Write a sentence, using each of the following gerunds as the part of the sentence named in parentheses.

Example: hiking (predicate noun) *My favorite activity is hiking in Wyoming.*

13. swimming (obj. of prep.)
14. traveling (direct object)
15. sculpting (obj. of prep.)
16. conversing (subject)
17. farming (predicate noun)
18. using (obj. of prep.)
19. cleaning (subject)
20. training (direct object)

(pages 367–370)

7 Gerund Phrases

- A **gerund phrase** can be a subject, a direct object, an object of a preposition, or a predicate noun.
- Use a possessive noun or a possessive pronoun before a gerund.

● Copy each underlined gerund phrase. Then label it *subject, direct object, object of a preposition,* or *predicate noun.*

Example: The decorator loved visiting the museum.
   visiting the museum   direct object

1. Looking at the prints was her favorite activity.
2. After walking through those rooms, she always had new ideas.
3. The Cooper-Hewitt Museum had a show on brushing your teeth.
4. Its aim was reviewing the history of the toothbrush.
5. Visitors would finish by rushing out for a new toothbrush.
6. Showing objects of daily life is the museum's purpose.
7. Visitors enjoy discovering the beauty of these objects.

▲ Write each gerund phrase. Label it *subject, direct object, object of a preposition,* or *predicate noun* to tell how it is used.

Example: Visiting a museum can be an exciting experience.
   Visiting a museum   subject

8. Your goal should be finding the right museum for you.
9. Some museums prefer concentrating on one type of collection.
10. Mary's favorite activity is visiting the Museum of Modern Art.
11. The Smithsonian aims at attracting all sorts of people.
12. Finding your way around that gigantic institution is not easy.

■ Write a sentence, using each gerund phrase in the way indicated in parentheses.

Example: designing houses (subject) *Designing houses is an architect's job.*

13. looking at artwork (predicate noun)
14. painting a realistic portrait (direct object)
15. being artistic (predicate noun)
16. sketching with charcoal (direct object)
17. framing a photograph (subject)
18. studying the history of art (object of a preposition)

(pages 373–375)

⑧ Verbals: Infinitives

- An **infinitive** is formed with the word *to* and the base form of the verb.
- An infinitive can be used as a noun, an adjective, or an adverb.

● Write the infinitive in each sentence.

Example: To learn is not usually easy. *To learn*

1. Some things are difficult to master.
2. To practice is often important.
3. Good athletes always find time to practice.
4. Have you always wanted to skate?
5. To skate requires a lot of practice.
6. To succeed, you usually must work long and hard.

▲ Write each infinitive. Then label it *noun, adjective,* or *adverb* to tell how it is used in the sentence.

Example: Both you and I have always liked to swim. *to swim—noun*

7. Swimming is not terribly difficult to learn.
8. To begin, you may go to a pool or to a lake.
9. The ocean is not a good place to start.
10. The ability to swim does not come naturally to people.
11. The first thing to do is to float.
12. To move, you kick your way to the other side of the pool.
13. For every new stroke, you need to concentrate and to practice.
14. Win or lose, the most important thing is to participate.

■ Write a sentence, using each infinitive as the part of the sentence or the part of speech named in parentheses.

Example: to learn (direct object)
   All her life my grandmother has loved to learn.

15. to fly (subject)
16. to go (adverb)
17. to drive (direct object)
18. to write (predicate noun)
19. to start (adjective)

20. to stop (predicate noun)
21. to ask (direct object)
22. to decide (subject)
23. to sail (adverb)
24. to expect (adjective)

(pages 376–378)

⑨ Infinitive Phrases

- An **infinitive phrase** is made up of an infinitive and the words that complete its meaning.
- Infinitive phrases act as nouns, adjectives, or adverbs.

● One sentence in each pair has an infinitive phrase. Write the sentence with the infinitive phrase.

Example: Jill is not going to summer camp this year. She plans to get a job. *She plans to get a job.*

1. Do you want to save money? You can take it to a bank.
2. Walk up to any window. The person to see is a teller.
3. To make a deposit, fill out a slip. Then give your money to the teller.
4. You can also go to an automated teller machine. To use the machine, read the instructions on the screen.
5. Remember to check your bank statement. One comes to you monthly.

▲ Write each infinitive phrase. If a sentence does not have an infinitive phrase, write *none*.

Example: In ancient times, some people liked to keep money in safes. *to keep money in safes*

6. Often you do not want to spend all your money immediately.
7. A bank is usually a good place to put your money.
8. A bank account makes it easier to pay bills.
9. When you give money to a bank, the bank uses it.
10. The bank's purpose is to make money for itself.

■ Write each infinitive phrase. Then write *noun, adjective,* or *adverb* to tell how it is used. If it is used as a noun, label it *subject, direct object, object of a preposition,* or *predicate noun.*

Example: This summer Ernesto wants to buy a new bicycle. *to buy a new bicycle—noun—direct object*

11. To earn some money, he found a good job.
12. To carry his money around might be dangerous.
13. Yesterday he went to the bank to open an account there.
14. He plans to deposit money in his account every week.
15. The bank must be able to return his money when he needs it.

As long as the wind blows, the rocks will continue to trace geometric patterns on the ground.

Clauses

Independent and Subordinate Clauses

Find the two clauses in this sentence. Which clause could stand alone as a sentence?

We had to stop when our hands ached fiercely from the cold.

—from *April and the Dragon Lady,* by Lensey Namioka

When you studied sentences, you learned that a **clause** is a group of words with a subject and a predicate.

Subject	Predicate
The air	grew cool.

1. There are two major kinds of clauses: main, or independent, and dependent, or subordinate. An **independent clause** expresses a complete thought. A simple sentence has one independent clause.

   The air grew cool.

   A compound sentence has two or more independent clauses.

   The air grew cool, and it rained.

2. A **subordinate clause** has a subject and a predicate but does not express a complete thought. It cannot stand alone as a sentence. It depends on, or needs, an independent clause to complete its meaning. A **complex sentence** has one or more subordinate clauses and an independent clause.

   subordinate   independent
   When the sun set, the clouds appeared.

   A subordinate clause may come before or after an independent clause.

   Before spring comes, it will snow.   It will snow before spring comes.

3. Clauses can be introduced by the same words that introduce phrases, such as *before, after, until,* and *since.* A clause always has a subject and a predicate; a phrase never does.

   Clause: I'll see you before spring comes.

   Phrase: I'll see you before sunset.

Speak Up Is each clause subordinate or independent?

1. he will arrive
2. since you aren't going
3. I didn't like it
4. after he flew here
5. soon Cary will leave
6. until he departs

Is each underlined group of words a phrase or a clause?

7. You'll need to stay here <u>until the end</u> of the storm.
8. <u>After the rain ended</u>, the traffic reporter watched the roads.
9. <u>From the helicopter</u>, he could see everything.
10. He would continue his work <u>until another shift came on</u>.
11. <u>Before he could leave</u>, he had to complete a lengthy report about the storm's impact.
12. <u>In some areas</u>, the storm had torn away large sections of pavement as it passed.
13. Many parts of the road system in the region became flooded <u>before the storm moved on to the northeast</u>.
14. <u>In spite of the intensity of the storm</u>, very little serious damage had occurred, and no trees had fallen.
15. The reporter finished his report <u>before the next shift began</u>.

Summing Up

- A **clause** is a group of words that has a subject and a predicate.

- An **independent clause** expresses a complete thought.

- A **subordinate clause** does not express a complete thought and cannot stand alone as a sentence.

On Your Own

Identify each group of words as a *subordinate clause*, an *independent clause*, or a *phrase*.

Example: if a tornado develops   *subordinate clause*

16. tornadoes do not last
17. before the wind blows
18. since they are strong
19. first you take cover
20. when a tornado hits

21. while the storm rages
22. you should stay low
23. in the safest place
24. during a powerful storm
25. soon the storm ends

26–30. The paragraph below is from an educational Web site on severe storms. Identify the underlined group of words in each of the five sentences as a *subordinate clause*, an *independent clause*, or a *phrase*.

Example: <u>Before a waterspout can form</u>, a center of low air pressure must develop.   *subordinate clause*

Web site

Storms

<u>When a tornado occurs over an ocean or lake</u>, it is called a waterspout. Winds <u>within a low-pressure center</u> begin to whirl, forming a rotating column above the water. Water vapor in the atmosphere condenses in the column, and <u>surface water is drawn up</u>, forming a waterspout. A large one can measure <u>about two hundred feet</u> in diameter. Most waterspouts occur in the tropics, <u>where they occasionally cause severe damage.</u>

Worldwide

Tropical

Writing Wrap-Up

WRITING • THINKING • LISTENING • SPEAKING

DESCRIBING

Write a Letter

Write a letter or an e-mail to a friend, in which you describe the scariest storm you have ever experienced. Use phrases and clauses. Exchange letters with a partner, and then discuss them. Did the letters make the experiences sound real?

2 Adjective Clauses

Identify the subordinate clause in this sentence. Which noun does it modify?

It had wet its forefeet and legs, and almost immediately the water that clung to it turned to ice.

—from *To Build a Fire,* by Jack London

Subordinate clauses, like phrases, can be used in sentences as if they were single units.

One Word:	The barking dog followed us home.
Phrase:	The dog, barking loudly, chased us.
Clause:	The dog, which was barking loudly, followed us.

1. You know that a word that modifies a noun or a pronoun is an adjective. An **adjective clause** is a subordinate clause that modifies a noun or a pronoun. Like all other subordinate clauses, an adjective clause cannot stand by itself. It needs an independent clause along with it to complete its meaning.

   independent   subordinate
   We need a dog that can guard.

2. An adjective clause usually follows the word that it modifies. Sometimes an adjective clause may interrupt the main clause.

   There must be someone who can tell us more about dogs.

   The dog that I like best is the Old English sheepdog.

3. Adjective clauses are often introduced by relative pronouns. A **relative pronoun** *relates* a clause to the word or words that it modifies. The most common relative pronouns are *who, which,* and *that.*

Relative Pronouns	
who refers to people	People who own dogs may exhibit them.
which refers to animals or things	Anyone could enter early dog shows, which were not regulated.
that refers to people, animals, or things	The group that regulates dog shows is the American Kennel Club.

Adjective Clauses **399**

4. You can also use the words *where* and *when* to introduce adjective clauses.

> This is the kennel where we left our dog.
> Friday is the day when we left it.

Try It Out

Speak Up Identify each relative pronoun and adjective clause. Which noun or pronoun does the clause modify?

1. A purebred dog is one that has parents of the same breed.
2. The American Kennel Club, which registers purebred dogs, is known as the AKC.
3. Those who own purebred dogs often receive pedigree papers from the club.
4. A dog that has a pedigree must have ancestors that are known and registered.
5. Peggy's dog looks like a beagle, which is a type of hound.
6. Peggy has a friend who raises pedigreed beagles in order to show them in dog shows.
7. The hound group, which has a large number of breeds of dogs, is often among the most amusing groups at a dog show.
8. Some of the dogs that attract the most attention are members of the working-dogs group.

Summing Up

- An **adjective clause** modifies a noun or a pronoun.
- A **relative pronoun** such as *who, which,* or *that* usually introduces an adjective clause.
- *Where* and *when* may also introduce adjective clauses.

9–20. Write the twelve adjective clauses in this part of a speech given to a group of dog-show visitors. Underline the relative pronouns and the words *where* and *when*. Write the words that the clauses modify.

Example: Dog breeds that are recognized by the AKC are in seven groups.
that are recognized by the AKC—breeds

PRINCETON
DOG SHOW

Welcome to the Princeton Dog Show, where all seven AKC groups are represented. The judging will begin at ten o'clock and finish at noon, when the show champion will be named. A lunch, which will celebrate the winner, will be held in the restaurant at the Atrium. The owners of the dogs that won best-in-class awards will also be invited.

People who like toy dogs can see many of the breeds that are tiny, among them the popular Yorkshire terrier. Anyone who admires a watchdog will appreciate the terriers, which include the fearless Airedale. The nonsporting group has dogs that are kept for show and companionship, such as the standard poodle. The working-dog group contains the herders, guard dogs, and sled dogs that were bred to serve people. The fifth group, sporting dogs, includes retrievers, which were bred to hunt. The last group, the hounds, includes the Irish wolfhound, which is the tallest breed.

Writing Wrap-Up

WRITING • THINKING • LISTENING • SPEAKING

EXPRESSING

Write a Journal Entry

In your journal, name the animal that you would like most to have as a pet. Describe what appeals to you about this animal. What is it that you especially might be able to give this animal? Include at least five adjective clauses in your journal entry. In a small group, read your journal entry aloud, and have group members identify the adjective clauses.

3 Adjective Clauses with *who*, *whom*, and *whose*

What is wrong with these sentences? How can you fix them?

Emily Dickinson, whom lived in Amherst, Massachusetts, is known for her poems about love, death, and nature.

She was a shy woman of who her devoted sister was fiercely protective.

You have already studied adjective clauses introduced by the relative pronoun *who*.

Emily Dickinson, who lived in the 1800s, was a poet.

The relative pronouns *whom* and *whose* are forms of *who* that you can use in an adjective clause describing a person.

Dickinson was influenced by the English writer Emily Brontë, whom she admired.

Ralph Waldo Emerson was another writer for whom Dickinson had great respect.

Dickinson, whose life was quiet and secluded, wrote with great intensity.

To decide whether to use the relative pronoun *who*, *whom*, or *whose* in an adjective clause, see how the pronoun is used *within* the clause.

Using *who*, *whom*, and *whose* as Relative Pronouns	
who Use as a subject in a clause.	Dickinson was a private person who did not travel far from home.
whom Use as a direct object or an object of a preposition in a clause.	She is a poet whom many admire. She had a small circle of friends to whom she was dedicated.
whose Use as a possessive pronoun in a clause.	Dickinson, most of whose poems were not published in her lifetime, is well known today.

Remember that the independent clause does not affect your choice of a relative pronoun. Decide how the relative pronoun functions in the adjective clause. If it is the subject, use *who*. If it is an object, use *whom*.

subj.

Emily Dickinson is the poet who wrote those lines.

obj.

Emily Dickinson is the poet whom I admire most.

Try It Out

Speak Up Complete each sentence with *who, whom,* or *whose.* What is the subordinate clause?

1. Everyone _____ knows Mr. Arno enjoys his company.
2. Mr. Arno, _____ has five brothers, has only one sister.
3. He lives next door to his sister, _____ children he adores.
4. The children, for _____ he writes poems, adore him.
5. He has become a serious poet _____ work is published.
6. He is a creative person _____ everyone likes.

Summing Up

- Use *who* when the relative pronoun is the subject of the adjective clause.
- Use *whom* when the relative pronoun is the direct object or an object of a preposition in the adjective clause.
- Use *whose* when the relative pronoun shows possession.

7–15. Write the sentences in this part of a biography. Correct the nine errors in the use of *who, whom,* or *whose.*

Example: Poe is a writer whom tales are often dramatic.
Poe is a writer whose tales are often dramatic.

Proofreading

Readers to who horror stories appeal enjoy the works of Edgar Allan Poe, who was a most imaginative writer. Those for who he wrote savored his supernatural tales such as "The Tell-Tale Heart" and "The Pit and the Pendulum." Poe, whom is often credited with originating the detective story, created memorable characters. In "The Murders in the Rue Morgue," he created C. Auguste Dupin, whom is said to be the model for later fictional detectives.

Poe, whom is well known for his short stories, is also known for "The Raven," "The Bells," and other famous poems. Among scholars, he is regarded as an important critic whom views influenced other writers of his time. Poe, whose private life was tragic, nevertheless had an admiring public by who he was considered the best writer of his time. To this day, those whom write short stories and poems owe an enormous debt to Edgar Allan Poe, whom work broke new ground.

Writing Wrap-Up   WRITING • THINKING • LISTENING • SPEAKING

DESCRIBING

Write Notes for a Script
Write notes describing several of the characters you will use in a TV mystery script. Use *who, whom,* and *whose* in several adjective clauses. Read your notes aloud with a classmate. Exchange papers, and check each other's use of pronouns.

4 Essential and Nonessential Clauses

Look at this picture of the Taj Mahal, a famous tomb built in India by Shah Jahan for his beloved wife. Write two sentences about it that contain adjective clauses, one clause beginning with *which*, the other clause beginning with *that*.

Taj Mahal

You may have noticed that some adjective clauses are set off with commas whereas others are not.

The Eiffel Tower was named after the man who designed it.
The tower, which was built between 1887 and 1889, still stands.

1. When an adjective clause is necessary to identify the word it modifies, do not set it off with commas. This kind of clause is called an **essential clause** because it is essential to the meaning of the sentence. Essential clauses are also known as restrictive clauses.

Essential: The Eiffel Tower is the building that defines the Paris skyline.
The man who designed this tower was an engineer.

2. When an adjective clause is not necessary to identify the word it modifies, do use commas to set it off from the rest of the sentence. This kind of adjective clause is called a **nonessential clause**. Another name for a nonessential clause is nonrestrictive clause.

Nonessential: Big Ben, which is the symbol of London, is a clock on a tower.
Big Ben sits atop the Houses of Parliament, which are London's government buildings.

3. Your decision whether to use commas with an adjective clause may depend on what you want the sentence to mean. Notice how commas change the meaning of this sentence.

Essential: People honored the architects who designed City Hall. (Only some architects were honored.)
Nonessential: People honored the architects, who designed City Hall. (All of the architects designed City Hall, and all of them were honored.)

Essential (no commas)	Identifies the noun or pronoun it follows and is needed for the sentence to make sense.
Nonessential (commas)	Adds optional information not necessary for the meaning of the sentence.

Try It Out

Speak Up Identify each adjective clause. Is it essential or nonessential? Where are commas needed?

1. People who move from place to place build temporary homes.
2. Such shelters which are easily built are made of various materials.
3. One shelter is the igloo which is made of ice, wood, or stone.
4. Igloos that are made of ice have long passageways for entrances.
5. The skins that cover the interior help keep in the heat.
6. The long passageways which are low and narrow help to keep wind from blowing into the igloo.
7. Ice igloos which would seem cold actually provide a quite comfortable indoor living space.

Summing Up

- An adjective clause is essential or nonessential.
- An **essential clause** identifies the noun or pronoun it modifies. It is not set off with commas.
- A **nonessential clause** gives extra information about the noun or pronoun it modifies. It is set off with commas.

8–16. Write each of the nine sentences in this part of a student's research report on castles. Underline the adjective clauses, and identify them as *essential* or *nonessential*. Add or delete commas as necessary.

Example: Some of the castles, that were built in the Middle Ages, still stand.

Some of the castles <u>that were built in the Middle Ages</u> still stand. *essential*

In medieval Europe, a lord who had territory to defend built a stone castle. Castles which were built for protection were strongly fortified. Massive walls which were made of stone, mortar, and iron chains encircled the castle. The walls were protected by a moat, that was crossed by a drawbridge. When possible, the castle was built on high ground, backed against a cliff—a site that limited the approach routes of an enemy. Openings in the parapets and walls allowed defenders to rain down lethal missiles on any enemies, who stormed the walls. Nevertheless, modern firearms which date from the fifteenth and sixteenth centuries ended the age of the medieval castle. Still, some castles, that have survived the years, continue to attract both tourists and potential buyers. Many people find castles which were built as fortified dwellings fine places to live.

Write a Caption
Find (or sketch) a picture of any kind of building that interests you. Write a few sentences as a caption for the picture, using as many adjective clauses as you can. Check to be sure that you have used relative pronouns and commas correctly. Volunteers can show their pictures and read their captions aloud, inviting comments. Which buildings and captions were the most interesting?

5 Adverb Clauses

One-Minute Warm-Up

A Street

Complete each of the following sentences:

Aaron became lost when . . .

Confused, he walked for several blocks until . . .

Identify the subordinate clause in each of your sentences. Which word does each one modify?

1. You have been learning about subordinate clauses used as adjectives. An **adverb clause** is a subordinate clause used as an adverb.

    We visited New York after we had seen Washington.

    In both cities we walked until our feet gave out.

    Like an adverb, an adverb clause modifies a verb, an adjective, or another adverb.

    You should check your camera before you take the picture.
    (modifies the verb *should check*)

    New York was still busy while other cities slept. (modifies the adjective *busy*)

    I walked faster in New York than I normally do. (modifies the adverb *faster*)

2. An adverb clause is introduced by a **subordinating conjunction**. The subordinating conjunction relates the adverb clause to an independent clause.

    adverb clause   independent clause
    When our visit ended, we returned home.

    independent clause   adverb clause
    We will travel wherever you want to go next.

Common Subordinating Conjunctions		
after	before	that
although	even though	unless
as	if	until
as if	in order that	when
as long as	provided (that)	whenever
as soon as	since	where
as though	so that	wherever
because	than	while

3. Different subordinating conjunctions express different relationships.

When: Whenever I see an airplane, I want to travel.

Where: My little brother wants to go wherever I go.

How: He acts as though I should take him everywhere.

Why: He cries because I do not always take him along.

Comparison: My sister is more patient with him than I am.

4. When you use a subordinating conjunction, think about the meaning that you intend. Choose the conjunction that best expresses that meaning. Using a different conjunction can change the meaning of a sentence. Notice that a comma is used after an adverb clause that begins a sentence.

Whenever the family visited Chicago, Sheila found it hard to calm down.

Before the family visited Chicago, Sheila found it hard to calm down.

After the family visited Chicago, Sheila found it hard to calm down.

Try It Out

Speak Up What is the adverb clause in each of the following sentences? What word or words does each clause modify? Where should commas be used?

1. From the top of the Sears Tower, I can see for miles when the day is clear.
2. When I move around the deck I see different views.
3. The city view is spectacular after the sun goes down.
4. Before I go there again I'll buy a new camera.
5. I'd like to take a snapshot while the sun is setting.
6. Chicago is lively because there is always plenty to do.
7. Because Chicago was near my home I visited the city often.
8. I love returning to Chicago even though I have visited many other cities many times.
9. As soon as I return to Chicago I immediately want to go back to each of my favorite places.
10. I am unable to leave Chicago until I see the river running through the city.

more ▶

Supply an appropriate subordinating conjunction from the chart on page 408 to complete each sentence.

11. Visitors to Arizona may be surprised _____ half the state is high and cool.
12. _____ I visit Arizona, I see its desert scenery.
13. _____ I go, there are interesting things to do.
14. No state has more spectacular sights _____ Arizona does.
15. Millions of people go there _____ they can see the Painted Desert and the Petrified Forest.
16. Residents can live _____ winter did not exist.

Summing Up

- An **adverb clause** is a subordinate clause used as an adverb.
- A **subordinating conjunction** introduces an adverb clause.
- Use a comma after an adverb clause that begins a sentence.

Write each sentence, adding commas where they are needed. Underline each adverb clause once and each subordinating conjunction twice.

Example: As long as the weather is warm enough tourists flock to Maine.
> *As long as the weather is warm enough, tourists flock to Maine.*

17. Maine becomes quieter when the weather turns cold.
18. However, Maine offers attractions whenever you go there.
19. Although winters are very cold they are also very beautiful.
20. Hikers like to visit Maine's forests while the summer sun shines.
21. Few forests are more beautiful than they are.
22. Wherever you go along Maine's rocky coast look for crashing surf and famous lighthouses.

more ▶

23–30. Write each of the eight sentences in this part of a travel brochure. Underline each adverb clause. Double-underline the word or words that each clause modifies. Add or delete commas as necessary.

Example: If you go to Maine visit its national park.
If you go to Maine, <u>visit</u> its national park.

Acadia
NATIONAL PARK

As soon as summer arrives eager visitors come to Acadia National Park on the Atlantic coast of Maine. Acadia is biologically rich, because it lies at the crossroads of northern and temperate zones. Since it contains about 150 species of birds and more than four hundred species of plants the park is a favorite with naturalists.

After visitors hike the trails on Cadillac Mountain they often go to the Anemone Cave and Sieur de Monts Spring. Many remain at the spring until they have seen the Nature Center and the Abbe Museum's Indian relics. When they walk through the forests of Mount Desert Island park visitors find beauty and food for thought.

Tourists also explore other regions of Maine because those regions serve as home to such rarely seen animals as moose, bears, and bobcats. Wherever they look, visitors to Maine can see an abundance of plants and animals.

Writing Wrap-Up
WRITING • THINKING • LISTENING • SPEAKING

COMPARING / CONTRASTING

Write a Comparison
You are about to come home after visiting a place that you especially like or especially dislike. Write a post card to a friend comparing this place with some other place. Use several adverb clauses. With a partner, read your post cards aloud. Were the comparisons clear and lively? Were adverb clauses used correctly?

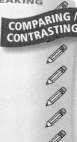

6 Noun Clauses

One-Minute Warm-Up

I didn't hear what you said.

Which clause in the first sentence is the direct object of the verb *did hear*? Which clause in the second sentence is the direct object of the verb *said*?

I said that I've lost my voice.

Uses for Noun Clauses

You have studied adjective clauses and adverb clauses. Another kind of clause is the noun clause. A **noun clause** is a subordinate clause that functions as a noun. You can use noun clauses in all the ways that you can use nouns.

	subject
Noun:	The message was clear.
	subject
Noun Clause:	What he said was clear.
	direct object
Noun:	I don't know his telephone number.
	direct object
Noun Clause:	I don't know how he can be reached.
	indirect object
Noun:	Give Claire Mahoney the message.
	indirect object
Noun Clause:	Give whoever answers the message.
	obj. of prep.
Noun:	I sent the notice to Rafael Lopez.
	obj. of prep.
Noun Clause:	I sent the notice to whoever was interested.
	pred. noun
Noun:	That is my intention.
	pred. noun
Noun Clause:	That is what I intend.

Words That Introduce Noun Clauses

how	what	where	which	whoever
if	whatever	wherever	whichever	whomever
that	when	whether	who, whom	why

Many words that introduce a noun clause can also introduce other kinds of subordinate clauses. To tell such clauses apart, determine how they are used in the sentence.

Noun Clause: Phil noticed that the phone was buzzing.
(The clause serves as direct object.)

Adjective Clause: The phone that was buzzing was off the hook.
(The clause modifies *phone*.)

Try It Out

Speak Up Identify each noun clause. Is it used as a subject, a direct object, an indirect object, an object of a preposition, or a predicate noun?

1. You know that the telephone uses electricity.
2. What you say into a phone creates sound waves.
3. An electric current carries the sound to whoever is listening.
4. Basically, this is how a telephone operates.
5. You can talk to whomever you like and say whatever you think.

Noun Clauses with who and whom

1. To decide whether to use *who* or *whom* in a noun clause, first decide how the relative pronoun functions within the clause. Use *who* or *whoever* as the subject of a verb within a noun clause.

Who is calling is not clear.   I know who is calling.
Whoever calls can talk to me.   Give the note to whoever answers.

2. Use *whom* or *whomever* as the object of a verb or the object of a preposition that is within a noun clause.

> Whom you meant is not clear. (You meant whom.)
> I don't know whom you called. (You called whom.)
> Whomever you called didn't answer. (You called whomever.)
> I'll give the message to whomever it was meant for. (It was meant for whomever.)

3. Look for how the relative pronoun is used in the clause, not how the clause is used in the sentence. The use of the pronoun within the clause tells you whether *who(ever)* or *whom(ever)* is correct.

Try It Out

Speak Up Identify the noun clause in each sentence. Which relative pronoun is correct?

6. Tell me (who, whom) is likely to run for that office.
7. (Whoever, Whomever) they nominate will probably accept.
8. I will vote for (whoever, whomever) will do the best job.
9. The candidate chosen was exactly (who, whom) you predicted.
10. The results of the election show (who, whom) the voters regarded as the most capable candidate.
11. Give my congratulations to (whoever, whomever) chose her.
12. I want to thank (whoever, whomever) was the campaign manager.

Voting booths

Summing Up

- A **noun clause** is a subordinate clause that acts as a noun.
- Use *who* and *whoever* as subjects in noun clauses.
- Use *whom* and *whomever* as objects in noun clauses.

Write each noun clause. Label it *subject, direct object, indirect object, object of a preposition,* or *predicate noun.*

Example: Do you know that telephones are important in elections?

that telephones are important in elections   direct object

13. Campaign workers use whatever helps them.
14. That telephones can be very helpful has been shown in many elections.
15. Who will win the election is what people want to know.
16. Telephoners ask whoever answers a series of questions.
17. Whether a candidate is popular is a vital matter.
18. Another question may be what the major issues are.
19. Voters usually give whoever is calling an answer.

20–24. Write each sentence in this part of a training manual for election campaign volunteers. Correct the five errors in the use of relative pronouns.

Example: Whomever called will call back.   *Whoever called will call back.*

Proofreading

Incoming calls should be taken by whomever is on duty. If a caller asks for someone by name, please say, "Whom shall I say is calling?" Whoever you talk to will probably ask about our candidate's views. Please learn the correct answers; answers should not depend on whom the caller speaks with.

Campaign workers will be asked to call whomever voted in the last election. Ask who the voter prefers in this election and why.

Writing Wrap-Up   WRITING • THINKING • LISTENING • SPEAKING

CREATING

Write Dialogue

Write some dialogue for a skit about a telephone conversation. (Perhaps the characters are confused about something.) Use noun clauses with *who, whom, whoever,* and *whomever.* With a partner, act out your skit. Invite the audience to comment on whether you have used relative pronouns correctly.

Forming Complex and Compound-Complex Sentences

Combining Sentences: Complex Sentences

You know that a complex sentence contains one independent clause and one or more subordinate clauses. You can combine short, related sentences to make a complex sentence. Make one sentence an independent clause. Turn the other sentences with supporting ideas into subordinate clauses.

> Remember that a subordinate clause can begin with a subordinating conjunction (such as *after* or *because*) or a relative pronoun (such as *which* or *who*).

We want the students to elect us.

We will fulfill our campaign promises.

Our promises include better communication.

subordinate clause
If the students elect us,
    independent clause
we will fulfill our campaign promises,
    subordinate clause
which include better communication.

Apply It

1–5. Revise this draft of a persuasive speech. Combine each set of underlined sentences to make complex sentences. Use the subordinating conjunctions *although, because, if,* and *when* and the relative pronoun *which.*

Revising

Other candidates want to be elected. They think it will look good on a future job application. Jaime is different. He sincerely cares about our school.

Jaime has no experience in student government. He can get things done. He has proved this many times.

The conservation club planted trees around the school last year. Jaime led this effort. This effort beautified the property. Adults respect Jaime. He worked with school committee members. They got the classrooms repainted. This was a big improvement.

Jaime will do more than improve our school's appearance. He wants all students to become more involved. New ideas and leadership are important to you. Elect Jaime.

Combining Sentences: Compound-Complex Sentences You can also combine short, choppy sentences into compound-complex sentences. A **compound-complex sentence** has at least two independent clauses and at least one subordinate clause. Use this type of sentence to vary your writing style and to group related ideas.

The word *telephone* was coined in 1849.

In 1876, Alexander Graham Bell made the first working telephone.

independent clause
The word *telephone* was coined in 1849,
independent clause
but there were no working telephones
subordinate clause
until Alexander Graham Bell made the first one in 1876.

In the sentence above, notice that no comma is needed between a subordinate clause and an independent clause when the independent clause comes first. When an independent clause follows a subordinate clause, remember to separate the clauses with a comma.

subordinate clause   independent clause
Before direct dialing was invented, telephone calls were connected by hand,
independent clause
and operators had to move wires to complete each call.

Apply It

6–8. Revise this draft of two paragraphs in a research report. Combine each set of underlined sentences to make a compound-complex sentence. Use the subordinating conjunctions *because, when,* and *while.*

Revising

The Telephone in Popular Culture

The telephone has a place in popular culture. Movie thrillers use the ominous ring of a phone to build suspense. Comedies play up the reactions of characters. This is while the characters are speaking on the phone.

Global Communication

Communication boomed in the twentieth century. We now rely on instant communication. Many people carry cellular phones. Many homes have more than one phone. Technology keeps changing. The fax machine and e-mail were developed. They revolutionized communication. The new technology continues to thrive.

Enrichment

Clauses!

CLAUSE CAPERS

Choose a subordinating conjunction from page 408. Write a subordinate clause starting with the conjunction. Make each following word begin with the next letter of the conjunction. Underline the first letter of each word. Then add an independent clause to form a complex sentence. How many sentences can you write using the same subordinating conjunction?

Unless   Unless Ned Lehman eats some supper, he won't have energy for the soccer game.

Challenge Start out with an independent clause. Then trade papers with a partner and add a dependent clause, following the rules above.

Clause-Clues Crossword

Create a crossword puzzle. Choose ten words for which you can write a clue that contains an independent clause and a subordinate clause. Write the longest word on graph paper—down or across—one letter per square. Each word must share a square with at least one other word in the puzzle. Number each word in the square of the word's first letter.

On a separate paper, write your clues. Check their accurateness in a dictionary. Each clue must be a complete sentence with a subordinate clause. Underline the subordinate clause. Number the clues and separate them into two lists, *Across* and *Down*.

On clean graph paper, copy the outline of the puzzle, leaving out the letters but including the numbers. Give the puzzle and clues to a classmate to solve.

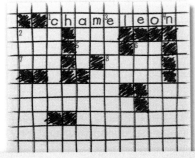

Across
1. It changes color when it is scared.

1 **Independent and Subordinate Clauses** *(p. 396)* Write each underlined group of words. Label it *phrase* or *clause*. Then label each clause *subordinate* or *independent*.

1. The gnu, <u>known also as the wildebeest</u>, is an African antelope.
2. <u>With its massive shoulders and thick neck</u>, the gnu is large.
3. <u>Despite its size</u>, the gnu stands on thin legs.
4. <u>It can travel fast</u> because it takes long strides.
5. <u>When they are disturbed</u>, gnu perform certain actions.

2 **Adjective Clauses** *(p. 399)* Write each adjective clause, and underline the relative pronoun. Then write the word or words that the clause modifies.

6. There are many cities that have popular nicknames.
7. Some are names that tell the city's most important industry.
8. Pittsburgh is a place that is called the Steel City.
9. Another major city is Detroit, which is known throughout the world as the Motor City.
10. The people of Dallas, who affectionately call their city Big D, express great pride in their hometown.

3 **Adjective Clauses with *who, whom,* and *whose*** *(p. 402)* Write each sentence, using *who, whom,* or *whose.*

11. There are many people _____ inventions improved our lives.
12. An inventor to _____ we are grateful is Alexander Graham Bell.
13. Bell, _____ invented the telephone, also designed devices to help deaf people.
14. This inventor, _____ was born in Scotland, lived in North America most of his life.
15. An inventor _____ many have praised, Bell also made discoveries about aircraft.

4 **Essential and Nonessential Clauses** *(p. 405)* Write each sentence, using the appropriate relative pronoun. Label each adjective clause *essential* or *nonessential.*

16. Most Eskimos call themselves Inuit, _____ means "people."
17. Some Inuit _____ live in the northernmost part of Canada use winter dwellings _____ are called igloos.
18. These winter homes, _____ are sometimes made from blocks of snow, are dome-shaped.
19. In summer, many Inuit live in tents _____ are made of canvas.
20. The kayak, _____ is a boat for one person, has a wooden frame.

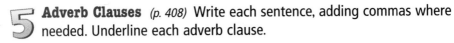

5 **Adverb Clauses** *(p. 408)* Write each sentence, adding commas where needed. Underline each adverb clause.

21. Because they were considered great delicacies oranges have been cultivated since ancient times.
22. Orange cultivation spread as the Roman Empire grew.
23. Before Columbus sailed orange trees grew in the Canary Islands.
24. Sweet, sour, and mandarin are the three main categories of oranges although there are many hybrids.
25. Although sweet oranges grow in warm areas some mandarin oranges can grow in the colder Gulf Coast region.

6 **Noun Clauses** *(p. 412)* Write each noun clause. Label it *subject, direct object, indirect object, object of a preposition,* or *predicate noun* to show how it is used in the sentence.

26. Studies show that dreams include sensations of sight, touch, and hearing.
27. Why images of smell and taste are rare in dreams is not known.
28. No one really knows what the purpose of dreams is.
29. One theory is that dreams help solve problems.
30. Ask whomever you know about their dreams.

Mixed Review 31–36. There are six errors in the use of clauses in these paragraphs from a physical therapy textbook. Write the paragraphs correctly.

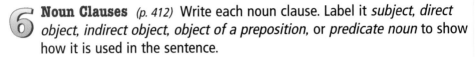

Proofreading Checklist
✔ incorrect use of *who, whom, whoever,* or *whomever* in adjective clauses and noun clauses
✔ incorrect punctuation of adjective clauses
✔ incorrect punctuation of adverb clauses

Proofreading

    The scapula which is also called the shoulder blade, performs six different motions. For example, it protracts and retracts the shoulder joint, that is attached to it. Because the scapula performs six joint motions it needs muscular support. Fortunately, the muscles that support the upper back, are strong and diverse.

    The shoulder blade must do its work well, especially for the person for who hard work or exercise is routine. Whomever has good posture uses the scapula to rotate the shoulder joint backward until the chest is thrust forward.

Test Practice

Write the numbers 1–4 on a sheet of paper. Read the underlined sentences. Then choose the best way to combine them into one sentence. Write the letter for that answer.

1 Zoe spoke loudly.
Zoe usually speaks more softly.

 A Zoe spoke more loudly than she usually does.

 B Zoe spoke more loudly which she usually speaks.

 C Zoe, who spoke more loudly than usual.

 D Zoe usually spoke more loudly than softly.

2 The newborn kangaroo stays in its mother's pouch for more than thirty weeks.
The newborn kangaroo is called a joey.

 F The newborn kangaroo whom stays in its mother's pouch for more than thirty weeks is called a joey.

 G The newborn kangaroo is called a joey, and stays inside its mother's pouch for more than thirty weeks.

 H The newborn kangaroo, which is called a joey, stays in its mother's pouch for more than thirty weeks.

 J The newborn kangaroo stays in its mother's pouch for more than thirty weeks because it is called a joey.

3 Frank Lloyd Wright was a great twentieth-century architect.
Frank Lloyd Wright designed a house called Fallingwater.

 A Frank Lloyd Wright, whom designed a house called Fallingwater, was a great twentieth-century architect.

 B Frank Lloyd Wright whom designed a house called Fallingwater was a great twentieth-century architect.

 C Frank Lloyd Wright who designed a house called Fallingwater was a great twentieth-century architect.

 D Frank Lloyd Wright, who designed a house called Fallingwater, was a great twentieth-century architect.

4 Please give this old coat away.
Please give it to someone who can use it.

 F Please give this old coat away, and please give it to whoever can use it.

 G Please give this old coat away, and give it to whomever can use it.

 H Please give this old coat away and to who can use it.

 J Please give this old coat away to whoever can use it.

Now write numbers 5–10 on your paper. Look at the paragraph. Choose the correct way to write the underlined part in each numbered line. Write the letter for that answer. If the part is already correct, write the letter for the last answer, "Correct as it is."

(5) New Zealand is a nation in the <u>Pacific ocean, East of Australia.</u>

(6) Originally <u>settling by the Maoris, a Polynesian people,</u> this country of

(7) islands <u>were colonized by the British in the 1800's.</u> Although the Maoris

(8) initially rebelled, they eventually signed the <u>Treaty of Waitangi, what gave</u> ownership of New Zealand to Britain. Today, this beautiful Pacific

(9) nation <u>has a real mixed population (Maoris individuals of British</u>

(10) <u>descent and</u> immigrants from other nations inhabit the islands.) <u>All considers theirself</u> true New Zealanders.

---

5 **A** Pacific ocean, east of Australia

   B Pacific Ocean, East of Australia

   C Pacific Ocean, east of Australia

   D Correct as it is

6 **F** settling by the Maoris a Polynesian people,

   G settled by the Maoris a Polynesian people,

   H settled by the Maoris, a Polynesian people,

   J Correct as it is

7 **A** was colonized by the British in the 1800s

   B was colonized by the British in the eighteen hundreds

   C were colonized by the British in the 1800s

   D Correct as it is

8 **F** Treaty of Waitangi which gave

   G Treaty Of Waitangi, which gave

   H Treaty of Waitangi, which gave

   J Correct as it is

9 **A** has a real mixed population; Maoris, individuals of British descent, and

   B has a really mixed population; Maoris, individuals of British descent and

   C has a really mixed population: Maoris, individuals of British descent, and

   D Correct as it is

10 **F** All consider themselves

   G All considers themselves

   H All consider theirself

   J Correct as it is

Unit 1: The Sentence

Sentences, Subjects, and Predicates *(pp. 34, 37, 40, 43, 46)* Write each sentence. Label it *simple, compound,* or *complex.* Draw a line between each complete subject and complete predicate. Underline simple subjects once and simple predicates twice.

1. People wrote on bones or clay before the development of paper.
2. Paper was first made from plants.
3. Plants and water were mixed, pounded, and squeezed into paper.
4. Paper was later made from wood.
5. Machines now produce paper, which people use extensively.

Compound Sentences, Conjunctions, Complex Sentences, Fragments, and Run-ons *(pp. 51, 54, 57, 63)* Rewrite the sentences, correcting the fragments and run-ons. Add conjunctions and commas where necessary. Label each new sentence *simple, compound,* or *complex.*

6. Kris's grandparents live in Stockholm he is visiting them.
7. Although they live there.
8. Stockholm is built on islands, it can be seen well from a boat.
9. As the guide points out sights.
10. A modern city with a long history.

Stockholm, Sweden

See www.eduplace.com/kids/hme/ for a tricky usage or spelling question.

Cumulative Review **423**

Unit 2: Nouns

Compound and Collective Nouns *(p. 85)* Write the compound and the collective nouns. Label each one *compound* or *collective*.

11. Cecilia Beaux was a painter who lived from 1855 to 1942.
12. When she was a small child, the family moved to West Philadelphia, where she was taught at home until she was fourteen years old.
13. She did not do very well in the classroom, and when she was seventeen years old, she entered art school instead.
14. Beaux became a successful painter, and in 1923 a committee named her one of the twelve greatest women in the United States.

Cecilia Beaux

Singular, Plural, and Possessive Nouns *(pp. 90, 94)* Copy each singular noun. Then write its singular possessive, its plural, and its plural possessive forms.

15. Morris
16. mouse
17. child
18. finch
19. fox

Unit 3: Verbs

Kinds of Verbs, Verb Phrases, Transitive/Intransitive Verbs, Direct and Indirect Objects, and Predicate Nouns and Adjectives

(pp. 112, 115, 137, 140, 144) Write each sentence. Then underline the verbs. Label each verb or phrase *action* or *linking* and *transitive* or *intransitive*. Then write *DO* (direct object), *IO* (indirect object), *PN* (predicate noun), and *PA* (predicate adjective) above the appropriate words.

20. How does a simple telescope work?
21. Some telescopes are reflective.
22. The lens gathers light from an object.
23. The light bends to a point, or focus.
24. At the focus, the original object becomes an image.

25. The eyepiece magnifies the image.
26. Then the human eye can see the enlarged image.
27. Willis gave his brother a telescope for graduation.
28. Willis's brother uses his telescope for stargazing.
29. No one knows the identity of the telescope's inventor.
30. With telescopes, people have made many discoveries about stars and planets.

Tenses; *be, have,* and *do* (pp. 118, 122)
Write the four principal parts of each verb.

31. hop
32. bathe
33. aim
34. play
35. worry
36. do
37. be
38. have

Irregular Verbs, Progressives (pp. 125, 129, 132) Write each sentence, using the correct verb or verbs. Underline that verb and any helping verbs. Label its tense and, when appropriate, its progressive form.

39. The human race (has, have) always studied the stars.
40. People (have, had) been gathering information about the heavens before anyone (make, made) telescopes.
41. Two thousand years before Columbus, a person (shown, showed) that the earth (is, are) a globe.
42. In the 1600s, Galileo (can, could) see details of the planets.
43. After this, scientists (was, were) still searching for better ways to make telescopes.
44. Isaac Newton (make, made) the first telescope that (produce, produced) a really sharp image.
45. By the 1800s, Alvan Clark (was, were) making powerful lenses that astronomers are still (use, using).
46. What will scientists (have, has) found by the end of this century?
47. Scientists will be (look, looking) for glass that can be large but will not (crack, cracks) when cooled.
48. A large telescope will (show, showing) the disk of a planet.

Unit 4: Modifiers

Adjectives, Adverbs *(pp. 190, 200)* Write each modifier, labeling it *adjective* or *adverb*. Then write the word or words that it modifies. Do not list articles.

49. Certain North American pioneers built wooden cabins.
50. Swedish settlers probably built log cabins in the 1600s.
51. Logs were not cut carelessly, for their size was important.
52. Carefully the builder fit the split logs together.
53. Few people could afford costly glass panes in their windows.
54. Most settlers used animal skins or greased paper to cover window openings.

Comparing with Adjectives and Adverbs *(pp. 196, 206)* Write each sentence, using the correct degree of each modifier.

55. One of the _____ castles in the world is in Bavaria. (elaborate)
56. Of all the castles he has seen, Marc likes this one, built by King Ludwig II, _____. (well)
57. Ludwig's Linderhof is _____ than his other castles. (unusual)
58. Linderhof has the _____ opera stage ever built. (strange)
59. Linderhof has _____ charm than Ludwig's other castles. (much)

Unit 5: Capitalization and Punctuation

Sentences; Proper Nouns and Adjectives; Commas; Dates, Addresses, Letters; Semicolons and Colons; Abbreviations *(pp. 239, 241, 245, 248, 253, 263, 268)* Write the following letter, using capital letters and punctuation where necessary.

60. 15 ridge st.
61. orange ca 92667
62. feb 18 2001

63. stamp masters inc
64. p o box 583
65. beaumont tx 77704
66. dear sir
67.   please send me the following items one stock book one pair of tweezers one stamp album and one box of hinges these were
68. advertised in your spring catalog
69.   i understand that you are opening a store in encino That will
70. please us customers in the west

71. sincerely yours
72. kirk o'brien

Quotations, Titles *(pp. 256, 260)* Write each sentence, adding the correct punctuation and capitalization.

73. What does the word *philately* mean Kirby asked.
74. It is the collection Barney responded of postage stamps.
75. Kirby then asked what was the first American stamp magazine?
76. Barney said that it was called the stamp collector's review.
77. Todd asked to borrow Barney's book, famous stamps of europe.

Commas *(pp. 245, 248)* Write each sentence, adding commas where necessary.

78. Paris the City of Light is a favorite tourist spot.
79. My friends you should visit this city.
80. Some people like Paris in winter but most prefer it in spring.
81. Looking from the top of Notre Dame you can see the entire city spread out before you.
82. The Paris Opera which has ceilings by Chagall is a spectacularly beautiful building.

Paris, France: Eiffel Tower

Paris, France: Arc de Triomphe

Unit 6: Pronouns

Pronoun Case, Choosing Pronouns *(pp. 308, 327)* Write each sentence correctly. Label the pronouns *subject* or *object.*

83. Mr. Cargill asked Ben and (I, me) to name a volcano in Italy.
84. Neither (he, him) nor (I, me) knew.
85. (We, Us) boys hadn't studied.
86. Lu and (she, her) mentioned Mt. Etna.
87. "Ask (she, her) and (I, me) the next question, please."

Indefinite Pronouns *(p. 318)* Write the form in parentheses that agrees with each indefinite pronoun.

88. All (has, have) completed (his or her, their) lists of state mottos.
89. Not everyone (has, have) defined *Eureka* as "I have found it."
90. Each of the teachers (has, have) checked the work.
91. Most of the students (has, have) remembered Nevada.
92. None of the answers on my test (was, were) wrong.

Antecedents, Kinds of Pronouns *(pp. 302, 312, 315, 323)* Rewrite each sentence, correcting any pronoun errors.

93. This here painting was done by Ron and myself.
94. Who's paintings are in the museum this month?
95. Sam told Dan that he visited the Brooklyn Museum.
96. Who did you take with you to the exhibit?
97. Who have you told about it besides herself?

Unit 7: Phrases

Prepositional Phrases as Modifiers *(p. 350)* Write each prepositional phrase and the word it modifies.

98. Periwinkles are a kind of sea snail.
99. You can find them off the coasts of the Atlantic and the Pacific.
100. Periwinkles depend on algae for food.
101. Algae are plants without stems, roots, or leaves.

Participles and Participial Phrases
(pp. 358, 361) Write the participial phrases and the words they modify. Underline each participle.

102. Letters sent to John Adams by his wife still exist.
103. Married fifty-four years, John and Abigail were a close couple.
104. The political advice given in Abigail's letters was usually sound.
105. Telling much about her times, her letters express strong feelings about women's education and freedom.

John and Abigail Adams

Gerunds and Gerund Phrases *(pp. 364, 367)* Write each gerund phrase, under-lining the gerund. Then label it *subject, direct object, object of a preposition,* or *predicate noun.*

106. You can learn a great deal by reading the newspaper.
107. Scanning the headlines daily will help you be informed.
108. Jason's favorite activity is doing the crossword puzzle.
109. Myra likes reading about travel.

Infinitive Phrases *(p. 376)* Write each infinitive phrase. Label it *noun, adjective,* or *adverb* to tell how it is used.

110. Now is the time to improve your diet.
111. To eat wisely is important to your well-being.
112. One way is to consume whole grains.
113. To have a better diet, you should consume less fat.

Unit 8: Clauses

Adjective Clauses *(p. 399)* Write each sentence. Underline each adjective clause once and each relative pronoun twice. Add commas if necessary.

114. *Madama Butterfly* which is an opera about Japan was written by a composer whose name was Puccini.
115. *The Girl of the Golden West* which is an opera about the Old West was written by the same composer.
116. Puccini also wrote an opera that takes place in Paris.
117. He never finished *Turandot* which some consider his finest work.

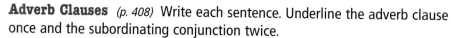

Adverb Clauses *(p. 408)* Write each sentence. Underline the adverb clause once and the subordinating conjunction twice.

118. Weather seems unpredictable because we have not yet learned enough about the forces affecting it.
119. Forecasters make use of sensitive equipment so that they can make accurate observations of the weather.
120. Better weather forecasts are possible because computer technology has advanced.
121. Weather forecasting is an important science as long as it is reasonably accurate.
122. Although they are often correct in their predictions, sometimes the weather surprises forecasters.
123. Even though a storm stays at sea, its effect can extend hundreds of miles.
124. Strong winds can unexpectedly develop while forecasters are measuring other storm variables.

Noun Clauses *(p. 412)* Write each noun clause. Label it *sub., dir. obj., indir. obj., obj. of a prep.,* or *pred. noun.*

125. Whoever is interested in the sea may enjoy visiting an aquarium.
126. The aquarium near the waterfront is where I'd like to go.
127. Beth suggested that we go there next Saturday.
128. We will first walk to wherever there are tropical fish.
129. Ask whoever has the guidebook where we should go.
130. We will follow whoever can take us on the tour.

(pages 396–398)

1 Independent and Subordinate Clauses

- A **clause** is a group of words that has a subject and a predicate.
- An **independent clause** expresses a complete thought.
- A **subordinate clause** does not express a complete thought and cannot stand alone in a sentence.

● Write each underlined clause. Label it *subordinate* or *independent*.

Example: <u>Because sea water is salty</u>, it is not drinkable.
      Because sea water is salty   subordinate

1. In general, <u>most sea water is about 3 percent salt</u>.
2. <u>Although some seas are saltier</u>, that is the average.
3. The Dead Sea, for example, <u>is 25 percent salt</u>.
4. <u>While it is the saltiest sea on earth</u>, it is small.
5. Nothing lives in the Dead Sea <u>because the sea is so salty</u>.

Dead Sea

▲ Write each underlined word group. Label it *phrase* or *clause*.

Example: <u>Before modern forecasting</u>, what did people know about the weather? *Before modern forecasting   phrase*

6. <u>Before people understood weather</u>, they observed and recorded it.
7. Sailors were the best observers <u>until modern times</u>.
8. <u>Since their lives depended on weather</u>, they watched it closely.
9. European ships met tropical storms <u>after new sea routes were developed</u>.
10. Most Europeans never knew such storms <u>before the fifteenth century</u>.
11. *Hurricane* is a name <u>based on a Carib word</u>.

■ Write *phrase* or *clause* to identify each word group. Change each phrase into a subordinate clause, and then write a complex sentence using each subordinate clause.

Example: before the end of the day
      phrase   Before the day ends, a major storm may strike.

12. before a hurricane occurs
13. until weather predictions became accurate
14. after a severe hurricane or other storm
15. after spotting a tornado in the distance
16. because of the severity of some storms

(pages 399–401)

2 Adjective Clauses

Remember

- An **adjective clause** modifies a noun or a pronoun.
- A relative pronoun such as *who, which,* or *that* usually introduces an adjective clause.
- *Where* and *when* may also introduce adjective clauses.

● Each adjective clause is underlined. Write the noun or pronoun that it modifies.

Example: The bloodhound, <u>which is used for tracking</u>, is a gentle dog.
     bloodhound

1. Bloodhounds came from England, <u>where they were well known</u>.
2. People <u>who are familiar with bloodhounds</u> know they are gentle.
3. Bloodhounds, <u>which are calm and friendly</u>, offer no protection.
4. Instead, they are used for their amazing noses, <u>which help them to track criminals and missing persons</u>.

▲ Write each adjective clause and the word or words that it modifies.

Example: The golden retriever, which is an attractive dog, is a breed that originated in England in the 1800s.
     which is an attractive dog—golden retriever
     that originated in England in the 1800s—breed

5. These dogs, which really are golden, are handsome.
6. It is one breed that is used for guiding people who are blind.
7. World War I was the time when dogs were first trained for this.
8. Morristown, New Jersey, is the place where many guide dogs are trained.
9. The golden retriever has a personality that is ideal for the job.

■ Add one or more adjective clauses to each independent clause to form a complex sentence.

Example: Some people prefer dogs.
     Some people who like pets prefer dogs that are good watchdogs.

10. People may want watchdogs.
11. Other people may prefer a different kind.
12. Animal shelters take in animals.
13. The shelters are usually full of animals.
14. Each of the animals will be right for someone.
15. An animal lover will probably go home with a new pet.

(pages 402–404)

3 Adjective Clauses with *who, whom,* and *whose*

Remember

- Use *who* when the relative pronoun is the subject of the adjective clause.
- Use *whom* when the relative pronoun is the direct object or an object of a preposition in the adjective clause.
- Use *whose* when the relative pronoun shows possession.

● Write each sentence correctly using *who, whom,* or *whose* to complete each adjective clause.

Example: Washington Irving was an author _____ wrote with humor.
    who wrote with humor

1. Washington Irving, _____ was born in 1783, was a New Yorker.
2. Irving was an American writer _____ Europeans admired.
3. Those _____ have heard of Irving know "Rip Van Winkle."
4. Rip Van Winkle was a person _____ life took a strange turn.
5. He was the man _____ fell asleep for twenty years.

▲ Write each sentence, using *who, whom,* or *whose.* Underline the adjective clause.

Example: People for _____ poetry is fun like to read poems aloud.
    People for whom poetry is fun like to read poems aloud.

6. Those _____ write poems use language in a special way.
7. There are poets _____ work has been read for centuries.
8. Anyone _____ has something to say can say it in a poem.
9. There are poets _____ poems tell a story.
10. There are some for _____ a poem expresses feelings.

■ Add an adjective clause introduced by *who, whom,* or *whose* to each independent clause to form a complex sentence. Vary the pronouns.

Example: People usually like to read.
    People who like to write usually like to read.

11. Shakespeare was a sixteenth-century writer.
12. One American poet is Emily Dickinson.
13. Edgar Allan Poe was a skilled writer.
14. Many people dream of creating great works of literature.
15. Writers have opportunities in the theater, movies, and TV.

(pages 405–407)

④ Essential and Nonessential Clauses

- An adjective clause is essential or nonessential.
- An **essential clause** identifies the noun or pronoun it modifies. It is not set off with commas.
- A **nonessential clause** gives extra information about the noun or pronoun it modifies. It is set off with commas.

● Write *essential* if the underlined adjective clause is necessary to the meaning of the sentence. Write *nonessential* if the clause only adds information.

Example: People have always needed shelters <u>that protect them</u>.　*essential*

1. At first, people lived in caves <u>that were in hills and cliffs</u>.
2. The first people <u>who moved out of the caves</u> built huts.
3. Soon huts were built for domestic animals, <u>which also needed shelter</u>.
4. Then came more shelters, <u>which were used for storage</u>.
5. Eventually, people built structures <u>that were large and strong</u>.

▲ Write each sentence. Underline the adjective clause. Label it *essential* or *nonessential*.

Example: The Egyptian climate, which is hot, requires cool homes.
　　　　　The Egyptian climate, <u>which is hot</u>, requires cool homes.
　　　　　nonessential

6. Ancient Egyptians built houses that were designed to be cool.
7. The windows, which were small and few, admitted little sunlight.
8. Doorways faced north to catch the breeze that came from there.
9. Outside walls, which were whitewashed, reflected the sun's heat.
10. Most houses had a lobby that led to a cool inner room.

■ Rewrite each sentence as a complex sentence that includes an adjective clause. Label the clause *essential* or *nonessential*. Use commas correctly.

Example: Kent designed two buildings. *The two buildings that Kent designed both won architectural awards.　essential*

11. The architect designed the house.
12. The house sits on a cliff above the beach.
13. The owners approved the design.
14. Visitors often admire the house.
15. The house next door is painted gray.

(pages 408–411)

5 Adverb Clauses

Remember

- An **adverb clause** is a subordinate clause used as an adverb.
- A **subordinating conjunction** introduces an adverb clause.
- Use a comma after an adverb clause that begins a sentence.

● The adverb clause in each sentence is underlined. Write each subordinating conjunction.

Example: <u>When city space became scarce</u>, people built skyscrapers. *When*

1. <u>Because skyscrapers extend upward</u>, they take up little land.
2. Skyscrapers became common <u>as the price of steel went down</u>.
3. <u>Before steel was used</u>, the walls had to support the weight.
4. Tall structures could not be built <u>unless the walls were very thick</u>.
5. Skyscrapers can have glass walls <u>if the steel structure is solid</u>.

▲ Write each adverb clause, underlining the subordinating conjunction. Write the word or words that the clause modifies.

Example: <u>Before</u> a skyscraper is built, engineers test the soil.
<u>Before</u> a skyscraper is built—test

6. If the test results are approved, plans can continue.
7. After the building site is cleared, the digging begins.
8. When the digging is done, the base and superstructure are begun.
9. Each piece of steel is numbered so that workers know its place.
10. The pieces are bolted until welders join them permanently.

■ Write a complex sentence by adding an adverb clause to each independent clause. Use a subordinating conjunction.

Example: I want to travel.
Whenever I see a plane or train, I want to travel.

11. I would first like to tour the United States.
12. There will be interesting things to see.
13. I can plan the trip in my imagination.
14. I will visit the southern states.
15. I plan to remain there.
16. My next visit will be to the southwestern states.

(pages 412–415)

⑥ Noun Clauses

Remember

- A **noun clause** is a subordinate clause that acts as a noun.
- Use *who* and *whoever* as subjects in noun clauses.
- Use *whom* and *whomever* as objects in noun clauses.

● Each noun clause has been underlined. Write *subject, direct object, indirect object, object of a preposition*, or *predicate noun* to tell how the clause is used in the sentence.

Example: Did you ever wonder <u>how other people answer the phone?</u>
       direct object

1. <u>How people answer the phone</u> varies around the world.
2. In Israel you give <u>whoever telephones</u> a big "Shalom."
3. "Bueno" is <u>what a person in Mexico says</u> on the telephone.
4. In Italy, "Pronto" means <u>that you are ready to talk.</u>
5. "Hello" is similar to <u>what people say in France and Germany.</u>

▲ Write each noun clause. Label it *subject, direct object, indirect object, object of a preposition*, or *predicate noun*.

Example: That telephones have changed is quite obvious.
       That telephones have changed   subject

6. Did you know that the first telephones were sold in pairs?
7. A direct wire ran between wherever the two phones were placed.
8. By World War I, a telephone was what many Americans wanted.
9. A telephone offered whoever used it a new way to communicate.

■ Write each sentence, using *who, whoever, whom*, or *whomever*. Then write *subject, direct object*, or *object of a preposition* to tell how the relative pronoun functions in the clause.

Example: Give the information to _____ calls.
       Give the information to whoever calls.   subject

10. _____ uses the telephone should thank its inventor.
11. _____ you should thank is Alexander Graham Bell.
12. Telephones are taken for granted by _____ uses them.
13. Without the telephone, how would you reach _____ you wanted to contact?
14. You could speak directly only to _____ you saw.

Part 2

Writing, Listening, Speaking, and Viewing

What You Will Find in This Part:

Section 1

Expressing and Influencing

What You Will Find in This Section:

Listening to an Opinion

An **opinion** states what someone thinks or feels about something. Opinions cannot be proved true or false, but they can be supported by facts, reasons, and examples. The main purposes for listening to an opinion are to learn what someone else thinks and to help yourself make up your own mind. The following guidelines can help you be a good listener.

Guidelines for Listening to an Opinion

▶ Listen for the topic. What subject is the opinion about?

▶ Notice terms such as *in my opinion, I believe, good, best, bad,* and *worst.* They signal that an opinion is being stated.

▶ Identify the opinion. What does the author think?

▶ Listen for reasons. Why does the author hold this opinion?

▶ Listen for details. What facts or examples explain the author's reasons?

▶ Evaluate the reasons and details. Are the reasons strong? Do the details support the reasons?

▶ Consider the author's purpose. Why is he or she sharing this opinion?

Try It Out Listen as your teacher reads aloud two *USA Today* editorials expressing contrasting opinions about community service for high school students. Take notes to help you answer the questions below.

● What is the topic of these articles?
● What are the opinions being expressed?
● What reasons do the authors give to support their opinions?
● What details do the authors give to explain their reasons?
● Why do you think each author wants you to know his or her opinion?

HELP 7 See page H33 for tips on taking notes while listening.

Writing an Opinion Paragraph

A **paragraph** is a group of sentences that work together to tell about a single main idea. A paragraph has a topic and a main idea. The **topic** is the subject of the paragraph. The **main idea** is what the author wants to say about this subject. The first sentence is always indented.

A paragraph that expresses an author's thoughts or feelings is an **opinion paragraph.** Its main idea is the author's opinion. What opinion is expressed in the paragraph below?

Indent —

Opinion — statement

> I support the school's decision to start teaching foreign languages in elementary school. First, studies prove that the younger you are, the easier it is to learn a new language. My cousin started Japanese lessons at age six, and now he speaks fluently. His parents began studying at the same time, but they still struggle in their intermediate class. Another reason is that learning a new language teaches more than just new words—it teaches awareness and tolerance of other people's cultures. The earlier this happens, the better. Finally, achieving fluency helps students find jobs when they're older. If two candidates have the same education and experience, the one who speaks a second language often gets hired. The only drawback to the school's decision is that I'm too old to benefit from it!

Supporting — sentences

Concluding — sentence

Opinion Statement

Supporting Sentences

Concluding Sentence

In the paragraph above, the topic is teaching foreign languages in elementary school. The main idea—the writer's opinion—is that it's best to begin teaching children foreign languages as early as possible. Which sentence tells the topic and the main idea?

The labels show the three parts of an opinion paragraph.

- The **opinion statement**, a kind of topic sentence, expresses the writer's opinion.
- The **supporting sentences** back up the writer's opinion.
- The **concluding sentence** wraps up the paragraph.

Think and Discuss Reread the paragraph about teaching foreign languages above. What reasons are given in the supporting sentences?

The Opinion Statement

You have learned that in an opinion paragraph the **opinion statement** introduces the topic and states the writer's thoughts or feelings about it. The opinion statement usually begins the paragraph.

Topic   Main idea

Example: The annual high school tour for eighth-graders helps most students feel less anxious about the transition.

Main idea

Occasionally, the opinion statement appears at the end of a paragraph. When this happens, it takes the place of the concluding sentence. Which is the opinion statement in the paragraph below? Which are the supporting sentences?

> Recently, our supermarket hired senior citizens as part-time cashiers. Hiring the seniors allowed the market to fill vacant positions. Low unemployment had been making it hard to find new employees, and long lines had been scaring away customers. Furthermore, the younger employees like working with their new coworkers. They learn from their elders' experience and enjoy hearing stories about the past. Finally, retirees who were bored at home now have a more interesting way to spend the day. My friend Raphael's grandfather explained, "I hated relaxing! I prefer feeling useful." Hiring senior citizens has benefited the whole community.

Try It Out Read the paragraph below. Alone or with a partner, write the topic and the main idea. Then write two possible opinion statements.

> _Opinion statement_ . First, you learn patience. When I started tutoring the younger students, I thought they were little pests! Eventually, though, I learned to put their energy to good use. Tutoring also teaches you to become more organized. You need to plan your lessons in advance and juggle your schedule to make time for the students. Most important, tutoring lets you feel proud of yourself. I don't know who is more excited when they finally understand a challenging math problem, me or my students!

Supporting Sentences

Supporting sentences usually follow the opinion statement in an opinion paragraph. They support the opinion with **reasons** that answer the question *Why?* about the writer's opinion. Each reason is supported in turn by details such as **facts** and **examples**. Facts are information that can be proved true. Examples are events or instances used to illustrate a point.

In the supermarket paragraph, the supporting sentences explain how hiring senior citizens has benefited the community.

Reason: The market was able to fill vacant positions.

Fact: Low unemployment had made it hard to find new employees.

Reason: Bored retirees have a better way to spend the day.

Example: Raphael's grandfather explained, "I hated relaxing!"

The paragraph below uses facts and examples in its supporting sentences.

Of all the musical instruments, the human voice is best. It's the most personal instrument there is. Like fingerprints and snowflakes, no two voices are exactly the same, even when they are singing the same notes. A more practical reason is that singing does not require any external equipment, so it's free, and you can take it anywhere. My mother loves to sing while she cooks—I'd like to see her try to cook while playing the tuba! Finally, singing offers complete freedom of expression. While a flute or an accordion has a limited range of sounds, the human voice can be manipulated in countless ways. I like to croon, wail, chant, hum, or harmonize, depending on my mood. Did you realize you were the owner of such a priceless instrument?

Think and Discuss Look at the supporting sentences in the paragraph above. What facts and examples are used?

more ▶

Ordering Details Reasons in an opinion paragraph are usually arranged from least important to most important or from most important to least important. **Transitional words and phrases**, such as *to begin with, next, for instance, furthermore,* and *finally,* connect the supporting details. What transitional words and phrases do the sample paragraphs on pages 443, 444, and 445 contain?

HELP? See page 20 for more transitional words.

Try It Out Complete the opinion statement below, and write three sentences to support it. Use at least one transitional word or phrase.

Opinion statement: _____ is the profession that deserves the highest salary.

GRAMMAR TIP *Use a possessive noun to express ownership or to show a relationship.*

The Concluding Sentence

The **concluding sentence** can restate the writer's opinion in an interesting way or make a final comment. In the foreign language paragraph on page 443, it makes a final comment. In the singing paragraph on page 445, it restates the writer's opinion.

Try It Out Read the following paragraph. On your own or with a partner, write two different concluding sentences.

> I believe that there are many advantages to preserving historical buildings. First, by giving future generations access to these special places, you allow people to learn about history firsthand. Saving older buildings also preserves a neighborhood's character. New neighborhoods built from scratch just don't have the charm found in a mix of old and new structures and different architectural styles. Finally, preserving historical buildings has economic advantages. Once a structure is renovated and reopened, it can bring jobs and money into the community. _____*Concluding sentence*_____ .

Write Your Own Opinion Paragraph

Now it's time for you to write your own opinion paragraph. First, choose a topic you care about. Then write an opinion statement that expresses what you believe. Finally, think of reasons and details—facts and examples—that support your opinion. After you have discussed your opinion and supporting ideas with a partner, you are ready to write!

Checklist for My Paragraph

✔ My **opinion statement** introduces the topic and expresses my opinion about it.
✔ My **supporting sentences** give reasons for my opinion.
✔ **Details** such as facts and examples explain my reasons.
✔ My **concluding sentence** restates my opinion in a different way or makes a final comment.

Looking Ahead

Now that you understand how to write an opinion paragraph, writing an opinion essay will be easy. It's organized in exactly the same way! The diagram below shows how the parts of an opinion paragraph correspond to the parts of an opinion essay.

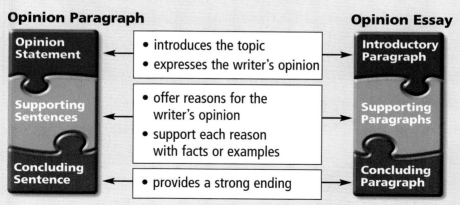

Opinion Paragraph

Opinion Statement

Supporting Sentences

Concluding Sentence

- introduces the topic
- expresses the writer's opinion

- offer reasons for the writer's opinion
- support each reason with facts or examples

- provides a strong ending

Opinion Essay

Introductory Paragraph

Supporting Paragraphs

Concluding Paragraph

Writing to Express an Opinion

Would you call it a junkyard or art?

In this opinion essay, Maya Angelou explains why she thinks Americans should become acquainted with other cultures and peoples. What reasons does she give to support her opinion?

Passports to Understanding

From *Wouldn't Take Nothing for My Journey Now*, by Maya Angelou

THE NEW YORK TIMES BESTSELLER

Maya Angelou

WOULDN'T TAKE NOTHING FOR MY JOURNEY NOW

Human beings are more alike than unalike, and what is true anywhere is true everywhere, yet I encourage travel to as many destinations as possible for the sake of education as well as pleasure.

It is necessary, especially for Americans, to see other lands and experience other cultures. The American, living in this vast country and able to traverse three thousand miles east to west using the same language, needs to hear languages as they collide in Europe, Africa, and Asia.

A tourist, browsing in a Paris shop, eating in an Italian *ristorante,* or idling along a Hong Kong street, will encounter

Maya Angelou

 Go to www.eduplace.com/kids/ for information about Maya Angelou.

more ▶

A Published Model   **449**

three or four languages as she negotiates the buying of a blouse, the paying of a check, or the choosing of a trinket. I do not mean to suggest that simply overhearing a foreign tongue adds to one's understanding of that language. I do know, however, that being exposed to the existence of other languages increases the perception that the world is populated by people who not only speak differently from oneself but whose cultures and philosophies are other than one's own.

Perhaps travel cannot prevent bigotry, but by demonstrating that all peoples cry, laugh, eat, worry, and die, it can introduce the idea that if we try to understand each other, we may even become friends.

Reading As a Writer

Think About the Opinion Essay

- What reasons does Maya Angelou give to support her opinion?
- What details support the reason given in the third paragraph of this essay?
- How do the introduction and the conclusion work together?

Think About Writer's Craft

- Find examples of exact verbs in this essay. What do they add to the essay?
- What image is used in the title? Why does it suit the essay?

Think About the Pictures

- Look at the photographs of people buying and selling things on page 450. What is familiar to you, and what is not?

Responding

Write responses to these questions.

- **Personal Response** Explain why you agree or disagree with Maya Angelou's opinion about travel. State your reasons clearly and support them with details.
- **Critical Thinking** According to the author, in what ways are all people the same? In what ways do people differ?

What Makes a Great Opinion Essay?

An opinion essay gives reasons and details that express how the writer thinks or feels.

When you write an opinion essay, remember these guidelines.

▶ Introduce your topic in a way that draws your readers into your essay.

▶ Clearly state your opinion about the topic. You may include two points of view if you wish.

▶ Give specific and interesting reasons to support your opinion.

▶ Use colorful details to elaborate, or explain, each reason.

▶ Organize your reasons from most to least important or from least to most important.

▶ Make smooth transitions between your ideas.

▶ Use engaging language to express your thoughts and feelings.

▶ Write a conclusion that leaves your readers thinking about your opinion.

GRAMMAR CHECK

When you add phrases to sentences, place each phrase close to the word it modifies.

WORKING DRAFT

Do you have a favorite subject in school? Joshua Crespo does. He wrote this opinion essay to explain why physical education class is his favorite. Here is his working draft.

Joshua Crespo

Physical education class always holds my attention because it is so exciting! All the activities are interesting, and we never get boring homework assignments. ~~Sometimes I get tired of the amount of homework I have to do.~~ Whether I'm swimming, shooting baskets, or even running and running on an endless track, I find myself totally involved in what's going on. This isn't always the case for history class or math class!

Another reason why I like P.E. is because it makes me use my brain and my body. You can't get this experience if you spend your whole life behind a desk. P.E. will help me stay healthy and fit. That makes P.E. class an important part of our education.

It's true that P.E. can cause some problems. It can be a pain to change into gym clothes, get all sweaty, and then clean up and change clothes again in time for the next class. For some reason, this always happens in a wild rush. It's easy to forget to put clean towels and clothes in your gym bag. It's really awful if you lose your deodorant.

~~By the way, things are a lot nicer since our school~~

> Will this introduction draw your readers into your essay?

> Could you state your opinion clearly?

> Could you give details to support this reason?

> You've explained this reason very well!

more

got a new gym. ~~The locker room is definitely an improvement. It was way too crowded before.~~

Is this a disadvantage? Should you move this paragraph?

P.E. gives me a change of pace in the middle of the day. I fidget when I have to study hour after hour, and sometimes I feel pressured. P.E. lets me leave all my problems behind. It gets my blood circulating and my mental gears moving again. When I go back to my studies, I feel wide awake. I can concentrate better. ~~It can be hard to concentrate in class on spring days when it would be so much better to be outdoors.~~

I don't understand. Could you tell me more?

P.E. can be a schedule problem. An extra study period could help me get ready for a test. The schedule says I have to go to P.E. I get tired. I wish I didn't have to go to P.E.

Still, I think the advantages of P.E. are truly greater than the disadvantages. I love this chance to break loose and get a good workout. I think it helps both my mind and my body, and that makes it an important educational experience. Best of all, it just makes me happy!

This is a strong conclusion.

Reading As a Writer

- What did Joe like about Joshua's essay? What changes did he suggest?
- Where might Joshua connect his ideas with transitional words or phrases?
- What details might Joshua add to support his reason in the second paragraph on page 453?
- In the first full paragraph on this page what reason did Joshua state? What are the supporting details?

FINAL COPY

Joshua revised his working draft after discussing it with a classmate. Read his final copy to see what improvements he made.

Sign Me Up for P.E.!
by Joshua Crespo

A basketball player races down the court, and his teammates shout with excitement as he gets close to the basket. Although opponents weave in front of him, he's got the ball totally under control. When he scores, he whoops and struts and exchanges "high fives" with his teammates. Is this scene a practice session of pro athletes or a college team? No—it's an average middle-school physical education class.

My favorite subject is definitely P.E. It always holds my attention because it is so exciting! All the activities are interesting, and we never get boring homework assignments. Whether I'm swimming, shooting baskets, or even running and running on an endless track, I find myself totally involved in what's going on. This isn't always the case for history class or math class!

Another advantage of P.E. is that it gives me a change of pace in the middle of the day. I fidget when I have to study hour after hour, and sometimes I feel pressured. P.E. lets me leave all my problems behind. It gets my blood circulating and my mental gears

> The introduction makes me feel the excitement!

> You've stated your opinion clearly.

> Smart move! This paragraph belongs with the advantages of P.E.

more

moving again. When I go back to my studies, I feel wide awake. I can concentrate better.

The most important advantage of P.E. is that it makes me use my brain and my body. This class isn't just physical. When I play sports, I have to work out strategies and experiment with better ways of doing things. Learning new skills in gymnastics or swimming makes me coordinate my mind and my body. You can't get this experience if you spend your whole life behind a desk. P.E. will help me stay healthy and fit. I don't want to get a potbelly! Any doctor will tell you that exercise is important to health, and students want to learn how to stay healthy. That makes P.E. class an important part of our education.

It's true that P.E. can cause some problems. First, it can be a pain to change into gym clothes, get all sweaty, and then clean up and change clothes again in time for the next class. For some reason, this always happens in a wild rush. It's easy to forget to put clean towels and clothes in your gym bag. It's really awful if you lose your deodorant.

Second, P.E. can be a schedule problem. For example, sometimes I'd give anything to have an extra study period to get ready for a test, but instead I have to

You've added good examples and details.

Exact words make your thoughts and feelings clear.

go to P.E. On days when I'm really tired, this class can be tough too. Now and then, I wish I didn't have to go.

Still, I think the advantages of P.E. are truly greater than the disadvantages. I love this chance to break loose and get a good workout. I think it helps both my mind and my body and that makes it an important educational experience. Best of all, it just makes me happy!

Your opinion essay is a success!

Reading As a Writer

- What changes did Joshua make in response to Joe's comments?
- What makes the title interesting?
- What transitional words and phrases did Joshua add to the last three paragraphs of his essay?
- How many advantages did Joshua discuss? How many disadvantages?

See www.eduplace.com/kids/hme/ for more examples of student writing.

Write an Opinion Essay

▶ Start Thinking

Make a writing folder for your opinion essay. Copy the questions in bold type, and put the paper in your folder. Write your answers as you think about and choose your topic.

- **Who will be my audience?** Will it be people I know well? people I have never met? Will my audience be readers or listeners?
- **What will be my purpose?** Do I want to entertain or inform? express my feelings and beliefs about a topic?
- **How will I publish or share** my essay? Will I read it aloud to my classmates? publish it in the school newspaper?

▶ Choose Your Topic

❶ Make a list of topics about which you have opinions. Avoid people as topics.

- Write at least one opinion for each topic. Give advantages and disadvantages, if you like. Make each opinion specific.
- Keep going until you have written at least five opinions.

❷ Discuss each opinion with a partner.

HELP

? Mind Gone Blank?

Do you like or dislike one of these?

- practicing a musical instrument
- living in the city (or the country)
- doing chores at home
- going to museums

See page 470 for more ideas.

- Is the opinion interesting? Does your partner want to know more?
- Do you have reasons and details to support this opinion?
- Is any opinion too broad? Could you write about just one part of it? Look at how Joshua narrowed his opinion.

School can be fun.

riding the bus   seeing all my friends   physical education class

❸ Ask yourself these questions about each opinion in your list. Then circle the one you will write about.

- Do I feel strongly about this opinion? Will I enjoy writing about it?
- Do I have enough to say about it?
- Can I keep my readers interested?

Supporting Your Opinion

Think of strong reasons to support your opinion. If you are presenting both advantages and disadvantages, give reasons to support both points of view.

Give real reasons. Don't just restate an opinion. *I learn a lot from school clubs* does not explain the opinion *Participating in school clubs is educational.*

Give reasons that relate to the opinion. Don't wander away from your main idea. Each reason must support your opinion.

Opinion: *Participating in school clubs is educational.*

Weak Reason	Strong Reason
Clubs have lots of parties.	Clubs increase understanding of school subjects such as French or computers.

Give specific reasons. Don't be too general. Say what you mean.

Opinion: *Participating in school clubs can bring down your grades.*

General Reason	Specific Reason
Clubs can take up too much time.	Clubs involve kids in frivolous activities that keep them from their homework.

Try It Out Work with a partner or small group.

● Think of two more strong reasons to support one of the opinions above.

▶ Explore Your Opinion

❶ **Decide** whether your opinion has one or two points of view. Make a T-chart for two points of view. Make a list for one point of view.

❷ **Brainstorm** as many good reasons as you can. Cross out any that restate your opinion or stray from your topic.

Advantages of P.E.	Disadvantages of P.E.
a great change of pace has exciting activities good for mind and body	can be a schedule problem a pain to get ready for class after P.E.

▲ Joshua's T-chart

 See page 16 for other ideas for exploring a topic.

Focus Skill

Elaborating Your Reasons

Show your readers exactly what you mean. Find thought-provoking details to elaborate, or explain, each reason.

Elaborate with facts. Back up your reasons with names, dates, measurements, or other facts. Exact facts are more convincing than general statements. Remember that facts can be proved true.

Reason: *Clubs teach social skills.*

Weak Detail: Too General	Strong Details: Specific Facts
Kids interact in clubs.	Members work together to make decisions and elect officers. Because clubs are run by elected student officers, they help kids develop leadership ability.

Elaborate with examples. Write about events, experiences, or observations that help make your point. Give enough detail to make a strong impression.

Reason: *Clubs don't always deepen your knowledge of a subject.*

Weak Detail: Too General	Strong Details: Specific Example
My French club didn't focus on learning.	My French club didn't focus on learning. When I joined, I thought members would work hard to converse in French. Instead, we sang French pop songs and wrote a French menu.

Sometimes all you need to do to strengthen a general detail is to add one or two sentences with additional details.

Think and Discuss Look at Joshua's final copy on page 455.

- Find two facts or examples Joshua used to elaborate one of his reasons about the advantages of P.E.
- Find two facts or examples Joshua used to elaborate one of his reasons about the disadvantages of P.E.

▶ Explore Your Reasons

❶ Make an opinion web for one or two points of view.

❷ Brainstorm details, such as facts and examples, to elaborate all your reasons.

- Try to anticipate and then answer questions your readers might ask about each reason, such as *Why?* or *How do you know?*
- Is each detail vivid and specific?

> Try doing a little research to find good facts and examples.

❸ Add these details to your web.

- Make sure you group your details with the reason they elaborate.
- If any reason needs more details, do some more brainstorming, perhaps with a partner.

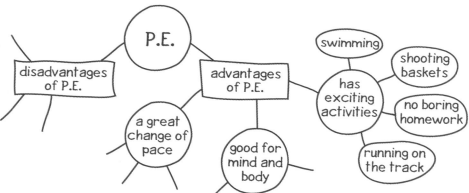

▲ **Part of Joshua's opinion web**

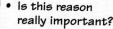

Focus Skill

Organizing Your Reasons

Choose what reasons to include. Use Joe's questions to help you decide.

- If you plan to discuss two points of view, give at least two reasons for each.
- If you plan to discuss one point of view, support it with three or four reasons.

> - Is this reason really important?
> - Will my readers understand this reason?
> - Do I have enough details to support this reason?

Plan your paragraphs. Each reason will be part of a different paragraph. Details will become supporting sentences for the reason they elaborate.

Arrange your reasons. Order your reasons either from most important to least important or from least important to most important. If you include two points of view, group the advantages, and order them. Group the disadvantages, and order them. Then decide which group you'll discuss first.

Think about connecting your ideas. Transitional words and phrases make connections between paragraphs. They can also show relationships between ideas within a paragraph.

Transitional Words and Phrases
in general, after all, eventually, equally important, in one case, afterward, specifically, despite the fact that, also, on the one hand, first, second, third, even though, on the other hand, in addition to, instead

Think and Discuss Look at Joshua's final copy on page 455.

- Where did Joshua tell his most important reason for the advantages of P.E.? his most important reason for the disadvantages of P.E.?
- How else might Joshua have organized his essay?

▶ Plan Your Essay

❶ **Review** your opinion web.

❷ **Circle** your strongest reasons. Delete any weak ones.

❸ **Number** the circled reasons for one point of view to show how you will present them. Do the same for your second point of view, if you have one.

Focus Skill

Writing with Voice

State your opinion with confidence. You might strike a serious tone, use humor, or express emotion.

Express yourself. Exact nouns and verbs, a well-chosen adjective or adverb, and interesting comparisons will enliven your writing. Try out a creative turn of phrase. Vary sentence length and structure.

Weak: Unexpressive	Strong: Expressive
Many things about French Club were good. I liked the French films and my French pen pal. Those things were fun sometimes.	Still, I liked many things about French Club. Watching classic French films transported me into the heart of French culture. Getting letters from my French pen pal was like having my own personal guide to Paris.

Avoid overblown language. Don't try to impress your readers by using difficult words that you really don't understand. Let your voice come through by choosing familiar words that say exactly what you mean.

Weak: Too Many Difficult Words	Strong: Clear, Direct Words
Club **aficionados** should not form **exclusive coteries**. Instead, they should **recollect** that they joined to **disseminate common enthusiasms** and not to prove themselves more **sagacious** than others.	Club members should not form cliques. Instead, they should remember that they joined the club to share interests and not to prove themselves more intelligent than others.

Think and Discuss Look at Joshua's final copy on page 455.

- Describe Joshua's voice. Point out examples of vivid, clear language.

▶ Draft Your Essay

❶ **Draft** your essay. Don't worry about mistakes. Use your web as a guide.

❷ **Write** at least one paragraph for each reason. State the reason in a topic sentence. Put the details in supporting sentences.

❸ **Express** your ideas and feelings with your personal voice.

HELP
I'm on a Roll!
Don't worry about neatness as you draft. Let your ideas flow! You can add new reasons and details as you write.

Focus Skill

Introductions and Conclusions

Start your readers thinking. You can state your opinion right away. You can also tease your readers by beginning with a scene, an example, or a question and then giving your opinion later, in the second paragraph.

Weak Introduction	Strong Introduction
Sometimes my bedroom gets dusty. Sometimes it gets all disorganized. Well, I'm busy with other things. Anyway, my room is my private space.	In my room lives a family of frightened animals called dust bunnies. What frightens them? The vacuum cleaner that invades and devours them all once a week. The results are tragic. These little creatures have only me to protect them! I like my room messy, and I want to clean it on my own schedule.

Leave your readers thinking. Conclude by summing up your reasons or making a final comment about your opinion.

Weak Conclusion	Strong Conclusion
I think that my bedroom is clean enough. I'm the one who has to put up with it. I've now told you all my reasons for thinking this.	I still believe that I should clean my room on my own schedule. It is, after all, my private space. By the way, I have good news about the dust bunnies. That vicious vacuum cleaner keeps trying to wipe them out, but these hardy little creatures keep coming back. I welcome them with open arms!

> In your conclusion, you might touch on something you mentioned in the introduction.

Think and Discuss

- Which technique is used in the strong introduction above?
- What links the strong introduction with the strong conclusion?

▶ Draft Your Introduction and Conclusion

❶ **Write** two introductions and two conclusions.

❷ **Choose** the introduction and the conclusion that best suit your purpose and audience.

Tech Tip

Dim your computer screen as you draft. This will help you focus on your ideas rather than on mistakes you might be making.

Evaluating Your Opinion Essay

▶ **Reread** your opinion essay. Use this rubric to help you decide how to make it better. Copy the sentences that best describe your paper.

Loud and Clear!

- The introduction will make my readers want to keep reading.
- I state my opinion clearly.
- At least three reasons support an opinion with one point of view; four reasons support an opinion with two points of view.
- Thought-provoking details elaborate each reason.
- My reasons are ordered well and linked with smooth transitions.
- My voice is engaging and sets a tone for my essay.
- My conclusion wraps up my essay in an interesting way.
- *There are very few spelling, punctuation, or grammar mistakes.*

Sounding Stronger

- My introduction could be more interesting.
- My opinion isn't quite clear.
- Some reasons are unimportant or stray off the topic.
- More details would help explain my reasons.
- One reason is out of order. Some transitions are weak.
- I need to sound more confident.
- My conclusion repeats what I've already said.
- *Parts of my essay have some mistakes.*

Turn Up Volume

- I forgot to write an introduction.
- I never clearly state what I think or feel.
- I lack strong reasons. I just restate my opinion.
- My details are vague and don't explain my reasons.
- The order of my reasons is confusing. I repeat myself.
- My voice gets lost. My language is bland.
- There is no conclusion. I just stopped writing.
- *Many mistakes make my essay hard to understand.*

See www.eduplace.com/kids/hme/ to interact with this rubric.

▶ Revise Your Opinion Essay

❶ **Revise** your essay. Use the list of sentences you wrote from the rubric. Work on the parts that you described with sentences from "Sounding Stronger" and "Turn Up the Volume."

❷ **Have a writing conference.**

When You're the Writer Read your essay aloud to your partner. Ask questions about any problems you are having. Take notes.

When You're the Listener Point out at least two things you like about the essay. Then ask questions about parts you think are unclear. Use the chart below for help.

HELP
? **Revising Tip**

Put a check mark by each supporting detail. Make sure you have at least two details for each reason.

What should I say?

The Writing Conference

If you're thinking . . .	**You could say . . .**
There's no real introduction.	**Could you begin with a question? an example?**
What is this essay actually about?	**What do you think or feel about _____?** **Tell me your opinion in one sentence.**
Where are the reasons?	**Why do you think or feel this way?**
This reason doesn't make sense.	**What do you mean by _____? What details might help explain this better?**
Wait! Stop! I'm lost.	**Could you make better transitions between your ideas?**
I need a dictionary to understand some of the words you use.	**What does the word _____ mean? Is there an easier word that would say what you mean just as well?**
The essay screeches to a halt.	**Could you write a strong conclusion?**

❸ **Make** more revisions to your essay. Use your conference notes and the Revising Strategies on the next page.

Revising Strategies

Elaborating: Word Choice If you repeat a word too often, replace it with a **synonym,** a word with a similar meaning. Find the synonym in a thesaurus, and check its meaning in a dictionary. Make sure its meaning is exactly right.

Not Quite Right	Exactly Right
Because of his **cheap** spending habits, Leo saved enough money to buy a new baseball glove.	Because of his frugal spending habits, Leo saved enough money to buy a new baseball glove.

▶ Look for repeated words in your essay and replace some with synonyms.

Use the Thesaurus Plus on page H96. See also page H14.

Elaborating: Details Add details to a sentence, or write more sentences.

Without Details	With Details
Riding a bike is good exercise. It makes you fit.	Riding a bike is good exercise. Pumping those pedals for mile after mile makes you fit to play any sport.

▶ Add at least three details to your essay. Use different types of details.

Sentence Fluency To give rhythm to your writing, vary your sentence structures. Try simple sentences, compound sentences, and complex sentences.

Simple sentences	We waste food. Often we forget about hungry people.
Compound sentence	We waste food, and often we forget about hungry people.
Complex sentence	If we thought more about hungry people, we might not waste food.

▶ Experiment with sentences in your essay. Use at least one simple, one compound, and one complex sentence.

GRAMMAR LINK ▶ See also pages 61 and 416.

GRAMMAR TIP ▶ When you connect two or more words, phrases, or dependent clauses with <u>and</u> or <u>or</u>, remember to use the same, or parallel, sentence structure.

▶ Proofread Your Opinion Essay

Proofread your essay, using the Proofreading Checklist and the Grammar and Spelling Connections. Proofread for one skill at a time. Use a class dictionary to check spellings.

Proofreading Checklist

Did I
- ✔ indent all paragraphs?
- ✔ correct sentence fragments and run-on sentences?
- ✔ use verbs that agree with their subjects?
- ✔ correct any misplaced phrases?
- ✔ use pronouns clearly?
- ✔ spell all words correctly?

 Use the Guide to Capitalization, Punctuation, and Usage on page H64.

Proofreading Marks
- ¶ Indent
- ∧ Add
- ℈ Delete
- ≡ Capital letter
- / Small letter
- ⸌⸍ Add quotes
- ∧ Add comma
- ⊙ Add period
- ∩∪ Transpose

HELP ? **Proofreading Tip**

Put a check mark above words that might be spelled incorrectly. Look them up in the dictionary.

Grammar and Spelling Connections

Phrases as Modifiers Check where you have placed a phrase in a sentence. Make sure it is close to the noun that it modifies.

	Unclear	Corrected
Dangling participial phrase	Walking through an art museum, the painting caught my eye. (Can a painting take a stroll?)	Walking through an art museum, I noticed the painting.
Misplaced prepositional phrase	Tara sang to her adoring audience in a striking red dress. (How did they all fit into it?)	In a striking red dress, Tara sang to her adoring audience.

Spelling the Prefix con- The prefix *con-* is spelled *com-* before the consonants *m* and *p*.

My neighbor first **controlled**, then **completely conquered**, his fear of air flight. He became a **committed** traveler.

See the Spelling Guide on page H80.

  Go to www.eduplace.com/kids/hme/ for proofreading practice.

▶ Publish Your Opinion Essay

❶ Prepare a neat final copy of your essay. Make sure to correct all errors.

❷ Title your essay to indicate the main topic and grab the reader's attention. For example, "Why I Like to Cook" is less interesting than "Call Me Chef!"

GRAMMAR TIP ▶ *Capitalize the first, the last, and each important word in a title.*

❸ Publish or share your essay in a way that fits your topic and your audience. See the Ideas for Sharing box.

Ideas for Sharing
Write It Down
- E-mail your essay to a friend. Ask him or her to respond.

Talk It Up
- Read your essay aloud to the class, and invite classmates to ask questions afterward.

Show It Off
- Create a magazine spread with pictures to elaborate your opinion. Show the pictures with your essay.
- Make a comic strip that illustrates your opinion. Display it with your essay.

Tips for Reading Aloud
- Read clearly, with expression.
- Pace yourself. Don't rush.
- Remember to breathe! Project your voice so everyone can hear you.
- Stand with good posture. Make eye contact with your audience now and then.

▶ Reflect

Write about your writing experience. Use these questions to get started.

- What was difficult about writing an opinion essay? What was easy?
- Which part most clearly expresses how you think or feel? What makes it work well?
- How does this paper compare with other papers you have written?

Writing Prompts

Use these prompts as ideas for opinion essays or to practice for a test. Decide who your audience will be, and write your essay in a way that they will understand and enjoy.

1 Do you prefer spending time in the natural world or in the city? Write an essay to explain your opinion.

2 What are the advantages and disadvantages of extracurricular activities? Write your opinion about balancing study time with time spent in team sports, music groups, and clubs. Explain both points of view.

3 Do you and your friends gossip? Do you think it is a harmless way of passing the time or a danger to people's reputations? Write an essay explaining your opinion about this issue.

4 Write your opinion about a school field trip you have taken. What did you like about it, and what did you dislike? Remember to include details.

Writing Across the Curriculum

5 **FINE ART**

What does this painting express that a more realistic portrait could not express? Write an essay explaining your opinion. Use details from the painting to support your reasons.

1939 Pablo Picasso. © Edimédia/CORBIS.

Head of a Woman, by Pablo Picasso (1881–1973)

✓ Test Practice

This prompt to write an opinion essay is like ones you might find on a writing test. Read the prompt.

> **Write your opinion about a school field trip you have taken. What did you like about it, and what did you dislike? Remember to include details.**

Here are some strategies to help you do a good job responding to a prompt for an opinion essay.

Remember, an opinion essay gives reasons and details that express how the writer thinks or feels.

❶ Look for clue words that tell you what to write about. What are the clue words in the prompt above?

❷ Write the clue words. Then choose a topic that fits them.

Clue Words	My Topic
your opinion about a school field trip you have taken, what did you like, what did you dislike	what I liked and disliked about going to the planetarium

❸ Plan your essay. Use an opinion web.

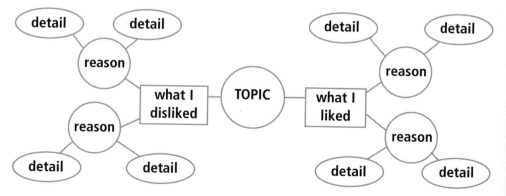

❹ You will get a good score if you remember the sentences under "Loud and Clear!" in the rubric on page 465.

Writing a Book Report

A **book report** provides the reader with a brief description of the book, as well as the writer's opinion. Read Ryan's report.

Title and
Subtitle — **Into Thin Air: A Personal Account of the Mount Everest Disaster**

Author ➤ by Jon Krakauer

Publisher/ ➤ Doubleday, 1998
Copyright

Introduction — Have you ever climbed a mountain? Did you have to carry oxygen to breathe at high altitudes? Although most people take oxygen when they try to climb Mt. Everest— which is 29,035 feet high—even that doesn't make it safe. Experienced climbers still die on the mountain. *Into Thin Air* is Jon Krakauer's personal account of the May 10, 1996 disaster on Mt. Everest.

Description — Krakauer gives a great picture of what climbing this massive mountain is like. He also describes the competition between the expeditions and guides to get as many climbers to the summit as possible.

When a storm came up, eight men and women died, including the very skilled guides. You may wonder why, and that's the main conflict of the book. Krakauer writes about mistakes made by different people that added up to a terrible tragedy. You can feel the sadness and hurt.

Opinion — This book grabbed me. It is extremely well written and has as much suspense as a novel. I think what intrigued me the most was the way Krakauer dealt with the situation. He blamed himself for a lot of things that happened, although he had no way of knowing what was going to unfold.

Conclusion — I would recommend this book. Whether you enjoy suspense, action, or thrillers, it covers them all and does it well.

See www.eduplace.com/kids/hme/ for more examples of book reports.

- The **title**, **author**, **publisher**, and **copyright** provide information others need to find the book you are describing. The copyright date is particularly important in nonfiction because it may help determine whether the information is out of date. *Who published* Into Thin Air?

- The **introduction** presents the subject of the report and captures the reader's interest. *How does Ryan engage the reader?*

- The **description** briefly describes the people involved, the location of the events, and what happens in the book. The writer may include a main point of interest.
  Why is the location of Into Thin Air *important?*

- The **opinion** tells what the writer thought about the book.
  What is Ryan's opinion of the book?

- The **conclusion** sums up the report and states whether or not the writer would recommend the book to others.
  How does Ryan conclude his book report?

How to Write a Book Report

1 **List** the title, author, publisher, and copyright date.

2 **Introduce** the book by engaging the reader. You may quote a particularly vivid passage. For nonfiction, you might list some interesting questions that the book answers or ask a question that refers to the reader's personal experience.

3 **Summarize** information that describes the book. Give highlights of the book, but don't tell too much. In the case of fiction, don't give away the ending.

4 **Give** your opinion and write a conclusion. Did the photos and illustrations help tell the story?

5 **Revise and proofread** your book report. Use the Proofreading Checklist on page 468. Use a dictionary to check your spelling.

6 **Display** a neat final copy of your book report in the school library for others to read.

Writing Poetry

Many poems are about people. Poets may write a tribute about someone they admire, or write to express their feelings about someone close to them, or they may describe a person whom they've observed. The images, sounds, and rhythms they create with words can communicate their thoughts and feelings about people.

Read these poems to see how poets create memorable images of people.

Martin Luther King Jr.

A man went forth with gifts.

He was a prose poem.
He was a tragic grace.
He was a warm music.

He tried to heal the vivid volcanoes.
His ashes are
    reading the world.

His Dream still wishes to anoint
    the barricades of faith and of control.

His word still burns the center of the sun,
    above the thousands and the
    hundred thousands.

The word was Justice. It was spoken.

So it shall be spoken.

So it shall be done.

Gwendolyn Brooks

Sailor

Mother,
    Do you know?

My calling to the sea came
when you sang me to sleep.

Alberto Forcada
Translated by Judith Infante

The Base Stealer

Poised between going on and back, pulled
Both ways taut like a tightrope-walker,
Fingertips pointing the opposites,
Now bouncing tiptoe like a dropped ball
Or a kid skipping rope, come on, come on,
Running a scattering of steps sidewise,
How he teeters, skitters, tingles, teases,
Taunts them, hovers like an ecstatic bird,
He's only flirting, crowd him, crowd him,
Delicate, delicate, delicate, delicate—now!

Robert Francis

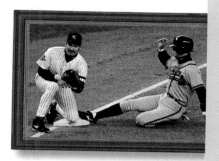

Thomas Paine, 1776

Tom Paine wrote a pamphlet called "Common Sense,"
and his words made the British feel quite tense.
In six months, half a million copies were sold,
spreading his words so strong, so bold.

He called King George a "Royal Brute."
The king did not think that this was cute.
"A new government is what we need.
If all of us try, we can succeed

to build a republic, so it's known
this land is no longer England-owned!"
The people took Tom's words to heart.
He contributed more than one man's part.

Elizabeth McCarthy
Student writer

Reading As a Writer

- What images does Gwendolyn Brooks use in her poem?
- What emotion do you think Alberto Forcada wanted to convey in his poem?
- What words and phrases does Robert Francis use to energize his poem?
- What is the rhyme pattern of Elizabeth McCarthy's poem?

more ▶

How to Write a Poem About a Person

❶ Choose a person to write about. Think about the kind of poem to write. Here are some ideas.

- Write about a person from history, as Gwendolyn Brooks and Elizabeth McCarthy did.
- Write a poem that shows your feelings about a family member, as Alberto Forcada did.
- Write about a person whose actions will be fun to describe, as Robert Francis did. You might choose a baby learning to walk, a basketball player, a tap dancer, or a restaurant cook.

> Here's another idea. Write a series of short poems about friends or family.

❷ Think about the person. Decide what you want your audience to see, appreciate, or understand about the person.

❸ Make a web to generate images for your poem.

- In the center, identify the person, and write the main impression that you want to make. Don't worry that this impression may change as you write the poem.
- Around the center, write details about the person. What is the person like? Describe the person's actions.
- Use vivid words and sensory details to note your impressions of the person.
- Add words the person has spoken that were memorable to you.

We trust her.

She turns pouts into laughter.

She stands up for little kids.

My Sister
She's courageous.

She's like a strong tree we can lean on.

"Do what's right, not what's easy."

4 **Highlight** your best ideas. Then think of ways that you can express them. Use figurative language to refine your images.

My sister is a tree of sparkling leaves.

Figurative Language	
simile	makes a comparison, using the word *like* or *as* Example: *Her words sailed like ancient ships.*
metaphor	states that one thing "is" another Example: *His brother was a granted wish.*
personification	gives human qualities to something that isn't human Example: *The mountain mocked them, but they kept climbing.*

5 **Write** your poem, using your web and any other ideas that come to you. Choose a pattern for your poem.

Poetry Patterns

Poetry can take different shapes on a page. Think about the ideas below, and review the poems on pages 474–475 for more possibilities.

- Write in stanzas, with a set pattern of rhymes and beats.
- Write a "skinny poem" with very short lines. Choose every word carefully.
- Mix short lines and long lines. The long lines will slow down your readers. The short lines will move the poem quickly.
- Write your poem in a shape, such as a triangle or the outline of a house.
- Skip a line when you want your readers to pause.

more ▶

6 **Revise** your poem. Ask yourself these questions, and make any changes that are needed.

- Have you said everything you want to say?
- Have you created a vivid picture of the person?
- Are any parts too wordy?
- Have you followed the pattern that you chose?

Read your poem to a partner. Discuss any parts that you still want to work on. Make further changes if you wish.

7 **Proofread** your poem. Use a dictionary to check spellings. Decide how you will use capitalization and punctuation. Remember that poets can play with the rules of grammar and punctuation, but if you do so, be sure you are improving your poem and not making it hard to understand.

8 **Publish** your poem. Create a collage to display with your poem. Include a photo or drawing of the person and drawings or cutouts of objects that tell something about him or her. Recite your poem aloud. Use background music that makes you think of the person.

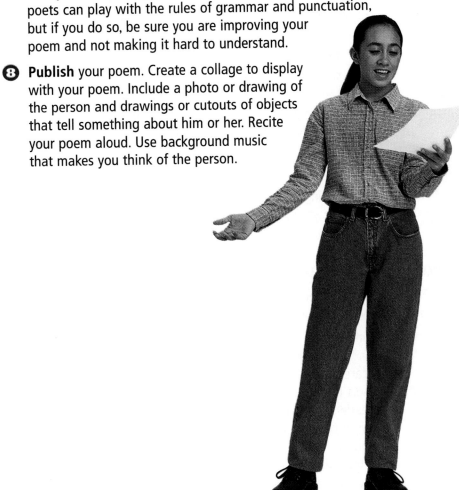

Singing the Blues

When you lose at sports or when a friend moves away, put your feelings into a poem made of **blues stanzas**. Created by African American musicians, blues songs have long lines that sound weary or sad. The stanzas can be humorous, though, despite the lamenting.

> Oh, the sun is so hot and the day is so doggone long...
> Yes, the sun is so hot and the day is so doggone long...
> And that is the reason I'm singing this doggone song.
> —from *The First Book of Jazz*, by Langston Hughes

Singer, Billie Holiday

Reading As a Writer

- What is the rhyme pattern of the three-line stanza?
- Which line is repeated?
- How many beats are in each line?

How to Write Blues Stanzas

1 **Choose** something to complain about—bad weather, missing someone, or a task that was hard to do.

2 **Draft** your poem.
  - Put five beats in each line.
  - Follow the pattern of repeated lines and rhymes in the model above.
  - Use straightforward, gutsy language. Blues artists tell what they really feel.
  - Add a twist of humor if it fits.

3 **Reread** your poem. Does it have the right beats, repeated lines, and rhyme? Does it send your message clearly? Revise problem spots.

4 **Proofread** your poem. Use a class dictionary to check spellings. You can use slang in a blues poem—it's meant to be informal.

5 **Publish** your poem in a Blues Stanza Bonanza, in which groups of four students perform their stanzas for the class. Speak with expression.

Conducting a Panel Discussion

A panel discussion is a way to showcase the ideas and opinions of informed people on a particular topic. Sometimes a panel discussion can provide a solution to a problem, or it can be used to plan a course of action.

To organize a discussion, you'll need a topic, a group of panelists, and a moderator. The panelists take turns presenting their information and ideas. Each has a limited time period to speak. The moderator introduces the panelists and makes sure that the discussion goes smoothly and stays on time.

How a Panel Discussion Works	
Panelists	**Moderator**
• give opinions or points of view on the subject • listen and respond to the ideas of other panelists • answer questions from the audience and each other	• keeps panelists to a time limit • keeps the panelists and the audience focused on the topic • introduces and summarizes the discussion

When you participate in a panel discussion, you need to speak effectively. You may have excellent ideas, but if you mumble, speak too softly, or speak in a monotone, the audience might miss what you are saying. Use the following guidelines to help you.

Guidelines for Being a Panelist

When You Are Speaking
- ▶ Clearly and confidently state your ideas or position on the topic.
- ▶ Give reasons for your opinions and support them with facts.
- ▶ Express your ideas so that others can understand them. Use language that is respectful of others' viewpoints.
- ▶ Be polite when you disagree with others. Keep your voice and facial expression pleasant.

It's important to listen carefully during a panel discussion so that you can respond appropriately to the opinions of other panelists. The following guidelines can help you sharpen your listening skills.

Guidelines for Being a Panelist

When You Are Listening
- ▶ Listen carefully to the speaker. Don't be distracted by wandering thoughts or the view out the window.
- ▶ Listen for the speaker's point of view. What reasons, supporting facts, and examples does he or she give? Are the reasons based on fact or opinion?
- ▶ Notice the speaker's facial expression and tone of voice. Is he or she confident about his or her ideas?
- ▶ Jot down notes to help you remember points you wish to respond to later.
- ▶ Wait to ask questions until the speaker has finished.
- ▶ Ask the speaker to elaborate or explain points that seem unclear.

more ▶

Observe Your Audience

As other panelists speak, observe the audience. Notice when they seem most interested in what a speaker is saying. At those moments, notice what gestures or tone of voice is being used. Be aware of how your audience is responding to what you are saying. Does your audience

- look puzzled? Choose another way to explain your idea.
- look bored? Say something lively or humorous.
- look restless? Make eye contact to help them connect to what you are saying.

Apply It

Choose a topic for a panel discussion. Research the topic and then write your ideas and opinions about it. Prepare notes. Use the Guidelines for Being a Panelist when you are speaking and listening. After the panel discussion, answer these questions.

> The best topics can be those that you and your classmates don't agree on—and those in which your audience can participate.

- What did you learn from the other panelists about the topic?
- Did you find yourself changing your views, based upon what other panelists said?
- Which guidelines were difficult to follow? Why?
- If you were the moderator, how would you conduct the discussion differently next time?

Identifying Points of View in Media

Many people are involved in creating images and messages in the media. Writers, producers, directors, photographers, artists, camera crews, and actors are only a few. Sometimes they present a point of view, or way of thinking about a subject, that is easy to identify. To identify more subtle points of view, you may need to compare media sources. Compare the photographs below.

Think and Discuss

- What did the photographer leave out of the first photograph?
- Why do you think he or she made this choice?

Seeing Is Believing—or Is It?

People tend to believe that what they see with their eyes is true. They may believe that photographs and news video footage provide reliable information. Photos give a sense of being real, but they are routinely manipulated to produce a range of meanings.

Photographers—including film, television, and video photographers—know how to create images that express a particular viewpoint. For example, by aiming up with a camera, a photographer can make people or buildings look taller or dramatic. By aiming up at an extreme angle, the same subject may seem to be looming or about to topple over.

more ▶

The chart below describes some common techniques used by photographers to produce particular effects.

Photographic Techniques and Their Effects	
Technique	**Effect**
A **cropped** photo is cut to show only part of the scene that the photographer shot.	focuses the viewer on the photographer's choice of subject
A **long shot** means the subject is shot from far away.	gives the viewer an overall impression of the subject rather than details about it
A **close-up** means a subject is shot from a very short distance.	makes the subject seem close to the viewer and gives the sense that the subject is credible; an extreme close-up can have a negative effect, however
A **pan**, or panorama, means the photographer moves the camera along the horizon.	gives a sense that the subject is wide or vast
A **crosscut** shot interweaves bits of two or more scenes.	makes two different subjects appear connected

Both a long shot and a close-up can leave out important information. Although a close-up lets you see details, you can't see the background. What information might the background provide?

Purpose and Viewpoint

Photographers and other media people usually have a purpose for making a subject look or sound a certain way. Sometimes their purpose is to clarify information. Sometimes it is to sell or to entertain. The purpose shapes the choices that people make when they create images.

Think of a television talk show you have seen. All of the show's visual elements—the set, the lighting, the video clips and photographs, and even the clothing of the host and the guests—are designed to give the show a particular image. Why do you think the set designer placed the guests, the audience, and the host in a certain way? What did the video photographers do to give the speakers credibility or to create drama?

Comparing Viewpoints

When you are unsure of the viewpoint in a photograph, a documentary, or a television show or newscast, find other media coverage on the subject and make a comparison. Also, when you present information from the media, be sure you have identified the viewpoint. Is it fair? Have you chosen the most accurate video or magazine article?

Here are some guidelines to help you identify the viewpoint in different kinds of media.

Guidelines for Identifying Points of View in Media

▶ Think about who created the media example and why they are publishing, showing, or broadcasting it.
▶ Find the purpose of the media example. Is it intended to inform, persuade, advertise, or entertain? How can you tell?
▶ Notice the photographic techniques that are being used. How do they influence the viewer's perceptions?
▶ Find the message of the media example. How would the message change if different photographic techniques were used?
▶ Think about the group of people the message is meant to reach. Who do you think the audience is? How can you tell?
▶ Consider whether any information is missing from this message. Can it be interpreted in more than one way?

Apply It

Watch the visual elements in two different network newscasts that report on the same event. If possible, videotape the newscasts. Turn the sound off and watch for different photographic techniques. Then, using the guidelines above, write two paragraphs that compare and contrast the viewpoint of each newscast. Use the following questions to help you.

● How were visuals used? What visual elements were common to both newscasts? What elements were different?
● What camera techniques were used? Describe shots that could have affected the audience's attitude toward an event or person.
● Did either newscast seem biased to you? Why or why not?

Unit 10

Writing to Persuade

Would this many runners show up if it weren't fun?

486

DDT is a chemical that was once sprayed throughout the United States to kill insects. Among the first people to speak out against DDT was Olga Owens Huckins, who wrote this persuasive letter to the editor of a Boston newspaper. Why does the writer want to stop the spraying of DDT?

A Letter to the Editor

January 1958
To the Editor of *The Herald*:

Mr. R.C. Codman, who wrote that he "is actively associated" with the Commonwealth of Massachusetts' aerial spraying programs for alleged mosquito control, also says that state tests have proved that the mixture used—fuel oil with DDT—last summer over Plymouth and Barnstable Counties was entirely harmless. These testers must have used black glasses, and the trout that did not feel the poison were super-fish.

Dr. Robert Cushman Murphy, distinguished scientist, observed after New York State sprayed Long Island in the same way, that no fish in still waters survived. All bees in a large section of the state were killed. Indeed, evidence of the havoc wrought by all air spraying of DDT is accumulating so rapidly that Mr. Codman's placid assurance becomes absurd.

The mosquito control plane flew over our small town last summer. Since we live close to the marshes, we were treated to several lethal doses as the pilot crisscrossed over our place. And we

Rust eats away an old pesticide can. The insecticide contained DDT, a dangerous toxin.

more ▶

consider the spraying of active poison over private land to be a serious aerial intrusion.

The "harmless" shower bath killed seven of our lovely songbirds outright. We picked up three dead bodies the next morning right by the door. They were birds that had lived close to us, trusted us, and built their nests in our trees year after year. The next day, three were scattered around the birdbath. (I had emptied it and scrubbed it after the spraying, but YOU CAN NEVER KILL DDT.) On the following day one robin dropped suddenly from a branch in our woods. We were too heartsick to hunt for other corpses. All of these birds died horribly, and in the same way. Their bills were gaping open, and their splayed claws were drawn up to their breasts in agony.

Mr. Codman also says that between DDT and mosquitoes, he prefers DDT. We had no choice; we have had both. All summer long, every time we went into the garden, we were attacked by the most voracious mosquitoes that had ever appeared there. But the grasshoppers, visiting bees, and other harmless insects were all gone.

The remedy of this situation is not to double the strength of the spray and come again. It is to STOP THE SPRAYING OF POISONS FROM THE AIR everywhere until all the evidence, biological and scientific, immediate and long run, of the effects upon wild life and human beings are known.

Air spraying where it is not needed or wanted is inhuman, undemocratic, and probably unconstitutional. For those of us who stand helplessly on the tortured earth, it is intolerable.

Olga Owens Huckins
Duxbury

A flagger is exposed to insecticide sprayed by a crop duster.

Reading As a Writer

Think About the Persuasive Essay

- What reasons does Olga Owens Huckins give to support her goal?
- What facts and examples does the writer give to support her reasons?
- Which of the writer's reasons is the most convincing? Why do you think so?

Think About Writer's Craft

- Find three places where the writer uses prepositional phrases to add detail to her writing.
- Read the last paragraph aloud. How does the author use repetition to add emphasis? What words does she emphasize?

Think About the Pictures

- Describe two ways each of the photographs on pages 487 and 488 supports the writer's view that spraying DDT is dangerous.

Responding

Write responses to these questions.

- **Personal Response** Olga Owens Huckins gives reasons to stop the spraying of DDT. Explain your viewpoint concerning the use of chemicals to kill insects.
- **Critical Thinking** The writer expresses strong emotions. Explain how this makes her essay more or less convincing.

What Makes a Great Persuasive Essay?

A persuasive essay gives reasons, supported by facts and examples, to convince an audience to take a specific action.

When you write a persuasive essay, remember these guidelines.

▶ Write an introduction that hooks your reader.

▶ State your goal clearly.

▶ Include at least three strong reasons that support your goal.

▶ Support, or elaborate, each reason with facts and examples.

▶ Anticipate possible objections, and answer them.

▶ Arrange your reasons in the most persuasive order.

▶ Use persuasive language that is appropriate to your audience.

▶ Write a memorable conclusion that summarizes your reasons and calls your audience to action.

GRAMMAR CHECK

Double-check subject-verb agreement when you use compound subjects joined by *and* or *or.*

Katie Clark

WORKING DRAFT

At Katie Clark's school an election for student council was approaching. Katie knew many good reasons why her friend Nicola Verona should be elected. She wrote this draft of her persuasive essay.

Nicola for Student Council

Student ~~government~~ council elections are coming soon to Northwood Middle School. We should elect Nicola Verona again.

> What about starting with an attention grabber?

One reason Nicola would be a ~~good~~ superb representative is her school spirit. She always participates in spirit days.

> Could you give facts or examples to support this reason?

Another reason for electing Nicola to student council is everything she has accomplished for us already. ~~A good representative must feel comfortable speaking in front of people.~~ Remember last year when Nicola's home base thought the gym uniforms were ~~stupid~~ ugly and unstylish? Nicola voiced our opinion at a student council meeting, and the student council decided to take action. Members talked to the school administrators, who are now looking into a new style for next year. Because of Nicola's initiative, more than a thousand students will be much happier on gym days when they slip into their uniforms.

more

If Nicola is elected again to student council, you can be sure that she will show her responsibility. When she gives oral reports, Nicola always knows exactly what she wants to say, and she speaks in a way that everyone can understand. Nicola has never missed a single student council meeting. She always takes excellent notes at the meetings and then tells us exactly what we need to know. Nicola also sets a good example. She is nice to everyone and always comes to school with a smile on her face. Moreover, Nicola is not the type of student who neglects her work. For two years Nicola has been on the honor roll every term.

School spirit is crucial, and Nicola ~~has~~ it obviously has it. A student council member must also be responsible, and this is certainly true of Nicola. All of her past accomplishments, such as changing the gym uniforms, are definitely proof of how much she can do for us in the future. Vote for Nicola as your student council representative.

> Does every example here support this reason?

> How might someone object to your goal?

> I like your persuasive language!

> Could your conclusion be more memorable?

Reading As a Writer

- What did Joe think works well in this persuasive essay? What revisions might Katie make to address Joe's questions?
- What is Katie's goal?
- What reasons did Katie give to support her goal? Will these reasons help persuade her audience? Explain why or why not.
- Which reason will be most convincing to Katie's audience? Why?

FINAL COPY

Katie revised her persuasive essay after discussing it with her classmates. Read her final version to see how she improved it.

The Right Student for the Job
by Katie Clark

Can anyone say Nicola Verona hasn't been an excellent student council representative in both sixth and seventh grades? Nicola can do an even better job for our home base as an eighth grader. Student council elections are coming soon to Northwood Middle School. We should elect Nicola Verona again.

The first reason Nicola would be a superb representative is her school spirit. She always participates in spirit days. For example, she dressed up as a baby on Halloween. She was a triplet with Brianne and Lisa on Twin Day in sixth grade and was a twin with me on Twin Day in seventh grade. On Slipper Day, she wore her favorite black slippers. She even went to the faculty basketball game, even though she does not really like basketball.

Second, if Nicola is elected again to student council, you can be sure that she will show her responsibility. Nicola has never missed a single student council meeting. She always takes excellent notes at

You start with a question. Interesting!

Examples support this reason very well now.

Transitional words and phrases now link your paragraphs.

more

the meetings and then tells us exactly what we need to know. Nicola also sets a good example. She is nice to everyone and always comes to school with a smile on her face. Moreover, Nicola is not the type of student who neglects her work. For two years Nicola has been on the honor roll every term.

The final reason for electing Nicola to student council is everything she has accomplished for us already. Remember last year when Nicola's home base thought the gym uniforms were ugly and unstylish? Nicola voiced our opinion at a student council meeting, and the student council decided to take action. Members talked to the school administrators, who are now looking into a new style for next year. Because of Nicola's initiative, more than a thousand students will be much happier on gym days when they slip into their uniforms.

Some may say that after two years on the student council, Nicola should give

> You moved your most convincing reason and put it last. Great!

> Raising this objection is smart.

others a chance to serve. However, Nicola is a valuable addition to the student council. School spirit is crucial, and she obviously has it. A student council member must also be responsible, and this is certainly true of Nicola. All of her past accomplishments, such as changing the gym uniforms, are definitely proof of how much she can do for us in the future. If we are interested in "new blood," there are two open seats for student council, and we can elect someone new to the other one. Our home base cannot afford to overlook what Nicola has to offer. Without her on the student council, we would all feel worse about our school. Vote for Nicola as your student council representative.

> This is a great conclusion. I'm convinced!

Reading As a Writer

- How did Katie respond to Joe's questions?
- What facts and examples did Katie use to support her reason about Nicola having school spirit?
- What possible objection did Katie introduce? How did she answer it?
- What is convincing about her answer?

See www.eduplace.com/kids/hme/ for more examples of student writing.

Student Model   **495**

Write a Persuasive Essay

▶ Start Thinking

Make a writing folder for your persuasive essay. Copy the questions in bold type, and put the paper in your folder. Write your answers as you choose and explore your topic.

- **What will be my purpose or goal?** What action do I want to persuade people to take? Why is this action important to me?
- **Who will be my audience?** Am I trying to persuade my friends? the president of a company? a senator from my state?
- **How will I publish or share my essay?** Will I reach my audience in a newspaper editorial? on a poster? in a speech?

▶ Choose a Goal

❶ Make a chart of topics for a persuasive essay. List five goals, or specific actions. Identify an audience and how you might reach this audience.

Goal	Audience	Publishing
Fix the tennis courts.	park officials	a letter
Elect Nicola Verona to student council.	my classmates	a speech
Buy school computers.	local and state officials	newspaper editorial

▲ **Part of Katie's chart**

❷ Discuss each goal with a partner. Can your audience actually do what you suggest? Does your audience already agree with any goal? If so, you don't need to persuade them.

❸ Ask yourself these questions. Then choose the goal you want to pursue.

- Do I feel strongly about this goal? Will my audience care about it?
- Do I have strong reasons? Can I support them with facts and examples?

HELP ? **Stuck for Ideas?**

Complete these sentences.
- It isn't right that . . .
- This town would be better if . . .
- My parents should allow me to . . .

See page 510 for more ideas.

Focus Skill

Supporting Your Goal

Provide specific reasons. Explain why your audience should do what you suggest. Think of three to five specific reasons that will support your goal.

Goal: *persuade officials to add sidewalks to the big streets in my town*

Weak: Vague Reason	Strong: Specific Reason
Most people like sidewalks.	Sidewalks are safer for pedestrians and joggers.

Elaborate each reason with facts and examples, not opinions. Facts give information that can be proved. You may need to research facts. Examples include events that you or someone else actually experienced.

Reason: *Sidewalks are safer for pedestrians and joggers.*

Weak Elaboration	Strong Elaboration
Opinion: It's scary to walk on the street. **Opinion:** Everyone deserves to be safe.	**Fact:** About fifty students could walk to our school if Route 21 had sidewalks. **Example:** Last year, our neighbor was hit by a car while jogging in the street.

Think and Discuss Look at Katie's final copy on page 493.

● What facts or examples does Katie use to elaborate her second reason?

▶ Explore Your Goal

Create a persuasion flow chart like the one shown. Elaborate each reason.

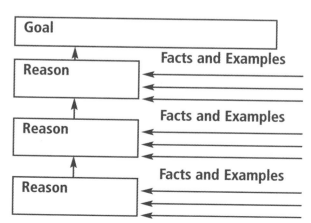

HELP ? See page 16 for other ideas for exploring a topic.

Focus Skill

Evaluating Your Reasons

All reasons are not created equal. Some are more convincing than others.

Does this reason directly support my goal? Each reason must explain, simply and clearly, why your audience should do what you ask.

Goal: *persuade my parents to let me take a part-time summer job at a cinema*

Weak: Doesn't Support Goal	Strong: Supports Goal
I'm not going to summer school this year.	I can earn money to buy books and clothes for school next fall.

Is this reason exaggerated? Be careful not to say too much. Choose accurate reasons that you can elaborate with several facts and examples.

Goal: *persuade business leaders to work with students to get classroom computers*

Weak: Exaggerated	Strong: Accurate
If we don't get computers, no one will learn anything.	Having access to computers will help us master the skills we will need later in life.

Does this reason matter to my audience? Different reasons work for different people. A reason that matters to a teenager might not persuade adults.

Goal: *persuade our teachers and our principal to allow more time for lunch*

Weak: Won't Matter to Them	Strong: Will Matter to Them
We need more time to talk to our friends.	We have to stand in line for so long we don't have time to finish eating.

Try It Out Work with a partner.

- Find another strong reason for two of the goals and audiences shown above.

▶ Explore Your Reasons

❶ **Reread** your flow chart. Which reasons best support your goal? have the most facts and examples? will matter most to your audience?

❷ **Star** your three strongest reasons. Make sure each one is different.

Using Persuasive Strategies

Try these techniques to make your essay more convincing.

Anticipate and answer possible objections. How might your audience disagree with your goal? Answer their objections before they make them.

Goal	*persuade town officials to build a basketball court in a local park*
Objection	Kids will hang around there and bother the neighbors.
Answer	Only organized leagues will use the court, and an adult will always be there when it's open.

Appeal to fairness. Connect your reasons to ideas your audience already has about what is right and what is wrong.

Goal	*persuade my classmates to volunteer for community service*
Appeal to fairness	Think of all the people in this community who have helped you— parents and grandparents, teachers and coaches. It's only fair to give something back to those who have done so much for you.

Appeal to emotions. Connect your reasons to feelings that you and your audience share.

Goal	*persuade town officials to repair the school building*
Appeal to emotions	One day the heater broke down, and we had to wear our winter coats in every class. We also had to wear gloves while taking notes. How would you feel if you spent a day like that at your job? Wouldn't you be upset? We feel the same way.

Knowing your audience will help you use persuasive strategies well. Turn the page for more techniques.

more ▶

Focus Skill continued

Cite precedents. A precedent is an earlier example of the action you are suggesting. Tell your audience, "If it was right then, it is right now."

Goal	*persuade my parents to let me take a part-time summer job*
Precedent	Both my older sisters had summer jobs when they were my age. They had fun and learned a lot too.

Explore consequences. Predict how your goal will benefit your audience.

Goal	*persuade a company to fix or replace a broken watch*
Consequence	I will buy my next watch from you. I will also tell other people that you care about your customers.

Think and Discuss Look at Katie's final copy on page 493.

● What persuasive strategies did Katie use in her final copy?
● As a class, think of other possible objections to three of the goals shown in this lesson. Then answer them.

▶ Explore Persuasive Strategies

❶ **List** possible objections to your goal and write answers for each one.

❷ **Decide** which of the other strategies listed above and on page 499 might make your essay more convincing.

❸ **Think** of reasons or facts and examples that would support these strategies. Add these to your persuasion flow chart.

**HELP
?** **Strategy Alert!**

Be sure to use persuasive strategies fairly. Don't weaken your argument by using tactics that encourage your readers not to think.

See page 514 and 516 to help you recognize unfair persuasive tactics.

Focus Skill

Organizing Your Argument

Your argument is your reasons, supported by facts and examples. Careful organization will make your argument more convincing. Keep these things in mind as you organize and write your essay.

Order reasons by importance. Choose one of these options.

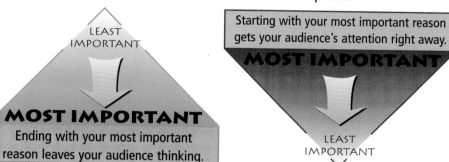

LEAST IMPORTANT

MOST IMPORTANT
Ending with your most important reason leaves your audience thinking.

Starting with your most important reason gets your audience's attention right away.

MOST IMPORTANT

LEAST IMPORTANT

Put each reason in a separate paragraph. State your reasons in topic sentences. Use facts and examples as supporting details. Use transitional words and phrases to link paragraphs, as well as sentences within a paragraph.

Transitional Words	Transitional Phrases
because, therefore, thus, consequently, however, although, similarly, too, another, besides, furthermore, moreover, better, best, finally, finest, worst, strongest	to begin with, as a result, so that, due to, for this reason, in response to, in conclusion, in addition, for example, above all, most important, less important

Check for coherence. Leave out facts or examples that don't support a reason. Think about a logical order for the details within each paragraph.

Think and Discuss Look at Katie's final copy on page 493.
- How did Katie order her reasons?
- Which of her reasons will leave her audience thinking? Why?

▶ Plan Your Persuasive Essay

❶ **Delete** weak or unimportant facts or examples from your flow chart.

❷ **Arrange** your reasons from most to least important and from least to most important. Which way works better?

Focus Skill

Introductions and Conclusions

Introductions

An effective introduction does more than clearly state your goal. It makes your audience sit up and pay attention. Here are three suggestions.

Ask a question. Start your audience thinking.

> **Strong Introduction**
>
> If there is one computer for each class, how much time does each student have to use the computer? However you do the math, it doesn't add up to much time. I urge you and other business leaders to work with us to get classroom computers.

Describe a scene. Create a mental picture that will appeal to your audience's emotions.

> **Strong Introduction**
>
> Imagine a park, clean and safe. Imagine a senior center filled with students and senior citizens talking and joking with each other. Imagine a program that enlists students to help others. A community service program is what our school needs.

Make a startling statement. Shock your audience with a surprising fact that supports your goal.

> **Strong Introduction**
>
> Over the last decade, Lake Winnepaug has claimed more lives from this town than car accidents have. At the end of last summer, the count was eleven lives. Our town should pay for a lifeguard to keep people safe.

Think and Discuss Look at Katie's final copy on page 493.

- Which of the techniques described above does Katie use to hook her audience?

502   **Unit 10:** Persuasion

Focus Skill continued

Conclusions

Make your concluding paragraph forceful. Summarize your goal and the main points of your argument. Then ask for the action you want.

Address your audience. Personalize your appeal to action.

> **Strong Conclusion**
>
> You can create a community service program. You can improve our students, our school, and our world. The costs are few and the benefits are priceless. Act now!

Use a figure of speech. Wrap up your argument with an unusual or thought-provoking comparison.

> **Strong Conclusion**
>
> Teachers and principals work hard to build the engine of our young minds. Without computer skills, however, we will be like cars without wheels. Our minds may have great power, but they won't take us where we want to go. Give us what we need to get ahead—easy access to computers.

See page H13 for more information on figurative language.

End with a warning. Predict problems that might occur if your audience rejects your goal. Don't exaggerate. Your prediction must seem reasonable.

> **Strong Conclusion**
>
> We cannot ignore this problem. Who knows which of our friends or family members will be lost next summer? Protect our town. Hire a lifeguard for Lake Winnepaug.

Try It Out Work with a partner to rewrite the examples above.
- Rewrite the first or third conclusion above to include a figure of speech.
- Rewrite the second or third conclusion above to address the audience.

▶ Draft Your Introduction

Write two introductions. Ask a question, describe a scene, or make a startling statement. Choose the one that works better for your audience and your goal.

Writing with Voice

In a persuasive essay your voice should be like a wise and trusted guide, leading your audience through your argument toward your goal.

Choose formal or informal language. Decide what level of language best suits your audience. The words and phrases that suit your friends might be different from the ones that suit your principal.

Informal Language	Formal Language
If you're on a bike, don't come screaming into the schoolyard at death-defying speeds. I know it's fun to blast through the gate without touching the brakes, but it isn't safe.	Some students achieve high speeds on their bikes before making the turn into the gate. This poses a grave threat to other students. As principal you should require students to walk their bikes into the schoolyard.

Strike a confident tone. Use persuasive language to help you sound certain of your goal and reasons. Avoid loaded language and name calling. A firm, quiet tone wins more arguments than shouting does.

Weak: Loaded Language	Strong: Persuasive Language
You call your watches reliable, but that's a **lie**. These **bizarre** products are so defective that they are **useless**. You're **crazy** if you think I will buy a watch from you again.	Computers are **clearly** indispensable to most jobs today. Having access to computers will **definitely** improve our computer skills. These skills cannot fail to make us better prepared to join the work force.

Try It Out Work with a partner.

- Rewrite the example of loaded language to make it persuasive.

▶ Draft Your Essay

❶ **Draft** the rest of your essay. Don't worry about mistakes. Just write.

❷ **Follow** your persuasion flow chart. Remember to elaborate all of your reasons. Write a forceful conclusion.

❸ **Think** about your voice. Pay careful attention to your language.

Evaluating Your Persuasive Essay

▶ **Reread** your persuasive essay. What do you need to do to make it better? Use this rubric to help you decide. Write the sentences that describe your essay.

Loud and Clear!

- The introduction hooks my audience and states my goal.
- At least three convincing reasons support my goal.
- Facts and examples elaborate every reason.
- My reasons flow logically from one to another.
- I've anticipated and answered all major objections.
- I write in a voice appropriate to my audience.
- A forceful conclusion restates my argument.
- *There are very few mistakes in grammar, punctuation, or spelling.*

Sounding Stronger

- The introduction states my goal but isn't interesting.
- One or more reasons won't matter to my audience.
- Some reasons need more elaboration.
- Transitional words would help my argument flow.
- I mention an objection but don't answer it.
- Some of my language isn't appropriate for my audience.
- My conclusion won't motivate anyone to take action.
- *Mistakes sometimes make my argument confusing.*

Turn Up the Volume

- I forgot to state my goal.
- My reasons are weak or unclear.
- Every reason needs more facts and examples.
- My argument needs more organization. I repeat myself.
- I haven't mentioned any possible objections.
- Most of my language is not appropriate.
- The conclusion doesn't restate my goal or reasons.
- *Mistakes make my argument very hard to follow.*

 Go to www.eduplace.com/kids/hme/ to interact with this rubric.

▶ Revise Your Persuasive Essay

❶ Revise your essay. Use the list of sentences you wrote from the rubric. Work on the parts that you described with sentences from "Sounding Stronger" and "Turn Up the Volume."

❷ Have a writing conference.

When You're the Writer Read your essay aloud to a partner. Ask questions about any problems you are having. Take notes.

When You're the Listener Say at least two things you like about the essay. Ask questions about any parts that are unclear. Use the chart below for help.

HELP ?

Revising Tip

Check your support.
- Underline reasons in one color.
- Underline facts and examples in another color.

What should I say?

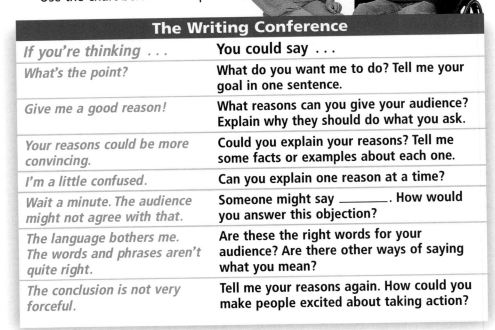

The Writing Conference

If you're thinking . . .	**You could say . . .**
What's the point?	**What do you want me to do? Tell me your goal in one sentence.**
Give me a good reason!	**What reasons can you give your audience? Explain why they should do what you ask.**
Your reasons could be more convincing.	**Could you explain your reasons? Tell me some facts or examples about each one.**
I'm a little confused.	**Can you explain one reason at a time?**
Wait a minute. The audience might not agree with that.	**Someone might say _____. How would you answer this objection?**
The language bothers me. The words and phrases aren't quite right.	**Are these the right words for your audience? Are there other ways of saying what you mean?**
The conclusion is not very forceful.	**Tell me your reasons again. How could you make people excited about taking action?**

❸ Make more revisions to your persuasive essay. Use your conference notes and the Revising Strategies on the next page.

Revising Strategies

Elaborating: Word Choice Two words with the same meaning can suggest different feelings. The feeling a word suggests is its **connotation**. Choose words with connotations that support your goal and match the tone of your essay.

Ineffective Connotations	Effective Connotations
Cleaning up the park will be easy! Just **haul** bags of garbage and **heave** them up on a truck.	Cleaning up the park will be easy! Just gather up bags of garbage and toss them up on a truck.
He should get paid more for that job. **Gathering up** furniture and **tossing** it up on a truck is a lot of work.	He should get paid more for that job. Hauling furniture and heaving it up on a truck is a lot of work.

▶ Find at least two places in your essay where you can use a word with a connotation that will help convince your audience.

📖 Use the Thesaurus Plus on page H96. See also page H15.

Elaborating: Details Precise, thought-provoking details will help your audience understand your reasons.

Few Details	Elaborated with Details
When you ride a bike on a busy street, **it is scary.**	When you ride a bike on a busy street, the wind from passing trucks makes your wheels wobble, and some trucks come so close that their mirrors almost hit you.

▶ Find at least three places in your essay to add precise details.

Sentence Fluency Be concise! Get straight to the point.

Weak: Too Wordy	Strong: Concise
I request your consideration of a rule allowing all students to vote on the choices available on the new cafeteria menu.	We should all be able to vote on what will be on the new cafeteria menu.

▶ Rewrite three of your sentences, using fewer words. Which way is more effective?

Proofread Your Persuasive Essay

Proofread your essay, using the Proofreading Checklist and the Grammar and Spelling Connections. Proofread for one skill at a time. Use a dictionary to check spellings.

Proofreading Checklist

Did I
- ✔ indent all paragraphs?
- ✔ use the proper end punctuation?
- ✔ check subject-verb agreement?
- ✔ use commas correctly with compound sentences?
- ✔ correct any spelling errors?

Use the Guide to Capitalization, Punctuation, and Usage on page H64.

Proofreading Marks

¶ Indent
∧ Add
⌐ Delete
≡ Capital letter
/ Small letter
∨∨ Add quotes
∧ Add comma
⊙ Add period
∩ Transpose

Tech Tip
Mistakes are easy to miss on-screen. Print out your essay to proofread it.

Grammar and Spelling Connections

Subject-Verb Agreement If the compound subject is joined by *and*, use a plural verb. If the compound subject is joined by *or* or *nor*, the verb agrees with the nearer subject.

Incorrect	Correct
Brenda **or** Yolanda **were** doing that.	Brenda **or** Yolanda **was** doing that.
Brenda **and** Yolanda **lives** on that street.	Brenda **and** Yolanda **live** on that street.

GRAMMAR LINK *See pages 152, 155, and 159.*

Spelling the Suffixes -al, -ile, and -ous The suffixes -*al*, -*ile*, and -*ous* form adjectives when added to base words or roots.

abnormal fragile continuous
manual hostile precious

See the Spelling Guide on page H80.

Go to www.eduplace.com/kids/hme/ for proofreading practice.

► Publish Your Persuasive Essay

❶ Make a neat final copy of your essay. Be sure you corrected all errors.

❷ Title your essay. Choose an attention-grabbing title, such as "A Software Famine" rather than "Our School Needs Software."

> **GRAMMAR TIP** ► *Capitalize the first, the last, and each important word in a title.*

❸ Publish or share your essay in a way that suits both your goal and your audience. See the Ideas for Sharing box.

Tips for Giving a Persuasive Speech

- Make a note card for each reason and the facts and examples that support it.
- Practice your speech beforehand.
- Speak in a confident tone. Make eye contact with your audience.
- Speak more loudly and slowly to a large group in a large room than to a small group in a small room.
- Use gestures and facial expressions that show your emotions.

📖 See page H7 for tips.

Ideas for Sharing

Write It Down
- Publish your essay as a newspaper editorial.

Talk It Up
- Read your essay as a persuasive speech.

Show It Off
- Display your essay on a poster. Use photographs or pictures to illustrate your reasons.
- Make slides that illustrate your reasons. Read your essay as you show them.

► Reflect

Write about your writing experience. Use these questions to get started.

- What was difficult about writing a persuasive essay? What was easy?
- What have you learned about reaching your audience? When might you use this knowledge in a different kind of writing?
- Compare this paper with other papers you have written.

Writing Prompts

Use these prompts as ideas for persuasive essays or to practice for a test. Some of them will work well for other subjects you study. Decide who your audience will be, and write your essay to convince them.

1 Computers do more harm than good in classrooms. Do you agree or disagree? Write an essay persuading your principal to add or remove classroom computers.

2 What is the legal driving age in your state? Do you think teenagers start too early or have to wait too long? Persuade your governor to raise or lower the driving age.

3 Persuade your classmates not to watch television or listen to the radio while doing their homework.

4 Should students be required to do community service? Write a letter to your school board arguing for or against such a requirement.

Writing Across the Curriculum

5 MEDIA
Teenagers should be allowed to see any movie they want. Persuade parents to agree with this statement, or persuade kids to disagree with it.

6 MATHEMATICS
Persuade your classmates that algebra is both useful and enjoyable. Remember to anticipate objections.

7 LITERATURE
Choose a book you love. Convince your friends to read it too. Use details and short quotations from the book to support your reasons.

8 HEALTH
Suppose your state legislature is considering a law that would prevent kids from buying junk food without permission from their parents. Persuade your legislators to vote for or against this new law.

✓ Test Practice

This prompt to write a persuasive essay is like ones you might find on a writing test. Read the prompt.

> **Computers do more harm than good in classrooms. Do you agree or disagree? Write an essay persuading your principal to add or remove classroom computers.**

Here are some strategies to help you do a good job.

❶ Look for clue words that tell what to write about. What are the clue words in the prompt above?

❷ Choose a topic that fits the clue words. Write the clue words that identify your audience, your goal, and sometimes your format.

> Remember, a persuasive essay gives reasons, supported by facts and examples, to convince an audience to take a specific action.

Clue Words	My Topic
essay persuading your principal, add or remove classroom computers	I will write an essay to convince my principal to remove classroom computers.

❸ Plan your essay. Use a persuasion flow chart.

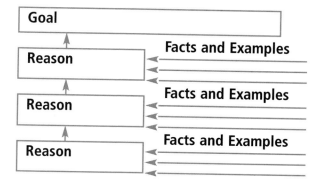

❹ You will get a good score if you remember the sentences under "Loud and Clear!" in the rubric on page 505.

Writing a Business Letter

A **business letter** is written to conduct business, such as to give or to request information, to purchase something, or to comment about a product or service. You may also write a business letter to persuade someone to do something. Business letters should be brief and direct, using formal and polite language. Read Dan's business letter.

Heading —
> 1478 Shawmut Street
> Winchester, IL 60531
> February 15, 2001

Inside address —
> Winchester Board of Selectmen
> Winchester Town Hall
> 12 Middle Street
> Winchester, IL 60531

Greeting → Dear Sir or Madam:

Body —

The planned construction of the Greentown Railroad is an issue that concerns me deeply. The effects of the railroad would be damaging to our town, and I appeal to you to cancel the project.

I have two main reasons for opposing the railroad. First, the noise a train makes is unbelievably loud. The train's whistles and squeals would distract people who work in Hindley Square. The noise would also be unbearable to people who live near the tracks.

My second reason is the potential effect on plants and animals. Trees within fifteen yards of the tracks would have to be cut down. This would destroy food supplies for animals. It would demolish their homes and invade more of their ever-shrinking habitat.

I believe that these are two good reasons why the Greentown Railroad should not be built. Please rethink the plans and save the town of Winchester.

Closing ————→ Sincerely,

Signature ————→ *Dan Griffin*

Dan Griffin

- The **heading** tells the sender's complete address and the date. *What is Dan's street address?*

- The **inside address** gives the complete name and address of the person, business, or organization that will receive the letter. *Who is to receive Dan's letter?*

- The **greeting** can include a specific name or, if the name is unknown, might say *Dear Sir or Madam* or *Dear (Title)*. The greeting is followed by a colon. *Why do you think Dan isn't writing to a specific person?*

- The **body** explains the purpose of the letter and should be written in a polite and formal style. *What is Dan's purpose in writing the letter?*

- The **closing** begins with a capital letter and ends with a comma. *How did Dan close his letter?*

- The handwritten **signature** appears above the typed name. *Why is a handwritten signature important in a business letter?*

How to Write a Business Letter

1 **Think** about your purpose and to whom you can write to accomplish it. Make notes about what you want to say, and organize them in sequence.

2 **Write** the body of your letter. Explain your purpose at the beginning.

3 **Use** formal language. If you are writing to persuade someone to support a cause or to act on an issue, politely offer strong reasons.

4 **Include** all six parts of a business letter.

5 **Revise** your letter if necessary. Be sure all the language is businesslike.

6 **Proofread** your letter. Use the Proofreading Checklist on page 508. Use a dictionary to check spellings.

7 **Address** the envelope accurately. Use a business-size (#10) envelope. Mail a neat final copy of your letter.

HELP

How Formal?

- Avoid slang.
- Be serious.
- Don't discuss personal matters.
- Use a respectful tone.
- Be as brief as possible.

Return address
Dan Griffin
1478 Shawmut St.
Winchester, IL 60531

Mailing address
Winchester Board of Selectmen
Winchester Town Hall
12 Middle St.
Winchester, IL 60531

Listening for Persuasive Tactics

When someone asks us to do something and gives clear and valid reasons for the request, we usually do it if we can. If the request would be against family rules or might be harmful in some way, we usually have no difficulty refusing. Some speakers, however, use persuasive tactics that can appeal to our emotions and prevent us from fully considering the request.

Look at the situations below.

Bandwagon   **Promises**

Other Tactics

A speaker may act superior by pointing out that he or she is older or more experienced than the listener. Another may suggest that the listener is afraid to do something. Still another may flatter the listener and suggest that his or her good points will be enhanced by doing what the speaker asks. What other persuasive tactics can you think of that play on your emotions before you've had a chance to think fully about what is being asked?

Decide for Yourself

Think carefully about what the speaker is saying. Then decide for yourself what to do.

- **Think about the goal.** What does the speaker want you to do? Why is this goal important to him or her?
- **Think about the reasons.** Why does the speaker think you should do this? Does each reason make sense to you? Do the reasons go against any rules?
- **Think about the support.** How does the speaker explain each reason? Does the speaker repeat an opinion or give facts and examples?
- **Think about person-to-person encounters.** Is it more difficult to refuse in person than it is over the phone or in a letter?

Guidelines for Listening for Persuasive Tactics

▶ Listen for bandwagon tactics. Is the speaker suggesting that you will be part of an important group if you do what he or she asks? Is the speaker specific about who he or she means by "everybody"?

▶ Listen for flattery. Does the speaker support the good things he or she says about you with examples? Even if what the speaker says is true, is it a good reason for doing what he or she asks?

▶ Listen for promises. Is the speaker promising something that seems desirable but is very vague? Does the speaker make it clear how doing what he or she wants will make these promises come true?

Apply It

Write a short speech using at least two persuasive tactics. Include emotional appeals. Then rewrite it, replacing all appeals to emotion with reasons that are supported with facts and examples.

- What persuasive tactics did you use?
- What emotional appeals were part of your tactics?
- Was it difficult to replace the appeals with facts and examples? Underline your facts and examples.
- How might using persuasive tactics help you recognize them?

Recognizing Persuasive Tactics in Media

Mass media go beyond television, movies, books, and the Internet. Coupons, advertising displays on public transportation, and skywriting are media. Promotional "freebies" are too. The messages of mass media are intended to inform or influence large numbers of people. Think about the points below.

About Media

- Media messages are constructed, meaning that they are made by people to send a particular message.

- Media use verbal and visual language. Different kinds of media use their own languages and special ways of presenting a message. For example, comic books do not follow the same rules as fashion magazines.

- Different people will not experience the same media message in the same way. Age and personal life experience each affect how a person views a message. For example, a teenager living in a large urban area might view an ad for a new mall differently than would a middle-aged person who lives in a rural area.

Advertising

Businesses pay advertisers millions of dollars to find out what target audiences like, don't like, and why. Then they use this market research to produce ad campaigns. The resulting ads are often loaded with bright images, popular music, snappy voice tracks, or catchy slogans.

The ads may also rely on persuasive tactics. The "testimonial" is a kind of tactic in which a famous person says a product or service worked for them. These and other tactics are intended to appeal to your emotions and to make you feel like you need the product. Advertisers want to keep you from thinking about factors such as how much the product costs or how durable it is.

Look at the following tactics. Do any seem familiar?

Persuasive Tactics	
Overgeneralization	An overgeneralization makes a general statement about something based on only a few facts.
Loaded language	Carefully chosen language is used to play upon your emotions or fears.
Flattery	Some ads compliment you. They tell you how smart you are to use the product, or they may say that you deserve the product. Exciting. Adventurous. A car just like you— the new XLQ!
Transfer	The transfer tactic connects a famous person, attractive image, or popular idea with the product.
Name-calling	Name-calling hopes to makes you feel superior to others by making them seem inferior. **Why drive their junkheaps? Call us: Safe Wheels, Inc.**

Stop and Think

Have you ever bought something that looked great in the picture but did not work well when you tried to use it? What claims did the advertiser make about the product? Did they seem too good to be true? Such claims are known as false advertising.

False advertising and unfair business practices are monitored by many public and private groups. The Federal Trade Commission, for example, is one government organization that protects consumers' rights and investigates complaints against businesses. When a company's claims about a product are proven false, the company may be forced to stop running an ad, to recall the product, to pay a fine, or to go to court.

more ▶

Propaganda

Some public and private organizations also monitor the spread of propaganda in the media. Propaganda is slanted and exaggerated information that attempts to win support for a particular view or belief. Often propaganda uses stereotypes, which are oversimplified ideas or images, usually about a group of people. These misrepresentations are unfair and can be dangerous.

Think and Discuss

- In what way is the Web page's message exaggerated? What is it trying to make you believe?
- What biases are shown? What beliefs are supported?
- How does oversimplification work in the image? What could you say in response?

Use the guidelines below when looking at advertisements or other media examples that promote products, people, or ideas. Then make up your own mind about what you see.

Guidelines for Recognizing Persuasive Tactics in Media

▶ Look carefully at the advertisement. Who paid for it? How does it want you to respond?

▶ Look at the images, music, and speech used. Why do you think they were chosen? How do they make you feel?

▶ Read the text or listen carefully to the words of the ad. Does the ad use facts or opinions? Do the words focus on the product or on a mood or an idea?

▶ Study the ad to see which persuasive tactics were used, if any. Why do you think the ones chosen were used?

▶ Study the layout. How are the people shown? Does the ad include stereotypes or make assumptions about a specific group of people?

▶ Look at the placement of the product. Does the ad try to distract you from thinking about the product? In what ways?

▶ Think about what the ad is trying to say. What does it ask you to believe?

Apply It

Keep a notebook for a week in which you watch for persuasive tactics in media. Focus on advertisements in different forms. Think about each ad's target audience and describe its overall effectiveness in appealing to that audience. Use the guidelines above to help you.

- Look in the classified section of magazines or newspapers. Find ads that make claims for such things as quick weight loss, instant money, or improving credit. Are these claims realistic? How do the magazines and newspapers protect themselves from complaints about the ads?

- As a class, make a list of promotional "freebies" you have seen or received, such as pens, calendars, magnets, and key chains. Discuss what each is promoting and the target audience. Why do you think the advertiser thought a "freebie" would help to promote a product?

Conducting a Debate

People can debate informally or formally. A formal debate involves two teams. One team argues in support of a proposition, or statement. The other team argues against it. Rules ensure that each team has a fair chance to make its case.

Before the debate begins, each side researches and organizes its ideas. The research is then pooled to prepare a persuasive speech.

The following chart shows one possible debate format. Each part of a debate has a time limit.

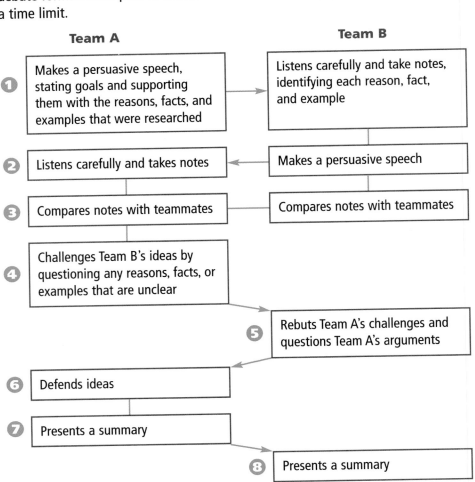

Team A

Team B

1 Makes a persuasive speech, stating goals and supporting them with the reasons, facts, and examples that were researched

Listens carefully and take notes, identifying each reason, fact, and example

2 Listens carefully and takes notes

Makes a persuasive speech

3 Compares notes with teammates

Compares notes with teammates

4 Challenges Team B's ideas by questioning any reasons, facts, or examples that are unclear

5 Rebuts Team A's challenges and questions Team A's arguments

6 Defends ideas

7 Presents a summary

8 Presents a summary

Use the guidelines below to support your speaking and listening skills in a debate.

Guidelines for Speaking in a Debate

▶ Choose exact words that support your position.
▶ Avoid using slang. Formal, but not difficult, language makes the speaker appear knowledgeable and believable.
▶ Use persuasive words, such as *clearly* or *certainly*, and speak persuasively but politely.
▶ Keep your voice low, calm, and confident. A high-pitched voice often sounds nervous.
▶ Speak slowly and clearly for a large audience in a large space. Pronounce each word carefully.

Guidelines for Listening in a Debate

▶ Think about each reason. Does it support the speaker's goal? Is it vague or exaggerated?
▶ Think about each fact and example. Does it elaborate a specific reason? Is it accurate?
▶ Watch the speaker's gestures and expressions. Are they relaxed and natural or stiff and awkward?
▶ Listen to the tone of the speaker's voice. Does the speaker sound confident or uncertain?
▶ Look at how the audience reacts to the speaker. Which reasons seem most persuasive to audience members?

Apply It

Hold your own debate. Use the guidelines above to help you get started. Then answer the following questions.

● What arguments were the most effective for each team? Give examples and tell why you think they worked.
● What materials did the teams use as sources for their arguments? Were the materials sufficient?
● What would you change in planning a future debate? Explain why.

Section 2

Explaining and Informing

What You Will Find in This Section:

- Listening for Information 524
- Writing Expository Paragraphs 525

Unit 11 | **Writing to Compare and Contrast** 534

Special Focus on Explaining
Writing Instructions 560

Communication Link
Viewing/Media:
Comparing Ways to Represent Meaning .. 566

Listening for Information

When you listen to a news report or to an explanation of how something works, you are **listening for factual information**. **Facts** can be proved true. Information can help you to increase your knowledge, to solve problems, and to make decisions. Here are some guidelines that can help you to be an effective listener.

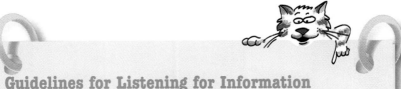

Guidelines for Listening for Information

▶ Identify the topic. What subject is the author discussing?
▶ Listen for the main idea. What does the author have to say about the topic?
▶ Listen for examples and for facts such as numbers or dates. How do they elaborate the main idea?
▶ Consider the source of information, if given. Is it reliable? Can you trust the facts to be accurate?
▶ Listen for the author's purpose. Why is the author writing about this topic?

Try It Out Listen as your teacher reads aloud from *The Importance of Thurgood Marshall,* by Deborah Hitzeroth and Sharon Leon. Take notes to help you answer the questions below.

- What is the topic of the expository piece?
- What is the main idea?
- What facts and examples elaborate the authors' main idea?
- Why do you think the authors wrote this piece?

📖 See page H32 for tips on taking notes while listening.

Writing Expository Paragraphs

An **expository paragraph** conveys factual information. The writer's purpose is to share information about a topic he or she knows well.

Remember to indent the first line of a paragraph.

An expository paragraph has a topic and a main idea. The **topic** is the subject of the paragraph. The **main idea** is what the author has to say about the subject. What is the topic of the expository paragraph below? What is the main idea?

Indent

Topic sentence

Supporting sentences

Concluding sentence

    Many different cultures have their own versions of lake or sea monsters. You've probably heard of the Loch Ness Monster, a giant, serpentlike creature that supposedly lives in Loch Ness, a lake in northern Scotland. Icelanders have the Skrimsl, a long, humped creature that moves from lake to lake. Swedes tell the story of a giant lightning-fast sea horse with a red and white mane. Although none of these monsters have ever been proved to exist, many people do believe in them. The next time you dive into the icy depths, just think about who—or what—might be paddling around with you!

Artist's idea of the Loch Ness monster

Topic Sentence

The topic is lake and sea monsters. The main idea is that different cultures have their own legends about these monsters. Which sentence tells the topic and the main idea?

Supporting Sentence

The labels show the three parts of an expository paragraph.

- The **topic sentence** states the topic and tells the writer's main idea.

Concluding Sentence

- The **supporting sentences** give facts and examples about the main idea.
- The **concluding sentence** wraps up the paragraph.

Think and Discuss What facts and examples are given in the supporting sentences of the paragraph above?

The Topic Sentence

You learned on the previous page that the **topic sentence** in an expository paragraph names the topic and tells what the writer wants to say about it. A strong topic sentence gets the reader's attention by stating the main idea in lively, clear language.

```
           Topic                 Main idea
         ┌───────┐┌──────────────────────────────┐
Example:  Minerva was the favorite child of Jupiter, the king
          of the gods in Roman mythology.
```

In expository paragraphs, the topic sentence is often first, as it is in the paragraph about lake monsters on page 525. Sometimes, however, the topic sentence comes elsewhere in the paragraph. If it comes at the end, it takes the place of the concluding sentence.

Which is the topic sentence in the paragraph below? Which are the supporting sentences?

Eleanor Roosevelt, a strong voice for many social causes, traveled extensively. When she wasn't on the road, she was conducting press conferences, writing her nationally syndicated newspaper column, or broadcasting her own radio program. In addition to serving as a U.S. delegate to the United Nations, Mrs. Roosevelt published several books and raised a large family. Eleanor Roosevelt was one of the most active first ladies in the history of the United States.

Try It Out Read the paragraphs below. On your own or with a partner, write the topic and the main idea of each paragraph. Then write two possible topic sentences for each paragraph.

1. Dancers have to practice long hours every day, often for years, before they are good enough to join a dance troupe. They have to keep dancing even when every muscle aches and every inch of skin is soaked with sweat. To the dancer, though, none of that really matters. ___*Topic sentence*___ .

2. ___*Topic sentence*___ . Good fit is important. Because your foot expands during exercise, it's best to try on new footwear within one hour of exercising. It also helps to wear the same kind of socks you'll wear while using the shoe. Another key consideration is design. For sports requiring frequent side-to-side movements, such as basketball and aerobics, stability is important. High-top sneakers can offer adequate ankle support. However, if you plan to walk or run, the priority changes. Extra cushioning and a lightweight sole are needed to protect feet from the constant pounding. Finally, the most important rule when you shop is to forget style. Cool colors and trendy logos will not help you when you are sidelined by injuries!

Supporting Sentences

Supporting sentences usually follow the topic sentence. They give details that help readers better understand the main idea. In informational paragraphs, these details can include **facts**, which can be proved true. They can include **examples**, which cite specific instances of the point being made. Details can also include **sensory words**, which tell how something looks, sounds, smells, feels, or tastes.

Fact: Many different cultures have their own versions of lake or sea monsters.

Example: Swedes tell the story of a giant sea horse.

Sensory words: giant, serpentlike, long, humped, lightning-fast, red, white, icy

Read the paragraph below. How do the supporting sentences explain the main idea stated in the topic sentence?

In New York City, it's possible to travel around the world and back in time without ever leaving one neighborhood. The Museum of Natural History, for example, has one of the most extensive dinosaur exhibits in the world. Inside, visitors marvel at the colossal skeletons of these prehistoric beasts. Across the street is Central Park, 843 acres of lush green space that draws over twenty million visitors from around the world each year. Visitors to the park entertain themselves riding in horse-drawn carriages, listening to the percussive music of steel drums, strolling down tree-lined paths, or rowing on the shimmering lake. Finally, on the other side of the park is the Metropolitan Museum of Art, which houses an ancient Egyptian temple and actual mummies. Visitors get to leave their passports and subway tokens at home on this tour!

Think and Discuss What facts and examples are in the paragraph above? What sensory words can you find?

Ordering Details Supporting sentences in an expository paragraph are organized in an order that makes sense. Different orders work better for different kinds of topics.

- Details about a sequence of events are usually told in **time order**.
- Details that describe are often told in **spatial order**, the order in which you might look at something.
- Still other kinds of details are told in **order of importance**, from most important to least important, or from least important to most important.

Transitional words and phrases, such as *first, finally, just beyond,* and *most important,* help readers follow these details and see how they are connected.

How are the details arranged in the New York City paragraph on page 528? What transitional words and phrases are used?

HELP ? See page 18 for tips on ordering details. See page 20 for more transitional words and phrases.

Try It Out On your own or with a partner, look at the diagram of the Hoover Dam below. Use what you see and the facts provided to write some supporting sentences for the topic sentence. Link at least two of your sentences with a transitional word or phrase.

Topic sentence: In addition to controlling floods and storing water, Hoover Dam generates hydroelectric power.

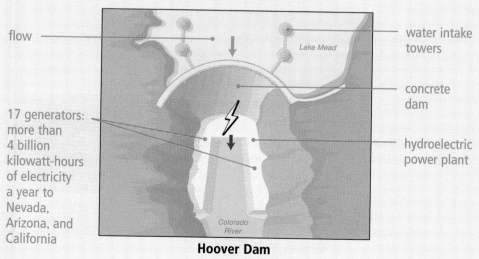

flow

Lake Mead

water intake towers

concrete dam

17 generators: more than 4 billion kilowatt-hours of electricity a year to Nevada, Arizona, and California

hydroelectric power plant

Colorado River

Hoover Dam

 GRAMMAR TIP Remember that time is shown by the **tense** of a verb. Use past tense, present tense, and future tense to express different times.

The Concluding Sentence

Unless it is the topic sentence, the **concluding sentence** of an expository paragraph can restate the main idea in an interesting way. It can also draw a conclusion or make an additional comment. In the sea monster paragraph on page 525, the author makes an additional comment. In the paragraph about New York City on page 528, the author restates the topic sentence in an interesting way.

What kind of concluding sentence does the writer use in the paragraph below?

> Just because the chance of becoming a supermodel, a rock star, or a professional athlete is small, you don't have to rule out careers in these fields entirely! There are hundreds of potential jobs that will allow you to pursue these interests behind the scenes. The fashion lover can design clothes, become a photographer, or edit a fashion magazine. The frustrated basketball star can write a sports column for a newspaper or coach a team and still be on the court daily. Young people fascinated by music videos can learn to produce them instead of starring in them. With a few small adjustments, it's possible to turn your fantasy job into a reality.

Try It Out On your own, read the paragraph below. Then write two different concluding sentences for it.

> Although alligators can be dangerous, many misconceptions surround this fearsome creature.  One myth is that alligators live for hundreds of years. With their scaly skin, hooded eyes, and razor-sharp teeth, they may look like ancient creatures, but alligators in the wild usually live to be only thirty-five to forty years old. Another misconception is that alligators are gigantic, over twenty feet long. In reality, the average alligator is thirteen feet long. It is true, however, that alligators move very quickly, at least over short distances, and that they occasionally attack family pets. _Concluding sentence_ .

Paragraphs That Compare and Contrast

Some expository paragraphs compare and contrast two subjects. When you show how two subjects are alike, you compare them. When you show how they are different, you contrast them.

A **paragraph that compares and contrasts** has a topic sentence, which usually comes at the beginning of the paragraph. It has supporting sentences that use facts and examples to show how the two subjects are alike and different. A concluding sentence ends the paragraph. Transitional words and phrases, such as *similarly, although,* and *on the other hand,* connect the supporting sentences.

Which sentences compare and which contrast in the paragraph below? What transitional words and phrases link the supporting sentences?

> If you have lots of similarities and lots of differences to discuss, write one paragraph for each set of details.

Topic sentence — My sister and I are both avid athletes and equally competitive, but that's where our similarities end. Our favorite sports are very different. I love anything that gets me in the water: swimming, water skiing, snorkeling, diving. My sister, Supporting sentences — on the other hand, loves to hit any kind of ball—a baseball, a tennis ball, a golf ball, even a croquet ball. I don't care if my form is not perfect. I just like to move! In contrast, my sister demands precision. Whether she wants a ball to fly perfectly down a fairway or slice over a net, she calculates each shot as if Concluding sentence — she were a mathematician. Although we both like sports, one thing is for sure—we'll never compete against each other!

Try It Out Choose one of the pairs listed below. On your own or with a partner, make a list of the subjects' similarities and differences. Then write at least three supporting sentences that compare and contrast the subjects.

- a radio disc jockey and a TV reporter
- a backpack and a locker
- a jumbo jet and a single-engine plane

Paragraphs That Show Cause and Effect

A **paragraph that shows cause and effect** explains why or how one thing causes another thing to happen. Its topic sentence, which usually comes at the beginning of the paragraph, introduces the cause, a result, or both. Supporting sentences give details that further explain the cause and its effects. Transitional words and phrases, such as *as a result, because of, consequently,* and *due to,* help the reader understand and follow what is happening.

Read the paragraph below. What is the cause? What are the effects?

Topic sentence —

Supporting sentences —

Concluding sentence —

> A violent rain storm can virtually paralyze a city's work force. When a storm floods the train tracks, it's impossible for the trains to get through. Thousands of suburban commuters end up stranded, waiting for trains that never come. City pedestrians who walk to work do not have an easy time either. As water overwhelms the storm drains, the streets become impassable rivers. As a result, thousands more are unable to reach their jobs, and businesses have to close. For some workers a storm brings a welcome vacation from work, but for others it creates a day of frustration.

Try It Out Choose one of the topic sentences below. On your own or with a partner, identify the cause stated in the topic sentence. Then write at least three supporting sentences that explain its effects. Use a transitional word or phrase to connect two of your supporting sentences.

1. Bad eating habits can have serious consequences.
2. Computers have brought about a revolution in the way we communicate.
3. The effects of an extended drought can be devastating.

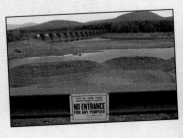  

Write Your Own Expository Paragraph

Now it's time to use what you've learned to write your own expository paragraph. You may choose to write a paragraph that explains what something is or does, a paragraph that compares and contrasts, or a paragraph that shows cause and effect. First, think about a subject that interests you. Choose the form most suited to that subject. Then make a list of details to include. After you share your ideas with a partner, you're ready to write.

Checklist for My Paragraph

✔ My **topic sentence** clearly states the topic and the main idea.
✔ My **supporting sentences** provide details, such as facts, examples, and sensory words, that elaborate the main idea.
✔ My **concluding sentence** restates the main idea or adds a final comment.

Looking Ahead

Now that you know how to write an expository paragraph, it will be easier to write a longer expository essay. As you can see by the diagram below, the parts of an expository paragraph match the parts of an expository composition.

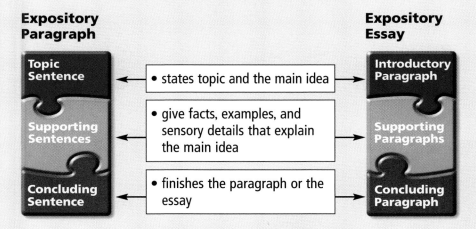

Expository Paragraph — **Expository Essay**

Topic Sentence	• states topic and the main idea	Introductory Paragraph
Supporting Sentences	• give facts, examples, and sensory details that explain the main idea	Supporting Paragraphs
Concluding Sentence	• finishes the paragraph or the essay	Concluding Paragraph

Writing to Compare and Contrast

Your teeth may be bigger, but do you really want to mess with these quills?

The Wright brothers, considered by many to be the fathers of modern aviation, had their first successful flight in a motor-powered airplane in 1903. What features does the author compare and contrast in this essay describing the two brothers?

THE WRIGHT BROTHERS
How They Invented the Airplane

Russell Freedman
With Original Photographs by Wilbur and Orville Wright

Wilbur and Orville

from *The Wright Brothers,* by Russell Freedman

"From the time we were little children," Wilbur Wright once said, "my brother Orville and myself lived together, played together, worked together and, in fact, thought together."

As they worked side by side in their bicycle shop, the brothers would sometimes start whistling or humming the same tune at exactly the same moment. Their voices were so much alike, a listener in another room had a hard time telling them apart.

People often remarked that Wilbur and Orville were as inseparable as twins. They shared everything from a joint bank account to their experiments with flying machines. Neither brother smoked, drank, nor married. Lifelong bachelors, they lived with their widowed father and unmarried sister in a modest frame house in Dayton, not far from the Wright Cycle Company, where they sold, repaired, and built bicycles.

After the invention of the airplane, the public was astonished to learn that the Wright brothers had no special training in science or engineering. Though they were good students, both left high school

See www.eduplace.com/kids/ for information about Russell Freedman.

more ▶

A Published Model   **535**

without receiving a diploma. Neither attended college. They learned more by teaching themselves than through formal schooling.

From boyhood on, each brother had a way with tools and a knack for solving problems. Even as grown men, they never lost their enthusiasm for mechanical playthings. The Wrights' favorite niece, Ivonette, later recalled: "When we were old enough to get toys, Uncle Orv and Uncle Will had a habit of playing with them until they were broken, then repairing them so that they were better than when they were bought."

They were as close as brothers can be, yet in many ways, they were different. Wilbur was four years older, an inch and a half taller, and a pound or two leaner. With a high domed forehead and long nose, he had striking hawklike features that set him apart from his younger brother.

Orville's most prominent feature was the reddish mustache he had grown in high school. Dapper and tidy, he was by far the more clothes conscious of the two. Even in the bicycle shop he wore sleeve cuffs and a blue-and-white-striped apron to protect his clothing. "I don't believe there was ever a man who could do the work he did in all kinds of dirt, oil, and grime and come out of it looking immaculate," said Ivonette. "When the job was finished he'd come out looking like he was right out of a band box."

Wilbur wasn't that fussy. Often he had to be reminded by his sister that his suit needed pressing or that something didn't match. Once she insisted that he borrow a shirt, cuff links, and an overcoat from Orville before going off to deliver an important speech.

It was hard to rattle Wilbur. He seemed very sure of himself and didn't say much. At a Fourth of July picnic one year, he put up the swings for the children, then stood aloof from the crowd for much of the day. "The strongest impression one gets of Wilbur Wright," said a friend, "is of a man who lives largely in a world of his own."

Orville was more impulsive, "bubbling over with ideas," according to his niece. Among family and friends, he had a reputation as a tease and a practical joker. Among strangers, however, he seemed uncomfortably shy. He would clam up and fade silently into the background.

Orville's greatest pleasure was to take something apart, see how it worked, and put it back together. Wilbur was more of a visionary, fascinated by the big picture rather than its individual parts. He was the one who first dreamed of building an airplane, but it was Orville's enthusiasm that carried the brothers along.

When their father was asked which of the two contributed the most and was the leader in their partnership, he gave this answer: "Wilbur in every respect was uncommon in his intellect and attainments—was a surprise to those near him. But he seemed not to care for notice. Orville's mind grew steadily, and in invention he was fully equal to his brother. They are equal in their inventions, neither claiming superiority above the other, nor accepting any honor to the neglect of the other."

more ▶

Reading As a Writer

Think About the Compare-Contrast Essay

- What features does the author compare? What features does he contrast?
- In which paragraph does the author introduce his subjects?
- Which paragraphs describe similarities? Which describe differences?

Think About Writer's Craft

- Where does the author use dialogue instead of reporting what people said? How does using dialogue improve his essay?
- What descriptive words help you to picture Wilbur and Orville?

Think About the Pictures

- The photograph on page 535 shows Wilbur on the left and Orville on the right. What physical differences between the two brothers can you see?
- The photograph on page 536 shows the house where the brothers lived. What item shown is directly linked to a detail mentioned in the essay?
- Explain why, for this particular essay, photographs work better to support the text than illustrations.

Responding

Write responses to these questions.

- **Personal Response** Which Wright brother is more appealing to you? Why?
- **Critical Thinking** What might have helped the brothers achieve their goal of motor-powered flight? (Consider experience, lifestyle, education, and character.)

What Makes a Great Compare-Contrast Essay?

A **compare-contrast essay** compares the similarities and contrasts the differences between two subjects.

Remember to follow these guidelines when you write a compare-contrast essay.

▶ Choose two subjects that have something in common.

▶ Compare or contrast the corresponding details for each subject.

▶ Write an attention-grabbing introduction that states your subjects.

▶ Choose a method of organization, and stick to it throughout your essay.

▶ Use topic sentences to state your main ideas.

▶ Use specific details to show similarities and contrasts.

▶ Use transitional words and phrases to help show similarities and differences.

▶ Write a conclusion that sums up your main ideas in a satisfying way.

GRAMMAR CHECK
Avoid double negatives. Remember that *hardly, scarcely,* and *barely* are negatives.

WORKING DRAFT

When Theo asked his father to pack his "board" for a family vacation, his father packed Theo's skateboard instead of his snowboard. His dad's mistake gave Theo the idea for this compare-contrast essay. Here is his first draft.

Theo Lipson

Working Draft

I'm both a skateboarder and a snowboarder. Both sports attract the same types of people. Although there are many differences, these two sports have many similarities.

The history of these two sports is actually quite similar. The skateboard was not invented by a single person, and nobody gives credit to any one person for inventing it. People all around in the 1960s were experimenting with the idea for the skateboard, especially people on the West Coast. Similarly, Sherman Poppen made an early example of a snowboard around 1965. By 1977, Jake Burton Carpenter was making snowboards out of fiberglass and wood.

Snowboarders and skateboarders are called "riders" because they ride a board. Both the snowboard and the skateboard are one plank, and the shape of the deck on each is similar, designed to be stable. The stability of the boards allows you to stand up. The snowboard has bindings to hold in the rider, but a skateboard has no straps—the rider stands on the deck of the board.

I love these subjects! Will your introduction grab your reader's attention?

Great! Each supporting sentence tells more about the main idea.

Does every sentence in this paragraph tell a similarity?

Working Draft

Since the boards have a similar shape, the tricks riders do on them are often going to be similar as well. There are many tricks that are the same in both sports.

Alike in many ways, snowboarding and skateboarding also have their differences. The terrain that you ride these two boards on is quite different.

When you look at a picture of each of these boards you would think that riding them would be a similar experience, but it's really not. Snowboarding is faster than skateboarding, and on a snowboard your whole body feels free because the terrain is so wide open. I spend much of my time cruising on the trails, but some people just enjoy doing tricks. With a skateboard, because you're not strapped in, your feet feel more free and you can do flip tricks. That's why I spend most of my time doing tricks when I am skateboarding.

With a skateboard, the rider has to create power. The snowboard has a flat bottom that is designed to ride smoothly on the snowy surface. The way that you move with a snowboard is just letting yourself ride in a downward motion.

> Can you add details about tricks and terrain?

> Can you state the main idea of this paragraph in a topic sentence?

> How can you make your ending seem less cut off?

Reading As a Writer

- What did Joe think works well in Theo's essay? What questions did Joe have? What revisions might Theo make?
- Where did Theo describe differences? Where did he describe similarities?
- Which sentence needs to be moved? Where does it belong?
- What additional questions would you like to ask Theo?

FINAL COPY

After Theo discussed his draft with his classmates, he made some changes to his compare-contrast essay. Compare the final version with Theo's working draft to see how he improved it.

Riding the Boards: Skateboarding and Snowboarding
by Theo Lipson

It's not unusual to find a skateboarder on the slopes in the wintertime or a snowboarder on a skateboard in the summer. Both sports usually attract young people looking for a seasonal thrill. That's why I'm both a skateboarder and a snowboarder. Although there are differences, these two "extreme" sports have many similarities.

The history of these two sports is actually quite similar. The skateboard was not invented by a single person, and nobody gives credit to any one person for inventing it. People all around in the 1960s were experimenting with the idea for the skateboard, especially people on the West Coast. Similarly, Sherman Poppen made the "snurfer," an early example of a snowboard, as a toy for his children around 1965. Jake Burton Carpenter, who is famous for designing the modern snowboard, liked Poppen's "toy." By 1977, he had moved to Vermont and was making snowboards out of fiberglass and wood.

> Now your introduction makes me want to read more.

> Hey, my dad never invented a "snurfer"! These details about snowboarding history are really interesting.

I'm glad you moved some sentences from this paragraph.

Snowboarders and skateboarders are both called "riders" because they ride a board. Both the snowboard and the skateboard are one plank, and the shape of the deck on each is similar, a long oval designed to be stable. The stability of the boards allows the rider to stand up in a slightly crouched, surfing position.

Descriptive details make the tricks sound exciting!

Since the boards have a similar shape, the tricks riders do on them are often similar as well. In a "tail grab," the rider grabs the back (tail) of the board. A "540" (a 540-degree spin) is a one-and-one-half spin involving both the rider and the board. These are just two examples of the many tricks that riders in both sports perform.

Alike in many ways, snowboarding and skateboarding also have their differences. These two boards are designed for quite different terrains. You need a snowy mountain to snowboard. However, you can skateboard wherever you can find a strip of pavement!

Although these two boards look very much alike, riding them is not. Snowboarding is faster than skateboarding, and on a snowboard your whole body feels free because the terrain is so wide open. I spend much of my time cruising on the snowy trails, but some people just enjoy doing tricks. The snowboard has to have bindings to hold in the fast-moving rider, but a skateboard has no straps—the rider stands on the deck of the board. In skateboarding the feet feel more free making it easier to do flip tricks. That's why I spend most of my time doing tricks when I am skateboarding.

more

The way each board moves is different too. With a skateboard, the rider has to create power by repeatedly pushing one foot against the ground. The strength of this push determines how fast the wheels spin on their axles. In contrast, the snowboard has a flat bottom that is designed to ride smoothly on the snowy surface. To ride a snowboard, you just let yourself glide down the slope.

> This topic sentence nicely sums up the paragraph's main idea.

Even though there are many differences between skateboarding and snowboarding, there are also many similarities. If you like one of these sports, you'll probably want to try the other. If you are not already a rider, grab a board! Who knows? Maybe you'll come up with a new way to ride the boards.

> Now your essay feels complete! I like how you tied the ending to the title.

Reading As a Writer

- What revisions did Theo make in response to Joe's questions?
- How did Theo improve his introduction? his conclusion?
- What new details describe the snowboard and the skateboard?
- What three transitional words or phrases did Theo use at the beginning of sentences to signal a contrast between his subjects?
- Which sentence did Theo move? Why?

See www.eduplace.com/kids/hme/ for more examples of student writing.

Write a Compare-Contrast Essay

▶ Start Thinking

Make a writing folder for your compare-contrast essay. Copy the questions in bold type, and put the paper in your folder. Write your answers as you think about and choose your topic.

- **Who will be my audience?** Will it be my teacher? friends? people reading a newspaper?
- **What will be my purpose?** Will it be to share information? to learn more about two subjects that interest me?
- **How will I publish or share my essay?** Will I submit it to a newspaper? read it aloud to my classmates? make a flap book?

▶ Choose Your Subjects

❶ **List** three people, places, or things that interest you. Then list another person, place, or thing that you could compare and contrast with each.

❷ **Discuss your ideas** with a partner. Which pair of subjects does your partner find most interesting? Why? Which pair has enough details to compare and contrast?

❸ **Choose** one pair of subjects. Write notes next to each pair of subjects, as Theo did. Then circle the pair you will write about.

> **HELP**
> **?** *Stumped?*
>
> Try one of these pairs.
> - two recent fads
> - you and a best friend
> - two school subjects
> - two foods
> - your bedroom and another room
> - two public figures
>
> **See page 558 for more ideas.**

> Be sure you have chosen subjects that have something in common.

football and ice hockey	know little about hockey
(skateboarding and snowboarding)	know lots about both—fun to write about
golf and car racing	too few similarities

▶ Explore Your Subjects

❶ Picture details of the two subjects you are going to compare and contrast.

❷ Make a chart with two columns like the one below.

❸ List all the details you can think of that relate to your subjects. Use these questions.

- How does each subject look, sound, taste, smell, and feel?
- Are there actions, equipment, rules, or advantages associated with each subject? What are they?
- What effects do your subjects have on each other? on you?

❹ Draw lines between the details in each column that are related. Cross out any details you have for one subject but not for the other.

> Try doing a little research to find more details. If you still can't think of enough details, choose another pair of subjects.

TV News	Newspapers
up-to-the-minute news	in-depth coverage
quick overview	one edition daily or weekly
daily: several broadcasts	printed the day before
~~cool trucks with satellite dishes~~	have time to get story just right
sometimes live: can't hide slip-ups	portable, can read anyplace
need TV, must be near one	must pay for each edition
reporters, editors, videographers	reporters, editors, photographers
local, national, and international stories	~~comics, crosswords, word games, classified ads~~
free	local, national, and international stories
visual, audio	visual only

5 **Draw** a Venn diagram. Write the name of one subject above each circle. Use the diagram below as a model.

TV News   Newspapers

Different
several broadcasts daily
up-to-the-minute news
can't hide slip-ups
quick overview
must be near a TV
free, if you have a TV
audio
videographers

Alike
local,
national, and
international
stories

reporters,
editors

visual

Different
one edition daily or weekly
printed the day before
time to get story just right
in-depth coverage
can read anyplace
costs money
no audio
photographers

6 **List** details about each subject in your Venn diagram.

- Use details from your chart and any new details that you think of.
- Write details that tell how the subjects are different in the outer circles. Write details that tell how they are alike in the space where the circles overlap.
- Try to write your details for both subjects in the same order.

> Look for interesting or unusual details that will keep your readers interested.

 See page 16 for other ideas about exploring a topic.

 Go to www.eduplace.com/kids/hme/ for graphic organizers.   Prewriting   **547**

Focus Skill

Organizing Your Essay

Select a method of organization, and stick with that organization throughout your essay. The examples below are taken from essays that compare and contrast the same subjects: news presented on television and news presented in newspapers. Each example shows one possible way to organize a compare-contrast essay.

Write about similarities, then differences. Use one or more paragraphs to tell how your subjects are alike. Then write one or more paragraphs telling how they are different. Here is part of an essay that is organized this way.

> Both newspapers and television news programs provide information about local, national, and world events. Both are produced daily, and both deal with factual material.

Similarities:
both subjects

> Despite these similarities, there are many differences between the two media…

Differences:
both subjects

Use feature-by-feature order. Select two or three features that your topics share. Then compare or contrast each feature.

HELP

? Paragraphing Tip

Group in one paragraph sentences that tell about one main idea, such as similarities, differences, or one particular feature. Begin a new paragraph for a new main idea.

> The same news item is presented differently in the newspaper than it is on television. TV news programs have just a minute or two to tell a story. They rely heavily on video and audio to deliver this story quickly. A newspaper can provide a more in-depth report, using words and photographs to tell what has happened. A reader can take more than a minute to get information.

Focuses on both subjects

Contrasts one feature: depth of coverage

Use subject-by-subject order. Describe features of one subject first and then features of the other subject. Write at least one paragraph for each subject, and present your details in the same order for both subjects.

> TV news programs can present the news in a number of different ways, using audio, video, and live action. Television news generally addresses a wide range of events in a short period of time. Separate segments cover local, state, and national news, as well as weather, sports, and business.

Focuses on one subject: TV news programs
Feature 1
Feature 2
Feature 3

> Newspapers are completely visual, using both art and type on newsprint. Newspaper type varies in size and shape, and its art includes photographs, charts, or graphs. Although it is possible to scan newspapers, reading the news thoroughly takes time. Finally, newspapers have sections covering national, state, and local news, as well as business, sports, and other topics.

Focuses on one subject: newspapers
Feature 1
Feature 2
Feature 3

Connect sentences and paragraphs. Whatever type of organization you choose, use transitional words and phrases, such as *despite, also, nonetheless, however, in addition, similarly,* and *as well.* These words and phrases can help clarify similarities and differences.

Think and Discuss Look at Theo's final copy on page 542.

- Which method of organization did Theo use? Did he stick to this organization throughout his essay?
- Work with a partner. Discuss how Theo might have used feature-by-feature order to organize his essay.

Plan Your Essay

❶ **Decide** which type of organization will work best for your essay: similarities and then differences, feature-by-feature order, or subject-by-subject order.

❷ **Create** an outline. Consider the organization you have chosen when you arrange the details.

See page H34 for information about outlining.

Focus Skill

Introductions and Conclusions

Introductions

The introduction of your essay is like an eye-catching store window display. If it's good, it attracts your readers' attention, rouses their curiosity, and might even make them laugh. Here are three different ways to begin.

Ask a question.

Weak Introduction	Strong Introduction
I know more about music than any of my friends. I probably know more about music than you, especially about rock and classical, two of my favorites.	What do the Beatles and Bach have in common? At first, their music seems about as alike as pizza and caviar. However, these two seemingly different kinds of music actually share some surprising similarities.

Share an anecdote. Recount an incident, from your own life or someone else's, that relates to the subjects you will compare and contrast.

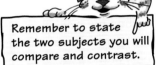
Remember to state the two subjects you will compare and contrast.

Weak Introduction	Strong Introduction
I worried about a lot of things when my family moved. I worried the most about attending a new school.	I was sure I'd arrived on a different planet. My new school locker kept jamming, my math class was really advanced, and people kept mispronouncing my last name. It was certainly different from my old school, but Goldberg Middle School had similarities that eventually made me feel right at home.

Tell a surprising fact.

Weak Introduction	Strong Introduction
In my essay, I will explain the surprising similarities and differences between the black widow spider and the tarantula.	Most people lump all poisonous spiders into the same fearsome category. Yet despite their similarities, these creatures differ in the harm they can do. The black widow's venom is deadly, but the tarantula's is only about as poisonous as a bee sting.

Conclusions

Write a powerful conclusion. The conclusion is where you make your final impression. Readers should leave your essay feeling satisfied. Sum up the major ideas in your essay in a memorable way.

Weak Conclusion	Strong Conclusion
See, I told you I knew a lot about music. Did you find that rock music and classical music have more in common than you imagined? That was the purpose of my essay.	As you can see, although rock music and classical music sound different and belong to different historical periods, both are respected art forms that will keep our feet tapping for years to come.

Did you make a surprising discovery while comparing and contrasting your subjects? If so, don't forget to summarize it in your conclusion as well!

Try It Out

- With a partner, rewrite the first weak introduction as an anecdote, the second as a surprising fact, and the third as a question.

▶ Draft Your Introduction

① **Write** three different introductions for your essay. Ask a question, share an anecdote, and tell a surprising fact. Make sure each introduction names the two subjects you will compare and contrast.

② **Choose** the best introduction, keeping in mind your purpose and audience.

Tech Tip
Use the Cut and Paste feature on your computer to try different introductions on your essay. Which one suits it best?

Focus Skill

Topic Sentences

State your main ideas in topic sentences. From reading just the topic sentence, your readers should know what the rest of the paragraph will be about. Here are paragraphs with topic sentences suited to each type of essay organization.

> The topic sentence usually comes first, but it can also appear later in the paragraph.

Similarities, Then Differences

Sure, crab and lobster taste great with butter, but that's not all they have in common. Both crustaceans have hard shells that protect their tender bodies. Like crabs, lobsters can escape danger by shedding limbs when trapped. They later grow new ones.

Feature-by-Feature

Neither sport is easy to pick up for people who are out of shape. Both jogging and cycling depend on well-developed lung capacity and cardiovascular strength. Without strong leg muscles, scaling even the smallest hill can be torture!

Subject-by-Subject

Reading a story in its original book form offers experiences that viewing the same story in a movie cannot give. A book contains the story as the writer originally intended it. Characters are more fully described. Plot lines develop at their own speed. Readers get to picture everything in their imagination.

Think and Discuss Reread the published model on page 535.

- Find three topic sentences. What does each sentence tell you about the paragraph that follows it?

▶ Draft Your Essay

❶ **Write a topic sentence** for each paragraph.

❷ **Add details** that support each main idea.

❸ **Write** a strong conclusion that sums up your ideas.

Tech Tip
Underline each topic sentence. Check that each detail in the paragraph relates to the topic sentence.

Evaluating Your Compare-Contrast Essay

▶ **Reread** your essay. Use this rubric to help you identify its strengths and weaknesses. Copy the sentences that best describe your essay.

Loud and Clear!

- ▪ My introduction states my subjects and hooks my readers.
- ▪ I compare or contrast corresponding details for each subject.
- ▪ I use one method of organization throughout my essay.
- ▪ My paragraphs are clear, with effective topic sentences and specific details.
- ▪ Transitional words make similarities and differences clear.
- ▪ My essay ends with a strong conclusion.
- ▪ *There are very few mistakes in grammar or spelling.*

Sounding Stronger

- ▪ My introduction states my subjects, but it's boring.
- ▪ I didn't always compare or contrast corresponding details.
- ▪ I slipped from one method of organization to another.
- ▪ At least one paragraph still needs a topic sentence or more specific details.
- ▪ More transitional words and phrases would make similarities and differences clearer.
- ▪ My conclusion could be more memorable.
- ▪ *Mistakes make my essay hard to follow in some places.*

Turn Up the Volume

- ▪ My introduction doesn't name my subjects.
- ▪ I describe many details about one subject without describing corresponding details about the other subject.
- ▪ I don't use any method of organization.
- ▪ None of my paragraphs have main ideas. All of them need more details.
- ▪ There are no transitional words or phrases to connect ideas.
- ▪ My essay just stops. There is no conclusion.
- ▪ *Too many mistakes make my essay hard to read.*

▶ Revise Your Compare-Contrast Essay

❶ Revise your essay. Use the list of sentences you wrote from the rubric. Work on the parts that you described with sentences from "Sounding Stronger" and "Turn Up the Volume."

❷ Have a writing conference.

When You're the Writer Read your essay aloud to your partner. Ask for feedback about the essay's strengths and weaknesses. Take notes.

When You're the Listener Tell your partner at least two things you like about the essay. Ask questions about anything that seems unclear. Use the chart below to help you.

What should I say?

The Writing Conference	
If you're thinking . . .	**You could ask . . .**
The beginning could be more interesting.	**Could you start with an anecdote, a surprising fact, or a question?**
Your ideas are great, but sometimes they're hard to follow.	**Have you stuck to one type of organization? Can you add transitional words or phrases?**
How do the details in this paragraph fit together?	**Can you write a topic sentence that states the main idea?**
I can't picture the similarities.	**Can you add more details to tell how _____ is similar to _____?**
I was a little surprised when your essay just stopped.	**Could you summarize the ideas in a conclusion?**

❸ Make more revisions to your essay. Use your conference notes and the Revising Strategies on the next page.

Tech Tip
Use boldface to identify transitional words and phrases. Replace any that are overused.

Revising Strategies

Elaborating: Word Choice Use **antonyms**, or opposites, to add meaning to or sharpen the contrast between your two subjects.

Repetitive	Elaborated with Antonyms
Watercolor paints are **light** and **transparent**, but oil paints are **not light** and **transparent**.	Watercolor paints are **light** and **transparent**, but oil paints are deep and opaque.

▶ Find one place in your essay where you can elaborate with antonyms.

📖 See also page H14.

Elaborating: Details Add vivid details that clarify the likenesses and differences between your two subjects.

Few Details	Elaborated with Details
Dogs are more companionable than hamsters.	My terrier likes to fetch and play catch, but my hamster can only run around in his cage and burrow in the woodchips.

▶ Find three places to improve your essay by adding details.

Sentence Fluency Vary the way your sentences begin. Your writing will sound more interesting.

Similar Beginnings	Varied Beginnings
All carnivorous plants eat insects. **All** secrete special enzymes to digest their prey. **Some** of these plants use bright colors to attract insects. **Some** use scented nectar.	All carnivorous plants eat insects and secrete special enzymes to digest their prey. Although some use bright colors to attract insects, others use scented nectar.

▶ Vary sentence beginnings in at least two places. Does your essay sound better?

GRAMMAR LINK ▶ *See also pages 61 and 371.*

▶ Proofread Your Compare-Contrast Essay

Proofread your essay, using the Proofreading Checklist and the Grammar and Spelling Connections. Proofread for one skill at a time. Use a class dictionary to check spellings.

Proofreading Checklist

Did I
- ✔ indent all paragraphs?
- ✔ begin and end sentences correctly?
- ✔ correct fragments and run-on sentences?
- ✔ correct double negatives?
- ✔ spell all the words correctly?

📖 Use the Guide to Capitalization, Punctuation, and Usage on page H64.

Proofreading Marks

¶	Indent
∧	Add
℘	Delete
≡	Capital letter
/	Small letter
ˇ ˇ	Add quotes
∧	Add comma
⊙	Add period
∿	Transpose

Tech Tip
If you typed your essay on a word processor, print it out before you proofread it. Small mistakes are easy to miss on-screen.

Grammar and Spelling Connections

Double Negatives A double negative is the use of two negative words to express one negative idea. Try using positive forms to correct double negatives.

Incorrect	I'm fairly outgoing, but my sister won't talk to **nobody**!
Correct	I'm fairly outgoing, but my sister won't talk to **anybody**!

GRAMMAR LINK ▶ *See also page 210.*

Spelling Plural Nouns Most plurals are formed by adding *-s* or *-es*. A final *f* or *fe* often changes to *v* before *-s* or *-es* is added. The key word in hyphenated or separated compound words usually becomes plural. The original plural form is kept in some foreign nouns.

stereos, thieves, brothers-in-law, data   📖 See the Spelling Guide on page H80.

Go to www.eduplace.com/kids/hme/ for proofreading practice.

▶ Publish Your Compare-Contrast Essay

❶ Make a neat final copy of your essay. Be sure you've fixed all errors.

❷ Choose a title for your essay that states your topic and makes readers curious, such as "Sailing the Oceans Black" rather than "Two Oil Spills."

GRAMMAR TIP ▶ *Capitalize the first, the last, and each important word in the title.*

❸ Publish or share your essay in a way that suits your audience. See the Ideas for Sharing box.

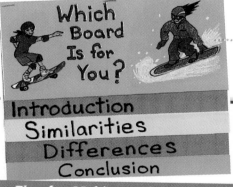

Which Board Is for You?

Introduction
Similarities
Differences
Conclusion

Tips for Making a Flap Book

- Fold sheets of paper horizontally to form flaps.
- Tuck the folded sheets inside one another. Put the shortest flap outside and the longest inside. Staple the sheets together along the crease.
- Write the title of your essay on the top flap.
- On the rest of the flaps, write labels such as *Introduction, Similarities, Differences,* and *Conclusion.* Use feature names if your essay is organized by feature.
- Transfer your essay to the appropriate sections.
- Add illustrations to your flap book.

Ideas for Sharing
Write It Down
- Send your essay with a cover letter to a local newspaper.
- Make a flap book.

Talk It Up
- Tape-record your essay. Add sound effects.
- Read your essay aloud. Include visual aids. See page 605 for help.

Show It Off
- Display your essay with a poster that compares and contrasts your subjects visually.

▶ Reflect

Write about your writing experience. Use these questions to get started.

- What is your favorite part of your compare-contrast essay?
- What was easy and what was difficult about writing the essay?
- How does this paper compare with other papers you have written?

Writing Prompts

Use these prompts as ideas for compare-contrast essays or to practice for a test. Some of them relate to other subjects you study. Consider who your audience will be, and write your essay in a way that they will understand and enjoy.

1 Compare and contrast two favorite holidays. What does each holiday celebrate? Are there foods, traditions, music, or clothing associated with each?

2 Compare and contrast eating at home and eating in a restaurant or cafeteria. How is the food prepared? presented? served? Consider the atmosphere and service.

3 Compare and contrast seventh grade and eighth grade. How are the responsibilities, privileges, and challenges similar? How are they different?

4 Choose a character from a book, a movie, or TV. Compare and contrast yourself with this person.

Writing Across the Curriculum

5 PHYSICAL EDUCATION
Compare and contrast the rules, equipment, and necessary skills associated with a water sport and a sport played on a field.

6 SOCIAL STUDIES
Compare and contrast two famous people. What field does each person work in? Why are these people important?

7 SCIENCE
Compare and contrast two minerals, such as gold and quartz. Include details about their texture, appearance, value, and usefulness.

8 LITERATURE/READING
Choose two different book categories, such as mystery and science fiction. Compare and contrast the characters, plots, settings, and language used in each.

 See www.eduplace.com/kids/hme/ for more prompts.

✔ Test Practice

Sometimes on a test you will be asked to write a paper in response to a picture prompt.

Remember that a compare-contrast essay compares the similarities and contrasts the differences between two subjects.

These pictures show the planet Earth and the moon. Look carefully at each picture. Then write one or two paragraphs comparing and contrasting the pictures.

Here are some strategies to help you do a good job responding to a prompt like the one on this page.

❶ Look at each picture and answer these questions:
- What images are shown?
- How are these images alike? How are they different?

❷ Plan your writing. Use a Venn diagram like the one shown on page 547. Compare and contrast the two pictures.

❸ You will get a good score if you remember the sentences under "Loud and Clear!" in the rubric on page 553.

Writing Instructions

Instructions explain how to make or do something. Read Edward's instructions on in-line skating. How easy are these instructions to follow?

In-line Skating: Getting Started

Introduction

What mode of transportation is efficient, fun, and good for fitness? Try in-line skating! If you're a beginner, it's not hard to learn how to use in-line skates. It just takes time and practice. Here's how to get started.

Materials

To start, it's usually a good idea to buy cruising skates if you're a beginner. Buy them one size larger than your regular shoe size. It's also a good idea to buy protective pads because, if you're like me, you'll take a few falls in the beginning. Knee pads and elbow pads are the most important. Make sure that when you buy them, they fit snugly. Also, you'll need a helmet to wear whenever you skate.

Steps

Now it's time to try out the in-line skates and pads. Put your skates on first and your pads second, keeping your joints relaxed and flexible. Although all in-line skates have unique straps, the how-to instructions with them are usually easy to follow.

After you've got the skates on, choose a smooth path or sidewalk with a handrail that you can hold onto for balance. Just practice standing at first. Keep your feet about shoulder-width apart and your toes slightly pointed inward. Next, ask a friend to push you off, so you get used to the movement and learn how to balance. Try to keep your feet pointed forward. Your knees should be slightly bent.

Order word

Then practice pushing yourself off and going without help. To push off, most people will place their right foot at an outward angle and push while keeping the other leg bent and pointed forward. As your body starts to move, pick up your push-off foot and bring it forward in front of your other foot. Remember to keep your feet about shoulder-width apart. Repeat this procedure back and forth, from foot to foot, to keep momentum going.

Steps

To turn, just lean a little to the left or right and slightly point your feet in that direction. Finally, to brake, point the toes of your right foot up and push the rubber at the heel of the blade gently to the ground. If you press the brake down too quickly and forcefully, you may lose your balance and fall. Watch experienced in-line skaters to see how they handle moving, turning, and braking.

Conclusion

In the beginning, your top speed may be only about five miles per hour. After six months to a year of skating, you'll probably be up to about thirteen miles per hour and be ready to trade in your cruising blades for more advanced blades. You'll be amazed at how much fun you have along the way.

Reading As a Writer

- The **introduction** states the purpose of the instructions and may give some brief, interesting information about the topic.
  What did you learn about in-line skating in the first paragraph?

- All **materials** are listed, including descriptions of them if necessary.
  What materials does Edward recommend for beginning skaters?

- All **steps** necessary to perform the task are described in order and in sufficient detail. *How does Edward describe braking?*

- **Order words** help the reader clearly understand the sequence of steps. *What order words does Edward use?*

- The **conclusion** can complete the instructions, restate the purpose, or include some interesting information about the subject.
  What does Edward predict in the last paragraph?

more ▶

How to Write Instructions

❶ Choose a task that you can do well. To help you decide which task to choose, ask yourself:

- Can I explain the task clearly in one or two pages?
- Does it require a demonstration or the use of graphics?
- Who is my audience, and what is my purpose?

❷ List all the materials needed and the steps to follow.

❸ Organize the steps in order. Make a flow chart like the one below or take notes on note cards. Explain each step with enough detail to make it clear to the reader. Ask yourself these questions.

- Why is this step important?
- Are the steps in the correct order? Can any steps be eliminated or combined?
- What details do I need to include?

Stuck for an Idea?

These suggestions might help.
How to
- make your favorite dessert
- grow tomatoes
- organize a field trip
- fish for trout
- design an invitation
- look for a summer job

> Try visualizing the steps to be sure the order makes sense.

Steps	Details
Buying skates	Get one size larger than usual.
Getting ready	Put skates on first, and then pads.
Standing	Point toes in and keep legs apart.
Skating	Push off with one foot, and then bring the other forward.
Turning	Lean left or right.
Braking	Press down on rubber heel.

4 **Write** a first draft of your instructions. Refer to your flow chart or note cards.

- State your topic and purpose in your introduction, keeping your audience in mind. Adapt your language to your audience.
- Use order words and phrases to help the reader follow your sequence of steps.

Order Words	Order Phrases
first	at first
before	prior to
next	after awhile
then	as soon as
when	later on
before	after several minutes
after	at the same time
now	the next day
finally	in the meantime

5 **Use** exact words to make your instructions as clear as possible. Notice how precisely Edward describes braking: *Finally, to brake, point the toes of your right foot up and push the rubber at the heel of the blade gently to the ground.*

6 **Write** a conclusion that suggests ways to share the instructions, or looks forward to the results of performing the task. For example, notice that the instructions tell readers that with practice they'll improve enough to get blades for more advanced skaters.

more ▶

7 **Revise** your draft. Use the Revising Checklist to help you assess and improve your instructions.

Revising Checklist

✔ Does my introduction state my topic and purpose and engage the reader's interest?
✔ Have I described in detail the materials needed?
✔ Did I include all necessary steps in the proper order? Would a different order be easier to follow? Is there anything I can take out to make the steps clearer?
✔ Have I used order words to help guide my reader through the instructions?
✔ Does my conclusion leave the reader feeling motivated or satisfied?

8 **Conduct** a writing conference.

What should I say?

The Writing Conference	
If you're thinking. . .	**You could ask. . .**
Your introduction is weak.	**Could you start with an interesting idea or fact?**
I can't figure out how to do this.	**Are all of the materials listed?** **Are all of the steps listed?** **Are they in the right order?**
I need to know more about this step.	**Could you give more details and exact information?**
This step doesn't tell me anything new.	**Is this step really necessary?**
The instructions end abruptly.	**In your conclusion, can you tell why the task is enjoyable or worthwhile?**

9 **Proofread** your instructions. Refer to the Proofreading Checklist on page 556. Use a dictionary to check spelling.

10 **Publish** or share a final copy of your instructions with an audience, such as children in a lower grade or friends. Illustrate your instructions for a class book or wall poster display. With a partner or by yourself, you can perform a demonstration in person or record it using a video camera.

HOW TO IN-LINE SKATE

1. Buying
- Choose skates one size larger than your shoe size.
- Select a helmet and elbow and knee pads.

2. Suiting Up
- Put on your skates first, pads second.

3. Standing
- Keep feet about shoulder-width apart.
- Point toes inward slightly.

4. Moving
- Keep knees slightly bent.
- Push off with one foot.
- Bring that foot forward and follow through.

5. Turning
- Lean to the left or right.
- Slightly point feet in that direction.

6. Braking
- Point up the toes of one foot.
- Press rubber at heel of blade to the ground.

Comparing Ways to Represent Meaning

The visuals you see in the media help to communicate and shape human understanding of the world. Visuals can extend meaning and provide ways to express ideas. The creators of visuals—photographers, illustrators, and filmmakers, for example—use different equipment and techniques to give images meaning. When they choose the same subjects, their "pictures" often reveal different viewpoints and a range of ideas and emotions.

News Photography

Photojournalists use images to tell news stories. They try to convey information in a clear and dramatic way. The choices they make about what to photograph and present to the public can be influenced by their emotions, their own opinions about a subject, or even their desire to sell their work. In the photo shown here, the photojournalist chose to record World War I soldiers at rest. What ideas about war does the photo convey?

What can a photograph show? It can show what happened and record details of a subject in context.

Illustrations

Illustrations are visuals that usually explain or interpret words, as in news stories, scholarly writing, fiction, and nonfiction articles. Illustrations of the same subject can vary greatly in style, emotional content, and viewpoint.

When you need to use a visual, think about whether a photo or an illustration would be better to express your ideas.

Look at the poster illustration. Its subject is similar to that of the photograph on the previous page, but its meaning is different. The photo suggests tedium and hardship, whereas the illustration offers a more patriotic vision of war.

What can an illustration show?
It can emphasize particular emotions or leave out information that might distract from the central focus.

Guidelines for Comparing Visuals

▶ Watch where your gaze goes first when you look at each image. What techniques have been used to attract your attention?
▶ Decide on the purpose of each visual. Is it intended to inform, persuade, advertise, explain, or entertain? How do you know?
▶ Think about what the photographer or illustrator is "saying." Compare techniques that enhance the artist's meaning.
▶ Imagine the message or information without the image. Compare how each visual affects your understanding of the subject.

Documentaries

A documentary is a narrated film or television program that presents political, social, or historical subjects in a factual manner. Most documentaries rely on a variety of images, such as historical photographs, news footage, scientific illustrations, or fine art. These images can convey different kinds of information and emotional meanings.

more ▶

Many people accept documentaries as purely factual. Most filmmakers ask historians or other experts to provide and check information. However, the images and the narration may not always work together accurately.

Think about the images in a documentary on Native American life in the 1500s. Illustrations could only provide an artist's educated guess about people's lives. Photography, which developed in the 1800s, often showed Native Americans in stereotypical ways. If used without explanation, these images would give a distorted view of life long ago.

Here are some of today's popular documentaries.
- "reality-based" police and crime shows
- nature programs
- filmed biographies
- news magazine shows
- history specials

Here are some guidelines to help you analyze documentaries.

Guidelines for Analyzing a Documentary

▶ Watch the presentation and think about its purpose and message.

▶ Pay attention to techniques that make the information more believable or more interesting. If you can view the film more than once, watch segments with the sound off and segments with the picture off. What do you notice about the images and the spoken words?

▶ If experts were interviewed, look at how they are presented. Are their credentials flashed on the screen? Are they in special dress or in uniform? Does the film include experts with different points of view?

▶ Notice sound effects and music. What are their purpose and effect?

Apply It

Watch two videotaped documentaries on the same subject. Use the guidelines and the questions below to analyze and compare them.

● Consider the visuals, spoken information, and other techniques. Which documentary was more interesting? Why?

● Which documentary seemed to you to be the more factual and accurate? Explain why you think so.

For more than four hundred years, the ruins of this ancient Incan city, Machu Picchu, remained buried under Peruvian dirt and a dense subtropical rain forest.

Writing a Research Report

Can plants grow on bare rocks? This article describes some that can. How does the writer organize facts and ideas so that they are easy to follow?

Lichens: The "Tough Guy" Plants

by Vince Brach, from *Highlights for Children*

Lichens (LIKE-ins) are among the weirdest-looking plants. And they live in strange places. You may find them growing on tree branches or brick walls. In the Arctic, they grow on the ground as a mat. Reindeer paw through the snow to find lichens, which are their most important winter food. Scientists have collected lichens from crevices in Antarctic boulders and from old skulls bleaching in the desert. Some lichens have been growing on old stone monuments for centuries.

Lichens are so hardy that they can survive even after they dry to a brittle crust in the sun. When rain falls, the lichens soak up water and begin growing again as if nothing had happened.

What makes lichens so different from other plants? Each type of lichen is a partnership between two forms of life. The first is a one-celled green plant called an alga. The alga lives inside the second partner. That partner is a fungus, which is related to yeast and mushrooms. The algal cells of a lichen capture the energy of sunlight and the carbon dioxide in the air to make food for both

partners. The fungus is a tough, moisture-holding house for the alga.

The name for this special kind of partnership is *symbiosis*. The lichen symbiosis allows the two different organisms to do things that neither could do alone. By themselves, one-celled green algae must live in water or as a thin film in damp places, such as a coating of green on a flowerpot. Fungi cannot make their own food. Most of them live on decaying things, like wood or leaf mold. But when they are together, the alga feeds the fungus and the fungus protects the alga.

In addition to being tough, lichens make acids that taste bitter to most animals. The fungus can produce these acids only when working together with its partner alga.

No one knows just how algae and fungi joined up to become lichens. Scientists can separate the algae from the fungi and grow them separately. But it's much harder to put the partners back together again.

In nature, most lichens spread without separating into algae and fungi. Instead, small bits break off and are carried away by rain and wind. When a piece settles onto a good spot, a new lichen grows.

However, a "good spot" for a lichen may be unfriendly to other plants. Lichens are called pioneer plants because they are often the first plants to grow in bare places. They are the tough guys of the plant world.

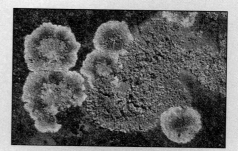

more ▶

Reading As a Writer

Think About the Article

- How are the facts organized to make them easy to follow?
- What is attention-catching about the introduction? the conclusion?
- What transitional words and phrases does the writer use?
- What keeps this article from sounding like a boring list of facts?

Think About Writer's Craft

- Which special terms did the writer define? Why do these definitions help?
- Where does the writer use comparisons to help make a point?

Think About the Pictures

- What do the pictures show about lichens that is not described in the article?

Responding

Write responses to these questions.

- **Personal Response** What did you find interesting about this article? What else would you like to learn about lichens?
- **Critical Thinking** The audience for this article is young readers. What might the writer have done differently if his audience were professional scientists?

What Makes a Great Research Report?

A research report presents factual information gathered through research.

When you write a research report, remember these points.

▶ Research your topic thoroughly, using a variety of sources. Organize the information before writing.

▶ Write in the third person. Focus on facts, not opinions.

▶ Introduce the topic and hook your readers in the first paragraph.

▶ Write a topic sentence for each paragraph. Support topic sentences with facts and examples.

▶ Guide your reader by using transitional words and phrases.

▶ Write in your own words, and use quotations correctly.

▶ Write a conclusion that sums up the report's main idea and makes a lasting impression.

▶ Provide a complete list of sources.

GRAMMAR CHECK

When you give an exact date in writing, use a comma between the day and the year.

WORKING DRAFT

Donna Guu wanted to understand more about Chinese culture. To do so, she researched the life and work of Confucius, a philosopher whose writings have greatly influenced China. Here is Donna's working draft.

Donna Guu

Working Draft

Confucius lived during a time of unrest and wars between the peoples of different parts of ancient China. He was deeply troubled by the confusion and distress of the Chinese people. He compared his own times to earlier, more peaceful days in Chinese history. Confucius believed that for society to become calm and orderly once again, the people had to return to basic values and moral behavior. To do that, the people of ancient China would have to ask themselves what would be the right thing to do and what would be the wrong thing to do. They would have to know the difference between good and bad. I think we all need to do this.

Confucius focused on correct behavior in five key relationships: ruler-subject, father-son, husband-wife, brother-brother, and friend-friend. People in these relationships had to behave properly. Those in the lower positions of society had to show respect and loyalty to those who had more power. Those with power had to be models of good behavior for their followers in the lower levels of society.

The principles of *jen* and *li* are two of Confucius's most important ideas. The principle of *jen* means acting with human kindness or humanity. For example, Confucius believed that if a person needed help with finding a lost possession, anyone who

> Could you introduce your main idea?

> Should this paragraph come after you define the term *li*?

passed that person should help find it. Also, if children on the street were ill or hungry, anyone who saw them should take them in and take care of them as if those lost and lonely children were their own. I think everyone should be more compassionate.

Could you add more supporting facts or examples?

The principle of *li* means behaving properly. According to Confucius, a person should try to be slow to speak but quick to take correct action.

Confucius contributed to China's government. He contributed so much to China's future. He affected China's future by giving leaders of China's dynasties an idea of how the people should be ruled. He believed that a ruler's most important duty was to serve as an example of the proper way to act. He said that the people's well-being was the ruler's responsibility. Confucius contributed to China's future by giving the future dynasties an idea of how China should be ruled.

Can you cut extra words and make smoother transitions?

Confucius had humble beginnings. His ideas have shaped Chinese civilization. His principles of *jen* and *li* are still ideals today. Though he died before he could see his ideas carried out, Confucius's teachings were important. These ideas became part of the very fabric of Chinese society. I think he was the greatest philosopher in history.

Could you write a stronger conclusion?

You've done excellent research!

Reading As a Writer

- What did Joe like about Donna's report? What revisions might she make?
- Find places where Donna let her opinion slip in.
- What unfamiliar terms did Donna define? How do they help you understand her report?

FINAL COPY

After getting feedback from her classmates, Donna revised her writing. Read her new, improved research report to see what changes she made.

> I like this title! It fits your report.

The Ageless Wisdom of Confucius
by Donna Guu

Although he was born poor in 551 B.C. and had only minor jobs in government, Confucius was probably the most influential person in Chinese history. He was an exemplary philosopher who became famous for his ideas on how to make society better. Confucius was also a brilliant teacher. His ideas were collected by his students and can be read in a book called *The Analects*. These ideas still have a big influence on China today.

> The introduction is informative and interesting.

Confucius lived during a time of unrest and wars between the peoples of different parts of ancient China. He was deeply troubled by the confusion and distress of the Chinese people. He compared his own times to earlier, more peaceful days in Chinese history. Confucius believed that for society to become calm and orderly once again, the people had to return to basic values and moral behavior. To do that, the people of ancient China would have to ask themselves what would be the right thing to do and what would be the wrong thing to do. They would have to know the difference between good and bad.

The principles of *jen* and *li* are two of Confucius's most important ideas. The principle of *jen* means acting with human kindness or humanity. For example, Confucius believed that if a person needed help with finding a lost possession, anyone who passed that person should help find it. Also, if children on the street were ill or hungry, anyone who saw them should take them in and take care of them as if those lost and lonely children were their own.

You've added a good example.

The principle of *li* means behaving properly. According to Confucius, a person should try to be slow to speak but quick to take correct action. For instance, two people with different opinions should take turns expressing their thoughts. They should speak politely and listen to each other's point of view. They should not shout, lose their temper, or be rude.

Confucius focused on correct behavior in five key relationships: ruler-subject, father-son, husband-wife, brother-brother, and friend-friend. People in these relationships had to behave properly. Those in the lower positions of society had to show respect and loyalty to those who had more power. Those with power had to be models of good behavior for their followers in the lower levels of society.

Confucius made a huge impact on China's government. He contributed to China's future by giving later dynasties an idea of how China should be ruled. According to *The Analects,* Confucius said, "To conduct government by virtue can be compared to the North Star: it occupies its place, and the many stars bow before it" (Confucius 301). In fact, he believed that a ruler's most important duty was to serve as an example of the proper way to act. In addition, he said that the people's well-being was the ruler's responsibility.

I like this quotation!

more

Despite his humble beginnings, Confucius was perhaps the most important shaper of Chinese civilization. His principles of *jen* and *li* are ideals the people of China still aspire to today. Though he died before he could see his ideas carried out, Confucius's teachings became part of the very fabric of Chinese society. In conclusion, Confucius influences the lives of millions of people to this day, even though he lived 2,500 years ago.

> This conclusion provides a fine summary.

Sources

Confucius. *The Original Analects: Sayings of Confucius and His Successors.* Trans. A. Taeko Brooks and E. Bruce Brooks. New York: Columbia University Press, 1998.

Rowland-Entwistle, Theodore. *Confucius and Ancient China.* Danbury, CT: Franklin Watts, 1987.

Wilker, Josh. *Confucius: Philosopher and Teacher.* Danbury, CT: Franklin Watts, 1999.

Yu, David C. "Confucius." *The Academic American Encyclopedia (1997 Grolier Multimedia Encyclopedia).* CD-ROM. Danbury, CT: Grolier, 1997.

> You've given complete information about your sources. Good!

Reading As a Writer

- What revisions did Donna make in response to Joe's questions?
- Which sentence tells the topic of the second full paragraph on page 577?
- What improvements did Donna make to the last paragraph on page 577?
- What examples illustrate important concepts in the report?

See www.eduplace.com/kids/hme/ for more examples of student writing.

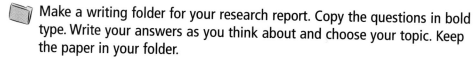

Write a Research Report

▶ Start Thinking

Make a writing folder for your research report. Copy the questions in bold type. Write your answers as you think about and choose your topic. Keep the paper in your folder.

- **Who will be my audience?** Will it be classmates? younger students?
- **What will be my purpose?** Do I want to learn more about a favorite topic? research something new? explore a time in history?
- **How will I publish or share my report?** Will I pose as the "resident expert" in an interview? make a visual display?

▶ Choose Your Report Topic

1 List five topics that make you curious. Think of your favorite subjects at school, your hobbies, or your career interests.

2 Discuss your ideas with a partner. Which ones interest your partner most? Which ones generate even more ideas? Choose three topics to think about carefully.

3 Check that you can cover your topics in the number of pages you have been assigned to write. Narrow or broaden your topics if you need to.

HELP

Can't Think of a Good Topic?

Try a topic in one of these broad categories.
- space travel
- television and film
- South America
- history of a sport
- reptiles

See page 598 for more ideas.

Too Broad	Too Narrow	Just Right
musical instruments	the drumstick	the percussion section of the orchestra
farm animals	what dairy cows eat	raising dairy cows
public monuments	the height of the Washington Monument	the history of the Washington Monument

4 Choose one topic, based on the information you have gathered. Keep your list of topics in case your first choice doesn't work out.

▶ Explore Your Topic

❶ Consider what you already know about your topic. What else would you like to learn? Make a K-W-S chart, and fill in the first two columns.

Here is part of Donna's K-W-S chart.

What I **K**now	What I **W**ant to Learn	Possible **S**ources
Modern Chinese society uses ancient wisdom.	How does Confucianism affect everyday life?	
~~Modern China has an improving economy.~~	~~How did this economy differ from that of the past?~~	
Confucius was a wise man.	What are the basic ideas of Confucianism?	
Confucius lived a very long time ago.	When did Confucius live?	
~~Marco Polo traveled to China.~~	~~What did he learn about Chinese philosophy?~~	
	What was China like during Confucius's life?	
	What did Confucius do for a living?	

❷ Use your chart to help you focus your topic.

- Cross out ideas that stray off the topic. Donna had to do this.
- To generate questions for the second column, ask *Who? What? When? Where? Why? How?* These questions will guide your research.

HELP

? **Empty Chart?**

If you can't think of ideas for your K-W-S chart, switch to one of the other ideas that you listed.

> To think of more questions, try browsing through a book on your topic. What would be interesting to research?

Go to www.eduplace.com/kids/hme/ for graphic organizers.

Focus Skill

Finding the Best Information

Locating Information

Be creative—explore a variety of sources.

Interview an expert. Does someone in your town or city know a lot about your topic? Set up an interview. You might speak with a police officer, an art teacher, a veterinarian, or an architect, depending on your topic. Quotations from an expert can spice up a report!

📖 See page H12 for information on interviewing.

Check print sources. To find print sources, use your library's catalog and the *Readers' Guide to Periodical Literature.* Review nonfiction books, encyclopedias and other reference works, and articles in newspapers, magazines, and journals.

📖 See page H25 for information on using the library.

Review primary and secondary sources.

- A primary source is a document, a book, or a person that provides first-hand information about a topic. Examples include government documents, recordings of speeches, diaries, autobiographies, and photographs of historic events.
- A secondary source uses information from primary sources and other secondary sources. Examples include textbooks, biographies, and reference works.

Use technology.

- Many reference works are available on CD-ROM. They usually include an index to make searching easy.
- Microfiche and microfilm store magazine and newspaper articles. Ask your librarian for help in finding what you need.
- The Internet offers many resources. Use search engines to find the specific information you need. Browse online encyclopedias. Find the Web site of a publication that specializes in your topic.

> Your librarian knows exactly where to find information! Make your research easier by asking for help.

📖 See page H51 for information on using the Internet.

more ▶

Focus Skill continued

Evaluating Information

Evaluate your sources. Not all sources provide trustworthy information. Ask these questions about each one you might use.

- Is the information related to my topic?
- Is the source reliable? Does the author have education or experience in the field? Is the magazine or newspaper a respected source? Ask your teacher if you're unsure.
- Is information from the Internet produced by a professional? Web sites created by amateurs often contain errors.
- Is the information current? Check for a recent copyright date.
- Is the information factual? Don't use sources that sound sarcastic or insulting. The writer may be biased.

Think and Discuss Look at Donna's final copy on page 576.

- What kinds of sources did Donna use? Discuss each one.
- Why would Donna choose recent sources to research a man who lived 2,500 years ago?

▶ Gather Sources of Information

❶ Get an overview of your topic. Read one encyclopedia article about it.

❷ Explore other library resources. Skim and evaluate each one. Eliminate those that don't meet the standards listed above.

❸ Choose at least four sources that fit your topic and the questions on your K-W-S chart. Write these sources in the third column of your chart. At most, use one general encyclopedia.

❹ Set up an interview if you can find a local expert on your topic.

> If you can't find good sources, choose a different topic.

 Go to www.eduplace.com/kids/hme/ for topic links.

► Research Your Topic

❶ Take notes. Use note cards or separate pages in a notebook.

- On a card, write one question from your K-W-S chart. Then write the related facts you find. Include examples and high-interest details. Don't pack too much on one card! You may have many cards for each question.

Tech Tip
If you have access to a laptop computer, you might use it to take notes.

- If you plan to use facts in your chart's *What I Know* column, check them in your sources. Add this information to your notes.
- Record complete information about your sources on a separate source card or somewhere else. Number each source. As you take notes, put on each card the number of the source that provided the information.

❷ Differentiate between fact and opinion. Take notes only on facts. A fact can be proved. An opinion cannot.

Fact	Source of Proof	Opinion
Abraham Lincoln was assassinated.	history book	Abraham Lincoln was greater than George Washington.
Jeff won the election.	number of votes	Jeff will be an outstanding class president.
The table is fifty inches long.	measurement	The table is too short.

❸ Paraphrase. Take notes in your own words. If a writer says something in a memorable way, copy the statement exactly, and put it in quotation marks. Note the page number. You may want to use the quotation in your report. If you copy someone's words exactly without giving him or her credit, you are plagiarizing.

Plagiarism isn't just tacky. It's illegal.

more ►

Here is part of a chapter on the early history of Texas and some notes a student took for a research report on Native American rock art. Only facts related to the questions have been recorded.

Texas: An Illustrated History

14

Paint Rock on the Rio Concho

There are more than 200 sites of Indian pictographs (drawings or paintings) and petroglyphs (carvings) in Texas. They are found on cave walls, cliffs, and rock shelters. Paintings vary from 1 inch to 18 feet in height and are usually red or black. They show human figures, hands and feet, animals, maps, religious symbols, dances, blanket designs, trees, the sun, shields, and masks. At Hueco Tanks, near El Paso, travelers attracted by pools of trapped water have decorated the rocks since the Archaic period. Near

there are 1,500 paintings on a limestone cliff that cover a 1,000-year span.

Reasons for the rock art are uncertain. Possibly they were meant to be religious signs, or perhaps they were attempts to record important events.

What are the subjects of rock art?
  –human figures, hands, feet
  –animals
  –maps
  –dances
  –religious symbols
  –trees and sun
  –blanket designs
  –shields and masks   4, p.14

Why did the artists make them?
  –no certain answers
  –might have religious meaning
  –might have been a way to tell about events

      4, p.14

4. McComb, David G. Texas: An Illustrated History. New York: Oxford University Press, 1995.

See page H32 for more information on taking notes and keeping track of sources.

Focus Skill

Organizing Your Report

The questions you have researched will form your report's **main topics**.
Sort your note cards. Make a stack for each main topic.

- Order the cards in each stack in different ways.
  Choose the most logical order. Try these ideas.
  - chronological order
  - from the most important
    to the least important
  - from the least important
    to the most important
  - from the familiar to
    the unfamiliar
  - from general to more
    detailed information
  - by cause and effect
  - in visual order, such as from bottom to top to write about a volcano

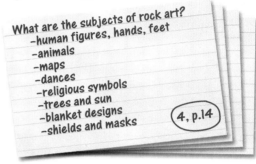

What are the subjects of rock art?
 -human figures, hands, feet
 -animals
 -maps
 -dances
 -religious symbols
 -trees and sun
 -blanket designs
 -shields and masks
(4, p.14)

- Remove cards that repeat facts. You need only one source for each fact.
- Remove cards that contain unimportant information.
- Then decide which stack you will write about first, second, and so on.

Make an outline from your notes. An
outline provides a map for you to follow as
you draft your report.

- Write each main topic after a Roman
  numeral (I, II, III, IV, …).
- Write each subtopic after a capital
  letter. Subtopics are the facts and
  examples that support the main topics.
- Write each detail after an Arabic
  numeral (1, 2, 3, 4…). Details give
  specific facts or examples about the subtopics.
- Give your outline a title.

HELP
?

**Is Your Stack of
Notes Too Thin?**

Make sure you have
answered each of your
K-W-S questions and
provided enough detail.
Continue your research
and note taking if
necessary.

GRAMMAR TIP ▶ *You don't need to write your outline in complete sentences.*

Here's how information from a note card can be written in outline form.

Life in Space
I. Effects of weightlessness
    A. Changes in body
        features
       1. Wrinkles eliminated
       2. Foot size reduced
       3. Height one or two
          inches taller
    B. Changes in posture
       1. Slight crouch when
          standing
       2. Backward lean
          when sitting

What does weightlessness do to
the body?
   — eliminates wrinkles
   — slight crouch when
      standing
   — backward lean when sitting
   — 1–2 inches taller
   — reduces foot size
              (2, p.102)

See page H34 for more information on outlining.

Think and Discuss

- What subtopics did the writer use in the outline above? Why do they make good subtopics?
- Describe the use of punctuation and capitalization in the outline above.

Plan Your Report

❶ **Organize** your note cards. Decide whether you need to gather more information.

❷ **Make an outline** for your report, arranging main topics, subtopics, and details. At least two facts or examples should support each main topic.

HELP

Information Overload

Do you have too much information for one report? Try deleting one of your main topics or cutting some details.

Writing from an Outline

Write topic sentences. For every main topic in your outline, write a topic sentence. Put each one on a separate piece of paper.

Write a paragraph for each topic sentence. Discuss the subtopics and details, writing in the third person.

Let your own voice come through. You don't have to sound stuffy or boring!

- Put the topic sentence at the beginning, in the middle, or at the end of a paragraph—whichever fits best.
- If you have lots of information on a main topic, break it into more than one paragraph. Each paragraph should have a topic sentence!
- If you include a quotation, follow it with the name of the source and the page number, in parentheses: (Wilker 23).
- Show your enthusiasm by writing expressively. Vary your sentence structure, and choose words that express your exact meaning. Have some fun!

Here is a paragraph written from part of an outline. The topic sentence is underlined.

Life in Space
I. Effects of weightlessness
   A. Changes in body features
     1. Wrinkles eliminated
     2. Foot size reduced
     3. Height one or two inches taller
   B. Changes in posture
     1. Slight crouch when standing
     2. Backward lean when sitting

One effect of weightlessness is an actual difference in physical appearance. Certain features change in noticeable ways. Wrinkles disappear, and feet become smaller. A person's overall height grows by one or two inches. Even the way someone stands or sits changes in space. A person stands in a slight crouch and leans backward when sitting.

Focus Skill continued

Use **transitional words and phrases**. These words will connect your sentences and paragraphs smoothly.

To introduce examples	for example, for instance, in one case, in fact, as proof, to begin with, in this instance
To show time relationships	after, before, next, eventually, first, in the meantime, not long after, as time passed, at this point, soon afterward, at the same time
To show causes or effects	because, therefore, consequently, thus, as a result, due to, for this reason, in response to
To compare or contrast	just as, like, similarly, on the other hand, on the contrary, equally important, unlike, the same as, different from
To connect ideas	though, moreover, yet, however, so, nevertheless, while, as well as, not only
To add another point	besides, also, in addition, furthermore, moreover

Think and Discuss Look at Donna's final copy on page 576.

- What transitional words and phrases did Donna use?
- Which is the topic sentence in the second paragraph on page 576?
- Reread the last paragraph on page 576 and the first full paragraph on page 577, where Donna broke one main topic into two paragraphs. What are the two subtopics? Why do you think she divided them?

▶ Draft the Body of Your Report

❶ **Write a topic sentence** for each main topic in your outline.

❷ **Write a paragraph** for each topic sentence. Create additional paragraphs for main topics with lots of information.

❸ **Use** examples, details, quotations, and comparisons as you write.

> Similes and metaphors aren't just for poetry! A good comparison can add sparkle to a report on any subject.

Focus Skill

Introductions and Conclusions

Write a focus statement. Write one sentence that expresses the main idea of your report.

Write an introduction. An introduction should present the main idea of your report and capture the reader's interest.

Weak Introduction	Strong Introduction
Let me tell you about an interesting event. Some scientists made a model of a flying dinosaur. There are many theories about why dinosaurs disappeared.	It must have been a strange sight—a dinosaur taking off and flying through the sky! A group of scientists and designers had launched a model of the extinct pterosaur, the largest creature ever to fly.

Write a conclusion. A conclusion should summarize your research and connect to your main idea. Strong conclusions are memorable.

Weak Conclusion	Strong Conclusion
The team worked hard, and it paid off. Everyone must have been really pleased. Models of other dinosaurs have been in movies. People never seem to get tired of learning about dinosaurs.	Thanks to a team of dedicated workers, the model was a success. Using fossil records, computers, electric motors, and imagination, the team put together a flying dinosaur that tells a lot about these extinct creatures.

Think and Discuss
- What makes the strong introduction above better than the weak one?
- What makes the strong conclusion better than the weak one?

▶ Draft Your Introduction and Conclusion

① **Express** the main idea of your report in a focus statement.

② **Draft** a lively introduction that presents the main idea.

③ **Draft** a conclusion that summarizes your research, touches on the main idea, and makes a memorable finish.

To capture attention, try putting an unusual fact in your introduction.

④ **Provide** a complete list of sources. Use page 578 as a model.

📖 See page H66 for help with formatting your sources.

Evaluating Your Research Report

▶ **Reread** your report. Use this rubric to help you revise. Write the statements that best describe your report.

Loud and Clear!

- The report is well researched.
- The strong introduction and conclusion present the main idea.
- Well-organized ideas are linked by smooth transitions.
- All sentences in each paragraph relate to the topic sentence. At least two facts or examples support it.
- I have written in the third person and presented facts.
- I have written in my own words and used quotations correctly.
- The list of sources is complete.
- *There are very few spelling, punctuation, and grammar mistakes.*

Sounding Stronger

- Parts of the report are well researched, but others aren't.
- Though adequate, the introduction and conclusion are boring.
- Though well ordered, the report needs better transitions.
- Most paragraphs have topic sentences. Some paragraphs stray off the topic. Some need more facts and examples.
- I give an opinion or two that should be deleted.
- I need to make sure that my quotations are written accurately.
- My list of sources is almost complete.
- *Mistakes make a few sentences confusing.*

Turn Up the Volume

- I have not done enough research.
- The report lacks an introduction and a conclusion.
- I jump from one idea to the next, without logical order.
- I have few topic sentences and need more facts or examples.
- My writing mixes opinions with facts.
- I have not used quotations carefully. I may have plagiarized.
- My list of sources is missing.
- *Mistakes make the report difficult to understand.*

 See www.eduplace.com/kids/hme/ to interact with this rubric.

▶ Revise Your Research Report

❶ Revise your report. Use the list of sentences you wrote from the rubric. Work on the parts that you described with sentences from "Sounding Stronger" and "Turn Up the Volume."

Tech Tip
Highlight each quotation as you reread your report on-screen. Then check it for accuracy.

❷ Have a writing conference.

When You're the Writer Read your report aloud to your partner. Ask for feedback about trouble spots. Listen and take notes while your partner is talking. Then decide which changes to make.

What should I say?

When You're the Listener Tell your partner at least two things you like about the report. As your partner reads, listen for places where the report is confusing or could be improved. When it's your turn to talk, ask about anything that was unclear. Use the chart below for ideas.

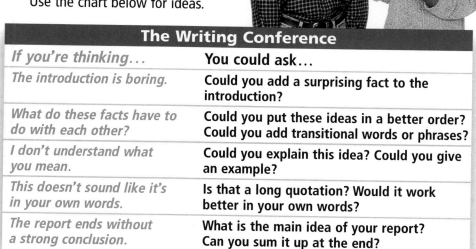

The Writing Conference

If you're thinking...	You could ask...
The introduction is boring.	Could you add a surprising fact to the introduction?
What do these facts have to do with each other?	Could you put these ideas in a better order? Could you add transitional words or phrases?
I don't understand what you mean.	Could you explain this idea? Could you give an example?
This doesn't sound like it's in your own words.	Is that a long quotation? Would it work better in your own words?
The report ends without a strong conclusion.	What is the main idea of your report? Can you sum it up at the end?

❸ Make more revisions to your research report, using your conference notes and the Revising Strategies on the next page.

Revising Strategies

Elaborating: Word Choice Define special terms to keep your audience informed.

Without Definition	With Definition
The **zeppelin** was named after its inventor.	The zeppelin, an airship that contained compartments filled with gas, was named after its inventor.

▶ Find two places in your report where you can define a term.

Elaborating: Details and Examples Without details and examples, your report will sound vague. Review your notes or sources to find ideas. Compare the sentence below from Vince Brach's article about lichens to the sentence with few details.

Few Details	With Details and an Example
By themselves, algae must live in water or in damp places.	By themselves, one-celled green algae must live in water or as a thin film in damp places, such as a coating of green on a flowerpot.

▶ Find three places in your report where you can add details or examples.

Sentence Fluency: Parallel Structure When discussing related ideas, use the same, or parallel, structure as Donna Guu did in her report. Often related ideas are linked with *and* or *or.*

Without Parallel Structure	With Parallel Structure
To do that, the people of ancient China had to ask themselves **what would be the right thing to do and wrong behavior**.	To do that, the people of ancient China had to ask themselves what would be the right thing to do and what would be the wrong thing to do.

▶ Find three places in your report where related ideas are joined by *and* or *or.* Check them for parallel structure.

GRAMMAR LINK ▶ *See also page 251.*

Adding Graphics and Visuals

To enhance your report, use visual aids to illustrate a point or to supply more information. Consider pictures, time lines, maps, charts, graphs, or diagrams that could be placed on the cover, within the report, or in a special section at the end.

> Every visual aid should have a caption or a title.

Not all topics lend themselves to visual aids. Don't try to force them into your report if they don't fit.

Pictures You can use pictures of people, places, and things discussed in your report. Photocopy drawings or photographs from books or magazines, and credit the source. You can also use your own drawings or photographs.

Astronauts in training float inside the KC-135 *Vomit Comet*. The plane flies to a high altitude and then falls freely to simulate a weightless environment. One of the men in this photograph is playing with a yo-yo.

▶ Add drawings or pictures to your report if they will enhance it.

Time Lines You might use a time line if your report includes events that happen over a stretch of time.

Early Women Aviators

| 1910. First woman pilot licensed to fly— Baroness Raymonde de la Roche of France | 1921. First black U.S. woman pilot licensed to fly—Bessie Coleman |

| 1910 | 1920 | 1930 | 1940 |

| 1911. First U.S. woman pilot licensed to fly—Harriet Quimby | 1932. First solo transatlantic flight by a woman—Amelia Earhart |

▶ Try using a time line if your report includes events from history.

more ▶

Maps Add a map if your readers need to know the locations of places you discuss. You can draw the map or photocopy one.

▶ Include a map if your report focuses on a particular place.

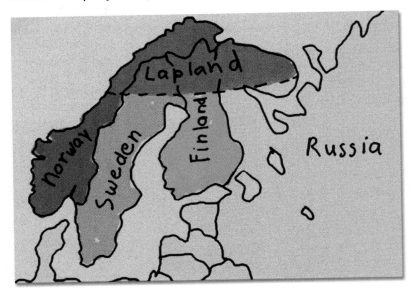

Diagrams Draw a diagram to show a step in a process or how something is put together.

Figure 1. The potter centers the clay on the wheel.

▶ Try using a diagram to show something that isn't easy to describe in words.

Charts and Graphs Use charts and graphs to organize complicated information. The visuals below show a bar graph and a pie graph.

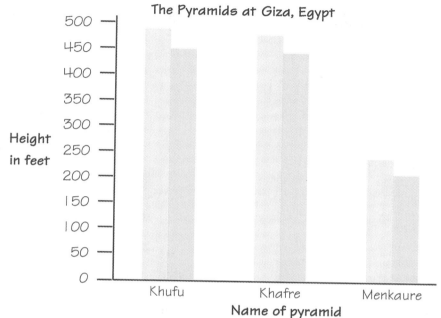

The Pyramids at Giza, Egypt

Height in feet

Khufu　Khafre　Menkaure
Name of pyramid

Height when built (feet)
Current height (feet)

China's Gross Domestic Product, 1997

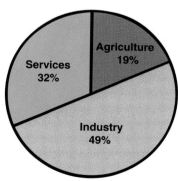

Agriculture 19%
Services 32%
Industry 49%

Visuals can't take the place of text. You'll still need to write text to fill the number of pages you've been assigned. Visuals will make your report even better!

▶ Think about using a chart or graph to show additional information.

Tech Tip
You may have a computer program that makes it easy to create charts and graphs.

For more information on using visuals see page H29.

Proofread Your Research Report

Proofread your report, using the Proofreading Checklist and the Grammar and Spelling Connections. Proofread for one skill at a time. Use a class dictionary to check spellings.

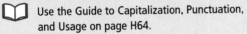

Proofreading Checklist

Did I
- ✔ indent all paragraphs?
- ✔ use verb tenses correctly?
- ✔ correct fragments and run-on sentences?
- ✔ use commas in dates and addresses?
- ✔ punctuate quotations properly?
- ✔ capitalize all proper nouns?
- ✔ spell all the words correctly?

📖 Use the Guide to Capitalization, Punctuation, and Usage on page H64.

Proofreading Marks
- ¶ Indent
- ∧ Add
- ⌐ Delete
- ≡ Capital letter
- / Small letter
- ⱽⱽ Add quotes
- ⋏ Add comma
- ⊙ Add period
- ∾ Transpose

HELP
? Proofreading Tip

Read one line at a time. Hold a ruler or a strip of cardboard under the line to help you focus on the spelling of each word.

Grammar and Spelling Connections

Commas in Dates and Addresses In dates, use a comma to separate the month and the day from the year. Add a comma after the year if the sentence continues. In addresses, use a comma between the city and the state. Add a comma after the state if the sentence continues.

> On October 19, 1879, Thomas Edison was working in his workshop in Menlo Park, New Jersey, developing what we now call the light bulb.

GRAMMAR LINK ▶ *See also page 253.*

Spelling Words with -logy The Greek suffix *-logy* means "study of." It is often used with Greek roots.

> To study ancient Mexico, the researcher used technology to find articles on archaeology and anthropology.

📖 See the Spelling Guide on page H80.

 Go to www.eduplace.com/kids/hme/ for proofreading practice.

▶ Publish Your Research Report

❶ Make a neat final copy of your report. Check that all spelling and grammar errors have been fixed.

❷ Title your report. Make your audience curious with a catchy title such as "Space Walkers" rather than "The Apollo Mission."

❸ Publish or share your narrative in a way that suits your audience. See the Ideas for Sharing box for ideas.

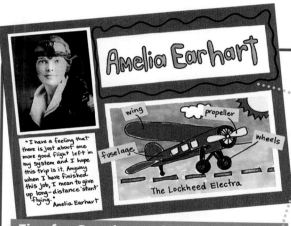

"I have a feeling that there is just about one more good flight left in my system and I hope this trip is it. Anyway when I have finished this job, I mean to give up long-distance 'stunt' flying." Amelia Earhart

Amelia Earhart

wing   propeller   wheels   fuselage

The Lockheed Electra

Tips for Creating a Visual Display

- Create large visuals to enhance your report. Use interesting lettering and art.
- Add creative touches such as magazine cutouts, objects related to your topic, quotations, or covers that can be lifted to get the answer to a question.
- Arrange your visuals on posterboard, as a standup big book, or as a tabletop display. Include your report.

Ideas for Sharing
Write It Down
- With classmates, post your reports on a class Web site.

Talk It Up
- Have a partner read your report and prepare questions. Then your partner can interview your as the resident expert on your topic.
- Deliver your report orally. See page 605 for tips.

Show It Off
- Make a visual display to show with your report.
- Make a multimedia presentation of your report. See page H53 for tips.

▶ Reflect

Write about your writing experience. Use these questions to get started.

- What did you find easy or difficult about writing a research report?
- What else would you like to research about your topic?
- How does this report compare with other papers you have written?

Writing Prompts

Use these prompts as ideas for research reports. They relate to other subjects you study. Think of a topic your audience will find interesting, and write your report in a way that they will understand and enjoy.

Writing Across the Curriculum

SCIENCE
Look at the landscape around you. Does a mountain, a desert, or other natural feature intrigue you? Write a report on how it was formed.

SOCIAL STUDIES
Choose a U.S. state, and research its history, important events, and people. Include a time line if you'd like.

MUSIC
Research how a musical instrument was developed and what it is like today.

MATHEMATICS/SCIENCE
Find out how something interesting was invented. You might choose the radio, the V-8 engine, or the printing press. Use diagrams if needed.

FINE ART
Qin Shi Huang Di declared himself emperor of China in 221 B.C. Write a research paper about his tomb and its life-sized terra cotta army of eight thousand soldiers and horses.

Terra Cotta Army, Qin Dynasty, 210 B.C. (detail)
Tomb of Qin Shi Huang Di, Xianyang, China

See www.eduplace.com/kids/hme for more prompts.

Writing a News Article

A **news article** reports information about a recent event. The first paragraph answers *Who? What? Where? When? Why?* and sometimes *How?* The rest of the article builds upon this information by adding details and quotations from people present. Read Christine's news article.

Headline → **Dolphins Swim to Triumph**

Lead paragraph or introduction

The Dynamic Dolphins swam to victory yesterday at Newbridge College, completing an undefeated season. By beating the Flying Sharks, the Dolphins won the district title for the fifth time in ten years.

Supporting details

The Dolphins led during the first three-quarters of the meet. After two losses, the Sharks tied the score with three races left. Each team won another race, putting the pressure on Lisa Torres to cinch the title in the final 50-meter freestyle. Torres, a junior, pulled past Shark Michelle Russo to win by three-tenths of a second. "It was a breathtaking effort, and she did it!" said Dolphin Fabiola Benicia.

Supporting details

To earn the district title, the Dolphins had to beat each of the nine other teams in the league. Coach Stephanie Kim said, "I am proud of this team, win or lose. They have great spirit. They practice like winners. We had a great season."

In a short ceremony after the final race, the smiling Dolphins held up the first-place trophy for photographs. Olympic champion Candace Scott met the Dolphins and Sharks and awarded medals. Smiling broadly at the Dolphins, Scott said, "Your victory sets the pace for all young swimmers. You are an inspiration."

Conclusion

more ►

Reading As a Writer

- The **headline** states the article's main idea in a few words.
  What is the main idea of Christine's article?
- The **lead paragraph** or **introduction** presents the most important facts to answer these questions: *Who? What? Where? When? Why?* and *How?*
  What questions are answered in the first sentence?
- Other **supporting details** are presented in the rest of the article.
  Who won the final race?
- The **conclusion** wraps up the news article with an interesting fact or a quotation from someone connected to the event.
  How does Christine end her article?

How to Write a News Article

❶ **Choose** an important upcoming event that will interest your audience.

❷ **Use** a pyramid structure to outline your article.

❸ **Take** notes at the event. Describe what you see and hear. Jot down quotations from eyewitnesses.

Who?
What?
Where?
When? Why? How?

Supporting facts

Other, less important, facts

❹ **Write** your article, keeping your audience in mind. Place the least important information at the end, in case your article is cut for space.

❺ **Think** of a headline that will attract your readers' attention.

❻ **Revise and proofread** your article. Are the facts clear? Are the names spelled correctly? Are your quotations accurate?

❼ **Make** a final copy. Post your article on a school or family Internet site, or work with other students to make a class newspaper.

Quotations may include opinions, but the rest of your article should include only facts.

Writing to Solve a Problem

When you write to **solve a problem**, you define the problem, identify and consult resources to help you solve it, and explain your solution. Read how Carla wrote to solve her problem.

Problem: How can I better organize my time?	Possible Sources of Information
I need time for • homework • drawing • exercise • after-school activities • scheduling with my family	• books or video • friends • older students • teachers

Problem

Resources

Summary

I need to organize my time better. I haven't been getting my homework done. Plus, I sometimes forget to coordinate my activities with my family. My sister wants to know why I can't let them know my plans in advance.

I decided to get advice from my soccer coach, who is very disciplined. She said I should plan my whole week in advance, not just one day. She showed me her datebook, which has all her appointments for the week, month, and year.

I discovered by talking to my friends that some of them keep calendars on their computers. A book I found in the library suggested using different colors for different kinds of activities.

Solution

I earned extra money so I could buy a weekly planner. I filled in my after-school activities in blue. I put tests and reports in red. I kept track of my homework and the time I wanted for drawing.

Now I can be sure I have time to do what matters and plan ahead when other people have to help me out. It's a lot more peaceful at home.

Reading As a Writer

- The **problem** is an obstacle you must overcome or a question you need to resolve. *What was Carla's problem?*

- **Resources** can be people, places, and materials that provide information to help solve the problem. *What sources did Carla list?*

- The **summary** restates the problem and describes the steps you take to arrive at a solution. *Which sentences restate the problem? What steps did Carla take to find a solution?*

- The **solution** is the action you take or the decision you make. *What actions did Carla take?*

How to Write to Solve a Problem

1 **State** your problem in one clear sentence.

2 **Write** a list of questions to be answered. Identify possible sources of information.

3 **Research** the answers to your questions. Organize your answers and sources in a chart.

MONDAY

7:00	
8:00	
9:00	Book report due
10:00	
11:00	
12:00	
1:00	
2:00	
3:00	
4:00	Soccer practice at 4.
5:00	
6:00	
7:00	
8:00	
9:00	
10:00	

Information	Source
Keep a datebook. Look at the big picture—a whole week at a time.	Ms. Nyu, soccer coach
Keep a calendar on a computer.	friends
Use color-coding to help balance schoolwork and other activities.	library book—*100 Ways to Organize Your Life*

4 **Solve** the problem, using the information you collected. Write a paragraph or two explaining what you decided and why you made the choice you did.

Completing a Form

When you **complete a form**, you provide specific information about yourself. You may be asked to give information when you want to enter a contest, sign up for a committee at school, or apply for a job. Read the form below.

Directions ———▶

Date ———▶

Personal information

Background information

APPLICATION
Assistant Dance Instructor

Complete this application. Please print.

DATE: _October 1, 2001_

NAME: _Henry Acosta_

ADDRESS: _4006 Erie Avenue_
Babson Park, Florida 33827

PHONE NUMBER: _(352) 555-2671_

AGE: _14_

1. How long have you been taking dance lessons? _9 years_

2. Mark the types of dance you feel most comfortable assisting with. jazz ___ tap ___ ballet _X_ lyrical ___

3. Mark the level(s) you feel qualified to assist with. beginning classes _X_ intermediate classes _X_

4. Mark the age group(s) you would prefer to work with. 4–6 years _X_ 7–9 years _X_ 10–12 years ___

5. Dance classes are held Monday through Friday from 3:30–5:30 P.M. Which days can you work? _____
Monday, Wednesday, Friday

6. What strengths will you bring to this position? _I enjoy_ _working with children, and I think I have a lot of patience with_ _them. I am also a hard worker, and I know how much time and_ _effort it takes to learn something._

> Think about the helpful qualities of teachers you have had over the years. Which of those qualities do you have?

more ▶

Reading As a Writer

- The **directions** tell how to complete the form. *Should Henry write in cursive or print?*

- The **date** gives the month, day, and year on which you fill out the form. *When did Henry fill out this form?*

- The **personal information** is often your name, address, and phone number. *Why do you think the dance school asks for Henry's age?*

- The **background information** asks about your past experience and qualifications for the position. *What are Henry's strengths?*

How to Complete a Form

1 **Read** the directions carefully.

2 **Date** the form.

3 **Complete** the form. Remember to print the information clearly.

4 **Proofread** for mistakes. Check that you have completed every part of the form.

Types of Forms

Catalog Order Form When you order an item by mail from a catalog, the form may ask you to supply the page number in the catalog where the item is featured.

Ship to:

Name _____

Address _____

City _____ State _____ Zip _____

Catalog Order Form

Music Catalog

Page #	Title #	Description (Please print and specify CD or cassette.)	Quantity	Price Each	Total
			Subtotal		
			Sales Tax		
			Order Total		

Internet Application Applications for workshops and courses are often available on the Internet. It may help to print out the application and read it before you fill out the application on-screen.

Giving an Oral Presentation

The goal of an oral report is to present credible information in a way that listeners can understand. After researching and writing your report, you can create or select visuals and other media to explain or enhance your information.

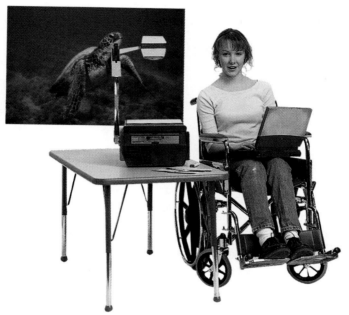

Choosing Media Tools

Audio and visual media can highlight key ideas and help your audience remember them. A handout, a list on the chalkboard, and information on a flip chart are simple and effective aids. Using a variety of media tools can hold your audience's attention, but too many can become distracting. Choose your presentation aids carefully.

A Career as a Naturalist

1. *Photos of wildlife*
2. *Videos—famous naturalists*
3. *Chart—accessible wilderness areas*
4. *Internet—bookmark the U.S. Fish and Wildlife Service site*

more ▶

Think about the options below. Would your audience better understand your topic if you used one or more of them?

Which Media?	
Models Showing a subject in three dimensions can be easier than describing it or using a photo. Models can also give a sense of scale. For oral reports on science and mathematics topics, models can be invaluable.	• dioramas, paper or clay models, papier-mâché objects
Photographs and Illustrations Choose simple images that can be seen from a distance. Charts and graphs that use a bold color and type that is easy to read can help to clarify complex information. When you show photographs or illustrations that others have made, be sure that you give them credit.	• posters, slides, photos from newspapers, magazines, the Internet, books 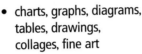 • charts, graphs, diagrams, tables, drawings, collages, fine art 
Technology Projecting images from CD-ROMs or from reliable Web sites can show viewers enlarged and detailed views of a subject. If possible, videotape actual events yourself, and then edit the tape for your presentation.	• audiotapes, videotapes, CDs, DVDs, the Internet, CD-ROMs, computer programs for tables and graphs, digital photography, and videotaping and recording systems.

See pages H53–H56 in the Tools and Tips Handbook.

Getting Ready

It's important to practice giving your report. Speak clearly, and adapt your language to fit the topic and your audience. If possible, record your talk, and then listen to it. Identify parts that need more practice. Repeat words that are hard to pronounce until you can say them easily.

You'll also need to practice using audio or visual aids. Mark your note cards at the places in which you will present your aids. Then rehearse your entire presentation. Will any of your movements be distracting to your audience? Will you need to avoid blocking anyone's view?

If you plan to show an Internet site, bookmark the site, and have it on screen and ready to go.

Use the guidelines below to help you use media aids.

Guidelines for Giving an Oral Presentation with Media Aids

▶ Plan what you need to do to set up equipment or to hang a poster or map in advance.
▶ When you make your own visuals using a computer, don't over-decorate them.
▶ Save and duplicate any computer files you use.
▶ Be sure that charts and graphs are free of errors.
▶ Point to the area of the visual that you are talking about.
▶ Keep a visual covered, or turned off, until you are ready to show it.
▶ Display the visual long enough for everyone to see it. Then put it away to avoid distracting from the rest of your report.
▶ Check the volume on equipment before you turn it on. Be sure everyone can hear.
▶ Keep audio and video clips short.

Apply It

Using the guidelines above, choose and prepare media aids for a report you have already written. Select only a section of your report if it is long. After giving your presentation, answer the questions below.

● Which media did you choose? Why?
● What was most successful about your presentation? Why?
● If you could present your report again, what would you do differently?

Evaluating Media Information

The mass media—including newspapers, magazines, books, radio, television, and the Internet—provide information about the world. Each of these sources serves different audiences, has different purposes, and gives different viewpoints.

The Internet

Almost anyone can set up and run an Internet site—and many people and groups do. Thousands of businesses, nonprofit organizations, universities, government agencies, groups, and individuals post a wide range of data, facts, and information on the Internet. Some of the material is reliable, some of it is flawed, and some of it is extremely biased.

The chart below compares some of the sources of news and information available on the Internet.

Information on the Internet	
Commercial and Nonprofit News	Magazines, newspapers, and television and radio news programs create and maintain, or are linked to, Internet sites. Some news sources, however, exist only on the Internet.
Government and Its Agencies	National, state, and local governments run a variety of Internet sites. These include the Library of Congress, the National Archives, and the Smithsonian Institution.
Public Institutions	Universities, libraries, and museums make available a variety of materials and information through the Internet.
Other Groups and Individuals	Groups and individuals post information at thousands of sites for a vast range of purposes. Many communicate through chat rooms and Internet bulletin boards.

Thousands of Sources

The Internet makes it possible for people to obtain information directly from thousands of sources. Having access to so many ideas and opinions can be both an advantage and a drawback. One drawback is that no one watches over the Internet to eliminate unreliable information. Also, due to the sheer volume of even reliable information, it's impossible for any one person to absorb all that is posted. When you use the Internet for finding facts, pay close attention to whether sources are accurate, unbiased, and fair. Use the guidelines below to help you evaluate the information provided on the Internet and in other forms of the mass media.

Guidelines for Evaluating Information in the Media

▶ Find the source of the information. What is the background or reputation of the person or organization? If you cannot determine the source, what might you conclude about the quality or reliability of the information?

▶ Think about the purpose of the information. Does it persuade? inform? sell? or inflame?

▶ Consider the fairness and accuracy of the message. Does the source provide several viewpoints or only one? Is the information biased or unfair? How can you tell?

▶ Examine the visuals used to illustrate the information. Why do you think they were chosen? What are they intended to convey?

Laws Govern the Media

The following types of expression are illegal.

• *Plagiarism*—the attempt to pass off someone's ideas or work as your own

• *Libel*—a published or broadcast statement that maliciously damages a person's reputation

• *Slander*—a false oral statement damaging to a person's reputation

Apply It

Compare and evaluate two Internet sites or two other media sources that publish information on the same subject. One should be a reputable source, such as the National Archives or the Library of Congress. The other can be any source you find on the same subject. Use the guidelines above and answer the following questions.

• What information was covered in both sources? How was it similar? How was it different?
• Why do you think some information was left out of one of the sources?
• Which source do you think gave better coverage of the subject? Explain why.

Narrating and Entertaining

What You Will Find in This Section:

Getting Started

Listening to a Narrative

Narratives are stories. They might be true experiences or imagined events. Listening to a narrative is different from listening to a news report or an editorial. Although a narrative may teach a lesson or reveal the author's opinion, the main purpose for listening to a narrative is enjoyment. Here are some guidelines for being an effective listener.

Guidelines for Listening to a Narrative

► Listen for the main idea. What is the narrative about?
► Identify the main people or characters in the narrative.
► Listen for the setting. Where and when does the narrative take place?
► Listen for the main events. What happens? in what order?
► Listen for details that describe and elaborate the setting, characters, and main events.
► Listen for the author's purpose. Does the author want to share a special experience? entertain you with an exciting tale? teach a moral?

Try It Out Listen as your teacher reads aloud from "Lucky to Be Alive," a true story by Carol Ann Moorhead about a frightening ordeal. Take notes that will help you to answer the questions below.

- What is the narrative about?
- Who are the most important people in the narrative?
- What is the setting of the narrative?
- What main events structure the narrative? Tell them in order.
- What details help you to picture the setting, characters, and events?
- What do you think is the author's purpose for telling this story?

HELP? See page H33 for tips on taking notes while listening.

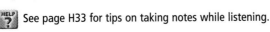

Writing a Narrative Paragraph

A paragraph that tells a true or imagined story is called a **narrative paragraph**. A narrative paragraph includes a topic and a main idea. The **topic** is the subject of the paragraph. The **main idea** is what the writer has to say about the topic. Every sentence in the paragraph tells something about the main idea. What is the topic of the narrative paragraph below? What is the main idea?

> Remember to indent the first line of a paragraph.

Indent

Lead sentence

    I was twelve years old before I finally learned to feel safe in the water. As a child, I had been afraid of the water. I would holler and thrash wildly whenever my dad tried to get me even to wade. As I got older, I always had an excuse to avoid swimming. Once I told my swimming instructor that I heard my mother calling me just after he told us to hold our breath under water. Then one day I decided to face my fear. I asked my older sister, who practically lived in the water, to teach me how to swim. We went to the lake. She told me to lie down in the water while she held my head and back with her arms. "Pretend you're a feather," she said. She had let go of me, and there I was, floating by myself. That was my first swimming victory. From then on I progressed quickly. Now I'm no longer the coward on the beach blanket.

Supporting sentences

Concluding sentence

Lead Sentence

Supporting Sentences

Concluding Sentence

In the paragraph above, the topic is fear of swimming. The main idea is overcoming that fear.

The labels show the three parts of a narrative paragraph.

- The **lead sentence** introduces the topic and summarizes the narrative's main idea.
- The **supporting sentences** follow the lead sentence and give details about what happens in the narrative.
- The **concluding sentence** ends the paragraph and finishes the narrative.

Think and Discuss Look again at the paragraph above. What details does the writer include in the supporting sentences?

The Lead Sentence

A paragraph usually begins with a sentence that states the topic and the author's main idea about the topic. In a narrative paragraph, this sentence is called the **lead sentence**. It introduces the narrative and may give a hint about the main idea or tell how the writer felt.

Hint about main idea   Topic

Example: I was twelve years old before I finally learned to feel safe in the water.

What might narratives with these lead sentences be about?

- "Riding a horse is easy," the instructor said in a hearty voice.
- Volunteering for my school's community-service program was a lot more exciting than I ever dreamed.

Try It Out Read the following paragraph. On your own or with a partner, write the topic and the main idea. Then write two possible lead sentences for the paragraph.

_____Lead sentence_____ . The moment their parents left, the children jumped all over me, babbling away nonstop. Each kid wanted me to do something different—bake cookies, play games, jump on the beds. They were relentless! Finally, I got them quiet by promising to tell a story. They gathered around me, and I began making up a story about a circus that needed a family to take care of its giraffe. I used a different voice for each character. The children were laughing one moment, sad the next, and begging for more. They told me I was going to be a famous writer. The way they said it made me believe it might be true. It also made me feel glad I had stuck with baby-sitting.

Supporting Sentences

Supporting sentences follow the lead sentence. They give **factual and sensory details** that answer one or more of the questions *Who? What? Where? When? Why?* and *How?* about the topic. They may also describe how things look, sound, smell, taste, or feel. In the swimming paragraph, the supporting sentences tell how the writer used to act in the water and how the writer learned to float.

Factual detail: Then one day I decided to face my fear.

Sensory detail: I would holler and thrash wildly...

Try It Out On your own or with a partner, choose one of the lead sentences below. List factual and sensory details that support it. Then write at least three supporting sentences, using details from your list.

1. Our dream day at the beach soon turned into a nightmare.
2. My parents told me the most amazing stories when I was working on my family tree project for my social studies class.

 Use an exclamation point after an interjection expressing strong feeling (Wow!). Use a comma after one expressing mild feeling (Oh,).

Keeping to the Main Idea Supporting sentences should give details only about the main idea.

Think and Discuss What is the main idea of the paragraph below? Which sentence does not keep to the main idea?

I panicked on my first day of carpentry class. The smell of sawdust made my palms sweat. A row of sharp, shiny handsaws sent a chill up my spine. My brother earned high marks in this class last year. When my teacher asked for a volunteer, I slumped down low, which wasn't easy on a shop stool. To my horror, she picked me! After demonstrating the proper cutting technique, she handed me the saw. My fear gave way to confidence as the sawdust drizzled steadily to the floor. When the block snapped in two, I decided this class was going to be a cut above the rest.

more ▶

Ordering Details Events in a narrative paragraph are usually told in the order they occurred. **Time-clue words and phrases**, such as *at first, after, later that day,* and *finally,* help readers understand when events took place.

HELP? See page 20 for more time-clue words.

Think and Discuss Which sentence is out of order? Where does it belong in the paragraph? What time-clue words and phrases link the sentences?

This year my parents' best friends invited us on a camping trip in the Arizona desert. When I first got there, the endless miles of sand amazed me. I learned a lot too. My parents' friends were desert experts, and they taught me all about lizards. I could run and run without running into anything. Best of all were our campfires in the cool evenings. As the sun sank into the shimmering horizon, we sat around the fire, sang songs, and talked about returning next year.

The Concluding Sentence

The **concluding sentence** ends a narrative paragraph. It can connect back to the lead sentence in some way, as it did in the swimming paragraph on page 613. It can explain how the writer felt, as it did in the carpentry paragraph on page 615. It can also simply tell a last event that wraps up the narrative, as it did in the camping paragraph above.

Try It Out Read the paragraph. On your own or with a partner, write two different concluding sentences.

When we moved from Dallas to San Antonio last year, I thought we would never get here. Two days before the move, the bathroom in our old apartment flooded, and the dog ran away. The next day my sister cut her finger while packing boxes and had to have stitches. Once we were on the road, our car broke down, and we had to wait for three hours for a tow truck. _____*Concluding sentence*_____ .

Write Your Own Narrative Paragraph

Now it's time for you to write a narrative paragraph about a personal experience. What was the most important thing ever to happen to you? the worst thing? What made it stand out? How did you feel? List details that describe the people, the setting, and each event. Practice telling your narrative to a partner. Then you'll be ready to write.

Checklist for My Paragraph

✔ My **lead sentence** introduces the narrative and hints at the main idea.

✔ My **supporting sentences** all develop the main idea and tell the events in order.

✔ **Factual and sensory details** help paint a picture of what happened.

✔ My **concluding sentence** connects back to the lead sentence, explains my feelings, or tells a final event.

Looking Ahead

Writing a longer narrative will be easy now that you understand how to write a narrative paragraph. This diagram shows how the parts of a narrative paragraph function the same way as the parts of a longer narrative.

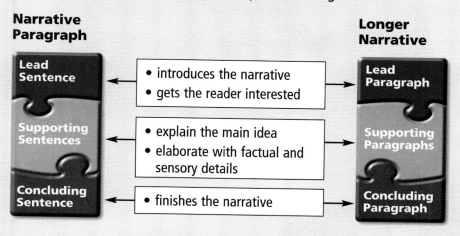

Narrative Paragraph

Longer Narrative

Lead Sentence
- introduces the narrative
- gets the reader interested

Lead Paragraph

Supporting Sentences
- explain the main idea
- elaborate with factual and sensory details

Supporting Paragraphs

Concluding Sentence
- finishes the narrative

Concluding Paragraph

Writing a Personal Narrative

We spent hours talking and laughing over pictures from last week's game. The game was one I'll never forget.

In this personal narrative, the writer shows, rather than tells, what he learned from an old man in his neighborhood. In what ways does the writer express his feelings about the man?

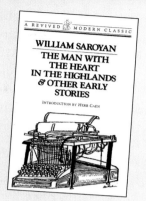

A REVIVED MODERN CLASSIC

WILLIAM SAROYAN
THE MAN WITH
THE HEART
IN THE HIGHLANDS
& OTHER EARLY
STORIES

INTRODUCTION BY HERB CAEN

The Hummingbird That Lived Through Winter

from *The Man with the Heart in the Highlands & Other Early Stories*, by William Saroyan

There was a hummingbird once which in the wintertime did not leave our neighborhood in Fresno, California.

I'll tell you about it.

Across the street lived old Dikran, who was almost blind. He was past eighty and his wife was only a few years younger. They had a little house that was as neat inside as it was ordinary outside—except for old Dikran's garden, which was the best thing of its kind in the world. Plants, bushes, trees—all strong, in sweet black moist earth whose guardian was old Dikran. All things from the sky loved this spot in our poor neighborhood, and old Dikran loved *them*.

One freezing Sunday, in the dead of winter, as I came home from Sunday School I saw old Dikran standing in the middle of the street trying to distinguish what was in his hand. Instead of going into our house to the fire, as I had wanted to do, I stood on the steps of the front porch and watched the old man. He would turn around and look upward at his trees and then back to the palm of his hand. He stood in the street at least two minutes and then at last he came to me. He held his hand out, and in Armenian he said, "What is this in my hand?"

I looked.

more ▶

"It is a hummingbird," I said half in English and half in
Armenian. "Hummingbird" I said in English because I didn't
know its name in Armenian.

"What is that?" old Dikran asked.

"The little bird," I said. "You know. The one that comes in the
summer and stands in the air and then shoots away. The one with
the wings that beat so fast you can't see them. It's in your hand.
It's dying."

"Come with me," the old man said. "I can't see, and the old
lady's at church. I can feel its heart beating. Is it in a bad way?
Look again, once."

I looked again. It was a sad thing to behold. This wonderful
little creature of summertime in the big rough hand of the old
peasant. Here it was in the cold of winter, absolutely helpless and
pathetic, not suspended in a shaft of summer light, not the most
alive thing in the world, but the most helpless and heartbreaking.

"It's dying," I said.

The old man lifted his hand to his mouth and blew warm breath
on the little thing in his hand which he could not even see. "Stay
now," he said in Armenian. "It is not long till summer. Stay, swift
and lovely."

We went into the kitchen of his little house, and while he blew warm breath on the bird, he told me what to do.

"Put a tablespoon of honey over the gas fire and pour it into my hand, but be sure it is not too hot."

This was done.

After a moment the hummingbird began to show signs of fresh life. The warmth of the room, the vapor of the warm honey—and, well, the will and love of the old man. Soon the old man could feel the change in his hand, and after a moment or two the hummingbird began to take little dabs of the honey.

"It will live," the old man announced. "Stay and watch."

The transformation was incredible. The old man kept his hand generously open, and I expected the helpless bird to shoot upward out of his hand, suspend itself in space, and scare the life out of me—which is exactly what happened. The new life of the little bird was magnificent. It spun about in the little kitchen, going to the window, coming back to the heat, suspending, circling as if it were summertime and it had never felt better in its whole life.

The old man sat on the plain chair, blind but attentive. He listened carefully and tried to see, but of course he couldn't. He kept asking about the bird, how it seemed to be, whether it showed signs of weakening again, what its spirit was, and whether or not it appeared to be restless; and I kept describing the bird to him.

When the bird was restless and wanted to go, the old man said, "Open the window and let it go."

"Will it live?" I asked.

"It is alive now and wants to go," he said. "Open the window."

I opened the window, the hummingbird stirred about here and there, feeling the cold from the outside, suspended itself in the area of the open window, stirring this way and that, and then it was gone.

"Close the window," the old man said.

We talked a minute or two and then I went home.

more ▶

The old man claimed the hummingbird lived through that winter, but I never knew for sure. I saw hummingbirds again when summer came, but I couldn't tell one from the other.

One day in the summer I asked the old man.

"Did it live?"

"The little bird?" he said.

"Yes," I said. "That we gave the honey to. You remember. The little bird that was dying in the winter. Did it live?"

"Look about you," the old man said. "Do you see the bird?"

"I see humming*birds*," I said.

"Each of them is our bird," the old man said. "Each of them, each of them," he said swiftly and gently.

Reading As a Writer

Think About the Narrative

- Describe the author's feelings about the old man. In what ways does the author express these feelings?
- What does the author do to catch your attention at the start?
- Which details show what the hummingbird and the old man are like?
- The writer tells this story in chronological order. What time clues help the reader move from event to event?
- How does the writer end his narrative? Discuss what you like or dislike about the ending.

Think About Writer's Craft

- Which parts of the narrative does the writer tell through dialogue? What kinds of information does the dialogue provide?
- The author uses some brief, one-sentence paragraphs. What effect do they have on the narrative?

Think About the Pictures

- The artist has used pastels, which are similar to chalk, to create soft lines and shapes in the illustrations on pages 620 and 622. Why do you think this style is appropriate for a personal narrative? Why is it a good style for this particular narrative?

Responding

Write responses to the following questions.

- **Personal Response** In your own life, who reminds you of the old man? Write about someone you have known whose actions and words show wisdom. How is this person like the old man?
- **Critical Thinking** Describe the old man's relationship with the natural world. Include examples of what he says, what he does, and how he is characterized in the narrative.

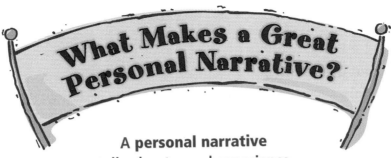

What Makes a Great Personal Narrative?

A **personal narrative**
tells about a real experience
in the writer's life.

When you write a personal narrative, remember to follow these guidelines.

▶ Start with a great beginning.

▶ Use the pronoun *I*.

▶ Focus on the important events in your narrative.

▶ Tell your personal narrative in chronological order. Begin with a flashback if it adds drama.

▶ Write with feeling, and let your personal voice come through.

▶ Elaborate your personal narrative with details to make it come alive. If possible, use dialogue.

▶ End in a way that wraps up your narrative.

GRAMMAR CHECK

Be careful not to run your sentences together. Rewrite them as separate simple sentences, compound sentences, or complex sentences.

Rachel Cipriano

WORKING DRAFT

Rachel Cipriano learned that she performed better in a sport when she had the support of a friend. She wrote this personal narrative to capture the experience of a special relationship. Read her working draft.

The Swim Meet

> More details and exact words would make this a super beginning!

I rolled over, looked at the time, and got out of bed. The temperature of the air woke me, and I went to get my bathing suit. ~~It was a blue racing suit.~~ This routine was well rehearsed from years of practice. It was 4:30 A.M. It was the day of my swim meet at the Good Games Pool.

> Could you cut some details?

Dad had agreed to drive me to all my meets, so we hopped into our station wagon and started out. Dad was sipping coffee from his travel mug. He looked a little tired. Driving to the meet, my dad got lost only once, a personal best for him. During this time I mentally prepared myself for the challenges ahead. My dad dropped me off and left to park the car. ~~He was gone a long time.~~

Katie showed me the way through the locker room. We found our coach waving to us, and we sat down next to her on very small bleachers. After stretching for about a half hour, we were ready to go.

> Are these events out of order?

After leaving my dad, I tried to find the pool deck, but I found Katie instead. My friend Katie and I were the only two kids from our swim team with times fast enough to qualify for the meet. Katie is really a good swimmer, and we've always been a support team for each other.

more →

My first event of the day was the 200 freestyle (eight laps of freestyle). I asked my coach for my heat and lane. She wrote 9–4 on my hand, which meant the final heat, lane 4.

I stretched some more, to stay loose. I was known to end a race fast, so my goal was to start out fast. It was time for my heat, so I stepped up to the block. I crouched down into the starting position. The person starting the race told us to go.

My legs flung me off the block. I was trembling, yet still moving, and remembering my goal, I picked up the pace. Katie didn't let me slack off. I took no breaths and charged the wall. I hit it and immediately looked at my time on the board. I threw a big smile at Katie, who had just finished, and she gave me a "thumbs up" sign. She meant I had gotten the fastest time. I signaled back and smiled, for she also had a new fast time.

Then we got out of the pool to greet each other, legs hurting, arms aching, but happy. We had accomplished something important.

Swimming has always been a win-win situation for me. Even if I don't win, I'm happy. When I'm not swimming, all I can think about is getting back into the water. Swimming is also something I can see myself doing all through my life.

> What does the person say?

> I can tell how great you feel!

> Does the ending stray off the topic?

Reading As a Writer

- What suggestions did Joe make? What revisions might Rachel make to address these suggestions?
- What do you like about Rachel's narrative? What would you improve?
- How would you describe Rachel's personality? What feelings did she share about the swim meet?
- What advice would you give to Rachel about improving her ending?

FINAL COPY

Rachel discussed her working draft with her classmates. Then she revised it. Compare her final copy with her draft to see how she improved her writing.

A Thrilling Race
by Rachel Cipriano

Beep! Beep! Beep! I groaned and then quickly shut off the dreaded noise otherwise known as my alarm clock. I rolled over, looked at the time, and slid slowly out of bed. The cold, dry air woke me immediately, and I quickly moved toward the bathroom to get my bathing suit. This routine was well rehearsed from years of practice. It was 4:30 A.M., and I was excited and nervous at the same time. It was the day of my swim meet at the Good Games Pool.

> This beginning will wake up your reader!

My dad drove me to the meet. During this time I mentally prepared myself for the challenges ahead. After my dad dropped me off and left to park the car, I tried to find the pool deck, but I found Katie instead. Her eyes were bright with excitement. My friend Katie and I were the only two kids from our swim team with times fast enough to qualify for the meet. Katie is really a good swimmer, and we've always been a support team for each other.

Katie showed me the way through the locker room. We found our coach waving to us, and we sat down next to her on very small bleachers. Music was blasting out of the loudspeakers, pumping me up. After stretching for about a half

> The events are now in chronological order.

more

hour, we were ready to go. My first event of the day was the 200 freestyle (eight laps of freestyle). I asked my coach for my heat and lane. She wrote 9–4 on my hand, which meant the final heat, lane 4. Katie and I were in the same heat.

I stretched some more, to stay loose. I was known to end a race fast, so my goal was to start out fast. "Heat 9, step up!" called out a voice. With heart thumping and knees knocking, I stepped up and calmed my legs, to get a sturdy grasp on the block with my toes. The block was clammy, wet, and rough like sandpaper. Katie and I made eye contact and wished each other luck. "Timers ready. Take your mark." I crouched in the starting position. "Go!"

What a vivid description!

As I shot like an arrow into the water, the only word that stuck in my head was *Go.* I was trembling, yet still moving, and remembering my goal, I picked up the pace. Katie didn't let me slack off. I went in and out of the walls seven times, watching my technique and hurting, but matching each lap's speed to the previous one's. Finally, there was one last lap, and seeing the wall ahead of me, I took no breaths and charged the wall. I hit it and immediately looked at my time on the board, but I was too dizzy to see it. I caught my breath and cooled down. I threw a

These are strong, smooth sentences.

big smile at Katie, who had just finished, and she gave me a "thumbs up" sign. She meant I had gotten the fastest time. I signaled back and smiled, for she also had a new fast time.

Then we got out of the pool to greet each other, legs hurting, arms aching, but happy. "Way to go!" we both shouted. We had accomplished something important, and it felt great!

Your ending is just right.

Reading As a Writer

- What changes did Rachel make to address Joe's questions?
- What details did Rachel add? How do they improve her narrative?
- What information did Rachel delete? What effect does this have?

See www.eduplace.com/kids/hme/ for more examples of student writing.

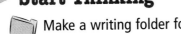
Write a Personal Narrative

▶ Start Thinking

Make a writing folder for your personal narrative. Copy the questions in bold type, and put the paper in your folder. Write your answers as you think about and choose your topic.

- **Who will be my audience?** Will it be friends? family? the school community?
- **What will be my purpose?** Will I entertain or inform my audience? share an insight gained from my personal experience?
- **How will I publish or share my narrative?** Will I put it on a poster? perform it as a reading? write it as a play?

▶ Choose Your Topic

❶ List at least five experiences that you might write about. Complete a chart like the one below by listing experiences in which you felt these or other emotions.

> **HELP**
> **?** **Need an Idea?**
> Ask family members and friends what interesting memories they have of experiences you and they have had together.
>
> **See page 642 for more ideas.**

SCARED	PROUD	EMBARRASSED	SAD
got lost in woods	won race	missed my entrance cue in school play	my dog hit by a car
the big storm	made a great dinner		

▲ **Part of Rachel's chart**

❷ Discuss each topic with a partner. Which idea is your partner's favorite? Is one idea too big? Should you focus on one aspect of an experience?

❸ Choose one topic. To help you decide, ask yourself these questions.

- Which experience do I remember most clearly?
- Which one will interest my readers most?
- Which one will I most enjoy writing about and sharing?

▶ Explore Your Topic

❶ Make a memory web for your personal narrative. Here is part of Rachel's memory web.

If your web fizzled out fast, try making a web with a different topic.

❷ Focus your topic.

- Have you generated too many ideas for one narrative? Cross out those that aren't related to the main topic.
- Add details to fill out the important ideas. Tell what you saw, heard, tasted, smelled, and felt.
- Include your thoughts and emotions.
- Add some dialogue to your web, if possible. What did people say?

HELP ? See page 16 for other ideas for exploring your topic.

Focus Skill

Using a Flashback

Personal narratives and stories usually proceed in chronological order, but sometimes a **flashback** can be effective. Here is one way to use a flashback.

Begin your narrative with an event that happens in the middle or at the end of the time period your narrative covers. Then "flash back" and tell your narrative's earliest event. From there, tell the rest of the narrative in time order.

Here is how one student used the flashback technique.

Event from middle of story

> Greg was incredibly surprised. His face wouldn't settle into one expression. First, his eyes popped wide open, and then he blinked twice, slowly. His mouth widened into an O and then turned up into a huge smile.

Flashback to beginning

> This was just the reaction that Lauri and I had hoped for when we first planned the party.

Think and Discuss

● How might Rachel have used the flashback technique? What events from the middle or the end of her narrative would have made an interesting beginning?

▶ Plan Your Narrative

❶ Look at your web. Determine the major events in your narrative.

❷ Order the events. Use a time line like the one below. Number your events in the order you will write about them.

❸ Choose details and dialogue from your web. Put each one on the time line under the related event. If you think of more details, add them.

> If you plan to use a flashback, put a star beside the event on the time line that you would like to use to begin your story.

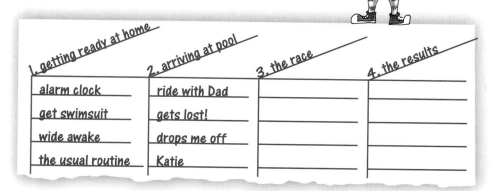

1. getting ready at home
   - alarm clock
   - get swimsuit
   - wide awake
   - the usual routine

2. arriving at pool
   - ride with Dad
   - gets lost!
   - drops me off
   - Katie

3. the race

4. the results

▲ Part of Rachel's time line

❹ Use time-clue words and phrases to help your reader understand the order of events. Use some from the chart below, or think of your own.

Time-Clue Words	Time-Clue Phrases
then	not long after
before	during that time
after	just before
last	two days later
meanwhile	the next summer
previously	earlier that week
until	at this point

Go to www.eduplace.com/kids/hme/ for graphic organizers.

Focus Skill

Good Beginnings

A strong beginning will make your reader want to dive into the rest of your narrative. Here are three ways you might begin.

Begin with something startling. Surprise your reader with an unusual statement, a noise, or a strange event.

Weak Beginning	Strong Beginning
I first met Duke, a huge Great Dane, on my paper route. Our encounter was really something.	Suddenly 150 pounds of Great Dane raced toward me.

Start with dialogue. Make the words sound natural, and show the speaker's personality.

Weak Beginning	Strong Beginning
I shouted for Henry. I needed his help with the popcorn maker.	"Henry, come here and help me!" I shouted. "Your popcorn maker has a mind of its own!"

GRAMMAR TIP ▶ *In dialogue, put the end punctuation inside the closing quotation mark.*

Use a flashback. Find an interesting or exciting part of your story. Start there.

Weak Beginning	Strong Beginning
Our art class was going to paint a mural on the cafeteria wall. This was going to take a lot of work and planning.	We stood, paint-spattered and tired, gazing at the finished mural. Our teamwork had paid off! Only five months ago, we were making sketches and trying to get organized. Our first project meeting was a disaster.

Try It Out

● With a partner, use a different technique than the one shown to improve each weak beginning above. Write the beginnings.

▶ # Draft Your Beginning

Use each technique to write three different beginnings for your narrative. Choose the beginning that best suits your purpose and audience.

Focus Skill

Writing with Voice

Sing to me!

Your style and personality are unique. Let them show when you write! Search for exact words to express a thought or feeling. To energize your writing, vary sentence type and length.

Compare the weak examples below with the strong excerpt from William Saroyan's "The Hummingbird That Lived Through Winter."

Weak Voice	Strong Voice
Example 1: The bird flew around the kitchen. It flew all over the place. It seemed to feel better. **Example 2:** Although heretofore that feather-laden creature had lain motionless, it now engaged in a great deal of flying.	The new life of the little bird was magnificent. It spun about in the little kitchen, going to the window, coming back to the heat, suspending, circling as if it were summertime and it had never felt better in its whole life.

Think and Discuss

- Describe the voice in each weak example, noting how word choice affects the voice.
- Which words and phrases in the strong example express the writer's feelings?

▶ Draft Your Personal Narrative

❶ **Write** your narrative. Don't worry about mistakes for now. Just write!

❷ **Follow** your time line as you work.

- Add or delete details. Make every word count.
- Use time-clue words and phrases to help your reader.
- Start a new paragraph whenever the speaker or the setting changes.

❸ **Put your voice** and personality into your writing.

Good Endings

A good ending smoothly ties up a story. Here are two ways you might end your narrative.

Echo an idea from the beginning. Your ending will make the story come full circle.

The Beginning	Beginning Echoed in Ending
Could we get along? We were five different kids, playing five different instruments. We all loved music, but we didn't always agree on how to play it.	Two weeks later, we were still five individuals, but we were also one cool quintet, making one cool sound. We were jamming!

Tell how the experience worked out. What was the final outcome, and what did it mean to you? Here are two endings to a narrative about baby-sitting.

Weak Ending	Strong Ending
I was glad when Mabel stopped screaming. I did homework and went home when her parents returned.	Suddenly Mabel stopped howling and started cooing. She smiled and then drifted off to sleep in her crib. "What a relief!" I thought. "Maybe I can be a baby-sitter after all."

Think and Discuss

- What makes the strong ending about baby-sitting more effective than the weak one?
- Look at Rachel's final copy on page 627. If Rachel had wanted her ending to echo her beginning, how might she have changed her narrative?

▶ Draft Your Ending

❶ **Write** at least two endings for your narrative. Try repeating a phrase or idea from the beginning. Tell how the experience worked out.

❷ **Select the ending** that seems perfect for your story. Make a great finish!

Evaluating Your Personal Narrative

▶ Reread your personal narrative. Use this rubric to help you improve it. In your notebook, write the sentences that describe your narrative.

Loud and Clear!

■ The beginning is catchy and intriguing.
■ If I used a flashback, it fits in smoothly.
■ I present the events in chronological order.
■ All events are important to the narrative. Nothing goes off track.
■ I bring the narrative alive with strong details.
■ My personal voice comes through clearly.
■ The ending wraps up my narrative.
■ *My writing has very few grammar or spelling mistakes.*

Sounding Stronger

■ My beginning could be more interesting.
■ If I used a flashback, it needs a smoother transition into the narrative.
■ Some events are out of order.
■ Here and there, the narrative wanders off the main topic.
■ I've used details, but I need more.
■ Some passages have voice, but others sound flat.
■ I need an ending that fits the narrative.
■ *I have some mistakes to correct.*

Turn Up the Volume

■ The beginning is dull.
■ If I used a flashback, it isn't working.
■ The sequence of events doesn't make sense.
■ Not much happens. I use few details. A narrative doesn't take shape.
■ My personal voice is missing.
■ The narrative trails off. It needs a solid ending.
■ *I have so many mistakes that the story is hard to read.*

Go to www.eduplace.com/kids/hme for more help with evaluating your writing.

▶ Revise Your Personal Narrative

❶ Revise your narrative. Use the list of sentences you wrote from the rubric. Work on the parts that you described with sentences from "Sounding Stronger" and "Turn Up the Volume."

Tech Tip

Boldface the words that describe the people in your narrative. You may need to add more details.

❷ Have a writing conference.

When You're the Writer Read your story aloud to your partner. Ask about parts that are giving you difficulty. Take notes.

When You're the Listener Tell your partner at least two things that you like about the story. If some parts are unclear, refer to the chart below and ask some questions.

What should I say?

The Writing Conference

If you're thinking . . .	You could say . . .
The beginning doesn't grab me.	**Could you start with something startling? with dialogue? with a flashback?**
What's going on? I can't follow the order.	**Are your events in the right order? How about using some time-clue words?**
There's no description to liven it up.	**Can you provide some word pictures— sights, smells, tastes?**
Some parts aren't really needed.	**Is the part about _____ really important?**
It sounds as if a machine wrote this.	**Can you put more of your personality and feelings into the writing?**
The end stops short.	**Could you tell how things worked out at the end?**

❸ Use your conference notes and the Revising Strategies on the next page to make more revisions to your personal narrative.

Revising Strategies

Elaborating: Word Choice Figurative language can paint a picture with just a few words. A **simile** uses *like* or *as* to compare one thing to another. A **metaphor** states that a person or a thing "is" something else.

Unelaborated	Lissa has a nice voice.
Simile added	Lissa's voice is as smooth and clear as a mountain stream.
Metaphor added	Lissa's voice is a smooth, clear mountain stream.

▶ Add a simile or a metaphor to your personal narrative.

📖 See also page H13.

Elaborating: Details Tuck new details into a sentence, or add a new sentence made up of elaborative details.

Few Details	Elaborated with Details
My father cooked the sauce the way I like it.	My father cooked the spaghetti sauce the way I like it. Lots of garlic, basil, and sliced green olives gave it a tangy taste.

▶ Add or revise details in three places in your narrative.

Sentence Fluency Give your writing rhythm by varying sentence structures. Too many simple statements can get boring! Try a combination of these kinds of sentences.

Simple sentences	I passed the ball to Hector. He stuffed it into the basket.
Compound sentence	I passed the ball to Hector, and he stuffed it into the basket.
Complex sentence	After I passed the ball to Hector, he stuffed it into the basket.
Introductory participial phrase	Grabbing my pass, Hector stuffed the ball into the basket.

▶ Rewrite four sentences in your narrative, varying the sentence structures.

GRAMMAR LINK ▶ *See also pages 34, 51, 57, 61, 371, and 396.*

▶ Proofread Your Personal Narrative

Proofread your narrative using the Proofreading Checklist and the Grammar and Spelling Connections. Proofread for one skill at a time. Use your class dictionary to check spellings.

Proofreading Checklist

Did I
- ✔ indent all paragraphs?
- ✔ write sentences correctly?
- ✔ correct fragments and run-on sentences?
- ✔ capitalize proper nouns?
- ✔ write dialogue correctly?
- ✔ correct all spelling mistakes?

📖 Use the Guide to Capitalization, Punctuation, and Usage on page H64.

Proofreading Marks

¶	Indent
∧	Add
⌐	Delete
≡	Capital letter
/	Small letter
⌄⌄	Add quotes
⋏	Add comma
⊙	Add period
∩	Transpose

HELP
? **Proofreading Tip**
Circle each word you need to check. Then add a mark to show you checked it.

Grammar and Spelling Connections

Complete Sentences Fix sentence fragments—your sentences should have both a subject and a predicate. Make sure no sentences are run together.

Fragment	After finishing my painting for the contest.
Run-on	I completed my painting it was almost midnight.
Complete sentence	I completed my painting just before midnight.

GRAMMAR LINK ➤ *See also page 63.*

Spelling Compound Words Check the dictionary to see if a compound word is spelled as one word, as a hyphenated word, or as two separate words.

When I baby-sat that night, I worked on my homework in the living room.

📖 See the Spelling Guide on page H80.

Go to www.eduplace.com/kids/hme/ for proofreading practice.

▶ Publish Your Personal Narrative

❶ Make a neat final copy of your narrative. Double-check for errors.

❷ Write a title that will arouse your readers' interest. Which is more intriguing—"The Day I Saved a Puppy" or "Rescue on In-Line Skates"?

GRAMMAR TIP ▷ Capitalize the first, the last, and each important word in a title.

❸ Publish or share your narrative. Consider your audience and purpose. See the Ideas for Sharing box.

Rescue on In-Line Skates
Based on the personal narrative by Sheila Boyle
THE MOVIE!

Tips for Making a Movie Poster

- Decide who will star as each of the characters in your narrative—famous actors, your friends?
- Choose which songs will be on the soundtrack.
- Make an eye-catching poster. Include "Based on the personal narrative by _____." Attach your narrative.

Ideas for Sharing

Write It Down
- Submit your narrative as an article in a class magazine.
- Write your narrative as a play.

Talk It Up
- "Broadcast" your narrative as a radio drama.
- Form a small group with other writers, and take turns reading your narratives aloud.

Show It Off
- Draw a picture of the story's high point.
- Make a poster advertising the movie version of your story.

▶ Reflect

Write about your writing experience. Use these questions as a guide.

- Which part gave you the most difficulty? Explain.
- Which part gave you the most satisfaction? Explain.
- What would you like to write about next time?
- How does this paper compare with other papers you have written?

Writing Prompts

Use these prompts as ideas for a personal narrative or to practice for a test. Some of them will work well for other subjects you study. Decide on your audience, and write a narrative that will be enjoyable for your readers.

1 Write about a proud moment in your life, such as receiving an award, accomplishing a task, or doing something for others.

2 Write about a time when your dream came true. How did this happen?

3 Tell about an outdoor adventure you had, such as completing a ropes course, taking a canoe trip, or visiting famous underground caves.

4 Write about a time when a special person helped you. Describe what happened. What are your feelings about the person?

Writing Across the Curriculum

5 **SOCIAL STUDIES**
Write about a time you helped others in your community. What did you do? What did you learn from doing it?

6 **PHYSICAL EDUCATION**
Tell about mastering an athletic skill you never thought you'd learn.

7 **SCIENCE**
Have you ever been puzzled by a natural event and then found the explanation for it? Describe what puzzled you. How did you solve the mystery?

8 **LITERATURE**
Think about a book you have read. Which character did you like the best? Why? Write about an experience you've had that was similar to this character's experience.

 See www.eduplace.com/kids/hme/ for more prompts.

✓ Test Practice

The following prompt to write a personal narrative is like ones you might find on a writing test. Read the prompt.

> Remember that a personal narrative tells about a real experience in the writer's life.

> **Write about a time when a special person helped you. Describe what happened. What are your feelings about the person?**

These strategies will help you do a good job responding to this type of prompt.

❶ Find the clue words that tell you what to write about. Identify the clue words in the prompt above.

❷ Choose a topic that fits the clue words. Write the clue words and what your topic will be.

Clue Words	My Topic
a time when a special person helped you your feelings	I will write about the day my uncle helped me learn to ride a bike.

❸ Plan your writing. Use a time line.

1. First event

detail

2. Second event

detail

3. Third event

detail

4. Fourth event

detail

❹ Your score will be good if you remember what kind of essay sounds loud and clear in the rubric on page 637.

Writing a Friendly Letter

A **friendly letter** gives you a chance to share thoughts, news, and feelings with someone you know personally. Read Dan's letter.

Heading —————— 33 Pine Road
Woodville, CO 80337
August 20, 2001

Greeting —Dear Yuka,

Body

    Hey, it's your buddy, Daniel. I just thought I'd write to tell you how it's going. We've been in Colorado for two weeks, and it's been a blast. We arrived really late the first day, so my uncle showed us to the guest house and we fell right to sleep. We got up early to see the sights. There was a public garden nearby where we had a picnic. The whole place smelled like Christmas trees. My cousin got his hand stuck in a pickle jar. It was hilarious.

    Yesterday we went to the mountains. We also went river rafting. It was really fun—even when I fell out of the raft! The scenery was so beautiful that I took a lot of pictures—all those jagged peaks towering above us. I'll show you the pictures when I get back. Write back!

Closing —————→ Your friend,
Signature —————→ Dan

Reading As a Writer

- The **heading** contains the writer's address and the current date. *What information does the last line of the heading contain?*
- The **greeting** usually begins with *Dear* and the name of the person receiving the letter. Capitalize each word and end the greeting with a comma. *To whom is Dan writing?*
- The **body** is the main part of the letter. *Why is Dan writing to Yuka?*
- The **closing**, such as *Your friend* or *Sincerely,* completes the letter. It is followed by a comma. *What closing did Dan use?*
- The **signature** is the writer's name. *Where is the signature written?*

How to Write a Friendly Letter

❶ Plan what you want to say.

❷ Write the letter. Include all five parts of a friendly letter.

❸ Proofread for mistakes. Use the Proofreading Checklist on page 640, and be sure to use a dictionary to check spellings.

❹ Make a neat final copy of your letter.

❺ Address the envelope, put a stamp on it, and mail it.

Return address
Daniel Riley
33 Pine Road
Woodville, CO 80337

USA

Mailing address
Yuka Takahashi
87 Tarpon Drive
Mill Springs, Florida 32608

Types of Friendly Letters

Thank-you Letter Writing a thank-you letter is a way to express your appreciation for something a person did for you.

> June 20
>
> Dear Mr. and Mrs. Kennet,
>
> Thank you very much for taking time from your vacation in California to get me the movie magazines. It was a very unexpected and wonderful gift. The magazines are amazing! They describe the technical effects in movies. They also tell about companies looking for artists. I'm writing to those companies to get more information.
>
> The magazines also helped me figure out a topic for my paper—how movie special effects are done. Again, I really appreciate your help.
>
> Many thanks,
>
> Philip

Invitation An invitation asks someone to come to an event such as a concert or a party. Most invitations include the name of the event, the place, the date, the time, and any special information, such as what to wear or bring. Invitations often give a phone number to call to respond.

Writing a Story

The falconer should have listened to the mysterious traveler's warning.

Sometimes a matter of life and death turns out to be a simple misunderstanding. Ernest Hemingway explores the quiet anguish of a boy with a high fever. How is the problem in this story resolved?

A Day's Wait
by Ernest Hemingway

He came into the room to shut the windows while we were still in bed and I saw he looked ill. He was shivering, his face was white, and he walked slowly as though it ached to move.

"What's the matter, Schatz?"

"I've got a headache."

"You better go back to bed."

"No. I'm all right."

"You go to bed. I'll see you when I'm dressed."

But when I came downstairs he was dressed, sitting by the fire, looking a very sick and miserable boy of nine years. When I put my hand on his forehead I knew he had a fever.

"You go up to bed," I said, "you're sick."

"I'm all right," he said.

When the doctor came he took the boy's temperature.

"What is it?" I asked him.

"One hundred and two."

Downstairs, the doctor left three different medicines in different colored capsules with instructions for giving them. One was to bring down the fever, another a purgative, the third to overcome an acid condition. The germs of influenza can only exist in an acid condition, he explained. He seemed to know all about influenza and said there was nothing to worry about if the fever did not go above one hundred and four degrees. This was a light epidemic of flu and there was no danger if you avoided pneumonia.

more ▶

See www.eduplace.com/kids/ for information about Ernest Hemingway.

Back in the room I wrote the boy's temperature down and made a note of the time to give the various capsules.

"Do you want me to read to you?"

"All right. If you want to," said the boy. His face was very white and there were dark areas under his eyes. He lay still in the bed and seemed very detached from what was going on.

I read aloud from Howard Pyle's *Book of Pirates*; but I could see he was not following what I was reading.

"How do you feel, Schatz?" I asked him.

"Just the same, so far," he said.

I sat at the foot of the bed and read to myself while I waited for it to be time to give another capsule. It would have been natural for him to go to sleep, but when I looked up, he was looking at the foot of the bed, looking very strangely.

"Why don't you try to go to sleep? I'll wake you up for the medicine."

"I'd rather stay awake."

After a while he said to me, "You don't have to stay in here with me, Papa, if it bothers you."

"It doesn't bother me."

"No, I mean you don't have to stay if it's going to bother you."

I thought perhaps he was a little lightheaded and after giving him the prescribed capsules at eleven o'clock I went out for a while. It was a bright, cold day, the ground covered with a sleet that had frozen so that it seemed as if all the bare trees, the bushes, the cut brush and all the grass and the bare ground had been varnished with ice. I took the young Irish setter for a little walk up the road and along a frozen creek, but it was difficult to stand or walk on the glassy surface and the red dog slipped and slithered and I fell twice, hard, once dropping my gun and having it slide away over the ice.

We flushed a covey of quail under a high clay bank with over-hanging brush and I killed two as they went out of sight over the top of the bank. Some of the covey lit in trees, but most of them scattered into brush piles and it was necessary to jump on the ice-coated mounds of brush several times before they would flush. Coming out while you were poised unsteadily on the icy, springy brush they made difficult shooting and I killed two, missed five, and started back pleased to have found a covey close to the house and happy there were so many left to find on another day.

At the house they said the boy had refused to let anyone come into the room.

"You can't come in," he said. "You mustn't get what I have."

I went up to him and found him in exactly the position I had left him, white-faced, but with the tops of his cheeks flushed by the fever, staring still, as he had stared, at the foot of the bed.

I took his temperature.

"What is it?"

"Something like a hundred," I said. It was one hundred and two and four tenths.

"It was a hundred and two," he said.

"Who said so?"

"The doctor."

"Your temperature is all right," I said. "It's nothing to worry about."

"I don't worry," he said, "but I can't keep from thinking."

"Don't think," I said. "Just take it easy."

"I'm taking it easy," he said and looked straight ahead. He was evidently holding tight onto himself about something.

"Take this with water."

"Do you think it will do any good?"

"Of course it will."

I sat down and opened the *Pirate* book and commenced to read, but I could see he was not following, so I stopped.

"About what time do you think I'm going to die?" he asked.

"What?"

"About how long will it be before I die?"

"You aren't going to die. What's the matter with you?"

"Oh yes, I am. I heard him say a hundred and two."

"People don't die with a fever of one hundred and two. That's a silly way to talk."

"I know they do. At school in France the boys told me you can't live with forty-four degrees. I've got a hundred and two."

He had been waiting to die all day, ever since nine o'clock in the morning.

"You poor Schatz," I said. "Poor old Schatz. It's like miles and kilometers. You aren't going to die. That's a different thermometer. On that thermometer thirty-seven is normal. On this kind it's ninety-eight."

"Are you sure?"

"Absolutely," I said. "It's like miles and kilometers. You know, like how many kilometers we make when we do seventy miles in the car?"

"Oh," he said.

But his gaze at the foot of the bed relaxed slowly. The hold over himself relaxed too, finally, and the next day it was very slack and he cried very easily at little things that were of no importance.

Reading As a Writer

Think About the Story
- What is the conflict, or problem, in this story? How is it resolved?
- Is this story told in the first-person or third-person point of view? What is the narrator's relationship to the boy?
- Where and in what season does this story take place? What details show this?
- What details show that the boy is struggling not to show his fear?
- What is the climax, or high point, of this story?

Think About Writer's Craft
- What does Schatz say that makes his father think Schatz is lightheaded? What phrase here foreshadows, or hints at, Schatz's misunderstanding?

Think About the Picture
- How does the artist capture the story's mood through the use of light and shadow?

Responding

Write responses to these questions.

- **Personal Response** Think of a time when you struggled to control a powerful feeling. In what ways was your experience similar to Schatz's? In what ways was it different?
- **Critical Thinking** Explain why, on the following day, Schatz "cried very easily at little things that were of no importance." Support your explanation with passages from the story.

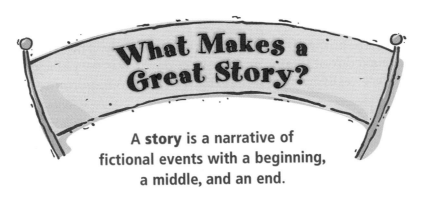

What Makes a Great Story?

A **story** is a narrative of fictional events with a beginning, a middle, and an end.

When you write a story, remember these guidelines.

▶ Create interesting, believable characters.

▶ Establish a setting by giving details that tell where and when the story takes place.

▶ Develop an engaging plot that includes a conflict and a resolution, as well as a climax, or high point.

▶ Tell the events in an order that makes sense, with a clear beginning, middle, and end.

▶ Include details and dialogue to bring characters, setting, and events to life.

▶ Tell your story from a single point of view.

▶ Use voice to create a mood, or emotion, for your story.

▶ Write a beginning that introduces characters and setting.

▶ Write an ending that resolves the conflict and answers any other questions your readers might have.

GRAMMAR CHECK

Remember that a pronoun must agree with its antecedent in person, number, and gender.

WORKING DRAFT

Andrew O'Sullivan wanted to write a story about overcoming fear. Here is his first draft.

Andrew O'Sullivan

Working Draft

At the Ropes Course

Patrick was not looking forward to climbing a wobbly rope ladder up to a forty-foot-high platform. The climb was part of a "ropes course" held at the community center. He had heard of the "high ropes" segment of the course, but he had figured if it meant getting out of a day of school he'd find a way to get through it.

> Could you make your beginning more exciting?

"I'm really nervous about the climb," Patrick told Scott on the bus ride to the community center. After getting up to that platform, he and his classmates were supposed to jump off it. "I don't want to jump either. I hate heights. Are you nervous?"

> Good! These details help me understand the setting.

"No. Not at all," said Scott.

Patrick was surprised. He didn't take Scott to be the kind of person to climb up to a forty-foot-high platform and then jump off it at a moment's notice. Then Scott told him that he wasn't climbing or jumping at all. He didn't even care if the other kids made fun of him. He wasn't going to do it.

> Dialogue would make this exchange more lively.

more

Working Draft

Somebody made fun of them both right then. This kid Ross popped up over the back of the seat and told them that if they didn't climb and jump they were both losers.

> Great! You pick one point of view and stick with it.

Patrick rolled his eyes at the obnoxious Ross and slouched down in his seat. He thought about staying on the ground, but he didn't want to look like a frightened little kid. He'd go up—he had to.

At the center, Patrick kept moving to the end of the line until he couldn't stall any longer. He hooked into a rope. He took a deep, raspy breath and grasped the first rung of the ladder with his already sweaty palms. Hand over hand he climbed. About three quarters of the way up, he made the biggest mistake of his life. He looked down.

> Vivid character details make Patrick believable!

He looked up, locked his eyes in that position, and continued. Even though the platform was now only inches away, he couldn't pry himself away from the ladder. Finally, he climbed up and onto the platform. He peered through a crack at the ground below and hung onto his rope as if there were no tomorrow.

> Isn't this the climax? Can you make it more suspenseful?

The instructor tried to lighten Patrick's mood. "Come on, Patrick, relax. The hardest part is over. It's downhill from this point on."

Patrick wasn't listening. Now he had to jump. He thought about closing his eyes and just sort of falling. Then what would the other kids think? He gathered up his courage and jumped—a full jump, not just falling off. When his feet touched the ground, he realized he had made it through alive.

Is this ending enough? What happens to Patrick?

Reading As a Writer

● What comments and questions did Joe have about this story? What revisions might Andrew make?

● What conflict, or problem, does Patrick face? How is it resolved?

● What details might Andrew add to make the climax, or high point, of his story more suspenseful?

FINAL COPY

Andrew revised his story after discussing it with a classmate. Read his final version to see how he improved it.

The Unreachable Platform
by Andrew O'Sullivan

Patrick grasped the first rung of the rope ladder. By no means was he looking forward to this part of the course. He had a fear of heights, and climbing a wobbly ladder up to a forty-foot-high platform while thinking to himself, "I am going to die RIGHT NOW," wasn't exactly on his "Most Fun Things to Do" list. The instructors had explained three times that the ropes could hold up to 6,000 pounds of weight and that as long as you were clipped to the top beam there was no way you could fall. Still, Patrick felt his stomach stick in his windpipe as he started to climb.

The climb was part of a "ropes course" held at the community center. He had heard of the "high ropes" segment of the course, but he had figured if it meant getting out of a day of school he'd find a way to get through it.

"I'm really nervous about the climb," Patrick told Scott on the bus ride to the community center. After getting up to that platform, he and his classmates were supposed to jump off it. "I don't want to jump either. I hate heights. Are you nervous?"

"No. Not at all," said Scott.

It's a flashback! You start with his climb and then go back in time.

Your word choice really helps to set the mood.

Patrick was surprised. "Really? I figured you'd be more scared than I am."

"I'm not climbing," said Scott. "I'm staying on the ground."

"Don't you know that kids will make fun of you?" Patrick asked.

"I really don't care," Scott replied. "Let them laugh. I'll be laughing when they're jumping off the top of that platform."

Dialogue makes this scene much more vivid.

"I can't believe you two are afraid of this thing," said Ross, who popped up over the back of the seat. "The only people not climbing and jumping are losers. I guess that's what you two are."

Patrick rolled his eyes at the obnoxious Ross and slouched down in his seat. He thought about staying on the ground, but he didn't want to look like a frightened little kid. He'd go up— he had to.

At the center, Patrick kept moving to the end of the line until he couldn't stall any longer. He hooked into a rope that didn't look thick enough to hold a large cat, let alone a hundred-pound kid. He took a deep, raspy breath and grasped the first rung of the ladder with his already sweaty palms. The rungs above him looked like oversized staples. Hand over hand he climbed.

more

These new details put me at the edge of my seat!

Well, actually it was slower than that, more like hand .... over hand .... over hand. About three quarters of the way up, he made the biggest mistake of his life. He looked down.

This exaggeration expresses well what Patrick is feeling.

He saw the ground, roughly forty miles away. His heart jumped, and so did he. Patrick hung in mid-air by his rope for a few seconds and then grabbed back onto the ladder, clutching it to him. He looked up, locked his eyes in that position, and continued. Even though the platform was now only inches away, he couldn't pry himself away from the ladder. Finally, he climbed up and onto the platform. He peered through a crack at the ground below, where his classmates looked like tiny figurines, and hung onto his rope as if there were no tomorrow.

The details you've added show how difficult this problem is for Patrick.

The instructor tried to lighten Patrick's mood. "Come on, Patrick, relax. The hardest part is over. It's downhill from this point on."

It was no use. Patrick could hardly hear what the instructor was saying. The time that he had dreaded had come. He had to jump, held only by a rope, from a forty-foot platform. He thought about closing his eyes and just sort of falling. Then what would the other kids think? He gathered up his courage and jumped—a full jump, not just falling off. When his feet touched the ground, he realized he had made it through alive.

On the way home Patrick sat next to Scott. Hardly anyone had made fun of Scott for staying on the ground. Thinking about this, Patrick decided that he was glad he had jumped but impressed with Scott for refusing to jump. He made up his mind then and there that he would never again let someone's lame insult force him into doing something.

You tie the story together by showing how Patrick resolves his problem.

Reading As a Writer

- How did Andrew respond to Joe's questions?
- What details did Andrew add to make the climax suspenseful?
- What did Andrew add to the end of the story to show how the conflict was resolved?

See www.eduplace.com/kids/hme/ for more examples of student writing.

Student Model   659

Write a Story

▶ Start Thinking

 Make a writing folder for your story. Copy the questions in bold type, and put the paper in your folder. Write your answers as you think about and choose your topic.

- **Who will be my audience?** Will I write this story for adults? my classmates? other kids I have never met?
- **What will be my purpose?** Do I want to amuse my audience? excite them with an adventure? teach them a lesson about life?
- **How will I publish or share my story?** Will I post it on an Internet site that publishes student writing? record a dramatic presentation?

▶ Choose Your Story Idea

❶ List five story ideas. Use a chart like the one Andrew used below.

Who and Where?	What Could Happen?
a boy in a school like mine	struggles against fear

❷ Talk with a partner about each story idea.

- Which idea is most interesting? Why?
- Is any idea too big? Look at how Andrew narrowed his story to one part of his original idea.

struggles against fear

- doesn't want to climb and jump at the ropes course
- worries about some bigger kids in the park
- nervous about a party

HELP ? **Need an Idea?**

Try one of these.
- learning to like an enemy
- surviving a flood
- rescuing an injured animal

See page 672 for more ideas.

❸ Choose the idea you will write about. Ask these questions.

- Can I think of specific details about people, places, and events?
- Will I enjoy writing about it? Will others enjoy reading it?

► Explore Your Characters and Setting

❶ List details about your characters—the people or animals in your story. Use the questions below.

Think About . . .	Ask Yourself . . .
Appearance	Is this character a hulk of a person or someone twiglike?
Thoughts or feelings	Does this character love a crowd? worry about making friends? brood over things people say?
Actions	Does this character shout at strangers? spend all weekend on the phone? ask for extra homework?
Interests	Does this character square dance? carve wooden sculptures? play football?

❷ Develop the setting for your story. List specific details about where and when the story happens. Use the questions below.

Think About . . .	Ask Yourself . . .
Place	Does this story happen in a forest? on a farm? at the mall? on a baseball diamond?
Time	Does this story take place during the 1800s? last winter? a hundred years from now?

HELP

? Stuck for Details?

If you can't think of specific details about character and setting, try another topic.

Characters	Setting
Patrick—afraid of heights, worries about what other kids think	school bus
	community center
Scott—also afraid of heights, doesn't care what people think	ladder and platform
Ross—makes fun of "losers"	

▲ **Part of Andrew's list**

See page 16 for more exploring ideas.

Focus Skill

Developing Plot

What Is Plot?

A plot is a series of fictional events that develop and resolve a conflict.

Create a conflict, or problem, that your main characters must solve. Introduce the conflict at the beginning of the story.

Kinds of Conflicts	
Person against person	• A star athlete is jealous of an honor student. • Two friends quarrel when one makes a new friend.
Person against nature	• A drought threatens a ranch family's livestock. • Family members are stranded in their car during a snowstorm.
Person against self	• A girl struggles to control her temper. • A talented swimmer worries about beating his older brother.

Build to a climax. Show your characters dealing with the conflict, but add obstacles as the story rises to its high point. Put your climax near or after the middle of your story.

Resolve the conflict. Make the solution believable. Tie up the plot's loose ends, and end your story soon after the resolution.

Plot Diagram: "A Day's Wait"

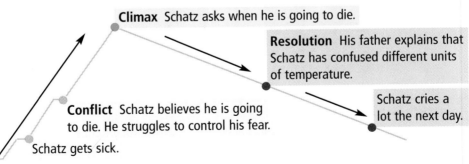

Climax Schatz asks when he is going to die.

Resolution His father explains that Schatz has confused different units of temperature.

Schatz cries a lot the next day.

Conflict Schatz believes he is going to die. He struggles to control his fear.

Schatz gets sick.

Think and Discuss

● Discuss one of the examples in the Kinds of Conflicts chart. Tell more about the problem. How might the character or characters resolve it?

Focus Skill

What Makes a Strong Plot?

A strong plot includes a conflict your readers want to see resolved. A weak plot has a weak conflict or no conflict at all.

Weak Plot	Strong Plot
Lisa brings her pet snake to school. She shows it to her classmates. She brings the snake back home.	On a dare, Lisa lets her pet snake out of its box at school, but within a matter of minutes the snake disappears. Lisa finds it wrapped around a hanging light in the cafeteria. Everyone panics. Her science teacher helps her set up a stepladder and get the snake down.

Here are some strategies for planning a strong plot.

Create suspense. Reveal information gradually. Make your readers wonder whether your characters will be able to solve the conflict.

Use foreshadowing. Keep your readers actively engaged by foreshadowing— dropping hints about what will happen later in the story.

Try a flashback. You don't have to tell your entire story in chronological, or time, order. You can start at the middle or at the end. Then go back to previous events and tell the rest of the story in chronological order.

Think and Discuss

● Reread the examples of plot above. What makes the strong plot better?

▶ Explore and Plan Your Story

❶ **Create** a story map. Brainstorm details to make a strong plot.

- Explore the conflict. What obstacles can you add? How can you build suspense?
- Explore the climax. What will be your story's high point?
- Explore the resolution. How will your characters solve the problem? How will the story end?

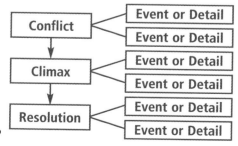

Conflict — Event or Detail / Event or Detail

Climax — Event or Detail / Event or Detail

Resolution — Event or Detail / Event or Detail

❷ **Number** details and events in the order you will write about them.

See www.eduplace.com/kids/hme/ for more graphic organizers.   Prewriting   **663**

Dialogue

Dialogue can help make characters and events seem real.

Show actions. You can tell your readers about an event. You can also let them listen in as characters talk about events.

Telling, Without Dialogue	Showing, with Dialogue
The monster came out of the cave. The two scientists were horrified.	"Ling!" yelled Dr. Briarly frantically. "The creature woke up! It's coming this way!" "Oh no! It sees us!" croaked Dr. Ling.

> **GRAMMAR TIP** Adverbs show <u>how</u> someone speaks.

Show personality and feelings. Dialogue can show what characters are like and how they think or feel.

> Use dialogue like spice—to add variety and life to your story. Don't overload your story with long conversations.

Telling, without dialogue	Kim was disappointed and annoyed that her brother hadn't come. Her friend Sandy tried to calm her, but Kim wouldn't listen.
Showing, with dialogue	"I can't believe he didn't come!" Kim cried. "He never comes to anything I do." "Don't be mad," Sandy said. "Of course I'm mad. I'm ripped! He can't do this to me."

> **GRAMMAR TIP** Begin a new paragraph of dialogue each time the speaker changes.

Think and Discuss

- What makes the passage that shows actions with dialogue interesting?
- Tell more about what happens by adding more dialogue to the conversation between Kim and Sandy.

▶ Draft Some Dialogue

Write dialogue between two of your characters about an important event in your story. Show their personalities and their feelings.

Focus Skill

Narrating Your Story

Choosing a Point of View

Decide what kind of narrator, or storyteller, you will use.

First-Person Point of View One of the characters narrates the story. For example, "A Day's Wait" is told by Schatz's father.

Limited Third-Person Point of View The narrator describes what only one character sees, feels, and thinks. Andrew told his story from this point of view.

Omniscient Third-Person Point of View The narrator knows everything about every character. This narrator can describe what any character in the story sees, feels, and thinks.

Pick one point of view and stick with it.

Here is the same event narrated from two different points of view.

Limited Third-Person	Omniscient Third-Person
The phone rang and woke Tara up. Then the ringing stopped. Her father must have answered it. She turned on her light and sat up in bed. She wondered whether someone was hurt. Then she heard her father's footsteps. "Is everything all right, Dad?" she called. He looked in the door. "It was just Uncle Don." She should have known. Uncle Don often forgot that normal people sleep at night.	The phone rang and woke Tara up. Then it woke up her father. He knew it would be his brother, Donald, who often forgot that normal people sleep at night. Tara turned on her light and sat up in bed. She wondered whether someone was hurt. Her father saw her light and came to check on her. He was surprised to hear her calling to him before he even looked in the door. "Is everything all right, Dad?" "It was just Uncle Don."

Try It Out

● Choose a topic and write several sentences about it in the first person. Exchange papers with a partner and rewrite the sentences in the third person. Use a limited or an omniscient point of view.

Voice and Mood

Your voice is the way you sound when you write. Your story's narrative voice is the way your narrator sounds. It creates your story's mood, or emotional effect.

Decide how you want your story to sound. Will it be funny, frightening, sad, regretful?

Create the feeling you want. Use exact words. Build different kinds of sentences—long or short, simple or complex.

Set the mood at the beginning of your story. These two beginnings describe the same scene but create different moods.

First Mood	Second Mood
Hearing a crowd, Meredith dashed to her window and discovered the square below filled with people. What could be happening? Was this the start of a parade? The mayor's face appeared in a window across the street, and the crowd gave a great whoop of joy. "I wish they were looking for me," Meredith said to her sister. "Wouldn't it be fun to be famous?"	In the square below, a mob had gathered. Hearing their yelling, Meredith crept to the window. What were they doing? Was this the start of a riot? The mayor's house was across the street. In a window, curtains moved. A pale face appeared briefly. The mob bellowed in fury. "I'm glad they're not looking for me," Meredith said to her sister. "They must be so frightened over there."

Think and Discuss Compare the moods in the passages above.

- Which words, phrases, and sentences establish each mood?

▶ Draft Your Story

HELP

 Ways to Begin

❶ **Choose** a point of view for your story.

❷ **Draft** two possible beginnings, each with a different mood. Which works better?

❸ **Draft** the rest of your story. Follow your story map. Use the dialogue you drafted if it still works. Include an ending that resolves the conflict and wraps up the plot.

- Describe the setting.
- Use dialogue.
- Try a flashback.
- Describe an action.

Evaluating Your Story

▶ Reread your story. What do you need to do to make it better? Use this rubric to help you decide. Write the sentences that describe your narrative.

Loud and Clear!

- ☑ The beginning introduces my characters and setting.
- ☑ Details show when and where the story takes place.
- ☑ My characters seem real. Dialogue shows how they think, act, and feel.
- ☑ The plot has a conflict, a climax, and a resolution.
- ☑ I chose one point of view and stayed with it.
- ☑ My language creates a definite mood that suits my story.
- ☑ My ending resolves the conflict in a satisfying way.
- ☑ *There are very few mistakes in grammar, spelling, or punctuation.*

Sounding Stronger

- ☐ I could help my readers by telling more at the beginning.
- ☐ Specific details would help make the setting clear.
- ☐ More dialogue would show how my characters think and feel.
- ☐ Some events stray from the conflict and the resolution.
- ☐ I change point of view once or twice.
- ☐ My voice is not strong, and so the mood is not clear.
- ☐ My ending resolves the conflict but is not believable.
- ☐ *Mistakes sometimes make the story hard to read.*

Turn Up Volume

- ☐ The beginning is confusing.
- ☐ My story has no clear setting.
- ☐ The characters don't seem real. There isn't any dialogue.
- ☐ What's the conflict? Many events are unnecessary.
- ☐ My point of view wanders. Who's narrating the story?
- ☐ The story is flat and has no mood.
- ☐ My ending doesn't resolve the conflict.
- ☐ *Many mistakes make the story very difficult to follow.*

See www.eduplace.com/kids/hme/ to interact with this rubric.

▶ Revise Your Story

❶ Revise your story. Use the list of sentences you wrote from the rubric. Work on the parts that you described with sentences from "Sounding Stronger" and "Turn Up the Volume."

❷ Have a writing conference.

When You're the Writer Read your story aloud to a partner. Ask questions about any problems. Take notes.

When You're the Listener Say at least two things you like about the story. Ask questions about any parts that are unclear. Use the chart below for help.

HELP ? Paragraphing Tip

- Look for paragraphs that tell about too many events.
- Start a new paragraph for each new event.
- Use transitional words or phrases when necessary.

What should I say?

The Writing Conference

If you're thinking . . .	You could say . . .
The beginning is a little dull.	How about starting with a bold action? some dialogue?
I can't picture the setting.	Tell me more about where and when this is happening.
Which character is the main character?	Which character has the problem? How does he or she try to deal with it?
What's this story about?	What is the conflict? How is it resolved?
Some information must be missing.	Tell me more about what happens. Are the events in the right order?
Why is this part here at all?	Does _____ move your plot forward? Do you need it to tell the story?
The ending seems really abrupt.	Tell me more about the resolution. What happens to the characters?

❸ Make more revisions to your story. Use your conference notes and the Revising Strategies on the next page.

Tech Tip
Use the Replace function to change the name of a character or the name of a place throughout your story.

Revising Strategies

Elaborating: Word Choice Choosing exact nouns, verbs, adjectives, and adverbs will make your writing clearer.

Without Exact Words	With Exact Words
The **woman looked** at Ron because he wasn't **doing** anything.	The librarian stared at Ron suspiciously because he wasn't reading anything.

▶ Find at least three places in your story where you can use more exact words.

📖 Use the Thesaurus Plus on page H96.

Elaborating: Details Use adverbs and prepositional phrases to add details. Show your readers exactly what is happening in your story.

Few Details	Elaborated with Details
He jogged. The wind blew. "I have to get back," he thought.	He jogged along the deserted beach in a business suit and leather shoes. The wind blew fiercely. "I have to get back to my family," he thought anxiously.

▶ Find at least three places in your story where you can add details using adverbs or prepositional phrases.

GRAMMAR LINK ▶ *See also page 204 and page 353.*

Sentence Fluency Don't overload sentences with clauses and phrases. Break stringy sentences into shorter ones of varying lengths.

Stringy Sentences	Smooth Sentences
Marlene turned on her flashlight, which she had bought just yesterday for six dollars, even though that six dollars was the last of her money, because she knew a flashlight would come in handy, and now it had.	Marlene turned on her flashlight. She had bought it just yesterday for six dollars, even though that six dollars was the last of her money. She knew a flashlight would come in handy, and now it had.

▶ Rewrite any sentences that have too many clauses and phrases.

GRAMMAR LINK ▶ *See also page 63.*

▶ Proofread Your Story

Proofread your story, using the Proofreading Checklist and the Grammar and Spelling Connections. Proofread for one skill at a time. Use a class dictionary to check spellings.

Proofreading Checklist

Did I

✔ indent all paragraphs?

✔ begin and end each sentence correctly?

✔ capitalize proper nouns?

✔ use pronouns correctly with antecedents?

✔ punctuate correctly with quotation marks?

✔ use correct verb forms?

✔ correct any spelling errors?

📖 Use the Guide to Capitalization, Punctuation, and Usage on page H64.

Proofreading Marks

¶	Indent
∧	Add
ℒ	Delete
≡	Capital letter
/	Small letter
ᵛ᷾᷾ᵛ	Add quotes
∧	Add comma
⊙	Add period
∿	Transpose

HELP ?

Proofreading Tip

Read your paper aloud to a friend. You may notice mistakes when you hear them.

Grammar and Spelling Connections

Using Pronouns Correctly with Antecedents A pronoun must agree with its antecedent in person, number, and gender.

> Jonelle was new to the game, but Coach Tom told her she was a natural.

GRAMMAR LINK *See page 302.*

Punctuating Dialogue Put a quotation mark around a speaker's exact words. Put end punctuation inside the quotation marks.

> "It's Mike," yelled my sister, running to the door. "I'll get it!"

GRAMMAR LINK *See page 256.*

Spelling Words with *ei* or *ie* Some words do not follow the rule "Use *i* before *e* except after *c* or in words with the |ā| sound, as in *neighbor* or *weigh*."

Follows the rule	yield, receipt, freight, reign
Exception to the rule	species, foreign, neither, seize

📖 See the Spelling Guide on page H80.

 670 **Unit 14:** Story   See www.eduplace.com/kids/hme/ for proofreading practice.

▶ Publish Your Story

❶ Make a neat final copy of your story. Be sure you fixed all your mistakes.

❷ Title your story. Make your audience curious, but don't tell them too much. "The Final Seconds" is a better title than "Winning in the Final Seconds."

GRAMMAR TIP ▶ *Capitalize the first, the last, and each important word in a title.*

❸ Publish or share your story. Consider your audience and purpose.

Tips for Tape-Recording Your Story

- Choose a quiet place where the tape recorder won't pick up unwanted noises.
- Ask a friend to help with sound effects. Practice with different objects. Choose music if it seems right to you.
- Rehearse your reading with sound effects before recording.
- Read slowly and clearly. Use a high or low voice to show different emotions.

HELP ? See page 680 for tips.

Ideas for Sharing
Write It Down
- Send your story to a magazine or Internet site that publishes student writing.

Talk It Up
- Tape-record a dramatic presentation of your story. Add sound effects and music.

Show It Off
- Illustrate your story with pictures of characters or key events.
- Film your story as a movie. Ask friends to play different characters.

▶ Reflect

Write about your writing experience. Use these questions as a guide.

- What was difficult about writing a story? What was easy?
- What is your favorite part of your story?
- What could you improve the next time?
- How does this paper compare with others you have written?

Writing Prompts

Use these prompts as ideas for stories or to practice for a test. Decide who your audience will be, and write your story in a way that they will understand and enjoy.

1 While an astronaut travels in space, the planet Earth changes drastically. Write a story about the astronaut's return to the world she once knew.

2 Two teenagers are hiking in the woods. It is nearly dark. They hear a screeching sound, a loud crack, and a strange laugh. What happens next?

3 Write a story that begins with the sentence *When I opened my eyes, I didn't know where I was.* Where is your character? How did he or she get there?

4 Two athletes train for a championship game. In what ways are they alike? different? What are their feelings about each other? about the game? Write a story about them that includes a conflict.

Writing Across the Curriculum

5 **FINE ART**
Thunder, lightning, and heavy rains arrive suddenly in the middle of a day. Who is caught in the storm? What problems does the storm cause? Write a story about how three characters resolve these problems.

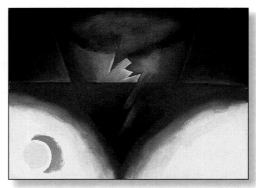

Anonymous Gift, 1981
The Metropolitan Museum of Art

A Storm, by Georgia O'Keeffe

Test Practice

This prompt to write a story is like ones you might find on a writing test. Read the prompt.

> While an **astronaut** travels in space, the planet **Earth changes drastically**. Write a story about the astronaut's **return to the world she once knew**.

Here are some strategies to help you do a good job responding to a prompt like this one.

Remember, a story is a narrative of fictional events with a beginning, a middle, and an end.

1 Look for clue words that tell what to write about. What are the clue words in the prompt above?

2 Choose a story topic that fits the clue words.

Clue Words	My Topic
astronaut, Earth changes drastically, return to the world she once knew	I will tell a story about an astronaut who returns to Earth and discovers that everyone speaks a strange language.

3 Plan your writing. Use a story map to organize your plot.

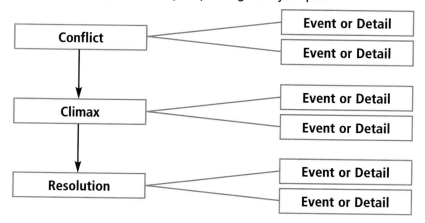

4 You will get a good score if you remember what kind of essay sounds loud and clear in the rubric on page 667.

See www.eduplace.com/kids/hme/ for more graphic organizers. Test Practice **673**

Writing a Play

A **play** is a story that is performed by actors before an audience. The playwright tells the story through the characters' dialogue and actions. Read this play to yourself or aloud with classmates.

Vocal Discord

Characters —
NARRATOR
DARREN, a high school senior
MR. BELLO, a teacher
MS. GREENISH, a teacher
CHORUS: JAKE, Darren's best friend
GRACE, Darren's girlfriend
VOICES, fellow students, male and female

Props — Pen and paper

Setting ——→ *(A high school classroom after school)*

(MR. BELLO sits behind his classroom desk, arms crossed, and DARREN stands facing him. The CHORUS stands on the opposite side of the stage. They all wear the same blank expression mask.) — Stage directions

NARRATOR: *(Crosses stage, speaking, and exits as he or she completes lines)* A high school senior named Darren wants so much to be who he isn't that he can't see how much he really is. Can we forgive him for thinking he should be better, smarter, richer, cooler, taller, faster . . . ? He has just finished singing, without permission, his latest composition over the school P.A. system.

CHORUS: (ALL) Darren! You hate the life you lead! Look at you. Darren, Darren, what do you need?

MR. BELLO: Darren, how could you do this?

DARREN: *(Uncomfortable, staring at the floor)* I know. I don't know what to do. If I just had . . . If I could just . . . If I were . . . . *(Voice trails off)*

MR. BELLO: If I were you, I'd—ugh. My dad used to say that to me. Never mind. You're fine, Darren, but . . .

Dialogue

DARREN: I know. It's my fault. I shouldn't have done it, and I can't sing. I really can't. I can't do anything.

MR. BELLO: Well, you just can't sing for beans, that's for sure.

CHORUS: (VOICES) Hey Darren, make yourself famous! . . . Get out there! Knock 'em dead! . . . You look good . . . They're gonna love you . . . Big bucks if you make it . . . Big bucks, buddy.

CHORUS: (GRACE) *(Reaching out to DARREN)* I've always wanted to go out with a musician.

CHORUS: (VOICES) *(Reaching out to DARREN, to copy GRACE)* Me, too. A musician, oooooooo.

MR. BELLO: *(Stands up as he speaks)* So many kids here at the school wish they were in a band. They watch TV and think, if I look like that or get into a band like that, my problems will be solved.

DARREN: What should I do?

CHORUS: (JAKE) So Darren, can you get me backstage?

MR. BELLO: *(Writes on a piece of paper and hands it to DARREN; MS. GREENISH enters)* Ms. Greenish, I'm glad you're here. We've got some serious business going on—with this one. *(Nods toward DARREN)*

MS. GREENISH: Oh boy, is that true. You have got one big serious problem. Plus, I'd say you sing like a screaming machine long out of gas.

DARREN: I made a mistake . . .

MS. GREENISH: So how do you plan to fix it?

DARREN: I can't do anything. What can I do?

CHORUS: (ALL) *(Parroting DARREN)* What can I do? What should I do? What can I do? What should I do?

CHORUS: (JAKE) Can you lend me a few bucks? Pay you back.

MS. GREENISH: So what does your friend Grace have to do with this?

DARREN: *(Looks toward GRACE in the chorus)* It's not her fault.

more ▶

MR. BELLO: Well, where'd you get the idea you can sing? You sure made it sound hard. I may not sleep tonight.

MS. GREENISH: *(To MR. BELLO)* We almost had a national emergency. Somebody called 911. Said, what's that noise?

DARREN: *(Obviously disgusted with the whole thing)* Okay. Okay.

CHORUS: (MALES) *(Singing, clapping)* Hey, Darren, you be smart, *don't* be a fool. Sing. Don't sing . . .

CHORUS: (FEMALES) *(Singing, clapping)* Hey Darren, hey Darren, you can play it cool. Sing. Don't sing . . .

DARREN: *(Waves them off)* Oh, shut up. *(Pause)* Except you, Grace. *(He looks at the paper* MR. BELLO *gave him.)* Lessons from you? You sing? You?

MR. BELLO *sings. (CHORUS claps hands over ears in pain.)*

NARRATOR: *(Recrosses stage, speaking to audience while* MR. BELLO *sings; the recorded sound of* DARREN *singing increases in volume, drowning out* MR. BELLO*)* Can Darren sing, ladies and gentlemen? Let's hear it. Do you want Darren to sing? Yes? Sing it, Darren! Sing!

BLACKOUT

Reading As a Writer

- The list of **characters** at the beginning of a play sometimes includes a brief description of them. *Who is in the chorus?*

- The **props** are items the characters will use in the play. *How are the props used in this play?*

- The **setting** tells the specific place and time of the action. *Where and when is the play set?*

- The **stage directions** tell, in parentheses, what the characters are doing or how they are speaking. *How are the characters on the stage positioned when the scene opens?*

- The **dialogue** is the conversation among characters that moves the story along and reveals their feelings. *What do you learn about Darren from his dialogue?*

How to Write a Play

1. **Think** of a story idea for a short play that would interest your intended audience. You will need characters who do a lot of talking. Include only a few characters and one or two settings.

   Use a T-chart to help you list details about your characters. Look at the sample T-chart below for Darren, Mr. Bello, and Chorus.

Need an Idea?
- Rewrite one of your own stories as a play.
- Write about a funny situation or a daydream.
- Write about two or more characters in competition for something.

Darren	Mr. Bello	Chorus
• longs to sing • has an awful voice • makes mistakes • is influenced by others	• tough critic • teases, but is sympathetic • also longs to sing	• eggs Darren on • taunts Darren

2. **Plan** your play. Using a story map like the one below will help you organize details about the setting, characters, and plot.

Character	Setting	Plot
		Beginning Middle End

3. **Draft** your play.
   - List your characters and describe the setting.
   - Write stage directions telling what the characters should do as the play begins.
   - Then write the rest of the play, using dialogue and stage directions. The action that takes place in a play is divided into scenes, just as a novel is divided into chapters.
   - If the action of your play moves from one setting to another or if time passes, begin a new scene. At the beginning of the new scene, write a setting description and stage directions. Then continue writing dialogue.
   - End your play in a way that resolves the main conflict. Does the central character get what he or she wants? How does this affect the characters in the play? When you have finished, write *CURTAIN* or *BLACKOUT*.

more ▶

4 **Revise** your play. Read your play to yourself or with classmates and ask yourself these questions:

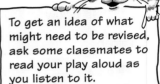

- Does my play include a title, list of characters, prop list, and brief description of the setting?
- Is the plot clear? Is there dialogue that seems unnecessary? Will the reader understand the characters' motivations?
- Does the dialogue sound realistic? Do I show the characters' thoughts and emotions through dialogue instead of relying on stage directions?
- Are stage directions used effectively? Will the actors know when to enter and exit the stage?
- Is the central conflict resolved by the end of the play?

5 **Conduct** a writing conference. Ask a friend or teacher to read over your play and give an opinion on what is clear and what can be improved.

Tech Tip
To indent dialogue under the first line, drag the bottom indent marker on the horizontal ruler to the location you want.

To get an idea of what might need to be revised, ask some classmates to read your play aloud as you listen to it.

The Writing Conference

If you're thinking . . .	**You could ask . . .**
This part of the play doesn't make any sense.	**Could you clarify this part for me?**
There isn't enough information about this character.	**Could you add some dialogue or action to explain more about this character? Why does he or she feel so bad?**
The ending of the play doesn't resolve the main conflict.	**Can you add a clearer resolution to the end of the play?**

6 **Proofread** your play. Did you enclose stage directions in parentheses and spell characters' names in capital letters? Is the dialogue punctuated correctly? Use a dictionary to check your spelling.

7 **Perform** your play for an audience.

- Invite guests to a readers' theater, or staged reading. This means the dialogue does not have to be memorized, but the performers should read their lines with feeling.
- Videotape your play. Consider asking the actors to put together simple costumes.
- Tape-record your play. Make sure someone reads the stage directions if the audience will be confused without them. Consider adding sound effects.
- Put together a class book of plays.

HELP ? See pages 680–681 for dramatizing tips.

Dramatizing

In a movie or a play, an actor dramatizes, or acts out, a character's role to bring the character to life. When dramatizing a story, a storyteller needs to think about how to change his or her voice to sound like different characters.

Using Your Speaking Voice

Actors and storytellers need to have expressive, flexible voices. It takes a lot of training for actors to get the control needed to make their voices different for each dramatic role. With little or no training, what can you do to prepare for a dramatic presentation? Think about each of the following points.

Pacing, or rate	Pacing, or rate, is the speed at which you speak. For example, an actor may slow down to stress an important point. At what pace would you need to speak to show excitement or boredom in a dramatic presentation?
Enunciation	Enunciation, or speaking clearly, is key to the listener's understanding of the actor's words. Try not to let phrases and words blend together. Saying words clearly and crisply may sound silly in everyday conversation, but in a performance it allows the audience to follow the plot.
Projection	Projection is a combination of volume and clarity. Projection allows everyone to hear and understand your words. Look at the performance space. Are there outside noises that may distract the audience? You may need to amplify your voice with a microphone or move around your audience as you speak.
Pitch	Pitch is how high or how low your voice sounds. Changes in pitch may be used to express a mood change. For example, if your character were happy about some good news, you could raise the pitch of your voice and increase the rate of speech.
Tone	Tone, or manner of expression, can show a character's mood or emotion. How does your tone of voice change when your emotion changes? With a change in tone, an actor can relate feelings of relief, anger, or excitement.

Use these guidelines to help you dramatize a story, a poem, a play, or a personal experience.

Guidelines for Dramatizing

1. Put yourself in your character's shoes. Is your character angry, proud, or confident? Decide why your character would act in a certain way.
2. Use your speaking voice. Change the volume, rate, pitch, and tone of your voice to express your character's feelings.
3. Use facial expressions. For example, closing your eyes while speaking could show deep thought or impatience.
4. Use gestures. A fist, a pointed finger, and an open hand all give different signals.
5. Enunciate. Be sure all of your audience can hear and understand you, even when your character speaks softly.
6. Practice reading your lines. You may want to practice with a partner or in front of a mirror to improve your facial expressions and gestures.

Apply It

Choose a speech, or part of a story or play, to dramatize. Then follow the Guidelines for Dramatizing as you practice it. Perform for a small group or the class.

- What was your character's mood?
- In what ways did you change your voice to express the meaning of different words?
- Was the audience engaged? Were they able to understand and hear your words?

 HELP ? **Stuck for an Idea?**

Try one of the following:
- a monologue from a play or story
- a scene from a play
- a poem that tells a story
- a personal narrative
- a student-written script based on a book, a short story, or a real-life event

Comparing Stories in Print and on Film

When filmmakers make movies from printed stories, they must decide how to interpret the stories for the big screen. Because print and film are different forms of media, movies often bear little resemblance to the original written stories. The chart below lists some of the differences between stories in print and on film.

Stories in Print	Stories on Film
Authorship Authors decide how to tell their stories, sometimes with the advice of editors. Authors use the written word to convey ideas about the characters, setting, plot, dialogue, and action.	**Authorship** Directors, producers, screenwriters, special-effects people, costumers, and actors influence how a story will be told. They may use sets, cameras, music, computers, and props to tell the story.
Audience • Readers form mental pictures of the characters, setting, and mood by using the author's words and their own imaginations. • Readers can carry books with them. They can read slowly or quickly, rereading or skipping parts.	**Audience** • Viewers see the characters and setting on the screen. Changing images, recorded dialogue, music, and special effects help the story unfold and set the mood. • Viewers cannot change the rate at which the story is told.
Length A written story may be told in several pages or several thousand pages.	**Length** Due to audience expectations, movies usually run about two hours.
Cost Books, magazines, plays, and newspapers are expensive to print, but they still cost much less to produce than most films.	**Cost** Producing movies costs thousands, even millions of dollars. Salaries for actors and staff, costumes, special effects, music, and much more add up to big budgets.

Think About It

A movie is only one interpretation of a story, so you may find that more than one movie has been based on the same story. Different filmmakers bring new ideas, technology, and special effects to a story.

Use these guidelines to compare a story in print to a story in a movie.

Guidelines for Evaluating a Movie Based on a Book

① Plot
- Were any scenes dropped, added, or changed?
- How do these changes affect the story? Why do you think they were made?

② Characters
- Were characters added, dropped, or changed?
- Were any characters in the book combined to make one character in the movie?
- How do these changes affect the story? Why do you think these changes were made? What else could the filmmakers have done?

③ Setting, Mood, and Costumes
- Are the movie's setting and costumes the same as that of the printed story? How do these affect the mood of the movie?

④ Technical Features
- What do camera angles, special effects, music, and lighting do to create the atmosphere of the movie?

Apply It

Watch the movie version of a story you have read. Use the guidelines above and take notes while you watch. Next, write one scene for your own film version of the story. Then answer these questions.

- Which version did you prefer—the book or the movie? Why?
- Was the filmmaker's interpretation "true" to the written story? Why or why not?
- What was missing from the movie that you included in your scene?

Books with Movie Versions
- Jane Eyre
- Great Expectations
- Man in the Iron Mask
- The Turn of the Screw
- The Diary of Anne Frank

3

Tools and Tips

What You Will Find in This Part:

Giving and Following Directions

Directions, or instructions, tell listeners how to do or how to make something. These guidelines will help you give good directions.

Guidelines for Giving Directions

1. Consider your audience. Use words a child younger than you is able to understand. Learn whether or not the person speaks English fluently or has a hearing problem.
2. Make the purpose of the directions clear.
3. Speak slowly so that your directions can be understood.
4. Give the directions in the correct order, step by step. Use words that signal this order, such as *first, second, next, then, now,* and *finally.*
5. Include all necessary details, such as materials, sizes, and amounts.
6. Use gestures, such as pointing, to support the directions, if appropriate.

It is also important to be able to understand directions when they are given to you. The following guidelines will help you to follow directions.

Guidelines for Following Directions

1. Listen for each step. Try to picture what to do.
2. Listen for order words, such as *first, next, after, when,* and *finally.*
3. Ask questions if any part of the directions is not absolutely clear.
4. Repeat the steps out loud so that the person giving the directions can correct any misunderstanding.

Apply It

Tell a classmate how to perform a skill. Have the classmate actually follow your directions. Adjust the directions until the classmate is successful. Then switch roles.

Resolving Problems

In the cartoon above, why did the discussion turn into an argument? What could the boy and girl have done to resolve the problem calmly?

Think about what pushes your anger button during a disagreement. If you follow the tips and guidelines here, you may find that instead of quarrels, you can resolve problems and have productive discussions.

Avoiding an Argument You don't have to get into an argument every time you disagree with someone. Check out a fact before you argue. Ask yourself if the disagreement really matters, and change the subject, if necessary. Don't take sides in other people's quarrels.

When you disagree with someone, choose your words carefully. Use words that show you are open-minded and willing to listen to another point of view.

Language to Use During a Discussion	Language to Avoid During a Discussion
Perhaps . . .	You're wrong!
I wonder if . . .	That's stupid.
May I suggest . . .	I'm positive . . .
Let's consider . . .	There's no way . . .
It occurs to me . . .	Definitely not!
I believe . . .	Forget it!
That's true, but . . .	That's impossible.

more ▶

Resolving Problems *continued*

Settling an Argument If an argument does begin, there doesn't always have to be a "winner" for it to be settled. You and the other person can reach a **compromise**, a settlement in which each of you gives up some of your ideas or wishes. If you keep an open mind, you may even realize that you are both right! If you follow the guidelines below and you don't insult each other personally, you will still be friends.

Guidelines for Resolving Problems

DO try to understand the other person's point of view.

DO express opinions in a way that suggests possibility rather than certainty.

DO point out the part of the other person's argument that you agree with.

DO give valid reasons for your point of view, and always offer alternatives.

DO stay calm.

DO try to be fair.

DON'T shout.

DON'T make personal remarks.

DON'T dismiss someone's ideas.

DON'T close your mind to compromise.

DON'T make statements that do nothing but express your anger or contempt.

DON'T act like a know-it-all.

Apply It

With a partner, role-play one of the situations below, or create one of your own. Follow the guidelines. Perform the scene in front of a group of classmates. Discuss how you handled the disagreement.

- You go to the movies with a friend and can't agree where to sit.
- You and your sister or brother disagree about which TV program to watch.
- You are doing math homework with a friend. You disagree with his method for solving one of the problems.

Listening and Speaking Strategies

Giving a Speech

To give a good speech, you must know your subject and audience, organize your thoughts, and rehearse the performance until it is smooth.

Guidelines for Giving a Speech

1 **Plan** your speech.

- Think about what your listeners know about your topic.
- Decide if the purpose of your talk will be to inform, to persuade, or to entertain.

2 **Prepare** your speech.

- Research your topic and find the information you need.
- Gather any graphics or visuals, such as maps or pictures, to display.
- Write notes on note cards to use as reminders while you speak. Use words and ideas that are appropriate for your audience.
- Be sure your talk has a beginning, a middle, and an end. Put your notes in the correct order, and highlight key words.

3 **Practice** your speech.

- Study your notes until you have them almost memorized.
- Rehearse in front of a mirror using your notes and visual aids. Practice gestures until they are smooth and natural.
- Practice how you say your words. Think about the rate, volume, pitch, and tone of your voice.
- Time your speech as you practice in front of family or friends. Make revisions if necessary after listening to their comments.

4 **Present** your speech.

- Use your voice and visual aids in the same way that you practiced.
- Stand in a comfortable position with your weight on both feet and your head up.
- Speak slowly, clearly, and loudly enough for everyone to hear you. Remember to adjust the volume of your voice to the size of the room.
- Avoid saying *um, ah,* and *well.*
- Make eye contact with people in the audience.
- Speak with expression. See the next two pages for tips.

more ▶

Giving a Speech *continued*

How to Speak Expressively

When you write, punctuation marks help you express your meaning. When you speak, you have several different ways to express your meaning. These are pitch, stress, volume, rate, gestures, and juncture.

Pitch You can change the meaning of words by letting your voice go up and down. Say these three sentences, and notice how their meanings change as your voice rises and falls according to the punctuation.

> Look at the moon.   Look at the moon!   Look at the moon?

Stress Giving emphasis to different words can also change a sentence. These three sentences change in meaning when a speaker puts emphasis on different words.

> **Maria** will sing.   Maria **will** sing.   Maria will **sing**.

Volume You can make an important point by speaking loudly or softly. If you have been speaking in a level tone of voice, a change in volume (louder or softer) signals to the audience that you are saying something important.

Rate Slowing your rate of speaking will also help you make an important point. Quickening your rate occasionally will add excitement to your speech.

Gestures An appropriate gesture, or movement, will not only make your meaning clearer, it will add a little drama to what you say. Try saying, "There's a car" as a statement, an exclamation, and a question. In each case, add a gesture. Notice that the meaning is now much clearer and stronger. You can learn more about movements, or nonverbal cues, on pages H10–H11.

Juncture This term refers to pauses in speech. You pause when one thought ends and another begins. Repeat the following sentences.

> Robert put the dog in its pen.   Robert, put the dog in its pen.

What changes the meaning in the written sentences? the spoken sentences?

Remember these guidelines for speaking expressively.

Guidelines for Speaking Expressively

① Vary the pitch of your voice when you make a statement, make an exclamation, or ask a question.

② Put stress on the most important words in the sentence.

③ Vary the volume of your voice to emphasize important points.

④ Change your rate of speech to draw attention to special ideas.

⑤ Use movements and gestures to clarify your meaning and make your speech more dramatic.

⑥ Use juncture, or pauses, in speaking for the same reasons that commas and other punctuation marks are used in writing.

Try It Out Here are some suggestions for speaking expressively.

A. Work with a partner. Say the following sentence as a statement, an exclamation, and a question. *There's a raccoon in the bushes.* Listen for, and discuss, the changes in pitch.

B. With your partner, practice saying the following sentences two ways by changing the juncture. Discuss the changes in meaning.
   1. Jennie let the baby crawl across the room.
   2. Can you hear Alfredo?

C. Repeat each sentence to a partner. Stress a different word each time. Then discuss the changes in meaning.
   3. I must finish this work.
   4. He decided not to go.
   5. Tasha will finish the report.

Apply It

Prepare a talk about a recent concert, magazine article, or topic of your choice. Practice different methods of speaking expressively. Have a partner listen as you say sentences with different pitch, stress, volume, and rate. Ask for feedback until you develop the most effective delivery for your speech.

Understanding Nonverbal Cues

Using Nonverbal Cues

Just like words, the nonverbal cues of facial expressions, body language, and gestures can convey what you think or how you feel.

Facial Expressions Your face can reflect or strengthen such strong emotions as anger and excitement; signal attitudes, such as boredom, disagreement, or approval; or convey tone, such as humor or seriousness.

Body Language Your body movements can send unspoken messages.

- Good posture, making eye contact, and using controlled movements show confidence. Slouching, looking at the floor or over someone's shoulder, shuffling, or fidgeting tend to signal nervousness, boredom, or lack of confidence.

Gestures Your hand motions can add to or distract from your message.

- You can use your hands to clarify a message, such as to point out something, to represent size or shape, or to demonstrate a task.
- You can use your hands for emphasis. For example, you could hold up three fingers to emphasize that you have three main points.
- Avoid using meaningless gestures.

  Warning! Keep in mind that your nonverbal cues may show feelings or thoughts that you don't want to share.

Interpreting Nonverbal Cues

You need to interpret a speaker's nonverbal cues in order to understand the complete message and to recognize the most important ideas.

Interpreting others' nonverbal cues will also help you to be sensitive to their feelings. A pained look may indicate someone's feelings have been hurt. A look of confusion may indicate a need for more explanation. A bored look may mean you need to change the subject or not talk so much!

Remember these guidelines for understanding nonverbal cues.

Guidelines for Understanding Nonverbal Cues

► Avoid unnecessary or distracting nonverbal cues.

► Use facial expressions, gestures, and other body language to support your spoken messages or to communicate nonverbally.

► Be aware of the nonverbal cues you are sending.

► Interpret speakers' nonverbal cues to understand their ideas fully.

► Use others' nonverbal cues to guide your actions.

Apply It

A With your class or a small group, take turns pantomiming and interpreting nonverbal cues to show different emotions or feelings.

B. Prepare a thirty-second message, such as giving directions, making an announcement, relating information, or describing an incident. Use nonverbal cues. Present your message to classmates, and ask for feedback about the effectiveness of your nonverbal cues.

Interviewing

Interviews with people knowledgeable about a particular subject are good sources of information. You can use interviews to gather information for a research paper, a news article, a persuasive argument, or just to satisfy your curiosity about a topic! These guidelines will help you be a good interviewer.

Guidelines for Interviewing

Planning the Interview

1. Brainstorm questions to ask. Use the five *W's—who, what, where, when, why*—and *how.* Avoid questions that can be answered with *yes* or *no.*

2. List your questions on paper in a sensible order. Leave space between questions so that you can fill in the answers.

3. Make an appointment for the interview. Be on time.

Conducting an Interview

4. State your purpose at the beginning of the interview.

5. Be courteous. If the person drifts away from your main purpose, bring the interview back in line tactfully.

6. Ask follow-up questions that show you are listening carefully. Don't be afraid to ask for an example or for a clearer explanation.

7. Take accurate notes. You may want to use a tape recorder instead.

8. You may want to quote important facts or comments. Ask the person's permission to use a quotation. Then write the quotation exactly and use quotation marks. Don't paraphrase.

9. Thank the person for his or her time and information. Send a follow-up thank-you note as well.

10. After the interview, review the notes to be sure they are clear.

Apply It

Write six questions for interviewing classmates about their first memory. Conduct two or three interviews and record the answers your classmates give you.

Listening and Speaking Strategies

Figurative Language

Figurative language paints vivid mental images, sometimes by making a comparison. In the sentence below, the word *like* is used to compare the summer air to a damp shirt. Figurative language that uses *like* or *as* to compare is called a **simile**.

The summer air clung to his skin like a damp shirt.
The tall trees swayed as gracefully as dancers.

The flowers peeked over the fence like curious faces.

Sometimes a comparison is more powerful if you can say that one thing is another. Figurative language that compares without using *like* or *as* is called a **metaphor**.

The summer air was a damp, clinging shirt.
The tall trees were swaying, graceful dancers.

Apply It

For each item below, form an image in your mind. It can involve any of your five senses—sight, sound, smell, taste, and feeling. Write a sentence using figurative language to describe your image. Create the kind of comparison (simile or metaphor) shown in parentheses.

1. a sunset (simile)
2. an ocean or body of water (metaphor)
3. a building (simile)
4. the moon (simile)
5. a plant or plants (metaphor)
6. a musical instrument (metaphor)
7. an athlete or dancer performing (simile)
8. an animal (metaphor)

Synonyms and Antonyms

Words that have nearly the same meaning are called **synonyms**. Using synonyms can help you avoid repeating the same word. Notice the two synonyms for *make* in the following sentence.

> We need at least a dozen talented people to create scenery and produce costumes for the play.

Here are some other synonyms for *make*.

> form   construct   fashion   develop   generate   build

Because each synonym usually has a slightly different meaning, you can choose the word that best expresses your idea. Use a thesaurus, either in book or electronic form, to find synonyms.

Words that have opposite meanings are called **antonyms**. You can use antonyms to show how things contrast or differ from each other.

> Instead of being satisfied with the results, we were really disappointed in the portrait the artist drew.

Sometimes you can change a word into its antonym simply by adding the prefix *un-* or *non-*, such as *known* and *unknown* or *flammable* and *nonflammable*.

Synonyms: canine   dog
Antonyms: miniature   huge

Apply It

A. For each numbered word below, write a synonym and an antonym from the word box. You may use a dictionary.

1. violent
2. precise
3. reckless
4. overcome
5. complex
6. glum

basic	prudent
elaborate	rash
elated	specific
fierce	surmount
melancholy	vague
mild	yield

B. 7–12. Choose two words from Part A above. Write sentences using those two words, their synonyms, and their antonyms.

Denotations and Connotations

When you write, you need to be aware of the two kinds of meanings of the words you use. The **denotation** of a word is the meaning that you find in a dictionary. The **connotation** of a word is the feeling or mental picture that you associate with that word.

Every morning Mr. Cassell trudged past our apartment on his way to the bus stop.

Every morning Mr. Cassell strolled past our apartment on his way to the bus stop.

Every morning Mr. Cassell walked past our apartment on his way to the bus stop.

TRUDGING   STROLLING

The words *trudge, stroll,* and *walk* have different connotations. *Trudge* has a negative connotation. It makes you think about walking with great effort, perhaps walking when you are very tired. *Stroll* has a positive connotation and suggests walking because you feel like it. *Walk* is neither positive nor negative. Its connotation is neutral.

Connotations can have an important effect on your writing by conveying certain meanings.

Apply It

A. Write each word in the pairs below. Label each one *positive, negative,* or *neutral* to describe its connotation.
   1. notorious, famous
   2. debate, quarrel
   3. reveal, expose
   4. odor, fragrance
   5. snoop, investigate
   6. attract, lure

B. For each of the following words, write the word from the word box that has a similar denotation but a different connotation. You may use a dictionary. Then write a sentence for each word in the pair.
   7. frank   8. pity   9. proud   10. request

concern	ask	vain	sympathy
blunt	pleased	demand	honest

Prefixes and Suffixes

You can increase your vocabulary by learning the meanings of prefixes and suffixes. A **prefix** is a word part added to the beginning of a word. A **suffix** is a word part added to the end of a word. The word to which a prefix or suffix is added is called a **base word**.

The doctor soon arrived for the postoperative examination.

Suppose you are unfamiliar with the word *postoperative*, but you recognize the base word *operate*. (Base words often lose a final letter or undergo other spelling changes when a suffix is added.) If you know that the prefix *post-* means "after" and the suffix *-ive* means "performing an action," you can figure out that *postoperative* means "after an operation."

Here are some common prefixes and suffixes.

Prefix	Some Common Meanings	Examples
dis-	not; opposite of	dissimilar; disapprove
inter-	between; among	interact; international
pre-	before	prearrange
re-	back; again	reclaim; remeasure

Suffix	Some Common Meanings	Examples
-ary	of or relating to	customary
-ate	characterized by; to act upon	fortunate; motivate
-ify	to become or cause to become	purify
-ation, -ion	action or process; state or condition	starvation; perfection

Apply It

Write each bold word, and underline the base word. Then write the meaning of the prefix and/or the suffix and the meaning of the whole word. Be sure the meaning fits the content.

1. Jake can usually count on his warm smile to **disarm** strangers.
2. The plot of the story revolved around an **interplanetary** mission.
3. This spinning wheel may **predate** the American Revolution.
4. The government purchased vast areas of farmland for **reforestation**.
5. Wait three hours for the mixture to **solidify**.

Noun and Adjective Suffixes

You have learned that a suffix is a word part added to the end of a word. Notice how the suffix -ment changes the verb amaze to the noun amazement.

The crowd gasped in amazement as the gymnast somersaulted through the air.

Here are other examples of **noun suffixes**.

Suffix	Meaning	Examples
-er, -or	one who does	governor
-hood	condition or quality	neighborhood
-ment	act, action, or process	amusement
-ness	quality of, state of	kindness
-tion, -ion	action, process, or state	subtraction

Many adjectives are formed by adding certain suffixes to words. Here are some common **adjective suffixes**.

Suffix	Meaning	Examples
-able	can be	agreeable
-al	of, relating to	comical
-en	to become, cause to be, or made of	wooden
-ful	full of	helpful
-ic	of, relating to	heroic
-ish	like, somewhat	childish
-less	without	worthless
-ly	like, resembling	lonely
-ous	full of	perilous

Apply It

A. Add a noun suffix from the chart to each of the words below. Check the new words in a dictionary. Then use each new noun in a sentence.
   1. plumb   **2.** reflect   **3.** thorough   **4.** nourish   **5.** adult

B. Add an adjective suffix from the chart to each of the words below. Use a dictionary to check the spelling of the new words.
   6. humor   **8.** reason   **10.** watch   **12.** flaw   **14.** mountain
   7. green   **9.** person   **11.** heaven   **13.** wool

Word Roots

fract, frag
"break"

"fraction"   "fragment"

If you were to remove all prefixes and suffixes from a word, in many cases the remaining word part would be a word root. A **word root** is a word part that contains the main meaning of the word. Unlike a base word, a word root cannot stand alone. It must be attached to a prefix, and suffix, or both. Learning the meanings of word roots can help you comprehend unfamiliar words and increase your vocabulary.

A profusion of gifts arrived on her one hundredth birthday.

If you know that the word root *fus* means "pour," you can combine this clue with the meanings of the prefix *pro-* ("forward") and the suffix *-tion* ("state of") to figure out that *profusion* means "a pouring forth."

Here are some more word roots and their meanings.

Word Root	Meaning	Example
duc, duct	lead, introduce	conduct
jud	judge	prejudice
cogn	know	recognize
pel	push	propel
rect	straight, right	direct, correct
fract, frag	break	fracture, fragile
cis	cut	incision
sequ	follow	sequel

Apply It

Use the chart to find the word root for each word below. Then write the definition of each word, and use it in a sentence. You may use a dictionary.

1. cognizant
2. compel
3. scissors
4. induce
5. infraction
6. judicious
7. obsequious
8. rectitude

Borrowed Words

English has a rich assortment of words from many places in the world.

Coiled in the grass, the frightened cobra raised its hooded head and prepared to strike.

Cobra comes from the Portuguese words *cobra de capello* meaning "snake with a hood."

When Modern English began to develop, the age of European exploration and discovery also began. The English sailed around the world and brought back not only material goods and new experiences but also new words, such as the Norwegian word *fjord*, which describes a narrow, steep-sided inlet. Many Native American words have also been added to the English vocabulary, such as *moccasin*.

Word	Origin
zany	Italian
chocolate	Spanish
ski	Norwegian
algebra	Arabic
pizza	Italian

Word	Origin
bayou	Choctaw
hurricane	Carib
zest	French
robot	Czech
cookie	Dutch

Apply It

Write the meaning and the language from which each word below was borrowed. Use a class dictionary.

1. pajamas
2. colonel
3. alligator
4. goulash
5. boss
6. taco
7. opera
8. parka
9. avalanche
10. piranha

Word Histories

Our language is always changing. Often we borrow words from other languages. We make up new words from old words and word parts. We give new meanings to old words. Therefore, languages and their individual words have histories. The history of a word is called its **etymology**.

Etymology can tell us many interesting and surprising facts about words and language. The word *eleven*, for example, originally meant "one left over after counting to ten." *Bovine* and *beef*, oddly enough, both developed from the same word root, *bos*. *Catch* and *chase* were once synonyms meaning "to chase."

Many dictionaries give complete or partial etymologies. There are also special dictionaries of etymologies. Knowing the history of language can give you a fuller understanding of English vocabulary.

Apply It

Below are parts of six etymologies. Write a word from the word box to match each etymology. You may use a dictionary.

1. This word comes from a Latin word meaning "winter."
2. This word comes from a French phrase meaning "spiny pig."
3. Long ago, this word meant "any food in general."
4. This word was named after the city of Tangier, Morocco.
5. This word and *Thursday* are both related to Thor, a god in Old Norse mythology.
6. This word comes from the same word root as *annual*.

meat
thunder
hibernate
anniversary
porcupine
tangerine

Regional and Cultural Vocabulary

In different parts of the country, people sometimes use different words to name the same thing. Using language that reflects local speech can make your writing more interesting to read. It can also make it sound more authentic if you are writing about a particular area.

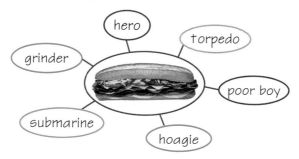

Let's say you are writing about a character who wants to buy a long sandwich filled with a variety of ingredients, such as meat, cheese, and vegetables. There are many names for this sandwich. If your story takes place in Philadelphia, it would be called a hoagie or grinder. But if the story takes place in New York or Los Angeles, the sandwich would be called a hero, or submarine.

Language can also reflect a culture. For example, in a Spanish-speaking family a pudding might be called flan. In a Jewish family it might be called kugel. What we call an elevator in the United States is called a lift in England.

Apply It

The words in each group below are used by different regions and cultures to mean similar things. Choose the word that is the most familiar to you, and use it in a sentence. Afterwards, compare chosen words and sentences with your classmates. What is the effect of the different words?

1. firefly, glow worm, lightning bug
2. soda, pop, tonic, phosphate
3. won ton, ravioli, kreplach, pelmeny
4. faucet, spigot, spicket, tap
5. expressway, freeway, motorway
6. crepes, palacsintas, dosai, tortillas, blini

Using a Dictionary

Your dictionary contains a lot of information. Learning to use it efficiently will help you to find facts quickly.

Guide Words At the top of each dictionary page, you will find the first and last words that are on that page. These guide words will help you to locate an **entry word**, such as the following entry for *forecast,* more quickly.

Guide words ——— **forced / foreigner**

Entry word ——— **fore•cast** (fôr′kăst′) *tr.v.* **fore•cast** or **fore•cast•ed, fore•cast•ing, fore•casts.** To tell in advance what might or will happen, especially to predict weather conditions: *forecast snow for the weekend.* —*n.* A prediction, as of coming events or conditions: *the weather forecast.* [First written down in 1400 in Middle English and spelled *forecasten,* to plan beforehand : *fore-,* before + *casten,* to throw, calculate, prepare.] —**fore′ cast′ er** *n.*

Syllabication Entry words are divided into syllables, which are separated by dots.

Phonetic Respelling To help you to pronounce an entry word, its phonetic respelling is given. Accent marks show where a word has primary (′) and secondary (′) stress. A **pronunciation key** at the foot of each or every other page explains the phonetic symbols. Check the pronunciation key for examples of the sounds shown in the respelling.

ă	pat	oi	boy
ā	pay	ou	out
âr	care	ŏŏ	took
ä	father	ōō	boot
ĕ	pet	ŭ	cut
ē	be	ûr	urge
ĭ	pit	th	thin
ī	pie	*th*	this
îr	pier	hw	whoop
ŏ	pot	zh	vision
ō	toe	ə	about
ô	paw	N	*French* bon

Parts of Speech The part of speech of the entry word is often abbreviated *n., v., adj., adv.,* or *prep.* This label can be a clue to choosing a definition that you need. Notice how the word *groom* is used in the sentence *Mr. Apple will groom Brian to be a salesperson. Groom* is used as a verb. Now check the verb definitions in the entry below. Definition 3 fits the sentence above.

groom (grŏom *or* grŏŏm) *n.* **1.** A person employed to take care of horses. **2.** A bridegroom. —*tr.v.* **groomed, groom•ing, grooms. 1.** To make neat and trim especially in personal appearance: *groomed themselves in front of the mirror before going to the party.* **2.** To clean and brush (an animal). **3.** To train (a person), as for a certain job or position: *groom a successor to the manager.*

Parts of speech

Definitions The meanings of a word form the main part of a dictionary entry. If there is more than one definition, each one is numbered.

Etymology The history or origin of a word—its *etymology*—often appears in brackets at the end of a definition. The definition of *gargoyle* below shows that the word comes from Middle English and Old French.

Part of speech

Definition

Etymology

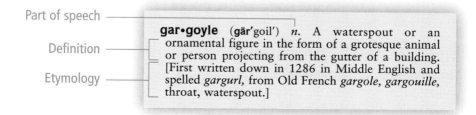

gar•goyle (gär'goil') *n.* A waterspout or an ornamental figure in the form of a grotesque animal or person projecting from the gutter of a building. [First written down in 1286 in Middle English and spelled *gargurl,* from Old French *gargole, gargouille,* throat, waterspout.]

Shown below is the entry for *insulate,* which comes from *insula,* the Latin word for "island." The present meaning of *insulate* is related to the Latin word because an island is land that is isolated or detached.

in•su•late (ĭn' sə lāt') *tr.v.* **in•su•lat•ed, in•su•lat•ing, in•su•lates. 1.** To cover or surround with a material that prevents the passage of heat, electricity, or sound into or out of: *We insulated our attic to keep out the cold.* **2.** To detach; isolate: *The mountain valley is insulated from outside influences.* [First written down in 1538 in Modern English, from Latin *īnsula,* island.]

Etymology

more ▶

Research and Study Strategies

Using a Dictionary *continued*

Homographs Some words have the same spellings but different meanings and origins. These words are listed as separate entries. In the following homographs, you can see that *sash*¹ and *sash*² have different origins. Notice that *sash*¹ comes from Arabic, and *sash*² comes from French.

Raised number

First homograph

Second homograph

sash¹ (săsh) *n.* A band or ribbon worn around the waist or over the shoulder as an ornament or symbol of rank. [First written down in 1599 in Modern English and spelled *shash*, from Arabic *šāš*, muslin.]
sash² (săsh) *n.* A frame in which the panes of a window or door are set. [First written down in 1681 in Modern English and spelled *shash*, alteration of French *châssis*, frame, chassis.]

Usage Labels The label *Informal* is used to identify words not suitable for formal writing but frequently used in conversation and ordinary writing. The label *Slang* identifies words appropriate only in casual speech.

sa•shay (să shāy′) *intr. v. Informal.* To strut or flounce. [Var. of French *chassé*, a dance step.]

Other Information A dictionary also can serve as a reference aid. You may find information about the population and location of many places. Maps may be included. Entries for famous people may include dates of birth and death, nationalities, and important accomplishments. Significant events, such as holidays and wars, may be listed as well. Various tables may show an alphabet such as Braille, the metric system, Morse code, and proofreading marks. Check the table of contents to see what other information your dictionary offers.

The Braille Alphabet

a	b	c	d	e	f	g	h
i	j	k	l	m	n	o	p
q	r	s	t	u	v	x	y
z	and	for	of	the	with	ch	gh
sh	th	wh	ed	er	ou	ow	w

Research and Study Strategies

Using the Library

Classification Systems

Most libraries have a systematic arrangement that makes it possible to locate any book in the collection. Fiction books are shelved by the last names of the authors. Nonfiction works are organized by the Dewey decimal system or the Library of Congress system. Most libraries use the Dewey decimal system.

Dewey Decimal System In this system, books are grouped into ten major categories. Each category includes a range of numbers, and every book in the category has its own number within that range. Decimals are used to indicate the smallest subdivisions. One history book might have the number 942.16, and another might be numbered 981.73. The number assigned to a particular book is its **call number.** The following table gives the numbers of the major categories and some of their subcategories in the Dewey decimal system.

000–099 **General Works** (reference materials)

100–199 **Philosophy** (psychology and ethics)

200–299 **Religion** (mythology)

300–399 **Social Sciences** (communication, economics, education, government)

400–499 **Language** (grammar books, dictionaries)

500–599 **Science** (biology, chemistry, mathematics)

600–699 **Technology** (engineering, medicine)

700–799 **The Arts** (music, painting, photography, sports)

800–899 **Literature** (essays, plays, poetry)

900–999 **History** (biography, geography, travel)

Call numbers

Indicates a reference book

more ▶

Research and Study Strategies

In addition to the call number of a book, you also need to know how the library arranges its books. Often, a sign at the end of each shelf shows the range of call numbers of the nonfiction books stored there.

The fiction books in a library are usually placed in a separate section and are arranged alphabetically by the authors' last names. Some libraries group autobiographies and biographies in a separate section. Although biographies are nonfiction, they are shelved alphabetically by the name of the person who is the subject, not by the name of the author.

The section of reference books, which cannot be checked out of the library, includes atlases, encyclopedias, dictionaries, and almanacs.

Library Catalogs

Using an electronic or traditional card catalog will enable you to find any book a library owns when you know the title or author. It will also help you find a selection of books when you just have a subject in mind.

Electronic Catalogs Many libraries use a computerized, or electronic, catalog that serves just the library itself, or it may be connected to a network of libraries. The World Wide Web is also a source of many library catalogs.

To search for a book using a computer, enter either the book's title, the author's name, a keyword, or the subject of the book. Do not enter the words *A, An,* or *The* at the beginning of a title.

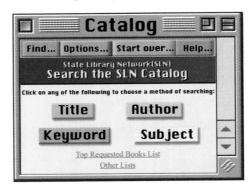

The computer will search its database of materials in the library's system for your request. If you enter an author's name, the computer will provide you with a list of all books written by that author. If you enter a subject or keyword, such as *bicycle touring,* the computer will provide a list of books on that particular subject.

From either of these lists, you can choose the title of a particular book and get more information. If an *R* or *Ref* appears with the call number, this indicates that the book is a reference work. Although libraries let you borrow other kinds of books, most libraries do not allow you to check out reference materials.

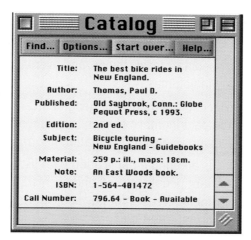

Card Catalogs If your library uses a card catalog in long wooden drawers, you will find title, author, and subject cards for every book in the library. Here are examples of each kind of card.

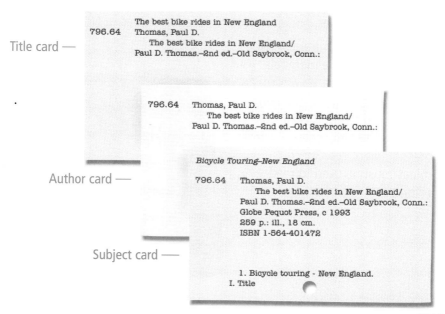

Title card —

796.64   The best bike rides in New England
Thomas, Paul D.
   The best bike rides in New England/
Paul D. Thomas.–2nd ed.–Old Saybrook, Conn.:

796.64   Thomas, Paul D.
   The best bike rides in New England/
Paul D. Thomas.–2nd ed.–Old Saybrook, Conn.:

Author card —

   Bicycle Touring–New England
796.64   Thomas, Paul D.
   The best bike rides in New England/
Paul D. Thomas.–2nd ed.–Old Saybrook, Conn.:
Globe Pequot Press, c 1993
259 p.: ill., 18 cm.
ISBN 1-564-401472

Subject card —

   1. Bicycle touring - New England.
I. Title

more ▶

Using the Library *continued*

Reference Materials

Reference materials in a library are full of information to help you write a research report or answer just about any question you may have. Most libraries devote an entire section to reference materials, such as the following sources.

See also "The Internet" on pages H51–H52 to read about using computers and the Internet to help you do research.

Encyclopedia An encyclopedia, which is a source of general information, contains articles about people, places, things, and events. The articles are arranged alphabetically in volumes.

Atlas An atlas is a collection of maps and geographical information. The atlas index provides the page number of each map and also gives the exact location of cities and towns as well as population information.

Almanac An almanac is an annual publication with lists, charts, and tables of information on important people, places, and events. The index in the front of an almanac gives all the references for any subject. The most recent almanac has the most current information.

Thesaurus A thesaurus is a reference book that lists synonyms and antonyms for each entry word. Some thesauruses have an index to locate entry words, and others are arranged alphabetically.

More Dictionaries In addition to the traditional dictionary, there are dictionaries that deal with specific topics. For example, there are dictionaries of geography, biographies, and even Native American tribes of North America.

Microforms Many libraries save space by storing some materials, such as newspapers, on pieces of film called microforms. If the film comes in rolled strips, it is called microfilm. If the film comes in cards, it is called microfiche. Special machines must be used to read microforms.

Using Visuals

Many articles and books include lists and drawings that present complex information in an easy-to-read form. These visuals show how things relate to each other and can be understood at a glance.

Tables

Facts and figures can be displayed in an organized way on tables. The vertical lines of information are called **columns**, and the horizontal lines are referred to as **rows**.

The table below lists the largest U.S. national parks in order of their size. The title tells you that only those parks with over one million acres are listed. Notice that each of the four columns is labeled with a caption, such as *Year Established.* Each row is labeled with the name of a national park. To find facts about Denali National Park, read down Column 1 until you find the name *Denali;* then read across Row 3 to get the information you need.

U.S. National Parks over 1 Million Acres			
Name	**State**	**Year Established**	**Number of Acres**
Wrangell-St. Elias	Alaska	1980	8,323,618
Gates of the Arctic	Alaska	1980	7,523,888
Denali	Alaska	1917	4,741,910
Katmai	Alaska	1980	3,674,541
Glacier Bay	Alaska	1980	3,225,284
Lake Clark	Alaska	1980	2,636,839
Yellowstone	Wyoming-Idaho-Montana	1872	2,219,791
Kobuk Valley	Alaska	1980	1,750,737
Everglades	Florida	1934	1,507,850
Grand Canyon	Arizona	1919	1,217,158
Glacier	Montana	1910	1,013,572

more ▶

Using Visuals *continued*

Graphs

Drawings that show numerical information are called **graphs**. There are several types: picture graphs, bar graphs, line graphs, and circle graphs. On a circle graph, or pie graph, a circle is divided like a pie into sections that represent a percentage of the whole circle. Usually each section is shown in a different color or a different pattern to make it easier to read.

Look at the circle graph below that shows water use in the United States in 1997. Notice that the sections are different in size. Each section represents a different type of water use.

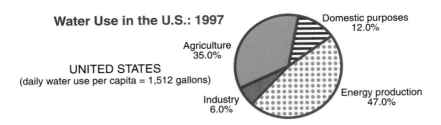

Water Use in the U.S.: 1997

UNITED STATES
(daily water use per capita = 1,512 gallons)

Domestic purposes
12.0%

Agriculture
35.0%

Energy production
47.0%

Industry
6.0%

Diagrams

Diagrams can be useful in helping you to visualize parts of something. A **picture diagram** is a drawing that shows how something is put together, how the parts relate to one another, or how the thing works. To understand a picture diagram, read each label and follow the lines to the parts being shown. Examine each part carefully.

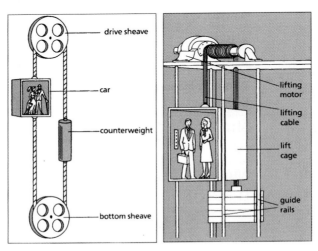

drive sheave

car

counterweight

bottom sheave

lifting motor

lifting cable

lift cage

guide rails

Fig.1 An early elevator   Fig. 2 A modern elevator

Research and Study Strategies

Maps

Look at the map of Albuquerque, New Mexico. It shows streets, highways, and important places.

Legend A box printed on a map that explains important marks and symbols is called a **legend** or **key**.

The legend below has symbols that explain various types of highways. You can see that the interstate highways are represented by dark yellow lines. All of the other highways and city streets are shown with white lines. Other symbols tell you whether a highway is an interstate, federal, or state route.

Compass Rose The directions *north, south, east,* and *west* are shown on a compass rose. Use the direction arrows to figure out how one place is related to another. For example, the Albuquerque airport is in the southern part of the city.

Scale You can determine the distance from one place to another by using the scale of distance. Scales differ from map to map, so be sure to refer to the scale on the map you are using. Use a piece of paper to mark the space between two places on the map, and then use the scale of distance to determine the actual distance.

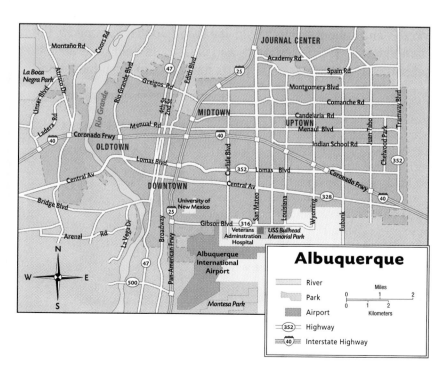

Research and Study Skills

Taking Notes

Whether you are reading, listening to a speaker, or watching a movie, taking good notes will help you recall what you read, hear, or see. Effective notes will help you remember much more than what you actually write down. These guidelines list important things to remember while taking notes.

Guidelines for Taking Notes

1. Don't copy material. Restate main ideas in your own words.
2. If you must use someone's exact words, use quotation marks and give him or her proper credit.
3. Write only key words and phrases, not entire sentences.
4. Following each main idea, list the details that support it.
5. Keep careful records of the sources you use.

Read this entry about eclipses from *The World Book Encyclopedia*. The note card that follows lists key words and phrases as main ideas and also lists supporting details. The card also lists the source of the information.

Eclipse is the darkening of a heavenly body. It occurs when the shadow of one object in space falls on another object or when one object moves in front of another to block its light. A solar eclipse takes place when the sun appears to become dark as the moon passes between the sun and the earth. A lunar eclipse occurs when the moon darkens as it passes through the earth's shadow.

Encyclopedia entry

Types of eclipses ——— Main idea
   –Solar eclipses
    sun appears to become dark
   –Lunar eclipses ——— Supporting details
    moon darkens
The World Book Encyclopedia, ——— Source
Volume 6, 1999 edition, page 51

Taking Notes While Listening If you are reading, you can look back and reread a section to check facts or recall information. But when listening to a speaker, it is important to take good notes, since you will not remember every word. Use the following guidelines to help you.

Guidelines for Taking Notes While Listening

1. Focus on the information presented. Don't let your mind wander. Shut out or move away from noises or other distractions.

2. Pay careful attention to the speaker's introduction and conclusion. A good speaker will outline the speech in an introduction and sum up the main points in the conclusion.

3. Listen for cue words, such as *first, the main point, most important,* or *in conclusion,* that signal important information.

4. Don't try to write everything you hear. Listen for important details, and write only key words or phrases. Read over your notes as soon as possible after the speech, and fill in missing details.

5. Record the speaker's name, the location, and the date.

Taking Notes While Viewing Taking notes while watching a film or event is more difficult than taking notes while listening or reading. Unless you are watching a video, there is no way to stop the action and see a section of the film again. Preparation is the key. In addition to the preceding guidelines for taking notes, the following guidelines will help you take good notes and still enjoy the viewing experience.

Guidelines for Taking Notes While Viewing

1. Prepare for the film or event by reading any related material ahead of time.

2. Listen to the dialogue or narrator even while you are taking notes.

3. Be aware of visual information, such as setting, body language, and facial expressions that add to your understanding of the film.

4. Check the credits at the end of the film for interesting information about the film's production.

5. Record the title of the film.

more ▶

Outlining

After taking notes, the next step in organizing your thoughts is to write an outline. You can use a **sentence outline**, which uses a complete sentence for each heading and subheading, or a **topic outline**, which uses phrases.

To make an outline, decide which kind of order will be most useful in organizing your facts. Chronological order tells the order in which events happen. Spatial order describes the location of things in a place. Logical order groups together related ideas, such as details, in order of importance.

An outline has a title, main topics, subtopics, and details.

- A main topic tells the main idea. It is set off by a Roman numeral followed by a period.
- Subtopics give supporting facts. A subtopic is set off by a capital letter followed by a period.
- Details give more information about a subtopic. A detail is set off by a number followed by a period. More precise details may follow.

Never use a single subheading. If an idea cannot be separated into two ideas, do not separate it at all.

Look at the following example of a topic outline.

Knots
  I. History of Knots ——————————— Main topic
    A. One of the oldest inventions ———— Subtopic
      1. Used with bows and arrowheads ⎤
      2. Used for clothing and shelter ⎦ Details
    B. Famous Gordian knot
  II. Tying Knots
    A. Language of knots to name parts of a rope
    B. Preparing rope for knots
      1. Work the rope to take out stiffness
      2. Whip the ends so rope doesn't unravel
    C. Useful knots
      1. Square knot
      2. Bowline
      3. Two half hitches

Skimming and Scanning

You do not always need to read every word of a nonfiction article. Depending on your purpose for reading, you can skim or scan to quickly find the information you need.

Skimming When you want just an overview, or a general idea, skim a selection. Follow these steps to skim effectively.

Strategies for Skimming

1. Read the title and any headings.

2. Read all of the first two paragraphs.

3. Read the first sentence or two and the last sentence of the other paragraphs. Look for key words.

4. Look at any illustrations, and read the captions.

5. Read all of the last two paragraphs of the article. These may provide a summary.

Scanning When you need to find specific information, scan a selection. To scan quickly, follow these suggestions.

Strategies for Scanning

1. Look for a key word or words that will help you to find the facts you need. For example, to answer a question about marine life, look for related terms, such as *ocean*.

2. Next, look for typographic aids, such as numerals, capitalized words, and words in bold or italic type.

3. When you think you have found the facts you need, read that section slowly and carefully.

Remember these two ways of reading when you want to locate information quickly. Skim to get an overview or the main idea. Scan to get specific facts.

more ▶

Summarizing

A **summary** is a shortened form of a longer article or story. By writing a summary, you can better understand fiction and nonfiction that you read.

Summarizing Fiction Below is a summary of "A Day's Wait," a story on pages 647–651 of this book. Read the story. Then read this summary. Notice how the writer was able to retell the story briefly.

> After being diagnosed with influenza, a boy learns that he has a temperature of one hundred and two. The boy won't sleep or have visitors. His father tries to comfort him but finally leaves for a while, thinking the boy is troubled because he is sick. When the father returns, he discovers why his son is so afraid. All day the boy has been convinced that he will die because he thought his temperature was 102 degrees Celsius instead of Fahrenheit.

Read a story carefully before you write a summary. Follow these guidelines for summarizing a fictional work.

Strategies for Summarizing Fiction

1. Identify the major characters and events. Decide what aspects of the story to emphasize. In "A Day's Wait," the plot is very important. For another story you might stress the characters.

2. Write clearly and briefly, but be certain that you tell enough about the plot to make the story easy for your reader to understand.

3. Include important names, dates, and places. The setting may be especially important in historical stories.

4. If possible, include information that captures the tone or the mood of the story. If you wish to quote a sentence or a phrase from the story, enclose it in quotation marks.

Summarizing Nonfiction Below is a summary of an article titled "Lichens: The 'Tough Guy' Plants" on pages 570–571.

> A lichen is made up of two organisms, algae and fungi, which have a partnership called symbiosis. This means that they work together to help each other. Living together, algae and fungi can survive in places where neither one could survive alone. Algae need a very moist environment and cannot live outside of the water. Fungi cannot produce their own food. Scientists don't know why the plants came together, but the result was that algae produce food for the fungi, and the fungi help keep the algae moist. Because of this special relationship, lichens can live in places that are extremely cold, dry, or barren. Sometimes they are the first plants to grow in bare places, so they are called pioneer plants.

Before you summarize nonfiction, be sure that you understand the major points of the article. Then follow these guidelines.

Strategies for Summarizing Nonfiction

1. Begin with a clear, brief statement of the main idea of the essay or article.
2. In the other sentences, give details that support and expand the main idea. It may help you to jot down the sentences that state the main idea of each paragraph in the article. Then you can combine and restate those sentences in shortened form.
3. Include important names, dates, numbers, and places.
4. If you are explaining events or steps, be sure to list them in the proper order.
5. Use as few words as possible. Try to put the facts into your own words, being careful not to change their meaning. If you quote directly from the article, use quotation marks to enclose the words from the article.

Word Analogies

Many tests ask you to complete word analogies. **Word analogies** compare two pairs of words in a special form using colons. In the example below, *near* and *far* are antonyms. *Polite* completes the analogy correctly because it is an antonym of *rude*. Both pairs of words now show antonyms.

> near : far :: rude : *polite*

It is easier to complete a word analogy if you think of it as a sentence.

> *Near* is to *far* as *rude* is to *polite*.

This chart shows some ways words can be related.

Word Relationship	Example
Word to its synonym	hide : conceal :: close : shut
Word to its antonym	rough : smooth :: persist : quit
Part to its whole	page : book :: tree : forest
Category to its member	fish : trout :: insect : ant
Object to its characteristic	whale : large :: guppy : small
Object to its use	pencil : write :: knife : cut
Person to his/her occupation	dancer : dancing :: pilot : flying
Worker to his/her tool	teacher : chalk :: dentist : drill
Worker to his/her product	gardener : flowers :: singer : song

Use these guidelines to help you complete word analogies.

Guidelines for Completing Word Analogies

1. Figure out the relationship between the first two words.
2. If you are asked to choose the second pair of words from a list, choose the pair that has the same relationship as the first pair.
3. If you are asked to choose the last word only, look at the first word in the second pair. Then try each of the possible answers in the blank. Decide which word creates the same relationship in the second pair as the relationship you identified in the first pair.
4. Double-check your answer. Say the completed analogy to yourself, substituting for the colons the words that explain the relationship.

A. Choose the pair of words that best completes each word analogy.

1. small : tiny ::
   a eager : bored
   b green : grass
   c frightened : scared
   d happy : angry

2. tailor : needle ::
   a baker : bread
   b farmer : plow
   c bone : dog
   d runner : running

3. knob : door ::
   a ocean : sand
   b hour : minute
   c willow : tree
   d wheel : car

4. potatoes : stew ::
   a lettuce : salad
   b ice cream : milk
   c warm : hot
   d car : automobile

5. sleepy : alert ::
   a happy : glad
   b tall : wide
   c willow : tree
   d timid : fierce

6. fast : swift ::
   a music : jazz
   b strong : powerful
   c sharp : dull
   d speed : runner

B. Write the word that best completes each analogy.

7. wool : scratchy ::
   satin : _____
   a cloth   c smooth
   b light   d sew

8. chef : meal ::
   poet : _____
   a pencil   c writes
   b magazine   d poem

9. apatosaurus : dinosaur ::
   Mars : _____
   a Pluto   c planet
   b planetarium d rocket

10. game : baseball ::
    color : _____
    a paint   c red
    b picture   d artist

11. broom : sweep ::
    stove : _____
    a hot   c kitchen
    b cook   d pot

12. barber : scissors ::
    gardener : _____
    a sunshine   c forest
    b shovel   d flowers

13. shirt : clothing ::
    typhoon : _____
    a windy   c blizzard
    b raincoat   d storm

14. star : constellation ::
    ship : _____
    a fleet   c engine
    b boat   d train

Open-Response Questions

On some tests you are asked to read a passage and write answers to questions about it. Use these guidelines to help you write a good answer.

Guidelines for Answering an Essay Question

1. Read the question carefully. Find the clue words that tell you what kind of answer to write, such as *explain, compare,* or *summarize.*
2. Look for clue words that tell what the answer should be about.
3. Write a topic sentence using words from the question. The rest of your sentences should give details to support the topic sentence.
4. Answer only the question that is asked.

Read the following passage and the question at the end.

The Modern Zoo

The word *zoo* is from the Greek word *zoion* meaning "animal." Zoos were originally owned by emperors or private citizens, and the animals were displayed and used to stage fights. It has been a long time since zoo animals were used for fighting, but other changes in zoos have come more recently.

In this country, zoos were once parks with fenced enclosures and buildings that contained caged animals. The animals were grouped by category, such as cats, monkeys, and birds. Often the cages were too small to accommodate the animals, and the lack of natural settings made it difficult for them to thrive. Now, however, animals are usually grouped by natural habitat, giving them adequate living space and allowing them more freedom and the chance to interact naturally with their surroundings.

The methods zoos use to get animals have also changed. Zoo directors used to buy animals from dealers who captured them in the wild. Today, however, with the threat of many animals becoming extinct, most zoo animals are bred in zoos.

Zoos are no longer just a place for people to learn about animals. Zoo workers want to save animals from extinction, so they breed animals for other zoos. They also breed animals so that they can be released into their native habitats.

All these changes have not only made zoo life better for the animals, they have made viewing the animals a more natural and educational experience for human visitors as well.

Summarize the changes in American zoos.

Read these two answers to the question. Which one is a better answer?

People used to capture animals and put them in cages. The cages were really small, and the animals didn't do well in them. It doesn't really seem right for people to catch animals and put them someplace where they don't belong. Do you think it would be comfortable to live in a cage? An animal in a cage can't be with any other animals. It can't roam around and get the food it wants. Worst of all, it can't run and play. People should leave animals where they find them.

There have been important changes in American zoos. Animals used to be in cages and kept separate from one another. Now they are placed in natural settings that allow them more freedom. Zoos used to buy captured animals, but now most animals in zoos are bred there. Sometimes they are even released into the wild. Modern zoos are not only places where people can come to see animals but also places that try to make sure that animals do not become extinct.

The first answer doesn't mention any of the changes that have taken place in American zoos. The essay tells about animals being captured and put in cages, but doesn't even mention that this is how they once lived in zoos. It merely gives the writer's personal opinion about keeping animals in cages.

The second answer does a better job of answering the question. It uses words from the question in the topic sentence, and the supporting sentences summarize the main points. The answer gives only the information asked for.

Open-Response Questions **H41**

Technology Terms

Computer Terms

Your school may be equipped with computers, or you may have one of your own. Try to become familiar with the following terms to understand how the computer works.

Floppy disk

Disk drive

Monitor

Hard copy

Keyboard

Printer

CD-ROM A flat round piece of plastic on which computer data or music can be stored and read with a laser; many computers come with built-in CD-ROM drives.

cursor The blinking square, dot, or bar on a computer screen that shows where the next typed character will appear.

disk drive A device in a computer that can read information from a disk or write information onto a disk; you insert a disk into a disk drive through a thin slot.

document A written or printed piece of writing.

floppy disk A somewhat flexible plastic disk coated with magnetic material and used to store computer data.

font Any one of various styles of letters in which computer type can appear.

hard copy A computer document that is printed on paper.

hard drive A computer disk that cannot be removed from the computer; hard disks hold more data and run faster than floppy disks.

hardware The parts of a computer system, including the keyboard, monitor, memory storage devices, and printer.

keyboard A part of the computer containing a set of keys.

menu A list of commands and other options shown on a monitor.

Using Technology

modem	A machine that allows computers to communicate with other computers over telephone lines. It can be inside the computer or an external machine.
monitor	A part of a computer system that shows information on a screen.
printer	A part of a computer system that produces printed material.
software	Programs that are used to operate computers.

Word Processing Commands

These commands are often used in word processing. You can give each command by typing a key or a series of keys or selecting it from a menu.

Close	Closes the displayed document.
Copy	Copies selected, or highlighted, text.
Cut	Removes selected, or highlighted, text.
delete	Removes selected, or highlighted, text.
Find	Locates specific words or phrases in a document.
New	Opens a blank document.
Open	Displays a selected document.
Paste	Inserts copied or cut text in a new location in the same or another document.
Print	Prints the displayed document.
Quit	Leaves the program.
return	Moves the cursor to the beginning of the next line.
Save	Stores a document for later use.
shift	Allows you to type a capital letter or a new character.
Spelling	Activates the spelling tool.
tab	Indents the cursor to the right.

Using E-mail, Voice Mail, and Faxes

E-mail

Writing an e-mail is different from writing a letter or talking on the phone. Follow these guidelines to write good e-mail messages.

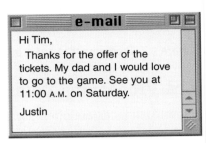

e-mail

Hi Tim,

 Thanks for the offer of the tickets. My dad and I would love to go to the game. See you at 11:00 A.M. on Saturday.

Justin

Guidelines for Using E-mail Effectively

❶ Give your message a specific title in the subject line. The recipient should know the subject before opening the e-mail.

❷ Keep your paragraphs short. Long paragraphs are difficult to read on-screen.

❸ Skip a line instead of indenting when you begin a new paragraph. Your message will be easier to read on-screen.

❹ Remember that special type, such as italics or underlining, may not show up on the recipient's screen.

❺ Be careful how you use humor. The other person can't hear your tone of voice and may not be able to tell when you're joking.

❻ Follow the rules of good writing. An e-mail may seem more casual than a letter, but what and how you write reflects on *you*.

❼ Proofread your messages, and fix all capitalization, punctuation, usage, and spelling mistakes.

❽ Be sure that an e-mail is the best way to send your message. Sometimes a phone call or a letter is better.

Voice Mail

Voice mail is an alternative to e-mail. Follow these guidelines for recording a message, which you leave for someone else, and a greeting, which you record to answer incoming calls.

Guidelines for Recording a Message

1. Make notes or mentally plan what you want to say beforehand.
2. Speak clearly when giving important information such as phone numbers or addresses.
3. Be concise.
4. Sign off in a pleasant manner.

Guidelines for Recording a Greeting

1. Speak clearly.
2. Record your greeting in a quiet place with no background noise.
3. Make your greeting short. Don't make your caller wait!
4. Tell the caller how to respond. For example, you can ask for the caller's name, the time of the call, a brief message, and a phone number where the caller can be reached.

Faxes

When you want to send a paper document or a document with complex graphics, a fax (short for *facsimile*) may be the best option. Follow these guidelines for sending a fax.

Guidelines for Sending a Fax

1. Make sure that the font used in your document is large enough to be read easily.
2. Use dark ink for any handwriting. Pencil does not show up well.
3. Fill out a cover sheet or label, including the total number of pages, the recipient's name and fax number, your name, and your phone number.
4. Call the recipient to make sure the fax has arrived.

Using a Spelling Tool

Your computer's spelling tool can help you proofread your writing. Having a spelling tool on your computer doesn't mean you don't have to know how to spell, though.

Look at this letter. Do you see any misspelled words? If you do, you're smarter than a spelling tool because it didn't find any of the mistakes.

A spelling tool can't find a misspelled word that is the correct spelling of another word.

A spelling tool can't tell the difference between homophones.

A spelling tool doesn't know whether two words are supposed to be one word.

Be careful of troublesome homophones that you use every day, such as *it's* and *its*, *your* and *you're*, and *they're*, *there*, and *their*.

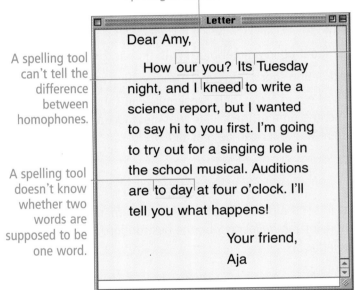

Letter

Dear Amy,

How our you? Its Tuesday night, and I kneed to write a science report, but I wanted to say hi to you first. I'm going to try out for a singing role in the school musical. Auditions are to day at four o'clock. I'll tell you what happens!

Your friend,

Aja

Think of a spelling tool as a proofreading partner. The spelling tool can help you find mistakes in your writing, but you still need to proofread to make sure the spelling tool didn't miss anything.

Computers and the Writing Process

Computers can help you plan, draft, revise, proofread, and publish your writing more efficiently. Here are some ideas for using a computer in the writing process.

PREWRITING

Type your thoughts as you think of them. Don't worry about completing your sentences or grouping ideas together. You can use the Cut and Paste commands to make changes later.

Dim the screen to help you concentrate on your thoughts rather than on correctness.

Create outlines, charts, or other graphic organizers to help you plan your writing. **Tip:** Some writing programs have ready-to-use graphic organizers that you just fill in.

```
┌─────────────────── Document ───────────────────┐
│  Life in Space                                  │
│  I. Effects of weightlessness                   │
│      A. Changes in body features                │
│         1. Wrinkles eliminated                  │
│         2. Foot size reduced                    │
│         3. One or two inches added              │
│            to body height                       │
│      B. Changes in posture                      │
│         1. Slight crouch when standing          │
│         2. Backward lean when sitting           │
└─────────────────────────────────────────────────┘
```

DRAFTING

Save your prewriting notes and ideas under a new name, and then expand a list or an outline into a draft.

Boldface or underline words you may want to change later.

Double-space your draft so that you can write revisions on your printout.

Save early and often!

more ▶

Computers and the Writing Process **H47**

Computers and the Writing Process *continued*

REVISING

Save a copy of your file under a new name before you begin making changes.

Conference with a partner right at the computer. Read your draft aloud and discuss any questions or problems you have. Then insert your partner's comments in capital letters. Later you can decide which comments you agree with.

Use the Cut and Paste commands to make changes. Move or delete words, sentences, or paragraphs with just a few clicks. **Tip:** If you're unsure about cutting something, just move text to the end of your document. You can always cut those "throwaways" later.

Rewrite problematic sentences or paragraphs under your original text. Boldface your new text and compare the different versions. Delete the version you don't want.

Use the Find and Replace commands to check for overused words. Enter words such as *and, then, pretty,* or *nice* in the Find function. When the word is found, click Replace and type in your change. You can also simply boldface the word and revise it later.

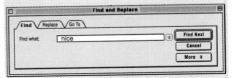

Use the electronic thesaurus in your word-processing program to find synonyms. Be careful to choose a synonym that has the meaning you want.

Thesaurus: English (US)	
Looked Up: nice	Replace with Synonym: pleasant
Meanings: pleasant friendly	agreeable likeable delightful superior good admirable pleasing

Insert   Look Up   Cancel   Previous

PROOFREADING

Use your word processor's spelling tool. Then check for errors a spelling tool won't catch! See "Using a Spelling Tool" on page H46.

Turn your sentences into a list. Place the cursor after each end punctuation mark, and press Return. Now you can easily spot sentences that are too long or too short, run-on sentences, and fragments. You can also make sure that each sentence begins with a capital letter. When you're finished proofreading, simply delete the extra returns.

Using Technology

Computers make publishing your writing a snap. Here's how you can create professional-looking final products.

Choose your fonts carefully. Designers suggest using no more than three fonts per page.

Times   Century   Helvetica

Choose a type size that can be read easily, but remember, type that is too big can look silly. Twelve-point type is usually a good choice.

10 point Times

12 point Times

14 point Times

Use bullets to separate the items in a list or to highlight a passage. On many computers, typing Option + 8 will produce a bullet (•).

Use other Option key combinations to make special pictures and symbols called *dingbats*. Many math and language symbols are included.

Design your title by changing the type size or font. Make a separate title page, if you like, and use your word processor's Borders and Shading functions to make the page fancy.

Add art to your paper or report.

- Use the computer's Paint or Draw functions to create your own picture.
- Cut and paste "clip art," which comes in a file on most computers.
- Use a scanner to copy images such as photographs onto your computer. You can then insert them electronically into your document.

If you don't have the equipment to create electronic art, simply leave a space in your document, print out a hard copy, and draw or paste in a picture.

more ▶

Computers and the Writing Process *continued*

PUBLISHING

Create tables, charts, or graphs to accompany your writing. For example, you can chart or graph the population growth in your town and include your findings in a research report.

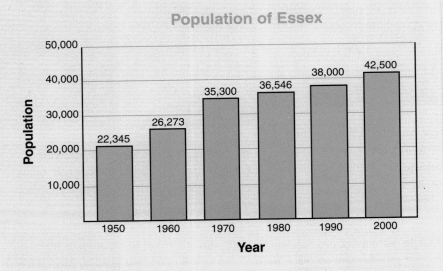

Population of Essex

Create newsletters, magazines, or brochures using word processing templates. Look at examples of real newspapers and magazines to see what kind of type to use, how big to make titles, and where to put pictures. Try combining electronic files to create a class newsletter that contains articles written by each of your classmates.

Choose your paper. White paper is always fine, but sometimes you may want to experiment with colored paper or stationery with borders or pictures. **Tip:** Check with an adult before changing the printer paper. Paper that is too thick or heavy can jam your printer.

Organize your writing in electronic folders. Create separate folders to store poems, stories, research reports, and letters. You can also make a folder for unfinished pieces.

Start an electronic portfolio for special pieces of your writing. You can create a portfolio folder on your hard drive or copy your files onto a floppy disk. Add pieces you choose throughout the year.

The Internet

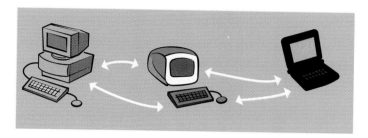

The **Internet** is a network of computers that connects people, businesses, and institutions all over the world. It lets computer users communicate with other computer users quickly and easily. Here are some of the many things you can do on the Internet.

- Do research on Web sites. You can watch a past president give a speech, take a tour of the White House, or hear music from the Great Depression. You can also search for current articles or historical documents.

- Visit an electronic bulletin board or chat room, where users "meet" to discuss specific topics. Here you can join an online book club, chat with other students who enjoy baseball, or debate current events.

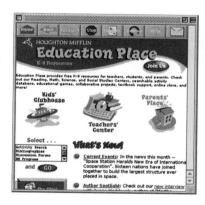

- Send e-mail to your friends and family. Anyone who is online is reachable. See "Using E-mail, Voice Mail, and Faxes" on pages H44–H45.

- Use special software to create your own Web site. You design the page, write the text, and choose links to other sites. Your school may also have its own Web site where you can publish your work.

Tech Tip Visit Education Place at www.eduplace.com/kids/hme/ for fun activities and interesting information.

more ▶

The Internet *continued*

Tips for Using the Internet

Although the Internet can be a great way to get information, it can be confusing. Use these tips to make the most of it!

- Search smart! Use a search engine to help you find Web sites on your topic or area of interest. Type in a key word or search by topics. Many search engines also provide tips on searching. Some search engines are designed just for kids.

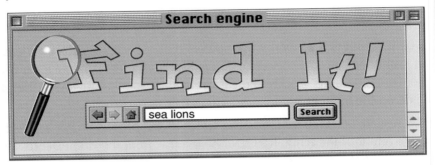

- Use quotation marks and words such as AND and OR to narrow your searches. Putting words in quotation marks tells the search engine to list only sites that contain those words in that order. Typing AND between words will bring up sites that contain all of those words. Typing OR between words will bring up sites that contain at least one of the words.

- Remember to write down the source of any information you find on the Internet just as you would do for a book. Along with the author, title, date of the material, and online address (URL), make sure you include the day you found the information. Information on the Internet can change daily.

- Check your sources carefully. The Internet is full of information, but not all of it is reliable. Web sites published by well-known organizations may be more trustworthy than those published by individuals.

- Protect your privacy. Never give your full name or address in a chat room.

Creating an Electronic Multimedia Presentation

An electronic multimedia presentation is a combination of text, images, and sound created on a computer. It lets you express much more than you could with just words. For example, an electronic multimedia presentation on volcanoes could contain a description of and animation showing the formation of a volcano, a recording of an interview with a geologist, photographs of Mount St. Helens and other volcanoes, and a video of an eruption.

Equipment

Here is what you need.

- a personal computer with a large memory
- high quality video and audio systems
- a CD-ROM drive
- a multimedia software program

Check with your school librarian or media specialist to find out what equipment is available.

Elements of an Electronic Multimedia Presentation

An electronic multimedia presentation may include text, photos and video, sound, and animation. Once you have created and selected the elements, an electronic multimedia authoring program lets you combine them.

Text The text of your presentation may include informative summaries, descriptions, directions, or photo captions. How the text appears on-screen is also important. You can adjust the font, size, and color of your text. **Tip:** Don't make your letters too small or put too many words on a single screen. Text should be easy to see and to read.

more ▶

Creating an Electronic Multimedia Presentation *continued*

Photos and Videos Images can be powerful, so choose them carefully. Here are some ways you can include pictures.

- Include a video that you film yourself.
- Scan in photos or artwork.
- Generate your own computer artwork.

Animation Computer animation lets you create objects and then bring them to life.

Two-dimensional animation lets you
- tell a story with animated figures,
- show an experiment being performed, or
- track changes in a chart or graph.

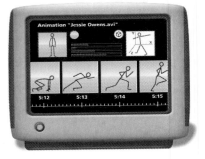

Three-dimensional animation lets you
- show how something is put together,
- show how something grows, or
- display an object from all sides.

Sound Sound can help make an image or text come alive. Imagine viewing a video of track star Jesse Owens. Then imagine viewing the same video while listening to the cheers of the crowd and the crackle of the announcer's voice. You're practically in the stands! Here are some suggestions for using sound in your electronic multimedia presentation.

- Add appropriate background sounds— birds calling, water dripping, bells ringing.
- Use music to set a mood or emotion.
- Include songs that represent a time in history or emphasize a theme.
- Include a button to let users hear the text read aloud.
- Include audio to accompany video clips.

Using Technology

Designing an Electronic Multimedia Presentation

The process of designing an electronic multimedia presentation is similar to that of creating a piece of writing, but here are some additional things to consider.

Types of Media If you are planning a presentation on Mars, you might come up with the following list:

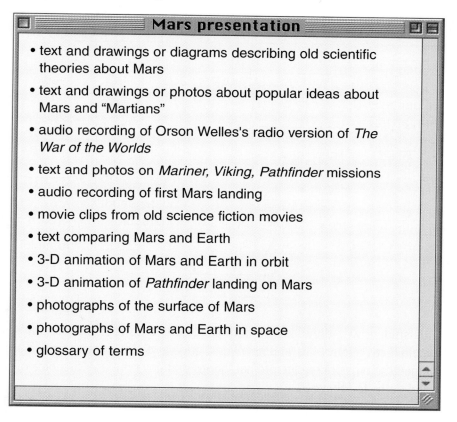

Mars presentation

- text and drawings or diagrams describing old scientific theories about Mars
- text and drawings or photos about popular ideas about Mars and "Martians"
- audio recording of Orson Welles's radio version of *The War of the Worlds*
- text and photos on *Mariner, Viking, Pathfinder* missions
- audio recording of first Mars landing
- movie clips from old science fiction movies
- text comparing Mars and Earth
- 3-D animation of Mars and Earth in orbit
- 3-D animation of *Pathfinder* landing on Mars
- photographs of the surface of Mars
- photographs of Mars and Earth in space
- glossary of terms

more ▶

Creating an Electronic Multimedia Presentation *continued*

Sequence Will the presentation have a specific order, or will you allow the user to choose his or her own path? A diagram, such as the one below, will help you plan.

Using Technology

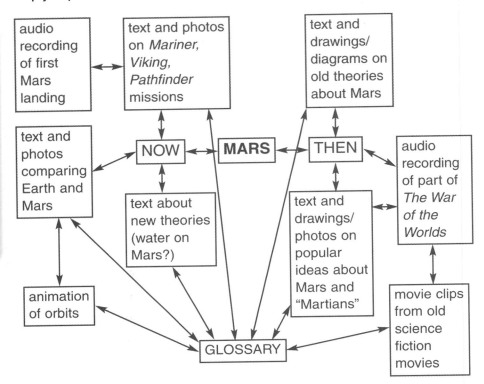

The student who drew this diagram planned two parts for his presentation: old ideas about Mars and new knowledge and discoveries. He then arranged the types of media into categories and gave the user a choice of several paths to follow.

Designing and creating an electronic multimedia presentation can be challenging and fun! **Tip:** As always, list your sources and write text in your own words. See the "Guide to Capitalization, Punctuation, and Usage" on pages H66–H67 for information on listing sources.

Keeping a Learning Log

A **learning log** is a notebook for recording what you learn in any of your subjects. It is a place to write facts and your thoughts about each subject.

Getting Started Write the date at the top of the page. Then use words, charts, or pictures—just get it all down on paper! Here's an example from one student's learning log.

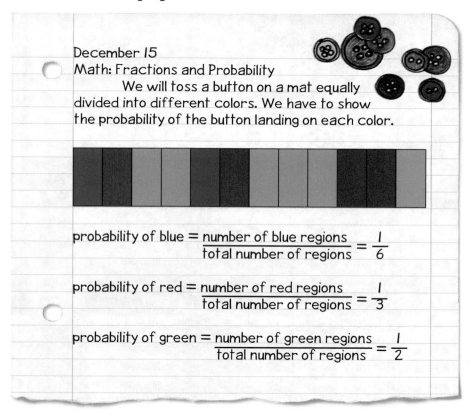

December 15
Math: Fractions and Probability
    We will toss a button on a mat equally divided into different colors. We have to show the probability of the button landing on each color.

$$\text{probability of blue} = \frac{\text{number of blue regions}}{\text{total number of regions}} = \frac{1}{6}$$

$$\text{probability of red} = \frac{\text{number of red regions}}{\text{total number of regions}} = \frac{1}{3}$$

$$\text{probability of green} = \frac{\text{number of green regions}}{\text{total number of regions}} = \frac{1}{2}$$

Try It Out Here are some suggestions for keeping a learning log.

- Make a vocabulary list for one subject. Include definitions.
- Work with classmates to record the results of a science experiment.
- Explain how fractions are similar to decimals. How are they different?
- Record your observations during a trip to a museum.
- Choose a country. Describe what it might be like to live there.
- Summarize what you have learned in a lesson in school.

Keeping a Writer's Notebook

A **writer's notebook** is a notebook you can keep just for writing. Make notes about ideas for stories, essays, or poems. List vivid words, record snippets of dialogue, or comment on authors you admire. Think of it as an artist's sketchbook. Write down whatever catches your eye.

When Do I Use It? Flip through your writer's notebook whenever you have a writing assignment. It can help you think of topic ideas, find exact words, recall details or dialogue, and develop support for a goal or an opinion. Parts of pages from one student's notebook are shown below.

Great Words

skewer Tom <u>skewered</u> the paper with his pencil and spun it around.

befuddle I woke up <u>befuddled</u> and ate breakfast in the middle of the night.

On the Way to Aunt Susan's

We are in the car. We can't find Aunt Susan's new house.

"I can't read this map," my dad says. "This is a terrible map."

"Why don't you drive, Dad? Let Mom read the map," my sister says.

"I like to complain. What would I complain about if I were driving?"

Try It Out Start your own writer's notebook. Try some of these suggestions.

- Write about something your school needs.
- Copy examples of effective writing from a book or an article.
- Describe a surprising, frightening, or funny experience.
- List descriptive words. Then write a sentence to show how each one can be used.
- Describe certain sounds, such as a faucet dripping into a pan of water.
- List reasons why you like a sport or other activity.

Graphic Organizers

Are you stuck for an idea to write about? Are you confused about how to organize your ideas? Try using these graphic organizers to help you explore and plan your ideas.

Clusters or webs are good for brainstorming topics, exploring ideas, or organizing information. Write your topic in a center circle. Write details about your topic, circle them, and connect them to the center circle. Add more details to each circle.

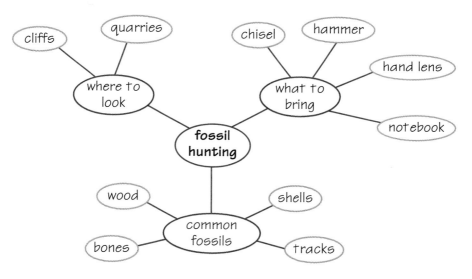

Inverted triangles can help you narrow topics that are too big. Write a broad topic in the first section of the triangle. Then write one part of that topic below it. Then write one part of the second topic. Keep going until you get a focused topic.

You can also use an inverted triangle to organize your details from most to least important.

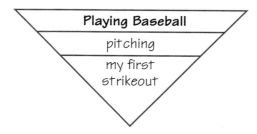

more ▶

Graphic Organizers *continued*

Planning charts help you organize your thinking about your purpose, your goals, and your audience before you begin to write.

My Topic _____

My Purpose	My Goals	My Audience
Circle one or more.	*Name at least one.*	*Answer these questions.*
• to tell a story • to explain • to persuade • to share • to plan • to learn • other _____		1. Who is my audience? 2. What do they know about my topic? 3. What do I want them to know? 4. What part would interest them most?

Time order charts are planning tools. They can be used after you have explored your topic by freewriting, listing, or using a cluster. Transfer the information from your brainstorming session into the boxes. Add more information where you see gaps.

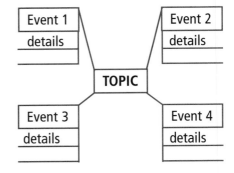

Story maps help you to gather details about setting, characters, and plot. Write notes in each section.

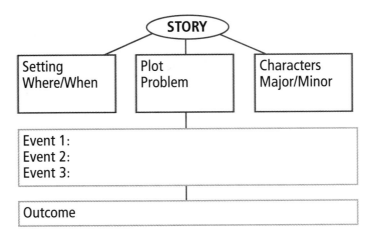

Observation charts organize details gathered through your five senses. Use them to add details to your writing. List details for your senses in separate columns. Depending on your topic, you may have more details in one column than another or no details at all.

Rainy Bus Ride				
sight	**sound**	**touch**	**taste**	**smell**
foggy windows yellow slickers water dripping wet hair	windshield wipers slapping wheels splashing	soggy lunch bag		wet clothes stuffy air

T-charts organize information into two groups. Use T-charts to lists details about two people, places, or things. They are also helpful for exploring two sides of an argument, showing likenesses and differences, or showing two points of view.

Draw a large T. Write your subjects at the top. Write details about each subject in the column below it. You may want to match the information in the columns.

me	my parents
listen to hip hop	listen to jazz
sleep late on weekends	get up early
always order French fries	ask for rice or baked potatoes

Step-by-step charts help you to plan your instructions. List the materials that are needed to follow your instructions. Then write each step in order. Include details your audience needs to know to complete each step.

Materials _____	
Steps	**Details**
Step 1 _____	_____
Step 2 _____	_____
Step 3 _____	_____

more ▶

Graphic Organizers *continued*

Venn diagrams are used to compare and contrast two subjects. Write details that tell how the subjects are different in the outer circles. Write details that tell how the subjects are alike where the circles overlap.

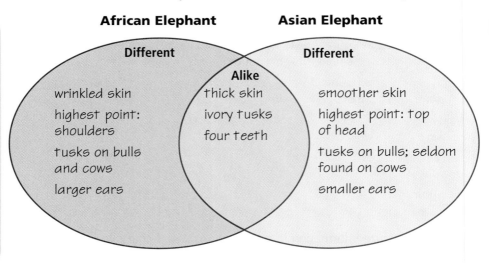

African Elephant   **Asian Elephant**

Different

wrinkled skin

highest point: shoulders

tusks on bulls and cows

larger ears

Alike

thick skin

ivory tusks

four teeth

Different

smoother skin

highest point: top of head

tusks on bulls; seldom found on cows

smaller ears

Persuasion maps can help you plan convincing arguments. Begin by stating your goal, a specific action you want a specific audience to take. Then write at least three reasons why your audience should do what you're suggesting. List facts and examples that elaborate your reasons.

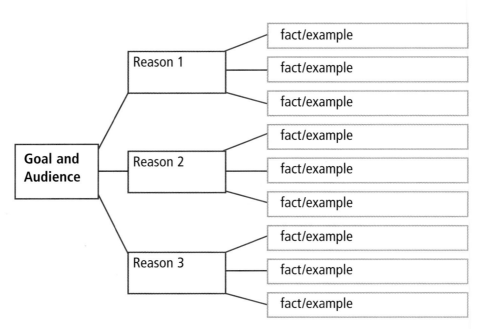

Goal and Audience

Reason 1 — fact/example, fact/example, fact/example

Reason 2 — fact/example, fact/example, fact/example

Reason 3 — fact/example, fact/example, fact/example

Writer's Tools

KWL charts show what you already **know** about a topic, what you **want** to know about it, and what you **learn** after doing research.

Mount Vesuvius		
What I Know	**What I Want to Know**	**What I Learned**
It's a volcano in Italy. It destroyed Pompeii.	Is this volcano still active? Do people live nearby?	The volcano is still active. Two million people live nearby.

ISP charts show **information (I)**, **sources (S)**, and, if appropriate, the **page references (P)** where you found the information.

Elephants		
I	**S**	**P**
largest teeth on the planet	Knowitall Encyclopedia	50
can weigh up to 7 tons	from the same source	102
don't drink through their trunks	zookeeper, Stone Zoo	

Time lines show events in order and tell when they happened. Draw an arrow, and write or draw events along it in order from left to right. Specify when each event took place.

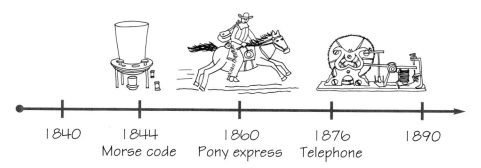

| 1840 | 1844 Morse code | 1860 Pony express | 1876 Telephone | 1890 |

Abbreviations

Abbreviations are shortened forms of words. Most abbreviations begin with a capital letter and end with a period.

Titles	Mr. *(Mister)* Mrs. *(married woman)* Ms. *(any woman)*	Dr. *(Doctor)* Sr. *(Senior)* Jr. *(Junior)*
	NOTE: *Miss* is not an abbreviation and does not end with a period.	
Initials	John F. Kennedy *(John Fitzgerald Kennedy)* E. M. Forster *(Edward Morgan Forster)*	
Days of the week	Sun. *(Sunday)* Mon. *(Monday)* Tues. *(Tuesday)* Wed. *(Wednesday)*	Thur. *(Thursday)* Fri. *(Friday)* Sat. *(Saturday)*
Months of the year	Feb. *(February)* Sept. *(September)* NOTE: Do not abbreviate *May, June,* and *July.*	
Time	A.M. *(midnight to noon)*	P.M. *(noon to midnight)*
Words used in addresses	St. *(Street)* Rd. *(Road)* Ave. *(Avenue)* Dr. *(Drive)* Blvd. *(Boulevard)*	Rte. *(Route)* Apt. *(Apartment)* Pkwy. *(Parkway)* Mt. *(Mount or Mountain)* Expy. *(Expressway)*
Words used in business	Co. *(Company)* Inc. *(Incorporated)*	Corp. *(Corporation)* Ltd. *(Limited)*
Other abbreviations	**Some abbreviations are all capital letters, with a letter standing for each important word.** P.D. *(Police Department)* R.N. *(Registered Nurse)* P.O. *(Post Office)* M.A. *(Master of Arts)* **Abbreviations for units of measure use neither capital letters nor periods. The only exception is the abbreviation for *inch*.** mph *(miles per hour)* in. *(inch)* l *(liter)* **Abbreviations of government agencies or national organizations do not usually have periods.** PBS *(Public Broadcasting Service)* NATO *(North Atlantic Treaty Organization)*	

Abbreviations *continued*

States	The United States Postal Service uses two capital letters and no period in each of its state abbreviations.
	AL *(Alabama)* LA *(Louisiana)* OH *(Ohio)* AK *(Alaska)* ME *(Maine)* OK *(Oklahoma)* AZ *(Arizona)* MD *(Maryland)* OR *(Oregon)* AR *(Arkansas)* MA *(Massachusetts)* PA *(Pennsylvania)* CA *(California)* MI *(Michigan)* RI *(Rhode Island)* CO *(Colorado)* MN *(Minnesota)* SC *(South Carolina)* CT *(Connecticut)* MS *(Mississippi)* SD *(South Dakota)* DE *(Delaware)* MO *(Missouri)* TN *(Tennessee)* FL *(Florida)* MT *(Montana)* TX *(Texas)* GA *(Georgia)* NE *(Nebraska)* UT *(Utah)* HI *(Hawaii)* NV *(Nevada)* VT *(Vermont)* ID *(Idaho)* NH *(New Hampshire)* VA *(Virginia)* IL *(Illinois)* NJ *(New Jersey)* WA *(Washington)* IN *(Indiana)* NM *(New Mexico)* WV *(West Virginia)* IA *(Iowa)* NY *(New York)* WI *(Wisconsin)* KS *(Kansas)* NC *(North Carolina)* WY *(Wyoming)* KY *(Kentucky)* ND *(North Dakota)*
Numbers	**Spell out numbers under one hundred and numbers at the beginning of a sentence. Use numerals for numbers over one hundred.** My team has twenty-five players. Two hundred sixty people were in the audience. There are 174 apartments in my building.

Titles

Italicizing	**Titles of books, magazines, newspapers, long musical works, plays, works of art, movies, and TV series are italicized. The important words and the first and last words are capitalized.** *In a Pickle (book)* *As You Like It (play)* *Miami Herald (newspaper)* *Mona Lisa (painting)* *Requiem (musical work)* *Nature (TV series)*
Quotation marks	**Titles of short stories, articles, songs, poems, and book chapters are enclosed in quotation marks.** "The Party" *(short story)* "If" *(poem)* "Crewelwork" *(article)* "Saxon Art" *(chapter)* "America" *(song)*

more ▶

Guide to Capitalization, Punctuation, and Usage *continued*

Quotations

Quotation marks with commas and periods	Quotation marks are used to set a speaker's exact words apart from the rest of the sentence. The first word of a direct quotation begins with a capital letter. Question marks and exclamation points that belong to the quotation are placed inside the quotation marks. Question marks and exclamation points that do not belong to the quotation are placed outside the quotation marks. Commas separate a quotation from the rest of the sentence. Always place periods and commas inside quotation marks.
	"Where," Saul asked, "did I leave my keys?"
	Did Joe say, "I am going to Miami on my vacation"?
	Linda replied, "I don't know what time it is."

List of Sources/Bibliography

The basic organization of a list of sources is alphabetical. If the author's name is not given, list the title first, and alphabetize it by the first important word of the title.

NOTE: Most online and CD-ROM references will not come with all bibliographical information, especially author names. In these cases, students should simply cite the information that is available.

Books	List the author's name (last name first), the book title, the city where the publisher is located, the publisher's name, and the year of publication. Note the punctuation.
	Sbordoni, Valerio, and Forestiero, Saverio. *Butterflies of the World.* Buffalo, NY: Firefly Books, 1998.
CD-ROM	Citations for entire CD-ROMs are similar to those used for print sources. For a complete publication on a CD-ROM, list the author/editor (if available), the title of the work (italicized), the electronic medium, version, place of publication, publisher, and date.
	Ancient Lands. CD-ROM. Vers. 1.0. Redmond, WA: Microsoft, 1994.
	For part of a publication on a CD-ROM, add the title of the part (in quotation marks) before the title of the work.
	Hoyt, Reginald A. "Zebra." *World Book Multimedia Encyclopedia.* 1998 ed. CD-ROM. Chicago: World Book, Inc., 1998.

Encyclopedia article	List the author's name (last name first), then the title of the article (in quotation marks). Next, give the title of the encyclopedia (italicized) and the year of publication of the edition you are using. Note the punctuation. Ferrell, Keith. "Personal Computer." *The World Book Encyclopedia.* 1997 ed.
	If the author of the article is not given, begin your listing with the title of the article. "Charles River." *Collier's Encyclopedia.* 1997 ed.
Internet	For information found on a Web site, list the author/editor, the part title (in quotation marks), the source (italicized), location of the source, the date of the material (*n.d.* indicates no date of publication given), and the edition. Next, list the publication information: medium (e.g., Online), the electronic address, or URL, and the date of access. Kientz, Sue. "What Is It Like on Saturn and What Are the Rings Made Of?" *NASA Kids Corner* Washington, DC: NASA, n.d. Online. http://www.jpl.nasa.gov/cassini/kids/kidscorner.html. 27 Sept. 1999.
	For a magazine or newspaper article found on a Web site, list the author, article title (in quotation marks), the magazine or newspaper title (italicized), the date, edition, pages or paragraphs, medium, the URL, and the date of access. "The Kosovo Conflict." *New York Times* 19 May 1999: 9 pars. Online. http://www.nytimes.com/learning/students/writing/articles/april99b.html. 28 Sept. 1999.
Interview	To cite an interview, list the name of the person interviewed, the kind of interview (personal interview, telephone interview), and the date. Perez, Lucinda. Personal interview. 23 July 2000.
Magazine or newspaper article	Study these examples carefully. Note the order and the punctuation. **MAGAZINE:** Lemonick, Michael D. "A Very Close Call." *Time* Sept. 27, 1999: 34–37. **NEWSPAPER:** Lilley, Ray. "Airlift Rescues Ailing Doctor at South Pole." *Chicago Tribune* 16 Oct.1999, sec. News: 1, N. **NEWSPAPER:** (no author) "Habitat for Humanity to Dedicate Home." *South Bend Tribune* 9 Oct.1999, sec.Local/Area: a4.

more ▶

Guide to Capitalization, Punctuation, and Usage *continued*

Capitalization

<table>
<tr>
<td rowspan="8">Rules for capitalization</td>
<td>

Capitalize geographical names such as cities, states, countries, continents, bodies of water, geographical features, and geographical areas. Do not capitalize small words like *the* and *of*.

Paris	Eastern Europe
Asia	Brazil
Rock of Gibraltar	Rio Grande
Vermont	the Northeast
Yangtze River	

</td>
</tr>
<tr><td>

Do not capitalize directions.

We live ten miles east of Philadelphia.

</td></tr>
<tr><td>

Capitalize titles or their abbreviations when used with a person's name.

Governor Bradford   Senator Smith   Dr. Lin

</td></tr>
<tr><td>

Capitalize proper adjectives.

We ate at a Hungarian restaurant.   She is French.

</td></tr>
<tr><td>

Capitalize the names of months and days.

My birthday is on the last Monday in March.

</td></tr>
<tr><td>

Capitalize the names of organizations, businesses, institutions, and agencies.

National Hockey League   The Status Company
Franklin Mint   Federal Aviation Administration

</td></tr>
<tr><td>

Capitalize names of holidays and other special events, streets, highways, buildings, bridges, monuments, historical events, periods of time, and documents.

Veterans Day	World Trade Center
Lincoln Memorial	Jazz Age
Route 9	Golden Gate Bridge
French Revolution	Bill of Rights

</td></tr>
<tr><td>

Capitalize the first and last words and all important words in the titles of books, newspapers, stories, songs, poems, reports, and outlines. (Articles, short conjunctions, and short prepositions are not capitalized unless they are the first or last word.)

Julie of the Wolves	"The Necklace"
"The Road Not Taken"	"The Exports of Italy"
The New York Times	"Over the Rainbow"
"Canadian National Parks"	

</td></tr>
</table>

Rules for capitalization *(continued)*	**Capitalize the first word of each main topic and subtopic in an outline.**
	
	I. Types of libraries
	    A. Large public library
	    B. Bookmobile
	    C. School library
	II. Library services

	Capitalize the first word in the greeting and closing of a letter. Dear Marcia, Dear Ms. Olsen: Your friend, Yours truly,
	Capitalize nationalities, races, languages, religions, religious terms, and specific school subjects followed by a number. Canadian Koran Buddhism Torah Old English Caucasian Spanish Geography 101

Punctuation

End marks	**A *period* (.) ends a declarative or imperative sentence. A *question mark* (?) follows an interrogative sentence. An *exclamation point* (!) is used after an exclamatory sentence and after an interjection that expresses strong feeling.** The scissors are on my desk. (declarative) Look up the spelling of that word. (imperative) How is the word spelled? (interrogative) This is your best poem so far! (exclamatory) Wow! (interjection) We've just won the essay prize.
Apostrophe	**To form the possessive of a singular noun, add an apostrophe and *s*.** sister-in-law's family's Agnes's
	To form the possessive of a plural noun that ends in s, add an apostrophe only. sisters' families' Joneses'
	For a plural noun that does not end in *s*, add an apostrophe and *s*. women's mice's sisters-in-law's

Capitalization / Punctuation / Usage

more ▶

Punctuation *continued*

Apostrophe *(continued)*	**Use an apostrophe and *s* to form the plural of letters, numerals, symbols, and words that are used as words.** *s*'s *i*'s *2*'s ***'s Fill in the questionnaire with *yes's* and *no's*.
	Use an apostrophe in contractions in place of dropped letters. Do not use contractions in formal writing. isn't *(is not)* they've *(they have)* it's *(it is)*
Colon	**Use a colon to separate the hour from the minute.** 7:30 P.M. 8:15 A.M.
	Use a colon after the greeting in a business letter. Dear Mrs. Trimby: Dear Realty Homes:
	Use a colon before a list introduced by words like *the following* or *these*. Do not use a colon after a verb or a preposition. Call the following: Hester, Wanda, Doyle, and Carl. Next year I am taking English, history, and math. He arrived with a suitcase, a coat, and an umbrella.
Comma	**Use commas to separate words in a series.** Clyde asked if we had any apples, peaches, or grapes.
	Use commas between two or more adjectives that come before a noun. Do not use a comma if the adjectives are used together to express a single idea. Her shrill, urgent cry was alarming. The tired British tourists decided to rest.
	Use a comma to separate the simple sentences in a compound sentence. Some students were at lunch, but others were studying.
	Use commas after words, phrases, and clauses that come at the beginning of sentences. No, you cannot avoid the deadline. Following the applause, the speaker continued. When you are in doubt, ask for advice.
	Use commas to separate interrupters such as *of course, however,* and *by the way* from the rest of the sentence. Maureen, of course, was late for the bus again. The driver, however, had forgotten the directions.

Comma *(continued)*	**Use commas to set off an appositive from the rest of the sentence when the appositive is not necessary to the meaning of the sentence.**
	The writer Charles Dickens created complex plots. *(The appositive is necessary to the meaning.)*
	Texas, the Lone Star State, borders Mexico. *(The appositive is extra, not needed for meaning.)*
	Use a comma to separate a noun in direct address.
	Joe, help me fix this. How was your trip, Pa?
	Use a comma to separate the month and day from the year. Use a comma to separate the year from the rest of the sentence. Do not use commas if a specific day is not included.
	January 12, 1987, is the date of the banquet. Halley's Comet appeared during April 1986.
	Use a comma after an interjection that expresses mild emotion.
	Gee, I hope the bus comes soon.
	Use a comma between the names of a city and a state in an address. If the address is within a sentence, also use a comma after the name of the state. Do not use a comma before the ZIP code.
	Does Chicago, Illinois, have the world's tallest building? Denise lives at 10 Palm Court, Lima, OH 45807.
	Use a comma after the greeting in a friendly letter and after the closing in all letters.
	Dear Deena, Sincerely yours,
	Use commas to set off a nonessential phrase or clause, which adds optional information not necessary to the meaning of the sentence. If a phrase or clause is essential, do not use commas.
	Emily Dickinson, who was born in 1830, was a poet. *(The clause is not necessary to the meaning.)*
	The man who read the poem is my father. *(The clause is necessary to the meaning.)*

more ▶

Guide to Capitalization, Punctuation, and Usage *continued*

Punctuation *continued*

Semicolon	**Use a semicolon to connect independent clauses that are closely related in thought or that have commas within them.** There were five movie tickets left; Ed needed six. He bought nuts, dates, and figs; we ate them all. **Use a semicolon to join two independent clauses when the second clause begins with an adverb such as *however, therefore,* or *consequently*.** It was growing dark; however, there were no clouds.
Hyphens, Dashes, Parentheses, Ellipses	**Use a hyphen to join the parts of compound numbers, inclusive numbering, to join two or more words that work together as one adjective before a noun, or to divide a word at the end of a line. Hyphens are also used in some compounds with *semi-, half-,* and *ex-*.** thirty-two long-range plans Raphael is known as one of Italy's many magnif- icent painters. semi-sweet half-mast ex-president
	Use dashes to show a sudden change of thought. The sky grew dark—it could mean snow.
	Use parentheses to enclose unnecessary information. Geraldine was reelected (once more) as treasurer.
	Use ellipses (three periods) to show omitted words or sentences. *(Complete quote)* "That is the last thing I remember about my walk last night. Then I woke up here." *(Shortened quote)* "That is the last thing I remember. . . . Then I woke up here." *(A period is added to the shortened sentence as well as ellipses.)*

Problem Words

Words	Rules	Examples
a, an	The indefinite articles *a* and *an* refer to any person, place, or thing. Use *a* before a word that begins with a consonant sound. Use *an* before a word that begins with a vowel sound.	a banana an apple

Capitalization / Punctuation / Usage

Words	Rules	Examples
the	The definite article *the* points out a specific noun or pronoun. Use *the* with both singular and plural nouns.	the apple the apples The books I like are long.
accept	The verb *accept* means "to receive."	The club accepted her.
except	The preposition *except* means "excluding."	They all went except James.
affect	The verb *affect* means "to influence."	The rain affected my plans.
effect	The verb *effect* means "to cause to happen."	They effected many changes.
	The noun *effect* means "result."	What effect has Sara had?
bad	*Bad* is an adjective. It can be used after linking verbs like *look* and *feel*.	This was a bad day. I feel bad.
badly	*Badly* is an adverb.	I play badly.
beside	*Beside* means "next to."	He is sitting beside me.
besides	*Besides* means "in addition to."	Who, besides Al, is going?
between	*Between* refers to two people or things.	I sat between Kyle and Pam.
among	*Among* refers to three or more people or things.	Talk among the four of you.
farther	Use *farther* to refer to physical distance.	Which town is farther away?
further	Use *further* in all other cases.	Please read further by tomorrow.
fewer	Use *fewer* or *fewest* with plural nouns.	Fewer boys are here today.
less	Use *less* or *least* with singular nouns.	I have the least money.
good	*Good* is an adjective.	The weather looks good.
well	*Well* is usually an adverb. It is used as an adjective only when it means "healthy."	She swims well. Do you feel well?
its	*Its* is a possessive pronoun.	The dog wagged its tail.
it's	*It's* is a contraction of *it is*.	It's cold today.

Capitalization / Punctuation / Usage

more ▶

Guide to Capitalization, Punctuation, and Usage *continued*

Problem Words *continued*

Words	Rules	Examples
lie	*Lie* means "to rest, recline, or remain in one place."	The dog lies in its bed.
lay	*Lay* means "to put or place something."	Please lay the books here.
raise	*Raise* means "to move something up," "to increase something," or "to grow something."	Please raise the window. The store raised its prices. Maggie raises sunflowers.
rise	*Rise* means "to get up or go up."	The elevator rises slowly.
shall	*Shall* is used with *I* and *we* in formal English.	We shall be there today.
will	*Will* is used in all other cases.	He will go tomorrow.
their	*Their* is a possessive pronoun.	Their coats are on the bed.
there	*There* is an adverb. It may be used to begin a sentence.	Is Carlos there? There is my book.
they're	*They're* is a contraction of *they are*.	They're going to the store.
theirs	*Theirs* is a possessive pronoun.	This dog is theirs.
there's	*There's* is a contraction of *there is*.	There's his tag.
them	*Them* is not a demonstrative pronoun.	These (not Them) are mine.
to	*To* used as a preposition means "in the direction of."	They are going to the city.
	To can be used to form an infinitive.	Now is the time to leave.
too	*Too* is an adverb that means "more than enough" and "also."	She ate too many grapes. Can my sister go too?
two	*Two* used as an adjective is a number.	I have two notebooks.
whose	*Whose* is an interrogative pronoun.	Whose tickets are these?
	Whose is also a possessive pronoun.	Jan, whose book I borrowed, is here today.
who's	*Who's* is a contraction of *who is*.	Who's that woman?
your	*Your* is a possessive pronoun.	Are these your glasses?
you're	*You're* is a contraction of *you are*.	You're late again!

Capitalization / Punctuation / Usage

Adjective and Adverb Usage

Comparing	**To compare two things, add -er to one-syllable adjectives and adverbs or use the word more.** This lily is taller than that one. It grew more quickly. **To compare three or more things, add -est or use the word most.** This lily is the tallest of all. It grew most quickly. **Add -er or -est to short adjectives or adverbs. Use more or most and less or least with most modifiers of two or more syllables.** thinner fastest less colorful most easily
Double comparisons	**Avoid double comparisons.** She is a better (*not* more better) skier than he. This is the deepest (*not* most deepest) snow ever!
Irregular comparisons	**Some adjectives and adverbs have special forms for making comparisons.**

Adjectives

good	better	best
bad	worse	worst
many	more	most
little	less	least
far	farther	farthest

Adverbs

well	better	best
badly	worse	worst
far	further	furthest
	farther	farthest

Position of adjectives and adverbs	**A modifier such as *almost, even, hardly, just, nearly, merely, only,* or *scarcely* should be placed as close as possible to the word that it modifies.** Just Mark wants to come to the library. (Mark is the only person who wants to come.) Mark wants to come just to the library. (Mark wants to come to the library and nowhere else.)
fewer, less, much, many	**Use *little, less,* and *least* with things that cannot be counted. Use *few, fewer,* and *fewest* with countable things. Use *much* with uncountable things. Use *many* with countable things.** Is there less interest in Sullivan than in Wright? Are fewer skyscrapers being built now? The John Hancock Tower caused much trouble. Many windows fell out onto the street.

Capitalization / Punctuation / Usage

more ▶

Adjective and Adverb Usage *continued*

real, really, sure, surely	*Real* and *sure* are adjectives. *Really* and *surely* are adverbs. This ring is made of real gold. Pat was sure of her answer. He is a really good skater. He surely is an excellent cook!

Negatives

Negatives	A double negative is the use of two negative words to express one negative idea. Avoid double negatives. *Barely, hardly,* and *scarcely* are considered negative words. INCORRECT: I didn't hardly have enough time. CORRECT: I hardly had enough time.

Pronoun Usage

Agreement	A pronoun must agree with the antecedent to which it refers. Kee bought a newspaper, but Mary read it first. Jeff and Cindy came to dinner. They enjoyed the meal.
Indefinite pronouns	An indefinite pronoun does not refer to a specific person or thing. When you use an indefinite pronoun as a subject, the verb must agree with it. Everyone is out. *(sing.)* Several were out. *(pl.)* Neither is here. *(sing.)* Many are here. *(pl.)* Pronouns must agree with indefinite pronouns used as antecedents. Each has its own name. Others forgot their books. Everyone should bring her own pencil.
Subject and object pronouns	A pronoun used as a subject or as a predicate pronoun (after a linking verb) is called a *subject pronoun*. It is in the *nominative case*. He composed many works for the piano. The writer was she. A pronoun used as an object is called an *object pronoun*. It is in the *objective case*. Clyde collected old coins and sold them. *(direct object)* Let's share these bananas with her. *(object of prep.)* She gave him a choice. *(indirect object)*

Compound subjects and objects	**To choose the correct pronoun in a compound subject or a compound object, say the sentence with the pronoun alone.** Pedro and I went hiking. (I went hiking.) Sara is visiting Al and me. (Sara is visiting me.)
Demonstrative pronouns this, that, these, those	**Do not use *this here, that there, these here,* or *those there*.** That (*not* That there) is a cute animal.
Incomplete comparisons	**To decide which pronoun form to use in an incomplete comparison, add the missing words.** Ben goes hiking more often than I (do). Lane gives him more help than (he gives) me.
Reflexive and intensive pronouns	**Do not use reflexive or intensive pronoun forms in place of personal pronouns.** INCORRECT: Ron and myself repaired the lamp. CORRECT: Ron and I repaired the lamp.
	Do not use *hisself* or *theirselves*. INCORRECT: Adam will do that hisself. CORRECT: Adam will do that himself. INCORRECT: They gave theirselves a head start. CORRECT: They gave themselves a head start.
I, me	***I* is used as a subject. *Me* is used as an object.** Jan and I are going to the show She is taking me.
	When using *I* or *me* with other nouns or pronouns, name yourself last. Beth and I will leave. Give the papers to Ron and me.
we, us	**Use the pronoun *we* with a noun that is the subject of the sentence or that follows a linking verb. Use the pronoun *us* with a noun that is an object.** We fans are proud. They saw us boys. It is we aunts again. He gave us girls a card.
who, whom	**Use the pronoun *who* as a subject. Use the pronoun *whom* as a direct object or object of a preposition.** Who was the surprise guest? *(subject)* Whom did you ask? (Did you ask whom?) *(direct object)* To whom did you speak? *(object of a preposition)*

Capitalization / Punctuation / Usage

more ▶

Guide to Capitalization, Punctuation, and Usage *continued*

Capitalization / Punctuation / Usage

Pronoun Usage *continued*

who, whoever, whom, whomever	The relative pronoun *who* or *whoever* can be used as the subject of a noun clause. The relative pronoun *whom* or *whomever* can be used as the object of a noun clause.
	Whoever calls can talk to me. I know who is calling. Whom you meant is not clear. I'll give the message to whomever it was meant for.
who, whom, whose	When the relative pronoun is the subject of an adjective clause, use *who*. When the relative pronoun is the object of a verb or a preposition in the relative clause, use *whom*. When the relative pronoun is possessive, use *whose*.
	Jan is the student who has contributed the most. Jan is the writer whom we should all thank. Jan, whose stories are funny, will be our editor.

Verb Usage

Active and passive voice	Use the passive voice when the doer of the action is unknown or unimportant. Use the active voice for direct, forceful sentences.
	I baked the bread. (*not* The bread was baked by me.) The Erie Canal was completed in 1825.
Agreement: compound subjects	A compound subject with *and* takes a plural verb.
	Jason, Kelly, and Wanda have new dictionaries.
	A compound subject with *or* or *nor* takes a verb that agrees with the nearer subject.
	She or her cousins are ready to help. Her cousins or Paula is ready to help.
Agreement: titles, names, collective nouns, plural forms	A title or name of a single thing takes a singular verb.
	McNally, Doyle, and Hennessey is a law firm. *Journey Through Bookland* was Sophie's favorite book.
	A collective noun takes a singular verb unless the group's members are referred to.
	The committee is meeting at eight o'clock. The committee have different opinions about that issue.
	A noun with a plural form that names a single amount or item takes a singular verb.
	Ten dollars is too much to pay. (the whole amount)

Agreement: inverted and interrupted order	**Subject and verb must agree, no matter where the subject is.** In the pond were several frogs. The show of photographs is now open.
Possessives with gerunds	**Use a possessive noun or a possessive pronoun before a gerund.** David's traveling took place on weekends. Their singing made the choir remarkable.
Tenses	**Avoid unnecessary shifts in tense.** The sun came out, and we were (*not* are) surprised.
	When a sentence describes actions that took place at two different times, use the past perfect for the earlier action and the past tense for the later action. Bob had trained hard, but he lost the match anyway.
	When a sentence describes two actions in the future, use the future perfect for the earlier action and the present for the later action. I will have left for practice before the sun rises.
	Use the present perfect for an action that occurred at an unspecified time in the past. She has ridden a horse only once.
Irregular verbs	**Irregular verbs do not add *-ed* or *-d* to form the past participle. Their forms must be memorized. Use a form of *have* with the past participle.**

Verb	Past	Past Participle
be	was	been
choose	chose	chosen
do	did	done
eat	ate	eaten
go	went	gone
lay	laid	laid
lie	lay	lain
shine	shone	shone
steal	stole	stolen
tear	tore	torn
throw	threw	thrown
wear	wore	worn

Capitalization / Punctuation / Usage

Words Often Misspelled

You probably use many of the words on this list when you write. If you cannot think of the spelling of a word, you can always check this list. The words are in alphabetical order.

A
acquaintance
again
all right
a lot
always
anxious
anyone

B
basketball
beautiful
because
before
beige
believe
biscuit
brought
bureau

C
campaign
cannot
can't
captain
caught
clothes
colossal
coming
cousin

D
didn't
different
don't

E
eighth
enough
everyone
everything

F
family
favorite
field
finally
friend

G
getting
going
guarantee
guess
guy

H
happened
happily
haven't
heard
here

I
instead
its
it's

K
knew
know

M
might
millimeter
minuscule

N
nuisance

O
o'clock
once
outrageous

P
people
playwright
probably

R
really
received
right

S
someone
stopped
stretch
suppose
swimming

T
their
there
there's
they
they're
thought
through
to
tongue
tonight
too
two

U
usually

V
vacuum

W
weird
we're
whole
wouldn't
write

Y
your
you're

Spelling Guidelines

1. Short vowel sounds are usually spelled with just one vowel in one- or two-syllable words. Long vowel sounds are usually spelled vowel-consonant-*e* or with two vowel letters in one- or two-syllable words.

craft	passion	filter	raven	preach	deceit	donor
strict	meddle	option	theme	raisin	climax	unit
scrub	pennant	luster	roam	legion	triumph	

2. The |ô|, |îr|, |oi|, |ou|, |o͞o|, |o͝o|, |yo͞o|, |är|, |î|, |ôr|, and |ûr| sounds in words of two or more syllables are usually spelled the same as in one-syllable words.

haughty	noisy	flounder	intruder	booster	dilute	commute
merely	fully	wooden	frontier	superb	carton	cordial

3. If a word ends with **e**, the **e** is usually dropped before a suffix beginning with a vowel, such as **-ed** or **-ing**. If a word ends with a vowel and a single consonant and the final syllable is stressed, double the final consonant before adding **-ed** or **-ing**. If the suffix begins with a consonant, the final **e** is usually kept.

bubbling	donating	propelling	amusement
separating	occurred	regretted	scarcely

4. Spellings of final unstressed vowel sounds with **l**, **r**, or **n** must be remembered.

sample	rural	grammar	gallon
channel	error	litter	kitchen

5. The pronunciation of an unstressed final ending does not always give a clue to its spelling.

storage	image	relative	recognize	generous
sausage	positive	organize	exercise	

more ▶

Spelling Guidelines *continued*

6. If a word ends in a consonant + **y**, the **y** changes to **i** when the ending -**es**, -**ed**, -**er**, or -**est**, or the suffix -**ness**, -**ful**, or -**ly** is added.

dair**ies**	appl**ied**	sunn**ier**	heav**iest**	dizz**iness**	merc**iful**

7. Some words have unusual consonant spellings. Double consonant spellings often occur when prefixes or suffixes are added to a word or word root and when two words are joined to make a compound word.

she**ph**erd	a**ff**ectionate	sta**rr**y	ove**rr**ate
wre**s**tle	a**gg**ravate	forbi**dd**en	u**nn**atural
de**bt**or	a**cc**ompany	contro**ll**er	mi**dd**ay
ra**sp**berry	fu**nn**y	tonsi**ll**itis	i**rr**egular

8. The vowel + **r** sounds can be spelled in different ways.

y**ar**n	**ear**th	sk**ir**t	pi**er**ce	th**or**n	**ur**ge

9. Compound words may be spelled as one word, as a hyphenated word, or as two separate words.

newsstand	long-lived	cold front

10. To find the syllables of most VCCV words, divide the word between the consonants.

shoulder	barrel	traffic	pattern	essay	sincere

11. When two different consonants in a VCCCV word spell one sound or form a cluster, divide the word into syllables before or after those two consonants.

laundry	mischief	although	complex	function	extreme

12. To find the syllables of a VCV word, divide the word before or after the consonant.

robot	closet	prefer	repeat	logic	laser

13. The |sh| sound is spelled **sh**, **ss**, **ci**, or **ti**.

cu**sh**ion	se**ss**ion	pre**ss**ure	an**ci**ent	par**ti**al	men**ti**on

14. The final unstressed |ĭk| sounds are often spelled **ic**. The final |əs| sounds are often spelled **ous**. The |chər| sounds are often spelled **ture**.

fantast**ic**	specif**ic**	curi**ous**	jeal**ous**	tor**ture**

15. The final unstressed |əns| or |ns| sounds in some words are spelled **ance** or **ence**. The final |āt| or |ĭt| sounds are spelled **ate**.

entr**ance**	influ**ence**	viol**ence**	fortun**ate**	separ**ate**
allow**ance**	sent**ence**	abs**ence**	associ**ate**	desper**ate**
inst**ance**	sil**ence**	audi**ence**	celebr**ate**	appreci**ate**

16. Final |īz| sounds can be spelled **-ise**, **-ize**, or **-yze**.

desp**ise**	anal**yze**	memor**ize**	paral**yze**

17. The rule "Use **i** before **e** except after **c** or when sounded as |ā|, as in **neighbor** or **weigh**" has exceptions.

bel**ie**f	f**ie**ry	y**ie**ld	d**ie**sel	rec**ei**pt	for**ei**gn
spec**ie**s	rev**ie**w	th**ie**f	dec**ei**ve	fr**ei**ght	l**ei**sure

18. The prefix **con-** is spelled **com** before the consonant **m** or **p**.

confirm	**com**ment	**com**plicate
contest	**com**motion	**com**plete

19. The Latin prefixes **pre-**, **pro-**, **post-**, **ab-**, and **ad-**, and the Greek word part **anti-** bring meaning to words and word roots. The prefix **ab-** is spelled **abs-** before a root that begins with **c** or **t**.

prejudge	**anti**social	**pro**pel	**abs**cess	**post**pone	**ad**journ

20. The prefixes **dis-**, **ex-**, **inter-**, **de-**, **ob-**, **per-**, **pre-**, and **pro-** begin many words. The prefix **ob-** is spelled **oc** when followed by **c**.

disappear	**ex**perience	**de**bate	**ob**lige	**pro**cess
discovery	**inter**fere	**de**velop	**per**suade	**oc**cupy
exclaim	**inter**view	**ob**serve	**pre**paid	**oc**casion

21. The Latin prefix **ad-** may be spelled **af**, **ac**, **ap**, or **as**.

addition	**af**fair	**ac**count	**ap**prove	**as**sist	**as**sume

more ▶

Spelling Guide

Spelling Guidelines *continued*

22. The prefixes **in-**, **un-**, and **non-** may mean "not." Sometimes **in-** is changed to **ir-**, **il-**, or **im-** to match the spelling of the following consonant. Sometimes the prefixes **ad-** and **con-** also change their spelling to match the following consonant.

inaccurate	**ir**regular	**ap**petite	**com**municate
uncertain	**il**legal	**ac**cessory	**col**laborate
nonsense	**im**mature	**al**legiance	**cor**rupt

23. Combining **uni-**, **bi-**, **tri-**, and **semi-** with a word usually does not affect the spelling of the prefix.

universe	**uni**fy	**bi**cycle	**tri**color	**semi**circle	**semi**final

24. The suffix **-ion** can change verbs to nouns.

except	excep**tion**	situate	situa**tion**	conclude	conclu**sion**

25. The suffixes **-ure**, **-age**, **-ion**, **-ment**, **-or**, and **-er** can affect the spelling of words or word roots.

tex**ture**	bond**age**	orna**ment**	opin**ion**	modera**tor**	lectur**er**

26. The suffixes **-ent**, **-ant**, **-ious**, **-ous**, **-able**, **-ible**, **-ile**, **-ial**, and **-al** form adjectives.

excell**ent**	prec**ious**	prob**able**	frag**ile**	artific**ial**
hesit**ant**	marvel**ous**	tang**ible**	fac**ial**	man**ual**

27. The noun suffixes **-ness**, **-dom**, **-ment**, and **-ian** sometimes affect the spelling of base words.

aware**ness**	free**dom**	king**dom**	argu**ment**	equip**ment**	come**dian**

28. The suffix **-able** is usually added to base words. The suffix **-ible** is usually added to word roots.

desir**able**	reli**able**	allow**able**	leg**ible**	divis**ible**	aud**ible**

29. The suffixes **-ory**, **-ary**, and **-ery** are often joined to word roots. When the sound is not clear, the spelling must be remembered.

laborat**ory**	ordin**ary**	myst**ery**

30. Think of a related word before spelling the suffixes **-ant**, **-ance**, **-ent**, and **-ence**.

> signific**ant** signific**ance** intellig**ent** intellig**ence** assist**ant** assist**ance**

31. The Latin prefixes **trans-** and **sub-** appear in many words. When **sub-** is added to a word or root beginning with **p,** the prefix becomes **sup-**.

> **trans**action **trans**fuse **sub**merge **sup**posedly
> **trans**late **sub**urban **sup**plement **sup**ply

32. The Greek suffix **-logy** means "study of." It is often used with Greek roots.

> socio**logy** zoo**logy** psycho**logy**
> geo**logy** mytho**logy** anthropo**logy**

33. Words that are related in spelling and meaning are easier to remember in pairs.

> severe   severity excel   excellence assume   assumption

34. Many English words came from ancient Greek, French, Spanish, and other languages. These words often have unusual spellings.

> sphinx fillet lariat kayak
> pharmacy brunette sierra ukulele

35. Some English words are formed from the names of people or places. Many of these words are no longer capitalized.

> Braille sequoia cologne cheddar
> tuxedo pasteurize silhouette Olympic

36. Some spelling problems can be solved through careful pronunciation.

> chimney governor probably temperament

37. The spelling of similar words is often confused. Note their sound, spelling, and meaning.

> access   excess dessert   desert coma   comma

Diagramming Guide

When you diagram a sentence, you show the relationships among all its different parts. These lessons are designed to lead you through the diagramming process. In the first lessons, you will diagram only the basic parts of the sentence. In these first lessons, you will find certain structures that you do not yet know how to diagram. Do not be concerned. Diagram only those words for which you have directions. As you progress, you will eventually learn to diagram all the given constructions.

Subjects and Predicates

The two main parts of the sentence are the subject and the predicate. In a diagram the simple subject and the simple predicate are placed on a horizontal line called the **base line**. The simple subject is separated from the simple predicate by a vertical line that cuts through the base line.

Each child wore a different costume.

child	wore

In an imperative sentence, a sentence that gives a command, the subject is understood to be "you." Notice how the simple subject and the simple predicate are diagrammed.

Look at the knight's armor.

(you)	Look

Practice

Diagram each simple subject and simple predicate.

1. Mr. Antonavich designed the gorilla suit.
2. Gus fanned his peacock feathers proudly.
3. Listen to the guitar music.
4. First prize went to the child inside the papier-mâché guitar.
5. Many costumes imitated the movie stars' clothes.

Compound Subjects and Predicates

The parts of a compound subject or compound predicate are written on separate horizontal lines. The conjunction is written on a vertical dotted line joining the horizontal lines. Study the example at the top of the next page.

Charlie Chaplin, Ike, and Napoleon chatted and laughed together.

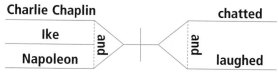

Practice

Diagram the simple or compound subject and the simple or compound predicate in each sentence.

1. Masks, makeup, and hats were popular disguises.
2. Babe Ruth and Eleanor Roosevelt wore authentic costumes.
3. Parents and teachers watched and enjoyed each child's act.
4. A clown, a giraffe, and a helicopter led the costume parade.

Predicate Nouns

Diagram predicate nouns by writing them on the base line after the verb. Between the verb and the predicate noun, draw a line slanting toward the subject to show that the subject and the predicate noun refer to the same thing. Study this example.

The automobile is a modern invention.

automobile | is \ invention

Notice how you diagram a sentence with a compound predicate noun.

The windshield is a protective barrier and a window.

Practice

Diagram the subjects, the verbs, and the predicate nouns in the following sentences.

1. Oliver Evans was an inventor and a steam engine designer.
2. Steam automobiles became the closest rival of the railroad.
3. Gottlieb Daimler and Karl Benz were the developers of the gasoline engine.
4. The trunk of a car was a large metal box originally.

more ▶

Diagramming Guide *continued*

Predicate Adjectives

Diagram a predicate adjective on the base line after the verb. Draw a line slanting back toward the subject to show that the predicate adjective modifies the subject.

Study these diagrams of predicate adjectives.

In the late 1890s, the electric car was popular.

Steam cars had been impractical, noisy, and smelly.

Practice

Diagram the subjects, verbs, and predicate adjectives.

1. The world's first gasoline-powered vehicle was clumsy.
2. These carriages were horseless.
3. In the 1900s a muddy road could be messy and dangerous.
4. By 1908 the parts for cars of the same model were interchangeable.

Direct Objects

Diagram a direct object by writing it on the base line after the verb. Separate the direct object from the verb by a vertical line, but do not let the line cut through the base line.

Tom and Diane designed their new kitchen together.

Study the diagram of a compound direct object.

They selected new appliances, cabinets, and fixtures.

Diagram each subject, verb, and direct object.

1. A carpenter and a plumber prepared the room for renovations.
2. Tom borrowed two ladders and some old canvas.
3. Tom, Diane, and her mother selected curtains for the windows.

Indirect Objects

Diagram an indirect object on a horizontal line below the base line. Draw a slanting line to connect it to the verb.

Mr. Talbot made us salads for lunch.

Mr. Talbot	made	salads

us

Diagram the following sentences, showing the subjects, the verbs, the direct objects, and the indirect objects.

1. Catherine baked us a loaf of French bread.
2. I offered Dad a piece.
3. Dad told us a story about a Paris restaurant.

Adjectives

Diagram an adjective or any of the articles *a, an,* or *the* by placing it on a slanting line under the word it modifies. Join a series of adjectives with a dotted line parallel to the base line. Note where *and* is placed.

Most supermarkets carry fresh, frozen, and canned foods.

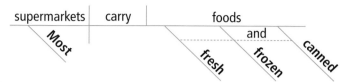

Diagram all of the words in the following sentences.

1. The produce section contains fresh fruit.
2. Broccoli and peas are nutritious green foods.
3. A tall, thin, blond man bought some green seedless grapes.

more ▶

Diagramming Guide *continued*

Adverbs

Diagram an adverb by placing it on a slanting line under the word that it modifies. Write the conjunction joining two or more adverbs on a dotted line between them.

The rather large wedding was planned quickly but carefully.

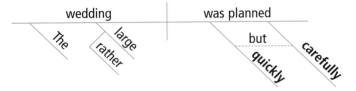

Practice

Diagram all of the words in the following sentences.

1. Some very traditional music was chosen finally.
2. The bride and groom made a relatively long guest list.
3. They discussed their rather complex plans frequently and happily.
4. Fortunately they found an outstandingly creative caterer.

Prepositional Phrases

Diagram a prepositional phrase by writing it under the word it modifies. Place the preposition on a line slanting from the base line. Place the object of the preposition on a horizontal line. Diagram its modifiers in the usual way.

The fancy lettering was done by the hand of a calligrapher.

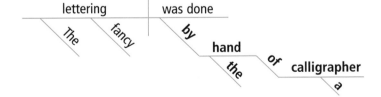

Practice

Diagram all of the words in the following sentences.

1. Calligraphers hold their pens at a certain angle.
2. The tip of the pen is selected for its width.
3. This nib is attached to an ink pen.
4. Calligraphers paint decorations in the margins of their parchments.

Participles and Participial Phrases

Diagram a participle like a prepositional phrase. In a participial phrase, the participle is followed by the word that completes the phrase.

Applauding the superstar wildly, they watched his hurried arrival.

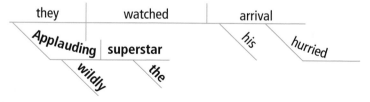

Practice

Diagram all of the words in the following sentences.

1. Happily, they saw him descending the airplane steps.
2. Shouting his name repeatedly, the crowd followed his every move.
3. The smiling film idol loved their totally unquestioning approval.

Gerunds and Gerund Phrases

Before you diagram a gerund, first write the other parts of the sentence on the base line. Then add the standard, or pedestal, for the gerund or the gerund phrase. Each gerund curves down "steps" in the standard, as shown in the example.

The key to managing Katie's puppy is daily training.

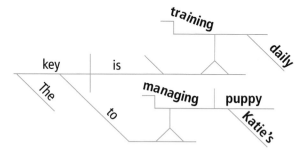

Practice

Diagram all of the words in the following sentences.

1. Developing good habits in her puppy was Katie's goal.
2. Repeating Daffy's name with each command was important.
3. Another important factor in pet rearing is being consistent.

more ▶

Diagramming Guide *continued*

Infinitives and Infinitive Phrases

When an infinitive or an infinitive phrase is used as a subject, a direct object, or a predicate noun, place it on a standard. If an infinitive is used as a modifier, diagram it as you would a prepositional phrase.

To publish a cookbook was hard to accomplish.

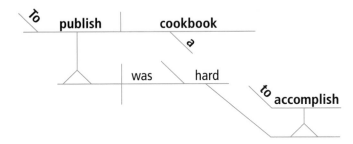

Practice

Diagram the following sentences completely.

1. To organize the recipes into categories seemed more logical to others.
2. To find a chicken recipe meant looking in the poultry section.
3. The reader uses an alphabetical index to locate each recipe.
4. The cookbooks to be sold at the bazaar will raise funds for the needy.

Appositives

Diagram an appositive by enclosing it in parentheses after the noun or the pronoun that it explains. Find the appositive in the sentence at the top of the next page. Then study how the appositive and its modifiers are diagrammed.

Dr. Carl Cohen, my periodontist, specializes in gum diseases.

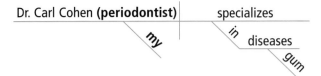

Practice

Diagram all of the words in the following sentences.

1. Debbie Carleton, a dental hygienist, taught me to floss correctly.
2. Gingivitis, a common periodontal disease, inflames the gum tissue.
3. Gums can be irritated by plaque, a sticky form of bacteria.

Compound Sentences

Diagram each clause of a compound sentence as if it were a separate sentence. Place the conjunction joining the clauses on a horizontal line to connect the verbs in the clauses.

William Shakespeare lived in Stratford-upon-Avon, but Anne Hathaway, his wife, grew up in Shottery.

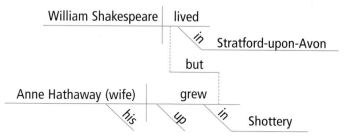

Practice

Diagram the following sentences.

1. Shakespeare began his career as an actor, but he earned his fame as a playwright.
2. His birthplace is on Henley Street, and many tourists visit it each day.
3. John Shakespeare, the writer's father, was a glovemaker, but he became mayor of Stratford-upon-Avon in 1568.

Complex Sentences: Adverb Clauses

Place an adverb clause below the word that it modifies in the main clause, and diagram it as if it were a separate sentence. Place the subordinating conjunction on a dotted line to connect the verb in the clause with the word that the clause modifies. Study the example below.

If the bus fare increases, some commuters will form a car pool.

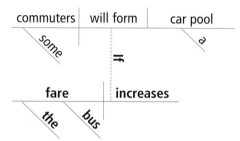

more ▶

Diagramming Guide *continued*

Practice

Diagram the following sentences.

1. Because they travel to the office on weekdays, they need five passengers.
2. Although the driving schedule is flexible, each person is responsible for one day of every week.
3. After the car pool was organized, Dave's day to drive was Thursday.
4. While some passengers nap during the commute, others read.

Complex Sentences: Adjective Clauses

Place an adjective clause below the noun or pronoun that it modifies in the main clause, and diagram it as if it were a separate sentence. Draw a dotted line to connect the relative pronoun in the clause with the noun or pronoun that the clause modifies. Study the example below.

Students who are going to the concert will be excused early.

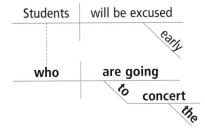

Practice

Diagram the following sentences.

1. The teachers who went on the field trip enjoyed themselves.
2. They all brought shoes that had extra support for walking.
3. The trip, which was paid for by the school, was very educational.
4. One museum that they planned to visit was closed.

Noun Clauses

A noun clause is diagrammed on a standard. First, write the other parts of the sentence on the base line, and then add the standard. Where you place the standard will depend on whether the noun clause is used as a subject, a direct object, an indirect object, an object of a preposition, or a predicate noun. In the following example, the noun clause is used as a direct object.

That girl always says whatever comes into her mind.

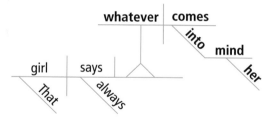

Practice

Diagram the following sentences.

1. The science class is what Roger likes best.
2. Students are often influenced by what they learn in class.
3. That Julianna is a good student is obvious to everyone.
4. Give whoever missed class the homework assignment.
5. Do you know why we are having a test tomorrow?

Nouns in Direct Address

A noun in direct address is diagrammed on a short line above and a bit to the left of the base line. This is its position no matter where the noun in direct address appears in the sentence.

Think, everyone, about our recent discussion and then try again.

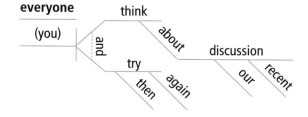

Practice

Diagram all of the words in these sentences.

1. Do you have any notes, Marcy?
2. I do not, sir.
3. She was sick, teacher, with the flu.
4. Now, George, I remember.
5. Children, form small groups and compare your notes.

How to Use This Thesaurus

When do you use a thesaurus? You use one when you want to make your writing more exact or more interesting. Suppose you wrote the following sentence:

After Ted cleaned the dirty window, it was clear.

Is *clear* the most exact word you can use? To find out, use your Thesaurus Plus.

Look up Your Word Turn to the Thesaurus Plus Index on page H98. You will find this entry.

clear, *adj.*

Entry words are in blue type. Because *clear* is blue, you can look up *clear* in the Thesaurus Plus.

Use Your Thesaurus The main entries in the Thesaurus Plus are listed in alphabetical order. Turn to *clear*. You will find the following entry.

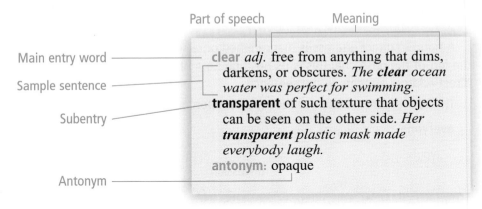

Part of speech Meaning

Main entry word —

Sample sentence —

clear *adj.* free from anything that dims, darkens, or obscures. *The **clear** ocean water was perfect for swimming.*

Subentry —

transparent of such texture that objects can be seen on the other side. *Her **transparent** plastic mask made everybody laugh.*
antonym: opaque

Antonym —

Other Index Entries There are two other types of entries in your Thesaurus Plus Index.

1. The slanted type means that *convey* is a synonym of *move*.

   convey move, *v.*
   convince persuade, *v.*
   cool cold, *adj.*

2. The regular type tells you that *corrupt* is the opposite of *good*.

   corrupt good, *adj.*

A. Use your Thesaurus Plus Index to answer these questions.

1. Is *trait* a main word or a subentry word?
2. What part of speech is *amble*?
3. What is the main entry word for *rugged*?
4. Is *support* a subentry word or an antonym?

B. Use your Thesaurus Plus Index and Thesaurus Plus to answer these questions.

5. What antonyms are listed for *dark*?
6. How many subentries are listed for *reason*?
7. What does *relocate* mean?
8. How many antonyms are listed for *exciting*?
9. What part of speech is *scrumptious*?
10. What does *undisturbed* mean?
11. What is an antonym for *tired*?
12. What color is *vermilion*?
13. What subentries are listed for *rely*?
14. What is an antonym for *sudden*?

C. Use your Thesaurus Plus Index to find the entry for each underlined word. Then use the Thesaurus Plus to rewrite each sentence, using a more exact or interesting word.

15. Because of the American Revolution, the United States is not a part of the British Commonwealth.
16. The Boston Tea Party occurred before the Revolution.
17. Angry colonists boarded British ships and threw chests of tea into Boston Harbor.
18. They were expressing their objections to British rule.
19. The argument was about the British tax on tea.
20. It was the colonists' belief that the tax was unfair.
21. Rapidly they banded together to rebel.
22. Only a small quantity of colonists were pro-British.
23. The Declaration of Independence was an effect of the colonists' dissatisfaction with England.
24. On July 4, 1776, the Declaration of Independence said that the colonies should be self-governing.
25. The Treaty of Paris of 1783 brought an end to the war.
26. This was no little achievement for the colonists.

Thesaurus Plus Index

conclusion, *n.*
conduct move, *v.*
confusing, *adj.*
conscientious good, *adj.*
consent refuse, *v.*
consequence, *n.*
consider think, *v.*
contaminated bad, *adj.*
continue persist, *v.*
contract, *v.*
contrast, *v.*
converse talk, *v.*
convert change, *v.*
convey move, *v.*
convince persuade, *v.*
cool cold, *adj.*
corrupt bad, *adj.*
corrupt good, *adj.*
courageous brave, *adj.*
cowardly brave, *adj.*
crawl hurry, *v.*
creep hurry, *v.*
cried said, *v.*
crimson red, *adj.*
crisp cold, *adj.*
cunning sharp, *adj.*
current ancient, *adj.*

damage fix, *v.*
damage harm, *v.*
damp, *adj.*
dark, *adj.*
dark bright, *adj.*
dash hurry, *v.*
dawdle hurry, *v.*
dazzling bright, *adj.*
dazzling exciting, *adj.*
decadent good, *adj.*
declared said, *v.*
decline refuse, *v.*
decline reject, *v.*
definite sharp, *adj.*
delay hurry, *v.*

delectable good, *adj.*
delicious good, *adj.*
delightful bad, *adj.*
deny refuse, *v.*
depart move, *v.*
depend rely, *v.*
depressed happy, *adj.*
deprived rich, *adj.*
destroy, *v.*
detail, *n.*
dewy damp, *adj.*
dexterous good, *adj.*
difference likeness, *n.*
different alike, *adj.*
differentiate contrast, *v.*
difficult easy, *adj.*
dim bright, *adj.*
dim dark, *adj.*
diminish increase, *v.*
dire bad, *adj.*
disagreeable bad, *adj.*
discuss talk, *v.*
disobedient bad, *adj.*
distinct sharp, *adj.*
distinguish contrast, *v.*
divide mix, *v.*
doubt objection, *n.*
drag pull, *v.*
dreadful bad, *adj.*
dry damp, *adj.*
dull boring, *adj.*
dull colorless, *adj.*
dull exciting, *adj.*
dull interesting, *adj.*
dusky dark, *adj.*

earlier after, *adv.*
earlier before, *adv.*
earnest serious, *adj.*
easy, *adj.*
edge, *n.*
effect consequence, *n.*
effortless easy, *adj.*
electrifying exciting, *adj.*

emerald green, *adj.*
enchanting exciting, *adj.*
end conclusion, *n.*
energetic tired, *adj.*
engrossing exciting, *adj.*
enigmatic confusing, *adj.*
enlarge increase, *v.*
entertaining interesting, *adj.*
enticing exciting, *adj.*
entreated said, *v.*
equivalent alike, *adj.*
ethical good, *adj.*
evacuate move, *v.*
even rough, *adj.*
even smooth, *adj.*
evidence detail, *n.*
evil good, *adj.*
examine, *v.*
example, *n.*
exceedingly very, *adv.*
excellent bad, *adj.*
exceptionally very, *adv.*
exciting, *adj.*
exciting boring, *adj.*
exclaimed said, *v.*
expand contract, *v.*
expedition trip, *n.*
experience, *v.*
expert, *n.*
expert good, *adj.*
expose, *v.*

fact detail, *n.*
faded colorless, *adj.*
faint colorless, *adj.*
fascinating exciting, *adj.*
fascinating interesting, *adj.*

more ▶

L

large small, *adj.*
later after, adv.
later before, *adv.*
law-abiding good, adj.
lead guide, v.
leading figure expert, n.
level rough, *adj.*
level smooth, adj.
light dark, adj.
light easy, adj.
light heavy, *adj.*
liken contrast, *v.*
likeness, *n.*
little small, adj.
long ago before, adv.
lug move, v.
lukewarm cold, *adj.*
lumpy smooth, *adj.*
luscious good, adj.

M

magenta red, adj.
main, *adj.*
mar harm, v.
maroon red, adj.
masterful good, adj.
meager small, adj.
melancholy sad, adj.
mend fix, v.
mesmerizing exciting, adj.
middle edge, *n.*
migrate move, v.
mingle mix, v.
minute small, adj.
misgiving objection, n.
mix, *v.*
moaned said, v.
modest shy, adj.
moist damp, adj.
monotonous boring, adj.

monotonous exciting, *adj.*
morose happy, *adj.*
motivate move, v.
motive reason, n.
mouth-watering good, adj.
move, *v.*
muggy damp, adj.
mumbled said, v.
murky confusing, adj.
murmured said, v.
muttered said, v.

N

naughty bad, *adj.*
needy rich, *adj.*
negligent careful, *adj.*
nippy cold, adj.
noble good, adj.
notable important, adj.
noted author expert, n.
notice see, v.
nubbly smooth, *adj.*

O

objection, *n.*
observe examine, v.
ominous bad, adj.
on account of because of, prep.
once after, *adv.*
once before, adv.
opaque clear, *adj.*
opinion, *n.*
opposite alike, *adj.*
opposition objection, n.
outcome consequence, n.
outgoing shy, *adj.*

P

paltry small, adj.
pass move, v.
patch fix, v.
peaceful smooth, adj.
penetrating sharp, adj.
pensive serious, adj.
perceive see, v.
perceptive sharp, adj.
persist, *v.*
persuade, *v.*
petite small, adj.
piercing sharp, adj.
pleasant bad, *adj.*
plod hurry, *v.*
point of view opinion, n.
poisoned bad, *adj.*
polished good, *adj.*
polished smooth, *adj.*
poor bad, adj.
poor rich, *adj.*
position argument, n.
preserve change, *v.*
previously after, adv.
previously before, adv.
primary main, adj.
primitive ancient, adj.
principal main, adj.
principled good, adj.
prior to after, *adv.*
prior to before, adv.
proclaimed said, v.
proficient good, adj.
pronounced said, v.
proof detail, n.
proper bad, *adj.*
provocative exciting, adj.
prudent careful, adj.
pull, *v.*

more ▶

Thesaurus Plus

push pull, *v.*
pushiness spunk, *n.*
puzzling confusing, *adj.*

Q

qualified good, *adj.*
quality characteristic, *n.*
queried said, *v.*
query ask, *v.*
questioned said, *v.*
quickly, *adv.*
quick-witted sharp, *adj.*
quit move, *v.*
quit persist, *v.*

R

radiant happy, *adj.*
rangy tall, *adj.*
rapidly quickly, *adv.*
reason, *n.*
reason detail, *n.*
reason think, *v.*
recall remember, *v.*
reckless careful, *adj.*
recollect remember, *v.*
red, *adj.*
refuse, *v.*
reject, *v.*
reject refuse, *v.*
relocate move, *v.*
rely, *v.*
remarked said, *v.*
remember, *v.*
repair destroy, *v.*
repair fix, *v.*
replied said, *v.*
reply ask, *v.*
requested said, *v.*
researcher expert, *n.*
resemblance likeness, *n.*
respectable good, *adj.*
responded said, *v.*
rested tired, *adj.*
restore destroy, *v.*

restore fix, *v.*
result consequence, *n.*
retorted said, *v.*
returned said, *v.*
reveal expose, *v.*
rich, *adj.*
righteous good, *adj.*
rim edge, *n.*
rise, *v.*
riveting exciting, *adj.*
roared said, *v.*
roasting cold, *adj.*
rocky rough, *adj.*
rose red, *adj.*
rough, *adj.*
rough smooth, *adj.*
rousing exciting, *adj.*
ruby red, *adj.*
rugged rough, *adj.*
ruin destroy, *v.*
run, *v.*
rush hurry, *v.*
russet brown, *adj.*

S

sad, *adj.*
sad happy, *adj.*
said, *v.*
satiny smooth, *adj.*
savory good, *adj.*
scarlet red, *adj.*
scientist expert, *n.*
scramble hurry, *v.*
screamed said, *v.*
scrumptious good, *adj.*
scrupulous good, *adj.*
see, *v.*
seething angry, *adj.*
sensational exciting, *adj.*
sense experience, *v.*
separate mix, *v.*
sepia brown, *adj.*

serene smooth, *adj.*
serious, *adj.*
serious funny, *adj.*
serious important, *adj.*
shaded dark, *adj.*
shadowy dark, *adj.*
shaggy rough, *adj.*
sharp, *adj.*
shift move, *v.*
shining bright, *adj.*
shoot run, *v.*
short tall, *adj.*
shouted said, *v.*
shove pull, *v.*
show expose, *v.*
shrewd sharp, *adj.*
shrieked said, *v.*
shy, *adj.*
significant important, *adj.*
silky smooth, *adj.*
similar alike, *adj.*
similarity likeness, *n.*
simple easy, *adj.*
sinister bad, *adj.*
sit rise, *v.*
skilled good, *adj.*
sleek smooth, *adj.*
slick smooth, *adj.*
slippery smooth, *adj.*
slowly quickly, *adv.*
small, *adj.*
smart sharp, *adj.*
smeared streaked, *adj.*
smooth, *adj.*
smooth rough, *adj.*
snapped said, *v.*
snarled said, *v.*
soggy damp, *adj.*
solemn funny, *adj.*
solution consequence, *n.*
some time back before, *adv.*

sorrowful happy, *adj.*
sound healthy, *adj.*
source expert, *n.*
speculate think, *v.*
spine-tingling exciting, *adj.*
spokesperson expert, *n.*
spot see, *v.*
spunk, *n.*
stabbing sharp, *adj.*
stammered said, *v.*
stand argument, *n.*
stand rise, *v.*
start conclusion, *n.*
stated said, *v.*
steaming cold, *adj.*
steer guide, *v.*
stirring exciting, *adj.*
streaked, *adj.*
striped streaked, *adj.*
study examine, *v.*
stuttered said, *v.*
subsequently after, *adv.*
subsequently before, *adv.*
sudden, *adj.*
superior bad, *adj.*
support objection, *n.*
sweltering cold, *adj.*
swiftly quickly, *adv.*

tainted bad, *adj.*
talented good, *adj.*
talk, *v.*
tall, *adj.*
teasing serious, *adj.*
tedious boring, *adj.*
tedious exciting, *adj.*
tepid cold, *adj.*
termination conclusion, *n.*
then after, *adv.*

thereafter after, *adv.*
therefore, *adv.*
think, *v.*
throw, *v.*
thus therefore, *adv.*
tiny small, *adj.*
tired, *adj.*
tiresome exciting, *adj.*
tiresome interesting, *adj.*
toasty cold, *adj.*
toss throw, *v.*
tote move, *v.*
touch move, *v.*
tour trip, *n.*
tow pull, *v.*
towering tall, *adj.*
trait characteristic, *n.*
tranquil smooth, *adj.*
transfer move, *v.*
transform change, *v.*
transparent clear, *adj.*
transport move, *v.*
trip, *n.*
trivial important, *adj.*
trust rely, *v.*
trustworthy good, *adj.*
tug pull, *v.*
turbulent smooth, *adj.*
turn down reject, *v.*

uncomplicated easy, *adj.*
undisturbed smooth, *adj.*
unfavorable bad, *adj.*
unimportant main, *adj.*
unmistakable sharp, *adj.*
unpleasant bad, *adj.*
unruffled angry, *adj.*
until now before, *adv.*
untroubled smooth, *adj.*

unwell healthy, *adj.*
unwrinkled smooth, *adj.*
upright good, *adj.*
upshot conclusion, *n.*
upstanding good, *adj.*

vacate move, *v.*
valiant brave, *adj.*
vast small, *adj.*
vermilion red, *adj.*
very, *adv.*
virtuous bad, *adj.*
virtuous good, *adj.*
vivid colorless, *adj.*

warm cold, *adj.*
watchful careful, *adj.*
weak healthy, *adj.*
wealthy rich, *adj.*
weary tired, *adj.*
weighty heavy, *adj.*
well healthy, *adj.*
well-behaved bad, *adj.*
well-defined sharp, *adj.*
well-to-do rich, *adj.*
whined said, *v.*
whispered said, *v.*
wicked bad, *adj.*
wicked good, *adj.*
win over persuade, *v.*
wintry cold, *adj.*
wreck destroy, *v.*
wretched sad, *adj.*
wrinkly rough, *adj.*

yelled said, *v.*
yummy good, *adj.*

Thesaurus Plus

Thesaurus Plus

after *adv.* behind in place or order. *You go ahead, and we'll come along **after**.*

subsequently following in time. *Sue started out taking French but **subsequently** dropped it.*

later after a particular time or event. *Let's eat now and hike **later**.*

once immediately after. ***Once** Michelle arrives, we can begin.*

thereafter from then on. *Jill learned to sew and **thereafter** made all her own clothes.*

then afterward. *I went to Paris and **then** London.*

antonyms: before, earlier, previously, prior to

alike *adj.* exactly or almost exactly the same. *His twin sisters look very much **alike**.*

similar related in appearance or nature; somewhat alike but not the same. *Your coat is **similar** to mine.*

comparable capable of being compared; having like traits. *A parakeet and a canary are **comparable** in size.*

equivalent equal in amount, value, meaning, force, measure. *A dime is **equivalent** to ten pennies.*

antonyms: different, opposite

ancient *adj.* very old, aged. *The abandoned house looks **ancient**.*

primitive of or in an early stage of development. *This museum has a collection of **primitive** sculpture.*

antonym: current

angry *adj.* feeling or showing ill temper. *The **angry** customer demanded a refund.*

furious full of extreme anger. *Lisa was **furious** when someone dented her new car.*

irritated annoyed; bothered. *Joel gets **irritated** when I call him Joe.*

seething violently agitated, disturbed, or annoyed. ***Seething** with anger, he stormed away.*

inflamed aroused by anger or other strong emotion. *The audience was **inflamed** by his unfair remarks.*

antonyms: calm, unruffled

argument *n.* a statement in support of a point of view; a reason. *The editorial listed several **arguments** against the proposed law.*

case a set of reasons offered in support of something. *She presented a strong **case** for buying a new bus.*

position a point of view or an attitude on a certain question. *The candidate's **position** on new taxes is well known.*

stand an opinion on an issue or question that one is prepared to defend. *The mayor took a strong **stand** against closing the school.*

issue a subject being discussed or disputed. *The new dress code is a hotly debated **issue**.*

ask *v.* to seek an answer to. ***Ask** Mrs. Jurigian if she saw anyone unusual outside her house.*

interrogate to question closely. *The police **interrogated** a suspect.*

inquire to seek information from. *They **inquired** about her job.*

query to question. *Officer Gould **queried** them about their whereabouts on June 10.*

antonyms: answer, reply, inform

B

Shades of Meaning

bad *adj.*

1. not good:
   poor, foul, inferior, unpleasant, disagreeable

2. morally evil:
   wicked, sinister, corrupt

3. causing distress:
   dreadful, unfavorable, ominous, dire

4. not behaving properly:
   disobedient, naughty, improper, insubordinate

5. diseased:
   infected, contaminated, tainted, poisoned

antonyms: good, pleasant, virtuous, excellent, superior, delightful, well-behaved, proper

---

because of *prep.* being brought on or made possible by. ***Because of** her strong will, she succeeded.*

on account of due to. ***On account of** rain, the band concert was postponed.*

as a result of being an outcome of. *She fell **as a result of** fainting.*

Word Bank

before *adv.* at an earlier time.

at one time	formerly
earlier	some time back
in the past	previously
back then	prior to
once	
long ago	
until now	

antonyms: after, afterward, subsequently, later

boring *adj.* not interesting. *The TV program was so **boring** that I fell asleep.*

dull lacking excitement. *Not one player scored during the **dull** soccer match.*

monotonous not interesting because of being always the same. *That very **monotonous** song just repeated the same words over and over.*

tedious tiresome because of slowness or length. *Copying my lengthy term paper was a **tedious** job.*

antonyms: exciting, interesting

brave *adj.* able to face danger or pain without showing fear. *The **brave** firefighter went calmly into the burning house to look for the family's pet.*

valiant showing great courage. *The emergency team made a **valiant** rescue in the blizzard.*

courageous able to face great challenges without showing fear. *The **courageous** knights protected the king.*

antonyms: afraid, cowardly

bright *adj.* radiant with light or color. ***Bright** umbrellas make a rainy day more cheerful.*

shining giving off or reflecting a steady light. *A **shining** lantern lit the path.*

brilliant glittering; sparkling with light. *The costume was **brilliant** with sequins.*

dazzling so bright as to be blinding; blazing with light. *The lifeguard squinted in the **dazzling** sunlight.*

antonyms: dark, dim

more ▶

Shades of Brown

brown *adj.* having the color of most kinds of soil.

beige:	a very pale brown, like that of sand
fawn:	a light, yellowish-brown, like a young deer
khaki:	a dull, yellowish-brown, like a soldier's uniform
bronze:	an olive-brown, like the metal bronze
russet:	a dark, reddish-brown, like a dark-colored apple
sepia:	a grayish-brown, like the color of an antique photograph

---

C

careful *adj.* using caution or care. *Looking for clues, the detective made a **careful** search.*

cautious not taking chances. *Kim is too **cautious** to try the difficult climb to the top.*

prudent having or showing good judgement; sensible. *We made a **prudent** decision to save our money for college.*

watchful being alert to trouble or danger. *The **watchful** German shepherd barked at every passerby.*
antonyms: casual, reckless, negligent

change *v.* to make or become different. *The new owners of the house **changed** the color from pink to yellow.*

transform to make very different in form or appearance. *The decorations **transformed** the gym into a colorful dance floor.*

alter to make somewhat different. *Al must **alter** his report to make it shorter.*

convert to make or be made into something different. *We **converted** the barn into a guest house.*
antonyms: keep, preserve

characteristic *n.* something that makes one person, group, or thing different from others. *One **characteristic** of racing cars is a streamlined shape.*

trait a distinguishing aspect, as of a person or an animal. *Eye color is an inherited **trait**.*

quality a general tendency or effect. *Many folk songs have a sad **quality** to them.*

feature a noticeable part or aspect. *An important **feature** of this radio is its small size.*

clear *adj.* free from anything that dims, darkens, or obscures. *The **clear** ocean water was perfect for swimming.*

transparent of such texture that objects can be seen on the other side. *Her **transparent** plastic mask made everybody laugh.*
antonym: opaque

How Cold Was It?

cold *adj.* having a low temperature.

1. slightly cold:
   cool, fresh, bracing, brisk, crisp

2. quite cold:
   nippy, wintry, chilly, frosty

3. extremely cold:
   icy, frozen, frigid, freezing, bone-chilling

antonyms: hot, tepid, lukewarm, warm, toasty, sweltering, broiling, roasting, steaming

Thesaurus Plus

colorless *adj.* without a distinct hue. *The moon's landscape is **colorless**.*

faint not clearly seen; dim. *A **faint** light flickered in the distance.*

faded without brightness, owing to gradual changes. *The old curtains were **faded** from the sunlight.*

dull drab. *The desert's **dull** colors change with spring rains.*

indistinct not clear or well-defined; fuzzy. *The boat was **indistinct** in the fog.*
antonym: vivid

conclusion *n.* the last part of something. *The **conclusion** of her speech made us cheer.*

end the final part or limit of something. *Labor Day marks the **end** of summer.*

close an ending or finish. *Her home run brought the game to a **close**.*

termination a formal or official ending. *His failure to pay his dues led to the **termination** of his club membership.*

upshot the final result; outcome. *The **upshot** of her efforts was a raise.*

finish a stopping point or end. *The race was thrilling from the start to the **finish**.*
antonyms: beginning, start

confusing *adj.* causing misunderstanding. *These **confusing** instructions won't help us learn how to wallpaper.*

murky vague; difficult to understand. *Her **murky** explanation was impossible to follow.*

puzzling hard to figure out. *The disappearance of the money is very **puzzling**.*

enigmatic not clear in meaning; mysterious. *We wondered how to interpret his **enigmatic** message.*
antonym: clear

consequence *n.* something that follows from an action or condition. *One **consequence** of the construction was traffic delays.*

effect something that has happened in response or reaction to something else. *Sunshine and a cool breeze always has the **effect** of making me feel energetic.*

result the outgrowth of a particular action, operation, or cause. *He slept late and, as a **result**, missed the bus.*

outcome a final product. *To most people, the **outcome** of the election was no surprise.*

solution the successful outcome of a problem. *Moving to a dry climate was the **solution** to my cousin's health problems.*
antonym: cause

contract *v.* to draw together; make or become smaller in length. *She **contracted** her muscles to swing the baseball bat.*

compress to put pressure on something so as to reduce the space it takes up. *Everyone **compressed** their clothes to fit into their backpacks.*
antonym: expand

contrast *v.* to compare in order to reveal differences. *The reviewer **contrasted** two modern films with two silent movies.*

distinguish to recognize differences. *Some people cannot **distinguish** between red and green.*

differentiate to understand or show the differences between. *Alison **differentiates** between spiders and true insects in her science report.*
antonym: liken

Thesaurus Plus

more ▶

damp *adj.* slightly wet. *Our bathing suits are still **damp**.*

humid having a large amount of water vapor. *The rain shower made the air **humid**.*

moist slightly wet with water spread thinly over a surface. ***Moist** leaves clung to the windows.*

muggy unpleasantly warm and humid, with little or no breeze. *The **muggy** summer made us wish for a cold fall.*

soggy softened with moisture. *Our heels sank into the **soggy** earth.*

dewy slightly wet with water droplets. ***Dewy** spider webs glistened in the morning sun.*

antonym: dry

dark *adj.* without light or with very little light. *He felt his way across the **dark** cellar.*

shaded screened from light. *Most frogs like **shaded** places.*

dim faintly lighted. *A **dim** shape appeared across the field.*

shadowy having scattered areas of shade. *A **shadowy** path led through the woods.*

dusky tending to darkness, as from the approach of night. *She lit a lamp in the **dusky** room.*

antonyms: bright, light

destroy *v.* to wipe out or demolish. *The tornado **destroyed** the town.*

ruin to damage beyond repair. *Her shoes were **ruined** in the rain.*

wreck to cause to break up. *Using heavy-duty equipment, the crew **wrecked** the old convention hall.*

antonyms: repair, restore

detail *n.* a part of a report or other composition that supports the main idea; an individual or specific item. *Adding more **details** will help your story.*

fact something real or known with certainty. *Pamela couldn't find the **facts** to back up her idea.*

evidence something that serves as proof. *The author presented little **evidence** of an unhappy childhood.*

reason a fact or cause that explains why something should or does exist. *The major stressed safety as a **reason** for widening the road.*

proof demonstration of the truth of something. *Our success is **proof** that the plan works!*

information facts about a certain subject. *This textbook on intelligence contains much **information** about the brain.*

easy *adj.* not difficult. *Tad solved the **easy** puzzle quickly.*

uncomplicated not hard to understand, deal with, or solve. *We followed Dad's **uncomplicated** directions without any problem.*

effortless easily done. *The athlete made weightlifting seem **effortless**.*

light needing little effort. *Because I am tired, I will just do **light** work.*

simple not complicated. *This game is **simple** enough for a young child.*

antonyms: complex, difficult

edge *n.* the line where an object or area ends. *The fence at the **edge** of the canyon prevents accidents.*

border the boundary where one thing ends and another begins. *The river forms the **border** of the land.*

rim the outside line or margin of something. *The cup's **rim** is chipped.*

antonyms: center, middle

Thesaurus Plus

examine *v.* to look at carefully. *The child **examined** the new toy.*

inspect to look at carefully in order to detect flaws. *You should **inspect** a used car before you buy it.*

study to look at closely in order to find out something. *He **studied** her face to see how she really felt.*

observe to watch with attention. *The bird watchers **observed** the eagles.*

example *n.* one item that is typical of a whole class or category. *The Irish setter is an **example** of an excellent hunting dog.*

case a particular condition or occurrence. *Sometimes you get a busy signal, in which **case** you can phone again later.*

instance an action or occurrence that is representative of a general subject. *Interrupting was just one **instance** of her rudeness.*

illustration something that serves as an example or demonstration. *A falling rock is an **illustration** of the effect of gravity.*

Word Bank
exciting *adj.* arousing, stimulating.

stirring	captivating
rousing	fascinating
inspiring	intriguing
gripping	mesmerizing
enticing	spine-tingling
riveting	breathtaking
engrossing	electrifying
absorbing	sensational
dazzling	provocative
alluring	compelling
enchanting	hair-raising

antonyms: boring, bland, dull, tedious, tiresome, insipid, colorless, monotonous, humdrum

experience *v.* to take part in; live through. *Almost everyone **experiences** failure at times.*

feel to experience physically or emotionally. *He **felt** anxious alone in the house.*

sense to become aware of by instinct. *The animals **sensed** the approaching storm.*

go through to experience with pain or displeasure. *I hope you didn't **go through** much difficulty.*

expert *n.* a person with great knowledge in a particular field. *Dr. Lee is an **expert** on animal behavior.*

source a person who supplies information. *In describing the accident, the reporter used a witness as her **source** of information.*

leading figure a very important person in a certain field. *Her great talent made her a **leading figure** among painters.*

noted author a well-known writer. *A book by a **noted author** draws great interest.*

researcher a person who studies a subject in order to contribute new knowledge. *Medical **researchers** have developed cures for many different illnesses.*

spokesperson a person who speaks as a representative for others. *The **spokesperson** announced that the governor would hold a press conference tomorrow.*

authority an accepted source of knowledge or advice. *Her mother is an **authority** on gardening.*

scientist a person who studies the laws of nature. *Newton was the **scientist** who discovered the laws of gravity.*

antonym: amateur

more ▶

Thesaurus Plus

expose *v.* to uncover; lay bare. *I **exposed** my back to the sun.*
show to make visible. *They **showed** us the way out of the jungle.*
reveal to make known; disclose. *The magician **revealed** her secrets.*

F

fix *v.* to set right. *This word processing program will **fix** the misspellings in my document.*
repair to put back in useful condition after damage, injury, or wear. *My uncle **repairs** old lawnmowers.*
mend to repair by joining torn, frayed, or broken parts. *Can you please **mend** this torn sleeve on my jacket?*
patch to cover a hole, rip, or torn place with a small piece of material. *She **patched** the nail hole in the bicycle tire.*
restore to bring back to an original condition. *The owner is **restoring** this historic house.*
antonyms: break, damage

funny *adj.* arousing laughter or amusement. *Rosa thinks that her practical jokes are **funny**.*
hilarious causing a great deal of laughter. *The cartoon had a **hilarious** scene with a silly pig in the mud.*
comical humorous. *The monkey's **comical** tricks made us laugh.*
antonyms: serious, solemn

G

Shades of Meaning
good *adj.*
1. of high moral quality: *honorable, ethical, noble, law-abiding, upstanding, conscientious, virtuous, principled, upright, trustworthy, scrupulous, respectable, righteous*
2. having much ability: *skilled, proficient, gifted, qualified, accomplished, adept, talented, polished, expert, dexterous, masterful*
3. pleasant-tasting: *delicious, scrumptious, mouthwatering, delectable, appetizing, yummy, flavorful, savory, luscious*
antonyms: wicked, evil, immoral, decadent, corrupt

green *adj.* having the color of most plant leaves and growing grass. *The fields turned **green** with the spring rains.*
chartreuse of a light yellowish green. *Most new fire engines are **chartreuse** instead of red.*
emerald of a dark yellowish green. *The cat's **emerald** eyes shone against its white fur.*

guide *v.* to direct the course of. *Our counselor **guided** us on our hike.*
lead to show the way by going ahead. *The captain always **leads** the team onto the field.*
steer to physically control the course of a vehicle, ship, or plane. *It is difficult to **steer** a truck on this winding road.*

happy *adj.* feeling satisfaction and pleasure. *She was very **happy** when the gift arrived.*

joyful feeling great happiness. *Their wedding anniversary was a **joyful** occasion.*

radiant glowing or beaming with happiness. *Her **radiant** face told us that she had won.*

blissful full of calm contentment. *He spent a **blissful** afternoon sailing.*

antonyms: depressed, glum, morose, sad, sorrowful

harm *v.* to injure; hurt. *Looking directly at the sun can **harm** a person's eyes.*

damage to injure something so that it is less valuable or useful. *Frost **damaged** the orange crop.*

mar to spoil the surface or appearance of. *Those rough crates **marred** the table top.*

healthy *adj.* free from disease or injury. *The **healthy** plants grew strong and tall.*

fit being in good physical shape. *Drew exercises and feels **fit**.*

sound having no damage or weakness. *Surprisingly, the shabby old house still had a **sound** frame.*

well not sick. *Even during the flu season, he stayed **well**.*

antonyms: ill, weak, unwell

heavy *adj.* having relatively great weight. *The rocks are very **heavy**.*

weighty having great weight. *This package is too **weighty** to carry.*

antonym: light

hurry *v.* to move or act with haste. *The students **hurried** to their seats.*

dash to race with sudden speed. *He **dashed** through the closing doors.*

rush to move or act with great haste. *The ambulance **rushed** to the accident scene.*

scramble to move quickly in a disorganized manner. *The players **scrambled** for the loose ball.*

fly to move swiftly. *The horses **flew** by in a cloud of dust.*

antonyms: amble, crawl, creep, plod, dawdle, delay

important *adj.* able to determine or change things. *Gettysburg was the site of an **important** Civil War battle.*

serious worthy of concern. *A **serious** engine problem prevented the car from starting.*

significant full of meaning. *The footprints are a **significant** clue.*

notable worthy of notice or comment. *There is only one **notable** exception to the rule.*

antonyms: frivolous, trivial

increase *v.* to make or become greater or larger. *The **increase** in pollution is dangerous to us.*

enlarge to make or become larger. *We had our photographs **enlarged**.*

antonym: diminish

interesting *adj.* arousing and holding attention. *I read **interesting** books quickly.*

intriguing arousing one's curiosity. *The disappearance of the rake is an **intriguing** puzzle.*

entertaining pleasing and enjoyable. *His **entertaining** stories kept us amused.*

fascinating extremely interesting. *Visiting my foreign relatives is always **fascinating**.*

antonyms: boring, dull, tiresome

more ▶

likeness *n.* a way in which things are the same. *I see a real **likeness** between the plots of those two mystery stories.*

similarity the quality of being alike but not identical. *The **similarity** among the three sisters was startling.*

resemblance a closeness in appearance. *There is a strong **resemblance** between those twins.*

antonym: difference

main *adj.* most important; major. *The **main** ride in the park is a water slide.*

principal first in rank or importance. *Willa is the **principal** soloist in the chorus.*

central having the most influence or control. *All orders come from the **central** headquarters.*

primary first or best; chief. *Her **primary** goal is to get into a good college.*

antonym: unimportant

mix *v.* to blend into a single substance. *We **mixed** blue paint with white paint to make light blue.*

blend to unite or join completely. *The two sounds of the instruments **blended** into one.*

mingle to join in with others. *We **mingled** with the crowd during intermission.*

antonyms: divide, separate

Shades of Meaning

move *v.*

1. to take something from one place to another:
   transport, carry, shift, transfer, convey, conduct, pass, bear, cart, haul, lug, tote

2. to leave one's location:
   depart, relocate, quit, vacate, migrate, evacuate

3. to cause an emotion or change of feeling:
   affect, arouse, touch, inspire, impress, motivate, influence

objection *n.* the expression of an opposing view or argument. *The committee explained their **objection** to the higher taxes.*

opposition the act of resisting or being in conflict. *The mayor's decision met with **opposition**.*

doubt worry; concern. *Mai had serious **doubts** about our plans.*

misgiving uncertainty about the wisdom of an action. *Leon now has **misgivings** about buying that used compact disc player.*

antonyms: agreement, support

opinion *n.* a belief not based on positive knowledge. *I don't agree with your **opinion** of the movie.*

belief something thought to be true. *The coach has **belief** in the team.*

point of view the position from which something is considered. *From this **point of view**, the decision was unfair.*

attitude a state of mind regarding someone or something. *Jeff has a positive **attitude** toward his job.*

feeling a belief based on emotion or instinct. *She had a strong **feeling** that we would succeed.*

judgment a decision reached after careful weighing of evidence. *The skipper's **judgment** was that the seas were too rough to sail.*

P

persist *v.* to insist or repeat obstinately. *She **persists** in practicing her saxophone.*

continue to keep on. *Even in snow or sleet, the mail carrier **continues** to work.*

antonym: quit

persuade *v.* to cause someone to do or believe something by arguing, pleading, or reasoning. *He **persuaded** us to wait another day.*

convince to cause someone to feel certain. *The lawyer had **convinced** the jury of her client's innocence.*

win over to appeal successfully to someone's emotions or sense of values. *His enthusiasm for the project **won over** the committee.*

influence to have an effect or impact on. *Our friendship did not **influence** my decision.*

pull *v.* to draw something forward. *I **pulled** a shirt from the closet.*

haul to draw or carry with effort. *The horses **hauled** the heavy load.*

tug to pull sharply. *A large fish **tugged** at the fish line.*

drag to draw or haul along the ground. *The dog **dragged** the branch across the yard.*

tow to draw along behind with a chain or rope. *A neighbor **towed** our car home after it broke down.*

antonyms: push, shove

 Q

quickly *adv.* with speed; right away. *The teller **quickly** counted the coins accurately.*

swiftly with great speed and smoothness. *The relay runner **swiftly** passed the baton to his teammate.*

rapidly in very fast sequence. *A hummingbird's wings beat so **rapidly** that you see only a blur.*

instantaneously immediately. *We **instantaneously** recognized the man in the photograph.*

antonym: slowly

 R

reason *n.* a statement or fact that explains why something exists or occurs. *Do you have a good **reason** for being late to this meeting?*

cause a person, thing, condition, or action that makes something happen. *The **cause** of the fire was faulty wiring.*

grounds the foundation for a belief or an action. *They have no **grounds** for claiming that we are responsible for the horrible mistake.*

basis an underlying cause, idea, or fact. *Belief in freedom is the **basis** of the Constitution of the United States.*

motive an emotion or desire that causes someone to act in a certain way. *His **motive** for working was to make money for a summer sports camp.*

more ▶

Shades of Red	
red adj. the color of ripe cherries.	
rose:	a deep pinkish-red
scarlet:	a bright orange-red
burgundy:	a dark reddish-brown
vermilion:	a bright red
cerise:	a dark red
ruby:	a very deep red
crimson:	a vivid purplish-red
maroon:	a dark purplish-red
carmine:	a deep purplish-red
magenta:	a strong reddish-purple

refuse *v.* to be unwilling to accept or agree to. *Sam was so tired that he refused to shovel more snow.*

deny to withhold or keep back. *The guard denied us permission to photograph the paintings.*

decline to refuse politely. *I invited her to dinner, but she declined.*

reject to refuse to recognize or accept. *The voters rejected the proposal for a new gymnasium.*
antonyms: agree, consent, grant

reject *v.* to refuse to accept, use, grant, consider. *My parents rejected my idea of a pet monkey.*

decline to refuse to accept or do. *He declined my offer to help him.*

turn down to refuse to accept. *The faculty turned down the principal's plan.*

rely *v.* to count on the ability or willingness of someone or something. *I'll rely on you to do the job.*

depend to count on for support or help. *You can depend on a friend.*

trust to have confidence in the soundness or honesty of. *I trust you because you tell me the truth.*

remember *v.* to think of again. *I just remembered to turn left.*

bring to mind to cause to think of. *Your dog brings to mind one that I had years ago.*

recollect to remember through deliberate effort. *I cannot recollect where I left my key.*

recall to bring back to memory. *Can you recall the names of all the Great Lakes?*
antonym: forget

rich *adj.* having much money, goods, land, or other valuables. *If I were rich, I'd travel all over the world.*

wealthy having a great quantity of money, valuable possessions, or resources. *The United States is a wealthy nation.*

affluent having plenty of money. *Large, beautiful houses can be the mark of an affluent community.*

well-to-do well-off; enjoying wealth or profit. *Their successful business has made them well-to-do.*
antonyms: deprived, needy, poor

rise *v.* to go up; ascend. *The moon rises quickly.*

stand to take or maintain an upright position on the feet. *I don't like to stand in lines.*
antonym: sit

rough *adj.* having an irregular surface. *The ocean looks rough on a windy day.*

bumpy full of lumps. *We laughed as we drove down the bumpy road.*

coarse not smooth or fine. *The coarse sand hurt our feet.*

rocky full of lumps from or as if from rocks. *It was hard to walk on the rocky path.*

rugged having an uneven surface or jagged outline. *Four-wheel drive vehicles can drive over rugged terrain.*

shaggy having long, rough hair, wool, or fibers. *The animals still had their **shaggy** winter coats.*

wrinkly puckered or creased. *An elephant's skin is **wrinkly**.*

antonyms: even, level, smooth

run *v.* to move on foot at a pace faster than a walk. *The hitter **ran** to first base.*

gallop to run at a fast, rhythmic pace. *We heard the mustangs **galloping** toward us.*

shoot to move swiftly and smoothly. *A meteor **shot** across the sky.*

S

sad *adj.* showing, filled with, or expressing sorrow or regret. *The losing team members had **sad** faces.*

forlorn pitiful in appearance or condition. *The **forlorn** kitten cried for its mother.*

wretched full of misery or woe. *Brad felt **wretched** when he lost the club's money.*

melancholy gloomy; depressed. *Long periods of rain make many people feel **melancholy**.*

antonyms: glad, happy, joyful

Shades of Meaning

said *v.* spoke aloud.

1. said quietly or unclearly:
   whispered, murmured, mumbled, muttered, grunted

2. said openly and clearly:
   stated, announced, declared, articulated, pronounced, asserted, remarked, proclaimed

3. asked:
   questioned, queried, inquired, requested, interrogated

Shades of Meaning (cont.)

4. answered:
   replied, responded, retorted, returned

5. said in a complaining way:
   whined, moaned, groaned, grumbled, griped

6. said in an angry way:
   snarled, growled, snapped, hissed

7. said loudly:
   yelled, screamed, shrieked, bellowed, hollered, roared, shouted

8. said in an excited or nervous way:
   exclaimed, cried, stuttered, stammered

9. said in a pleading way:
   begged, implored, entreated, beseeched

see *v.* to become aware of by sight. *In the distance, he **saw** clouds of black smoke.*

spot to detect; recognize; locate. *We **spotted** a fawn under the bush.*

notice to become aware of casually or by chance. *On my way home, I **noticed** a hat on a park bench.*

perceive to recognize or understand information gathered through any of the senses. *He said he was fine, but I **perceived** he was very upset.*

serious *adj.* not joking or speaking casually. *Are you **serious** about moving to Chicago?*

earnest showing or expressing deep, sincere feeling. *The police chief made an **earnest** plea for help.*

more ▶

Thesaurus Plus

grave extremely serious; solemn. *The doctor's face was **grave** as she gave them the bad news.*

pensive in a thoughtful mood. *Jan was not unhappy, but she was quite **pensive**.*

antonyms: fooling, teasing

Shades of Meaning
sharp *adj.*
1. clearly outlined: *clear, distinct, unmistakable, in focus, well-defined, definite*
2. able to think quickly and well: *intelligent, smart, bright, astute, shrewd, clever, canny, perceptive, cunning, alert, quick-witted*
3. felt suddenly and strongly: *piercing, penetrating, keen, acute, stabbing, intense*
antonyms: blurry, fuzzy, foggy, hazy

shy *adj.* quiet and withdrawn in manner. *He was too **shy** to speak.*

bashful timid and embarrassed. *Sam felt **bashful** when he suddenly became the center of attention.*

modest tending to play down one's own talents, abilities, or accomplishments. *The concert pianist was **modest** about her talent.*

antonyms: bold, outgoing

small *adj.* slight in size, number, quantity, extent, volume, or importance. *Kate's room is too **small** for two people.*

little below average in size, quantity, or degree. *They have **little** faith in his promise.*

tiny extremely small. *The **tiny** ant looked like a speck.*

petite small and dainty. *One girl is tall, while the other is **petite**.*

paltry insignificant; small in power or value. *He earned a **paltry** sum.*

meager lacking in quantity or richness; scanty. *We looked for beans, but the crop was **meager**.*

minute exceptionally small. ***Minute** flecks of gold glittered in the sun.*

antonyms: big, great, huge, large, vast

Shades of Meaning
smooth *adj.*
1. flat: *even, level, unwrinkled*
2. having a fine-textured surface: *sleek, slick, satiny, silky, slippery, glossy, glassy, polished*
3. calm: *undisturbed, untroubled, peaceful, serene, tranquil*
antonyms: hilly, coarse, bumpy, rough, grainy, nubbly, lumpy, turbulent

spunk *n.* spirit; courage. *My friend showed real **spunk** by calling for help when I broke my arm.*

pushiness aggressiveness. *Your brother's **pushiness** is annoying.*

streaked *adj.* marked with irregular lines of color. *The sky was **streaked** with long, pink clouds.*

striped marked with straight, even lines of color. *His tie had a simple **striped** pattern.*

smeared marked with messy-looking streaks. *His apron was **smeared** with spaghetti sauce.*

sudden *adj.* happening without warning. *The rainstorm was surprisingly **sudden**.*

abrupt unexpected. *Later, we made an **abrupt** change of plans.*
antonym: gradual

talk *v.* to have a conversation. *At dinner Jill and Ray **talked** about the day's events.*

chatter to speak rapidly and without much purpose; jabber. *A noisy parrot **chattered** in a cage.*

gossip to start or spread rumors. *Mary **gossiped** about the mysterious visitor.*

discuss to speak together about. *We can **discuss** the issue at dinner.*

converse to speak informally with others. *Mark, who reads a lot, can **converse** on many subjects.*

tall *adj.* of greater than average height. *The redwood is one of the **tallest** trees in the world.*

colossal extreme in size, extent, or degree; enormous; gigantic. *From a distance, the people climbing the **colossal** pyramid looked like ants.*

rangy long-legged and thin. *The **rangy** girl stepped over the fence with ease.*

towering of impressive height; very tall. ***Towering** trees hid the sun.*
antonym: short

therefore *adv.* for that reason. *He was sleepy and **therefore** took a long nap.*

thus consequently; as a result. *They broke the tie, and **thus** they won the game.*

hence thereby. *This necklace is gold; **hence**, it is expensive.*

think *v.* to form an idea in one's mind. ***Think** about your purpose before you start writing.*

believe to suppose or to expect. *I **believe** that it will rain later today.*

consider to think over carefully. *She **considered** moving to Chicago.*

imagine to form a mental picture, idea, or impression of. *Can you **imagine** the world without colors?*

reason to think clearly and logically. *Try to **reason** out what must have really happened.*

speculate to think deeply on a particular subject; to ponder. *Scientists have **speculated** about why dinosaurs died out.*

throw *v.* to send something through the air with a swift motion of the arm. *The catcher **threw** the ball.*

hurl to throw with great force. *She **hurled** the javelin a long distance.*

toss to throw lightly. *He **tossed** the keys onto the desk.*

tired *adj.* having little physical or mental energy. *The **tired** dog paddled slowly to shore.*

weary feeling worn out. *We were **weary** after the long drive.*
antonyms: energetic, rested

trip *n.* a journey from one place to another. *We took a **trip** to Ohio.*

expedition a trip made by an organized group for a definite purpose. *The scientists made an **expedition** to study the eclipse.*

tour a trip to or through a place for the purpose of seeing it. *The geologist provides guided **tours**.*

very *adv.* to a high degree. *A chimpanzee is a **very** unusual pet.*

exceedingly to an extreme degree. *Computers can do mathematics **exceedingly** quickly.*

exceptionally to an unusual degree. *Jo is an **exceptionally** fine singer.*

Glossary of Language Arts Terms

abbreviation   the shortened form of a word.

abstract noun   a word that names ideas, qualities, and feelings.

active voice   when the subject of a verb is the doer of the action.

adjective   a word that describes a noun or a pronoun.

adjective clause   a subordinate clause that modifies a noun or a pronoun.

adjective phrase   a prepositional phrase that modifies a noun or a pronoun.

adverb   modifies a verb, an adjective, or another adverb. It tells how, when, where, or to what extent.

adverb clause   a subordinate clause used as an adverb.

adverb phrase   a prepositional phrase that modifies a verb, an adjective, or an adverb.

agreement   the use of a singular verb with a singular subject and a plural verb with a plural subject.

antecedent   the noun that a pronoun replaces.

appositive   a noun or a noun phrase that directly follows another noun and explains or identifies it.

articles   *a, an,* and *the.*

audience   the person or people who read or listen to something.

auxiliary verb   a helping verb used with a main verb to form a verb phrase.

brainstorm   to think of ideas.

clause   a group of words that contains both a subject and a predicate.

collective noun   a word that names persons, animals, or things that act together as a group.

common noun   names any person, place, thing, or idea.

comparative degree of an adjective   used to compare two things.

comparative degree of an adverb   used to compare two actions or qualities.

complete predicate   includes all the words in the predicate.

complete subject   includes all the words in the subject.

complex sentence   includes at least one subordinate clause combined with one independent clause.

compound-complex sentence   a sentence that has more than one independent clause and at least one subordinate clause.

compound noun   made up of two or more words that act as a single noun.

compound predicate   formed by combining the predicates of two or more simple sentences with the same subject.

compound sentence   two or more independent clauses with related ideas joined by a comma and a conjunction.

compound subject   formed by combining the subjects of two or more simple sentences with the same predicate.

concrete noun   names things that can be seen, heard, smelled, tasted, or touched.

conjunction   a word used to connect words or groups of words.

contraction   a word formed by combining two words and replacing missing letters with an apostrophe.

conventions   the standard rules of spelling, grammar, usage, capitalization, and punctuation.

coordinating conjunction connects words or groups of words of equal importance (*and, but, or*).

correlative conjunctions used in pairs, such as *either/or*.

declarative sentence a statement that ends with a period.

demonstrative pronoun points out particular persons and things (*this, that, these, those*).

details exact facts about a topic.

direct object the noun or pronoun that receives the action of a verb.

direct quotation a speaker's exact words enclosed in quotation marks.

drafting the part of the writing process when the writer first attempts to put his or her ideas on paper in the form of a composition.

elaborate to give more details.

essential clause identifies the noun or the pronoun it modifies and is necessary for the sentence to make sense. It is not set off by commas.

exclamatory sentence expresses strong feeling and ends with an exclamation point.

future perfect tense used for an action that will be completed before another future action.

future tense shows something that will happen later.

gerund the present participle of a verb used as a noun.

gerund phrase functions as a noun.

helping verb an auxiliary verb used with the main verb.

ideas thoughts that form the main points of a composition.

imperative sentence gives a command or makes a request and ends with a period.

indefinite pronoun does not refer to definite persons or things and does not always have antecedents.

indent to begin the first line of a sentence a few spaces in from the margin.

independent clause a group of words that can stand by itself as a sentence.

indirect object tells who or what was affected by the action of a transitive verb.

indirect quotation what a person says without using the person's exact words.

infinitive formed with *to* and the base form of the verb. It is used as a noun, an adjective, or an adverb.

infinitive phrase made up of an infinitive and the words that complete its meaning. It acts as a noun, an adjective, or an adverb.

intensifier an adverb that tells to what extent.

intensive pronoun emphasizes a noun or another pronoun.

interjection a word or a group of words that expresses feeling. It is followed by a comma or an exclamation point.

interrogative pronoun used in questions (*what, which, who, whom,* and *whose*).

interrogative sentence asks a question and ends with a question mark.

interrupted order when other words come between the subject and the verb of a sentence.

intransitive verb does not have an object.

inverted order when a subject follows all or part of a predicate.

irregular verb a verb in which the past and past participle forms do not end with *-ed.*

linking verb links the subject with a noun or an adjective in the predicate that names or describes the subject.

more ▶

Glossary

main idea the most important thought or point.

main verb in a verb phrase expresses the action or the state of being.

modifier a word that describes other words.

negative a word that means "no" or "not."

nonessential clause gives extra information about the noun or the pronoun it modifies. It is set off with commas.

noun a word that names a person, place, thing, or idea.

noun clause a subordinate clause that functions as a noun.

object of the preposition the noun or pronoun that follows the preposition.

object pronoun used as a direct or indirect object.

order words words that signal sequence, such as *first* or *next*.

organization the structure of a composition.

paragraph a group of sentences that work together to express one main idea.

participial phrase made up of a participle and its accompanying words.

participle a verbal that is used as an adjective.

passive voice when the subject of a verb is the receiver of the action.

past perfect tense used for an action that was completed before another past action.

past tense used to show something that already happened.

perfect tense made up of a form of *have* and the past participle.

personal pronoun classified by person (first, second, or third) and by number (singular or plural). Third-person singular pronouns

are also classified by gender (masculine, feminine, or neuter).

phrase a group of words that does not contain a subject and a predicate.

plural referring to more than one.

possessive noun a noun that shows ownership.

possessive pronoun replaces a possessive noun.

predicate tells what the subject is, has, does, or feels.

predicate adjective follows a linking verb and describes the subject.

predicate noun follows a linking verb and identifies or renames the subject.

preposition relates a noun or a pronoun to another word in the sentence.

prepositional phrase begins with a preposition, ends with the object of the preposition, and includes any words that modify the object.

present perfect tense used to show action that took place at an indefinite time in the past.

present tense used to show something happening now.

presentation the way in which writers share their compositions.

prewriting the part of the writing process when the writer chooses a topic and plans the composition.

principal parts the verb, the present participle, the past, and the past participle.

progressive form a verb form that expresses continuing action. It is made up of a form of the verb *be* plus the present participle.

pronoun a word that takes the place of one or more nouns.

proofreading the part of the writing process when the writing is checked for mistakes.

Glossary

proper adjective formed from a proper noun and capitalized.

proper noun names a particular person, place, thing, or idea.

publish the part of the writing process when writers make a final copy of their composition.

purpose the goal of a composition.

reflexive pronoun refers to the subject.

regular verb a verb in which the past and past participle forms end with -*ed*.

revising the part of the writing process when the writer tries to improve the working draft.

run-on sentence expresses too many thoughts without correct punctuation.

sensory words words that describe how something looks, sounds, feels, tastes, or smells.

sentence a group of words that expresses a complete thought.

sentence fluency the structure and order of sentences so that a composition reads smoothly.

sentence fragment a group of words that does not express a complete thought.

series three or more items listed together in a sentence.

simple predicate the key word or words in the complete predicate. It is always a verb.

simple sentence an independent clause that stands by itself.

simple subject the key word or words in the complete subject. It is usually a noun or a pronoun.

singular referring to one.

subject tells whom or what the sentence is about.

subject pronoun used as a subject or a predicate pronoun.

subordinate clause a group of words that cannot stand by itself as a sentence.

subordinating conjunction a word such as *before* used to introduce some subordinate clauses.

superlative degree of an adjective used to compare three or more things.

superlative degree of an adverb used to compare three or more actions or qualities.

supporting sentences tell more details about a main idea.

tense of a verb tells when the action or the state of being occurs.

topic the subject of a discussion or a composition.

topic sentence a sentence that states a main idea about a subject.

transitional words words that connect sentences or ideas, such as *also, however,* and *for example*.

transitive verb expresses action that is received by a noun or a pronoun in the predicate.

verb expresses physical action, mental action, or a state of being.

verb phrase consists of a helping or auxiliary verb and a main verb.

verbal a word that is formed from a verb but used as a noun, an adjective, or an adverb.

voice in writing, the personality of the writer conveyed through the written words.

word choice the selection of interesting, exact words.

working draft a composition that is not yet final.

writing conference a discussion between a writer and a reader about the writer's composition.

writing process a series of steps that a writer follows to write a composition.

Glossary

Glossary of Language Arts Terms **H121**

Index

Index

Index

Index *continued*

Index

Index *continued*

types of
Interviews, 39, 48, 158, H12
Introductions, writing,
451, 452, 453–457, 464, 473, 491–495, 496–503, 537, 542, 550–551, 561, 589
Italics, 260–261, 292

J

Journals, 93, 131, 136, 212, 244, 274, 401

L

Language
choice, 490, 504, 656
formal, 32, 504, 513
informal, 32, 504
loaded, 517
tone, 490, 504, 656
Letters, 42, 279, 290, 301, 305, 398, 426
activities for writing, 42, 96, 121, 124, 135, 167, 250, 255, 278, 301, 305, 398
parts of, 253–255, 278, 290
types of
business, 167, 250, 278, 290, 512–513
friendly, 66, 96, 124, 135, 163, 255, 290, 301, 398, 644–645
newspaper (letter to editor), 42, 278, 305
Libel, 609
Library, 581, H25–H28
Linking verbs. *See* Verbs
Listening

for author's purpose, 524, 612
for details, 24–25, 442, 466, 506, 554, 591, 638, 668
for information, 524
to interpret, 524
to interpret nonverbal cues, H10–H11
for main ideas, 443, 458, 524, 612
to a narrative, 612
to an opinion, 442, 443, 447, 458, 506, 520–521
for persuasive tactics, 514–515
to predict outcomes, 317
responding to a speaker, 36, 39, 42, 45, 60, 84, 93, 96, 134, 143, 146, 154, 163, 238, 240, 247, 250, 262, 265, 301, 317, 349, 352, 357, 360, 366, 378, 380, 398, 401, 404, 407, 411, 415, 447, 458, 481, 506, 520–521
and taking notes, 442, 524, 612
to understand ideas, 39, 442, 458, 466, 480–481, 506, 524, 554, 591, 612, 638, 668
Listening, speaking, thinking strategies
distinguish between opinion and fact, 442, 443, 444, 445, 447, 453–457, 458, 471, 481, 496–509

identify persuasive techniques, 45, 87, 88, 146, 238, 250, 277, 305, 322, 366, 378, 491–495, 496–509, 514–519, 524
Listing, 15, 458, 579
Literary terms
character, 652, 654, 661, 674–679, 683
dialogue, 674–679
fiction, 652
foreshadowing, 663
metaphor, 477, H13
mood, 656, 666, 683
personification, 477
plot, 652, 662, 663, 677, 683
setting, 134, 652, 653, 661, 676–677
simile, 477, H13
Literature
discussing, 653–659
fiction, 652, 653–659
responding to, 653–659

M

Main idea
keeping to, 452, 453–457, 458
listening for, 443, 447
of paragraphs, 20, 443, 444, 445, 447, 453–457, 526, 539, 552, 573
Main topics, in outlines, 585–588
Main verbs. *See* Verbs
Maps, 593, 594, 663, H31
Mechanics, 34–36,

Index

Index

Index *continued*

Index

Index

Acknowledgments *continued*

"To the Editor of The Herald" by Olga Owens Huckins from *The Boston Herald.* Reprinted by permission of The Boston Herald.

"Lichens: The 'Tough Guy' Plants" by Vince Brach from *Highlights for Children Magazine,* June 1998 issue. Copyright ©1998 by Highlights for Children, Inc., Columbus, Ohio. Reprinted by permission of the publisher.

"Passports to Understanding" from *Wouldn't Take Nothing for My Journey Now* by Maya Angelou. Copyright ©1993 by Maya Angelou. Reprinted by permission of Random House, Inc.

From *Texas: An Illustrated History* by David G. McComb, New York: Oxford University Press, 1995.

From "Wilbur and Orville" from *The Wright Brothers: How They Invented the Airplane* by Russell Freedman. Copyright ©1991 by Russell Freedman. Reprinted by permission of Holiday House, Inc. All rights reserved.

Poetry

"The Base Stealer" from *The Orb Weaver* by Robert Francis. Copyright ©1960 by Robert Francis, Wesleyan University Press. Reprinted by permission of University Press of New England.

"Blues Stanza" from *The First Book of Jazz* by Langston Hughes. Copyright ©1955, 1976, 1982 by Franklin Watts, Inc. Reprinted by permission of Franklin Watts, Inc.

"Martin Luther King, Jr." from *Blacks* by Gwendolyn Brooks. Copyright © 1991 by Gwendolyn Brooks Blakely. Reprinted by permission of the author.

"Sailor" originally published as "Marinero" by Alberto Forcada. Copyright ©1992 by Alberto Forcada and CIDCLI, S.C. All rights reserved. English translation copyright © Judith Infante. Reprinted by permission of CIDCLI, S.C. and the translator.

Book Report

Into Thin Air: A Personal Account of the Mount Everest Disaster by Jon Krakauer. Copyright ©1997 by Jon Krakauer. Reprinted by permission of Villard Books, a division of Random House, Inc.

Student Handbook

Definitions of "forecast," "gargoyle," "insulate," and "sash" from *The American Heritage® Student Dictionary.* Copyright ©1998 by Houghton Mifflin Company. Reproduced by permission of *The American Heritage Student Dictionary.*

"Eclipse" excerpt from *The World Book Encyclopedia,* Volume 6. Copyright ©2000 by World Book, Inc. By permission of the publisher. www.worldbook.com.

Pronunciation key on page 399 from *The American Heritage® Student Dictionary.* Copyright ©1998 by Houghton Mifflin Company. Reproduced by permission of *The American Heritage Student Dictionary.*

"Water Use in the U.S." from *World Eagle,* September 1999 issue. Copyright ©1999 by World Eagle/IBA, Inc. Reprinted with permission from World Eagle, 111 King Street, Littleton, MA 01460 U.S.A. 1-800-854-8273. All rights reserved.

One Minute Warm-up

8/1 *The Great Dimpole Oak* by Janet Taylor Lisle, drawings by Stephen Gammell, published by Orchard Books, 1987. Used by permission.

8/1 *The Life and Times of the Peanut* by Charles Micucci, published by Houghton Mifflin Company, 1997. Used by permission.

8/2 *Ospreys* by Dorothy Hinshaw Patent, photographs by William Munoz, published by Clarion Books, 1993. Used by permission.

8/3 *Black Diamond: The Story of the Negro Baseball Leagues* by Patricia C. McKissack and Frederick McKissack, Jr., published by Scholastic Inc., 1994. Used by permission.

8/3 *Passport on a Plate: A Round-the-World Cookbook for Children* by Diane Simone Vezza, illustrated by Susan Greenstein. Text copyright ©1997 by Diane Simone Vezza. Illustrations copyright ©1997 by Susan Greenstein. Reprinted with the permission of Simon & Schuster Books for Young Readers, an imprint of Simon & Schuster Children's Publishing Division.

8/3 *The Barn* by Avi, published by Avon Books, 1994. Used by permission.

8/3 *The Phantom Tollbooth* by Norton Juster, illustrated by Jules Feiffer. Text copyright ©1961 and renewed 1989 by Norton Juster. Illustrations copyright ©1961 and renewed 1989 by Jules Feiffer. Reprinted by permission of Random House Children's Books, a division of Random House, Inc.

8/3 *Ultimate Sports: Short Stories by Outstanding Writers for Young Adults* edited by Donald R. Gallo. Copyright ©1995 by Donald R. Gallo. Used by permission of Random House Children's Books, a division of Random House, Inc.

8/4 *Althea Gibson* by Tom Biracree, published by Chelsea House Publishers, 1989. Used by permission.

8/4 *Martha Graham: A Dancer's Life* by Russell Freedman, published by Clarion Books, 1998. Used by permission.

8/5 *Alvin Ailey, Jr.: A Life in Dance* by Julinda Lewis-Ferguson, published by Walker and Company, 1994. Used by permission.

8/5 *Kid Cash: Creative Money-Making Ideas* by Joe Lamancusa, published by TAB Books, 1993.

8/5 *Restless Spirit: The Life and Work of Dorothea Lange* by Elizabeth Partridge, published by Viking, 1998. Used by permission.

Acknowledgments *continued*

8/6 *Salamandastron: A Novel of Redwall* by Brian Jacques, illustrated by Gary Chalk, published by Philomel Books, 1992.

8/6 *The House on Mango Street* by Sandra Cisneros. Copyright ©1984 by Sandra Cisneros. Reprinted by permission of Ballantine Books, a division of Random House, Inc.

8/6 *The Journey Back* by Johanna Reiss, published by Thomas Y. Crowell, 1976. Used by permission.

8/7 *Collecting Baseball Memorabilia* by Thomas S. Owens. Copyright ©1996 by Thomas S. Owens. Used by permission of The Millbrook Press.

8/7 *Oracle Bones, Stars, and Wheelbarrows: Ancient Chinese Science and Technology* by Frank J. Ross, Jr., illustrated by Michael Goodman, published by Houghton Mifflin Company, 1982. Used by permission.

8/7 *Within Reach: My Everest Story* by Mark Pfetzer and Jack Galvin, photographs by Dutton Books, 1998. Used by permission.

8/8 *April and the Dragon Lady* by Lensey Namioka, published by Harcourt Brace & Company, 1994. Used by permission.

8/8 *El Bronx Remembered: A Novella and Stories* by Nicholasa Mohr, published by HarperCollins Publishers, 1975. Used by permission.

8/8 *To Build a Fire* by Jack London, illustrated by Byron Glaser, published by Creative Education, Inc., 1980. Used by permission.

Student Writing Model Contributors

Bethany Braun, Rachel Cipriano, Katie Clark, Christine Coe, Joshua Crespo, Daniel Griffin, Julia Gruberg, Donna Guu, Philip Howard, Daniel Riley Kershner, Edward Lin, Theo Lipson, Elizabeth McCarthy, Ryan Moore, Andrew O'Sullivan

Credits

Illustrations

Special Characters illustrated by: Joe, the Writing Pro by Rick Stromoski; Pencil Dog by Jennifer Beck Harris; Enrichment Animals by Scott Matthews.

John Bendall Brunello: 37, 113, 141
Ann Bissett: H30 (left)
Chris Demarest: 34, 46, 54, 63, 236, 239, 241, 248, 268, 272, 275, 346, 361
David Diaz: 11-13
Jim Gordon: 206
True Kelley: 203
Rita Lascaro: 502, 518
Andy Levine: 142
Ethan Long: 517, H15
David Marshall: 1-4, 6-8
Beth Peck: 620, 622
Trevor Pye: 85 (bottom)
Tim Robinson: 94
Claudia Sargent: H105, H106 (top), H112-H116
Lauren Scheuer: 25, 43, 51, 67 (center), 99, 129, 138, 162 (bottom), 166, 278 (center, bottom), 302, 323, 355, 477, 482, 514, 634, 636
Alfred Schrier: 308
Michael Sloan: 82, 85 (top), 118, 125, 152, 367, 373, 408, 412
David Soman: 648, 651
Jim Stout: H30 (right)
George Thompson: 403
George Ulrich: 119, 194, 204, 210, 317, H106 (bottom)
Matt Wawiorka: 67 (bottom), 140, 155, 159, 162 (top), 167 (bottom), 200, 216, 217 (bottom), 330, 379, 380 (center), 418 (center)
Bill Whitney: 211, 324
Amy L. Young: 377
Debra Ziss: 217 (center)

Maps

Ortelius: 66, 96, H31

Photographs

iv © Jan Butchofsky-Houser/CORBIS. **ix** © Bojan Brecelj/CORBIS. **x** © J. Sneesby/B. Wilkins/Tony Stone Images. **xi** © Arnulf Husmo/Tony Stone Images. **xii** © Ron Chapple/FPG International. **xiii** (t) © Paul & Lindamarie Ambrose/FPG International. (b) © Adam Woolfitt/CORBIS. **28** © PhotoDisc, Inc. **33** © Telegraph Colour Library/FPG International. **35** © Jack Vartoogian. **37** © David R. Frazier/Tony Stone Images. **39** © Walter Bibikow/FPG International. **41** © Margot Conte/Earth Scenes. **42** © Rick Gayle/The Stock Market. **44** © The Newberry Library/Stock Montage, Inc. **45** © Popperfoto/Archive Photos. **46** © Tony Freeman/PhotoEdit. **48** © Popperfoto/Archive Photos. **49** © Don Smetzer/Tony Stone Images. **50** © Jim Whitmer. **52** © Museo Capitolino, Rome, Italy/ET Archive, London/SuperStock, Inc. **55** © Tim Davis/Tony Stone Images. **56** © SuperStock, Inc. **58** © SuperStock, Inc. **60** © PhotoDisc, Inc. **62** (l) © Noah Satat/Earth Scenes. (c) © Karen Tweedy-Holmes/Earth Scenes. (r) © Charlie Ott/Photo Researchers, Inc. **63** © Richard Hutchings/PhotoEdit. **64** © Underwood and Underwood/CORBIS. **72** © Tim Fuller/Photo Network. **73** © Hulton-Deutsch Collection/CORBIS. **74** © Paul Avis/FPG International. **75** © Hulton-Deutsch Collection/CORBIS. **76** © CORBIS. **79** © PhotoDisc, Inc. **81** © Jan Butchofsky-

Acknowledgments *continued*

Houser/CORBIS. **82** © Cindy Charles/PhotoEdit. **83** © David M. Jennings/The Image Works. **86** © Robert Ginn/PhotoEdit. **89** (t) © Owen Franken/CORBIS. (b) © Owen Franken/Stock Boston. **91** © Manoj Shah/Tony Stone Images. **92** © Stephen J. Krasemann/Photo Researchers, Inc. **93** © Corel Corporation. **95** © Bruce Gaylord/Visuals Unlimited. **97** © Duncan Smith/Artville. **98** © PhotoDisc, Inc. **105** © SuperStock, Inc. **106** © PhotoDisc, Inc. **107** © PhotoDisc, Inc. **111** © Chris Hamilton/The Stock Market. **112** © David Young-Wolff/PhotoEdit. **114** © Mitch Hrdlicka/PhotoDisc, Inc. **116** © Matthew Stockman/Allsport USA. **117** © Bettmann/CORBIS. **119** © Nicole Katano/Tony Stone Images. **120** © Aneal Vohra/Unicorn Stock Photo. **122** © Burke and Triolo/Artville. **123** © Martha McBride/Unicorn Stock Photos. **127** © Frank Cezus/Tony Stone Images. **128** © Digital Vision/Picture Quest. **130** © Mary Kate Denny/PhotoEdit. **132** (t) © Gerard Lacz/Animals Animals. (b) © Ann Purcell, Carl Purcell/Words and Pictures/Picture Quest. **134** © Ian Cartwright/PhotoDisc, Inc. **135** © David Forbert/Stock Connection/Picture Quest. **136** (r) © Zig Leszczynski/Animals Animals. (l) © Clive Druett; Papilio/CORBIS. **139** © Corel Corporation. **145** © Christel Rosenfeld/Tony Stone Images. **146** (t) © CORBIS. (b) © Comstock, Inc. **147** Image provided by MetaTools. **148** © Gamma-Liaison. **150** © Culver Pictures. **151** © Bettmann/CORBIS. **152** © Darrell Gulin/Tony Stone Images. **153** © John Warden/Tony Stone Images. **154** (t) © PhotoDisc, Inc. (b) © Peter Weimann/Animals Animals. **155** © Bettmann/CORBIS. **157** © Anna E. Zuckerman/PhotoEdit. **158** © 1998 North Wind Pictures. **160** (t) © Jeff Greenberg/Visuals Unlimited. (b) © N/A/Archive Photos/Picture Quest. **161** © Mike Johnson Photography. **163** © CORBIS. **164** (t) © Duomo/CORBIS. (b) © David Young-Wolff/PhotoEdit. **170** © Kathi Lamm/Tony Stone Images. **173** © PhotoDisc, Inc. **174** © Roger Ressmeyer/CORBIS. **176** © CORBIS. **177** © PhotoDisc, Inc. **179** © Corel Corporation. **180** © Corel Corporation. **182** © PhotoDisc, Inc. **183** Image provided by MetaTools. **184** © Joe McDonald/CORBIS. **186** © Gianni Dagli Orti/CORBIS. **189** © David Fleetham/FPG International. **191** © Paul Bennett; Eye Ubiquitous/CORBIS. **193** © Bettmann/CORBIS. **195** © PhotoDisc, Inc. **196** (t) © Tibor Bognar/The Stock Market. (b) © Jan Moline/Photo Researchers, Inc. **198** © Richard Schulman/The Gamma Liaison Network. **201** © David Young-Wolff/PhotoEdit. **202** © Roger Viollet Gamma Presse. **205** © Scott Barrow/International Stock/Photo Network. **206** © Tony Freeman/PhotoEdit. **208** © Hulton Getty/Liaison Agency. **209** © Paul A. Souders/CORBIS. **213** © Anthony Edgeworth/The Stock Market. **214** © Science VU/Visuals Unlimited. **216** Image provided by MetaTools. **225** © George Bernard/Earth Scenes. **226** (t) © Jeffrey L. Rotman/CORBIS. (b) © Bettmann/CORBIS. **227** © Express Newspapers/Archive Photos. **228** © Comstock, Inc. **229** © PhotoDisc, Inc. **230** © David Barnes/The Stock Market. **233** © PhotoDisc, Inc. **234** © Vladimir Pcholkin/Black

Star/Picture Quest. **235** © Ellen B. Senisi/The Image Works. **237** © Bob Daemmrich/Tony Stone Images. **239** © Hulton Getty/Liaison Agency. **240** © Hulton-Deutsch Collection/CORBIS. **242** (t) © Stuart Westmorland/Tony Stone Images. (b) © Vic Bider/PhotoEdit. **244** © Bob Thomas/Tony Stone Images. **246** © Art Wolfe/Tony Stone Images. **247** © Collection of Kean E. Wilcox. **249** © Amy C. Etra/PhotoEdit. **253** © Siede Preis/PhotoDisc, Inc. **254** © Arthur Gurmankin and Mary Morina/Visuals Unlimited. **255** © Library of Congress, Washington D.C./SuperStock, Inc. **256** © Turner and Devries/The Image Bank. **257** (t) © Cartesia. (b) © Steve Vidler/Tony Stone Images. **261** © Liaison. **262** © Eric R. Berndt/Photo Network. **264** © Pablo Corral, V/CORBIS. **267** © PhotoDisc, Inc. **269** © Roy Corral/Tony Stone Images. **270** © David Young-Wolff/Tony Stone Images. **273** © Michael Newman/PhotoEdit. **276** © Bill Aron/PhotoEdit. **277** © The Granger Collection, New York. **281** © PhotoDisc, Inc. **285** © Yoav Levy/Phototake/Picture Quest. **286** © Joe Atlas/Artville. **287** © PhotoDisc, Inc. **289** © PhotoDisc, Inc. **290** © Tony Roberts/CORBIS. **295** © The Granger Collection, New York. **297** © Barbara Peacock/FPG International **299** © John Welzenbach/The Stock Market. **300** © Hulton Getty/Liaison Agency. **303** © Hulton Getty/Liaison Agency. **304** © Hulton Getty/Liaison Agency. **305** © Artville. **306** (l) © SW Productions/PhotoDisc, Inc. (c) (r) © Stockbyte. **309** © Kunsthistorisches Museum, Vienna, Austria/SuperStock, Inc. **310** © Hulton Getty/Liaison Agency. **313** © The Granger Collection, New York. **316** © Art Wolfe/Tony Stone Images. **319** © Paul Avis/Liaison International. **320** © PhotoDisc, Inc. **326** © Corel Corporation. **327** © Bob Daemmrich/Stock Boston. **328** © Charles Gupton/Tony Stone Images. **337** © PhotoDisc, Inc. **339** © Bettmann/CORBIS. **340** © SuperStock, Inc. **341** (t) © Robert Maier/Animals Animals. (b) © Richard Alan Wood/Animals Animals. **342** © Joe Atlas/Artville. **343** © PhotoDisc, Inc. **345** © Terry Husebye/Tony Stone Images. **347** © Jack Vartoogian. **351** © Ed Malitsky/Liaison International. **352** © Kelly-Mooney Photography/CORBIS. **353** © Ron Dorsey/Stock Boston. **354** © Tom Tracy/FPG International. **355** © Gjon Mili/Time Inc. **356** © Archive Photos. **357** © Erik Butler/Tony Stone Images. **359** © Mark Newman/Visuals Unlimited. **360** © Jess Stock/Tony Stone Images. **362** © Eadweard Muybridge Collection/Kingston Museum/Science Photo Library/Photo Researchers, Inc. **365** © Chris Cheadle/Tony Stone Images. **368** © Tony Freeman/PhotoEdit. **369** © Bill Bachmann/Stock Boston. **371** © PhotoDisc, Inc. **372** (t) © C Squared Studios/PhotoDisc, Inc. (b) © CORBIS. **374** © Jeff Greenberg/Visuals Unlimited. **378** © Comstock, Inc. **379** © Michael Newman/PhotoEdit. **386** © Jack Vartoogian. **387** © Southern Stock/Picture Quest. **389** © CORBIS. **390** © Bojan Brecelj/CORBIS. **391** © Sacha Ajbeszyc/The Image Bank. **393** © David Ulmer/Stock Boston/Picture Quest. **395** © Jack Dykinga/Tony Stone Images. **397** © John

Acknowledgments

Neubauer/PhotoEdit. **398** © C.C. Lockwood/Bruce Coleman, Inc. **400** © Tim Davis/Tony Stone Images. **402** (inset) © The Granger Collection, New York. © Image Farm/Picture Quest. **404** © Bettmann/CORBIS. **405** © Luis Villota/The Stock Market. **406** © Jeff Schultz/Alaska Stock Images. **407** © Michael Busselle/CORBIS. **409** © Mark E. Gibson/Visuals Unlimited. **411** © Neil Rabinowitz/CORBIS. **414** © Bob Daemmrich/Tony Stone Images. **423** © Macduff Everton/CORBIS. **424** (t) © The Granger Collection, New York. (b) © Thomas Brummett/PhotoDisc, Inc. **425** © Bob Torrez/Tony Stone Images. **427** (l) © SuperStock, Inc. (r) © Paul Thompson; Eye Ubiquitous/CORBIS. **428** © Jim Mejuto/FPG International. **429** (t) © Patti Murray/Animals Animals. (l) (r) © Bettmann/CORBIS. **431** © Carmona Photography /FPG International. **432** © R. Packwood/Earth Scenes. **434** (inset) © Hulton Getty/Liaison Agency. Image provided by MetaTools. **436** © David Muench/CORBIS. **437** © Arthur Tilley/FPG International. **440** © Don B. Stevenson/Index Stock Imagery. **440-1** © Bojan Brecelj/CORBIS. **441** (b) © Sylvain Grandadam/Tony Stone Images. **442** © Mug Shots/The Stock Market. **445** © Mug Shots/The Stock Market. **446** (l) © Comstock, Inc. (c) © Ken Chernus/FPG International. (r) © The Stock Market. **448** © Don B. Stevenson/Index Stock Imagery. **449** © Chuck Burton/AP Photo. **450** (tl) © Owen Franken/Stock Boston/Picture Quest. (tr) © Kevin Fleming/CORBIS. (bl) © Owen Franken/CORBIS. (br) © David Samuel Robbins/CORBIS. **457** © Michael Heron/The Stock Market.

470 © *Head of a Woman,* 1939 Pablo Picasso. © Edimédia/CORBIS. **474** © Associated Press. Frame provided by Image Farm. **475** (t) © Ron Frehm/Associated Press. (b) © CORBIS. Frames provided by Image Farm. **479** © Bob Parent/Archive Photos. **483** (tl) (tr) © Rick Doyle/CORBIS. (c) © Ric Ergenbright/CORBIS. (b) © Kit Kittle/CORBIS. **486** © Sylvain Grandadam/Tony Stone Images. **487** © Galen Rowell/CORBIS. **488** © David H. Wells/CORBIS. **522** © J. Sneesby/B. Wilkins/Tony Stone Images. **522-3** © Arnulf Husmo/Tony Stone Images. **523** (b) © Telegraph Colour Library/FPG International. **524** © Bettmann/CORBIS. **525** © UPI/CORBIS-Bettmann. **526** © Bettmann/CORBIS. **527** © Peter Beck/The Stock Market. **528** Given to the United States by Egypt in 1965, awarded to The Metropolitan Museum of Art in 1967 and installed in The Sackler Wing in 1978. (68.154) Photograph © 1998 The Metropolitan Museum of Art. **530** © Raymond Gehman/CORBIS. **531** (l) © Bob Daemmrich/Tony Stone Images. (r) © Patti McConville/The Image Bank. **532** (l) © Barbara Alper/Stock Boston/Picture Quest. (c) © T. Kerekes/Sovfoto/Eastfoto/Picture Quest. (r) © Matthew McVay/AllStock/Picture Quest. **534** © J. Sneesby/B. Wilkins/Tony Stone Images. **535** © Smithsonian Institution. **536** © Wright State University, Dayton, Ohio. **560** © Paul Barton/The Stock Market. **566** © Culver Pictures. **567** (t) © The Granger Collection, New York. (bl) (bc) (br) © Culver Pictures. **569** © Telegraph Colour Library/FPG International. **570** © David Muench/CORBIS. **571** (l) © Sally

A. Morgan/Ecoscene/CORBIS. (r) ©
Kevin Schafer/CORBIS. **582** © Jeff
Greenberg/PhotoEdit. **584** © Joseph
Sohm; ChromoSohm, Inc./CORBIS.
593 © Jim Sugar Photography/
CORBIS. **597** ©
Bettmann/CORBIS. **598** © Tomb of
Qin shi Huang Di, Xianyang,
China/The Bridgeman Art Library.
599 © Bob Daemmrich/Stock
Boston/Picture Quest. **605** (inset) ©
Kennan Ward/CORBIS. **606** (t) ©
RO-MA Stock/Index Stock. (b) ©
CORBIS. **608** (inset) Courtesy
National Park Service, Department of
Interior. **610** © Ron Chapple/FPG
International. **610-1** © Paul and
Lindamarie Ambrose/FPG
International. **611** (b) © Adam
Woolfitt/CORBIS. **612** © CORBIS.
614 © Chuck Carlton/Index Stock
Imagery/Picture Quest. **615** ©
David Young-Wolff/PhotoEdit. **616**
© Bob Rowan; Progressive
Image/CORBIS. **618** © Ron
Chapple/FPG International. **629** ©
Dan Helms/Newsport. **646** © Adam
Woolfitt/CORBIS. **655** © Bob
Daemmrich/Stock Boston. **659** ©
Bob Daemmrich/Stock Boston. **661**
© Jane Sapinsky/The Stock Market.
666 © 2000 Chien-Chi
Chang/Magnum Photos, Inc. **672** *A
Storm,* Georgia O'Keeffe 1922, Pastel
on off-white laid paper, mounted on
illustration board, 18 x 24 1/8 inches.
Anonymous Gift, 1981, The
Metropolitan Museum of Art, New
York, NY (1981.35) **680** © Bob
Daemmrich/Stock Boston. **H8** ©
Greg Kuchik/PhotoDisc, Inc. **H13** ©
ChromaZone Images/Index Stock.
H14 © David Allan Brandt/Tony
Stone Images. **H16** © Kunio
Owaki/The Stock Market. **H19** ©
Michael & Patricia Fogden/CORBIS.
H21 © PhotoDisc, Inc. **H28** ©
David Burnett/Contact Press/Picture
Quest. **H32** Courtesy NASA. **H35**
© Jeff Zaruba/The Stock Market.
H54 (t) © Bettmann/CORBIS. (b) ©
Brown Brothers.

Cover Photograph

© Telegraph Colour Library/FPG
International.